As Chief of Staff for President Richard Nixon from 1969 until 1973, H. R. Haldeman was one of the very few who observed the inner workings of the Oval Office during this tumultuous period. It was revealed only recently that he spent those years keeping a detailed, day-by-day account of Nixon's presidency: Vietnam, China, the Kent State killings, the power struggles, the ''dirty tricks''—and, ultimately, the Watergate break-in, cover-up, and national scandal. *The Haldeman Diaries* offer a valuable and rarely seen picture of one of the most controversial figures of our time—and an important document of four crucially important years in our nation's recent history.

The Haldeman Diaries

"NEW INSIGHTS INTO NIXON'S COMPLEX PERSONALITY."
—*Los Angeles Times*

"ALMOST EVERY ENTRY IN THE *DIARIES* could have made the front page of *The Washington Post* the next day . . . There are also ground-zero insights into how Washington really works, how bureaucrats and courtiers act when the cameras are gone and they think no one is paying attention."
—*Washington Monthly*

continued on next page . . .

Most Berkley Books are available at special quantity discounts for bulk purchases for sales promotions, premiums, fund-raising or educational use. Special books, or book excerpts, can also be created to fit specific needs.

For details, write or telephone Special Markets, The Berkley Publishing Group, 200 Madison Avenue, New York, New York 10016; (212) 951-8891

The Haldeman Diaries

Inside the Nixon White House

H. R. Haldeman

Introduction and Afterword by Stephen E. Ambrose

B

BERKLEY BOOKS, NEW YORK

THE HALDEMAN DIARIES

A Berkley Book / published by arrangement with
G. P. Putnam's Sons

PRINTING HISTORY
G. P. Putnam's Sons edition / May 1994
Berkley edition / May 1995

ISBN: 0-425-14827-0

BERKLEY®
Berkley Books are published by The Berkley Publishing Group,
200 Madison Avenue, New York, New York 10016.
BERKLEY and the "B" design
are trademarks belonging to Berkley Publishing Corporation.

PRINTED IN THE UNITED STATES OF AMERICA

10 9 8 7 6 5 4 3 2 1

To Bob's family
who always came first in his heart
and who, each in his own way,
contributed to bringing this publication to fruition

In Appreciation

There is no way that this project could have been completed without the invaluable assistance and contribution of Scott Klososky, who worked both with Bob in organizing, reviewing, and editing an incredible amount of material and with me in bringing the raw manuscript to publication.

Jo Haldeman

Contents

Prefatory Note

> "Until he has been a part of a cause larger than himself, no man is truly whole."
> RICHARD M. NIXON
> Inaugural Address, January 1969

Handwritten by President Nixon at my request and presented to Bob upon the commencement of his White House tenure, this quotation hangs today on the wall of Bob's Santa Barbara office. Without question, serving as Assistant to the President and White House Chief of Staff gave Bob the opportunity to participate in "a cause larger than himself."

Before moving to Washington, Bob and I discussed his new role and the total dedication to the President it would require. We knew that this commitment would put a strain on our marriage and on the family, but we also recognized the great privilege and opportunity the experience would provide. As anticipated, Bob and President Nixon did have an intense one-on-one working relationship, although they were never personal friends.

During his years in the Nixon Administration, Bob kept a personal daily record of the events in which he was involved. After 12- and 14-hour workdays, he would return home and faithfully chronicle his observations. At first he wrote the entries in longhand; later, he switched to dictating, and I would hear the steady drone of his voice coming from his den late each night.

At the time, Bob had no intention of ever publishing these accounts. He considered them as a potential resource for historians and scholars of the Nixon Presidency. It was not until long after he left the White House that he even had the material transcribed.

At Bob's request I read the diaries for the first time just last year (1993) and found them very interesting for a number of reasons. For the most part, the daily entries are much longer than I expected. Bob was a great note-taker; however, recording each day's events in detail was particularly tedious work for him. He was unusually self-disciplined, as is evidenced by these accounts.

Despite the volume of material produced, Bob made no attempt to document the entire fabric of the Nixon Presidency. He wrote from the perspective of Chief of Staff; consequently, his diary covers solely, and fully, his experience in that role. Therefore, even personality issues, such as the ongoing conflict between Bill Rogers and Henry Kissinger, are covered in detail, even though discussing other individuals was not characteristic of Bob. When a particular issue consumed his time, it consumed his journal pages as well.

It was revealing to read how often Bob expressed his opinion on matters of foreign and domestic policy. He usually described himself as a "sounding board" and avoided playing an active role in the policy-making process.

Surprisingly, very little direct mention is made of Bob's organization of the White House staffing system. Wanting to maximize the efficiency of his operation, Bob studiously researched the job of Chief of Staff and the staff structures of previous presidents. I know that he was very proud of his system and continuously worked on perfecting it.

There is a dramatic difference between the postinaugural attitudes of 1969 and 1973. Bob's early entries are fresh and naive, with a feeling of expectation and excitement of the first term. In contrast, despite the tremendous election victory of 1972, the later entries reveal a tired and negative attitude, compounded by an uncooperative Congress and press, the President's absorption with the reorganization of the Executive Branch, and the growing effect of Watergate.

Indeed, Watergate slowly crept into the journal entries until it was all-consuming. It was poignant for me to see Bob document his own diminishing involvement with the President. This culminated in his entry of April 30, 1973, describing President Nixon's last awkward telephone call which followed his televised speech announcing Bob's resignation:

> [The President] said to me: you're a strong man, you've got to keep the faith, you're going to win this, God bless you. Then he asked me . . . if I could do some checking around on reaction to the speech . . . and I said no, I don't think I could. He realized that was the case. . . .

These are some of my observations in reading the 1,521 entries in the full text. Each reader will have his or her own reactions, and noted historian Stephen Ambrose has shared his theories in his introduction. Bob was pleased to know that Mr. Ambrose had agreed to contribute to the book; however, he did not have a chance to see his material, and I feel that he would not have agreed with a number of Mr. Ambrose's conclusions. Bob had planned both to write an afterword and to do a promotional tour. These were to have provided forums for him to explain some of the controversial issues touched on in his diaries. Unfortunately, he did not have the opportunity to do either.

Twenty years after he left the White House, Bob decided to review the transcripts of his records. He realized then their historical value as an unprecedented account of the inner workings of the office of the President of the United States and became committed to their publication. He was working full-time on this project up until one month before his death. At that time contract negotiations were almost complete for the publication of the diaries both in their entirety on CD-ROM and in a condensed book version. He was excited about the undertaking, and I deeply regret that he did not live to see the end result.

On November 12, 1993, my life was shattered by the unexpected death of my husband of almost forty-five years. Suddenly, among much unfinished business, I was left with the decision of whether to pursue his commitment to the journal or to withdraw from the contract negotiations. My unsure emotional state made me question taking the project onto my own shoulders. As Bob knew only too well, I always had deep-seated reservations about "revealing" more inside stories of the Nixon White House. I was also sensitive to the diary's effect on individuals for whom Bob had great admiration—the President, Bill Rogers, and Henry Kissinger, among others. On a more personal level, our children and I were not anxious to reopen old wounds.

On the other hand, there were strong mitigating factors which favored proceeding with the project. First and foremost was Bob's belief in his commitment and his request to me to continue where he had to leave off. Second was the historical value of the material. Third was the desire to give a full, annotated presentation of the diaries, rather than having them released by others in a piecemeal or out-of-context format.

At first, my immediate personal loss overwhelmed any other

interests and my heart was not in the project. However, in taking it on, I became involved in the process of editing and worked diligently with the editors at Putnam's to produce a balanced condensation for the book version which fairly represents the substance of the full text.

Watergate, however, is the one topic which is included in its entirety in the book. There may be less on the subject than the reader would expect, but this reflects its initial relative unimportance to Bob and the President rather than any editing. Not a single reference to Watergate has been omitted.

There is no doubt that Watergate was a very humbling experience for Bob, which he accepted—as he did *all* challenges—as a means to grow and to acknowledge the positive. While the pinnacle of his life was his service in the White House, the nadir was his time served in Lompoc Federal Prison. The testimony of Bob's true nature is that he handled *each* with equal fortitude and saw *each* as an equally challenging opportunity.

Regrettably, H. R. Haldeman was someone most Americans knew only through his limited exposure in the media. In reality, Bob was a businessman who had a wide range of interests outside of politics. He was especially interested in young people and held a number of positions in the field of education: President of the UCLA Alumni Association, Regent of the University of California, and Trustee of the Coro Foundation, among others. At the request of the Disney family, he was the first Chairman of the California Institute of the Arts. He entered politics not as a career, but for a limited time and purpose. He accepted the position of Chief of Staff because he felt it provided him with the opportunity to put his management skills to use in serving Richard Nixon and his country. Throughout his career, he was actively involved in serving both the community and our church.

I was married to a remarkable man, whose devotion, integrity, and strength of character I will always treasure. As father to our four children and ''Grandpa'' to our five grandchildren, he stood solidly at the head of a close-knit family.

My husband lived and died ''truly whole.''

JO HALDEMAN
Santa Barbara
February 1994

The Nixon White House
January 21, 1969–April 30, 1973

The Cabinet

Spiro Agnew—Vice President, January 1973, to October 10, 1973

Winton (Red) Blount—Postmaster General, January 22, 1969, to July 1, 1971

Peter Brennan—Secretary of Labor, February 2, 1973, to March 1975

Earl Butz—Secretary of Agriculture, December 2, 1971, to November 1976

John Connally—Secretary of Treasury, February 11, 1971, to June 1971; later ran the Democrats for Nixon during 1972 campaign

Fred Dent—Secretary of Commerce, February 2, 1973, to May 1975

Bob Finch—Secretary of HEW, January 22, 1969, to June 23, 1970; later stayed on as Counselor to the President until 1972

Clifford Hardin—Secretary of Agriculture, January 22, 1969, to November 11, 1971

Walter Hickel—Secretary of Interior, January 24, 1969, to November 25, 1970

James Hodgson—Secretary of Labor, July 2, 1970, to February 1973; formerly Undersecretary of Labor

David Kennedy—Secretary of Treasury, January 22, 1969, to February 1, 1971; later Ambassador-at-Large; Ambassador to NATO

Richard Kleindienst—Attorney General, June 12, 1972, to April 3, 1973; formerly Deputy Attorney General Department of Justice

Melvin Laird—Secretary of Defense, January 22, 1969, to February 1973

John Mitchell—Attorney General, January 22, 1969 to June 1972; later chairman of the CRP

Rogers Morton—Secretary of Interior, January 29, 1971, to June 1975; formerly Congressman from Maryland

Pete Peterson—Secretary of Commerce, February 21, 1972, to February 1973; formerly Assistant to the President for Foreign Economic Policy

Elliot Richardson—Secretary of HEW, June 24, 1970, to February 1973; Secretary of Defense, February 1973 to May 1973; Attorney General, May 25, 1973, to October 20, 1973; formerly Undersecretary of State, State Department

Bill Rogers—Secretary of State, January 22, 1969, to September 3, 1973

George Romney—Secretary of HUD, January 22, 1969, to February 1973

George Shultz—Secretary of Labor, January 22, 1969, to July 1, 1970; Director of OMB, July 1970 to June 1972; Secretary of Treasury, June 12, 1972, to May 1974

Maurice Stans—Secretary of Commerce, January 22, 1969, to February 1972; later finance committee for the CRP

John Volpe—Secretary of Transportation, January 22, 1969, to February 1973

Caspar Weinberger—Secretary of HEW, February 12, 1973, to August 1975; formerly Deputy Director of the OMB, then Director

Staff and Other Administrative Personnel

Roy Ash—Head of the President's Advisory Council on Executive Organization

Pat Buchanan—Assistant to the President; speechwriter

Arthur Burns—Counselor to the President, economics

Alex Butterfield—Deputy Assistant to the President; aide to H. R. Haldeman

Dwight Chapin—Deputy Assistant to the President; appointments secretary

Kenneth Cole—Haldeman staff aide; later Ehrlichman staff

Chuck Colson—Special Counsel to the President

John Dean—Counsel to the President

Harry S. Dent—Special Counsel to the President

Lee DuBridge—Science Advisor; later State Department

John Ehrlichman—Assistant to the President for Domestic Affairs

Peter Flanigan—Presidential Advisor on International Trade

Leonard Garment—Counsel to the President

Patrick Gray—Acting FBI Director

Erwin Griswold—Solicitor General

Alexander Haig—NSC Deputy; 1972 Vice-Chief of Staff, Army

H. R. Haldeman—Chief of Staff

Bryce Harlow—Political Counselor to the President

Larry Higby—Assistant to H. R. Haldeman

J. Edgar Hoover—Director of the FBI

General (Don) Hughes—Head of Ad Hoc Interagency Group Concerning POWs

Howard Hunt—Consultant to the White House

Herbert Kalmbach—President's personal attorney; campaign fund-raiser

James Keogh—Assistant to the President; speechwriter

Henry Kissinger—Assistant to the President for National Security Affairs

Herb Klein—Director of Communications

Egil (Bud) Krogh, Jr.—Deputy Assistant to the President for Domestic Affairs

Gordon Liddy—General Counsel of the CRP

Clark MacGregor—Congressional liaison; chairman of the CRP after Mitchell

Jeb Magruder—Haldeman aide; Deputy Director of White House Communications; Deputy Campaign Director, CRP

Frederick Malek—White House aide; reelection-campaign leader

Mike Mansfield—Senate Majority Leader

Paul McCracken—Chairman of the Council of Economic Advisors

Admiral Thomas Moorer—Acting Chairman of the Joint Chiefs of Staff

Patrick Moynihan—Director of the Urban Affairs Council; White House Counselor

Lyn Nofziger—Director of Communications for RNC; Director of Reelection Committee in California

Ray Price—Assistant to the President; speechwriter
Bill Safire—Assistant to the President; speechwriter
Manolo Sanchez—President's valet
John Scali—Senior Consultant on Foreign Affairs; U.S. Ambassador to the U.N.
Hugh Scott—Senate Minority Leader
General Brent Scowcroft—NSC Deputy; replaced Haig
Gordon Strachan—Haldeman aide/General Counsel of the USIA
Bill Timmons—Chief of White House liaison to Congress
Dr. Walter Tkach—White House Physician
Rose Woods—President's personal secretary
Ron Ziegler—Press Secretary to the President

Family and Friends

Robert Abplanalp
Walter Annenberg
Ed Cox—Son-in-law
David Eisenhower—Son-in-law
Billy Graham
Don Nixon—Brother
Ed Nixon—Brother
Julie Nixon (Eisenhower)—Daughter
Pat Nixon—Richard Nixon's wife
Tricia Nixon (Cox)—Daughter
Bebe Rebozo

The Haldeman Diaries
Inside the Nixon White House

Introduction
by Stephen E. Ambrose

For anyone interested in modern American politics, H. R. "Bob" Haldeman's diary covering his four and a half years as President Richard M. Nixon's Chief of Staff is a priceless document. It puts the reader within the innermost circle of power. It gives new information and provides new insights and perspectives on all the major and many of the minor events of the period January 1969 to May 1973. Because it is all true, and because readers know the players (Nixon, Henry Kissinger, John Mitchell, John Ehrlichman, John Connally, Ross Perot, George Bush, Ron Ziegler, Pat Buchanan, and so many more), it makes for gripping reading, better than the best political novel.

We know what is going to happen, but of course Haldeman doesn't, so the tension builds as we see Kent State coming in the wake of the Cambodian incursion or Nixon and Kissinger sweating it out as the United States bombs Hanoi and mines Haiphong Harbor on the eve of the 1972 Moscow Summit. Will the Soviets cancel or not? The unfolding of Watergate, from the ho-hum attitude within the Administration at its inception to the crisis of April 1973 that led to Haldeman's resignation, is absolutely absorbing.

This is a unique document. No other Presidential chief of staff has gone to such lengths to make a record in anything approaching such detail. No other Presidential chief of staff spent as much time with his boss, or was so deeply involved in discussions and decision-making about such a wide range of subjects. So this diary is exactly what Robert Rutland told Haldeman it would be, when he urged Haldeman to make it (see Haldeman's foreword): "An invaluable asset to historians and scholars of the future."

Dwight Eisenhower's press secretary, James Hagerty, kept a diary for the first couple of years of his term, and it is a valuable document for historians, but it is not as extensive or informative as Haldeman's. General Andrew Goodpaster, Staff Secretary to Eisenhower, kept notes on private conversations and conferences Eisenhower had in the Oval Office that were extensive and invaluable, but Goodpaster wasn't present when the subject was politics or domestic policy. Sherman Adams, the first of the modern chiefs of staff in the White House, was important to Eisenhower, but nowhere near as critical to the President as Haldeman was to Nixon. And none of Haldeman's predecessors or successors as chief of staff worked for a president who was involved in such high drama or low skulduggery.

This is politics at its cutting edge, tough as nails. When American Jews boycotted French President Pompidou during a visit to New York because the French had sold some jet fighter planes to the Arabs, and Mayor John Lindsay and Governor Nelson Rockefeller joined the boycott, Nixon was embarrassed and furious. He struck back by postponing an arms shipment to Israel and by telling Kissinger to tell American Jewish leaders to "go talk to Lindsay and Rockefeller about whether *they* can provide arms for Israel." We see Nixon tell the IRS to start doing audits on Democratic campaign contributors; Nixon manipulating George Wallace both before and after he was shot, using money and IRS threats to keep Wallace out of the 1972 race; Nixon helping McGovern win the 1972 Democratic nomination by putting out fake polls showing McGovern doing well in trial heats; Nixon in October 1972 making "the interesting point" (as Haldeman put it) "that after the election we will have awesome power with no discipline, that is, there won't be another election coming up to discipline us," so all of Nixon's enemies—Democrats, bureaucrats, reporters, publishers, television networks, and so on—had better brace themselves.

We see American politics at the most practical level. In 1970 Nixon had a welfare reform program called the Family Assistance Plan. He told Haldeman "to be sure it's killed by Democrats and that we make big play for it, but don't let it pass, can't afford it."

And we see bureaucratic infighting and turf battles at the most petty level; Haldeman's diaries are filled with stories about the struggle between Henry Kissinger and Secretary of State William Rogers for power and influence. Haldeman writes: "P realizes K basically is jealous of any idea not his own, and he just can't swallow the apparent early success of the Middle East plan [in 1970] because it is Rogers'. In fact, he's probably actually trying to make it fail for just this reason."

Kissinger made Haldeman's life miserable with his constant complaining and his continuous threats to resign if Rogers wasn't fired. Haldeman called his bluff on a number of occasions, best of all on December 7, 1971, a couple of months before the historic trip to China. "I talked again with Henry and played it a little brutally by saying that if he was going to announce his resignation in December, he should resign in December. He couldn't just announce it and then hang on, and he said, oh no, he couldn't do that because he couldn't leave the P alone to go to China, and I said you couldn't go to China with him having announced your resignation." Kissinger folded.

The old Nixon is here, on every page—the hatred and jealousy of the Kennedy family, the contempt for bureaucrats, liberals, professors, the educated, and others, the obsession with Alger Hiss, the amazing memory. In January 1972 Nixon had Haldeman bring him a copy of a book by H. G. Wells "and found a devastating quote about the military mind and the fact that it is by definition mediocre because nobody with any real intellectual talent would submit himself to the military career." The President added, "Of course Wells has the feeling that the solution to all problems is education for everyone, and that's a terrible idea, especially for women, says the P."

Obviously the P said things to Haldeman he said to no one else. On another occasion, Nixon got into "a sort of a long philosophical thing, making the point that . . . in this period of our history, the leaders and the educated class are decadent. Whenever you ask for patriotic support, they all run away. The college types, the professors, the elite, etc. So he concludes the more a person is educated, he becomes brighter in the head and weaker in the spine. When you have to call on the nation to be strong, on such things as drugs, crime, defense, the educated people and the leader class no longer has any character, and you can't count on them. We can only turn for support to the non-educated people."

One more preview. Here is Nixon, musing to Haldeman about American youth. "We should be understanding of upper- and middle-class parents because they really do have great problems with their kids because they've been given so much. It's a mistake to think that the way to greatness is to make it easy to get there. . . . He said we must not destroy the character of children by permissiveness, permissiveness that denies the child the opportunity to look in a mirror and finally realize that the problem is me, not my teachers, not the war, not the environment, but me."

Nixon's private views on the Republican Party were as scathing as were those of two of his predecessors as Republican presidents, Theodore Roosevelt and Dwight Eisenhower. TR abandoned the party as hopeless in 1912 and ran against President William Howard Taft as the candidate of the Progressive Party. Ike indulged himself in the fantasy of cutting loose from the Old Guard of the Republican Party and forming a new party, made up of moderate Republicans and Southern Democrats. Nixon, too, liked Southern Democrats more than he did most Republicans—John Connally most of all. Haldeman's diaries make crystal clear what was only sensed before—Nixon regarded Connally as "the best man in the country," the only one who was fit to follow him into the White House. Nixon was constantly hatching schemes to get Connally the vice-presidential nomination for 1972. He tried to persuade Spiro Agnew to resign before the convention so that he could appoint Connally. It is amazing how completely Nixon trusted and admired Connally. After 1970, at virtually every critical moment Nixon told Haldeman to check with Connally for his advice—on economic matters, political and Vietnam War crises, relations with China and the Soviet Union, everything.

Nixon told Haldeman that after the election he wanted to "move to build a new party, the Independent Conservative Party, or something of that sort, that would bring in a coalition of Southern Democrats and other conservative Democrats along with the middle-road Republicans. By structuring it right, we could develop a new majority party under a new name. Get control of the Congress without an election, simply by the realignment, and make a truly historic change in the entire American political structure."

In the 1972 campaign, Nixon rarely used the word "Republican," nor did he go out of his way to campaign for Republican candidates—a fact that caused the Republicans to complain bitterly, and a fact Nixon denied. The day after the election, which he won in a landslide while the Republicans lost both the House and Senate, he vindictively expressed to Haldeman his concern that he get the party before it got him. (A disastrous decision; when the crunch came in Watergate, precious few Republicans were ready to come to Nixon's defense.)

Nixon's well-known hostility toward the media is highlighted here by casual and spontaneous comments to Haldeman, such as: "The White House press is totally dedicated to screwing us rather than getting the facts and reporting them." He hated leaks, yet as Haldeman records he was the all-time master leaker. He hated *The New York Times* and *The Washington Post* and CBS-TV and PBS and a host of others, but above all he hated *Time* magazine (which over the course of his political career has had him on its cover almost fifty times, far more than any other individual).

All his political life, Nixon complained about the double standard of American reporters. When *Time* failed to select him as Man of the Year in 1969, Haldeman recorded that Nixon commented that "it was the first time they haven't selected the P in his first year. [I] checked and this is not true. They didn't pick DDE until 1959. They *did* pick FDR, HST, JFK, and LBJ in their first years."

So far as Haldeman was concerned, that *Time* had picked every Democratic president in his first year, but not Ike or Dick, proved the double standard.

Nixon was terribly worried that *Time* might name Kissinger Man of the Year—he said it would be very bad for Henry. (In 1972 *Time* named Kissinger *and* Nixon as Men of the Year. Having to share the honor infuriated Nixon—and probably Kissinger as well.)

In January 1972 *Time* columnist Hugh Sidey remarked that the President had too much access to television, which made it difficult for other candidates. "The P's reaction," Haldeman wrote, "was that we ought to explore the question of whether Sidey ever deplored Nixon's problem for eight years while he was out of office. When he traveled around the world alone with his briefcase, got no coverage, a lot less than even Scoop Jackson gets now, and did Sidey at that time complain about

Kennedy dominating news? Did he argue for equal time for the Republicans?''

The President found it easy to feel sorry for himself, for the battles he had to fight, alone, without support, with the media always out to get him. In one White House interview, a president said, ''That is the press's fault, too, damn it. I have fought more damn battles here for more things than any president has in 20 years . . . and not gotten one damn bit of credit from the knee-jerk liberal press, and I am sick and tired of it. . . . You get no credit around here for fighting and bleeding.''

That is vintage Nixon, but it was not Nixon speaking—it was President Bill Clinton, in a 1993 *Rolling Stone* interview. That Clinton sounded so much like Nixon makes an obvious point, but it needs to be added that not all presidents feel that way. Certainly Roosevelt didn't, nor Truman, nor Kennedy, nor Eisenhower. At his last press conference as president, Eisenhower was asked if he felt the press had been fair to him over the past eight years. Ike laughed and replied, ''Well, when you come down to it, I don't see that a reporter could do much to a president, do you?'' (When I quoted that line to Haldeman in 1988, he almost choked. He absolutely refused to take the remark seriously.)

If most presidents feel put upon by the press, all presidents indulge themselves in self-pity. One day in 1955, Eisenhower cleared an afternoon schedule so he could play golf, only to have a rainstorm come on. Standing at the window in the Oval Office, watching the rain, he told his secretary, Ann Whitman, that sometimes he felt so sorry for himself he could just cry. Haldeman records the day in 1970 that Nixon wanted to go to a good restaurant for lunch, only to have Kissinger talk him out of it and instead have a working lunch at the White House. ''The P then sulked about never gets to do anything fun that he wants to do, always has to do what's right.''

All presidents feel frustration. Political philosopher Hannah Arendt once remarked that the President of the United States is simultaneously the strongest and the weakest of all national leaders. The strongest because he is Commander in Chief and has the power to destroy the world at his fingertips, a characteristic of the Presidency that is constantly present in Haldeman's diaries, either right up front with ''Nixon the mad bomber'' (as Nixon sometimes called himself) or implied in every sentence describing dealings with the Chinese and Soviet leaders. The weakest because the House controls the money, the Senate controls the treaties, the Congress as a whole has the power to make war, the next election is always just around the corner, the bureaucracy is always there, and so on.

Shortly before Eisenhower's Inaugural, Harry Truman gave a warning: "Poor Ike," he said. "He'll sit here and he'll say, 'Do this! Do that!' *And nothing will happen.* It won't be at all like the army." Nixon could fill in the details. He couldn't get the FBI to do some investigating for him because J. Edgar Hoover was getting cold feet in his old age. He couldn't get the IRS to spy on the Democrats. He couldn't get the CIA to do his bidding. (The smoking gun that did Nixon in was his order to the CIA to tell the FBI to back off the Watergate investigation—an order the CIA refused to carry out.) He couldn't get the military to go all out in Vietnam. And so on.

Nixon wanted to start a New American Revolution. It would include welfare reform, more power to the states, less to the federal government, energy independence, national health care, education reform, and more. Haldeman recorded Nixon's pessimism about his chances for success: "There are only 537 elected officials here. All the other people are career diplomats and career bureaucrats who you can't get rid of and who you can't change. The enemy, then, is the invisible bureaucracy, the self-perpetuating people that are not elected and that blatantly brag that they'll be here, and are not going to change regardless of who comes in and out. They'll bury the new recommendations under a mountain of paperwork."

Oh, how those bureaucrats drove him up the wall. At a 1971 Cabinet meeting, Nixon declared that the people in the Civil Service "are out to get us. This is true of all administrations, but it's worse now, and it's strange because I've been much more permissive than any other P. . . . 96% of the bureaucracy are against us, they're bastards who are here to screw us."

At that meeting, Nixon also said, "You've got to realize the press aren't interested in liking you, they're only interested in news or in screwing me." For his part, Nixon was concerned with manipulating the reporters. He was obsessed with the coverage he received, and thus spent a great deal of his time—and therefore Haldeman's—focusing on the Presidential image. "Mystique is more important than content," he told Haldeman. The PR was always more important than the policy.

Politicians did not use the word "spin" in Nixon's day, but Nixon was an active practitioner of the spin (but not the first: JFK and LBJ were spinners of the worst sort). Nixon was continually urging Haldeman to get the press to cover his courage, his warmth, his depth, his human side. In this regard I am reminded of a comment Ann Whitman, Ike's secretary, once made about then Vice President Nixon to the effect that Nixon spent too much time trying to act like a nice guy instead of just being one.

The President was frequently influenced by what he read, one time latching on to a theory that it was a waste of time to sleep. Haldeman has an entry in February 1969 that speaks to the point. Nixon, he wrote, was "fascinated by [White House physician Dr. Walter] Tkach's report of people who need no sleep at all. Hates to waste the time. Feels . . . that people take breaks to avoid the problems and decision, not because they need rest. Thinks you have to be 'up,' not relaxed, to function best. He's thought a lot about this and is pretty firm in his views."

When Henry Kissinger reported that peace was at hand in Vietnam (erroneously as it turned out), Nixon invited Haldeman to join in a celebration dinner. "The P told Manolo [his houseman] to bring the good wine, his '57 Lafite-Rothschild, or whatever it is. To be served to everyone. Usually it's just served to the P, and the rest of us have some California Beaulieu Vineyard stuff."

The Haldeman diaries are replete with such incidents and anecdotes, but revealing as they often are, and funny as they usually are, they are not what makes the document so compelling and important. Haldeman covers the major events of a tumultuous time. The walk on the moon. Vietnamization. Chappaquiddick. The Vietnam Moratorium. My Lai. Senate rejection of the nominations of Clement Haynsworth and G. Harrold Carswell to the Supreme Court. The Cambodian incursion and Kent State. The invasion of Laos. The Pentagon Papers. The China trip. The 1972 North Vietnamese offensive. The bombing of Hanoi and the mining of Haiphong Harbor. The Moscow Summit and SALT I. The 1972 election.

On these and all other issues and events, Haldeman portrays Nixon at work, doing what he did all his life, being a politician and statesman. Haldeman's long account of the August 1971 meetings at Camp David, where Nixon decided to impose a wage-and-price freeze and to take the United States off the gold standard, is a classic piece of reporting that shows Nixon at his very best. So too the accounts of Nixon in China and Nixon at the Moscow Summit.

All are integral to the diaries. On all of them, Haldeman adds to what we know. And there is so much more here. I've already written a three-volume life of Nixon, using nearly 1,000 pages to describe the period covered in Haldeman's diaries—and I'd like the opportunity to write another entire book on the basis of what is revealed in the diaries. But the raw diaries themselves are better than anything I or any other historian could produce.

A few words on the Nixon-Haldeman relationship are in order. "From now on," Nixon told his Cabinet in 1971, "Haldeman is the lord high executioner. Don't you come whining to me when he tells you to do something. He will do it because I asked him to and you're to carry it out."

Bob Haldeman was not only the Chief of Staff closest to his President, he was also the most powerful. First of all, he played an active role in policymaking. He denied it, but it was so, not only with regard to politics, but in military and foreign policy as well. He urged the President to bomb Hanoi in the spring of 1972, for example, and to go into Cambodia in the spring of 1970.

Second, more than any other person—more so even than Rebozo, or Pat Nixon, or Julie, or Tricia Nixon, or David Eisenhower—Haldeman was the one Nixon could talk to about any subject. About his personal taxes. About opening to China. About the nature of the American family. About screwing his political enemies. About making sure John Connally would be his successor. About anything.

This was because Haldeman was completely trustworthy. He did not leak to the press, or to Ehrlichman, or to Kissinger. What Nixon told him stayed with him—until now, with the publication of his diaries.

Third, Haldeman was completely devoted to the President. Not to Nixon personally so much as to the Office of the President. He never forgot that his job was to make it possible for Nixon to work as effectively as possible. He could be ruthless in meeting his responsibilities; he had no soft curves; he was all sharp edges and corners. He was rough on his subordinates, just as Nixon could be very rough on him. Though Haldeman was often praised for his efficiency, no one ever thought to praise him for his humanity, and he wanted it that way. He was tough enough to stand up to the slurs and pounding that went with the job of being the President's son of a bitch, the man who would have to say no to requests to see the President or for other favors far more often than he would be able to say yes.

Nixon once said that Haldeman's job was to be "the gate-keeper of the Oval Office." He certainly was that. Haldeman's diaries are replete with instances of his telling Agnew or a governor or a Cabinet member that he could *not* see the President. Haldeman kept the President's schedule—an immensely difficult job for any chief of staff, especially so for Nixon's, as Nixon was often changing his mind about whom he would see, where he would go, when he would depart, what group he would speak to, which state or city he wanted to visit next.

Haldeman was also the chief hand-holder. Almost every day, certainly at least every week, he had to reassure Henry Kissinger that the President really did love him and appreciate him and couldn't get along without him and would someday fire Bill Rogers.

Haldeman was always available. Seven days a week. In the 1,561 days he served as Chief of Staff, he was with the President all but twenty or so of those days—and in telephone contact with him on most of the twenty days.

Haldeman was with Nixon, often just the two of them, for more time than any other human being. It was not unusual for them to have a working lunch together, and sometimes dinner. Haldeman attended almost any State dinner he wanted (more often than not dining in the housekeeper's office to avoid the dinner conversation). He was ordinarily the first person Nixon saw in the morning, the last one he talked to before bed.

But it was strictly a working relationship. There was not the slightest hint of friendship. Haldeman had managed Nixon's 1962 campaign for governor of California, yet after a decade of the most intimate association, Nixon did not know how many children Haldeman had. At their last meeting, at Camp David on April 29, 1973, when Nixon told Haldeman he would have to resign, Haldeman records: "The P was in terrible shape. Shook hands with me, which is the first time he's ever done that."

Nixon needed Haldeman not just during working hours. He

would call at any time—midnight, two A.M., four A.M.—to discuss the reaction to a speech, a personnel problem, the latest poll, a television program, anything.

Haldeman could match Nixon's almost superhuman energy level, as these diaries demonstrate beyond all doubt. Haldeman put in long days, very often followed by long evenings. Yet before going to bed on every one of the 1,561 days he served, he wrote or (after December 2, 1970) dictated an entry for his diary. Sometimes they were as long as ten or more typewritten pages. He based the dictation on his handwritten notes taken during the day, and on his memory. It was a simply incredible accomplishment.

The most dramatic setting for a dictation came on May 24, 1972. Haldeman was in Moscow for the Summit. He had hardly slept for three days. His bedroom, like all rooms in the American quarters, was bugged, so he went to the President's car, parked in the yard of the Kremlin, to dictate an entry covering the past three days.

As Haldeman relates in his foreword, he was the one who classified his journal Top Secret. That led to the National Security Council doing a review and removing so-called sensitive national-security-related material. Haldeman states that only a small amount was deleted, and I have no reason not to believe him, but I also have no way of knowing how much was involved, nor how important it was.

In the full text version of the diaries on May 20, 1971, most of which was removed, Haldeman explains an annotation: "The deleted material covers P's briefing of the Cabinet on the SALT announcement. He reviewed the history leading up to the agreement, explained the deadlock that had held it up for some time, outlined in detail the Soviet opposition, all in a great deal of detail. The deletion runs for 9½ minutes on my recorded tape because I made extensive notes, sensing the historic importance of this background—but, unfortunately, I am prohibited from passing it along."

For the historian, this kind of censorship by the government is worse than frustrating, it is infuriating. Haldeman's entry concerns events of a quarter-century ago, a treaty long since ratified with a government that no longer exists, about arms-limitation agreements that have long since given way to arms-reduction agreements that render the SALT I treaty completely out-of-date. Yet somehow it would hurt national security to make the record available to the public. (These deletions appear in the full text, and are commented on by Haldeman in the foreword.)

The first thing to notice when reading the Watergate material is that when Haldeman made these entries, no one except Haldeman's assistant Alexander Butterfield, a couple of Secret Service technicians, Haldeman, and Nixon knew that there was a voice-activated taping system in the Oval Office, the Cabinet Room, Nixon's Executive Office Building (EOB) office, and on the telephones in the Oval and EOB offices, the Lincoln Sitting Room at the White House, and on the office phone at Camp David.

In February 1971 Nixon ordered Haldeman to set up the system, secretly. The President had earlier told Haldeman to remove the less-complex system he had inherited from Johnson, then changed his mind. Nixon wrote in his memoirs that he intended to use the tapes to prepare the memoirs and to protect himself from "revisionist histories."

Because the taping system existed, and because Haldeman and Nixon were the only men in the conversations who knew a tape was running, everything Haldeman and Nixon say could be suspect. Were they speaking the truth? Or for the record? To explore options? Or to provide protection for themselves? Haldeman told me in 1988 that he often forgot the system was in place; as proof he pointed out that he certainly would not have said some of the things he did say after the Watergate break-in had he remembered. Thanks to these diaries, readers can judge for themselves.

Haldeman's first entry on the break-in, June 18, 1972, shows that he did not know in advance about the scheme to bug the Democratic National Committee office and that if he wasn't exactly shocked, he was disapproving of the break-in. The next conversation between Haldeman and Nixon about the break-in came on June 20. This was the conversation that contains the infamous 18½-minute gap on the Watergate tapes. In his diary entry, Haldeman relates what was said. He made his remarks on the basis of his handwritten notes made during the conversation, notes made on a yellow legal pad. I've studied those notes in the Nixon Presidential Materials Project and can attest that Haldeman's diary entry corresponds exactly with the notes he kept that morning. The point being that there was little that was sinister in the conversation. (Who erased that tape remains a mystery. Al Haig said it was done by "some sinister force." Nixon's secretary, Rose Mary Woods, said she did it, accidentally. Haldeman told me years later that Nixon might have done it inadvertently, which Nixon has always denied.)

Haldeman's June 20 entry needs to be read with great care. It is in the second paragraph that he describes his conversation with the President. In the first paragraph, Haldeman begins in the fifth sentence to describe a meeting with Ehrlichman, Mitchell, Attorney General Richard Kleindienst, and Nixon's counsel, John Dean. Nixon was not present. It was in this conversation that the cover-up began: "The conclusion was that we've got to hope the FBI doesn't go beyond the necessary in developing evidence and that we can keep a lid on that as well as keeping all the characters involved from getting carried away with any unnecessary testimony."

At this stage, Nixon felt that to some degree Watergate could be redirected to his advantage. On June 21 he told Haldeman, "Every time we have a leak in our organization we should charge that we're being bugged. Even if you plant one and discover it."

On June 23, Haldeman and Ehrlichman told the CIA to tell the FBI that the bugging was a CIA operation and the FBI should back off. "We talked to [CIA Deputy Director Vernon] Walters and had that worked out."* They had started down the slippery slope; from here on there was no turning back. But as the entries make clear, the President's aides felt they had little if anything to fear. In mid-August, Billy Graham reported—and Haldeman recorded—that Lyndon Johnson "laughed about it [Watergate], said it won't hurt a bit." So the two smartest politicians in the country, Nixon and Johnson, agreed that Watergate wasn't going anywhere. If those two agreed, why should Haldeman worry?

And Watergate never became an issue in the campaign, and Nixon was triumphantly re-elected, but he failed to bring Congress along with him, and after "peace is at hand" and then the Christmas bombing, and after the various dirty tricks in

---

*However, the CIA refused to do as instructed, i.e., tell the FBI to stay away from the case because of CIA involvement.

the campaign, the Democrats were determined to use their control of Congress to get Nixon.

Nixon's move to head them off is to me the most tantalizing item in the diaries. On January 11, 1973, Nixon told Haldeman to go to Johnson aide George Christian to get him to "get LBJ to use his influence to turn off the Hill investigation." Nixon wanted Haldeman to bring Connally in on the effort to get Johnson to get the Democrats in the Congress to back off. Nixon was threatening that if Johnson did not kill the Congressional investigations into the 1972 campaign, he would reveal that Johnson had bugged Nixon's airplane in the 1968 campaign and put out some revelations about contributors to Hubert Humphrey's campaign.

Johnson heard about the prospective blackmail, and on January 12 Haldeman records that Johnson "got very hot and called Deke [DeLoach of the FBI], and said to him that if the Nixon people are going to play with this that he would release . . ." and at this point the diaries contain a notation: "deleted material—national security." (This is the only place in the book where an example is given of a deletion by the NSC during the Carter Administration.)

Eight days later Nixon was inaugurated for his second term. Ten days later Johnson died of a heart attack. What Johnson had on Nixon I suppose we will never know.

On February 7, the Senate voted 70-to-0 to establish a seven-member select committee to investigate Watergate and related activities in the 1972 campaign. Chairman Sam Ervin and the other Democrats turned back Republican attempts to broaden the inquiry to include the 1968 campaign.

Over February and March, Nixon spent an increasing amount of time on Watergate; by April the scandal and cover-up were taking virtually all his time—and thus Haldeman's. Nixon, Haldeman, and Ehrlichman struggled to wiggle out of the net, first relying on and then against John Dean. They were like three men in a rubber boat, with no rudder, no paddle, no motor, no sail, in the middle of the Atlantic, with a storm bearing down on them, discussing their options.

They had no options. Haldeman's diary entries make this crystal clear. They try one scenario after another, only to realize that nothing could withstand the slightest scrutiny. They were powerless. They were trapped.

Some highlights. On March 24 Haldeman records that at

Nixon's instruction he called Bill Rogers "to raise the question with him first of where he feels we now stand in the public eye and second what his advice is on our general Watergate approach." What intense satisfaction this must have been for Rogers. After all the humiliation the Nixon White House had caused him over the preceding four years, now they turn to him to ask, "What do we do?"

Rogers told them the truth, that now that the case was in the courts, and the FBI was investigating, and the Senate was investigating, they were being besieged by "the forces of righteousness." Rogers forthrightly added, "The real problem on this is what's been done after the event, not the Watergate event itself."

It is all here—the money for the burglars, for their bosses Howard Hunt and Gordon Liddy, the destruction of evidence by Pat Gray, Acting Director of the FBI, the made-up stories to the grand jury, John Dean's desertion and threat to appear before the Ervin Committee.

Ehrlichman wanted to "destroy Dean." Nixon commented that "there's no sense in aggravating Dean." Ehrlichman's response was that Dean would force a resolution of impeachment "on the ground that the P committed a crime and there's no other legal process available." Nixon thought it could never come to that.

It might, however, come to Haldeman and Ehrlichman, as it was obvious the Ervin Committee wanted some big trophy. Nixon swore he would never throw them overboard. Toward the end of the first week of April, Nixon told Ehrlichman, "Haldeman is more important to me than Adams was to Ike. For example, the K situation, which only he can handle. I can handle the rest, probably, but I can't do that. So protecting Haldeman . . . is a major consideration. He is the P's closest confidant . . . and we can't let him be tarred as a dirty SOB."

Kissinger weighed in. Haldeman writes, "If the P does let me down or does let the situation develop to the point where I have to get out, he *(Kissinger)* too will leave because he would refuse to serve in a White House that would permit such a thing to happen."

On April 9, for the first time since the system was set up, Nixon talked to Haldeman about the taping apparatus. "Had a long discussion about the monitoring facilities in his offices and he wants them all taken out. But then he later changed his mind and said to leave them in on a switch basis. He's obviously concerned about having everything covered and wants to set up some kind of limited means of coverage.''

On April 18, as the pressure for a Haldeman resignation mounted, ''The P had me in at eight o'clock this morning. Said that if this thing goes the way it might, and I have to leave, he wants me to take all the office material from his—ah—machinery there and hold it for the library [meaning the prospective Nixon Presidential Library].''

On April 25 the tapes came to the fore. Dean was preparing to testify. ''What would you fellows answer,'' Nixon asked Haldeman and Ehrlichman anxiously, ''if Dean testifies that there was a discussion in which I said Hunt's lawyer had to get paid off?'' When the tapes were eventually made public, they did in fact include the President's asking about the options regarding a payoff.

Haldeman volunteered to review the tape of that meeting. He did—the first time, so far as I can tell, that either he or Nixon had listened to a tape—and returned to report that it wasn't too bad. He was putting the best possible face on what was in fact a smoking gun, digging up sentences that Nixon could use to exonerate himself. The best of these, the one Haldeman emphasized, was Nixon's statement with regard to clemency for Hunt and the others, ''But that would be wrong.''

Nixon latched on to that. ''That's not bad,'' he said enthusiastically.

But Nixon knew he had told Dean he could get a million dollars for Hunt, that the problem wasn't getting the money but finding a way to get it to Hunt. He asked Haldeman how he would answer that one.

Haldeman suggested that Nixon was just feeling Dean out, trying alternatives, exploring options. ''You ask people questions on the basis of . . . to try and see what direction they're going.''

Nixon brightened up. ''It's his word against the President's.''

Then he grew worried. ''I hope to God he didn't have a tape recorder in his pocket.'' (On at least two dozen occasions thereafter, Nixon anxiously asked Haldeman to reassure him that Dean didn't have a hidden recorder.)

Back to ''would be wrong.'' Nixon worried that perhaps he

had said "wrong" about the timing of clemency, not about the promise of clemency or the million dollars in hush money. (History has recorded that indeed he had.)

Haldeman, who had just listened to the tape, inexplicably replied, "No, you said getting the money was wrong."

That is also what Haldeman told the Ervin Committee when he testified. When the tape was finally made available, it was that inexplicable answer that got Haldeman his conviction for perjury.

I have gone into this in some detail to give readers an opportunity to check Haldeman's diaries against the critical parts of the actual transcript of the conversation (on the Watergate tapes made public in 1974) he summarizes in his entry for April 25.

In his April 26 entry Haldeman said that "The question he [Nixon] has is, did the P at that time order Dean to do anything? And the answer is no." This is a quibble, to say the least. Twelve times Nixon told Dean the hush money had to be paid to Hunt. The next day it was paid (via John Mitchell). But it was technically true that Nixon did not order Dean personally to pay over the money.

Later, "[Nixon] questioned me again on whether Dean had any basis to feel that he'd been instructed by the P to go out and get the money and I said no. That wasn't the case." Haldeman did not add that what the P had said was he knew where he could get the money and in the process was not doing Nixon a favor.

By this time it hardly mattered. Nixon had decided to try to save himself by tossing Haldeman and Ehrlichman overboard. He had them come up to Camp David. Haldeman's account of the firing is moving, revealing, infuriating, sad, maudlin, and pure Nixon. With that entry, the diaries come to an end.

Foreword
by H. R. Haldeman

With the inauguration of Richard Nixon as the 37th President of the United States, I became Assistant to the President and White House Chief of Staff. Little did I realize that this would lead me into a major role in the most controversial, tragic, and least understood Presidency in the history of our country.

I did sense that this would be a momentous period in my life and that the Nixon Presidency would be a significant one. I knew that I would be at the very eye of the storm for the next four years—with all the challenges and opportunities of being integrally involved in virtually every decision and act of the President.

When my appointment to the White House was announced, Robert Rutland, a close personal friend and eminent Presidential scholar, urged me to record faithfully in a journal the major events of each day and my thoughts regarding them. He believed that this had never been done by someone working so closely with the President. At the least, my "diaries" would provide a fascinating account for my children and grandchildren; more importantly, they could prove to be an invaluable asset to historians and scholars.

Not fully realizing what this would involve, I decided that the commitment was worth the effort, and for the next four years and three months, I did maintain a daily diary. Initially, I wrote in a bound journal; later, I switched to dictating onto cassettes. It was not an easy assignment, and it required a tremendous amount of self-discipline to sit down every night and record the major actions and thoughts of a long day.

For safekeeping, as each journal book and tape cassette was completed, I marked it "Top Secret" and placed it in a safe in the office of the White House Staff Secretary. These recordings were not read or heard by anyone, including me, until well after I had left Washington.

On April 30, 1973, as the Watergate crisis mounted daily, the President announced my resignation as Chief of Staff. When I arrived at my office the next morning, I found that it had been secured by the FBI, with orders that I could enter only under their surveillance. I was not permitted to remove anything—including whatever I brought in with me. This order even applied to my personal papers, files, and diaries.

After seven years of legal action, the diaries finally were admitted to be my personal property; however, they had to remain in the custody of the National Archives, where they had been stored upon removal from the White House safe. A negotiated settlement with the Archives resulted in my being provided copies of each handwritten journal book and oral cassette in return for my "giving" the originals to the Archives (which was a little ironic, since they already had them under lock and key).

Because I unofficially marked the diaries Top Secret, they had to be reviewed by the National Security Council for classified national security material. Before I could receive my copies, all entries deemed "sensitive" were deleted. Once in my possession, the copies of the journals and tapes were put aside, and I did nothing with them until almost twenty years after my resignation, when I had them transcribed.

The diaries are my personal record of each day's amazing array of events, conversations, decisions, and actions: an admixture of enormously important and incredibly insignificant matters with which the President, and I, dealt each day. The people involved are intelligent, hardworking and, at times, very human.

As a daily documentation, the diaries "tell it like it is" without benefit of hindsight or foreknowledge. Recorded are my thoughts at the time. Included are actions I would now prefer had not been taken, conversations I would now like to forget or disavow, and opinions with which I now strongly disagree. In the interest of historical accuracy, the content remains unchanged from the day it was written.

Since I now deeply believe that my diaries do, in fact, provide valuable insights for historians, journalists, and scholars, as well as the general public, I have decided to make them public. The full text of the diaries is almost 750,000 words and is a little too much for the average reader. There is an enormous amount of repetition, trivia, and ephemera, and the sheer bulk is unmanageable. Therefore, I have looked for entries which I consider the most significant, insightful, colorful, or simply the most representative of life in the Nixon White House, to produce this book. Nothing has been deleted to hide the truth, painful as it sometimes is. For instance, although the book represents only about 40 percent of the full text, it includes virtually every word I wrote about Watergate. Where appropriate for clarification, I have added annotations. These appear in boxes or italics to distinguish them from the original text.

For historians and those who wish to pursue the subject further, I have also used the technology of CD-ROM to publish the diaries in their entirety, fully indexed and cross-referenced. The availability of the full text on CD-ROM should answer any questions or doubts as to its accuracy or the fairness of the account.

When I originally wrote the diaries, I used initials and acronyms wherever possible. With the exception of the President (P), Henry Kissinger (K), John Ehrlichman (E) and defined acronyms, these shorthand abbreviations have been spelled out in the transcribed text. There are instances, however, when first names are used.

In these pages, the reader is given an overall view of the White House and the Nixon Presidency as seen and felt by the one person who was with the President far more than anyone else during his first term, and who was involved on a broader and deeper basis in all respects. It is my strong hope that this book will, once and for all, put those years into perspective.

1969

First Quarter: January–March

After the election victory in November 1968, the Nixon Campaign Organization wound down its business and was immediately replaced by the Nixon Transition Organization, based at the Pierre Hotel in New York. At that point we had seventy-five days in which to conceive, construct, and implement the entire initial plan for staffing and operating the Executive Office of the President of the United States, which had to take over full operation at noon on January 21, 1969. This task was completed, to the best of our abilities, by January 18. It was time to move to Washington, D.C., and get ready to take on the job ahead. My diaries begin on that day.

Saturday, January 18, 1969
I arrived last night from New York via Presidential Jet Star with all my bags and boxes. Met the family at the Statler-Hilton—all here for the Inaugural. Today went house-hunting with *(my wife)* Jo and settled pretty much on Spring Valley, where Nixon had told us to go. Dinner at Trader Vic's, saw Billy Graham, who had been at the White House last night with LBJ. Johnson told him the Nixon Cabinet was the best in history, with HEW Secretary Robert Finch and Secretary of State William Rogers the stars. He had met and talked with each one separately.

Then to the gala—a disaster!

Sunday, January 19, 1969
Another day of house-hunting, this time with the family and in a White House car. Nixon arrived late afternoon. Concert at Constitution Hall, great success. Nixon looked great, thor-

oughly enjoyed every minute. A great feeling among the gathering crowds. All the old Nixon troops, the new Administration officials, etc. Lots of last-minute "getting ready" at the White House so we can move in with minimum disturbance. Things appear to be pretty well set, all plans working out reasonably well. Larry Higby *(my personal assistant)* really snowed with office assignments, equipment, phones, etc. Tough job for a 23-year old, he's doing great. Rose Woods *(RN's longtime personal secretary)* said she cried all the way in from Andrews AFB, crowds along the streets, triumphal return vs. departure eight years ago.

Monday, January 20, 1969, The Inaugural

Great excitement at the Capitol, Jo and I sat on the platform, first row behind the Cabinet in front of the diplomatic corps. Cold, but no rain. Family all down in front under TV stand.

Most outstanding moment: fanfare, Nixon and Pat Nixon come to top of steps, stand at attention for musical salute. Expression on his face was unforgettable, this was the time! He had arrived, he was in full command, someone said he felt he saw rays coming from his eyes. Great ovation. Then slowly, dignified, down the steps to the front of the platform.

Ceremony very good, address outstanding. So many quotable lines, it will be used over and over. Then "Hail to the Chief" for The President, almost impossible to believe.

Then to Room 206 for signing the first official papers. P, Mrs. Nixon, John Ehrlichman *(Counsel to the P)*, Secret Service and clerk. Nominations for Cabinet and UN. No one had a pen so he used my Pentel to sign them all. Awkward, no one knew what to say. P very pensive, quiet, drinking cup of coffee.

Then luncheon, P with Inaugural Committee, we with Cabinet. Secretary of State William Rogers asked Commerce Secretary Maurice Stans to say grace.

The parade, P exuberant, reacting to bows, bands, floats, greeting VIP's in stand. Very cold.

Then to White House—offices pretty well set up. P to family reception in Mansion. P called me on the phone, I urged him to come to West Wing to see his office, fires in fireplaces. That intrigued him, paused, asked like a little kid "Is the dog there?" (reference to Irish Setter we gave him, not here yet).

The six Inaugural Balls, carried through in fine form. Good

witty speeches, very enthusiastic, friendly, P obviously relishing it all.

And to the White House for the first night.

Tuesday, January 21, 1969

The first day on the job, pretty hectic, family all came to the White House.

Staff reception. P and Mrs. Nixon down grand staircase, "Hail to the Chief" at the landing. Marine Band in hall, into East Room for brief remarks.

Back to the office, papers to get ready. E and I in with P for an hour, general discussion before swearing in of staff.

Staff swearing in by Chief Justice Warren. P brief informal remarks, mainly directed to families of staff. Then lunch with Jo and kids in the Mess *(the White House Staff Mess, a dining facility for the senior staff and their guests)*. Good-bye, family back to California.

At end of day P decided to see his office in EOB, so we headed over with no notice. First took swing through West Wing. Higby led EOB tour. P agreed on the old Vice President's office, after looking it all over and checking out the old *(LBJ's Consumer Affairs Advisor)* Betty Furness corner office. Took tour through first floor, chatted with staff that were still there (7:00).

The Old Executive Office Building (EOB) is right across a narrow closed drive from the West Wing of the White House. P had decided he wanted to have a separate office in that building as a hideaway working office where he would not be interrupted by the constant activity in and around the West Wing and the Oval Office. This tour was to select the specific office suite he would use, and the one he picked was right at the top of the entry stairs and easily accessible. He used this office a great deal for working alone and for small private meetings with staff members, as contrasted to his use of the Oval Office for ceremonial and official meetings.

Wednesday, January 22, 1969

The day started with the Cabinet swearing-in, in the East Room, coffee at 7:30, ceremony at 8:00. I didn't go. Then the first Cabinet meeting at 8:30. P told me at last minute I should attend. Plan was for me to stay out of these, but he felt I had to be there. I was called on for several administrative items near the end. P roared in right on time, announced by Appointments Secretary Dwight Chapin. Took immediate command, and started on the agenda full tilt with no nonsense. The Governors distinguished themselves by their compulsion to talk, whether or not they had anything to say.

> There were several former state governors in the new Cabinet:
> George Romney of Michigan, John Volpe of Massachusetts,
> and Walter Hickel of Alaska, and they all seemed to have
> trouble adjusting to their new status as members of the Cabinet
> instead of chief executive officers.

I was in with P for an hour in the afternoon on myriad of general items, mainly details. He used the little office for a while. I don't think he liked it.

> There was a small office next to the Oval Office along a short
> corridor connecting the Oval Office to the office I originally
> used before moving to my permanent corner office. This short
> corridor also had a bathroom for the P, and a small cubbyhole
> from which a steward operated to provide coffee and refreshments
> for the Oval Office.

Teddy White saw him for an hour, for the final session *(concerning White's current book on the making of the President)*. Then I spent another half hour getting papers signed. Our staff system is working remarkably well, the staff work is in on time and usually right. Ken Cole *(Staff Secretary, responsible for all paperwork and follow-through)* is doing a very fine job. Chapin has yet to get on top of his role, but he's not blowing anything.

This morning I had a fire in my fireplace, and it was a disaster! The chimney didn't draw, and smoke poured into the office. They had to break through years of accumulated paint to get my windows open. Rose was furious, smoke all through the West Wing. Fortunately, I went to the Cabinet meeting and missed it all. Pat Buchanan *(Presidential speechwriter)* had his first meeting with P this afternoon, and discovered when he left after an hour session about press and TV briefings that his fly was open.

Thursday, January 23, 1969

Our first morning staff meeting with P. Bryce Harlow *(Assistant to the P for Congressional Liaison)* and E for about 45 minutes. Mainly about schedule and general operations. P still getting the feel of the whole thing, but remarkably well adjusted.

> For the P, as well as for all of us, life in the White House was like entering an entire new world, although he had been on the periphery for eight years during his Vice Presidency. He stepped right into the role of president with great ease, but it was still a totally different position from that of VP. There were lots of new things to learn every day, and he clearly enjoyed the process.

Then the first meeting of the Urban Affairs Council and the first major breakdown of the staff system. Council Director Daniel Patrick Moynihan wanted the P to sign an Executive Order creating the Council, with pictures, etc. But he didn't pre-staff the order so we ended up with the Council members cooling their heels in the Cabinet Room, while E calmly reviewed the order before approving it for the P.

Friday, January 24, 1969

Interior Secretary Walter Hickel sworn in finally. P had some very good gags. All his own notes. Meeting with Harlow and E, added *(Special Advisor to the President Arthur)* Burns and Paul McCracken *(Chairman of the Council of Economic Advisors)* about procedures for developing programs. Agreed Burns would develop directives to implement his program points by the departments. Also need a Presidential message to Congress about reorganization authority renewal. P ordered all of us to read Burns' book tonight. Very determined to get things moving—wants action. Burns is great, has good effect on P.

Economic Policy group meeting delayed by E, who was held up at the Mansion with Mrs. Nixon, and was late to P's office to review two executive orders, one holding up a CAB route case (major impact, first big decision, E sat on couch in Oval Office imperturbably reviewing the papers while P, determined to be at Economic Policy meeting on time, fidgeted) and the other formalizing the Economic Council, which became the Cabinet Committee on Economic Policy. The order had been drawn at the last minute because this Committee wanted same status as Urban Affairs and *they* had an executive order.

P ready for haircut tomorrow, but worried about the White House barber, wanted to know if he really did LBJ and JFK, did he really have full instructions from the P's California barber, etc. Finally set appointment for 3:00 Saturday.

P came up with the idea of a writer type in each major meeting to do a memo for his file on the tone and flavor of the meeting, and to consult about what to say to press and how to get follow-up mileage.

Wants all ambassadors to resign *(as a means of making all posts available for new Nixon appointees)*.

Discussed procedure for press-conference preparation. *(Briefing)* book to P 6:00 Sunday.

Saturday, January 25, 1969
Six and a half hours of NSC *(National Security Council)* with break for lunch. The first haircut turned out fine. P says Martini is the best barber yet. I took huge stack of letters down to barbershop *(located in the basement of the West Wing of the White House, just down the hall from the Situation Room),* he signed during haircut, after calling Harlow to ask how to sign letter to Congress (RN, Dick or Richard Nixon). Liked the barber so much he invited him to church tomorrow.

President received beautiful silver cigarette box from Bob Gray. Presidential seal and name on top, date on front, plays ''Hail to the Chief'' when lid lifted, *most* appropriate! Flap in the early morning about Mississippi tornadoes. President called me at breakfast, wanted some action. We released a statement and I called the Governor to tell of President's concern. Can't declare a disaster because requirements not met.

P wandered into my office and around to others to see what everyone was doing. Stopped by Press Secretary Ron Ziegler's office on way up from haircut, during briefing, P spoke to press, said he'd had his first press conference as VP in this room, so maybe Ziegler will be president some day.

P met my new Deputy Assistant, Alex Butterfield, briefly, for first time. Rather awkward. Will take time to develop.

(National Security Advisor Henry) Kissinger was *very* enthusiastic about the way P handled the NSC, K is really impressed with overall performance, and surprised!

Sunday, January 26, 1969

The first White House church services. Very, very impressive. People all seated in East Room at 10:45, organist playing. Then piano solo. Then Mrs. Nixon, Tricia, and Mrs. Graham entered from front of room, all stood. A little more music. Then President and Billy Graham and soloist George Beverly Shea entered. All stood. President to rostrum for brief opening remarks. Graham conducted service. Lots of kids. White House phone operators. Most of Cabinet. Short reception in State dining room after—coffee, juice, and rolls.

Chapin and Alex and I took tour of mansion in the afternoon when President and family went out for a short drive.

In the evening I took the briefing book to President in his bedroom. He was sitting by the fire with papers all around, doing his homework.

Monday, January 27, 1969

The first press conference. Staff group met at 7:30 in Cabinet Room (Buchanan arrived late, and then sat in the P's chair). I presided. Two hours of discussion, developed an opening statement (which he did not use) and added seven or eight Q&A's to the book. Small group (E, Harlow, chief speechwriter Jim Keogh and K) met with P at 9:30. Supposed to be a half hour but they stayed until time for press conference.

P *very* tense at opening, but loosened up and did great job. Excellent reaction from all sides.

President changed his schedule and went early to the Pentagon, had lunch with Defense Secretary Mel Laird before briefing.

Formal call by Dean of Diplomatic Corps, Sevilla-Sacassa. His entrance was hysterical. Stood at rigid attention in doorway of Oval Office, clicked his heels, boomed out "Mr. President!" then went rigid again, with all chins trembling. Stood that way until P moved forward and broke the spell. Then came in with big abrazo.

Long discussion about Europe trip plans. P feels must go

early before Vietnam problems set in and Paris talks bog down. Didn't like the picture of himself that's all over the Defense Department. Too severe.

Pushing for action, wants a barrage of messages to Congress, one a day for 20 days. Wants a plan of what we'll be doing. Wants decision on whether to give State of Union, or not. Advisors divided.

Wants people meeting with him to bring their staff people in with them when appropriate. Wants Chapin to send the girls in with messages, etc., so he sees more people on the staff more often.

Still loves every minute, and shows it all the time.

Brought the new dog in for a preview visit. P pretty awkward about how to handle him, basically embarrassed.

Tuesday, January 28, 1969

Formally presented the new dog, King Timahoe, in Rose Garden after Leaders Meetings, they all watched. Rose and I brought Tim up to P, press all there. Lots of gags about picking him up by the ears *(as LBJ once did with his beagle)*, housebroken, etc. P explained Irish origin of name.

Visit to the House of Representatives. First, small group in Speaker's office, then on to the floor, long ovation, then members lined up to shake hands.

Meeting with Atomic Energy Commission Chairman Glenn Seaborg, who is very concerned about report about new discovery that nuclear bomb can be made much more easily than had been believed. No one knows this yet, Seaborg has only told members of the AEC. Could have enormous effect on world power balance if smaller nations find out, because would give them potential for nuclear capability without need for stockpile of uranium, etc., as previously believed. Also long discussion about Plowshare and peaceful use of atom. P very interested in this, asked lot of questions. Wants to go forward fast on peaceful uses.

Wednesday, January 29, 1969

Staff meeting, mainly concerned with getting out reaction to Inaugural. P wants PR staff to read incoming mail and get a feel of what the people think and what they react to. Is afraid they *(PR staff)* are too much influenced by the columnists, should read and react to people, not columns. Don't get out of touch. White House provides almost total isolation from the real world. Need to know what moves and concerns the average guy. Must not be overbalanced by Washington reaction.

Furious when he discovered there are *two* prayer breakfasts tomorrow. Long tirade about self-promoters, etc.

Had Tim in the office, both of them pretty nervous.

King Timahoe, an Irish setter, was a gift from the White House staff. It took Nixon and Tim quite a while to adjust to their new life together. Neither one was quite sure how to handle a dog in the Oval Office, but it all worked out well.

Disaster of the day was a leak by Communications Director Herb Klein about the European trip, made the headlines in the *Star* tonight. Came out of a backgrounder breakfast. Herb, of course, denies the quote. Strangely, P not too upset even though he's been very concerned about keeping the trip a secret.

Visited the Senate, and the State Department. Both great successes according to all reports.

Thursday, January 30, 1969

Busy day, the two prayer breakfasts first. (Bob Finch said P was best he had *ever* seen him. I told the P later, and he laughed it off, said he had just given them some "church stuff".) Then the astronauts for a picture and announcement of *(former astronaut)* Frank Borman's goodwill tour. Then a CIA-State meeting. Then appointments, K, Max Fisher (wants to be head of Jewish relations and handle that whole area), Science Advisor Lee DuBridge with heads of National Science Foundations (they were ecstatic afterward and especially impressed with P's understanding and genuine interest).

Finally got Alex in for several sessions. P pretty awkward with stranger there, but tried to cover it up. He's not very good at that.

P really handles new people well, i.e., the NSF group. Knows just how to lead them on and establish rapport. Build their interest.

This skill in handling new groups is in stark contrast to his awkwardness, mentioned above, in having a stranger sit in on meetings with others. One of many interesting contrasts in Nixon's nature.

Friday, January 31, 1969

Staff meeting with Ehrlichman and Alex. President called me in about the day's schedule. Upset about visit to reconstruction site. President did reconstruction site visit (great press) and trip to Pentagon, returning at noon. Had long session about schedule and called Kissinger and me in. Started by shifting schedule and personnel responsibilities regarding State from Kissinger to me, to get Kissinger out of trivia. Lots of problems today. President takes them on one by one, no sweat.

Great show as three ambassadors arrive to present credentials, troops along South Drive, trumpeters fanfare from balcony. P went out on porch to watch departure. Had Tim in the office, can't get him to come over by P's desk, he's trying dog biscuits, no use.

Long session with Harlow to schedule meetings with congressmen and senators. P still groping to find orderly schedule plan that he likes. Also covered some appointment problems, reviewed mail signing procedure, he goes back and forth on how much mail he wants to do. Problems with Rose, not in on things, and the Pat Nixon staff bitching.

Diplomatic reception in the Mansion at 9:00, white tie. P's entrance spectacular. All guests in East Room. Color guard goes up to second floor, precedes P and Mrs. Nixon down stairs and into Cross Hall with band playing processional. P like a little kid, or a wooden soldier, arms stiff, trying not to look as tickled as he obviously was. Stands behind colors in Cross Hall, is announced, "Hail to the Chief," follows colors into and through East Room to Green Room, where he receives. P really ate it up, as at all ceremonies. He loves being P!

Saturday, February 1, 1969

NSC this morning. Then a session with K about the *(upcoming)* trip to Europe.

Session in afternoon with K and Harlow, mainly about ambassadors and key appointments. Upset by press reports that he's not changing people, especially in State. Ordered me to

have resignations of all non-career ambassadors and all LBJ political appointees on his desk Monday. Said he'll write them and
"accept the resignation with pleasure." Feels we haven't done
enough to get in good new people that are ours. He's right.
Problem is need to deal with Democratic Congress, and P isn't
tough enough with his Cabinet officers. Won't *make* them fire
incumbents and/or take our political recommendations. Ehrlichman now in charge of this, we'll see how he can produce.

Included me in stag dinner at Mansion, 8:00 black tie. Bebe
Rebozo, Hobe Lewis, Jimmy Crosby, Bob Abplanalp, Bob
Finch. Tour of second floor after dinner conducted by P. Gave
all historical highlights, thoroughly enjoyed himself. Remarked
tonight is "just our close friends—all six of them."

At the dinner P frequently returned to the subject of thought-
fulness and appreciation toward the "little people," i.e., house
staff, drivers, etc. Great contrast from the LBJ family, who
gave rise to all kinds of tales about their terrible arrogance.

> This point on the LBJ family reflects constant comments we
> heard from all levels of the permanent White House staff peo-
> ple regarding the way they felt they were treated during the
> Johnson years.

Talked about astronauts' comment that the mood of the
White House was so different, that they felt really uncomfortable when there with LBJ. He (Johnson) was in a "black
mood."

Sunday, February 2, 1969
Church at the White House. Bigger crowd. P added 100 seats.
Includes House and Senate leaders and White House drivers
and guards.

P came over to office after lunch, cleared up papers, called
me in to talk about Key Biscayne plans, Bebe there too. He
wants to go down this coming weekend, but only two days
available unless we can clear Monday. Also wants to go the
following weeks. Then immediately starts trying to think up
excuses and covers. He's constitutionally unable to say he's
taking time off, has to appear he's working. Said, though, that
LBJ told him he spent one year of his five in office at the
ranch. Also DDE *(Eisenhower)* told him to take time off. He

just can't bring himself to do it. We'll keep trying. Then he starts worrying about whether Ziegler has gotten out the story of how hard he's been working, long hours, etc.

> Nixon felt that he should not ever appear to be taking time off from the job for relaxation or rest. We were therefore required to provide evidence of constant ongoing activity on the P's part, and in most cases there *was* almost constant activity because of the P's preoccupation with his work. This viewpoint did change somewhat over time as more and more people advised him of the necessity of not working all the time.

Monday, February 3, 1969

P called tonight very upset by column quoting Klein that we'll be relying heavily on polls. This problem is always with us. P most anxious to avoid any appearance of being like LBJ.

P backed off on his threat to Rogers to accept all ambassador resignations (non-career) today. Did sign a few, put off the rest. Has E working directly with Rogers, and making some progress.

Still trying to get Tim by his desk, dog biscuits are starting to work. P decided to use the pool today for the first time, and had me get him a size 36 bathing suit, and a bathing cap because the barber told him the chlorine was bad for his hair. We got three of each. Also had Chapin's office get a supply of dog bones and a water dish, etc.

Tuesday, February 4, 1969

Day started with a problem. He thought a tape from his house dictating machine was blank, but it turned out to be all right.

Concern about oil quota and Maine free port. Wants to get it out of Hickel's hands and back to White House.

Decided after talk with CIA Director Richard Helms to visit CIA as well as AEC. Feels agency and department visits have been *very* productive. Amazed no president has done it before (except for official ceremonies).

Also, got to tossing dog biscuits around the office for Tim. One hit the grandfather clock.

Strange problem with Agnew, who's hired LBJ's top advance man as an administrative assistant. No one seems to be able to dissuade him, the guy has turned out to be a total spy, has all the inside poop, etc.

Wednesday, February 5, 1969

Afternoon free for preparation for press conference. P couldn't get right to work on it though, came into my office, then to Rose's, to try on six pairs of new shoes. Got the briefing book at 2:00 and started to work about 3:00. Left for dinner at 6:30, back at 8:10, still there when I left at 10:45.

E and I had knock-down with VP, about his staff and office facilities. Hard to get anywhere. Afraid we made things worse, and that it will have to go to P. VP has no concept of P's view of how he should handle the role, and I don't think he ever will. Real problem about his hiring LBJ advance man. He sees no reason not to, and apparently intends to buck us all the way.

P also upset because VP got into act at legislative Leaders Meeting and sided with Congressmen vs. Postmaster Red Blount and the P. *(P planned to take the Post Office out of politics and turn it into a nonpartisan corporation.)* Just doesn't get it yet.

Thursday, February 6, 1969

Morning preparation for 11:00 press conference. Another coup. Big concern about ABM *(Anti Ballistic Missile program)*. Laird had halted program, announcement in press (leak), but had not discussed with President or NSC, and had not included this fact in his departmental Q & A material. President got a question on it and had to toe-dance it, which he did very well, but not very happy about it afterward.

Met with Pennsylvania Governor Shafer, who came in loaded with two huge color pictures for P to sign. Had a bundle of things he wanted, and got most. P very inclined to agree with whatever these guys propose, may become an enormous problem. Someone has got to be in all meetings, if only to shortstop Presidential commitments.

Met with Congressman Teague about Santa Barbara oil in the ocean. *(P)* overreacted again, ordered troops, stop drilling, pull out all stops. Called John Mitchell and asked him to "bend the law" to permit Hickel to order halt (it was done).

Friday, February 7, 1969

The busiest day yet for sheer volume of activity. All before 5:00, when we took off for Key Biscayne. Left by helicopter from White House back lawn, pretty exciting. Poor Tim scared to death. Called me in near end of plane trip to say he wanted *no* special cars flown to Europe, and the Secret Service detail cut way down. Doesn't want to look overprotected. I spent the day getting decks cleared for Key Biscayne trip. Had long lunch meeting with Ken Cole and Larry about operation of our group. Problem is how to keep work, people, and calls away from me and handled by others, and how to avoid the feeling or the fact that people can't get to me. Also need to improve our internal communication.

Saturday, February 8, 1969

Key Biscayne, beautiful weather and almost a day off! Spent the day relaxing, went out for a short boat ride, says he slept two hours last night and another two hours on the beach today. P *very* relaxed, great humor. Impressed by fresh flowers in all rooms of his house, realized need for this kind of weekend off, and especially the need for sleep.

President signed his first bill today, House Joint Resolution 414 appropriating extra funds for ex–Federal employees. I kept the pen. We won't announce it until tomorrow because Ziegler has "the lid on" for today.

Sunday, February 9, 1969

(*At Key Biscayne*) Bebe called to say P wanted me and Dr. Walter Tkach (*White House physician*) to join them for dinner at 9:00, but I was to come over then (7:00) to go over some things.

Drinks until almost 10:00, when we ate. Then cigars and coffee in living room, and talk until midnight. Discussion of daily schedule for P. He's interested in working out best plan, his primary goal to eliminate as much sleeping time as possible. Agreed to try daily nap after lunch, plus swim, sauna, sun lamp and osteopath at 5:30. Doesn't think it will work.

Fascinated by Tkach report of people who need no sleep at all. Hates to waste the time. Acutely aware of the necessity of being sharp all the time. Feels, though, that people take breaks to avoid the problems and decision, not because they need rest. Thinks you have to be "up," not relaxed, to function best.

He's thought a lot about this and is pretty firm in his views. States no feeling of value of vacation or rest, but realizes that he probably has to have it.

Tuesday, February 11, 1969

Usual bits and pieces in the morning meeting. Problems with signals on his Menzies dinner last night. Served just champagne when should have had cocktails, 12 in black tie. Also was in family dining room upstairs, so Pat Nixon and Tricia trapped in their bedrooms. Wants the best decorator to do EOB office, etc.

Another pretty heavy day, but some time to kill at the end; he wandered into my office as Larry and I were talking and fireplace was backing up and smoking. Asked me to take him to K's office, we walked in, startled the secretaries and interrupted K conference with the German Ambassador. P joined them. Late night for me, stacks of paperwork, talked with Alex about system. Have to work it out.

Wednesday, February 12, 1969

P called Moynihan, Finch, Burns, Harlow, and me in at end of day for long discussion of OEO *(Office of Economic Opportunity)* and welfare. Did masterful job of forcing them to move to direct action instead of studies. Will announce next week moving Job Corps to Labor and Head Start to HEW. Determined to show action, be different. At one point Burns said "just one word of caution," P quickly said "not too many!"

Thursday, February 13, 1969

Each morning K and I start with breakfast to rework schedule and plans for *(upcoming European)* trip. Quite a project.

P told me to have *(Presidential Assistant Robert)* Ellsworth seated next to Rogers at dinner so Bob could make some hay about NATO. Plan is to appoint him ambassador. I talked Rogers into it yesterday, but he's not really sold on it.

I spent another day haranguing Cabinet officers about firing people. Went pretty well. Also got most of backlog cleaned up. Have started evening staff meetings with my crew, soon as the P leaves for his swim. Should help. Will try to set routine, and then get P to let me use the pool, massage, sauna, and sun lamp.

Friday, February 14, 1969

P pushing at staff meeting for plans to get things rolling. Wants weekly program with plan for major event every day, especially now a major legislative proposal every day. Game plans instead of reaction.

More discussion of Presidential action about campus disorders. Feels Congress will overreact, and we should get the jump with our own plan.

Later, family, Julie and David, Tricia and Pat Nixon, all came over to office, P discussed decor, etc., lots of advice, all conflicting.

Saturday, February 15, 1969

Big item was meeting planned for Monday with the Soviet Ambassador *(Dobrynin)*. Problem arose because P wanted me to call Rogers and tell him of meeting, but that Ambassador and P would be alone. I did, Rogers objected, feeling P should never meet alone with an ambassador, urged a State Department reporter sit in. Back and forth, K disturbed because Ambassador has something of great significance to tell P, but if done with State man there word will get out and P will lose control. Decided I should sit in, Rogers said OK, but ridiculous. Ended up State man and K will both sit in, but P will see Ambassador alone for a few minutes first, and will get the dope in written form. K determined P should get word on Soviet intentions direct so he knows he can act on it. May be a big break on the Middle East. K feels very important. *(In fact, at the meeting, Dobrynin did indicate a willingness to move ahead on several fronts. Soon, K and Dobrynin had set up a private channel for meetings.)*

Sunday, February 16, 1969

P at Camp David this morning. We met with Williamsburg people about redecorating West Wing. They're very interested, and P wants them to go ahead. Idea would be to get good authentic reproductions in all staff offices, antiques in Oval Office. Redo Fish Room, Cabinet Room, etc. Also debated whether to change my office with Dwight's. Hard to decide which is best.

On return P came to office to work on briefing books. After getting them all spread out, and his briefcases open on the back table, he called me in and said we should have thought of this as a good picture possibility. So we called in photographers. He had called me earlier from Camp David about story in *New York Times* saying Secret Service was shipping bulletproof cars to Europe. He has *ordered* no cars to be sent, and was upset. Later had E come in (just home last night from Europe) to discuss this. John talked him into using our Secret Service cars with communications, but not the bulletproof ones. He's determined not to create image of oversecurity.

P came back to office after dinner, walked into my office, sat down, and chatted about California summer White House possibility, P *very* interested. Also the Williamsburg decorator idea, he thinks it's great and says to go ahead.

I left at 8:30, P still in office poring over briefing books. This week will be a tough one because he'll really want to concentrate on getting ready. Glad I'll be gone.

Monday, February 17, 1969
Lot of talk about demonstrations on the trip. P wants E to hold backgrounder, and explain we expect them, but are determined not to let a few dissidents get in the way of the imperative need to communicate.

Friday, February 21, 1969
P still wants to do something about campus disorders problem. Said to have *(conservative speechwriter Pat)* Buchanan work on it independently of *(Presidential Speechwriter Ray)* Price, who's doing radio address. Also very anxious to get out letters about Job Corps and Head Start to *(Labor Secretary George)* Shultz and Finch to demand *changes.* Kept returning to these points during the day and into the evening.

Also got cranking on political problem. He's obviously concerned about reports (especially Buchanan's) that conservatives and the South are unhappy. Also he's annoyed by constant right-wing bitching, with never a positive alternative. Ordered me to assemble a political group and really hit them to start defending us, including Buchanan, *(White House aide John)* Sears, Harlow, E, *(Legislative Liaison Assistant Bill)* Timmons, *(Legislative Liaison Assistant Ken)* BeLieu, Ellsworth, *(Political Affairs Assistant Harry)* Dent, *(Cabinet Secretary John)* Whitaker, Ziegler, Klein, *(Staff Assistant Bud)* Wilkinson. Will meet tomorrow morning.

P planning dinner for Duke Ellington's birthday, wants to

have "all the jazz greats, like Guy Lombardo"—oh well!

P wants me to hold regular staff meetings like Sherman Adams did, feels we need the participation level raised in the staff. Probably right, but I hate to do it.

P came into my office in the evening to chat about the California residence possibility. He's very interested and I think he'll go ahead.

Saturday, February 22, 1969

P pushing hard for student statement, decided finally to release a letter to *(Notre Dame President)* Father Hesburgh. Also annoyed that positive Republican response unit in Congress is not working. No good reaction to OEO move, electoral reform, etc. Harlow slipping on this.

P spent most of the day on the briefing books again. I had to interrupt a number of times with things to be signed. Noticed one time that the book he was diligently studying was a hardware catalogue open to the section on shower heads.

Cloud on the horizon. DDE having problems with intestine. They were going to operate, but decided not to, because they are afraid he'd die on the table. Talked to P, he decided we'll abort the *(Europe)* trip if and when anything happens. Truman also has been ill, but is apparently OK now.

Have everything pretty well cleared up for departure tomorrow. Looks as if I'll have a fairly free ride on the trip. Others have everything under control.

Sunday, February 23, 1969

The high point of the day was Haldeman's disaster. The P's helicopter was scheduled to depart the White House lawn at 7:28 for Andrews—then departure ceremonies—then take off at 8:00. I ordered a car for 7:00 since we (staff) were due at White House at 7:20. Set my clock for 6:30 and went to bed.

In the morning my signal phone rang and woke me up from a dead sleep. It was the garage asking if I still wanted my car to stand by. I looked at the clock—it was 7:30. I frantically leaped up, still in a daze, and started throwing clothes on. The phone rang again at 7:31. *(Military Assistant)* Don Hughes from the helicopter asking where I was. Told him I couldn't make it for at least five minutes and to go ahead without me. He said he'd send another helicopter back for me—in five minutes.

I finished dressing, slapped on some shaving cream and gave a quick once-over with the razor, ran down to the car, and headed for the White House. En route, driver said they had an escort ready to drive me out to Andrews, we checked on radio to confirm helicopter and canceled escort. It was snowing—slushy type.

As the car drove up the South Drive, the helicopter was just landing on the lawn. I jumped out, ran to helicopter, the door opened, Marine saluted, I sat down, door closed, we took off. Fastest helicopter takeoff I've ever seen. Barreled to Andrews, landed by Air Force One, Honor guard was just dispersing. P was aboard. I ran up rear ramp into P's cabin, they closed the door, and we took off. Airborne at 7:58, less than a half hour from when my phone first rang. Naturally, everyone was in great state of glee, although all were most understanding. P just said good morning as I walked through his cabin.

P worked all the way, mostly alone, a little with K and Rogers. K very impressed with P's complete grasp and understanding of briefing materials and the fact he had drawn his own conclusions—contrary to those in briefings.

Arrived Brussels precisely on time at 9:00. King Baudouin and many dignitaries on hand. Fairly large crowd of students (?) on roof of terminal chanting in French. We thought they were unfriendly at first, especially when they kept chanting all through National Anthem. But they stopped when King and P spoke, and cheered both. Then they reviewed the troops.

At the end of the line of troops a lovely white tent had been erected for the VIP reception. After return to hotel, P went to bed but not to sleep. Staff stayed up working on schedule and speeches and cards for tomorrow. As I walked out of Hughes' room at about 2:15 AM, P opened his door across the hall, in his pajamas, and asked me to get the speaking copy of his address to NATO tomorrow. I just happened to have it in my hand, having just picked it up from Rose, and handed it to him forthwith, which dumbfounded him. He stayed up, sitting in bed working, until well after 3:00 AM, as I took in several schedules, etc., that he wanted.

Monday, February 24, 1969—Brussels

I slept in, the P left at 9:00 for NATO. I guess it went well, although K felt he was too verbose in his responses. He stayed ½ hour beyond scheduled time, so was late for Tomb and

Palace. *(A wreath-laying at the Tomb of the Unknown Soldier and an "intimate" lunch with the King and Queen and 100 others)*

I went to airport with K and *(my travel secretary, Elmer)* Juanich for a special meeting in plane (only secure area). Very interesting discussion about important future possibility—can't be identified until later.

> This meeting on Air Force One, parked at the Brussels airport, was so secret at the time that I was afraid to say anything more than the above entry, even in this highly secret and protected diary. At the meeting K, his deputy, Al Haig, and a Pentagon planning officer worked out guidelines for a proposed plan for bombing North Vietnamese sanctuaries in Cambodia. P had decided on the plane to Belgium to order this bombing as a response to the North Vietnamese countrywide offensive that they launched the day before we left. I was not normally a participant in this sort of meeting, especially in these early days of the Administration—but in this case I attended in place of the P because it was felt he could not attend himself without attracting attention—and he and K wanted someone present other than the military planners.

Then departure ceremonies at the airport and we're off for London, with the lost time made up.

Arrived on time at Heathrow, met by Prime Minister Wilson and military honors. P left direct from airport with Prime Minister to Chequers for dinner. Too foggy to use helicopters so had to drive.

Beautiful hotel accommodations. Real old-fashioned elegance. Lovely suites, huge bathrooms with directly overhead showers, monstrous tubs, heated towel racks, bidets, etc. Great service and real style. I am in part of the P's suite, with a separate hallway, bedroom, sitting room, and bath. Great!

Feels like we're in an armed camp. Threats of demonstrations in Grosvenor Square have brought out more police than even New York produces, many of them on horses, all unarmed. Group of us, with State Department officials, had dinner in hotel dining room, then went out to scout demonstrations. Pathetically small and ineffectual group, contained in a little square, totally surrounded by police who outnumber them at least 50–1.

They are shouting and will be a real problem for sleeping if they keep it up. This is going to be a problem from here on, I guess.

P arrived about an hour late *(from dinner with Prime Minister Wilson),* got into the hotel with no problem, and the demonstrators all dispersed. Now we're left with just armies of cops.

He called me in to review the trip so far, was in his pajamas. Made point that two major purposes of trip are: 1) to establish with the free world leaders a clear picture of Nixon as the leader and 2) to present to people of United States the clear picture of Nixon as free world leader and so accepted. Thus far he's sure accomplishing this in fine fashion.

> The next several days saw a whirlwind of meetings and ceremonies with British leaders in London, German leaders in Bonn, and Italian leaders in Rome. All went well at all official stops, the crowds were enthusiastic, and we were little troubled by demonstrators for the rest of the trip. At one stop in Berlin, for instance, my diary notes "The antidemonstrations never materialized. Perhaps because of the huge numbers of police. There was one group of Maoists (we were told) with anti-war signs and somewhere someone threw a brick that hit Dan Rather. But this was really insignificant against the overall day."
>
> The highlight of the trip was our visit to Paris.

Friday, February 28, 1969—Paris

Arrived in midafternoon. De Gaulle very cordial. Greeted P in English which is very unusual. Usual ceremonies, only the French do it with more style. De Gaulle, in welcoming speech, referred to his people's and his personal pleasure with the statesman the American people had selected as their leader. P responded with very warm words, about American relations with France and ended with "Vive la France." De Gaulle started to applaud at English version, then waited for translation.

On drive in from airport, many police, as everywhere, all roads completely cleared in both directions, kind of eerie. Huge motorcycle escort. A few people along the way, but not many. Went directly to Quai D'Orsay, beautiful palace and lovely quarters. I have a corner room, blue cloth walls, white and gold trim, huge room, high ceilings, great chandelier. Bathroom is also a corner with huge windows. Big bathtub with rack holding sponge, Chanel soap, and thermometer. Really luxurious living. Also an array of French cigarettes and a beautiful leather holder with Cuban cigars.

Left shortly after arrival for Arc de Triomphe. While waiting for departure *(US Ambassador to France, and Kennedy brother-in-law)* Sargent Shriver introduced me to Foreign Minister Couve de Murville, and we had quite a chat. Drive down Champs Elysées was disappointing to me, not very many people, and even less enthusiasm. Quite a contrast to Berlin, and even to Rome. A few hecklers along the way, the police really pounced on them. Barricades on all streets and lots of police.

Ceremony at Arc went well, usual routine. Then P went to meet with de Gaulle. E and I went to Embassy to do some business, then back to Quai. Apparently meetings went well, P in great spirits when he returned.

Tonight may well have been his finest hour. At de Gaulle's dinner, the General's toast was warm, eloquent, and way beyond the need of protocol. The P's response was absolutely superb. He really built up France and de Gaulle in beautiful style. I was seated next to Madame Billotte, wife of the General who was de Gaulle's Chief of Staff during the war. She said at the end of dinner that she felt we had seen the making of history tonight, and she was quite overcome and most sincere. It would appear that at least a giant step has been taken toward the principal goal of this trip.

The dinner was the best of all. The French seem to handle things the best of any country we've visited. Eighty-eight were at the one long table, small orchestra in the wings for dinner music. All guests at their places, then de Gaulle and P made their entrance with music playing. Very impressive.

Before dinner we assembled in the salon. The two Presidents came into the next room, we went in one by one, announced with title, to meet them, then into next room for drinks, champagne, port or martinis. After dinner they first served liqueurs, then trays of orange juice and grapefruit juice, then champagne. Only two hors d'oeuvres before dinner and those very skimpy (there were none in Italy or Germany).

Beautiful palace courtyard entrance, guards with swords at salute, red carpet up steps, etc. I sat between Mme. Billotte (above) and Mme. Lucet, wife of the Ambassador to the

United States. Both spoke perfect English, but I had an interpreter (pretty young girl) who sat behind me all through dinner—and before and after. Would have sure helped last night in Rome.

Saturday, March 1, 1969
We left the Quai by motorcade (after breakfast in State Dining Room) for Versailles. All the roads en route completely closed off in both directions, and uniformed guards at attention every fifty yards, the entire way. Also many plainclothesmen along the route and scattered back through the woods, especially in Bois de Bologne.

Arrived at Le Grand Trianon, met at steps by de Gaulle. He and P went right in to start their talks.

P didn't get back to the Quai until after 6:00, so put in a nine hour working day, before the U.S. State Dinner at the Residence. Then left at 7:45 for the dinner. K says that talks went extremely well and that our mission is accomplished.

The big issue now is the Berlin blockade. They lowered the gate, and so we are now sending extra convoys down the autobahn at an increasing rate to call their bluff. We are prepared to fight our way through if necessary. Four convoys got through today and we're sending eight tomorrow, and then 100+ vehicles on Monday. The point is to build up our average daily volume, so if there is a civilian blockade, we'll have a higher level of allowable military traffic which we feel they will not try to cut off.

The East Germans had threatened a new Berlin crisis if the West Germans held an election for their new President in West Berlin. The Soviets refused to allow the East Germans to create a crisis, however, so they basically made a pain of themselves by blocking the autobahn and conducting joint maneuvers on the border. They also stopped some shipments from going across the border, calling them "military goods."

As for the future possibility referred to in Brussels, it has had to be called off because State will not accept responsibility, and risk otherwise is too great. K very disappointed.

> This refers to the plan for bombing Cambodia which was developed at the Brussels airport. While it was, at this point, called off, it was later implemented.

Dinner at the Residence worked out pretty well, but there were too many people (about 80) for the house to handle comfortably. Toasts were again very warm and considered very significant. De Gaulle said this visit had increased his admiration of P—if that were possible. Interesting to watch Eunice Shriver last night and tonight, she obviously hates seeing Nixon as President. She talked to herself and winced all through the toasts, both nights, and must have been thinking back to JFK. His visit here was all ceremony and no substance. But it was a great show and made an indelible impression. Tomorrow we leave for Rome (a meeting with the Pope), then home.

Sunday, March 2, 1969
(After fascinating morning meeting with the Pope and Vatican staff members), trip home was uneventful. P slept a little but spent most of the time talking to Rogers and staff. Some of us tried the bunks, they're pretty good.

Colorful arrival ceremonies at Andrews, with Cabinet, Congress leaders, troops, etc. Poor Agnew slipped on the icy runway during troop review and smashed his nose. Then went on TV to introduce P with huge cut on nose bleeding profusely. Then helicopter to White House.

Couple of sidebars: K's great delight in finally "one-upping" Hughes by asking him during troop review at Paris if his "bag of gold" got on the plane all right. K's reaction to announcement of Apollo shot tomorrow, "Well, I'm not going." K's note to Ziegler at some meeting that said, "Don't worry, they're taking the speakers in alphabetical order." Henry swings from very tense to very funny. He's getting into the swing of things pretty well.

Wednesday, March 5, 1969
Long staff meeting with E and Harlow and Alex this morning because P involved with NSC. Decided on some major changes in operations. Will start daily staff meetings of all top staff, for a half hour in morning, to see if we can solve com-

munication problem. Probably will shift fairly quickly to Monday, Wednesday, Friday. Also agreed we need a czar for domestic like K in national security and decided it should be E. Now have to implement.

Spent lot of time with P as he floundered through the day. Letdown from trip and press conference has set in. NSC was about all he could handle, he canceled a couple of appointments. Was rambling on about lots of trivia, wants Lincoln portrait over fireplace instead of Washington, discussed plans for EOB office, staff odds and ends.

Came up with idea of going to Manchester, New Hampshire, on March 12, anniversary of New Hampshire primary.

Still worried about PR side, thinks we need another man to propagandize while Ziegler handles straight briefings.

Got great telegrams reacting to press conference last night. But thinks we don't adequately get out the story.

Good meeting with Rogers Morton. Pepped the P up with his enthusiasm. He needed it. Decided to walk around at EOB, see people. Dropped by Klein's offices and the writer group. Looked at his space again, and said to go ahead with plans for redecorating.

Friday, March 7, 1969

P presented his first Congressional Medals of Honor today. Ceremony in the East Room, with the Marine Band, families, etc. He did a marvelous job of personalizing the presentation, and broke from the script to have the families each come up for a picture afterward.

Sunday, March 9, 1969

E and I to P's *(in Key Biscayne)* at 10:00, long two hour talk on his personal finances, the California property, and a few brief notes on business. K called me early in *great* distress because Rogers had reversed United States policy in his talk with Dobrynin yesterday. K feels it is disastrous and is really upset, but will spend today developing recovery plan and come down tomorrow to see P. K feels the policy question is so serious that if continued he'll have to leave. Can't preside over destruction of Saigon government. Feels we have great chance to take hard line and Rogers gave it away. Spent rest of the day in the sun and sailing. Tough.

> K felt that Rogers had given Dobrynin the stance that the U.S. wasn't fully backing the Thieu government, by alluding that we would stop the private talks with the North Vietnamese. K also felt this would lead to the destruction of Saigon, and was against current policy.

K called to say had canceled Sunday strike *(the Cambodia bombing)* and *(Deputy Defense Secretary David)* Packard very disturbed, wanted to call P, feels we're wrong, should go ahead. K will figure out recommendation and call P this afternoon. Rogers still opposed and he reflects establishment press view. K feels better to be clobbered now by *Times* etc. if it will help end war sooner. He thinks it will. Rogers is right about immediate reaction, but not for long haul. Have to do it before starting private talks.

Monday, March 10, 1969
Still in Key Biscayne. K came down this morning to meet with P. K and I had talk first. He is still very upset about the Rogers/Dobrynin meeting because he feels Rogers, in reversing our policy about private talks with North Vietnam about political matters as well as military, has seriously jeopardized our negotiating ability and our chance to end the war. Especially bad because it follows right on their shelling of Saigon, and at a time when Soviets are in trouble with China at the border.

I suggested he try to turn this to advantage by a maneuver designed to totally confuse the Soviets, and he thinks this may be possible. K agreed not to raise with P the question of his leaving. The matter at hand has to be settled on its merits, then if he loses he's got that one additional move. Real problem is his conviction that Rogers' self-interest is so paramount that he can't adequately serve the P. K suggests only solution is to put Rogers in as Chief Justice. Too bad this situation exists. I feel K is basically right, and don't know how he'll handle it to his own satisfaction, but there must be a way.

Tuesday, March 11, 1969
Well, the first crisis appears to be building. ABM decision will be tough.

> P felt that the construction of an antiballistic missile defense
> system was a crucial bargaining chip in the forthcoming Soviet
> arms control talks. The doves hated it, though, and many mod-
> erates were disturbed by the cost. It was shaping up to be a
> real donnybrook.

He has to go ahead from defense viewpoint but pressure
against is enormous and growing under great pressure. Du-
Bridge was in today to argue scientist's viewpoint that small
increase in defense doesn't justify huge expenditure and popular and political risk. Harlow has advised P that Congressional passage is in real doubt, and will require all-out battle
on part of P. Question whether he's really willing and ready
to fight.

P urged me to cut schedule back as much as possible to give
him time to talk with key individuals, instead of meetings and
trivia. He's realized it's tough. Plans now for a Friday morning
press conference to announce decision. Even canceled NSC
for tomorrow. Part of problem is Congressional receptions
every night that cut into working time.

Hard for P to stay on the big issues, he keeps hacking away
at PR concerns, especially in the domestic program area. Moynihan points out that he *can't* have a Domestic Program. Not
any money available, and politically impossible anyway. Better just to try to get rid of the things that don't work, and try
to build up the few that do.

Wednesday, March 12, 1969
Big flap about proposed Ambassador to Canada. Turned out
to be a guy P had met in '67 in Argentina. He was Ambassador
there, and Nixon stayed at residence, he left anti-Nixon liter-
ature and Herblock cartoons on bedstand. So now P has
blocked this appointment, or any, for this guy. Shows how
things can come back to haunt you.

Thursday, March 13, 1969
Started out badly. P overslept and didn't get into the office
until after 9:30. Immediately buzzed for me to raise hell because the press conference briefing book (due at the Residence
at 8:00 last night) had not arrived, but was on his office desk.
I had blown it by going out to dinner with Higby before Buch-

anan brought over the book. Pat just left it on my desk, assuming I'd be back, and it was still there in the morning. I explained to P. Then he discovered he had 10:00 appointment with *(AFL President)* George Meany (which he thought had been canceled). Then there was the problem of the Labor Manpower statement which he refused to approve and ordered rewritten, with hardly any time left. Then he had to meet with Laird (just back from Vietnam) and put out a wire to the astronauts (after deciding not to phone them). All this when he *thought* he was going to have the day free to prepare.

When this was finally all done, about 12:45, he buzzed and told me he was not to be disturbed for the rest of the day. We left him alone. Did go in once to give him Bryce's message from DDE (Bryce had been summoned to the hospital) that he totally disapproved of ABM and urged no deployment. This after I'd been chewed out in the morning for giving him *(Special Consultant Len)* Garment's anti-ABM memo (didn't want arguments after decision made).

I had a key staff meeting in the afternoon to "game plan" the whole ABM reaction program. Assigned contacts, etc. Fascinating to see scope of what we have to cover to lay adequate groundwork for using our support and blunting the opposition. Tension fairly high as everyone realizes explosive potential of the whole issue. I think if we handle it right we'll come out OK, but this is clearly the first tough test. P is concerned and edgy, but I'll bet he brings it off well, although it will be a pretty unpopular decision.

Friday, March 14, 1969

Today was ABM day, finally! P started with bipartisan Leaders Meetings to give them the background. Then an hour of preparation, then the press conference at noon. P had heavy afternoon of appointments and was obviously pleased with his performance. The tension of the last few days was gone and he was really relaxed and cheery. At one point I got in for fifteen minutes to check quickly on a couple of items, and in that period he signed at least 20 to 25 commissions, nominations, etc., and talked to five congressmen to thank them for their ABM support, and approved the whole plan for the California trip. Really amazing what he can accomplish when he really cranks, vs. the usual time-wasting. And he was great on the phone, hitting exactly the right point with each guy.

Sunday, March 16, 1969
Another day off, more or less. Took Jo to White House Church
Service, then some time in West Wing with the Williamsburg
people about decorating. Then off for a little more house-
hunting before the ladies' replay of the Gridiron. Then from
there to White House for surprise birthday party for Pat Nixon.
Beautiful party, she was really surprised. Made grand entrance
with family to what she thought was stag party. Had all the
close friends, receiving line, dinner at round tables in State
dining room. Highlight was Singing Strings during dessert,
then toasts. As P started first toast after cake came in, Pat said,
"Wait until I blow out the candles." Tricia and Julie arranged,
and it worked out very well!

Monday, March 17, 1969
St. Patrick's Day. Received Irish Ambassador in Roosevelt
Room.
    Historic day. K's "Operation Breakfast" finally came off
at 2:00 PM our time.

> This was the working title for the Cambodian bombing oper-
> ation that had been set up at the airport in Brussels, then turned
> on and off several times in view of new developments. The
> final decision was made at a meeting in the Oval Office Sunday
> afternoon, after the church service

    K really excited, as was P. Early reports only that it was
underway.
    Still can't get a P statement about campus problems put
together. Widely varying views within staff. Also great confusion in trying to get volunteer program squared away. Poor
E has to untangle all this and Arthur Burns is now driving him
nuts, as he did me (and still does).

Tuesday, March 18, 1969
K's "Operation Breakfast" a great success. He came beaming
in with report, very productive. A lot more secondaries than
had been expected. Confirmed early intelligence. Probably no
reaction for a few days, if ever.
    Tough (posthumous) Medal of Honor ceremony when a
mother broke down, and so did everyone else. Apparently P

closed formal remarks with typical Nixon very personal remark that did it. Hughes had to come into my office to recover.
P furious with press for taking pictures of her.

Wednesday, March 19, 1969

P had tried to start his ''clear Wednesday'' policy today, but
we had to load in a batch of appointments this morning. Afternoon *was* clear. Problem with giving the P free time is that
he hauls me in for hours on end, about four total today. Lots
of little details, and the two always present big ones, ABM
and budget. Plans to hit the Cabinet hard tomorrow on budget
after *(Budget Director Robert)* Mayo's briefing, P will call
executive session and really push for cuts. He's particularly
bothered by Finch, because he's apparently not cutting at all.
Feels most of the others are at least trying.

Romney really stirred up, wants appointment, but P won't
see him until his volunteer program is fully worked out. Poor
E has to handle and George ain't easy. Is reaching the crisis
stage, with threats of quitting, etc.

Long discussion about ABM battle plans. P feels we aren't
really organized to push it through. Wants a complete plan.
He's right!

Then on to need for a domestic program, the other of the
week's big three problems. E promises the raw material for
review on the plane to California, but I think we're a long
ways from what P wants, i.e., a specific legislative program.
According to Moynihan, this is neither feasible nor desirable,
time now to consolidate, not to innovate. But Congress pressures (and the columnists) for action, and P reacts.

Planning to take more time off, per the last advice from
DDE. Hope he does it.

Thursday, March 20, 1969

Cabinet meeting, mainly to hit them on the budget. First a long
briefing and discussion about ABM. Laird briefed, then P got
into quite a dialog with various members. He went a bit far in
his desire to convince them that we have very valid reasons
for the decision and revealed a lot of highly classified information about pictures. I interrupted and pointed out the nature
of the material.

It was sometimes a problem for P to sort out in his own mind
the various levels of classification of the information he received. This was perfectly understandable because he was the
constant recipient of all sorts of information from all sorts of
sources. Much of it was classified material, and much of that
was classified at the highest level of secrecy. When P got into
a heated or intense discussion of some issue, he occasionally
used highly classified material to make his point, without realizing that his audience at the moment was not cleared for
this level of secrecy. This, in effect, declassified the material,
much to the consternation of the "keepers of the flame" of
national security.

Main thrust was that we have to have real military superiority and defense as a base for negotiations. P stated flatly that
war will be over by next year, but that it must be understood
that next four to five months will be very tough because we
have to take public position that outlook is tough, etc., while
we negotiate in private. Rogers said his answer to criticism
that we have no planned strategy is that we do have one and
that it is that we will not tell anyone what it is. Based on
position that the only productive negotiations are the private
ones, and as soon as we tell anyone about them, they're not
private.

Still a stir about Domestic Program. Not organized right yet.
Burns and Moynihan both feel strongly that P not putting
enough time or attention on this and that nothing will be settled
until he does. I think they're right. This morning he flatly
rejected Head Start and Job Corps proposals without even really reading them. Just wants them changed—or preferably
abolished.

P comments to Cabinet, about the need for military strength
as a basis for successful negotiating, the intellectuals are all
opposed to this approach, "It's only us nonintellectuals who
understand what the game is all about."

Monday, March 24, 1969
Trudeau arrived via the "inclement alternate" because of rain.
*(Inclement alternate refers to having to use the North Portico
of the White House for State arrivals instead of the South
Lawn.)* P had called me at home three or four times last night

about assignments for State dinner, to change from round tables to "E" *(formation)*.

Doctors say DDE failing fast, probably go today or tomorrow. Family has been called to hospital. Tricia and Julie are going to go over.

A few periods of sort of spare time. He called me in and just kind of chatted. Complained in a way about some speech material, but in a very understanding way. Pretty mellow. As he left in the evening, he said, "Well, I have to go rest a little before tonight's ordeal *(the State dinner)*." Actually I think he'll really enjoy it.

Flap with Chapin over lousy staffing of proposal for P to drop by NAB meeting tomorrow. I overreacted as usual, but we do need to tighten up.

Tuesday, March 25, 1969

5:00 meeting with Devine's dissident GOP congressmen *(Samuel L. Devine was a conservative Republican congressman from Ohio)*. P opened with 35 minute oration on the office, emphasized priorities, first, settle the war; second, establish law and order; third, stop inflation and settle the economy. Said P must concentrate on these, can't worry about all the little side issues. Pointed out that if these settled, all else will be well, if not, nothing will be well. Got into long discussion of OEO and poverty war, determined to change it, and so committed.

E and I had a knockdown with Arthur Burns at lunch. Pretty bitter discussion, still didn't settle the problem of getting a domestic program. Burns determined to run the show, but it's obvious he can't manage. Tough one for John. P later said again E has to ride herd on this, because Arthur will never get it done. We're at a period of internal dissension. Bryce is worn to a frazzle and so is Burns. John and I are probably pushing too hard, as a result of P pushing on us. Need to get back together, but hard to do when everyone is tired and edgy.

Friday, March 28, 1969

This was the day Dwight Eisenhower died.

The morning was occupied with details and an NSC meeting. The afternoon had been left clear for personal time. P had me in quite a while before NSC, mainly on wanting to take stronger action on obscenity. Wants to move ahead with Justice on strong program, fast. Even decided he'd go to a play in New York where they take off clothes, and get up and walk out, to dramatize his feeling.

After NSC, at about 12:20, he went into Oval Office with Mel Laird. 12:25, I had just stepped out into the hall, ran into Tkach who said DDE had died. The two of us went into the Oval Office through the hall door. I went on in. P was at his desk, Laird in chair at the side. Laird started to say something, P asked if he'd heard Tkach, he hadn't. P told him. Both were quiet for a minute. Then P started talking about some funeral details. He then got up, said to have Rogers, Harlow and K come in, then stood looking out the window. I told Chapin to get the others. P then started to cry, just standing there. Then he walked slowly, still crying, into the little hall, stood there and sobbed, said "He was such a strong man," went into little office for a few minutes. Then came back into Oval Office, others were there by then, standing awkwardly. P still had tears, and red eyes, talked with them aimlessly then sat on the edge of the desk, half crying and described in detail his last visit to DDE. Harlow commented on how DDE has seen all his checkpoints, the nomination, the election, the wedding *(of David Eisenhower and Julie Nixon),* the Inaugural, the P's success and John's *(his son's)* appointment as Ambassador. So he could go freely now. Rogers by now also has tears.

Things then turned to plans and arrangements. P decided to go right to hospital to see Mrs. Eisenhower. Then found Pat Nixon had not been told, so he called her. Also talked to Tricia. Asked others in room to go with him to hospital. Had to wait until public announcement, at 12:45. Then we left. I rode in staff car. Pat Nixon and Tricia with P. Some people on streets, but most didn't know yet.

At the hospital I stayed downstairs and used the time on the phone about arrangements. Set up details about timing, plan for Camp David this afternoon, guests for funeral, etc.

I rode with Nixons on the way back. Pat Nixon strongly opposed going to Camp David, but P firm and had me argue for it. Swung Tricia over. Not Mrs. Nixon!

Back at White House all regrouped in Oval Office for further discussion about foreign visitors, and overall plans. Some confusion, but all pretty well organized. No way to know how many coming.

Interesting sidelight, before going to hospital had to sign

proclamation, etc.: Debate about which day for official mourning. P had previously decided on Sunday. Others argued for Monday. So I changed the proclamation *after* he had signed it, and had him initial the change.

Also we decided, and P approved, to let employees off for balance of day. Later found there's a law that prohibits P giving time off in honor of death of former government official. Got around it (after the fact) by using basis that DDE is five-star general and died in office since it is a permanent rank. So we're legal.

At Camp David, P took me into Aspen *(cabin at Camp David)* for brief tour.

This was my first of what were to become many visits to the Presidential retreat at Camp David in the Catoctin mountains of Maryland. Weekends at Camp David became a regular presidential routine when we were in Washington. This beautiful, rustic facility is a Navy base, with all the needed communications and services backup for the P, and was an ideal spot for the P and his family to relax or work in comfortable quiet and seclusion. It also turned out to be a great place for the senior staff to work uninterrupted by the many diversions that inevitably arose at the White House.

Asked to have barber brought up (on chopper with Bebe). Then settled down, and I left for my cabin.

He called me over to give him the texts of the proclamation, etc. Talked for a few minutes about arrangements. He was in sport jacket, sitting by the big window. Fire crackling.

He called Julie, at the White House, to ask about time of TV specials. Mrs. Eisenhower was there and came on phone. Thought P was in his office. When he said he was at Camp David, she said that was Ike's favorite spot in the world and she was so glad the P was there. P explained he was working on eulogy, and wanted to get away. They had a fairly long and good chat, which obviously affected him emotionally.

Sunday, March 30, 1969
The first Eisenhower funeral day. Dawned bright and sunny at Camp David. Chapin and I took *long* walk after breakfast around whole camp perimeter. Brisk, cold, a little snow left

from last night. Lots of exercise (bowled four lines yesterday afternoon with Chapin and Chuck Larson and the Camp Commander). Then Chapin and I had a long talk about operations, people, etc.

P slept fairly late, then worked with Ray *(Price)*. Feeling better but still obviously under the weather. Chopper back at 1:00. Brief spell in office.

Left in P motorcade at 2:45 for National Cathedral, streets cleared, light snow, dreary. People all along way. Impressive ceremony to bring casket out of cathedral into hearse. I rode in second car behind P, with Tkach and Ziegler. Ahead of P were 15 Eisenhower family cars. Motorcade back to Washington Monument, stopped there to change to caisson. Lots of people on all the streets. No great sadness, mainly appeared to be curious. *Lots* of cameras. Impressed by many who saluted P car as it passed (flags on bumpers, with black streamers above). Constitution Avenue was jammed for cortege route.

Someone really screwed up on schedule, ended up one and a half hours late. Allowed no time for getting into and out of cars, and motorcade was a mile long, all the heads of state, Cabinet, etc. Arrived at Capitol for another impressive ceremony as casket carried up steps. Great hymn, 21 gun salute, poor bearers had tough job on steps.

P very good on eulogy in rotunda. Read it (had called me this morning to be sure he had lighted podium). Hughes said he broke down in hall after leaving rotunda. The whole thing has been pretty tough on him, topped by not feeling well.

Monday, March 31, 1969
The second Eisenhower funeral day. The official day of mourning. General de Gaulle arrived at ten for his appointment. Semiformal arrival, no troops on the drive or trumpets, just a cordon at the diplomatic entrance. The P met the car at the driveway, they posed for pictures briefly, de Gaulle gave the signal to move, and they went in for the meeting. It lasted almost an hour, was scheduled for a half hour. Just barely got de Gaulle out the drive before *(King)* Baudouin *(of Belgium)* arrived.

Same arrival ceremony for the King, and in for his meeting. Both of these scheduled today because they can't stay until tomorrow.

Then on to the funeral. Picked up casket at Capitol, with

full honors, drove to Cathedral, full honors, good service, back out, full honors, to Union Station, full honors, and on to train. P had no part except to move along, at the back of the motorcade. I again rode in staff car. I was right there at every step of the way.

Back to White House just in time for reception. We did a good job of organizing and it went very well. P received heads of all delegations, about an hour, then went upstairs for private meetings with key people who aren't coming in tomorrow. Mme. Ky was spectacular in purple outfit; Russian Marshall equally so in his uniform with rows and rows of ribbons. De Gaulle came and was first through the line. He stayed until the P went upstairs, but left that instant. Stickler for the "right" thing. Battle of striped pants went on, State Department-types wore theirs, P didn't.

P pretty tired, but in good mood. Taking all this in stride. Tomorrow will be tough.

Second Quarter: April–June

Tuesday, April 1, 1969
Chiefs of State day. P came in late, and buzzed. E and I went in, reviewed quite a few things right up to 10:00 when the first visitor was due. P spent the whole day until 6:30 seeing the main heads of state that were here for the funeral.

E came in at 7:00 (P was due then at house for dinner with Don Nixon and his daughter), to report on problems with Don Nixon. Don Kendall had spent half the day on this. Don Nixon still holding out for more dough, plus extracurricular earnings and fees.

Don Kendall, head of PepsiCo, had agreed to provide suitable employment for the P's brother, Don Nixon, as a favor to P. As has often been the case, the P's brother found it difficult to live in the limelight and shadow of his brother and Kendall was trying to help alleviate this problem.

Wednesday through Sunday, April 2–6, 1969
Palm Springs and Key Biscayne. *No* contact with P for the entire period. E covered through Friday night, Harlow through the weekend. Good break. P had whole family down for the weekend. Big domestic policy meeting Friday, apparently quite successful.

This was the Easter period, and a chance for P to get to Florida for a few days of needed rest. I took advantage of the opportunity to join my family, who were still in California. They

did not move to Washington until after the end of the school
year in June.

Monday, April 7, 1969
Wants to write off the senators that oppose ABM, i.e., Percy
(Illinois), Goodell *(New York),* (already written off Javits) and
Congressman Mac Mathias. E suggests way to ''get'' Percy is
not to let him be chairman of his housing foundation.

Press trying to build up idea of internal feud: E vs. me. Hard
to sell, but Evans and Novak giving it a try, to great glee of
some White House Staff. I think we'll shake down into better
defined roles, but don't feel that is really necessary. We have
excellent rapport now and move in and out of overlapping
areas with no real problem.

Long session tonight with Larry and Chapin about Haldeman image. They're concerned by Evans and Novak, and other
adverse publicity, feel we need to get our line out, and that I
have to move more into public eye. Problem is to define first
the exact view we want to project. They had some good ideas,
had put in a lot of time and thought. Also Bill Safire working
on general suggestions. Probably do need to do something to
avoid letting the ''von Haldeman'' concept become firmly en-
trenched.

Tuesday, April 8, 1969
Biggest challenge at the moment is the ABM. Apparently P
has decided not to fight all-out. Strange. He told me in some
detail of the importance of not getting too overinvolved in each
day-to-day problem. Should not feel each issue is life-or-death
matter, need long range perspective. All on staff feel battle is
vital, and should not drop to P's idea of letting us lose in
Senate and then winning in conference. They feel this is first
battle of '72, vs. Teddy Kennedy, and we *must* win. So I've
set up project groups with Alex as coordinator. Main trouble
at the moment is Bill Rogers' constant public undercutting of
Administration position, and unclear line. We'll see what we
can do.

Wednesday, April 9, 1969
NSC this morning. P arrived late at office, 8:40, and E and I
went right in as he came in the door. He looked annoyed, said

he had some things to do, so be brief, then we couldn't get the meeting to end.

Some discussion of ABM battle, and question of best platform for P. He feels strongly that the press conference is overall the most effective, and a set speech to an audience at a banquet is the least. The "5:00 Group" basically agreed.

> The "5:00 Group" was an informal collection of staff members who met on a regular basis to review general PR matters and make recommendations for action.

We had quite a discussion at staff meeting about ABM, and Alex is trying hard to get battle plan set and going.

Late afternoon P called me in, kind of rambling, he'd spent a lot of time clearing up paperwork and had read Buchanan's memos about party needs, and wanted some actions taken as a result. Then E came in and there was some general discussion. We went into Cabinet Room to look at jewelry giveaway samples.

> One of the peculiar customs in the Oval Office is for the P to give his visitors souvenir mementos of their meeting. These range from ballpoint pens imprinted with the Presidential seal and/or signature to fairly elaborate pieces of jewelry, i.e., bracelets, tie clips, etc.
>
> A constant source of amusement for the staff was the P's awkwardness in making these presentations, which required him to go around to the front side of his desk to get the desired item from a drawer. He clearly never felt at ease in this process.

Monday, April 14, 1969

Lot of appointments and meetings. Went to Pan American Union for OAS meeting, brief speech. Decided as we drove away to go see the cherry blossoms at Jefferson Basin. Good touch. P and Pat Nixon got out of car and strolled along the path. Really surprised the tourists and the police. We only had one escort car, they had to radio for reinforcements, including the mounted park police, who galloped alongside the car.

P finally has agreed to need for policy to stay on top of

public attitudes. Wants a quick reading now, overall and on specific issues. Will work out a plan with Derge, via the RNC *(Republican National Committee)*.

> David Derge was the poll taker used by the WH, with funding by the RNC, to provide ongoing polling data as requested by the P. As noted above, it took some persuasion to convince P of the importance of getting this information on a regular continuing basis in order to keep in close touch with general public reaction to ongoing events.

ABM planning meeting this afternoon, P has committed now to fighting the fight, and will work on individual senators where needed. Plan was okay with him, but needs a lot more work.

Have agreed to put *(former advance man and scheduler Nick)* Ruwe in overall charge of White House social events. Should help pull this together.

P had *long* session with bipartisan Congressional big 8 about budget, which goes up tomorrow. Released domestic message today. Not nearly the reaction we'd hoped for, at least initially.

K about to launch another project. Started last Friday with program of mining Haiphong to look tough. K meeting tonight with Dobrynin to say we'll take only one more try at settlement, then will have to move. Putting two month deadline on results. Really tough move. K very impressed with P's guts in making this hard decision. Also P sent *really* tough memo today to Laird and Rogers, about need to back Administrative position and importance of loyalty to decision once made. Again K surprised he'd take this hard line.

K so pleased with his plan, like the earlier one, that he can't resist telling someone outside his shop, so he goes over it with me.

Tuesday, April 15, 1969

> An unexpected crisis started on this day. North Korean jets shot down one of our Navy reconnaissance planes, with 31 men aboard. The plane had been outside their territorial waters, so we were plainly being tested. But how to respond?

Koreans shot down our plane, gave K a big issue for the day. He wants to bomb the airfield where the MIGs came from. P agrees, thinks we need to show strong reaction. K also worried that this louses up our mining operation temporarily, because it will look like reaction to this.

Cabinet meeting, with wives for first time in history. Pretty dull session until P's windup for a half hour at the end. He followed the budget presentation and did superb job of explaining to wives what their husbands had to go through, and in the process, what a load he has to carry. Then gave his pitch about patience on Vietnam. Did say hoped we would have it over in a few months. Indicates he has some real faith in K's plan. About civil rights and equal opportunity, P said don't expect any credit for what you do, or any real PR gains, just do what is right and forget it. Also he warned them press would attempt to build up stories of internal divisions, etc. Said must keep perspective and don't worry about it.

Wednesday, April 16, 1969

The plane shot down by Korea dominated the day. P had NSC in the morning, followed by long session with K, Laird and Rogers. Later in afternoon another with the same, plus General Wheeler. Trying to decide on United States course of action. P almost has to retaliate in some fairly strong fashion.

Thursday, April 17, 1969

Main thrust is on the Korean incident. Building up to first really major decision, whether to retaliate. K told me after meeting with P that we would bomb the North Korean airfield at noon on Monday, and move in four carriers, plus a lot of other strength. He's uptight on this, Rogers opposing as usual. K furious because Rogers doesn't openly oppose, just stalls for time then takes steps to make strike impossible, i.e., refer to UN.

Fascinating problem. Only two viable alternatives. Bomb airfield or not retaliate but continue reconnaissance flights but with fighter cover, or, of course, do nothing but protest. Argument for bombing is show of real Nixon strength, especially to Soviets. Problems are public and world reaction, and possible danger of opening a Korean ground war or air battle. Will be a very strong move, dangerous, but potentially very productive toward ending Vietnam. Would sure back up K's earlier conversation this week.

(Later), as I was getting in the shower, K called to talk about Korea, and make sure he had my opinion accurately. I'm for the strike, but with the caveat that we have to know what we'll do, and be willing to do it, if the North Koreans counterattack South Korea by air, or open up a ground attack.

We talked over the alternatives again. This is really tough for K, because the risk level is enormous and he is the principal proponent. He feels strongly that a major show of strength and overreaction for the first time in many years by a United States P would have an enormous effect abroad, and would mobilize great support here. But it would sure lose the doves and might screw up the ABM battle.

Friday, April 18, 1969
K in to go over Korean plans. Then buzzed me in again, long chat about Korea mainly, exploring alternatives, weighing risks. He's determined to make a big positive move, but *not* convinced this is the best time and place for *us*. Knows that if we don't retaliate in Korea we'll have to either find another similar incident in three to four weeks, or go with Operation Lunch *(the planned follow-up to Operation Breakfast, the initial bombing program)* in Cambodia. Feels relative gains and risks may balance better for us there. No decision, but I'd bet now *against* Korea strike, reversal of last night's view.

Saturday, April 19, 1969
P came in late, canceled meeting with K and NSC group because decision already made, *not* to go ahead with Korean plan, primarily because all his advisers are opposed. K called me at home early in morning to discuss this, and his general concern that P had been let down, and thus had failed to make a strong decision at opportune time. But K had also come to the conclusion P could not go ahead.

(P) had me in for quite a while in the morning, just to talk. Reviewed decision and reasons. Real problem was risk of second war, which public wouldn't buy. Also felt reaction to incident was so mild that people didn't want, or expect hard retaliation.

Decision now to go ahead on Cambodia on Tuesday to provide necessary show to Soviets to back up K's talk with them.

P well recognizes K's thesis that a really strong overt act on part of P is essential to galvanize people into overcoming slothfulness and detachment arising from general moral decay. K feels this was ideal time and place, P concerned that it's not. That an act related to ending Vietnam war will be better accepted than one that risks another land war, which this does. E took this view and P said, "So you've sold out to the doves too."

It's been a tough period, and P has moved with total command and self-assurance, while thoroughly canvassing and probing alternatives. I think he's now fortified to move very strongly on next incident, and has learned a lot from this one about our weaknesses. Especially in area of lack of military contingency planning and readiness, i.e., we couldn't strike back for five days because we didn't have enough force available, and no plan.

K also really fed up because military had no plan and spent all the decision time arguing what planes to use, in interservice rivalry, and Rogers spent Friday morning lining up a golf date for Friday afternoon. K also plans to force whole range of contingency plans. So some good has come out of it.

P rather surprised by first wave of telegrams after press conference. They were strongly disapproving of his lack of positive steps to retaliate.

Sunday, April 20, 1969
Left for Camp David yesterday afternoon. P invited Mitchells to dinner at Aspen and the rest of us for movie later. Saw *Dr. Zhivago*. Strange to sit in room with leader of free world and Commander in Chief of Armed Forces and watch the pictures of the Russian revolution, Army overthrow, etc. We all had the same thought.

Wednesday, April 23, 1969
Several discussions about how to handle Cabinet officers. Volpe wants regular monthly appointment (also wanted Secret Service protection) and Agnew wants regular weekly appointment. P says we have to have a Sherman Adams *(Eisenhower's Chief of Staff)* to handle this and keep them away from him, so E and I are it, divided, I take big four, he takes rest. P said he can see why all presidents want to be left alone. The routine baloney really bores him and annoys him.

Decided Burns should explain to Agnew how the Vice Presidency works.

Friday, April 25, 1969

To Camp David at 4:00, Mitchell and J. Edgar Hoover as guests. All of us at Aspen for dinner and movie. Talk centered around all the bad guys "they" have infiltrated into everywhere, especially State. Hoover full of hair-raising reports about all this, plus terrible problem in the courts, etc. He is a real lobbyist, and never quits. And never hesitates to chop everyone else in the process.

VP called just before dinner and said had to talk to P. He took the call. Later called me into bedroom to report, furious, that all he wanted was some guy to be Director of Space Council. May turn out to be the straw that breaks the camel's back. He just has *no* sensitivity, or judgment about his relationship with P. After movie we were walking home and P called me back, again to ponder the Agnew problem, and that of general area of Cabinet relationships. He's not really sure how to handle. His instinct is to be very distant and unavailable, but people tell him he needs more contact and this bothers him, because he thinks he may be handling wrong. Real problem is that none of them except Mitchell really knows how to relate to him.

Monday, April 28, 1969

Got into a deep discussion of welfare, trying to think out the Family Security decision, with E and me *(welfare reform had been one of P's campaign issues)*. P emphasized that you have to face the fact that the *whole* problem is really the blacks. The key is to devise a system that recognizes this while not appearing to. Problem with overall welfare plan is that it forces poor whites into same position as blacks. Feels we have to get rid of the veil of hypocrisy and guilt and face reality.

Pointed out that there has never in history been an adequate black nation, and they are the only race of which this is true. Says Africa is hopeless, the worst there is Liberia, which we built.

Tuesday, April 29, 1969

A day full of little appointments, but still quite a little free time in between, especially during the noon break. Called me in several times to talk about position about student disorders. Became clear he was toying with the idea of using this as the subject of his Chamber of Commerce appearance this afternoon. He was completely disenchanted with the suggested remarks prepared for him, so felt he had to do his own, and has been anxious to speak out again about students, because things have gotten much worse and more widespread since his last statement.

Net result was that during noon break he tried out his ideas on me, I made some suggestions, and he hit it hard at the Chamber of Commerce. Great success with the audience, and P got a tremendous reception. Made very clear case, government must not get into running institutions, students have right and need to express dissent and we should listen; but they have no right to use force, disrupt campus, threaten violence and carry weapons. When they do this, faculty, administration, and trustees (my addition) must have backbone to stand up against this kind of action. Afterwards he was quite pleased. Had taken the press by complete surprise, and got terrific coverage. Had a long talk about it in office, trying to analyze whether this is a good technique. It was.

Tonight was the Duke Ellington seventieth birthday dinner at the White House. Unbelievable. High point was Duke's sister, who came down the stairs with him and the Nixons, in long flowing blonde hair. Duke kissed all the men twice, on each cheek (mother's kiss) as they went through the receiving line. Party ended after 2:00 AM.

Wednesday, May 7, 1969

I ended up with six pages of notes on follow-up for Defense luncheon, Arthur Burns' latest problem, some ambassador possibilities, Mrs. Doyle *(an interior decorator hired by Pat Nixon)*, the need to investigate foundations (he's fascinated by the Fortas case, has found from Mitchell that he not only took $20,000 fee, but signed contract for $20,000 for life and his wife after that, shocking), possible appearance at Building Union meeting next week.

The previous June, LBJ had nominated Associate Justice Abe Fortas as Chief Justice of the Supreme Court. Shortly there-

after, various financial and potential conflict-of-interest problems surfaced, and the nomination was withdrawn. Fortas
would soon resign from the Court.

Huge Burns flap because he didn't get in to see P about two
sentences in "hunger message." E kept him out so he came
to me, then wrote long memo to P. Feels if he can't get in
when he wants to he'll have to quit. No more need for him.

Sunday, May 11, 1969
Rockefeller was late for his meeting, so I went over at 10:00
for yesterday's canceled Schedule Meeting. Nothing very important, but P had obviously been doing a lot of general thinking about planning his time. Feels we haven't adequately
weighed priorities in each week's schedule (problem is, we do,
but then he cuts schedule up by changes, and we get screwed
up while trying to regroup).
   Has decided to go with peace plan announcement on
Wednesday evening, either as statement, or press conference.
K all stirred up because he thinks Hanoi may be folding, has
had some feelers. Also problem because Rogers wants to announce the peace plan, instead of P, also wants to modify.
   We are canceling all possible schedule through Wednesday
to allow time for preparation. He's really preoccupied with
this. Hope it works.
   Came back to DC from Key Biscayne on the Airborne Command Post, and they staged a briefing and a test exercise. Pretty
scary. They went through the whole intelligence and operational
briefings, with interruptions, etc., to make it realistic.

The Airborne Command Post is a Top Secret aircraft facility,
which is on constant ready standby for the use of the P in case
of a national emergency requiring his immediate evacuation
from Washington. It is fully equipped with everything P needs
to conduct his official business and to function as Commander
in Chief, and can stay in the air for a relatively unlimited
period by refueling in air.

Fascinating plane, with command room setup, all kinds of
communications, display boards, rear projection, etc. Took P
a while to get into the thing (his mind was on the peace plan),

but he finally did, and was quite interested. Asked a lot of questions about our nuclear capability and kill results. Obviously worries about the lightly tossed-about millions of deaths.

Tuesday, May 13, 1969

Another supposedly clear day. Started with GOP leaders, mainly about the draft message sent up today (should do some good with students); then UAC *(Urban Affairs Council)* had Ralph Abernathy *(President of the Southern Christian Leadership Conference)*. Pretty ridiculous. He brought six, or eight, of his cohorts and read a long list of demands. Tried to trap P into meeting with the rest of his group, or ordering Cabinet officers to do so. No luck. P handled beautifully. Abernathy went out and stabbed us on TV. Proved again there's no use dealing honestly with these people. They obviously want confrontation, no solutions.

Despite the best of intentions, these efforts at establishing communications with the black leadership were rarely successful. They usually ended up, as this one did, with the black leaders using the White House forum as a platform to attack the P and his policies. The meetings themselves tended more to confrontation than communication. This was unfortunate.

Rest of day pretty clear. Very relaxed at 5:30 called E and me in. Great humor, quips etc. Think he feels this is a good week, with some strong news stories, especially Vietnam peace plan for tomorrow. He'll read the speech. Lot of discussion about network time, we wanted 10:00, they wanted to give 8:30. We won. P feels we should take best possible. Haven't asked up to now. I agree. Pretty fed up with blacks and their hopeless attitude.

Wednesday, May 14, 1969

The Big Speech on Vietnam.

P holed up at the Residence all day, in the Lincoln sitting room, working on the speech. Called over three times—in the morning to say he wasn't coming over, in early afternoon to say he wanted small steaks served at the breakfast tomorrow because "they don't do eggs very well," and in the late afternoon to be sure I had solved the problem of the podium light. (I assured him I had, but later discovered it was still totally inadequate.)

P met with the bipartisan leaders about the speech, in the treaty room. He had a call during the meeting from Chief Justice Warren (I assume about Fortas), who said it was urgent. So P came out of meeting to return the call. A little later a letter arrived from Warren. Can only assume it's the Fortas resignation.

K did briefings all afternoon about the speech. They did some good with the commentators. He realized by late today, though, that we had made a mistake in trying to make a major diplomatic move, requiring checking with other governments, etc., in the form of a TV speech. Instead should have done a paper, gotten it cleared, etc., and sent it. Then go on TV to explain it, instead of presenting it there. Whole thing was too complex with too many nuances that are totally unintelligible to the ordinary guy.

> The basic proposal was for the major part of all foreign troops—both U.S. and North Vietnamese—to withdraw from South Vietnam within one year after a signed agreement. An international group would supervise the process.

Staff meeting this morning was mainly about reaction to Abernathy yesterday. We were had, and now they all realize it. Hope a lesson is learned.

Lunch with E about treachery in the State Department. Reports show all kinds of staffing skulduggery at end of last Administration. We have to figure out a way to get on top of this. Obviously it's all over, not just in State.

Thursday, May 15, 1969
Interesting day after the speech. Started with Armed Forces/Defense breakfast. All top brass and civilians. P gave spectacular speech about America's commitment and world role, and need for true patriotism, etc. Really cranked 'em up. Great consternation, because it wasn't recorded.

Then the Fortas resignation broke, and poor Ziegler was in huge flap between releases from the Court, etc. P really discouraged by whole affair.

Then Cabinet/NSC meeting. P had all key people speak

about last night's speech. All high in praise for the speech and its importance. P wrapped up with a semireplay of the breakfast speech, with more detail on the ''why'' of Vietnam position. Was great, got long ovation (as at breakfast). Then said ''I didn't mean to make a speech to the Cabinet. I wasted that one, and I don't have many.''

K and I both feel last night's TV would have been *much* better if he'd used the morning speech and done the diplomatic stuff by a white paper. But K feels he had to do this one this way, and that in the process he really became his own man in foreign policy.

Discussion about plan for Ohio State speech. Decided to cancel on basis of strong recommendation from John Mitchell and concern of Secret Service about demonstration. Will use plan of having Vietnam President Thieu and Vietnam people come to meet P in California that day and drop OSU.

Friday, May 16, 1969
P in great mood, coasting through a hectic day of bits and pieces types of appointments: session with Mitchell about Court and getting Fortas matter settled. Book closed as far as P concerned, but Justice and Congress to go ahead with full investigation. P feels *(there is)* probably much more than has been revealed.

(Session with) Ross Perot about his ideas on student conference this summer, good guys and key government officials to try to find *positive* answers for a change, and on his buying $50 million worth of TV time to present our story in prime time. Discussion about format, town meeting, telethon, panel, etc. P anxious to do something, not sure what. Perot the same. P pretty reluctant on student idea but said to go ahead, have to try some risks.

Saturday, May 17, 1969
Expected a late start, but P came in at 8:00 raring to go. Had me in for long session about *pages* and pages of little scraps of notes, some must have been accumulated for months.

Had read Hoover's report on bad guys in State and Defense, ordered a few specific ones to be fired or transferred. Wants to get some follow-up on anti-ABM Senators who spoke *for* Vietnam speech, distressed that this had not been programmed (he's putting a lot of thought against ABM battle). Very anxious to follow up fast on Fortas, be sure our story out clearly to avoid Jewish establishment and press reaction, because they are horribly embarrassed and backed against the wall. We acted very responsibly, but aren't getting credit for it.

Had some ideas for decorating the Oval Office, led to a little more discussion about Mrs. Doyle. Afraid we just have to go with her, I won't buck Pat Nixon.

Definitely decided to scratch Ohio State, meet Thieu at Midway. Wants me to handle notifications. Wants receptions in California and Hawaii to show public support.

Presented two Congressional Medals in full military ceremony on South Lawn. Very impressive. Then he went back out to shake hands with crowd. Then kept me in office (almost missed chopper) to go over some more things before leaving for *Saratoga*. Demonstrations on *Saratoga* for Armed Forces Day were spectacular. First we reviewed fleet by air, then landed on *Saratoga*. Had firepower demonstration. Launched all kinds of jets, fighters, bombers, tankers, and intelligence. Chopper from there to Camp David for the night.

Sunday, May 18, 1969

At Camp David. Slept late. Worked for a while after breakfast, then to pool for sun, swim, lunch TV of Apollo X launch. Interrupted by word P was ready to leave. Chopper back to White House. P into office and buzzed me in for two hours. First concern was White House staff. He'd been doing a lot of thinking about feeling that we don't do an adequate job of selling our story. Feels Ziegler is a superb mechanic, but not a designer. He had read all the Sunday papers pretty thoroughly and found just what he had expected and had predicted to K, all comments about his speech were either neutral, or negative. Not one line about the fact that 98% of the foreign press had acclaimed the speech, or the strong positive reaction in Congress. Makes point that if JFK had made the speech they would have all been ecstatic. (Afraid a good part of this is a fact of life, but I'm sure we could do a lot better.)

Real problem, as he says, is that we don't have a real PR operator, at a very high level, who really works at this all day, every day. *(Herb)* Klein and *(Bud)* Wilkinson are both very inadequate, and not *in* enough.

P is reading Patton's book and quoted point that a successful commander has to have leadership and be a superb mechanic, but most important be ruthless in analyzing his staff and throwing out the people that are not up to it. Another quote, that there are more tired division commanders than there are tired divisions, and all tired men are pessimists.

Overall, we just haven't done an adequate job of building up the P, even though the press has been generally good. The accurate story of how hard he works, etc., is not getting out, i.e., about how he wrote his speech. He says the staff are all doing as well as they can, considering their limitations.

He wants E, K and me to try to figure this all out. Says we are the only people on the staff smart and strong enough to do it. Would like to have Mitchell involved also, but feels he's too involved. Hope we can do something.

Thinking about schedule, he feels he should be more aloof, inaccessible, mysterious, i.e., de Gaulle feels overexposure detracts from impact. Shouldn't be too chummy, etc.

Monday, May 19, 1969

Has decided to announce Thieu meeting tomorrow at 10:00, after some debate about coordinating with Thieu. Discussion about procedures, especially about notifying Ohio State, etc. Strange turn of events. Now the big news will be the important meeting, when actually the whole thing came about as an idea for a way to get out of Ohio State because of planned disorders. Will go to Hawaii Saturday, June 7, Midway for meeting June 8 and back to Hawaii. Return to DC nonstop on Monday.

Also has decided on Chief Justice and will announce on Thursday (assuming he'll accept). Even E was caught by surprise. I figure it will be Warren Burger. E agrees.

Lots more talk about schedule and staff and the problem. E and I discussed reason behind this new obsession, both feel he senses end of the easy going and is getting ready to deal with adversities, both internal and external, plus bad press coming up. Is really pushing staff reassessment and more thorough planning of his time.

I think we're in a new phase, or just closing out the first phase. Have really finished the shakedown cruise, now ready to tighten up and handle the big stuff. This seems to be his feeling, and the reason for the intro-analysis. Will probably be some pulling and tugging in the staff. We have a lot of people we could do without. Need to reevaluate the real role of the White House staff. Now try to *do* too much instead of catalyzing, prodding, inspiring, checking others.

Big flap with Arthur Burns on AID *(Agency for International Development)* this time vs. K. Resulted in necessity to postpone bill to Congress until fully staffed. Burns completely end runs the system, but this time K was the reason. His staff system is in bad shape, just not getting the work out, but P doesn't know it, still thinks they're superb.

Tuesday, May 20, 1969

Announced the Thieu meeting at Midway this morning. P really furious because *Washington Post* had leaked the story, especially because our agreement with Vietnam was for simultaneous release. He said he hadn't reacted to other leaks, but this endangered national security and was serious.

He's now banned White House communication: with the *Times* (for their editorial yesterday about the Nixon Foundation related to the Fortas Case and for their coverage on the Cambodian bombings); the *St. Louis Press Democrat* (for Ottenad's inside story on Administration problems, pure phony); and *The Washington Post* (for today's leak). Says won't tell Ziegler or anyone his plan about Chief Justice announcement, to avoid leak.

As last few days, had me in for several long talks ranging over personnel and PR, more of the process of getting ready for what's to come. He's in a very introspective kind of mood. Mad for a little while this morning, then right back on course. Same line of discussion about need for really strong overall PR man, and the TV problem.

While home writing this at 10:00 he just called me back to office "to go over a few things." He was there when I left, but I didn't check out.

It's now midnight, just returned from an absolutely fascinating two hours with the P in the Oval Office. Walked in, he was pacing the floor in blue velvet smoking jacket puffing on a cigar. Said he'd decided to really dramatize the Chief Justice announcement. Move it up from Thursday to Wednesday, and do it in East Room with whole Cabinet, on live TV at 3:00. Have to announce to press at 11:00. I suggested 7:00 for prime time. P agreed. We talked on and on about the new Chief Justice, the plan for announcing, etc. Called Mitchell at the Iranian Embassy to have him come in first thing in the morning to discuss plan. He'll have to speed up his tax and security checks, but says he can. Once again, P comes up with the right answer, after we all struggle with it.

He rambled on about the kind of Justice Burger will be, etc. Had me bring in *Who's Who,* and read his, as well as Burger's. Just wanted to sit and talk, like the good old days when he was picking a VP and a Cabinet. Also went over the Klein, etc. stuff, the need for a TV man, etc. And the plans for building up the Thieu meeting, and hope for a major announcement at the end. Hope it all works out.

Wednesday, May 21, 1969

Chief Justice day, and a very strange day. I spent almost the entire day on the Chief Justice announcement. It worked out very well, following basically the plan P and I worked out last night.

Lots of discussions in P's office on various details. A real project to pull everything together. Had to let networks know by 1:00 at latest to get set up by 7:00. Mitchell met with Burger at noon, and didn't call me until just before 1:00. Barely made it. Used all the troops, had *(TV aide)* Roger Ailes down to produce (He blew things pretty well, mistimed "Hail to the Chief," forgot the flags on the podium, etc. Probably would have done better without him, but CBS producer was a real nervous type). In general, staging was excellent, P very good, also Burger. We had to whip up a biography during the afternoon, Buchanan did it by phone interview.

Main coup was that it was really a *complete* secret until actually announced. Pretty hard to do in this business. We told no one on the staff, and press got no leads. Sneaked Burger and his family in through the Treasury Building tunnel, so no one saw them at White House gates. Brought Cabinet into East Room on live TV, then family, then P and Burger.

P zinged Fortas pretty well by saying Burger was above reproach in business and personal. Burger zinged political appointees pretty well by saying what an honor P had bestowed on all sitting judges. We did a good job of pre-programming, and it worked. Wires are loaded with favorable comments. Now we'll see if the papers will carry them.

P, in talking about need to understand press and especially *New York Times,* said "I know our guys will say Bob Semple *(of the* Times) is a nice guy, and Kosygin is probably kind to his mother, but all that is totally irrelevant."

Friday, May 23, 1969

The Minnesota Concert Band played this morning in the Rose Garden. A remarkable event. They had just returned from a cultural exchange tour of Russia, so the Soviet Ambassador was invited. Great concert, and impressive kids, all rose and clapped enthusiastically when P came out, and all sang Alma Mater with genuine feeling and enthusiasm. P very impressed, felt there may be some hope for our kids after all.

To Camp David midafternoon, with Bebe and Pat Nixon. P bowled 204 and was really pleased. Best he's ever done, by far. The new ball helped.

Dinner at Aspen. Movie was *Man for All Seasons.* Would have been great, but projectionist screwed up again, with the topper of getting the reels in the wrong order. Poor guy was panic-stricken.

Monday, May 26, 1969

Flap about Midway trip because Thieu is insisting on coming to Hawaii after the meeting, which blows the reason for going to Midway. P says he won't go to Hawaii, will fly direct to Midway instead. Have to work something out. K says Thieu has a girl in Honolulu and that's the problem.

Wednesday, May 28, 1969

Long meeting in Cabinet room this morning with group of young GOP congressmen, who have been out talking to students at colleges. P called me in to listen, I had planned to skip it. Also had K come in. K sent me a note saying "These fellows sound just like the French aristocracy two years before the revolution." And they did. They take the radicals at face value, vastly overrate their influence. Only George Bush seemed to understand their desire for confrontation, not solution.

Monday, June 2, 1969

Decided late in afternoon to have K go to Texas and brief LBJ on his way to California. Picked up phone and called LBJ to set up. We've been trying to get him to call for two weeks. He waited until he had something to offer in return for ABM support. (He'll also send Harlow to cover ABM status.)

> This is fairly typical strategy—to hold off on a contact requesting something like ABM support until he could open with a positive report, or offer. The old political game of "You scratch my back and I'll scratch yours."

Tuesday, June 3, 1969

Big flap about Okinawa leak in *New York Times*. Rick Smith had complete and accurate story about contents of an NSC decision memorandum *(regarding negotiations with the Japanese about Okinawa)*. P really upset because of jeopardy to national security. Had me call Cushman, Richardson, and Laird, have them get complete internal report on who had access etc. (I had to make the calls from Air Force One en route to South Dakota.)

Long talk with K about his leaks. E and I had breakfast with him and advised him to move out the suspect people. He later told P this is what he's doing. Set up detailed plan for tapping all suspects, not carried out. *(Not then, but it later would be.)*

Left White House at noon for trip. Used the remodeled Air Force One. Tricia, Julie, David, and Mrs. Nixon all along. New configuration is great. Puts press way in back, allows staff privacy. Chopper to Mundt Dedication, over plowed field that said "Hi Nixon." Smalltown crowd, solid Americans, good but not wild reception. One heckler, and the crowd was going to beat him up until police saved him. Motorcade with big crowds and lot of bands along the street. Then to Colorado Springs. Good airport arrival, lots of "fence-working."

Problem on release of speech. P called me at dinner and said to hold until 9:00 AM. Ziegler unreachable, so I told Jerry Warren. Ziegler had promised 10:00 PM, agonized all night, finally we agreed on 6:00 AM, and overrode P's order.

Lot of discussion on plane about security problems. P really concerned, issuing all kinds of orders, hope we won't have to follow.

> A couple of examples in this day illustrate a challenge I faced frequently—which was to decide whether or not to follow a specific Presidential order. I sometimes decided not to, on the basis that it was not an order that was really intended to be carried out, but rather a letting off of steam, or that it was

clearly not in the P's interest that it be carried out. Usually I later informed P that the order had not been followed, and he usually agreed that was the right decision. There were times, however, when he intentionally would end-run me with an order to someone else who he felt would do his bidding when I wouldn't.

Wednesday, June 4, 1969

Air Force Academy speech, defending military. Pretty controversial. P didn't like Don Hughes functioning as personal aide, in hotel, crowds, etc. Had me in plane on way to California to discuss in detail. Also feels he did too much at the airport fence. Wants better coordination between speechwriters and advance crew. Should have had TV man along. Speech and Academy show very good.

Decided no more NSC meetings. Result of leak. Can't trust to papers. Will make decisions privately with K.

Lot of discussion on plane about broad distribution of Air Force speech. Feels it will do a lot of good. Wants whole NASA and Defense apparatus to promote it.

New security flap about troop withdrawal story leak. *(The Washington Star had reported that we had decided to begin troop withdrawal—we'd promised Thieu it would be announced jointly.)* Had me call all departments again, this time to say we know someone gave a backgrounder, wants report on who. Of course all denied it. Then wanted more detailed push on NSC Okinawa investigation. By evening was really mad. Kept calling me from San Clemente house with new orders to investigate. K advised me not to go too far. Would be counterproductive, so I ignored some of the orders. Still called Richardson and Laird several times.

Thursday, June 5, 1969

At the practice Summer White House at the Newporter. P arrived early and beat E and me there for the staff meeting. Gave orders he is not to be given cables anymore, wants them retyped.

Long lecture about leaks and how reporters get their stories. But he had really simmered down from last night, and it was good I followed K's advice. Firm orders, all *New York Times* reporters off limit, to punish the institution. Also had us get reports on leaks from OEP and VP about Okinawa leak.

Saturday, June 7, 1969

Left first thing in morning for Honolulu. Few sessions en route with the P, just little odds and ends. Then he took a long nap. *Lousy* airport arrival. Chopper to hotel. Meeting of the Midway delegation at hotel. P moved it up an hour, confused everyone. Took Rose to dinner at Trader Vic's. Terrible! Poor P tried to get family out to dinner but Tricia wouldn't go. Julie and David did. Family had room service.

Sunday, June 8, 1969

The Midway Conference. Flew out in morning, whole delegation on Air Force One. Meetings all the way. Good operation there. All went as planned. Morning conference. Announcement of troop withdrawal *(of approximately 25,000 men)*. Complete surprise to press corps, as to timing and amount. Then formal group session in afternoon. P in great form. Obviously enjoyed whole deal. Rose, E, Chapin, and I went swimming at great beach. Farewell ceremonies and back to Honolulu.

Monday, June 16, 1969

Back to the White House. P had canceled all of morning schedule for no apparent reason. Spent most of the day buzzing me in for odds and ends. In good spirits, trying to do some long-range planning. Several long sessions with K. Lots of follow-up type projects for me. Back and forth on press conference plans. Will do one on Thursday evening. Feels he should go for prime time and get maximum audience, prohibit networks from selecting just the parts they want for the news.

This was a very key element in our general PR strategy. It was based on the fact that if P did a public event to make an important statement, or announcement, it would be covered by the TV networks, but only a small and highly selective portion would actually get on the air. If he did a press conference or special event, with the request for live TV coverage, the networks generally complied, and the result was a much better and more complete presentation from the P's standpoint. Also, since these were live events, all the networks carried them at the same time, forcing a large portion of the TV audience to watch, since there was no network alternative.

This tactic also made it possible for us to force coverage in prime time by scheduling the event at whatever time we wanted it to air. After a while, the networks got smart and quit providing simultaneous coverage on all three, but it was great while it lasted.

Worried about K's overreaction to leaks in his office.

Decided to expand *(Israeli Prime Minister)* Golda Meir dinner and make some hay with Jewish community and congressmen who need Jewish support. Rose's idea.

Thursday, June 19, 1969

Press conference day. P stayed at residence all day. Came out at 5:45 to greet the First Lady on return from her trip. Called over frequently on specific questions, number of Vietnamese killed, number of Negroes in America, etc.

Rather startling answers on some Vietnam questions. Said he hoped to beat *(LBJ Secretary of Defense)* Clark Clifford's goal on withdrawals (all out by end of next year); there would be more withdrawals this summer, decision in August; he wasn't "wedded" to Thieu regime; he was not opposed to a cease-fire, etc. Also said we'd like to start SALT talks July 21 and they might be in Geneva, or Vienna.

All this shook K pretty badly. He feels that it will probably mean collapse of South Vietnam government in near future and will result in South Vietnamese troops fighting us. Thieu will consider it a betrayal, as will all South East Asia, and it will be interpreted as unilateral withdrawal. K thinks maybe P has decided to pull out, and is taking this step knowingly. I don't think so. I feel he just wanted to hit back at Clifford, and overplayed his hand. If this is the case, K feels we'll have monumental and maybe impossible job in trying to build around P's statements and reshore up our own previous position. Poor K gets really shook by these things, and for good reason. He's been pushing the opposite approach. He's been discouraged deeply the last few days, because he feels Vietnam plans aren't working out right. P knows this and may have reacted. K says we won't know real effect for about two weeks. Tough.

Will be interesting to see what tomorrow brings, his mood was great today, which usually indicates he's made a big and tough decision, and maybe he has. I hope not, for K's sake.

P called at home later, riding high, feels he was very effective. Likes prime time idea.

Friday, June 20, 1969

P couldn't sleep, stayed up late last night calling people about press conference. Was up early this morning, into office before 7:30. Took Tim and went for a walk in the South Grounds, through EOB, and back along Pennsylvania Ave. In the front entrance of West Lobby, and came into the staff meeting at 8:00, just as we were starting. Really startled the troops!

Pretty routine day of meetings and appointments. I had a session with K, after he saw P, and he's quite depressed. Feels P has made decision to reverse the Vietnam plan, and hasn't told K, or discussed with him. Feels P has been up to something all week. K has modified his view since last night, but is still very worried, mainly because he feels maybe P has lost confidence in him. Swore me to tell him if this ever happens, in my judgment. He's really quite insecure, for no reason, I believe.

Yesterday I went through a similar exercise with Harlow, who feels (and rightly, I fear) that his working relationship with the P has badly deteriorated and is continuing downhill, and this in turn is eroding his personal friendship. He knows P well enough to be able to read the signs, and it's hard to try to convince him otherwise. He's convinced he should leave soon, to prevent further decline, and I'm not sure I can change his mind. I'll try, on the basis of his duty to the P and the country. Real trouble is, he's right, and only the P can change the situation, and then not just by a little quick therapy. He'll have to bring Bryce back into the real inner councils. And I'm not sure he'll do it.

Tuesday, June 24, 1969

Went with the political group on the *Sequoia* for dinner, VP, Morton, Mitchell, Finch, Harlow, Dent, E, and me. Good meeting, concerned with RNC progress, Morton's plans and ideas, patronage problems, finally starting to get solved.

Mitchell told me about Drew Pearson story, via J. Edgar Hoover, when we got back to hotel.

Hoover had reported to Mitchell that columnist Drew Pearson had a report that Ehrlichman, Chapin, and I had attended homosexual parties at a local Washington hotel. Pearson was checking before running the story. E and I told Mitchell the report was totally untrue in every respect and implication, and at Mitchell's suggestion, we agreed to be deposed by the FBI to clear this up. We did so, as did Chapin, and that was the end of the episode.

Thursday, June 26, 1969
Had dinner on the terrace with Jo and Adele, then sat there talking.

I had a small terrace just outside my original office, next to the Oval Office, which I frequently used to get some fresh air—and even on occasions like this one, to have dinner with my wife and her mother.

Looked up to see P in my office, prowling in his smoking jacket. Had me come in, long talk. He's worried about the surtax.

The P requested an extension of the surtax past its June 30 expiration date. However, he was receiving opposition both from liberals (who wanted tax reform) and conservatives (who opposed the increased federal spending implied by higher taxes).

Especially feels Harlow not really handling Congress right. I told him of Bryce's real concern that he has lost P's confidence, he is aware but doesn't know how to handle. Discussed ways and means of beefing up Bryce's operation. Have to do it. Talked about possibility of taking Congress on and making it the issue. May *have* to if Democrats decide to play straight political obstructionist game. But then P has to get into '70 battle hard and early and he doesn't want to (and he shouldn't).

Very introspective and subdued mood. Just sat and talked and pondered. Realizes problems are coming up, wants to see his way through them, but doesn't. Not discouraged, just very pensive.

Saturday, June 28, 1969

Interesting sidelight. P called me about 9:30 about program for Sunday worship at White House. First was upset because the rabbi was from New York, while he had ordered that Senator Scott (of Pennsylvania) select the rabbi. (Turned out that Finkelstein had been committed before the order.) Then wanted Scott invited upstairs to coffee before service with rabbi to give him some political mileage. (Turned out Scott was in Philadelphia for the week and couldn't come anyway, but was very appreciative.) To get this far I tried to call Wilkinson, finally got him at football stadium in Atlanta for all-star game. He didn't know the situation. Said *(Presidential Assistant Peter)* Flanigan did. So I got Pete in New York. He didn't know, said Bud and Atwater did. So I put a call in to Atwater *(James Atwater, Special Assistant to the P)*. He was out at a party. Finally got him, but too late, I had already talked to Scott in Philadelphia.

Next call from P was concern whether Cye Halpern, the only Republican Jewish Congressman, had been invited. Tried to get Lucy, she was out. Rose was out. Got Marge and she *thought* Halpern was invited. Got Timmons, he had checked list with police, Halpern not on. Talked to Bryce about Scott matter and Halpern. He didn't know, so we concluded he'd been invited and declined and I so advised P.

Next call from P was about program. He was afraid they had included the doxology, which would be an affront to the Rabbi. I tried Atwater again, he was on way to airport to meet Rabbi, left word out on car radio, never connected. Called Lucy, she didn't know, but called usher and found doxology *was* on program. So she called Sandy Fox and got printers on stand-by to reprint programs tonight. (It was then 11:30 PM.) Finally got Atwater at home, 12:15, and he said the Rabbi had reviewed the program including the doxology. So we called off the troops at 12:30 and all went to bed. Another day at the White House.

Third Quarter: July–September

Wednesday, July 2, through Sunday, July 6, 1969
P and E In Key Biscayne, I at Camp David with Chapin and Higby. Called frequently with developments. P really on track to come up with big "first six months" story about accomplishments. Hard to put together. Will start tomorrow at staff meeting.

Monday, July 7, 1969
(Ethiopian Emperor) Haile Selassie arrival at North *(Portico)* because of rain.

Rough lead article in *Newsweek*—really cracks P for lack of leadership and direction. Discussed with him this morning, in regard to his plan for six months summary battle plan. Clearly we need to reverse the PR trend and get our own line out. Record is not spectacular, but not nearly as bad as *Newsweek* says. We have another flood of legislation and activity coming. Then will put the heat on Congress to pass some of it. P thinking of moving on Family Security Plan, originally was going to wait until after surtax and ABM votes. Now feels we need the domestic momentum and leftward balance before he leaves for Asian trip.

Problem is to get the positive story of proposals and legislative successes (haven't lost a vote yet) across to counterbalance press play of negatives. Plus problem still of right wing Republican unhappiness, because we're not adequately cutting spending, welfare, etc., and they feel we're softening in Vietnam.

At the same time, K is discouraged, because his plans for ending war aren't working fast enough and Rogers and Laird are constantly pushing for faster and faster withdrawal. K feels this means a "cop out" by next summer, and that, if we follow that line, we should "cop out" now. He wants to push for some escalation, enough to get us a reasonable bargain for a settlement within six months. Hope he prevails. Big meeting tonight about this on the *Sequoia*.

Wednesday, July 9, 1969

NSC and Selassie farewell. Wednesday afternoon off didn't work out, as activity built on trip planning *(on around-the-world trip slated to begin on July 23)* and Senate problem. Ended up with a *long* session in EOB office with Quadriad *(an unofficial advisory group consisting of the Treasury Secretary, Chairman of the Council of Economic Advisors, Director of the Budget Bureau, and Chairman of the Federal Reserve Board)* about surtax. They, or some, felt P should go on TV to nation and say must have surtax extension *now,* or else he will order $6 billion cut in spending. Harlow also with them. Also they opposed Family Security or any other spending plan until after surtax settled. Real question is how essential it really is. Bryce sees it as absolutely imperative that P win this as a major test of his strength and urges pulling out all stops and using full prestige. P seems to feel surtax will eventually pass anyway, and that he can afford to sit out the delay and accept the tax reforms. Does appear now, however, that there is some chance of tax actually being defeated.

Thursday, July 10, 1969

Cabinet meeting. P said on phone last night to be sure they stick to agenda, and *don't* get into surtax question. He was late to meeting, because of session with former Secretary of the Treasury Fowler. When he came in, he brought up the surtax. Gave an overall appraisal of the situation and a great argument for immediate passage, for Secretaries to use in speeches, etc. Is going to have a bipartisan Senate group meeting Monday evening, with three former Secretaries of the Treasury to put the heat on.

P met with Senator Russell and Senator Long about ABM and surtax. Tomorrow breakfast with Mansfield. Bryce really pushing for all-out fight, and discouraged because P won't take it on totally. I think he (P) feels it can be won without total involvement on his part, and he wants to save as much equity as he can. Bryce doesn't agree. Real problem is lack of adequate action by others. All rely on P to carry the main load. He'd be more willing to do so if he felt all other stops had been pulled out first. Trouble is, they always start with his part, then add the others instead of vice versa. Bryce's point is that P ends up having to get in anyway, and that the same effort is far more effective early than late.

P went bowling at EOB this evening with Julie and David. Julie upset because her trip to Chicago not well enough planned for TV and interviews, etc. Now P wants me to supervise all these activities. Rough!

> Julie had an exceptionally good sense of the value of her public activities and the need to get maximum benefit from them. She was absolutely right in her criticism—but it is hard to cover all the bases.

Saturday, July 12, 1969
At Camp David. P called me over about 11:00 and I was there until after 3:00. In the study at Aspen. Spent most of the time on surtax vs. Family Security question. Point is, Family Security is for '71, not '70. Long discussion of strategy, etc. Then into plan for a domestic council with E as head. Then into long analysis of his daily schedule. Wants more time free, especially at the end of the day, when he wants to leave office at 6:00. I told him *he* was the problem, not the schedule, and he agrees. Wants pool converted to bowling alley. Says he'll use it every night.

Monday, July 14, 1969
P really rolling on the new domestic plan with E in command, although E says he was a bit vague at the domestic group meeting today.

Had a session about planning overall for Apollo XI. P decided to do his TV from the White House Sunday night, instead of going to Houston or the Cape (P planned to speak live to the astronauts on the moon). Really a much better idea; it was Rose's. Met with Frank Borman. P all excited about Sunday service. We'll have Borman do scriptural reading, same as he did from moon. Also all cranked up about playing "Star-Spangled Banner" when flag placed on moon. Borman opposed, because astronauts would lose three minutes at attention, and possible adverse reaction about overnationalism. P really intrigued with his participation in the whole thing.

Now ready to go with Family Security *before* the trip, pressured by Finch and Shultz. Will lose a lot of impact, overshadowed by moon shot *plus* trip. Much better to wait until the week we get back. Drop it plus, revenue-sharing, plus Moynihan's ten new cities, and really send Congress home with a bang. Oh well.

The renamed Family Assistance Plan was a work-for-welfare program. It expanded Federal aid to the working poor, as well as the unemployed poor, but everyone who accepted aid also had to accept work or job training. It would be expensive to begin with, but gradually the incentive to get better jobs would take people off the welfare rolls. Or so we hoped.

Friday, July 18, 1969

At Camp David, all day and overnight. I slept until 10:00, P until nearly noon. Great. I was at pool sunning when P called me over to Aspen to talk. I put on tie, no coat because it was so hot and humid. He was out on lower terrace, and we sat and talked for two hours in the sun. I darn near melted. Was dripping and had a horrible time trying to take notes.

Went round and round on the plan for announcing domestic program. P had obviously already thought a lot about it, and had plan pretty well in mind. Wants E to get a new high-level lawyer to handle the counsel's job and free John up for domestic. (*On July 28, 1969, John Dean accepted this position.*)

Saturday, July 19, 1969

At Camp David. All slept late again. (*My son*) Hank and I went up to bowl around noon, had to leave because P coming. Then he went to pool. Called me up there, and it was rainy, he sitting under umbrella in trunks. Rain stopped. Talked for about a half hour. Mainly about his concern that we didn't get out tax reform word. And wanted action about *New York Times* editorial about his moon telecast plans.

Returned to White House at 3:00. P came to office for a while, with E and Ziegler. Cleaned up the loose ends, schedule details, E's items, etc. Then he returned to Residence for dinner.

Called me over to tell family about Teddy Kennedy's escapade. Very strange news coverage as they try to cover up real implications of what happened. Kennedy, late last night in Martha's Vineyard, drove his car off a bridge into a pond, left girl in it to drown. She was a former secretary of Bobby's. Lot of peculiar possibilities, but wires carry no sensationalizing, or speculation. E has investigators, etc., working on what really happened.

Wants to be sure he doesn't get away with it, but of course no reaction from us. Real concern is realization of what they'd be doing if it were one of *our* people. Obviously (P feels) he was drunk, escaped from car, let her drown, said nothing until police got to him. Shows fatal flaw in his character, cheated at school, ran from accident.

Sunday, July 20, 1969

Moon landing day, fantastic. P to EOB for solo work most of the day. I worked at hotel, packing. Back to White House at about 5:00. Some trip details finalized, a few phone conversations with P in EOB about details for telecast tonight. P came into office about 8:45, went into little office, because Oval filled with TV gear and crew. Had me in for discussion of the Teddy Kennedy matter. Reviewed today's developments. He is *very* interested in the whole thing, and feels it marks the end of Teddy. Had E working on investigation, etc.

Then had Frank Borman in to describe what was happening, as the men got ready to leave the LEM *(lunar excursion module)*. Borman, P, and I watched on little TV in little office. When Neil *(Armstrong)* hit the surface, P clapped and said, "Hooray." He's very much excited by the whole thing. Was fascinated with watching moon walk, etc. Then went into Oval Office for TV, and did a *great* job on split screen with the moon. He wrote his own remarks instead of using the suggestions. All in all, a great day, and he was very elated as he left for the house. Julie, David, and Tricia were waiting in the Rose Garden and walked him home.

He's going to push hard on the Ted Kennedy thing, mainly because he feels it greatly reduces Teddy's influence in the Senate and may help us on ABM and surtax, as it takes wind out of opposition's sails. The whole thing really is *very* strange, and it will be interesting to see how they maneuver to cover it up.

P has canceled press trip briefing schedule for tomorrow afternoon, because moon shot overshadows it. Will do it in Guam Thursday evening instead. Actually much better anyway, and will get far better ride and set stage for the trip. We have a rough period ahead, but everyone is ready and eager and I think it will go well.

Monday, July 21, 1969

Big thing today was a meeting with P, K, E and me. Kept getting put off, finally started about 5:00 and went for three hours. P outlined his thinking about need to get into gear. Feels all we have really accomplished in six months is to learn how to run the place. Need now to establish the mystique of the presidency, and wants the three of us to function as the hardcore inner circle. Wants us to zero in on hard-nosed basis and take charge. Feels where we have failed is where we've temporized.

Main thing is we haven't used the power of the White House, to reward and punish. Haven't inculcated in all the staff the view that their job is to build the P, *not* themselves.

All led up to his idea of using the word "GO" as the theme, much impressed by astronauts last night. Means all systems ready, never be indecisive, get going, take risks, be exciting. Can't fall into dry rot of just managing the chaos better. Must use the great power of the office to *do something*. Boldness. Now is the time to go. We've organized things, now use them. Go for broke now, on what's right. If that loses us 1972, I accept that.

Power of the United States must be used more effectively, at home and abroad or we go down the drain as a great power. Have already lost the leadership position we held at end of WW II, but can regain it, if fast! Looking for a sense of history and a sense of drama. Wants this group also to concentrate and decide on what the P should use his time for.

Usual discussion during the day and at this meeting about Harlow problem. And lots of talk about Ted Kennedy episode. General agreement that it has killed him as presidential candidate.

Also wants to set up and activate "dirty tricks"—with Buchanan, *(Lyn)* Nofziger, *(aide Clark)* Mollenhoff, Woods, and *(Director of Communications Herb)* Klein. Back to the ban on *The New York Times*. Mainly due to moon TV editorial, which *was* uncalled for.

> "Dirty tricks" as used here refers to the general political campaign activity of harassment and needling of the opposition, planting spies in their camp, etc. In other words, hardball politics.
>
> The *New York Times* editorial berated the President for "sharing the stage with the astronauts" and wasting their precious time with his direct link conversation. It also voiced the opinion that Nixon had very little to do with the program, giving most of the credit to Kennedy and Johnson.

And so to our round-the-world journey.

Tuesday, July 22, 1969
All day at the White House in preparation for the trip. P had horrendous schedule—mainly Congressional—starting with bipartisan leaders breakfast. Several ABM sessions with senators. A long session with E about work to be done while P is gone. Flew to San Francisco tonight. Overnight at the St. Francis, then on to Johnston Island tomorrow.

P still fascinated with Kennedy case, and covered some things about it with E also. Had me into his cabin on Air Force One for a good part of the trip covering details and mainly just chatting.

Wednesday, July 23, 1969
Landed at Johnston Island and transferred to helicopters for trip to the USS *Arlington* where we stay overnight while steaming to the pickup area *(for the Apollo XI astronauts)*. We'll leave here by helicopter at 4:40 AM for the *Hornet* and the splashdown due at 5:50. Just Bill Rogers, K, Hughes, Borman, and me with P plus Ziegler and five-man press pool.

Long talk with P at the hotel this morning, mainly about need for cutting back on expenses and staff.

Thursday and Friday, July 24–25, 1969
We crossed the dateline so one day covers two.

This is the day the men came back from the moon. After a

sleepless night on the *Arlington* for me (my cabin was next to the radio shack and a banging door) we were up at 4:00 for 4:40 departure. It was beautiful on the flight deck, absolutely dark, millions of stars, plus the antenna lights on the ship. Borman said it looked more like the sky on the back side of the moon than any he had ever seen on earth. Helicopter left in the dark and flew over the ocean to the *Hornet.* Landed and went through quick briefings on the decontamination setup and the recovery plan. Then waited on the bridge for the capsule to appear.

It did, in spectacular fashion. We saw the fireball (like a meteor with a tail) rise from the horizon and arch through the sky, turning into a red ball, then disappearing. Waited on bridge an hour or so until we could see the helicopters over the capsule and raft in the sea. We steamed toward them. Watched the pickup, first through binoculars, then with naked eye. P was exuberant, really cranked up, like a little kid. Watched everything, soaked it all up. Showed everyone his fancy binoculars (actually Don Hughes').

Then the pickup helicopter landed on deck. P ordered band to play "Columbia the Gem of the Ocean." (*The name of the spacecraft was* Columbia.) Presented gifts in flag plot—then down to hangar deck for P chat with astronauts in quarantine chamber. Great show. He was very excited, personal, perfect approach. Then prayer and "Star-Spangled Banner." Then "Ruffles and Flourishes" and "Hail to the Chief," and we left.

Had a short hop to Johnston Island because splashdown closer than planned. A brief stop there and on to Guam.

Huge crowd at Guam airport, lot of kids. Usual honors. P worked fence and spoke. Then to quarters. Then the press backgrounder at the Officers Club.

And so to bed early after lots of lack of sleep. Pretty historic and fascinating day!

More historic than I knew. P's remarks at that "backgrounder" became known as the Nixon Doctrine. In the future, he said, we would supply arms and assistance only to those nations that would supply their own manpower to defend themselves. No more automatically rushing in our men.

Saturday, July 26, 1969

Started the day in Guam by taking notes over the phone of Ted Kennedy's TV speech while Cole held his phone to the radio in DC. Then got a report and evaluation from E in New York. P still very interested. Discussed it with him on the plane *(to Manila)*, and he still has a lot of theories. Also long talk about White House staff, the need to shake things up and really get people down to work. Also need to get rid of some that don't carry their load. His mind very much on these things instead of the trip.

Also concerned about report that I was calling reporters about the Kennedy case. Feels White House board may be tapped, or operators listen in.

Sunday, July 27, 1969

Manila to Djakarta. Woke up during the night to discover we were in the middle of a typhoon. Very heavy winds, and rain really pouring down. This canceled helicopter plans for this morning and created problems as streets flooded and the river rose. Long flight to Djakarta. Standard arrival, but with smaller crowds and even more military control. Dinner was in a pavilion at the palace. White jacket. Building was not air conditioned, and the heat was almost unbearable. Everyone dripping wet. Most of the Indonesians, men and women, had fans and spent all evening fanning themselves. Dinner was pretty good, French style. Entertainment after dinner in adjoining hall, also very hot, was superb. The Siamese-type dances with 27-man gamelan, with opening ceremony including strewing flower petals and serving seeds and cold drinks. Didn't end until nearly midnight.

Monday, July 28, 1969

Arrived in Bangkok, and rain started as plane door opened. Really poured and we all were soaked to the skin as we stood in it for the arrival ceremony, including the King and the P. Rain stopped just as ceremony ended and we went into building. King and P received diplomatic corps and privy council, etc. All ladies deep curtsy, men deep bow, to King. He doesn't acknowledge in any way, looks over their heads. Queen very gracious, smiles and nods at each one.

Palace, where we are staying, is unbelievable! Dinner of King's was superb. Beautiful hall, the throne room, for head table of sixty. Rest of guests, about 150, in next room. Thai Army band played during dinner. Lady singer entertained after with songs composed by King. Troops out in front and band to play national anthems on arrival and departure. Trees all lighted along route.

Wednesday, July 30, 1969

The trip to Vietnam. Very exciting, interesting, and worthwhile. Left *(Bangkok)* first thing in morning, by chopper from Palace to airport, then by 970 *(the tail number for Air Force One backup)* to Tan San Nhut Airport at Saigon. Flew low over Saigon and could see the little fortifications in triangle shape, scattered throughout the countryside. No airport ceremonies. Chopper direct to front lawn of Palace. Good view of city. Huge, crowded, typical of South East Asia. Big river *full* of boats.

Ceremonies on arrival at Palace. Thieu and P spoke from front steps and P decorated some Vietnam soldiers. Then in for private talks. I sat in on the session with the advisors. Not much accomplished, reviewed the military situation and public morale and our commitments, etc. Very hot, but not so bad in air conditioned areas. Most of palace is open-air.

After talks, P and Thieu made departure statements and then we left by helicopter for Xi Nam, the base for First Army. Did a tour of the bunkers and helicopter revetments, by open jeep. Fascinating. P was great with troops. Pushed away the microphone, got off the stand and moved among the men, talking to individuals. Made several stops at guard posts, helicopter areas, etc., always talking directly to individual men. Really impressed them, the press, and even General Abrams. Then helicopter back to airport, rejoin Pat Nixon, who had busy and very successful day at an orphanage, a palace tea, and a veteran's hospital.

On plane back, P was elated with visit and very much impressed. Gave quite an emotional charge to me never to let the hippie college-types in to see him again. He was really taken by the quality and character of the guys he talked to, and by reaction really fed up with the protesters and peaceniks. Also some talk about plans for Domestic Program when we return. This continued in his room at the Palace when we got back to Bangkok. Had some late reports on status of the surtax, which keeps going up and down. Hard to keep in touch because of the time difference.

New Delhi and Lahore followed, but Romania was the high point.

Saturday, August 2, 1969

Lahore to Bucharest and a real day to remember! Left Lahore first thing, long flight. P really on edge, anticipating Romanian reception. Bucharest welcome exceeded all expectations. Was really unbelievable. People massed along entire route except where prohibited. *Very* enthusiastic, clapped as whole motorcade went by, threw flowers into P's car, shouted, "Hurrah" and "Nixon," really spectacular. P elated and really cranked up. Stood up in car with President Ceausescu almost all the way. Stopped and got out several times, drove the Romanian security man up the wall.

Guest house is beautiful modern building with all kinds of facilities, pool, theater, staff dining room, banquet room, etc. P went by car to State Building for talks, and returned in driving rain. *Huge* crowds along the streets both ways still clapping and cheering. Then out for the dinner, same thing, and then to reception at 10:30, still crowds. Really great.

On return home at 11:30, P called me down, then K, had on pajamas, went out on his huge garden and walked and talked and smoked a cigar for over an hour. Reviewing the day and its significance. Feels history was made, the turnout and emotional reaction was enormous and showed the real feeling of the people under Communist rule. Said the dinner group was reserved, etc., because they are the officials and they are scared, sitting on a tinder box. Don't have the guts of their P. P feels Ceausescu is extremely shrewd and bright, and was *very* much impressed by him. The talks were apparently most useful. P still concerned about our PR weakness and afraid we're not adequately getting the story out. Especially concerned that the significance of story is fully understood and reported.

He sat on a concrete bench by the lakeside in his garden and expounded on all this, and it was quite a session. He sees the great historical first of United States P here, topped by the fantastic reception of the people, as highly significant.

Great music at dinner. Three folk bands, singers, mostly Romanian music.

Sunday, August 3, 1969

Romania. More crowds, clapping, cheering, even early Sunday morning, as we went out for brief tour of city. Ceausescu decided at last minute to come along. (Probably aware of crowds.) Streets lined even more heavily, and people leaning out of all balconies and windows. Really a show. Visited farmers' market, apartment development, model village. Then back into talks. Then our luncheon at the guest house which turned out very well. Little hard to talk through interpreter especially when the other party is the Minister of Defense and *very* close-mouthed.

Left immediately after lunch for the airport and the departure ceremonies, which became quite effusive as the two Presidents ended up with their arms around each other. Remarkable! President was understandably riding high on the flight to England. Felt Romania had been a truly historic visit, very impressed with Ceausescu and feels we have a real opportunity through him for communication to the Communist world. Still really concerned that we aren't adequately selling the accomplishments, keeps grinding away on this. Got heavily into the need for a PR man again.

It was obviously hard for the P to go through this truly spectacular trip while feeling that the real picture and understanding of it was not getting through to the American people. A valid concern.

Also some discussion about Domestic Program and the plan for this. Everyone pretty well pooped on the long flight home, not much accomplished. Arrival at Andrews with full ceremonies. VP did excellent job in his welcoming speech. Chopper to White House. Julie and Tricia both *very* enthusiastic about the TV coverage etc. Helps. Good crowd, even in the rain.

Monday, August 4, 1969

Back to the White House. P came in early about 7:00. P had long meeting with bipartisan leaders to report on trip. Then had Ted Kennedy into his office. Told him he understood how tough it was, etc. Said he was surprised to see how hard the press had been on him, especially because they like him, but have to realize they are your enemy at heart even if they *do* like you, because their prime motivation is the story.

Spent the rest of the day talking to the troops one by one. Harlow in to recap legislative situation. Basically a victory on surtax. Bad erosion of *(Senator Everett)* Dirksen's leadership in the process, because he opposed Administration position. Agnew led fight against, which will create some future problems.

Moynihan for one more go around on the Welfare Program. He's still sold on it. Pat is great, because he provides the up-beat shot in the arm that the rest of the staff lacks.

Tuesday, August 5, 1969

At Camp David. Planned to sleep in, but P called me over at 8:30, no breakfast, was there three hours. Mainly on the PR need. Concerned about the Harris poll, shows huge drop. I checked via Chapin with *(pollster George)* Gallup who says it can't be valid. Long harangue on staff spirit, and on and on with PR. Dinner in the evening with the Cabinet at Aspen. P gave long and very good report on his trip, explaining all the background and zinging State for opposing both Vietnam and Romania.

August 6 saw the ABM vote come before the Senate. The result was an even split, 50 to 50, and so Agnew cast his vote to end the tie, 51 to 50. A razor-thin margin, but we took it. Meanwhile, in Paris, Henry Kissinger had begun the top-secret meetings with the North Vietnamese, which would extend over the next three years.

Sunday, August 10, 1969

(P's first visit to the Western White House.) San Clemente. P called fairly early in the morning, was at the office. Was really excited about the setup and the remarkable job done. Wants

to bring the old Cabinet table out for the conference room. Said this whole project, and his house and landscaping, show the high level of competence you find here in California, and nowhere else in the world. Very impressed by executive mess *(dining room)* and patio.

Called late in the afternoon to be sure we watched Pat Nixon special on TV and called her afterward. Wants to be sure we get good treatment for the Cabinet officers while here, social stuff plus TV coverage. Very concerned about lack of coverage in *LA Times,* especially about no follow-up on Bucharest, or the Domestic Program. Feels strong need to maintain our momentum while at crest. Reviewed plans for the Astronaut dinner and Johnson visit.

We went down to look things over. It's all beautifully done, Higby deserves great credit. The setup should be darn near ideal. P came over. Had me in for a while, then over to see the house. He's really happy with the whole setup.

Monday, August 11, 1969

First day at the Western White House. All went well. P in good spirits, arrived early with Tim. Right to work, long session with Rumsfeld, then Don did press briefing about OEO reorganization. Not much for me to work on, review again of *(astronaut)* dinner plans. Wants Borman to come in and go over it with him. Worried because Mitchell doesn't have a pool for his little girl. Wants everyone to be happily situated. Quit around 1:30 and went back to the house, trying to set the pattern.

Tuesday, August 12, 1969

Shultz in for his briefing on manpower. P at work early again, can't get readjusted to time changes from trip. More detailed discussion of the dinner. He's determined to have it just right. Tried the ocean, pretty hard to get in because of rocks, but water is great!

Wednesday, August 13, 1969

The day of the big dinner. Borman in this morning for final plans. Ronald Reagan also. Dinner was a truly smashing success. P handled emcee role to perfection. Staging was superb. Dinner and service adequate. Astronauts very good. Highly emotional and patriotic evening that completely succeeded in meeting all the P's objectives. Well worth all the work. P called about 1:30, still really cranked up.

Thursday, August 14, 1969

Bad night. Went to bed about 2:10, after P's call. Phone rang at 3:30, Bill Rogers very concerned because P has just called him saying he was not well, had Tkach there, feared a heart attack and might have to go to hospital. Bill not sure what to do, I told him to get over to P's house, see what's happening and call me. He did. Problem is gas, due to overexcitement. Bill and Tkach left a little after 4:00, both called me from home to say probably all OK. So I ended up with darn little sleep.

P came into office almost on time. Only planned schedule was NSC meeting, which he attended. Seems to feel OK, still some trouble, and looked sleepy. He spent some time with Borman thanking him for dinner, etc., then went home, probably for a nap.

Had a reception at Residence for press at 6:00. Worked out fine. Then down for the day.

Friday, August 15, 1969

Phone rang at 5:00, Tkach saying same problem as night before, at 3:00 again. Is getting a specialist out to try to cure it. No schedule today. P didn't come to the office at all. Played golf with Bebe, kids and Bill Rogers. Called in late afternoon to see what's going on, very relaxed. No problems.

Monday, August 18, 1969

At *(speech)* writers meeting P discussed whole approach to the future, mainly in regard to his speech to the National Governors Conference. Question whether to take on the Democratic Congress. If so, can lay the basis with speech on all the items he has put before Congress, with no action. P said he's not about to take on Democrats, but can't say this to *(due to)* politics. Reason of course, is that if he didn't win, he'd have an impossible situation for next two years. Said no president since FDR has gained in Congress in an off-year, and even FDR in 1934 was just continuation of the tide that swept him in. Down deep, though, I think he feels he does have a chance to get a Republican Congress if he ends the war, etc., but won't follow the attack route, at least not now. Makes sense.

At K, E meeting we talked about Vietnam alternatives. Obvious that we have to end it in six to nine months, and that the process will be difficult. K has scenario, now with Mitchell. Feels P has to make total mental commitment and really be prepared for the heat. I think he realizes this and is getting ready. This is at least part of the reason for the efforts to build strong nationalism with space thing, and certainly the reason behind the push for better PR capability, and also, I think, the reason he's really taking a vacation, to get ready for what lies ahead. Hope it will do the job.

(Presidential Speechwriter William) Safire came up with his idea for the New Federalist Papers, to play off New Federalism. To be used as the basis for knocking down the zig and zag theory about Nixon, and establish basic theme for Administration. To be written anonymously, under name of Populus.

Tuesday, August 19, 1969

Pretty active morning. E and me, then K. Then a meeting with Wallace Sterling about Bicentennial Commission. Then the new Indian Commissioner, then six new ambassadors. Concerned about Ziegler telling press about his golf, and having them follow him around. Still trying to get some freedom and privacy. Also wants aides to find a sandy beach for swimming, unfortunately the rocks (boulders) on his beach make it almost useless.

Wednesday, August 20, 1969

Meeting with Ash's Reorganization Group. *(P had asked California industrialist Roy Ash to study Executive Branch reorganization.)* Very good session about their basic approach to Executive Office of President. P was quite interested and responsive, and seemed to buy his ideas. Did launch into a half hour sidebar on the whole foreign policy problem of State vs. Defense vs. K. Called K in to cover this. Hard to figure exactly why, except as filibuster, and to dazzle them with a little taste of the "big stuff" as they wallowed around in petty problems. P does seem to recognize, though, the need for a new organizational approach and buys the idea of a Domestic Policy Council and an Office of Executive Management. Now have to figure out how to implement the whole thing. Will break a lot of china, especially at Bureau of Budget because really cuts across their lines of responsibility. Must be done. P took group on tour of Residence after meeting. Darn good session overall.

Monday, August 25, 1969

E and I had lunch meeting with Ted Braun and Cliff Miller about PR. They agree with us we should not add a PR staff man, but rather a policy board using outside counsel, for which they volunteered. Cliff makes a lot of sense and can be brought into this.

Also a number of meetings and talks about staff reorganization, and I settled the deal with Jeb Magruder. He'll probably be the staff man for me on PR, which we'll call "PO" instead, for Presidential Offensive. Need to finalize a recommended plan for the whole structure, then try to sell it to E. He's the key at this point and question is whether he'll take on the domestic responsibility. I think he will, but reluctantly, because he hates to give up his options, which are numerous at present.

Wednesday, August 27, 1969

LBJ's birthday. P had personally planned the whole production for today, from the original idea down to the details of a mariachi band at the helipad.

P and Pat Nixon went out to pad in golf cart to greet them. Mariachis played Happy Birthday, and all the staff and press were ordered out to sing. Pat Nixon took the family to the house. P took LBJ to the office for briefing. Called me in as soon as they got there. LBJ had launched immediately into a discussion of his problems with adequate staff, funds, GSA snooping and press leaks, etc. He's really psychopathic. Raved on and on about how humiliating it all was. Had *(aide to LBJ)* Tom Johnson bring all the press clips, official records, etc., and went on for 45 minutes. K and E were called in the meantime. Fortunately, LBJ knew and approved of my memo ordering support for him, main complaint was that it isn't being implemented.

He also wove in several times references to his decision not to run, which he implies was firmly made long before he announced it. Cited examples of papers he's working on, i.e., his Vietnam troop decisions; his memo to JFK about moon program feasibility that led to the decision, etc. Is obviously completely absorbed in writing history the way he wants it to be. Especially about the war, the bombing pause, etc.

On plane to redwoods he urged P not to listen to the critics, cited mistakes he had made in this regard. Gave excellent extemporaneous remarks at dedication ceremony, think he was genuinely and deeply pleased. Setting and ceremony were great, whole idea of P's was well worthwhile.

P had me meet with Tom Johnson to work out all the problems, and I think we can settle it all satisfactorily. They really do have a problem about mail and declassifying the 32 million pieces of paper. We will provide manpower through K operation. LBJ makes valid point that our interests are very much involved, in that there will be many of his papers we will not want made public, but general interest is, of course, to release as much as possible.

P, in usual stage-managing fashion, completely screwed up the plane seating arrangements as soon as we were aboard Air Force One. Decided to reverse family, staff, and VIP locations and had everything in a complete turmoil. He was cranked up with the whole deal, and I think really enjoyed having LBJ on his new plane.

Thursday, August 28, 1969

(P) talked a little about reaction to LBJ and his peculiar concern with costs, etc. Feels he's hypersensitive because of all he has taken down to Texas plus all the criticism about how much money he's made while President.

Reviewed K's contingency plan for Vietnam tonight. Will be a tough period ahead if we go to it. K feels strongly that he, E and I, plus Mitchell, must hang tight and provide the backup. Also feels we need a domestic plan to go with it, covering actions and reaction here.

Friday, August 29, 1969

E, K, and I had long session with Mitchell, primarily about Rogers problem, but also the general situation of Cabinet officers' failure to take the heat, and to sell the line. Mitchell has agreed to hit Rogers head on, on basis of scenario from K.

Saturday, August 30, 1969

Supposedly a day off. Started with continuing flurry of phone calls. Chairman of Pitney-Bowes, and of the United Fund, was camped at the compound entrance in long black chauffeured limousine. Would not leave until he saw the P about doing a

TV spot for United Fund, which we had consistently turned down for months. Cole tried to get him settled, but failed. So we put it to the P via E, and he, of course, capitulated, will do the film Monday morning. The guy ended up sitting in the car four hours, and in the office another hour. E finally saw him and settled it.

The Western White House operation has really worked out sensationally well, but there are now signs of the P starting to become restless. I'm amazed it's taken this long. Part of the problem now is that Julie and David have gone back, so he doesn't have them as diversions. Also he's talking more and more about operating routine in Washington, etc. Nonetheless, it has been great relaxation for him, *and* for all of us and the press. And it will pay dividends. The going will get very tough very fast when we get back, and everyone will need this reservoir.

Friday, September 5, 1969

Morning meeting of the "group" (Haldeman, Harlow, K, E). Started slow but P got in gear and roared through all his PR points: need for a PR man; need to sell Nixon Doctrine as a major breakthrough in foreign policy; need to get over the importance of Bucharest as rejection of Doctrine of Limited Sovereignty; need to show reestablishment of American leadership around the world; need to use more unconventional approaches; need to work more closely with the governors, especially the liberal ones; need to realign Congressional liaison and use the guys who are really with us; then a long harangue about the whole subject of press relations, who to boycott, etc.

Would have gone on and on, but was interrupted by Rogers/Yost meeting, then a photo session, then a haircut, then off for golf with John Mitchell for his birthday. First, though, another session with E and me. Nothing special. Changed into golf clothes in the office, after his usual pineapple and cottage cheese lunch. All quiet through the afternoon.

Sunday, September 7, 1969

The last day at Western White House, and all was quiet. P went to church in San Clemente and laid low the rest of the day. Beautiful day. *(I)* had a long sail with Chapin. Then packed up. *(Everett)* Dirksen died, so lots of phone calls setting things up.

This extended stay at the Western White House was an experiment to see whether it really worked as a way to slow down a little for a while. It followed closely after the return from the exhausting trip around the world and lasted for four weeks, which I thought was amazing. It did work well, but probably extended too long.

One factor that made it feasible was the actual setting up of a working Western White House on a Navy compound just adjacent to the P's new residence in San Clemente. All the necessary facilities and backup support were available and functioned well. Cabinet officers and others who came out for meetings with the P seemed to greatly enjoy the opportunity.

Monday, September 8, 1969

Back to work. A busy day, early take off for Del Rio, Texas, and joint bridge dedication with President of Mexico. Hot as Hades, all went well. Will never forget the Mexican band's rendition of their national anthem, unbelievably horrible! Luncheon after, with sensational entertainment. Mariachis, dancers, rope spinners, etc. Then on to fly over Louisiana and Mississippi flood and hurricane damage. Landed at Gulfport, great crowd. P really fired up, great enthusiasm, about 40,000, waited for hours, only one road in.

Several sessions on the plane en route. Urged us to make the tough staff moves now. Doing some thinking about the Dirksen eulogy, which reminded him to worry about the relationship with Ogilvie *(the Governor of Illinois, who would be appointing Dirksen's successor to the Senate)*.

Arrived at DC, went to White House to see the new office designs, late at night. P's office is really bright blue and yellow. Most dislike it immensely. I kind of like it for what it is, with the exception of some of the furnishings. It is at least colorful and controversial now and certainly can't be called dull. My office is great, but still a lot to do. Desk turned out very well.

So the San Clemente era closes for the year. It was a good idea and worked out well. Did all of us good to have the changes, especially the P. And now it's back to the DC operation, but with my family here. The house looks great, and I do think we'll all greatly enjoy it.

We have a lot of revamping to do now, and I hope the HEHK *(Haldeman, Ehrlichman, Harlow, Kissinger)* operation will work out. It should be our best approach.

Tuesday, September 9, 1969

Back at the White House. A little time to get used to the new decor. Some problems about lighting and color, etc., but overall a great step forward except for the Oval Office. P says he likes it, and keeps analyzing why. Maybe he really does. A generally undistinguished day of getting back to work.

Friday, September 12, 1969

The big Vietnam meeting. The key NSC types plus Vietnam Commanders and Ambassador. Top secret, to lay plan for next troop withdrawal. Also big flap over 36-hour halt of B-52 raids in South Vietnam. Meeting lasted all morning in the Cabinet Room, then P had military and *(Ambassador Ellsworth)* Bunker over to EOB for additional session.

Then back to Oval Office for some general stuff and routine signing. Off to Camp David at 4:30, with Julie and David plus HEHK.

We had our first Camp David session tonight. It worked out only fairly well. Problem was too many phone calls, plus a great difficulty in getting to the point. A lot of meandering. Most of the pre-dinner and a good part of after was devoted to the Green Beret case. *(The Green Berets stood charged with murdering a Vietnamese who was believed to be a double agent.)* A real PR problem for the P and Administration. Army plans to go ahead with court-martial which will bring out a lot of secret activity, but worse it will give great fodder to the antiwar types, which is just what we *don't* need as school opens.

Tried to call Admiral McCain to get his view, and Laird found out, and called K, very upset that we hadn't gone to him instead.

The fact that Laird apparently knew immediately of our attempt to call McCain from Camp David gave us something new to worry about. Were the Camp David phones tapped for the Defense Department? Way back during the transition period, J. Edgar Hoover had warned the P and me that the Army Signal Corps, who operated the White House Communications Agency, were known to listen in on supposedly secure phone communications that they were handling.

Monday, September 15, 1969

Sort of hit the fan this morning as Ziegler came in to say *(Vietnam Vice President Nguyen Cao)* Ky had leaked the troop story in Vietnam *(we'd planned to announce the withdrawal of 35,000 more by December 15)*. Spent quite a while with K and E and Ziegler and P trying to work out our approach, and wording of statement. Decided we had to go today, not let Ky story ride alone. Problem is in working out the details of the statement. Hard to get the actual figures squared away in simple, but accurate form. Ky figure of 40,000 is misleading in a way because it refers to authorized troop level, instead of actual number in country. Now we have to explain, which becomes confusing.

As the day went on K was unable to get a satisfactory statement, so decided to stay with plan for Tuesday announcement. Moved bipartisan leaders to this afternoon late, and GOP leaders tomorrow morning.

P canceled a lot of today's appointments and meetings in order to go over things with K, and to get ready for leaders. It's hard for him to shift from the current crisis to the relatively meaningless routine type things, and the way out is just to cancel the latter. Understandable. Actually it works out pretty well the way we set up the weekly schedule because we leave a lot of time open, which provides flexibility. A little rough sometimes on those we shift around.

Our system is going to build up gradually. He's dividing more between E and me, instead of using us interchangeably. Unfortunately E leaves Friday for a ten-day vacation which will put a major crimp in progress. Harlow seems to be tracking well and will be valuable, also it will help him to see some of the rest of the picture besides just Congress.

P called at home to say he wanted to be sure the call he's expecting from Governor Ogilvie is put right through. Trouble is Ogilvie hasn't called. Probably will appoint Dirksen successor in next couple of days.

Wednesday, September 17, 1969
Day clear for speech work *(for the opening of the UN General Assembly)*. Did add a signing session for an old-age bill to use as staging for an announcement of intention to raise Social Security 10%. P especially pleased that we had analyzed and planned whole event for TV, and did it all on basis of getting what *we* wanted on the TV news.

Problem at the UN because podium light is not adequate and they won't permit us to add anything. Important because he'll read the speech and it will all be on TV.

P spent all afternoon at EOB working on the speech. K concentrating all his efforts on the UN speech and the plans for the Foreign Minister meetings afterward. No major activity about Vietnam, although the withdrawal announcement yesterday is still reverberating, with lots of interpretations arising from K's background.

P came back to office in late afternoon, from EOB, and had some points to cover about staff organization. Think we're making progress.

Also P wanted progress report on plans to convert *(White House indoor)* swimming pool to press facility. He's really determined to go ahead with that, and it would sure help clean up the West Wing.

Thursday, September 18, 1969
UN Day. P didn't come in to the office. We left at 9:30, to New York. He gave a very good speech and was very good at reading it *(urging the nations to persuade Hanoi to negotiate seriously)*. Reaction was pretty lukewarm. They did finally stand and clap when he was introduced and came in, but there was no applause during the speech and they did not stand at the end.

Then to the Waldorf for private meetings with Foreign Ministers. Worked very well on our schedule of 15 and 20 minute appointments. Really had to hustle. Decided to go to "21" for dinner after our reception. Ran into Zsa Zsa *(Gabor)*, Gina Lollobrigida, Dorothy Lamour, and Henry Ford. Shook hands after with crowd waiting in the street. Interesting, because LBJ couldn't even appear in public in New York. Our reception most friendly and enthusiastic all through the city, and no anti demonstrators.

I spent the whole flight back with Pat Nixon, about her

White House Preservation Committee, and her staffing thoughts. She's determined to run her own operation in the East Wing, which is the right approach, but she will *have* to have a better staff to do it right. Good first step is her increased interest. Can build from there.

> The White House Social Office and the needed office facilities for the First Lady's other activities are usually located in the East Wing of the White House, and thus the phrase "East Wing" has come to mean the First Lady's Office (until the Clintons) just as the "West Wing" refers to the President's offices.

Harlow called in New York to urge P take over Laird's plan to announce draft cuts. Feels it will be the best news we've put out yet. *(Because of the troop withdrawals, draft calls for November and December had been canceled.)* I talked to P and he agreed, and was very pleased to learn Laird was willing to do it. So we swung into action and switched Laird's press conference tomorrow to the White House. Press all intrigued with what's happening. The shift itself built up interest.

P called K late tonight *really* upset by the Green Beret announcement of court-martial, which topped his UN story in the *Star* headlines. Justifiably furious with Defense for letting this happen. And feels it's my fault because no PR control, but K told him I didn't even know about it.

Saturday, September 20, 1969
At Camp David. P slept late. We left at noon. Had to wait awhile on chopper while they tried to find Vicki *(Tricia's dog)*. Reception in East Room for student body and College Presidents. P disturbed afterward, felt it was useless, and that we should not have done it. One kid gave him a lecture on how to be a good president and start leading the country, this set him off. Another example, maybe, of our letting the bad guys use us as a forum. We'll see how the press comes out and how the kids react.

Then he had an appointment with Bob Hope, and after saying yesterday he could not play golf ever on Saturday, they went off to Burning Tree for the afternoon.

Tuesday, September 23, 1969
Some morning appointments, including fairly long session with Mitchell after a meeting with him and Senator Griffin about Haynsworth appointment. Appears it may be in some actual trouble.

On August 18 we had nominated Judge Clement Haynsworth of South Carolina to replace Justice Fortas on the Supreme Court. He was immediately accused by liberal groups of being "racist" and "anti-labor" and of having "conflicts of interest."

Minor flap at start of the day because there had been no speech material prepared for Tricia for her trip to Philadelphia to open a museum exhibition. Problem is still almost complete lack of communication between East and West wings. Hope Stuart's return will resolve this.

P is all of a sudden enamored with use of the Dictaphone and is spewing out memos by the carload, plus about double the volume of news summary marginal comments.

He was delighted this morning that pool dismantling was under way, and worked out a plan with Ziegler and me to take a few press through the whole new press setup. Ziegler had a long session with P in the late morning and succeeded in talking him out of his plan to meet a small group of press for a backgrounder, and instead to have a full press conference Friday. Then P spent about a half hour telling me how to re-juggle the schedule to accommodate it.

After lunch hour he took UPI reporter Merriman Smith and two others on complete tour of West Wing, pointing out how awful the lobby, Roosevelt Room, and West Basement are, then showed how the press setup will work out in the pool area. They basically bought the idea, and he was absolutely right in approaching it this way. Now it's a fait accompli except for details.

Wednesday, September 24, 1969
Big military morning. P had breakfast meeting with Joint Chiefs of Staff to let them cover their views on military budget cutbacks. First time he's met with the Joint Chiefs of Staff.

Called me in once to find out who the Republican senators

had elected as leader, but they hadn't voted yet. A little later Scott was elected, and I went in and told P. He was very pleased, feels Hugh *(Scott)* will be effective leader, and that he can bring the liberals along, where *(Howard)* Baker could not have, and we can hold the conservatives by ourselves.

P spent most of the afternoon at the EOB working on his briefing books for the press conference. Called, as usual, several times about need for more material on specific questions. Then had a haircut and went over to the Residence. Called me at home on need to plan weekly outside activity for Tricia, and concern about Nelson Rockefeller *(who was)* mad because junior staff man called him. Can sure jump fast from the monumental to the totally infinitesimal.

Thursday, September 25, 1969

Harlow came up with an interesting approach to the Congressional logjam problem. Have P pay personal call on *(Speaker John)* McCormack and Democratic leaders in Speaker's office, to discuss ways and means of getting things moving. Would be first time this ever done, lay groundwork for later attack on Democratic Congress, with base of saying have done *everything* possible to work with them, but no luck. Also might actually produce something.

K feels he finally has the Green Beret problem under control. The CIA has been ordered to refuse to let their men testify as witnesses. *(CIA Director Richard)* Helms really dragged his feet, but finally gave in. Now Laird has to get *(Army Secretary Stanley)* Resor to cancel the trial for lack of case. Will be hard to do, but should have been done months ago, the publicity, especially TV, is really damaging. Laird could have closed it up, and said he was doing so, but didn't, in face of Resor determination to go ahead.

Golda Meir dinner tonight, she used her toast to recount all the problems of the Jews over the centuries, but did really praise P strongly for his understanding, listening, during talks today. She got a standing ovation at end of remarks, without even waiting for the toast.

Saturday, September 27, 1969

At Camp David. In afternoon a political session with House and Senate leaders, Whips and Campaign Chairmen, plus Morton, Dent, Harlow, Nofziger and Buchanan. P in great form, as he cranked them up to get out and hit hard on the offensive. Then gave them insight into Vietnam plans, long discussion of October 15 plans and our need for counteraction *(antiwar demonstrators had called for a Vietnam War Moratorium rally in Washington, D.C., that day)*. Pointed out in Vietnam the enemy misjudges two things, the time (P still has three years and three months) and the man (he won't be first President to lose a war). Emphasized importance of the next 60 days (first said 30), need for unity, have to take the P's assurance that we know what we're doing.

Regarding October 15, he says they are prolonging the war by this attack, because our only hope for negotiation is to convince Hanoi we are ready to stay with it.

Monday, September 29, 1969

Big review of all our PR activity and follow up on his memos, etc. Said his real concern is that whole staff is not zeroing in on the big issues and really getting things done. Says he really feels frustrated, because he knows people disagree with his orders and just don't carry them out. With others in the office, he several times cracked that "Your staff never follows up on anything, so of course this won't be done," etc. Trouble is, he's generally right, and so it's hard to argue. As Harlow says, all presidents go through periods of "Nobody is doing anything but me," and I'm sure he really has that feeling to a degree.

Keeps coming back to the October 15 Moratorium Plan, although he says it doesn't concern him. Told me, secretly, he's thinking of doing a one hour press conference that night at news time, to preempt coverage of the day's activities. Not a bad idea! Also is interested in the Day of Prayer idea *(to show our sympathy with peace)*, which I discussed today with Billy Graham. Looks feasible if we move quickly. Need to build leadership. Realizes war support is more tenuous every day and knows we have to maintain it somehow. Turned the House hawks loose today, demanding we resume bombing, etc., as a counter on the right to all the pressure on the left to cop out. K got his Green Beret trial turned off, with Resor dropping the charges because no CIA witnesses.

Tuesday, September 30, 1969

Presented Unit Citation to 1st Marines, and used the occasion for an appeal to national unity behind the war. One more step in the LBJ direction of using every occasion to plead for support. More of the reaction to the situation closing in. Not good, but hard to avoid.

Several miscellaneous appointments in the afternoon. A session with K and E about the Symington hearings problem, on which they had been meeting most of the day in the Situation Room. Problem is his men (staff members) *(Walter)* Pincus and *(Roland)* Paul, who have been scooping up secret data all over the world and leaking it to press plus building big antiadministration case.

Symington was the chairman of the Foreign Relations Subcommittee that was investigating activities at all foreign military bases; Pincus and Paul learned of secret American involvement in Laos, and Symington made it public.

Question now is how to avoid having our key people testify, big issue of executive privilege. Dick Allen had been working on this for months and is really concerned about the possibilities. Mollenhoff also heavily involved and distressed.

P called tonight, says may cancel Key Biscayne because he has too much to do, then spent rest of the time trying to figure out something to fill Wednesday and Thursday schedule.

Fourth Quarter: October– December

Wednesday, October 1, 1969
Harlow concerned about Haynsworth, as is E, so they were told to work it out with Mitchell. Bryce recommended to P that the nomination be withdrawn. Mitchell later persuaded him otherwise.

P had several pages of lists on yellow pad that he checked off as we covered the ground. Also has been cleaning out all his old briefcases, etc., because there are piles of stuff in the out box every day, way beyond what goes in, some going clear back to the transition period. Hope it eventually all gets cleaned out.

Thursday, October 2, 1969
Big stir on Haynsworth. P even decided to leave Harlow in DC to work on it over weekend. P feels that our Congressional staff have not handled this adequately. At first had blamed Justice, but meeting today with *(Assistant Attorney General)* Rehnquist convinced him they had done their part, but White House had not. This is not completely fair, because Mitchell has blithely relied on his reports that everything was OK, while it was falling apart behind the scenes. Real problem is not the merits of Haynsworth, but a combination of reaction against the Fortas matter, plus a strong anti-Southern move, plus pure partisan politics.

Met with Mitchell and group of Congressmen in the morning, and with some of the NSC later. Then a batch of diplomatic credentials, which we tried in the Residence in an effort to speed up the process. Did five in less than an hour, not bad.

One of the more onerous ceremonial chores of the President in his role as Chief of State is the protocol requirement that he personally receive the credentials of each foreign ambassador upon his posting to the United States. With some 120 nations recognized by the United States, each with an Ambassador in Washington, and with each new appointment requiring a detailed ritual of introductions and niceties, this was a very time-consuming addition to the heavily loaded Presidential schedule.

Richard Nixon viewed this procedure, cherished and expanded by the Diplomatic Corps, as a complete waste of time. So he sought all kinds of ways to avoid, or at least curtail it. The first idea was to shift the burden to the VP, but this was totally unacceptable in the rules of protocol. So we kept working on ways to speed up the procedure.

On the plane (to Florida) he had E, K and me up for long staff session. Still hammering on Haynsworth. Had some ideas on other follow-through steps. Then a lot of odds and ends, wants General Chapman of Marine Corps used on TV, change Ambassador to Paris, get Buchanan to blast peaceniks about Russian and Chinese atom tests, stop use of Harris for departmental polls, make Rogers and Laird start selling Vietnam policy, need for internal discipline, etc.

Friday, October 3, 1969
At Key Biscayne.

The Nixon routine on these weekend, and sometimes longer, stays at Key Biscayne became pretty well established. In the early part of the term, the President stayed at one of several rented or borrowed houses on the Bay side of the Key. Later, he bought his own house on the Bay, which was equipped with a helicopter landing, complete security and communications facilities, and working and living quarters for the President and his family.

The senior staff stayed at the Key Biscayne Hotel on the ocean side, just across the Key from the President's residence. Our facilities at the hotel were also equipped for security and communications. We were at all times reachable by the White House Communications Agency, by either phone or walkie-talkie (cellular phones had not arrived yet), and so always directly available to the President and vice versa. The press was housed at the Sonesta Beach Hotel, about a quarter mile down the beach from our hotel.

The President generally spent most of his time working alone or relaxing with his family or Bebe Rebozo. As needed, he had staff people or invited guests, who were also usually housed at the Key Biscayne Hotel, come over to his house for working meetings and sometimes for dinner.

Day dawned bright and clear, hot and humid, after last night's storm. All quiet through the morning, then P called E and me over for about a two-hour session at his house. He was in trunks and a sport shirt. Sort of one of those mystic sessions, which he had obviously thought through ahead of time. Said for next six weeks he'd have to concentrate on foreign matters, and we would have to handle most of the domestic without him. Wants all staff to understand and wants large free chunks of schedule time to work on Vietnam decisions. Long general talk about all this. We reviewed our plans and ideas, especially about need to game-plan Vietnam alternatives and start buildup for whatever actions he decides to take.

Then had session with K, and he is of course very concerned, feels we only have two alternatives, bug out or accelerate, and that we must escalate or P is lost. He is lost anyway if that fails, which it well may. K still feels main question is whether P can hold the government and the people together for the six months it will take. His contingency plans don't include the domestic factor. E feels strongly we can and should pre-program several routes on a PR basis, and start getting ready. It's obvious from the press and dove buildup that trouble is there, whatever we do.

Monday, October 6, 1969

Several sessions with individual senators and one group, about Haynsworth. Big blow came this afternoon in letter from *(Senator)* Bobby Griffin saying he could not support the appointment. Odd position for the Whip *(the party floor leader in the Senate)*. I told the P just before his meeting with the group of senators; he was quite startled since Harlow had assured him earlier of Griffin's support.

Had E, Harlow, and me join him at Executive Office Building at 6:45 for a one and a half hour discussion of the whole thing. Result was to have Harlow talk to Romney and try to get him to return the letter to Griffin and shape him up. He'll try. Also talked a lot about general handling of senators, etc. P really disturbed, will destroy Griffin as Whip.

Some good news too. *(Selective Service chief Lewis)* Hershey is ready to retire, and to announce it this week. Will help with campuses.

Didn't get home until 8:45, then P called and wanted a research project about problems other Supreme Court Justices had in getting confirmed. Plans to use it somehow tomorrow.

Wednesday, October 8, 1969

NSC this morning. Session first with Harlow and E and me about Haynsworth and odds and ends. Had a bunch of notes from last night's party, as always. After NSC did the Bicentennial Commission, which we had cranked up as a TV opportunity to do a high level non-war pitch to the people. Worked out fairly well but he didn't have enough time to prepare, so rambled and repeated a bit. Lost some of the potential effectiveness, but still a good idea.

Asked me about news magazines, because Cronkite had mentioned them last night. I told him just how they had hit us. He reacted very well. Said it was to be expected, that we had not sold his accomplishments as well as we should have and had let the Cabinet dissensions get out of hand, but it would have happened anyway. Main problem is Vietnam, and we've bought nine months, but can't expect to get any more time. Kept doves at bay this long, now have to take them on, first Agnew etc., then later the P. Problem is that this does make it his war.

This was what Pat Moynihan was constantly warning against. From the start of his Presidency, Nixon focused primarily on Vietnam, recognizing that it was his overriding major challenge. On one hand, he was determined to reach a conclusion of the war on a basis of "peace with honor" and not a "cop out" that would result in abandoning South Vietnam and a collapse of South East Asia along the lines of the "domino theory." On the other hand, he knew the domestic dissatisfaction with the ongoing "impossible war" would inevitably increase daily and become more and more unmanageable.

He had fully expected that an acceptable, if not totally satisfactory, solution would be achieved through negotiation within the first six months. But this was not to be, unfortunately.

Decided today to make Moynihan a Counselor to P, with Cabinet rank. Really best way to position him. Gets him out of operations, and into free-wheeling idea-generating, plus working as a prod to all others, good use of great talent. And it vastly simplifies E's problem in staffing.

Prominent Democrat Daniel Patrick Moynihan's initial appointment as Assistant to the President for Urban Affairs and staff head of the Urban Affairs Council was designed to take full advantage of his expertise and advice in that field. But it came to involve a great deal of operational responsibility as well, which was not Pat's real talent.

Flap today about TV, when P filmed spots for Cahill and Holton (*two Republican gubernatorial candidates*). Al Scott had camera mounted high, and P knows this is bad angle. So this proved to him we have to have a full time top level TV man at White House. He called me twice during afternoon, and twice at home about this. He's right on need for top pro as supervisor, but we'll never get one to come here full time at any pay. New problem. They never end.

Thursday, October 9, 1969

Had me in at lunchtime, long talk about things in general, especially K's concern about Rogers and his *(K's)* obsession with *total* compliance and perfection, which needs to be modified somehow. (K had talked to me earlier, felt maybe we were trying to ease him out, had heard rumors he was leaving and thinks P has decided finally against his plan for Vietnam.) Then on to whole Vietnam problem; he still is pondering the course. Does *not* yet rule out K's plan as a possibility, but *does* now feel Laird-Rogers plan is a possibility, when he did not think so a month ago. Low casualty rate now has changed his mind. (Also K still thinks Hanoi may negotiate this month.) P discussed the alternatives, ruled out the dramatic cop-out blaming the dove senators. Said that would be a great way out for him, but terrible for the country. Worry about K's plan is that it will take six to eight months, and fears can't hold the country that long at that level, where he could hold for some period of withdrawals.

Wants me to work with K and try to keep him on an even keel, and stop his worrying.

E and I spent most of the afternoon in PR meeting with Cliff Miller, mainly about Vietnam plans and alternatives. Agreed we have to concentrate all efforts on maintaining P's credibility, so he can move the people with him when he is ready to make the overt move on Vietnam.

P met with Democratic House leadership at 5:00, about the Domestic Program shopping list. Does Senate tomorrow. Decided to drop World Series visit, bad PR, will do Joint Chiefs of Staff at Camp David instead.

Sidenote: My guess as of today on Vietnam outcome: P will go on TV November 3, with some prior buildup about major announcement, and will enumerate all the secret moves he has made for peace, with names and dates. Point out he's done everything possible to resolve with Hanoi to no avail. So has ordered Paris talks ended and brought team home. Will send personal envoy to Hanoi if they want to talk. Will also announce no further United States offensive action, and withdrawal of troops in December, about 40,000. And continuous United States withdrawal until all are out, at fastest rate South Vietnam can handle.

Will then sit tight for two to four weeks to await reaction. If they continue lull, or de-escalate, we withdraw. If they escalate heavily we move *fast* to heavy retaliation, mining etc., with this bad faith as basis. Could then probably bring United States opinion around to support level of fighting to get military victory in three to six months. We'll see!

Friday, October 10, 1969

Busy and complex day. Private breakfast with Hugh Scott and Attorney General Mitchell about Haynsworth; long visit with Hubert Humphrey (who then went out and strongly backed P on the war); a ''Congressional half hour'' *(a scheduling device we had developed to process a maximum number of brief visits, or presentations, from congressmen and senators who*

needed to be able to say they had met with the President) and
a batch of diplomatic credentials; a meeting with Finch that
went on and on into the lunch hour. (I had to interrupt at end
of lunch period to get the "laundry list" message to Congress
OK'd, and the statement about Hershey change); meeting with
General Hershey to work out his reassignment; then he taped
the whole message to Congress for radio; a meeting with K;
an hour with Mansfield; then a spell with me for signing, and
out at 7:00.

Called me several times at home, odd range of topics. First
wanted 100 wires sent to Hubert commending his support; then
a plan to give *(Senator Charles)* Goodell *(of New York)* et al.
a going over for their opposition; then concern about schedule
for next week after October 15, not strong enough. Discussed
inflation letter, and he had excellent idea to make it to 1000
leaders, instead of one man, ask their views, etc. Then do radio
speech for housewives. Then need a major move for Friday,
maybe a Rogers press conference (I urged nothing on Vietnam,
rather let mystery build from the Bunker-Wheeler-Lodge meetings).

He says now he'll announce his November 3 speech *(a major televised address on Vietnam)* on Monday, then use that to
hold off any other Vietnam question, i.e., in press conference
the following week. I urged him not to say in the announcement that he would cover all the secret moves, etc., let that be
the opening impact on November 3. He agreed.

Then some discussion of Haynsworth. Then a call about
ashtrays for California press group and some concern that
(swimming) pool conversion isn't moving fast enough. Shows
how the Presidential attention can jump from the momentous
to the insignificant.

Saturday, October 11, 1969

Lot of little project stuff and some philosophical discussion in
the office. He's concerned about K's attitude and wants to be
sure we keep him upbeat. Can't let him overreact to each little
aberration of Rogers, or Laird. (K argues that you have to
maintain tight discipline on the little things or you can't control
the big ones, P feels you should lose the ones that don't matter
and save your strength and equity for the big battles that really
count.) Also feels we have staff well shaped up now, but must
constantly keep on them.

Some planning about overall Vietnam strategy. He's getting into the final decision stages, and wants to talk through alternatives, will go ahead with November 3 speech plan, agrees with my recommendation to stay clear of war from now until then.

Monday, October 13, 1969

Lot of concern about plans for Moratorium Day as it nears and heat builds. May want P to participate in some way, generally by going to church. His firm view is to avoid any involvement and to maintain a normal routine on other activities.

Another long introspective talk at the end of the day. I sense a growing intolerance of K's attitudes and habits. He overreacts and this bothers the P. Tendency now more and more to keep him out, and K senses this, which builds up the frustration and accelerates the overreacting. Also K is getting heat for his staff inefficiency, which is really just his bottlenecking. Maybe my prime contribution for a while will be to get this straightened out, because he is extremely valuable and effective and any deterioration would be damaging to the overall operation.

Tuesday, October 14, 1969

Pre-Moratorium Day. P had Leaders Meeting this morning, main thrust on tactics for follow-up of message about reforms and priorities, plus Haynsworth.

Big deal for the day was arrival of intelligence bulletin at noon reporting release of a letter by North Vietnamese Prime Minister Pham Van Dong to American people in support of Moratorium, in very flowery red rhetoric. K called me and said thought we should get it out. I agreed and we started a hectic process of deciding how, by whom, etc.

Harlow argued for a Presidential TV appearance to say Hanoi was wrong and that Moratorium Day demonstrators were not trying to aid the enemy, but rather to express desire for peace. K strongly opposed this, wants no involvement of P. E mainly agreed, feels P is positioned right as a result of the college letter Sunday. (*P had written to a Georgetown student that government policy based on street demonstrations "would destroy the democratic process."*) P decided he would not get into it, but wanted VP to take it on, to get maximum possible coverage. So we set him up, had Buchanan do a statement,

frantically got him into a review with P and barely got before
the cameras in time for the evening news. Also cranked up
great Congressional action and even some commentators. Result was we got the coverage, question now is whether it helps
or hurts. Point is to try to make the innocents see they are
being used, and to blunt the effect of tomorrow. Hard to do
much because momentum is tremendous and broad based.

Wednesday, October 15, 1969

The Vietnam Moratorium Day, finally here. After weeks of
planning, concern, and discussion. Didn't turn out nearly as
bad, or good, as expected. Crowds were pretty big, but not
anywhere near what they might have been. News media were
obsessed with the whole thing, but have been reasonably fair
in pointing out that hundreds of thousands were participating,
but millions were not.

Had Rogers and Laird in after NSC to try to get them in
line about Vietnam and November 3 speech. Apparently this
uncovered all their problems with K, because P called me in
to discuss it. Says he'll have to bring Mitchell in more because
K can't deal with Rogers and Laird, has problem of communicating with them, and has become an issue. Wants me to
make all this clear to K, hard to do. Problem is his insistence
on perfection and total adherence to the line in every detail.
Also injects himself too much into everything, between P and
Cabinet officers, and they just won't buy it, so he becomes
ineffective even at getting them to do what they already were
ready to do.

P commented that Cabinet members shouldn't have to be
told to stay in line. He thinks back to the DDE days when all
staff and Cabinet concentrated on keeping the P "up" and
never came in with a problem without a solution. Wonder if
it was really that way.

Thursday, October 16, 1969

The day after Moratorium Day, and a great sigh of relief because it wasn't nearly as bad as everyone had feared. Great
debates rage on the tactics for the future and analysis of how
this one was handled. Basic lines are drawn on question of
whether VP should have used the Dong letter and called for
repudiation. Many feel this was the prime factor in toning the
whole thing down, the others feel it was the final step in co-

alescing the opposition, as follow up to P's press conference that he wouldn't be affected in any way.

I talked to P about Rogers' view that he should make a statement about our pleasure that the demonstration had been peaceful and that it showed country is for peace.

P got going again on necessity for hard line and no concession to the left. Yet sees merit of Rogers' view. Moynihan goes much further, and is especially concerned about the November 15 exercise *(when the next Moratorium was scheduled)*. We have to start preparing because it may be a real disaster. Problem is still to separate the good guy dupes from the hard-core organizers.

Friday, October 17, 1969

The "high prices" radio speech. After several rejections because of non-people-type language Safire finally got the inflation speech down to a "high prices speech." P read it for live radio at 1:00 on all four networks. Then shot one minute on film for TV news. Made all the papers, all radio cuts live and replay, and all TV net news. Darn good parlay. Plus we're mailing and have an intensive follow-up plan for promotion. Did this one right all the way, for once. P very pleased, though earlier in day he said he wouldn't do the TV.

Saturday, October 18, 1969

At Camp David. P in great mood, had a few things he wanted to cover, then went over all our stuff. E raised point of need to answer question about P's attitude towards religion and the role of prayer in his life, using the National Day of Prayer Wednesday. He agreed, and wants Billy Graham to be there, then talk to press and explain P's view of this as private personal matter, not a public function, etc. I talked to Graham and he agreed to do it, but wants to talk to P first.

Monday, October 20, 1969

Haynsworth press meeting. P stayed at Residence till late, then had all the press into Oval Office for briefing on Haynsworth. E says it went very well. P had, as always, really done his homework, and was on the offensive all the way.

Met Dobrynin for about an hour this afternoon.

> At that meeting, P really blasted him for Soviet intransigence
> on Vietnam and other matters.

Tuesday, October 21, 1969

Big to-do because no staff follow-up on P's Haynsworth press
conference yesterday. Especially bad because *(Senator Birch)*
Bayh hit him for "gutter politics," and we had no response
or counterattack. So I had several head-banging sessions. Just
the same old problem. We don't have a built-in automatic re-
flex action.

E and *(his assistant Bud)* Krogh and I were in for a while
on plans for the November Moratorium and march. P wants
to be sure we don't use too tight a rein, better to let the nation
see what these people really are, and let them do their thing,
not make martyrs of them or appear to be afraid. He's right.

> P's thinking on this point was that the marchers would be their
> own worst enemies in terms of public reaction, so it would be
> better not to restrain them any more than absolutely necessary;
> instead, let them show their true colors on the TV and let the
> public draw their own conclusions.

Wednesday, October 22, 1969

John Connally said LBJ had told him to tell P he could reorganize everything all he wanted, but he had three main problems, 1) press 2) Congress 3) disloyal people in State and CIA.

Thursday, October 23, 1969

Busy day. Started with another of our schools for congressmen, this time on narcotics. Had Art Linkletter come in to
make part of the presentation. E said it was *very* successful.
Democratic leaders outdid themselves in jumping on the band-
wagon. P extremely impressed and is now much more "up"
on the whole problem, and fully determined to charge ahead
and get something done. (That is proving to be a very valuable
fringe benefit of these sessions.) P now wants education funds
tripled, huge attack on media for going along, exploration of
all ways to stop traffic, tie in dope with organized crime, etc.

Fourth draft of Vietnam speech in today. P had no time to
review it. Big problem building, as liberals have (very clev-

erly) shifted ground away from blasting P to saying they're with him. The main result is a massive buildup of hopes for major breakthrough in November 3 speech. Problem is there won't be one, and the letdown will be tremendous. Obvious they are intentionally building him up for the biggest possible fall. Even the stock market is soaring up on peace hopes. Speech will be good and will clearly state the case and would under normal circumstances be very effective, and probably buy us another couple of months. Under the present situation, a massive adverse reaction could conceivably be developed the next day, and built up over ten days into the November 13–15 demonstrations with horrible results. No real way to stem this now. White House and Laird are trying to squelch specific speculation, i.e., Hugh Scott's call for a unilateral ceasefire, etc., but it doesn't have much effect, and clear general impression is being created that something big is brewing.

> The concern at this point was that expectations were being built up so much that the speech could end up producing a negative reaction that could be snowballed into developing major momentum for the upcoming demonstrations.

Sunday, October 26, 1969

About the plans for SALT announcement tomorrow, secret has been well kept. Rumors just now starting. Big flap between K and Rogers, as to where and who does briefing. Ended up that Ziegler makes announcement at White House, then Rogers briefs at State. K very upset, feels he should brief and P should get all the credit. P pleased with secrecy, but he told Mansfield and practically told *(Senator Gordon)* Allott and McCormack. Then can't understand why it leaks.

Monday, October 27, 1969

The K problem came to a head today. P had me in early to review some items, then got into problem of K vs. State, and especially Rogers, which we had discussed last week and which K had churned up some more over the weekend in phone calls with P. As we were talking, K and Ziegler came in for morning briefing. K got going on State. This time saying he had decided not to force *(Assistant Secretary of State Joe)*

Sisco to cancel appointment with Dobrynin, because that would be worse than keeping it, but then went on and on about what a terrible mistake it was. Then got into Lebanon problem, Israel jets, etc. Finally P said, "Well that's all for today, have to get to work," and got up and walked out into his little office. K then said he wanted me in the noon meeting because he had to get into the Rogers problem with P. I took him into my office and tried to point out the fallacy of his technique, regardless of merits of case. I think he saw it a little, at least. P called me in to restate his concern with this as latest example. Feels K is impairing his usefulness, and is obsessed beyond reason with this problem. Later P called Mitchell and me in to discuss further, and asked Mitchell to have a talk with K. Tough one, because there *is* some real merit to K's concern about Rogers' loyalty.

Saturday, November 1, 1969

P at Camp David. Called in the afternoon, very relaxed, said well, the "baby's been born," worked until 4:00 this morning, have final draft *(of the Vietnam speech)*. K had gone up after meeting with us in the morning. Had been pleased with direction speech was going yesterday and *much* more so today. Says it is really good.

> As the scheduled November 3 Vietnam speech day approached, Nixon spent incredible hours alone finalizing the drafts and intentionally encouraging wide speculation as to what the big announcement would be. There was great divergence within the top echelons of the Administration as to how hard or soft a line he should take. His position was always the hard line—no cop-out, hang tough but negotiate.

Monday, November 3, 1969

The big day. P stayed at Camp David until 1:00. Arrived at White House and went right to EOB office for the whole afternoon. Called many times. Several shifts in plans about makeup, etc. Called and ordered me to take personal responsibility for the Oval Office, keep everyone out. Lot of questions about lighting, only one camera, etc. Did a great job on the air, content superb, delivery very good, with a few fluffs. Commentary after was mixed. After telecast, stayed *very* briefly for photos, then shot out and over to Residence.

Then started a long night of phone calls. From 10:15 to 1:15, he was on and off at least 15–20 times. Started wanting to know what we were doing for all-out counterattack (while networks were still commenting). Then asked for reactions, what did people around the office think? Then broader reaction. By 10:30, phones were ringing off the wall, all staff taking calls, and making checks around the country, and I reporting every few minutes to P whenever there was a new item. Got a lot of just ordinary people, and some bigshots. Then pressure about what is Klein doing to get reaction. Reports on editors around country. Then orders to get out wires and letters story in morning fast. Then the *New York Times* ad idea again. Then hit network management for biased reports. Then call Rogers and Laird, be sure they know about big reaction, shore them up. Then get reports from West (by now too late to call in East). Then a plea, if only do one thing get 100 vicious dirty calls to *New York Times* and *Washington Post* about their editorials (even though no idea what they'll be).

We had fun pumping the line onto LA TV in the late hours. And big crisis about getting the telegrams in. Couldn't get the supply line unplugged.

This process of immediate follow-up after a major TV address to the nation became established routine. It evolved from the President's sense of the need to know what effect the speech had on both the media and the people. This was especially true in the case of Vietnam speeches, because the raison d'être for them was the need to keep the nation informed as to what he was doing and why, in order to maintain as strong a level of public support as possible, and to deflate the opposition as much as possible. These were essential in order to carry out the ongoing negotiations with any hope of success.

The plea for "vicious dirty calls" to the papers was to keep pressure on them from the public in the hope that they would consider the other viewpoint occasionally.

Tuesday, November 4, 1969

Reaction day, and a spectacular one! Wires pouring in all day as fast as machines could process them. Piled them all on P desk. He greatly enjoyed going through them all through the day as the pile steadily grew. Showed his favorites to all comers. Almost all favorable, and about 43 referred to "quiet majority" *(P's phrase from the speech which would become famous as the "silent majority.")* Bill Hopkins *(White House Staff Administrator through many previous administrations)* says biggest telegram response to a president's speech.

P especially pleased at the reaction from the speech because he succeeded in moving people to action without demagoguing. His view is that you fire people up with a tough loud speech, but you win them over and change their minds only by calm reasoning.

Then the Prince Philip dinner, and the election returns. I came home and rode herd by phone. Great evening!

P called several times after I'd gone to sleep about followup on election results. Said rather thoughtfully and wistfully, "There probably has never been a day like this. Here was the press last week that we were in the dumps, lack of ideas, etc., but now look at things." Started each call with, "It's been quite a day," and it sure has!

Thursday, November 6, 1969

The euphoria continues. Reaction runs high, even the bad guys have finally agreed the P scored heavily with the speech and the election results. The worst the *Washington Post* could do was complain editorially that he shouldn't have been so happy about it. Now the telegrams are fading out and the letters starting, 30,000 today, amazing! Ended up with about 50,000 wires.

Had another talk with Borman today about his role and discussed it with P. Frank wants to come in, but has personal problems about moving and money, solution may be to have him work with Perot to set up a new institution that we can use as an outside arm to do a lot of the PR things, polling, distribution, mailing lists, etc., that we just can't handle from within.

P said this afternoon he really needs the weekend off, hasn't slept much recently, first getting ready for speech, then trying to unwind. Said this week brought a greater turn-around in public attitude than at any time since the Fund Speech in 1952 *(the so-called Checkers speech),* and interestingly both were brought about solely by a solo TV talk to the people, and both by Nixon.

Had a session with Pat Nixon and Bob Taylor of Secret Service about Julie's insistence that she not be protected. Hard to work out, but she is really insistent, can't stand the lack of privacy.

Monday, November 10, 1969

Main concern was to be sure we are maintaining the momentum, and not letting up. Again quoting General Patton about no tired divisions, just tired commanders.

> Nixon constantly preached the importance of not letting down in the euphoria of success and the necessity of driving hard to capitalize on it while it was hot. This seemingly odd attitude prompted K to comment to me once that Nixon was absolutely superb in dealing with defeat, and terrible in handling success.

Tuesday, November 11, 1969

Veterans Day, and focal point for National Unity Week, one of our several pro-Administration efforts. P observed it by visiting a veterans' hospital, which came off pretty well, after he called me in before leaving to emphasize no press coverage and no one to accompany him on ward tour. Feels very strongly about capitalizing on another's misfortune and just won't do it. Then he had a full day of general appointments.

Considerable discussion of Buchanan's idea of VP doing a major speech blasting network commentators. P feels it's a good idea. I discussed it yesterday with VP and he too is interested, but felt it was a bit abrasive. (Kind of humorous with all the attention he's getting for his recent "hatchet man" tactics.) Needs to be said and he's the one to do it.

Ross Perot just called about his United We Stand. Running more ads and a full TV show, really almost unbelievable. He is *really* determined and will get some results. Problem is his *total* lack of sophistication. But that doesn't stop him, our real need is to find a way to channel the energy and money productively. It's an amazing resource.

> Apparently this is when Ross Perot started his conception of "United We Stand," which was resurrected into a major political movement in the mid-1990s.

Wednesday, November 12, 1969
P really pleased and highly amused by Agnew speech for tomorrow night *(which took on the "unelected elite")*. Worked over some changes with Buchanan and couldn't contain his mirth as he thought about it. Will be a bombshell and the repercussions may be enormous, but it says what people think.

Had a busy afternoon (it was supposed to be clear) as P received 17 congressmen, senators, and staff who had worked the "Support the President" Resolution through the House and letters through the Senate. Got 300 in House and at least 58 in Senate, unprecedented support for a P on a divided and critical issue. P called *(Henry Cabot)* Lodge in Paris and then talked to him, on basis of effect this support would have at talks tomorrow when Hanoi presents its answer to the speech.

P called me in three or four times to discuss his "Evenings at the White House" idea, which is rapidly becoming an obsession and I can't figure out why. He insists on getting started with them and is full of specific ideas for what to do and how. Add diversion at a time like this.

P pushing Harlow on Haynsworth as the vote draws near. While he claims to want to avoid meetings and personal involvement, he keeps asking Bryce who he should see. All of a sudden he called Mansfield this afternoon and invited him to breakfast tomorrow morning. He knows it's virtually lost, but keeps thinking maybe a little more effort will push it over. Not really much hope, and he's already thinking about how we handle the defeat. Too bad, because this one was really bobbled by Mitchell and Justice in the early stages, and to a degree by Harlow.

Thursday, November 13, 1969
The *(Vietnam)* march started tonight at 6:00. No problems at the White House. Just single file of candle carriers with name placards of war dead. E and I stayed at White House all night, he in his office, I in the shelter. Not too bad. Went out and watched them for a while, mostly kids, some very young. Mostly solemn and quiet, a few kooky types. P not interested, spent two hours at the bowling alley.

Friday, November 14, 1969
Moon shot day. We left at 8:15 for Cape Canaveral, arrived in good, solid rain. Choppered to viewing area, waited in the rain for a half hour, got absolutely drenched. Saw the shot, but because of low clouds rocket disappeared right after launch, so not too spectacular. Then back to DC. Sessions on the plane both ways.

(P) was really pleased with VP talk last night *(attacking TV network newscasters)* and feels he's now become a really good property, and we should keep building and using him. Wants to be sure we keep riding the Congressional support story hard. Very anxious to get the *New York Times* ad run, hitting them for not carrying support story. Talked with Borman and is all set to have him go the Perot-route, to build a pro-Administration external organization to utilize Perot's money and steam for productive purpose. Frank also really hot on this.

After return, had three solid hours with P in Oval Office, since he had no afternoon schedule and wanted to just sit and talk. Covered Christmas plans for White House social events, wants it to be gay and fun, went through all the types of functions and people to cover. Discussed California vs. Florida for after Christmas. General ideas about State of the Union.

(Vietnam) march and mob grew violent tonight as groups tried to march on Vietnamese embassy. Police busted it up with tear gas, but they roamed streets breaking windows, etc. We were in E's office working phones, etc. when P came in, about 9:00, stayed until 11:00. Interested in whole process. Had helpful ideas like using helicopters to blow their candles out, etc. *(The marchers were all carrying candles in the night as a dramatic gesture for TV.)* Very relaxed. Said was like watching an old movie, keep thinking something interesting will happen. We stayed overnight again.

Saturday, November 15, 1969
Mobe Day. *(We referred to this day as the Mobilization or Mobe Day.)* The big march turned out to be huge. Official estimate was 250,000. By our photo count, it was 325,000. Anyway, it was really huge. E, Krogh, and I went out in helicopter to look it over in the morning, very impressive. Weird around White House because they have a cordon around two-block area, so no people, cars, or anything can get by the solid barricade of buses lined up end to end.

More violence in late afternoon as they mobbed Justice. Krogh there, said tear gas bad in Mitchell's office. Also very strange emotional impact as they took down American flag and ran up Viet Cong. Whole business is sort of unreal. They massed at 15th and Pennsylvania after dark and we went out on North Lawn to see them. No action, all just stood there, facing massive lines of police, jeeps, etc. Most with gas masks and helmets.

Sunday, November 16, 1969
White House church this morning, then to Redskins game, then to Camp David for the night.

Monday, November 17, 1969
P at Camp David until noon. Spent most of afternoon with me, about schedule plans, White House parties, especially for Christmas, a little Mobe postmortem, and his dream of having our own monster rally, with 500,000, to outdo them once and for all.

Tuesday, November 18, 1969
Main area of attention was Haynsworth. Vote now set for Friday. As we go into the stretch, it all of a sudden appears he might have an outside chance. Would still be a minor miracle, but it could happen. P is all set for a loss, and actually at this point that might well be preferable. Wouldn't lose much, and if he gets in he'll be a continuing problem. Especially would work out OK if P can find a good clean conservative Southerner to put in.

The debate on Agnew rages on, with P fully convinced he's right and that majority will agree. I talked to Stan Blair and told him to tell VP to keep up the offensive, and to keep speaking, now is major figure in his own right. P wants him to get maximum exposure right away.

Wednesday, November 19, 1969
Huge problem late today as Ziegler tells me of the VP's speech for tomorrow night, a real blast, not just at TV, now he takes on newspapers, a lot of individuals and the kids again. Pretty rough, and really does go too far. Problem is Agnew is determined to give it and won't listen to Ziegler, or Klein. Blair said, "Only I could turn it off," so I said he should. Now

we'll see what happens. All are at *(Japanese Prime Minister Eisaku)* Sato dinner tonight.

Thursday, November 20, 1969

Day starts deep in the Agnew problem, as we try to decide what position to take. Finally E, Harlow, and I agreed the original speech would be harmful, to a substantial degree. So we told P about it (since Blair had made it clear to me that nothing short of P would cause VP to make any change). P agreed, after I skimmed through the objectionable area, then said only way to handle was through whoever had written it. I didn't know. P looked at first page and said obviously it was Buchanan. He was right. I spent a long time with Pat, but as the final version came out it didn't do very much good. It still hits very hard, especially at the *New York Times*. I did get out the highly personal and defensive segments.

P made point that Agnew must be cool and calm and never defend against attacks from a lower level.

Friday, November 21, 1969

Bryce in for last-minute discussion about Haynsworth. Clear that it will be lost, estimate 54–46, but might lose one or two more when they know there's no hope. Chapin brought the news in at about 1:30. 55–45. P not at all disturbed, because had expected it. Did make the point to Harlow that we had failed to win any of the ones he'd had P really work over.

P called Haynsworth, asked him to stay on bench, and says he will.

In analyzing it, P concludes principal fault is Mitchell's. First for not having all the facts; second, for coasting on assurances from Eastland and Hollings instead of really working (they were assuming we had GOP fully locked), and keeping Harlow out of it until too late, and failing to see Griffin and others. Then at the end he overplayed, with excess pressure on some, which backfired, was too heavy-handed. So we learned something and politically probably come out ahead.

One Presidential reaction from Haynsworth was to decide to leave Griffin and Scott out of briefing meeting Tuesday about CBW *(chemical-biological warfare)*. Will have some big repercussions if he goes through with it. Also wants me to cover Cabinet officers Finch, Rogers, E and the others, about don't give anything to the 12 senators who went against us on both ABM and this one without White House clearance. Wants to play it very tough, and this I think we should do.

Saturday, November 22, 1969
Pretty funny day. P to dentist in morning, then back for meeting on budget with K, E, and Mayo. But he found out about Ohio State–Michigan game, and so cut the meeting at 1:00 to retire to his little office to watch. Wanted to shift afternoon dentist appointment, but we put a TV in the dentist's office, and he took a portable radio along, then regrouped with them for about an hour, then zipped off for Camp David in time to be sure to see start of SC-UCLA game. So the budget got squeezed in between the dentist and football on TV.

Also learned Gallup poll tomorrow will show popularity up to 68%, highest yet, and the Moratorium obviously didn't hurt us.

Monday, November 24, 1969
Have to plan foreign trip to avoid Julie's graduation because of bad guys. (Like Midway to miss Ohio State graduation last year.)

> This last point refers to the scheduling of the Midway meeting with President Thieu of Vietnam to coincide with the Ohio State graduation, which the P had earlier committed to attend. It was actually earlier this year, not last year. In both cases, the scheduling process was used to create a conflict which would provide a reason for not attending an event that would cause problems because of demonstrators.

Tuesday, November 25, 1969
Had a surprise session this morning when a free half hour came up and P had VP over for a chat. Mainly about his forthcoming trip. P wants him to go on around the world since he'll be halfway at Afghanistan. VP already has itinerary set and very reluctant to change. P told him he should now stop talking about the media except for some light quips, and said the VP could now talk about all those things he had been talking about before but no one was listening, and now they'll listen because he's become a national figure. Sort of a backhanded compliment, not intended that way. Main point was to

get the VP back on to constructive ground and stop him from riding the media issue to death. He got the point.

Question of astronauts going to Vietnam came up and P was furious because NASA said they shouldn't go because of political consequences or relations with Russia. P ordered that anyone expressing this view be fired immediately. He is sending Borman over in early December, and wants Armstrong to go for Christmas with Bob Hope.

P called tonight, wants me to call a staff meeting tomorrow, to have K explain significance of recent accomplishments, make point that Johnson couldn't have gotten NPT *(non-proliferation treaty)*, CBW, Okinawa, and draft because didn't have the confidence of the people or the world leaders. Thinks this gives our house liberals something to think about.

Wednesday, November 26, 1969

Had a session with E, K, and me. Said he had studied budget carefully and had decided we have to bite the bullet and move hard on a 25% personnel cut. Is going to work out a plan with Hampton of Civil Service to accomplish this throughout the departments. Feels we are in a terrible bind on budget and inflation and that the heart of the problem is personnel, all offices are overstaffed, especially at the upper levels. Recognized there are some areas that really can't be cut, but most can.

P comment when K told him of wires from Harvard congratulating on germ warfare move, "The wires would really pour in from Harvard if I surrendered the United States to Kosygin."

Thursday, November 27, 1969

Thanksgiving, and no word from P. He had a dentist appointment at 8:30, no advance press notice, and it worked out OK. Then the big White House dinner for the old folks, which was a great press success. Then the family left for Key Biscayne. Peace and quiet here.

Monday, December 1, 1969

P concentrated on the "hunger speech," because he'd decided the *(Ray)* Price draft was not right. Then the second try, following his instructions, turned out to be worse. Price worked on it all night last night, and he and Moynihan both called today to say it is a disaster, and that P will be booed if he uses it. I passed this on to P who, by midmorning, had E in with him redoing the whole thing. So he had E get the latest version to Pat and Ray, and they worked it into an acceptable, but camel-like, final version. The whole Hunger Conference is a disaster, due mainly to *(nutritionist)* Jean Mayer, who is clearly not on our side.

Tuesday, December 2, 1969
P didn't come in this morning, left right from Residence at 10:00 for Hunger Conference. Went pretty well, no boos, and adequate though not overwhelming applause. At least it's done.

Skipped morning budget meeting to have a long session with E and me, first on miscellany, then got down to the point, concern about speechwriter. Feels he just doesn't have the right guy. Needs a *(Kennedy speechwriter Ted)* Sorensen, a real craftsman who can produce compact, well-organized literate speech. Says he must have the knack of organizing a structure, making it speak well (not just read well), add the gimmicks for memorability and emphasis, and finally give it moving power. Feels our people are all too intellectual and are ashamed of using the devices and approaches that move people. Need is to reach folks, not intelligentsia.

Thursday, December 4, 1969
GOP Leadership, and P really rocked them. He started out pretty mad, due to Haynsworth and the current anti-White House bitching on the Hill. Charged in and told them Congress was totally irresponsible. That he understood why they individually had to take certain stands, but that he as P *had* to be responsible, and do what is right. When Rhodes said P might have to call a special session later, P said it will start December 27. Took them all completely by surprise. When Griffin objected, P said it will start December 26. Was really tough and they realized it. Both McCormack and Mansfield later responded favorably, and got right to pushing for action.

Had long session with Perot and Borman about Ross's ideas on outside support operations. While he wants to remain independent, and has a lot of project ideas, especially for TV, he's fully willing to support our need of a highly professional PR operation, and agreed to fund it. Went through his other

ideas and P generally agreed, so we will have Borman go
ahead and set it all up with Perot. Can really be productive if
it gets on track.

Friday, December 5, 1969

P came in this morning boiling mad about press and TV story
that *(Illinois Senator Charles)* Percy had released a letter tying
Chuck Robb *(LBJ son-in-law)* to Vietnam atrocities. Wanted
Ziegler to blast Percy and demand apology, etc. Simmered
down a bit as we found facts were not quite so bad, but tried
to call Robb, later got Linda, to express his concern. Had me
call Tom Johnson, and Tom put LBJ on the phone. Got a little
rough, because he was obviously very upset. Did greatly appreciate the P's concern, and wanted us to be sure and have
facts investigated. Wants Robb fully cleared. Implied strongly
he felt it was deliberately and politically motivated. Did say
he didn't want P worrying about his troubles, knows he has
enough of his own.

Problem with Congress, especially Republican senators,
deepens daily. Scott seems to go out of his way to take on the
White House at every opportunity. P is determined now to hold
to his line of the cold shoulder for those who don't stick with
us, and then to work closely with the good guys. Also is ready
to take Congress on, and not cajole them into each vote. Let
them vote us down and then stand on their record.

Saturday, December 6, 1969

P to Arkansas for the Texas game. All pleased with his plan
to present Presidential plaque to winner as number one team
in 100th year of collegiate football. Great combination of circumstances to make this possible, as final game of season is
between number one and number two teams on national TV.
He did a great job and TV covered it thoroughly, the arrival
by helicopter, the half-time interview in the press box, the
plaque presentation to Texas (15–14), the crowd scene outside
the locker room, the consolation visit to the Arkansas locker
room.

Great stuff. Especially at half-time, when P gave thorough
analysis of the game so far, and outlook for second half, which
proved 100% accurate. And some really good stuff in the
locker rooms, talking to the players. A real coup with the
sports fans.

Wednesday, December 10, 1969

NSC, on the Middle East. Ran way over time. Then P spent the afternoon at EOB. Had *(Wilbur)* Mills and *(Representative John)* Byrnes come down to discuss tax bill plans for Conference. P was going to tell them he'd veto any bill that had an increase in personal exemption, but Arthur Burns called me and said he now felt P could permit an increase, because other factors would counterbalance the revenue loss. I told him to get memo to P, which he did, and as a result P didn't take an unfavorable position, much to Harlow's horror. Real problem is to determine how far P can go in permitting amendments, or whether he'll have to veto bill and get no reform, and kill Social Security increase.

Thursday, December 11, 1969

LBJ day. Came for private breakfast and stayed over two hours. Apparently went pretty well, mainly because we've more or less ironed out his problems about pilot project for reviewing his papers and getting the geriatrics home back on track.

I had meeting with Stans, Dent, and Gleason about setting up our own funding for backing the good candidates in hot races. A little tricky to handle outside the RNC *(Republican National Committee)* but looks pretty good.

This plan, which was ultimately carried out under the designation of Operation Townhouse, was to develop a means of raising and allocating campaign fund support for candidates considered to be ''good'' by the White House. It came about because there were a number of GOP candidates coming into the field that were not considered ''good,'' and P felt we should do what we could to help those who would be most likely to support the Administration when elected.

Friday, December 12, 1969

Another breakfast, this time McCormack and *(Carl)* Albert. Then a meeting with POW wives, who really impressed the P. He now has a great interest, amazing what a little personal exposure will do. He now wants all sorts of action. All this got the morning schedule pretty well screwed up and had to juggle because of appointments. P pretty upset that we let it get screwed up. Overlooks fact that he added the breakfast, which was what threw it off.

Saturday, December 13, 1969

P wants a big meeting with Rumsfeld, Finch, Shultz plus E, Moynihan, Burns, Mayo and Nathan about whole area of overlap of OEO, fight it out and decide where and how to locate all the overlapping programs. A number of items today put over to that meeting. Feels all agencies proliferate too much, and should have one department in total charge of each program so everything clears through one place and there is some degree of control.

P took, as usual, very tough line on cutting, especially in personnel. Particularly zeroed in on PR people. Also moved hard on cutting the OEO programs he doesn't like, i.e., Legal Services, Head Start, etc.

Monday, December 15, 1969

Another Vietnam TV announcement day. P came in a little late and started out with complaint about inadequacy of speech preparation. In this case, K's, which he says is great on analysis, but turgid. Pretty full morning schedule, mainly with Quadriad. That started things snapping, because he realized economic outlook still bad, so told Mayo to cut all budgets 25% (he's been saying this for weeks and not really meaning it, but now feels he's really got to push the cuts as far as possible).

Chatted a lot before lunch, then he ate, gave Rose final changes in speech draft, then went to EOB for the afternoon, while they set up his office for TV. Came over just in time to go on the air, did a great job, probably his best-read speech yet, paced slowly and very relaxed and confident. Not great news, is withdrawing 50,000 more troops. Decided against really big chunk now in order to save some for spring.

Talking about moves to approach youth. He says to forget it, that if we are alienating youth it is because we have to, can't give in and coddle them. We do have to take them on, silence would be approval or at least acquiescence.

Tuesday, December 16, 1969

This afternoon, P lighted the national Christmas tree. Not very anxious to do it. Cold as the dickens, and windy. Fairly large group of peace demonstrators in the crowd with Viet Cong flags, etc. Started shouting when P started to speak, he plowed right ahead, ignoring them, but it was pretty bad. Called me in as soon as we got back, felt strongly we shouldn't have gone, will either do it by remote, or not at all, in future years. Feels, and rightly, that President of United States should not be subjected to this kind of indignity. Problem is there's really no way to control it, and you can't just stay locked in the office. Actually he took it pretty well in stride, but it obviously rankled him.

General reaction to speech last night has been very good, but not too many people saw it because of the early hour. Seems that P has pretty thoroughly gotten into the position of calming down the war opposition, killing the mobilizations and assuring the people that he has a plan and that it's working. Can probably keep it that way for a while. Problem will be if Viet Cong mounts a big offensive, or some other turn-around.

K is still cranking on his meetings with the Communists. Tomorrow is the Romanian emissary, still no clue as to what they, the North Vietnamese and the Chinese are up to, but it still looks as if there's some pattern.

Big problem persists on oil import quotas. Have to make some decision, and can't win. If we do what we should, and what the task force recommends, we'd apparently end up losing at least a couple of Senate seats, including George Bush in Texas. Trying to figure out a way to duck the whole thing and shift it to Congress.

Wednesday, December 24, 1969
Great political coup! P toured White House offices after buying 150 lbs. of candy to distribute.

Wednesday, December 31, 1969
San Clemente. Long session with P, partly with Ziegler and E. He had a lot of odds and ends stored up to run through. Set the plans for tomorrow. He'll sign the Environment Bill which was going to be done next week, so I am having it flown out tonight by special plane. At one point he thought he'd sign it at midnight as a special way to start new decade. Fortunately got off that kick. Big problem on setting time for bill signing was to avoid conflict with any of the football games on TV. He's really become a total addict.

K also in for a while. Discussed Perot's adventures in trying to get food, etc., to the POW's. He and his people have been calling K, E, and Haig all through the night to ask for various kinds of help. P said, "Well, he's no worse than the State Department."

P was displeased with *Time* Man of Year, said it was the first time they haven't selected the President in his first year. Checked and this is not true. They didn't pick DDE until 1959. They *did* pick FDR, HST, JFK, and LBJ in their first years. Interesting!

It would appear that being a Democratic president substantially increases the chance of being selected by *Time* in the first year. It was "coincidences" like this that helped to develop our feeling that it was very difficult to get a fair shake from the clearly liberal press.

Did a little pushing about our operations, said, "We can't be satisfied with just doing well, we have to do better. We have so little time. While you've got the power, you have to move quickly, especially now when we're up, build a mythology."

1970

First Quarter: January–March

> The first week of the year was filled with schedule plans, a trip to Bob Hope's house in Palm Springs for a meeting on the GI Bill and a few rounds of golf for the P.

Wednesday, January 7, 1970

(San Clemente) P all cranked up last night with K about reports that Peace Corps men were demonstrating against Agnew in Afghanistan. Then today similar reaction to Stuart Loory story in *LA Times* about cost of Western White House. Wants me to move ruthlessly to get him *(Loory)* removed from White House. Really mad in the evening, when he called me.

Fairly light day. P and Bebe went for drive and walks along the beach to the south. First had a session on trivia.

Came up with big plans for having government use Western White House as year-round conference center when P not here. Wants to have base for justifying the cost, not really necessary since virtually all the major expenditures have been on government property.

Thursday, January 8, 1970

Back to DC. Long sessions in the late morning, going through all his notes, schedule guidance plans for Western White House government use. Called E and me up for long session on the plane. Heavy dose of political strategy review, need to build our own new coalition based on Silent Majority, blue collar, Catholic, Poles, Italians, Irish. No promise with Jews and Negroes. Appeal not hard right-wing, Bircher, or anti-

Communist. Need to study the real base, and the reason for Agnew upsurge. Feels he's getting coverage on his trip because he attacked the press and forced them to pay attention.

Then a long analysis of PR, and where we've failed. P's main thrust is that we haven't adequately developed the image of him and his role and the office. Need to build image now while going good, in order to carry over when going badly. Ideas for new year, wants to hold aloofness theory, and build on it.

Great quote, "No leader survives simply by doing well. He only survives if the people have confidence in him when he's *not* doing well." Basis of his reasoning about need to move fast and hard now to build up mystique. Have to build the equity now on the personal side so when the attacks come the person stays above the attack.

Feels 1970 will be the worst year, have to ride it through. Will have inflation/recession, no turn on crime, election attacks, etc. But will improve in '71 and build up to '72. Must be prepared.

P called me back up with Bebe about problem of personal household staff, lousy food of wrong kind, etc. Wants me to solve it. Also wants to change personal family cooking, but Pat Nixon approves the menus. Gave orders about wines, no French or California white, only Moselle or Rhine, Johannesburg, only Bordeaux red or *very* good light French Burgundy. Salad, wilted lettuce and Camembert.

Friday, January 9, 1970

P's birthday. Had a staff card, and talked him into a press photo shot with Rose and new secretary presenting it. Worked fine, but P his usual awkward self, just can't cope with personal-type situations. Explained the whole card (*Washington Star* front page) in minute detail. But the photographers couldn't have cared less. In late afternoon went up to Julie's for dinner, wouldn't let us announce it ahead because of probable demonstrators. All was fine on arrival, but during dinner a bunch of bad guys arrived and chanted outside the apartment. Julie cried, P left abruptly, really too bad. Press pretty good on it, but tough on the family.

P reviewed Price's first real draft of the State of the Union and said it was eloquent, and a complete disaster. No substance, no cheer lines, no organization. Led to a new harangue on need for a speechwriter who can write a Nixon speech. Tough. Hard for Ray to hit it right when he has no direct contact with P and no real guidance. Led further to discussion of need for P to spend most of next week writing his own speech. Feels it is more than twice too long. Said, "Now I can see why I decided not to do it last year," and is very happy that he's doing this one at noon instead of prime time. *(P did not give a State of the Union address in 1969.)*

Saturday, January 10, 1970

P really slept in, up about 11:00, and not in to the office until 12:30. Met with K for about two hours. Big problem in Biafra. We have secret word that they have collapsed. K feels there's a real danger that all six million Biafrans will be massacred or starved to death. K in and out all the rest of the day on this. P had me stay to discuss the household problems again. Told him of my talks today with Walter and Lee Annenberg. May borrow Annenbergs' cook to solve the family problem.

P was bringing me more and more into the area of East Wing operations, those of the First Lady's office, because of his dissatisfaction with specific factors from time to time and his unwillingness to get directly involved himself. This was a difficult role for me, and one I resisted but not always successfully. I did try to work with the Pat Nixon staff to get the P's problems handled, but this was sometimes a cause of friction.

Sunday, January 11, 1970

White House church, Vienna Boys' Choir. No word from P.

K bounced in with word Biafra was about to fall, P ended up calling Prime Minister Wilson to discuss plans for flying food, etc., for the refugees.

P jumped all over me about progress on converting the pool to press facilities. Said he hoped the contractor was a Republican because he must be making a fortune.

He watched the Super Bowl most of the afternoon. Made a lot of calls about Biafra.

Monday, January 12, 1970

Limited schedule to provide time for work on the State of the Union, but he didn't use any of it for that. Did have several long sessions with me, and with E and me.

(P) spent most of the afternoon sessions reviewing and reverting to the new Derge poll. Was fascinated with the findings and had made a lot of notes on analysis. Especially interested in the strength of the Silent Majority, the weakness of the Moratorium, the decline of the Republican Party. I suggested change in party name as a start on new realignment and P very seriously took me up on it.

All set to bring Chotiner in as inside White House man for political campaigns. Mixed blessing.

> Murray Chotiner was an extremely able, shrewd political strategist and operative of the old school of politics and in many ways a real asset. But many felt he lacked the finesse and appreciation of the far-reaching importance of Presidential political actions that were a basic requirement in the White House.

Concluded we can't really stop inflation in this year, the only real solution is controls and that is unpalatable, so you just make the best of it. In this case form is more important than substance.

Tuesday, January 13, 1970

Another day supposedly cleared for work on State of the Union, but no work done. *(Instead, the day was filled with a series of appointments and a Cabinet meeting.)* I think this is a classic example of forced procrastination. The draft he has is totally unsatisfactory, and he dreads getting started to work on it, so keeps inventing excuses. Will have to get at it pretty quick and he knows it, so I will bet on Camp David tomorrow afternoon, stay until Saturday and that he'll waste a couple of days, then get it pretty well started. This will mean a rough week next week as he tries to wrap it up.

Wednesday, January 14, 1970

Since P was supposed to go to Camp David last night, he had *nothing* on the schedule for today. Managed to fritter away the morning, mostly by reviewing a long list of things with me. Then spent about a half hour at noon trying to settle on a departure time and whether to go over to EOB first. Settled on 4:00 and no EOB, then got bored and left at 3:30. Finally decided to get Safire and Buchanan cranking on the speech, as well as Price. Says he needs more input, at first wanted bits and pieces by noon tomorrow. Then called me at dinner, and said to have them each do a draft. He'd read the book of past State of the Union speeches and decided he wanted his to be Wilsonian, which apparently means short. Maximum 3000 words, 25 minutes. Thematic instead of programmatic, with strong uplift, etc.

> All this hemming and hawing about getting to work on a major speech is pure Nixon. This had been a pattern during the campaign, the convention, the transition, and now the White House period. I tried to develop a basic plan for handling it more efficiently, but found it was usually best just to clear the decks and let the process run its course. There did not seem to be any way to change Nixon's personal modus operandi. This is one of the basic essentials of the job of White House Chief of Staff, as I understand it. That is, to adapt to the individual P's ways of working, and make them as easy, efficient, and comfortable for him as possible.

Concerned about use of K's time, especially with press. Wants me to take over his schedule guidance for public and PR things, get him to see the right press people and not waste time on the unwinnables.

Had long PR staff session on philosophy and approach and told P about it, he was fascinated with the whole discussion. This is always at the top of his interest level.

Friday, January 16, 1970

P at Camp David, still alone. Called several times, about schedule and miscellaneous stuff. Some ideas on speech, said he's going to hit on uplift theme about what's ahead, and can just hear the intellectuals grinding their teeth and saying why doesn't he talk about pollution in the rivers.

Saturday, January 17, 1970

P at Camp David, still alone. Long call at noon with a bundle of instructions for the speech. Feels he's ready now to zero in, apparently is getting a general feel of what he wants to do, but still not really writing his own draft. Looking for statistics, etc., and also doing some background reading. Has been sleeping late in the mornings and working very late at night. Breaks at noon and dinnertimes and spends an hour or so on the phone. We've done very well at keeping calls and interruptions away from him.

Sunday, January 18, 1970
Had all the drafts he wanted waiting for the P in EOB at 10:00, and I waited in my office for his arrival. He didn't get up until about 1:00, and went to the office a little before 2:00. He'd gone to bed last night at 12:05. At 12:30 there was a fire alarm, and the ushers discovered the P in the Lincoln sitting room trying to light the fire. He worked there until after 2:30.

Monday, January 19, 1970
Another day of speechmaking. P at EOB all morning and afternoon except for couple of meetings at midday. Appointed Carswell to the *(Supreme)* Court, called him to confirm it.

This was Judge G. Harrold Carswell of Florida. Shortly thereafter, his nomination began running into trouble because of a statement he had made back in 1948 supporting segregation.

Made point of wanting Justices to balance out regarding the Constitution, and said after you are appointed I'll never talk to you except socially, but I must appoint men who will bring the balance, and your decisions show you will.

Had me keep K out all day again, doesn't want to get distracted.

Tuesday, January 20, 1970
Inaugural anniversary. Hard to believe a year has passed. Late in the afternoon P came back over to Oval Office and buzzed for Rose and me. When we came in he was standing by the desk in his overcoat, he reached over and opened his silver cigar box and it played "Hail to the Chief," he just stood there with a sheepish smile, and then said, well, it was there a year ago.

Thursday, January 22, 1970
State of the Union. Big flurry this morning about final changes.
Speech was great success, *very* well delivered. Covered all the
Democrats' issues and left them having to agree in general and
carp about lack of specifics. No really strong opposition so far,
may come in next few days when they figure it all out. Also
was short, 35:20. I timed with stopwatch.

Had a little staff session in P office to present anniversary
gifts. He was as awkward as usual, but everyone enjoyed it,
good touch! A few afternoon appointments, then had K and
me in to rehash the speech a bit. Feels good about it, knows
he did well.

Called me at home several times. First to report on his phone
calls around, all reaction had been very good (what else is
anyone going to say to him?). Then a little later with some
specific changes in the budget message, so apparently he's
gotten back to work. I thought he'd fold early.

K called all disturbed because Laird is skipping the NSC
meeting tomorrow where he's supposed to hit the hard line on
ABM; wants to be able to say he wasn't present when decision
was made to go ahead. Dedicating a nuclear frigate instead. K
really mad.

Friday, January 23, 1970
NSC meeting about ABM, and VP's report. K and P really
startled by State position on ABM, backing off. K had expected Defense problems, Laird didn't even come to the meeting. K very agonized, finally late today told P that State and
Rogers were engaged in all-out systematic effort to destroy
NSC apparatus. He feels this strongly, and ties it in to current
heavy PR program at State to build up Rogers. Feels he'll have
to have confrontation and threaten to leave, or have Rogers
take over full responsibility.

Tuesday, January 27, 1970
A loaded day, trying to catch up. Prime Minister Wilson arrival
with usual fanfare. Big feature was the new uniform of the
White House police.

The new uniforms were designed by Jimmie Muscatello. They
included double-breasted white tunics, trimmed with gold,
gold buttons and a stiff military hat with a high crown and
plume. The idea was inspired by Nixon's exposure to foreign
police during his '68 European tour. The press thought the
uniforms were inappropriately formal and military-looking.

At midday break did all the signing and then chatted about
being worked too hard, especially in having to do so much
speechwriting. Busy afternoon with a bunch of cats and dogs.
Finished at 5:00 right on schedule. Decided to drop TV press
conference on Friday and do one in the office instead. Feels
he's overexposed and doing too much. Real reason is problem
of having to get "up" again after State of the Union and veto
speeches *(the appropriations bill for Labor and HEW was too
high, and the P vetoed it).* Obviously is anxious just to let
down a little. We talked him into leaving it on, partly because
Ziegler had already announced it, but also because he knows
he really should do it. But then he really lashed out about how
hard he has to work, and the inadequate staff support again,
especially about speechwriting. Flared up a bit for a few
minutes, then simmered down, and obviously realized he had
little choice. K encourages the view that he should limit his
exposure, E argues just the opposite. After they had left and
he was on the way out he made the point that E et al. will
always push to do more, and that I must hold the line. State
dinner tonight for Prime Minister *(Wilson).*

Wednesday, January 28, 1970

This afternoon P had an hour with *(Democratic Senator)* Harry
Byrd, about his possible shift to Republican Party. Don't know
the outcome. Then filmed an interview in the Oval Office with
Art Linkletter and four kids. Then to the Residence for a reception for all the congressmen who voted to sustain the HEW
veto. Got 191, a great victory! And a sensational way to start
off the second year, with strong action and a major Congressional coup.

P holed up tonight at EOB with the press conference briefing books, no word from him.

Good meeting today with the PR group, really have a pretty
good system rolling and the results show it.

Thursday, January 29, 1970

Press conference preparation. P really blew a fuse when he came in just on schedule to meet the Environmental Council of Advisors and discovered he was supposed to go before press with the group and announce them. Had not prepared remarks, etc. A classic staff goof in setting up the meeting. Really amazing how few of these we have. He rallied to the cause all right and did very well.

Had first of the "Evenings at the White House," with (Comedian) Red Skelton. Was a smashing success and will be a great new program.

Flap on new White House police uniforms is building. E doing great job of backing out of it, and apparently Secret Service approved the headdress all by themselves after E had okayed the tunics. It looks like a long-lasting point that they'll keep bringing up in cartoons, etc. Can't hit us on substance so they pick away at the fringes.

Friday, January 30, 1970

Press conference tonight. No schedule all day in preparation. P spent whole day at EOB till one hour before airtime, then to the house to get dressed. Called couple of times on specific questions.

Good press conference, he was more combative and hit harder than in others. Afterwards called me in Mess to get an evaluation, and asked that E, K, and I do a total evaluation of the whole drill. Made point that there are 178 questions in his briefing books, and only did 18 on air. So a lot of extra work. Said why don't we do it like de Gaulle, who would talk for thirty minutes then answer four questions that he had ordered asked, and only once or twice a year.

Also wants to see how many press conferences LBJ and JFK did in their later years, after they wised up to fact they were doing them no good. Feels it would be much better to get exposure on *our* ground and with *our* issues, i.e., mini press conferences once a week or so, one subject only, and look for other better ways of exposure.

Huge flap today over leak of budget in *Washington Post*. P not too upset, but staff meeting was a real blow. Ziegler and K both pretty shook, and E really rough on Ziegler especially. Turns out leak was probably GPO. I called McCracken because it appeared CEA (*Council of Economic Advisors*) was the source, and he immediately offered to resign.

P later made point that these leaks are a real problem because they will necessitate his eliminating the planning and discussion meetings which he doesn't like anyway and only holds for therapy. Says LBJ and other presidents have overreacted, and he won't. But still is a problem.

Saturday, January 31, 1970

P met for an hour privately with Arthur Burns before his swearing-in *(as Chairman of the Federal Reserve Board)* this morning. Called me a couple of times for factual data about Fed *(Federal Reserve Board)* for his remarks and to set up, in front of Arthur, a new plan for regular meetings of the Quadriad. Then had David's swearing-in for the Navy, in Don Hughes' office. P off to Camp David with David and Julie, Pat Nixon in Key Biscayne with Tricia, who has the measles.

Sunday, February 1, 1970

P at Camp David, then down for White House church, then meeting with Ross Perot. Guess he worked all afternoon—I had left a lot of stuff in his office and he had a full briefcase at Camp David.

Monday, February 2, 1970

Discussion with me on wide range of ideas. P was quite impressed by his talk with Perot yesterday, especially Ross's idea that the only way to get things done is to have for each project one manager with total responsibility for results. Get rid of boards, advisory committees, etc.

About staff, he is fascinated with our plan to reduce White House staff by moving *our* people into departments and agencies, which we badly need. Said like in poker game, don't leave in anyone you have to feel sorry for, get down to hard group, lean and tough.

Talk about press conference strategy. P fully convinced he should do only two or three a year on TV, because of basic problem that they are not to our advantage because they don't feature our issues. A lot more on need for better press on P's image and leadership. Says trouble with all our backgrounders was that they were all on *what* we accomplished, nothing about personality of the man. Point of JFK did nothing but appeared great; LBJ did everything and appeared terrible. Taft infinitely more effective than Teddy Roosevelt. Teddy Roosevelt had personality. Taft just *did* well.

Wednesday, February 4, 1970

Rather a slow day, with some juggling of the morning schedule (afternoon clear, Wednesday plan).

Staff meeting mainly about obvious move by the "Establishment" to reopen the Vietnam debate. All the magazines hit it this week. Clear that they gave us 90 days after the November 3 speech and are now back at it. Also lot of effort to revive Moratorium activities. Have to remobilize the Silent Majority and get our own fires burning.

P issued strict orders that Ziegler and White House staff are to say *nothing* about Vietnam until further orders. Has to keep complete control and not let an inadvertent comment play into their hands. Also has embargoed ABM.

Hit me again on failure to redirect our hiring from New York, Harvard, Ripon types to South, Midwest, and West. Is really determined to change the balance. Told the Congressional staff group he would reappoint Haynsworth if we picked up three senators and could get him confirmed.

Told me to tell E he plans to take on the integration problem directly. Is really concerned about situation in Southern schools and feels we have to take some leadership to try to reverse Court decisions that have forced integration too far, too fast. Has told Mitchell to file another case, and keep filing until we get a reversal. Told E to get *(HEW Office for Civil Rights Director Leon)* Panetta's resignation by Friday. (E already has it, has been holding it, undated.)

The school desegregation issue was becoming more important as enforcement strategies and tactics were debated between the White House, Justice, and HEW. P's very strong view was that the major impediment to successful desegregation was the liberal establishment's determination to interpret the law as requiring total integration rather than desegregation. He felt that pushing too hard and too fast would just continue to lead to more and worse confrontations, whereas a policy of moderation and steady progress would bring far greater and earlier success. Panetta was a leader in the push for speed and rigid enforcement and the P ordered him removed. Panetta had suc-

cessfully resisted earlier efforts to remove him, so P took the
route at this time of simply announcing Panetta's resignation
at a meeting.

Saturday, February 7, 1970

P had farewell breakfast for Bill Rogers, who is off to Africa.
Then came to office about 8:45 and no one in yet.

Going again on his determination *not* to play to blacks and
professional civil-righters. Is convinced we gain nothing. Key
is to limit all our support and communication to the *good*
blacks and totally ignore the militants, etc. Afternoon meeting
with the Cabinet group working on Southern school problem.
Then off to Camp David with the whole Mitchell family, plus
Rose and Chotiner.

Tuesday, February 10, 1970

Morning was set aside for preparation and filing of a brief
summary of the big environment message, which went to the
Hill today. Worked out well, as P used a lot of the time productively, had makeup, and did an unrushed TV shot for the
networks in the Oval Office, and it was good.

A discussion with E about school problem, with the result
of at least considering a P statement directly taking on the
courts for ruining the school system in their zeal for full integration. A dangerous step, but maybe not as dangerous in
the long haul as doing nothing. Late in the day Harlow came
in about mass rally tonight in Charleston to try to block busing
decision. Shaping up into real crisis, and P will ultimately
probably act on his own personal conviction that forced integration is wrong.

Wants a lot of planning and thought given to question of
how and when to use TV. Back now to idea of more frequent
press conferences, etc.

Gave me a little lecture to cover with key staff. Wants us
always to approach a tough problem with great confidence, and
only tell the P *once* that it's a hard battle. Don't keep on
telling him over and over that it's a real problem. Obviously
a reaction to K's incessant hand-wringing, and Harlow's
overdramatic statements that "This means real big trouble."
He says he *knows* the problems are hard, but wants us to worry
about how to solve them, not about how bad they are.

Wednesday, February 11, 1970

K got P all stirred up about State Department recommendation that P not issue his Foreign Policy message because it would conflict with State's. P rejects this out of hand and ordered me to call *(HEW Secretary)* Elliot Richardson to transmit his very firm view (Rogers is in Africa).

Also very concerned about a story that Administration was considering a shift on voting rights. Wants to be sure we don't let anyone back off on any of the civil rights positions.

Ordered me to have *Portnoy's Complaint (an allegedly pornographic best-seller)* removed from White House library and put out story he'd done it.

Left for Key Biscayne after Business Council dinner.

Thursday, February 12, through Sunday, February 15, 1970

At Key Biscayne. P stayed out of work, called me two or three times a day, but had no meetings. K also down finishing up his foreign message. Settled the flap with State, as they decided not to do a report. Rogers very upset, wanted to talk to P, but never got a phone connection.

Long chat on trip home about recession-minded Cabinet members, like those of DDE's in '57 and '58. P more inclined to follow Shultz as only really knowledgeable economist.

Monday, February 16, 1970

First flap of the day, about VP school desegregation group. Rump session this morning decided to overrule decision last Saturday and set up big meeting in Atlanta tomorrow night. All signs indicate a historic turning point, away from all-out integration programs, with recognition they don't work. Great break for us. Agnew made big pitch for his using a new Buchanan speech, about end of desegregation movement. Wants to give it in Atlanta this week. Others all opposed in varying degrees. P agrees with Buchanan thesis, but feels Atlanta the wrong place, and doesn't want VP to get out beyond his own position, and thus become oversold as the Southern strategy man. Afraid to dilute or waste the great asset he has become.

Tuesday, February 17, 1970

A long discussion of school problem, with even *(Senator)* Scott agreeing we should go for another Congressional vote against busing, to try to impress the Courts and deflect their present trend toward ordering end to de facto segregation nationwide at any cost.

P made *very* strong statement of his position and his real concern that we may be headed for total chaos unless the courts let up. They all seemed to agree. This has become the major cause of the moment, and may really be very serious. Great advance political possibilities.

Couple of long talks during noon and late afternoon, as he broods over the school problem and some other current issues, especially recession. These clearly are the two big ones now. Great detail about Agnew speech. He's inclined now to think he should do it, especially on Harlow's recommendation, based on talk with VP at lunch, which convinced him that VP has valid point that if we don't move out on this, a Southern Democrat like Russell will, and might unite the right and left-wing Democrats on a strange basis, both against the Courts, but for opposite reasons. Feels we can preempt the proper position by going first, and also must avoid being trapped in the position of having to enforce integration by busing or gerrymandering in the North.

K all cranked up about his secret trip to Paris, fully covered, and no one knows he's going. He loves the intrigue, and P enjoys it too.

Wednesday, February 18, 1970
Cabinet meeting. McCracken gave a brief report, then P launched into his antirecession pitch, which set off Romney, who was not supposed to get into his wage-price-policy pitch but did.

P finally really whapped him by saying wage-price-policy had never worked; Romney said it had in England; P laid him low saying, "Don't talk to me about England," and explained differences. Pretty sharp alignment of Romney, Volpe, Blount (and Stans, who was absent) against the Shultz-McCracken view, which is to handle things by fiscal and monetary policy.

P had Shultz and me in after meeting, and covered the subject further, trying to lock up George's view, which made George fear that P thought he was a wild man on the subject.

P spent most of afternoon at EOB. Had Harriet Elan, Chapin's Negro secretary, come over to talk about problems and viewpoint of a responsible intelligent Negro. Obviously P deeply concerned. Later kept saying to me there's really no adequate solution and nothing we can do in the short haul to settle this, it will have to take one hundred years, but people don't want to wait.

Really mad at the Jews because of Pompidou reaction and is saying so pretty loudly.

French President Georges Pompidou had sold Libya over 100 Mirage jet fighters, and many in the Jewish community had announced a boycott of his upcoming State visit.

Thursday, February 19, 1970

Another day of concentration on the school/race problem. Was really mad about report that DC school board had caved in and fired a white principal and put in a black. Afraid if we let all this go on it will result in adverse counteraction that will build a monstrosity, i.e., Wallace. Is convinced, though, that Northern liberals, Ribicoff and Bayh, are going anti-busing only to trap the Administration politically. Is really afraid we're in a dilemma. If we strongly oppose de facto integration, Court may still go against us, and then P has to enforce order he has opposed. But if we don't lead in opposing the trend, we'll have impossible decisions. Way out is that government can interpret the Court in a very narrow way, and we must.

As one idea, wants to get a right-wing demagogue into some tough race and have him go on basis of anti-integration, would get enormous reaction, might even win.

This is a fairly typical strategy on Nixon's part—i.e., to set up, or hope for, an external extremist view to be launched which would in turn bring counterpressure on the extremists of the other side instead of letting the current activist element dominate the debate and the action.

Feels now we have to develop a careful plan for the whole approach to schools. Can't go on fuzzing the issue forever.

Wants Agnew to go ahead with his speech, but doesn't want Buchanan to write it. Wants to work on revision of it himself.

Started pushing again on wide range of general follow-through items.

Meeting in EOB with Tower et al., late afternoon, about Senate races. Andrew Wyeth dinner, great success, with Rudolf Serkin as entertainment. One of the best functions, key seems to be a homogenous group.

Friday, February 20, 1970
Cleaned up some odds and ends, with fairly light schedule. K left this morning on his secret mission, obviously all cranked up, going in Air Force One, elaborate cover, etc. He really thinks it may mean something. In typical K fashion, with all the secrecy, he then leaves by chopper from the *Ellipse.*

Change of view about the Agnew speech, based on memo from Garment and Price. Now decided P must make the speech, and that it needs a *lot* more work. P *very* impressed with column in *Post* by William Raspberry (black) about school problems and idea that forced integration won't work. Met with group of Catholic educators which got him really going on support for private schools. Had *(Special Counsel Chuck)* Colson in and gave him orders to "break the china" and get things done.

Told *(speech)* writers this *(school desegregation)* is a very historic crisis, and the country must not move in the wrong direction. We must hit it effectively in a way that will affect the Court. Says there's only mileage in this for demagogues. Fine for a man who *wants* to be Governor but not for a man who *has* to be President. Must mobilize the *decent* opinion, but not throw down gauntlet to Court.

Volunteer dinner tonight.

Saturday, February 21, 1970
Another day of long talks. Then he left for Camp David at 3:30 and I spent three hours just trying to get my notes cleared up so I'll have a slew of appointments with staff next week.

Really got into a harangue on follow-up. Especially distressed about Carswell, because we are apparently not doing anything positive, while the opponents are charging ahead just as they did with Haynsworth.

It's been a long week. Tried to set up new office procedures with my move to the corner office, but I spent most of the week in the Oval Office listening.

Sunday, February 22, 1970
P at Camp David. Called once.

Monday, February 23, 1970
Defense Panel and NSC meetings in morning. K back from his journey Saturday night. Reported to P Sunday at Camp David. Is pretty pleased, feels made a start towards some real progress. Long talks and he was (he says) very tough. Quite a stir about P's orders to Colson to charge ahead on the Catholic school thing. He did, and there are some problems, with Moynihan especially opposed. Wants E and group to submit a proposal for strongest possible forward position, but *some* action.

Chuck Colson was originally brought into the White House to work in the Congressional liaison area, but his assignments were expanded to include general relations with outside interest groups, i.e., labor, ethnics, special causes. He also became more and more of a special assignment man for the P, primarily due to his eager willingness to carry out any Presidential order with great zeal.

This inevitably created major problems from time to time because it often involved an end run around the system that had been carefully set up to be sure that all orders were properly staffed and the concerned parties notified and given the opportunity to provide alternative views or recommendations, or to express opposition for stated reasons.

Late afternoon got into quite a long talk probing whether we need to get tougher, both on the rest of government and on our own staff. Feels maybe we aren't hard enough on backsliders and I agreed. Problem is that P is not willing to stand tight on unpleasant personal situations and won't back us if we do. He has a great way of "working it out" instead of confronting head-on. We need to make and win some challenges to get real control, but can't yet.

Tuesday, February 24, 1970
Pompidou. Good arrival ceremony, extra fanfare, and larger crowds laid on to compensate for snubs, etc., expected elsewhere. P *very* anxious to do all we can.

Good busy afternoon of appointments, including meeting with Rogers to report on his African trip. K scared to death he wouldn't be asked to sit in and afraid to ask for fear of turndown. All worked out fine. Then had me in for another long one at 5:45.

Main subject was introspective rumination about his role and use of his time. Said had done a lot of thinking over the weekend about his three classic roles, leader of party, chief of state, head of government.

Wants to have more concentration on thinking deeply about the important decisions, and time to read and think, and to rest enough to be always in best physical condition.

Doesn't like relying so much on staff for major decisions, wants staff to do *all* minor ones, but feels he should get much more deeply into the major ones and know what he's doing.

Also emphasized need to concentrate overall thinking about public stuff on TV; that's all that counts. Says he can't spend his time just signing his name and reading briefing papers someone else has prepared.

So, a lot of soul-searching that indicates an uneasy feeling that he's not really going at it the best way. I think he's right. Main problem is how he'd use the time if it were made available. Right now he generally wastes it in trivia.

Wednesday, February 25, 1970
Governors' Conference.

Thursday, February 26, 1970
Really raged again today against United States Jews because of their behavior toward Pompidou. Has decided to postpone Jewish arms supply for their "unconscionable conduct." Also said, in front of K, not to let any Jews see him about Middle East. Said they can go talk to *(New York City Mayor John)* Lindsay and *(New York Governor Nelson)* Rockefeller about whether *they* can provide arms for Israel *(they were boycotting Pompidou's New York dinner)*. As mad as he's been since we got here.

P did later postpone delivery of our jets to Israel, as threatened above.

Called *(Representative)* Wilbur Mills to thank him for getting Family Assistance through *(House)* Ways and Means *(Committee)*. P played it straight although Democrats did this to try to trap P with unworkable program. Will backfire on them as P succeeds in getting first major social legislation in decades.

P spoke at White House Radio/TV Correspondents dinner, and was a hit with brief and funny remarks. Had some good gags, several of them his own, and delivered them beautifully. Tough crowd, virtually all against him, but he made some points. Called me at home after and was pleased with himself. Also delighted because he had just called Reagan, who will stand up to the Jews and escort Pompidou in California.

Friday, February 27, 1970
Started off the day by refusing to sign a decision about glass imports. Wants E to move fast on developing a constitutional amendment about schools. Feels we should bite bullet now and hard, if it's called racism, so be it! Feels we have to take a black or white position (didn't even notice the pun), can't be on both sides because we just get hit from both and please no one. Feels the only good thing we've done in this area is to fire Panetta. Says an *act* is better than a statement, because it comes through loud and clear.

Saturday, February 28, 1970
P came in late, brief meeting with me on miscellany before conference with group Moynihan assembled about black problem.

Very interesting session, three hours in Cabinet Room, with professors from Harvard, Berkeley, Columbia. P in good listening form as well as participating.

Group all felt P should shift policy to helping and backing the strong instead of putting all effort into raising up the weak.

Sunday, March 1, 1970
All quiet until just after church when P called from Camp David, had report from *(Protocol Chief Emil)* Mosbacher about treatment of Pompidou by Jews in Chicago. P furious. Will announce cancellation of Israel arms tomorrow, wants legislation to provide protection for foreign visitors, and he will go to New York dinner tomorrow night to add an extra touch.

Really disturbed because Mrs. Pompidou has decided to go home tonight, wants to try and stop her. So we swing into immediate action this afternoon and have all the wheels grinding. Fun to have a crisis, if only a little one.

P also cranked up about two major leaks in *New York Times* today, especially one of Moynihan memo about blacks. Wants a complete freeze on *Times,* etc.

> Moynihan had urged a cooling of overheated racial rhetoric—a period of "benign neglect" during which progress could quietly continue. The phrase was immediately taken out of context.

Monday, March 2, 1970

Pat Nixon left this morning on her college tour. P had light schedule all at midday because day had originally been kept clear for press conference tonight which was dropped. He had a meeting with Raspberry, black columnist, about his thoughts on the school problem. This continues to be the main item of interest, plus work on the Laos statement.

At 2:30 we left for New York and the Pompidou dinner, moving the departure up an hour to confuse the demonstrators and the press. Trip turned out a huge success. We went right to the Waldorf, spent balance of afternoon there, P meeting with K about Laos, and a private meeting with Pompidou who was deeply touched and impressed by P's gesture of coming to the dinner. P got great reception at the dinner and scored with his remarks. A darn good maneuver. Had to reroute motorcade into Waldorf because of threat of man with gun on FDR Drive, so went through crummy area of lower Manhattan. P went into quite a harangue at the hotel about the miserable city of New York, and the whole impossible problem of how to make such cities livable, really can't be done.

Tuesday, March 3, 1970

Full schedule today, but not dinner tonight (was going to have a private one), so he can work on Laos statement. Leaders Meeting this morning on education message. P had long meeting with VP about their plans for Gridiron and then into other areas. (They're going to do a piano duet, which should be great.) Quadriad meeting in late afternoon.

Wednesday, March 4, 1970

NSC meeting this morning. Cabinet and Subcabinet groups about reorganization this afternoon. P canceled Irving Kristol dinner tonight to have afternoon and evening to work on Laos statement.

Wants us to move hard on Larry O'Brien now that he's back as DNC chairman. P feels this is clear signal that Teddy is back in control, all the maneuvering was just a dodge to cover this. Is worried about O'Brien's effectiveness, especially as a spokesman, will say anything and has great ability to get on TV. Wants Chotiner to manage Operation O'Brien.

I don't know what this was specifically, but it was a plan to discredit O'Brien.

Some more long talks with me about his internal analysis and planning and need to get to concentration on priorities. Will really push to have all secondary matters handled without his involvement. Wants second level staff to step up to this and act for White House and P whenever they need Presidential strike; should feel free to do it by proxy. Is prepared to deal with mistakes and bad decisions as inevitable so long as lower level staff handles.

Made point that Churchill's technique was to make little notes on every little item as a way to create a sense of movement and keep things happening.

Thursday, March 5, 1970

(Budget Director Bob) Mayo session. Bob launched into an extensive anti-E diatribe full of petty complaints. Topped it off by saying he'd probably better resign, since he and E were at an impasse on question of where policy is to be made. He contends Budget (or OEM) cannot be divorced from policy development. P handled whole thing beautifully, putting off decision until next week. Said afterward real problem is Mayo doesn't realize policy must be controlled by the P's men, and they aren't in the Budget Bureau. P is apparently ready to let Mayo go. He had a good session with John Connally and is

strongly of the view that he would be ideal head of OEM. This may turn out to be the solution.

In the Connally meeting, P outlined his whole line of thinking about delegation, etc., much to Connally's approval. Connally made point P must be totally ruthless inside the Oval Office, but firm and human outside. Also said he should not pay any price to mollify Cabinet members. Should be tough with them, and let them go if they don't like it. Connally tracks well with P and would be an excellent addition if we could get him in.

P gave dinner for NAB Regional Chairmen, a motley collection of high- and low-level types and a real waste of time and effort except as a sop to Don Kendall. Then off to Key Biscayne for the weekend. Spent most of the afternoon trying to keep P on track about Key Biscayne, he decided he didn't want to go because of bad weather, but finally agreed to give it a try. Then had to wait one half hour on plane because of starter problem, pretty late night. E and I in cabin for whole flight, K in and out about Laos.

Friday, March 6, 1970
In Key Biscayne. Beautiful cool sunny day. No word from P. K did backgrounder on Laos and we released the statement. Went out on Bebe's boat for an evening cruise.

Saturday, March 7, 1970
Still at Key Biscayne, weather okay in morning, clouded up after the eclipse and rained at night. Still no word from P. He did talk to E a little about schools. Went out on the *Julie* in afternoon, press boat got up close and caused a major flap.

Monday, March 9, 1970
We got back into the Laos flap which, in K's absence, took an enormous amount of P's time.

Problem arose because of discrepancies in terms and in numbers of men killed over the years. K had given out more specific information than he should have in the briefing Friday, and then had guided the press group in giving out some more on Sunday. Turned out today it was inaccurate. So poor Ziegler had to explain, in two long involved briefings. P spent a lot of time with him working it all out.

Apparently came out reasonably well, but the whole episode

shows more clearly than anything yet how the White House press is totally dedicated to screwing us rather than getting the facts and reporting them. They bent every effort to tangle it up and prove a credibility gap instead of trying to get it straight. P called me at home tonight to have me call K to tell him not to nitpick Ziegler and Haig's work while he was gone. They had done outstanding job.

I was in for three and a half hours this morning, alone except for Ziegler in about a half hour. Went through my whole pile of schedule and information material and got a lot decided. Nothing very important. Worried about Mitchell's image and need to get crime action going; plan for GOP dinner and need to avoid P getting partisan; meeting on economy and need to get interest rates down; some long-range trip plans; some press guidance for Connie Stuart; some songs he wants Johnny Cash to do at his "Evening at White House"; and the need to build up Herb Klein.

Tuesday, March 10, 1970
P met with Timmons' attack group first thing, not too impressed with either the group or Timmons' planning.

> This was an informal team set up to find and capitalize on Democratic weaknesses—including any tax problems they might have.

Had me in after for long talk about how to build up the whole attack operation. Wants a new group set up to go hard on this. Also wants to be sure we are doing an all-out hatchet job on the Democrat leaders, through IRS, etc.

Call from Chapin, saying K *had* to see P, new break in Mideast. P won't see him, K very upset. Problem continues. P wants me to try to untangle him too. I learned from Haig this morning that K had really battled with Rogers on phone yesterday about Laos, and the whole deal is really building up. P's refusal to see K today won't help, but it is just because he doesn't want to get into Middle East with K. Going to be hard to keep this on track.

We left EOB after another hour, P to the Residence. I was confronted first by Garment, wanting to know what was wrong; E had dealt him out of school statement, then got into whole Jewish problem and gave me a handwritten letter from Golda Meir to P. Then in came Moynihan with a new internal memo that has been leaked to *New York Times,* this time from clear back in January '69. Someone's really rolling on the memo leaks.

Wednesday, March 11, 1970

K finally got in, after not seeing P at all yesterday. He's still shook about Laos, and credibility story is still riding. K wanted to do another backgrounder on the theory that he could straighten it all out and get the subject back to the merits of the case, instead of nitpicking statistics. We said he shouldn't, at staff meeting, then he took it up with P, who also shot it down. Later in day P had E, K, and me in for a little lecture about how we all will have problems and we must take them in stride, etc. All directed at trying to get K to quit beating a dead horse and move on the more constructive efforts. Trouble is, there really is a problem. Epitomized by Laird's statement yesterday that Defense had given P the wrong figures on Laos casualties on purpose to cover up secret operations. Pretty shocking.

K is in pretty bad shape, feels he goofed and thus let P down and was taken in and had, by both Defense and State, and has lost P's confidence. The lecture was designed to undo this, and to get him back in gear, but I don't think it worked. Will probably have a continuing problem on this, and will just have to play it day by day.

The whole situation occupied most of the day for most of the key staff.

P had to do State Department drop-by and GOP fund-raiser dinner tonight. Is pushing for more free time to work out his civil rights/school position.

Another Moynihan memo leaked today, and P wants me to clamp down on leaks. Problem is how. He's extremely well controlled on this, but doesn't think we should just let it go on. Wants to try the five men against a wall technique.

This refers to the story about the five suspects who were lined up against the wall and told that the one who had done the wrong must step forward immediately and admit it or all five would be shot.

Thursday, March 12, 1970

P had a bipartisan Congressional session about Consumer Affairs, then a meeting with GOP Governors Executive Committee. Then had piano practice with VP, for Gridiron, great idea doing duo piano practice routine as complete surprise. This afternoon a long talk with Moynihan and interview with Dick Wilson for feature article in *Look*. I was only in a couple of times and then very briefly.

Tonight P stag dinner with key staff and *(conservative writer)* Irving Kristol. Got off to slow start and through dinner P talked with Shultz about labor matters, Kristol just listened. Sort of a waste of time and talent. In Oval Room after dinner the talk heated up, about whole subject of condition of the country, focused on radicalization of large number of college students, strength of nihilistic groups (in influence, not numbers), and how to deal with it all. Attorney General was incredible. Has an absolutely fixed point of view. Wouldn't even listen, and when he did, he didn't hear. Insisted on expounding on and on. P finally turned him off so we could hear a little from Kristol. Must say, Kristol didn't add much.

I had two hour private session with Mayo about his concerns on OEM, now OMB *(Office of Management and Budget),* and E. Turns out his real basic problem is purely personal and is based on his conviction that E is obsessed with determination to acquire total control over government. Can't talk him out of it. Also a very strong vein of pure egotism and status worry involved. Trouble is, he's a really top budget man, but a woeful choice for this new top management job. I think he knows it, and that may be the real overriding cause of his trouble, although he sure won't admit it.

Friday, March 13, 1970

A last-minute decision first thing this morning to go out and visit Washington Technical Institute, all-black vocational college. Lots of risk as building bombing threats continue and all DC schools suspend classes. But all went well, a few anti-demonstrators, most of students friendly.

Off to Camp David in late afternoon. K thinks he's working out a deal on Mideast. He is fascinated by complexity of P's mind and approach. K loves this kind of maneuver as does P, and K is amazed by P's ability at it.

K also still hopeful of a deal in Paris. He goes back again tomorrow. Thinks if the North Vietnamese have anything positive this time, we'll be on the way to a settlement this year. A real coup if it works out. Problem is to maintain balance in United States, and this is getting tougher as Senate critics fire up again, especially about Laos. Also we have a Gallup *(poll)* that shows P down 11 points on handling Vietnam.

Lot of concern growing about terrorism and left-wing plans for violence. Many in staff feel it is a real and major threat and that it extends to the P and top officials, assassination or kidnapping. Feel we are not taking adequate preventive measures and that we have totally inadequate intelligence.

Saturday, March 14, 1970

Very funny, P has secret plan to do a piano duet with VP at Gridiron tonight, and didn't want *anyone* to know about it. Midafternoon, VP called Chapin to be sure P had arranged for two pianos, said he had through me. Called me to check. P had said nothing, I had done nothing. So I had Chapin call P and sure enough he hadn't made the arrangements. Would have been quite a fiasco! Anyway, Chapin worked it all out. P's idea was an absolute smash hit as he and VP did a stand-up dialogue first, then played favorite songs of past presidents, with VP coming in each time with "Dixie," climax, "God Bless America." The whole audience rose and sang along with them. They also played "Auld Lang Syne" with Marine Orchestra and soloist, for the finale. Great idea and beautifully executed.

P called me after we got home, was really pleased with how it had come off, as he should have been. Feels he'll never be able to top it, and won't even go next year.

Sunday, March 15, 1970

P meets this afternoon with *(Reverend Billy)* Graham's group of black ministers.

Tuesday, March 17, 1970

Biggest problem of the day came via phone call from P after I got home. K had apparently hit him again on the Rogers problem, said Rogers is out to get him and takes a stab two or three times every day. Probably comes from Rogers having a meeting with P yesterday while K in Paris. P trying as usual to stay out of it, and K as usual obsessed with discussing it in detail. P wants me to try and get him turned off, and to take a vacation for a while to simmer down.

I had long talk with K this morning about Paris. He's still very optimistic because North Vietnam was at least willing to discuss mutual withdrawal, which is first admission they even have troops in. K playing tough, uneager role, and they keep going for the next step. He wanted to wait four weeks for next meeting, they said no, must be in two weeks. So maybe there's hope. K says if we can hold here in United States for two to four months he thinks we'll have it.

Wednesday, March 18, 1970

Cabinet meeting with the new tables, chairs, and decor. Looks great. First juggling Cabinet around. Would love to get rid of Kennedy, Romney, Volpe, and especially Hickel. But not much hope. Wanted Morton to take a stab at getting Hickel to go back to Alaska to run for Governor again. And maybe Romney to do the Senate after all.

Then finally got to the real point, K. He's really worried about his obsession with the idea that Rogers is out to get him, and even more by his inability to stay out of the Israel problem. Talked about how we could help by trying to get K to stick to priorities, etc.

P worked at EOB all afternoon on press conference briefing books. Called me over at 6:30, to talk about book from K too thick. Problem is as staff gets bigger their work gets more voluminous and less valuable and less imaginative and more careful.

I brought up George Murphy problem again, which I had spent several hours on in the afternoon (*the ex-actor was running for the Senate in California*). The *LA Times* ran a horrible editorial against him and that reopened the efforts to get him not to run, but no one thinks it can be done, except possibly by the P. He's perfectly willing to try if we want him to. So we have to get more information.

Thursday, March 19, 1970

The morning was kept clear to prepare for filing a statement on education, so P had E and me in for a long session, then a longer one with me after E left.

School statement still in great agony, major internal staff division. P doesn't want to indicate in any way that we'll move on *de facto* segregation or imply that we'll spend money on buses. Said to leave out "maintain momentum" and "morally right" type phrases. But then says Buchanan is just as far off on the right as Garment is on the left.

Also wants to move on hard legislation hitting people who plan bombings—fast, and hijackers. Wants death penalty for both.

Start of a postal strike today that could spread beyond New York, wants to be sure we do what we should.

Alabama poll we took indicates Brewer can beat Wallace for Governor, so we'll put in $100,000 to make sure. P has slogan for him, "Forward with Brewer, Not back to Wallace."

The $100,000 would be contributed by the outside campaign fund group that was set up for the purpose of raising and distributing funds for candidates designated as key prospects by the White House.

P loaded with appointment schedule for afternoon. I spent most of it on the phone about George Murphy problem. Still going back and forth on whether P should call and try to get him to pull out. Finally concluded he should at least call and get Murphy's evaluation and give him a chance to react by pulling out. P called after the "Evening at the White House," Murphy said he'll win and that's that.

Friday, March 20, 1970
Day kept clear for press conference preparation. But postal strike in New York is still on, and P got into some lengthy sessions with E on it. He spent whole day at EOB. P's first reaction was for really tough stand, examine the law, if people can be fired, fire them, if troops can be moved, move them; wants to do something now, this morning, not going to tolerate Federal employees strike. Says suspend them if we can't fire them, all-out attack, not worried about the mail, it's the principle. Wanted E to get this all worked out and bring over an order for P to sign. Then got worried that E should be working on school statement instead, must have by 5:00 today, after

press conference. Later called over, all upset because K making an issue out of State reluctance to bomb Laos. Rogers wanted a meeting, to argue P's decision. P told me to tell K to go ahead and bomb, don't make announcement or notify State, just do it and skip the argument. K in a bind because he's committed to Rogers to notify him before any strikes.

At midday, as P got better feel of seriousness and complexity of postal problem, he decided not to have the press conference today. Will probably do it tomorrow morning. In discussing items with Ziegler for briefing, P said, "Hard-nose it at the moment, we'll have some good news before long." Wants to be sure not to express concern, etc., about postal strike because that implies we're not in control, lack of leadership, etc.

P talked with Shultz on phone, said he'd do anything he wanted about meetings, statements, etc. He's anxious to get in command of the situation.

Spent the balance of the day working on briefing. P later decided to hold the school statement until next week partly because it's still not really ready, and because he'll do press conference tomorrow.

Postal problem settled in late afternoon when union leaders agreed to get workers back in, then negotiate. At least E thinks this settles it. I doubt that leaders can get workers back, since it's a wildcat strike to begin with.

Saturday, March 21, 1970

P in early, to EOB, to work on briefing books. Had to spend quite a little time on postal problem. The settlement didn't work, because rank and file won't go back, have rejected leaders, and now SDS (Students for a Democratic Society) types involved, at least in New York. Walkout has spread to many other cities, including Chicago, where they voted a strike. Real danger of national strike, with need then to call in troops to deliver mail, and police to disperse pickets. Strategy is to do the least we have to do, but to insure the delivery of the mail.

P had a press conference in the Oval Office at 11:30. Canceled plan to go to Camp David, to stay on top of mail crisis. Threat now is of radicalization, a national strike, other walkouts, i.e., Teamsters, Air Traffic Controllers, etc., to cripple whole country at once. Would provide a real opportunity for leadership, but how to handle it? Overreaction could bring a real disaster.

Sunday, March 22, 1970
A busy day as the postal strike issue got worse. Most of us were in several sessions with P and with Shultz, etc. No action today, will see what the workers do in the morning. If they don't come back, P will move with troops, consequence may be bad. P spent whole day at EOB on this and with Harlow on the school statement. Wants tomorrow cleared to finish statement and be prepared to act on strike.

Monday, March 23, 1970
Maybe an historic day. P ordered troops into New York to take over essential mail services. Started with a long early morning session in my office with Blount, Shultz and E, plus Klein and Ziegler. Went round and round on what to do, and all the possible consequences. Finally, inevitable that he use troops. Shultz was the last holdout but finally agreed we had to do it. E, Ziegler and I went over to EOB and told P. He fully agreed. Set time and plan for announcement on national TV, with top leaders meeting first. Got a statement prepared. Amazing how little leadership in the group, but finally got them divided up and onto work.

P alternated between strike and segregation, still trying to get school statement out tomorrow. Hung in balance until 5:00 and then decided to go. Harlow riding herd on it, with E jumping between the two projects. P obviously thoroughly enjoying the pressure and need for fast action. Stayed at EOB all day except to come over for Leaders Meeting, that lasted so long he had to postpone TV fifteen minutes. Rushed into little office, quickly read final draft over (Rose was late getting it typed), and then went on the air, with excellent seven-minute statement. Had signed State of Emergency and Order for troops at Leaders Meeting. Went right back to EOB and to work on school statement. There until 5:30, back for meeting with labor group, building trades, then Harlow and E about statement until 7:35, when he left to get dressed for 8:00 African dinner. A really busy and maybe momentous day.

First results appear to show some success as some of the

big locals vote to go back to work. But New York still out, and troops moving in tonight. Strike could easily spread back out across country and into other unions.

(Postmaster General Winton "Red") Blount got into a flap with the Army over who's giving orders. E had revised Red's timing and quantity of original troop movement. I had to call Army and tell them to take orders from PMG *(Postmaster General)* only. E of course concurs.

P again completely cool, tough, firm and totally in command; fully aware of it, and loving it.

Tuesday, March 24, 1970

School desegregation day. After weeks, the statement is finally out.

> P reaffirmed his support of desegregation and his opposition to busing. Emphasis was put on local authorities and voluntary compliance rather than Federal enforcement. P also said he would request $1.5 billion over two years for local desegregation.

P had bipartisan leaders for breakfast and a briefing. Said Teddy K asked the only smart question, "Where will you get the money?" Then E et al. had a one-and-a-half-hour press briefing on it. No reaction yet, but P pleased with final result.

Blount and his Deputy, Ted Klassen, trapped me in late morning about White House staff interference in Post Office negotiations, especially Colson. They were really mad. Three-hour meeting this afternoon at Post Office. Finally got Blount to agree to Usery (Labor) as the chief mediator in charge. Hard to beat the Post Office down, they are determined to have full control in their hands.

At meeting looked as if we were in pretty good shape externally, problems all internal, mainly ego. All unions basically back, except New York, and their leaders are here and anxious to meet. We seem to have the upper hand. Problem is to keep it, and move on from here. Also air traffic controllers threaten walkout tomorrow, a disaster if they do.

Poor K, no one will pay any attention to his wars, and it looks like Laos is falling.

Wednesday, March 25, 1970

Had planned on Key Biscayne at noon today, but Congress is staying in session at least until tomorrow, and the postal negotiations start at 2:00, so decided to wait until tomorrow.

P had NSC meeting this morning, then spent rest of day at EOB until meeting with Senator Cooper about ABM and Carswell at 5:00 in Oval Office; after that to Residence.

Made point in meeting this morning that under no circumstance would he declare a national holiday for Martin Luther King.

Some more discussion about Carswell, still worried for good reason as he continues to decline, lose a few senators each day.

Easter weekend spent in Key Biscayne. Continuing concern re Carswell nomination, postal negotiations, and the possibility of a "sick-out" being called by the air traffic controllers.

Monday, March 30, 1970

Now K is all stirred up. Had him stashed away at Paradise Island for a week's vacation, but he's afraid to be away if crisis breaks, and Cambodia is brewing one. After numerous calls, I finally talked him into staying, much to P's relief. He knows K needs time off and rest.

On March 18 General Lon Nol had overthrown Cambodia's Prince Sihanouk, which was all right with us, but Lon Nol's troops were having a tough time against the Khmer Rouge and the North Vietnamese.

P met with Blount and E at 5:00 when we arrived at White House. Fairly encouraged about postal negotiations. Spent evening at house on phone. Getting caught up after absence. Toured new press facilities and seemed pleased.

Tuesday, March 31, 1970

Back to work in earnest. Fairly light schedule resulted in my spending hours in Oval Office on all sorts of odds and ends.

Moynihan in to see me, disturbed about staff leaks designed to screw him, especially via Mollenhoff. Made point he's ruined in Democratic party because of the "benign neglect" memo. He's really distressed, mainly because he has nowhere left to go. A tough day for me, pages of notes of details for follow-up. Got them all done, though.

Second Quarter: April–June

Wednesday, April 1, 1970

(P) had a meeting with Rogers this morning, and concluded
he's got to have more of these without K. Feels K doesn't give
him accurate picture of Laird's and Rogers' views. Always
puts it in black and white. P talked a long time with E and me
about this problem, trying to figure out how to handle this.
Basically, it's impossible because of the characters, especially
K. But Rogers clearly maneuvers to clobber Henry. Haig is
doing great job in K's absence, and P agrees. Has had several
long sessions with him. Ordered a big retaliation move because
North Vietnam hit us, wants to knock out a SAM *(surface-to-
air missile)* site; Haig feels this is wrong, told P so. Wants to
wait until Saturday so as not to screw up K's secret talks in
Paris.

P also got into problem of where you find people for government service. Must have judgment, character, loyalty, patriotism. Most lack at least two of these, especially the Eastern
intellectuals.

Thursday, April 2, 1970

Settlement day. Postal agreement. Knew we had it at noon
when Usery made deal with *(George)* Meany, but had to go
through motions of negotiating session. Now have to sell it to
Congress. Came out pretty well, P especially anxious to get
positive interpretation on it.

P interested in basic political and philosophical problems,
as outlined in Kevin Philips' thesis about lack of a conservative elite, and the Pusey report about the problems at Harvard.
Trying to figure out where to put together our base. Broods
frequently over problem of how we communicate with young

174

and blacks. It's really not possible, except with Uncle Toms, and we should work on them and forget militants.

The air controllers problem goes on, and the plan now is to fire a bunch of them, especially after postal settlement, to prove government employees can't win by striking. Theory is that the mailman is a family friend, so you can't hurt him, but no one knows the air traffic man. Also they make a lot more money, hence invoke a lot less popular sympathy.

Haven't told him about the latest Gallup, he's down another 3 points after an 8-point drop a week ago, that wasn't published. Confirms a downward trend, probably due to a general lack of positive exposure. He has really been out of view, but doesn't seem to realize it.

Friday, April 3, 1970
Pretty busy schedule up to departure time for Camp David, so not too much chitchat today. Carswell battle moving ahead a little better.

Wants to consider letting (*Teamsters' leader Jimmy*) Hoffa out of jail. I'm to have Mitchell talk to Shultz and work out a plan.

Called me from Camp David, still on subject of postal deal. Wants more action on setting the tone. Especially keep Congressional people on it. Try to get our people on Sunday TV. Also worried about who's throwing the first baseball. Wants to have David do it.

Saturday, April 4, 1970
P at Camp David. I stayed home to do taxes. P kept calling all day. Mostly with more thoughts on postal settlement. K has his Paris meeting today and back here this evening. Will want to get right to P, who will be tied up with Duke of Windsor dinner.

Sunday, April 5, 1970
K called, back from Paris. Meeting went OK, but no breakthrough. Thinks Cambodia has thrown them completely off balance. They think we engineered it (*the coup*) and can't figure it out. K thinks they would have been ready to deal but are now confused. But they didn't close things off; K did say he wouldn't meet again unless they had something positive to offer. He's going to stay on a tough line. Hard to tell how

well K evaluates these sessions. He tends to be all one way, optimistic or pessimistic, and colors everything based on his basic reaction.

Monday, April 6, 1970
Breakfast with LBJ. Nothing startling.

Another long talk about poll situation. Gallup will be out Thursday with the big drop. P trying to analyze why. Feels we have proven that a lot of activity, i.e., messages, stunts, etc., doesn't do any good about national popularity, only events affect this. Strongly says we shouldn't worry about doing something every day. It doesn't make any difference, so not worth all the effort and expense. Instead should be sure to do *more* to follow up and capitalize on the big events that *do* make a difference. Ordered an immediate phone poll to see effect of past two weeks.

P decided to go to opening ball game in about 5th inning.

Made point again that we need to change the Agnew approach. He is a very effective salesman for himself but not for the Administration. Has become too much of an issue and a personality himself.

Tuesday, April 7, 1970
Too much open time in schedule, plus E gone through Wednesday, plus setbacks in polls, etc., resulted in my getting caught for hours of conversation and analysis. *(P)* very cranked up about final stages of Carswell battle, feels staff is not adequate. Then a lot of talk about lack of enthusiasm, in the Administration and especially in White House staff. No one takes the offensive, all just lie down (except Garment and Moynihan, who aren't really on our side). Don't radiate enthusiasm, because really don't feel it. Said I should see movie *Patton*. He inspired people, charged them up, chief of staff has to do this. Pointed! Said everyone works long and hard and all comes out blah, no fire except after November 3, and then didn't follow up. Thinks we rely too much on P for all this, wants to see some leadership in others.

Wants a complete analysis of all Presidential activity and TV coverage and its effect on polls this year, to prove his point that doing stuff doesn't help.

Wednesday, April 8, 1970

Carswell day, and he went down the tubes! Too bad. As the day started we had a pretty good chance. P's immediate reaction was to decide not to submit another nomination until after the elections, and then go for Bob Byrd of West Virginia. I urged an early start to the effect that if it was obvious this Senate would not approve a Southerner, then put in a good Northern constructionist. May do that. P did feel we had not done adequate job in our Congressional group, but that main fault was Justice. He called Carswell, good brief chat. No substance except urged him to stay on Court. He will.

P very concerned that staff, et al., not overreact to this and to tomorrow's Gallup poll, that shows a new low of 53. Will have another one Sunday, back up to 56. Odd! Lot of talk about the polls, had our quick phone poll that gives him 59.

He decided to go out on the boat for dinner, with Mitchell and me. Very nice cruise to Mt. Vernon, and chopper back. Long talk about plans for next appointment.

K in for a while this afternoon, discussing Dobrynin talks about preliminary plans for Summit this fall. P wants to go to Berlin, Leningrad or Warsaw. P also said we've saved Laos for four weeks at least, and maybe we can hold a few weeks more. Set plans for troop withdrawal announcement on 16th, 150,000, big!

Thursday, April 9, 1970

Started the day by canceling Cabinet meeting this afternoon to keep the time clear to work on new justice, etc. Decided to go with troop announcement Thursday night 16th, prime time TV. Set up Monday meeting with Laird, Rogers, Wheeler, and K to finalize. But will not tell them the real plan. Wants a program set up to leak 40,000 reduction to *Post* and *Times,* then go with 150,000.

Wants to step up political attack. Investigators on Kennedy and Muskie plus Bayh and Proxmire. Also get dope on all the key Senatorial candidates, and especially crack the anti-Carswell groups.

By "investigators" P is referring to E's two men that were used to handle investigations that were outside the normal scope of the Federal investigative agencies. The two former New York policemen were Jack Caulfield, who was on E's White House staff handling special assignments, and Tony Ulasciewicz, who was paid by outside campaign funds.

Wants to capitalize on Carswell defeat by really moving on our contributors, to get new Senate. Have to declare war.

Decided to do a strong crime statement, maybe tomorrow on TV. Again looking for the offensive to counteract defeat. Have to find some way to get across the point that he can't appoint a judge from the South, find a way today to do this on TV. My suggestion was to go on TV for two minutes with very simple statement, no questions. He decided to do it. Met first with Mitchell, then really cut loose in press room. Probably too strong, but he doesn't think so.

Then turned into a demon for the rest of the day, on follow-up. Knows he really banged the Senate and partly wants justification, partly thinks he's scored.

Then had political group in to charge them up. Read statement, chortled with glee over the tough parts.

Friday, April 10, 1970

(German Chancellor) Willy Brandt day. Usual State Arrival and private meeting. Had me in first about more battle plans for follow-up on his statement. Started really mad because Semple in *New York Times* said his statement was "bitter." (I think he knows it *was* bitter and thus doubly resents it.) Set up meeting with Mitchell and *(Minnesota judge Harry)* Blackmun, the new Justice for this afternoon, *completely* off record. But the name leaked from Justice, and was in *Evening Star.*

Saturday, April 11, 1970

Brandt farewell, and SALT delegation farewell. Then a little chitchat about "it's noon and another week over." Took off with Bebe for boat ride, then to Camp David. Called to see if anything new. Pretty calm, thinks he got things cranked back up. Planning a hot week, with Justice on Monday, postal deal on Tuesday, crime blast on Wednesday, Vietnam Thursday.

Monday, April 13, 1970

Another of those days of hours alone with P in Oval Office, just talking. A few appointments in morning, and a Cabinet meeting on the economy in the afternoon. Lot of talk about new justice and plans and timing for announcement.

P got K's draft of Vietnam speech, and had me take it to read vs. his December 15 speech. K's new one completely negative, three times too long and misses point. I convinced P to let Buchanan take a stab at boiling it down. P feels K is lost cause as writer, also in reading his Paris report it's obvious he can't negotiate, he makes debating points instead.

Some concern about Mitchell, and especially what can be done about Martha.

> Martha's behavior was sometimes outlandish, due to both emotional and drinking problems. It was a source of embarrassment to both John and the Administration. However, John was always patient with her, even later when it became a public issue.

At about midnight, K called about problems of Apollo XIII on way to moon.

> A fire and power failure had knocked out the Command Module's systems. The astronauts would see if they could cram into the Lunar Module and make it back to Earth.

He wanted to discuss all the possible problems that the abort and possible disaster would raise. Also very concerned as to whether we should notify P. I decided no, on basis there was nothing he could do. Then Chapin called with advice from Safire. And K a couple more times. And finally to sleep.

Tuesday, April 14, 1970

Apollo 13 day. And the Danish Prime Minister. P had to spend two hours on arrival and meeting, and was furious that visit had even been scheduled. After that the rest of the day was spent on Apollo XIII, starting with E urging an instant trip to Houston, which we managed to avoid, after getting Borman to recommend against it. Then a whole review of other alternatives to show P's concern and interest. Finally ended up going out to Goddard Space Center for a briefing; good move and it worked out fine. Whole deal still pretty shaky, but there's apparently an even chance that they'll get back. P resisted all grandstanding ideas. Decided to postpone Vietnam speech because of Apollo abort. Will wait until Monday. P called Laird and Rogers to tell them, and order no discussion.

I got into a bind with VP by ordering him to halt on runway at Des Moines as he was leaving for Houston. Made him sit and wait for over an hour while P was with Prime Minister, then raised question with P, and he fully agreed VP should not go to Houston for same reasons P shouldn't, *plus* upstaging P. VP mad as hell, but agreed to follow orders and go to Florida and wait.

Overall a crisis day that came out OK but showed we aren't really geared for it. Too much confusion and duplication as everyone gets into the act. Need more discipline and routine. Not too bad.

Wednesday, April 15, 1970
Long morning session on schedule, as we rejuggle the next couple of weeks and set up for various contingencies about Apollo. Lot of discussion about various options for P about Apollo return; go to Houston, go to splashdown, etc. P determined to find exactly right way for his getting into it. Wanted to be first one on the air to announce safe landing. I reviewed a whole range of these with Borman, then back to discussion with P. Out of that developed my plan for P going to Houston to greet ground crew and take wives to Hawaii to meet astronauts. Give them Medal of Freedom. P spends as much time discussing the problem he has of shortage of time, as he does doing the things he says he doesn't have time to do. Seems to have lost a lot of the basic "feel" of the job that he had. Partly a result of multiple unsolvable problems bearing in, and partly a function of less newness in the job. He really needs crises to deal with, and is not at his best with a period of general erosion such as this. Moved well on postal strike, Pompidou, etc., but not good on self-initiated momentum. This is undoubtedly perfectly natural and, I suspect, represents a normal doldrum period through which we'll pass.

Thursday, April 16, 1970
Big news activity day. P briefed Congressional leaders on SALT, then another session on postal deal, then this afternoon the House passed Family Assistance. Plus continuing suspense about Apollo, although no new developments on it today.

Apparently he did outstanding job in morning meetings because he was concerned about getting out the line about decisiveness, command, etc. Feels gist of an operation is ability to command a group and he has it to much greater degree than Kennedy, Johnson, or DDE, but we don't ever tell anyone. Compares to Teddy Roosevelt, Wilson, and de Gaulle, whose staffs all got enormous coverage of the mystique, without participation by the principal. Feels his main strength is his ability, but he gets no credit for it, which is necessary to build up and thus make it even more effective.

Fascinating discussion about his ideas for his own funeral plans. I raised subject during discussion of astronauts. He wants simplicity, only one DC service, at Rotunda, no horse. Need a layman for the eulogy, no ideas. Graham and *(Norman Vincent)* Peale for prayers. All contributions to Boys Clubs. Burial at Rose Hills near parents, simple service. Told me to work up all the details, he didn't care about them.

Friday, April 17, 1970
Apollo XIII day. They made it back and P was really elated! Ordered cigars for all on success when learned that was Chris Kraft tradition at NASA. Put through calls to wives immediately, then waited to call astronauts till they were aboard *Iwo Jima* and had called wives. Meanwhile P called all the Congressional leaders and George Meany, saying to all, "Isn't this a great day." He was really excited. Even told Ford to give his best to Justice Douglas (whom Ford is trying to impeach). Then talked to astronauts and told them of trip plans, then out to press to do likewise, then over to EOB at about 3:30, with no lunch. Took a nap and was ready for GOP drop-by, then "Evening at White House" with Johnny Cash. Lots of people, enthusiasm. It *was* a great day.

Saturday, April 18, 1970
More Apollo XIII, as we flew to Houston to thank the backup ground team and give them a Medal of Freedom. Good ceremony. At end of flight an awkward little session where he gave wives pearl pins, with press in.

Hawaii ceremony very good, our guys did a spectacular advancing and logistics job, and it all went perfectly. Very brief, touching and impressive.

On to Kahala Hilton. P had Rose and me in for drinks and

dinner with him and Pat Nixon. Nice chat, mainly about how bad the press people are, usual topic, treat them with complete contempt.

Overall an extremely good day, but a lot of work and a lot of air time, 11 hours, to bring it about. Probably worth it, because it was completely a TV story and thus will override any adverse reporter reaction.

Sunday, April 19, 1970

In Hawaii. P up early, due to time difference. Called me at 7:00 about reaction to yesterday's events. Told him I didn't have a report yet. He went for a walk on the beach with Don Hughes and the Secret Service. Then a 7:30 breakfast with CINCPAC for a briefing on Vietnam, etc. Then to a special service at the Kawaiahao Church. Very fascinating with the old Hawaiian ladies in their long black dresses, etc. Minister was excellent with his use of ukulele in the sermon and a wonderful choir. Then to the airport and back to California.

Monday, April 20, 1970

In San Clemente. P up early, charged into the office and announced we'd leave early for DC tonight right after the TV *(the televised troop withdrawal speech)* at 6:15.

Got word today that Carswell will run for Senate in Florida, told the P later in day when he was relaxing. Quite a surprise, but P tickled by the prospect. Would be a real vindication if he wins.

P overruled Ziegler plan for K backgrounder on general foreign policy on grounds that it would help the press, but wouldn't do us any good and would only divert from speech. Gave K a lecture about playing only to your friends in the press, those that give you a 40–50 percent chance of a fair story.

Good speech, best reading he's done. No great dramatic appeal. Left right afterward for DC.

Long session on plane. Mainly pushing on speech follow-up. He made some phone calls from the plane, got very strong positive reaction. Wants to be sure, as usual, that we cover all the bases, set the line right, especially in Congress. Had K in, talked about problem of dealing with Cabinet people. Wants to set up back channel to issue orders to military not through Secretary of Defense. Said he's not going to let Laird kill this by pulling out too fast. Said will pull all together tomorrow, will decide without Rogers. P will personally take over responsibility for war in Cambodia.

Tuesday, April 21, 1970
Thought we'd start late today. But he was up at 6:00, in office at 7:05. I got in at 9:00 and he was cranking in full gear.

All the commentators, etc., still off balance about speech. Weren't expecting 150,000 withdrawal, and it left them without a line. One time we really kept a secret. Only way is not to tell anyone.

Wednesday, April 22, 1970
Another busy day, as P roars on, in his new energy, with still little sleep. He was up at 5:00 this morning dictating. Really in high gear when he got to the office, wanted everything possible canceled so he could concentrate on Cambodia decisions.

By this time the Communists controlled a quarter of "neutral" Cambodia. Something had to be done. Under consideration were plans for a South Vietnamese push into an area called the Parrot's Beak, and a joint American/South Vietnamese push into another Cambodian territory called the Fishhook.

Gradually simmered down as the day went on. As he followed K into NSC meeting, turned back to me with big smile and said, "K's really having fun today, he's playing Bismarck." They have moved South Vietnam troops up to Cambodian border and are going ahead with a strike on Saturday.

Long sessions with K, and another one with Helms, getting the whole project under way. K said he was great in NSC; funny, just when K is getting really low and discouraged a new break comes along and cranks him back up. Big white-tie dinner tonight for Medal of Freedom winners in press.

Thursday, April 23, 1970
Leaders Meeting first thing, about new Draft-reform Bill. Then he had me in for most of the rest of the morning.

A long afternoon with K, about Cambodia primarily. Will move ahead on putting South Vietnamese troops in on Saturday; follow-up with United States tactical air support and blockade of Sihanoukville, if Lon Nol government collapses, which it will if North Vietnam takes Phnom Penh.

He's very much absorbed in Cambodia and realizes he's treading on the brink of major problems as he escalates the war there. Will have to do a masterful job of explanation to keep the people with him. And there'll be a monumental squawk from the Hill. Before he left the office tonight he was standing looking out the window and said, "Damn Johnson, if he'd just done the right thing we wouldn't be in this mess now." This refers especially to the bombing halt, which P regards as great mistake, because we could have closed the whole thing down if we'd stayed with it in 1968. He still feels he can get it wound up this year if we keep enough pressure on and don't crumble at home. K agrees.

Not much interest in domestic affairs as the whole focus is on the war. He finds it much more absorbing at any time, and especially when things are tight and he has to make major decisions, going against the bureaucracy. He left early for the house, called me over for quick schedule review with Pat Nixon.

Friday, April 24, 1970

He's still really driving about Cambodia. Had K assemble Helms and Moorer and Cushman at 7:15 this morning. Has told them to go ahead with planning for second phase next Wednesday, following Phase I on Sunday, which moves South Vietnamese troops into Cambodia to cut off the Parrot's Beak, with some tactical air support. No great problem because no United States troops, at least at the outset. But it only cripples North Vietnam, doesn't really knock out their sanctuaries. That comes with Phase II, which does use United States troops and could be a real problem.

K was very worried last night, and still is to a lesser degree, that P is moving too rashly without really thinking through the consequences. Also Ziegler disturbed because of his problem in getting adequate briefing from K so that he's prepared to handle questions.

Quite a discussion in staff meeting this morning about P's loss of momentum and leadership in public eyes. E and Harlow and Ziegler and Klein all feel there is a substantial problem, and that P's theories of isolation and remoteness are badly aggravating it. Hard to get them to come up with positive ideas to counterbalance this, but they do feel strongly. They argue for more public Presidential presentation, press conferences, speeches, review trips, etc. Not so much to sell programs, but to demonstrate P cares and is interested and will *try* to do something. Whole thrust is on need for appearance, not substance. Took off for Camp David with Bebe at about 3:00. All quiet.

Saturday, April 25, and Sunday, April 26, 1970

(P) wants to lay groundwork for big moves on Cambodia this coming week. He had a big Sunday meeting of the NSO types, no word out of that. All still quiet.

Monday, April 27, 1970

P started right in on Cambodia this morning. Called me in at 8:30, and I was there until 1:00, moving over to EOB at 9:15 with a detour to look at the crabapple blossoms in the Rose Garden. Canceled NSC, left other minor items on schedule in early afternoon. Had a few notes from over the weekend to clean up first. Then to EOB, had K join us. Went through a review of need for a strong offensive on Cambodia announcement, which will be Thursday night. Decision made last night *after* meeting. First move today on Parrot's Beak (later moved to Tuesday). Second move on COSVN *(the Communist headquarters for all operations in the South)* Thursday, and P goes on TV to announce.

Then K reported Rogers disturbed by decision, wanted to call P. P called Rogers, said decision was made, but OK to come over right now. Had me call Laird to come too, since Rogers said he was also disturbed. See report below. Then got report back from Abrams confirming his full support. Called me at home, wants to use Map Room for speech Thursday night. Historic significance, etc. I don't think that's a good idea.

Meeting, P, Rogers, Laird, and K. EOB 11:00–11:53

Rogers opposed to COSVN decision, taken without consultation. He clearly tried to hang K for inadequate information to P about consequences. Feels will cost great United States casualties with little gain. Not significant, not permanent base, not a really crippling blow.

Laird not really opposed to COSVN, but very upset about NSDM *(a Kissingerism for National Security Decision Memorandum, the mechanism he used for controlling National Security Council actions)* making WSAG *(another Kissingerism for Washington Special Action Group, an informal working group within the NSC apparatus used to do preparatory work for planned actions)* responsible for implementation, says that must be Secretary of Defense responsibility. Did try to say Abrams opposed to COSVN, but waffled several times as K answered back.

Became clear on questioning by P that Rogers' real problem was his testimony this afternoon on Hill. He doesn't want to say we're sending United States troops into Cambodia, but he can't say otherwise with NSDM out without lying, which he won't do (P agrees). Rogers obviously quite upset, emotional, mainly played on high casualties, little gain.

K laid low, injecting only factual points about Abrams' views, to correct Laird. In each case Laird backed down.

P raised question of alternatives. Made clear his position that Parrot's Beak alone not adequate. Willing to consider an alternative to COSVN if all agree, including Abrams. Problem with alternatives is all would require United States troops, but would be lesser benefit to us.

Rogers and Laird reiterated their arguments several times. Rogers saying if decision made he'll support it, but feels all these decisions are being made without adequate consultation, and he doesn't like it.

After meeting, P told K to suspend orders for 24 hours, cable Abrams and get his true views and recommendations, convene meeting of group tonight to review again. Said he's committed to two operations, but will consider alternatives to COSVN if Abrams recommends. P made clear he understood basis of both Rogers and Laird in meeting. Rogers playing against any move, in reaction to Senate, establishment press, etc. Laird trying to figure P's position and be with it, without his prerogatives cut. K pushing too hard to hold control.

K said afterward, Helms warned him Rogers would not go along. K takes whole deal as test of P's authority, and I think would go ahead even if plan is wrong, just to prove P can't be challenged. P recognizes maybe need another look. Even if change plan, will still do two, and his authority is maintained but he shows he's willing to listen.

Tuesday, April 28, 1970

Sort of at loose ends today. Had a 10:15 session with Rogers, Laird, and Mitchell to lay down the law to Rogers and Laird. He's decided to go ahead with the full plan and told them so, with darn good salesmanship according to Mitchell. Then roared into Cabinet Room for meeting he had me set up with E and Flanigan about economy.

End of morning, after couple of quick appointments, had VP in for briefing on Cambodia, with K and me. Gave him quick outline of plan, which he bought enthusiastically. Will be a good salesman for it.

Spent some time wandering around, haircut, etc. Took E for long walk on South Lawn to discuss general economic and domestic matters. E feels P in effect told him to take over the domestic side for the time being while P concentrates on the crisis. Is clearing the decks and gearing up for the whole thing to hit hard, which it may. Called me about whether OK for him to go to Camp David tomorrow to work on speech. I said yes, after it has been announced. If we go the route of letting this build as a major crisis, instead of downplaying it as we have in the past, that will add to the atmosphere. I think his action will greatly surprise most of the country. Good or bad will depend heavily on how he sells it on TV. Today he told patriotic group heads the general gist of it, and I guess tried out the approach. It went well with them, anyway.

P really worked me over on the phone about CBS filming of "Tricia White House Tour," which was set as a 20 or 30 minute segment on the "60 Minutes" show. P feels she should have full 60 minutes or nothing, says he controls the film and they can have full hour, or nothing. Really mad, and said so, chewed me out worse than he ever has as P. Basically a release of tensions on the big decision, but potentially damaging if he starts flailing in other directions. Think this one is under control.

Wednesday, April 29, 1970

Speech preparation day. No schedule. Started by giving Ziegler a rundown on how to handle press for the day. The story of last night's attack didn't break until a Thieu announcement at 9:30 *(South Vietnam's announcement of the Parrot's Beak move)*. Then speculation built fast, and Defense released their prepared statement. P told Ziegler to continue to lead speculation down the path that we are considering Cambodia's aid request. Wants a planted story that he will ask $35 million aid. Say the troop movement has no relation to Lon Nol request, just another border action, only bigger. Then say P will discuss entire situation on TV tomorrow. Set timing of procedure for tomorrow night, Congressional Cabinet, staff, press briefings, advance calls to Reagan and Rocky, etc.

Then had E and Flanigan in for a review of economy and their stock market meeting. Agreed we needed to get a briefer up to Wall Street to calm their fears after the TV. Then K and Ziegler back in for more briefing instructions, based on adverse senatorial reaction, especially Mansfield. Then worked out what he wanted for TV map setup, etc. Then sat back and relaxed with K and me. Reviewed DDE's Lebanon decision and JFK's Cuban missile crisis. Decided this was tougher than either of those, especially since it didn't have to be made. But P is convinced it had to be this now, or get out now, no chance to go along the same path. All this ran till about 1:00. I was in for three and a half hours. Then he went to EOB to work on speech, stayed all afternoon and into evening.

Called me, to have Bebe come up to be with family, and have Rose get Julie and David home, away from campus problems. Called again to discuss problem of locating his new pool table. Decided it won't fit in solarium, so wants a room in EOB. Absolutely astonishing he could get into trivia on brink of biggest step he's taken so far. Thinks speech is coming along well, as does Rose. Usual problem of trying to get it short enough, he only wants ten minutes. But he has a lot to say.

Had a session with E this afternoon about probable violence at Yale this weekend. Debate whether to send troops up on standby. E and I oppose on grounds it will only incite them and we'll be accused of repression. Mitchell and *(Deputy Attorney General)* Kleindienst are determined to go ahead, on grounds that will take 14 hours lead and potential for damages is too great to ignore. Will settle tomorrow.

In earlier debate, Rogers and Laird both said we could do Parrot's Beak with no trouble, COSVN was big problem. Now Parrot's Beak has busted Hill wide open.

Will be a tough couple of days.

Thursday, April 30, 1970

Cambodia speech day. P up until about 1:00 AM, to bed for an hour, up again till about 5:30. Then in to office at about 8:00. Not much sleep before a big day. He spent the day at EOB, finishing up the speech, and keeping in touch by phone during breaks while Rose was typing.

P called frequently about ideas for follow-up tonight, queries about our plans and readiness, especially to be sure we are ready to hit the networks, etc., for bad coverage; activity in Congress for support; be sure we kill or deflect Reid Amendment that would stop efforts in Cambodia; shore up Rogers; keep Congressional criticism about Parrot's Beak muted, wait till you hear P tonight; be sure to crank on target Senators, etc.; amending list for Congressional briefing tonight, etc.

Called me over at 3:00, K already there. Read us the speech, making a few corrections along the way. (Same as he did on November 3 speech, a new procedure.) Very strong and excellent wrap-up. K and I both felt it will work. Some more discussion on follow-up and how to handle reaction.

P left EOB about 7:20 to go to Residence, I walked over with him. Then came down to leaders and Cabinet briefing at 8:15. (Cabinet met first, with VP presiding, for brief pitch from Rogers, who did only moderately well. He's obviously not the least anxious to go ahead with this and it's very hard for him to back it.)

P did excellent briefing, quite personal. Understanding of those who would oppose, but laid it pretty hard to them he was doing this to end war and save lives. Odd to watch Fulbright, Mansfield, Aiken, Ted Kennedy, all of whom had blasted him yesterday and today. They all stood and applauded at end.

Then to Oval Office for TV. A horrifying moment when he lost his place on the script, but recovered beautifully. Left for Residence right after, strolling slowly through Rose Garden. Stayed up late, 1:30, taking phone calls, Cabinet and key staff, reports from me on reaction, etc. Had Chief Justice up for couple of hours, when he came by to drop off a letter about 10:30.

We set up a well-organized operation for phone calls, reaction, etc. Worked pretty well. Kept P posted, and generated some key calls to him. Reaction was more mixed than November 3, but a lot of strong favorable response. Not as violent and anti-TV commentators played it *very* straight, no real adverse shots.

Friday, May 1, 1970

Reaction day. P in at 7:30. Had me in at 8:00, gazing out at Rose Garden and musing about how short a time the spring lasts. Then K and Ziegler in for review of line for today. Cold steel, no give, nothing about negotiation, Hanoi can now choose between peace and war. Mainly stay strong, whole emphasis on "back the boys," sell courage of P.

Then he took off for Pentagon briefing. Very pleased when he returned by the reception he had received from secretaries, etc. Battle is going well. Meanwhile I had series of staff meetings to get all cranked up and rolling on the offensive.

P back at 11:00, had me in, reviewed progress. Made a lot of phone calls, thanking people. Then took off for boat ride lunch with family, then to Camp David. Afternoon was pretty calm, kept the follow-up going. P was really beat, but still riding on reaction. Really needs some good rest.

Called couple of times from Camp David about specific follow-up.

Thought he'd fold early, but he watched movie and called me again afterwards, at 10:30, just to chat a little and get updated.

Saturday, May 2, 1970

Fortunately our poll came out darn good, so I had good news for P when he called about 9:30. I was on the phone solidly from then until 3:45, on follow-up. Never even hung up phone between calls. Got a lot going. Analyzed the negatives in news and moved to try to counteract.

Everyone in good shape and working hard, getting pretty good response.

P called about 2:00 and said to let everyone go home and relax, I said "No, not now, when we've got things rolling. Will let them up later." He was pleased.

Sunday, May 3, 1970

Another busy day on the phone working on the reaction. P called several times with ideas for follow-up. Later had K call me to cheer me up, K uptight, and I think P was working on him indirectly. K was concerned because I had given P information on campus problems, etc., is worried he will toss babies to the wolves instead of hanging tight.

Monday, May 4, 1970

And the repercussions roll on. Discussed with P the plans for the week. He says he's ready to move to domestic matters, but then keeps coming back to things related to "The Decision" (Cambodia).

K in for review of situation, especially report on the strikes against North Vietnam. Going well. Then added Ziegler for review of line for the day. Then some quizzing about follow-up activity, basically *very* calm and undemanding.

Then he went over to EOB for rest of the day. A long session with E to get caught up on domestic. A nap. Then had me over, reviewed trip plan. Then I told him of four students killed at Kent State. He's very disturbed. Afraid his decision set it off, and that is the ostensible cause of the demonstrations there. Issued condolence statement, then kept after me all the rest of the day for more facts. Hoping rioters had provoked the shooting, but no real evidence they did, except throwing rocks at National Guard.

Talked a lot about how we can get through to the students, turn this stuff off. Really sad to see this added to all his worries about the war. He's out on a tough limb, and knows it. This makes it a lot worse, as he has to take the heat for having caused it. There's an opportunity in this crisis as all others, but it's very hard to identify and know how to handle it. Main need right now is maintain calm and hope this serves to dampen other demonstrations rather than firing them up. Hard to tell yet which will result. I moved to try to cover all our people, and congressmen and Cabinet officers to keep a firm position, but not inflammatory. Lots of rumors and strong probability of major march on DC on Saturday. Also student strike starting tomorrow.

P is troubled by all this, although it was predicted as a result of the Cambodian move.

Tuesday, May 5, 1970

Another day of reaction. P had his big meetings with Congressional leaders, the House and Senate Armed Forces Committee for breakfast and the House and Senate Foreign

Relations Committees at 5:00. Both covered military briefings on progress so far, some darn good news about material discovered, and P really pushing to get this out. P did superb job at each meeting of presenting his case and the reasons behind it. Questioning was tough but he handled very coolly. Probably didn't change any minds, but at least he met with them and told his story.

Big problem today is the whole student disorder situation. Not much hard news or specific developments but a lot of planning for strikes and marches for the rest of the week. Reaction very tough to the four killed at Kent State yesterday. All our people trying to figure how best to handle, and whether P can perform any useful role.

P had a long meeting at noon with his top economic types, Kennedy, Shultz, Mayo, McCracken and Flanigan, about what seems to be a budding financial crisis, mainly because of major continuing drop in stock market. Got Fed to reduce margin requirement, made decision not to hold to balanced budget in '70, or '71, will go ahead with deficit this year due to revenue shortfall instead of trying to recoup by accelerated tax collections, etc. P much more concerned with upgoing economy in fall because he feels that's the only chance to make gains in the elections, and that in turn is the only way ultimately to get control of the economy.

> This line of reasoning is easily misinterpreted as crass political manipulation of the economy for personal political benefit. It should instead be understood as a valid recognition of the necessity to make political gains, in terms of gaining favorably inclined congressmen and senators, so that there are enough votes to take the necessary economic moves.

Big thing now is to ride out all the crises with a show of cool strength and no inflammation, but no waffling. Then to make one or two good firm moves to maintain leadership. Real test is how the Cambodia venture turns out. If it can be proclaimed as success and we can get out in six weeks, it will set him up pretty well for a while. If not, we're in for a bundle of trouble.

Wednesday, May 6, 1970

Another day of watching and waiting, except for a meeting with Arthur Burns and a group of Kent State students. The Kent State 6 were a good group and meeting went very well. No concrete results. Their main pitch is need for better communication and more student participation in major decisions. Did confirm that Cambodia was not the basic cause. Wants VP to stop saying anything about students. *Very* disturbed by Rogers-Laird story that they disagreed with the decision.

As day went on, concern from outside about campus crisis built rapidly. All of us had lots of calls and memos, etc. P came to grips with it this afternoon. Obviously realizes, but won't openly admit, his "bums" remark very harmful.

> In his visit to the Pentagon the past Friday, P had referred to the people who were "blowing up the campuses" as "these bums." This comment was widely reported out of context as referring to all students, and consequently produced an enormous adverse reaction.

He agreed to plan of action, meet university presidents tomorrow, press conference Friday night, call in all governors Monday. Wants to hold off on appointing special commission about Kent State. Feels it may be a mistake, so wait a little.

Very aware of point that goal of the Left is to panic us, so we must not fall into their trap.

Thursday, May 7, 1970

And the reaction goes on. The Hickel story broke big today. He wrote P a letter about need for communicating with young, shutting up Agnew, meeting more with Cabinet members. It leaked to *Star* yesterday and was the big news today, along with resignation of Youth Head at Department of Education. All designed to enhance the "collapse of the Presidency" theory. P pretty calm about it last night, pretty cold-blooded today. Feels Hickel's got to go as soon as we're past this crisis. This led to a rising "anti-Cabinet" feeling as he thought more about it. Went back to deep resentment that none called him after speech and none rose to his defense on this deal. So he struck back by ordering the tennis court removed immediately.

Feels Cabinet should work on own initiative to support P, and they haven't.

> The decision to remove the tennis court was simply a spiteful way to take a jab at the Cabinet by removing one of the "perks" many of them enjoyed—the use of the White House tennis court. Since the P didn't play tennis, the court was of no use to him and he diligently pursued this plan for a while, then let it drop.

Distressed about continuing failure to get out word of Cambodia successes, he keeps pumping the story to everyone, and they all are surprised.

An Agnew problem, result of the Hickel letter, and stories that P is muzzling him. Wants VP to avoid any remarks about students, etc., VP strongly disagrees. I passed the word. VP said he would act only on order of P.

P met with university presidents. Then took me on tour of South Grounds to discuss tennis court removal and life in general. Feels very concerned about campus revolt and basically helpless to deal with it. It's now clear that many are looking to him for leadership and to calm it down, and there's really no way he can do it. Also have the omnipresent media problem, as they build up everything to look as bad as possible. P said the university presidents were all scared to death, feel that this now includes the non-radical students, and agree with Moynihan's theory that the whole university community is now politicized, and there's no way to turn it off. All blame Agnew primarily, then the P's "bums" crack. General feeling is that without Kent State it would not have been so bad, but that even without Cambodia there were a lot of campuses ready to blow.

P went to Camp David late this afternoon to work on press conferences. He's pretty tired, and he knows it. Went to bed early, after a bunch of phone calls.

Friday, May 8, 1970
The big press conference with an awful lot at stake as the tension mounts in the nation. Media have built it up very big, and it really is. An awful lot of schools closed, a lot of rhetoric, a major threat of violence, etc. P spent the day at Camp David

working on the briefing book. Called down several times about specific questions and logistics. Came down in time for dinner and to dress, then went right to East Room, back upstairs afterward. Had said absolutely no phone calls after (because he was really concerned and unsure about this one), but changed that afterward when he knew he had done extremely well. Then he stayed up until after 1:00 on the calls, and we ran a batch through. He was very tired and rambled on a lot.

All through the day the advice poured in from all sources, as everyone feared the P would either be too belligerent and non-understanding of the dissenters, or would be too forgiving and thus lose strength and P leadership. All depends on your point of view. I gave all the pertinent advice on both sides to the P, the hard line was mainly from K who feels we should just let the students tear it for a couple of weeks with no effort at pacification, then hit them hard. Most of the others leaned the other way and wanted a full apology for the ''bums'' and a tight muzzle on Agnew's rhetoric. Fortunately P was shrewd enough to accomplish both objectives without giving in on either.

Whole press conference was masterful. He really zinged the bad guys by promoting ABC, the *Star,* etc., and worked in all the points he wanted to make. Even got a great laugh out of turning the Hickel letter thing around, and zinged Wally pretty good at the same time. The aftermath on the White House staff was a mood of great relief and almost exhilaration. My crew stayed until about 12:30 handling calls, then left. P called several times after I was home, last at about 2:00.

In trying to leave we were jammed in by the troop trucks unloading the Third Army into the EOB. A very strange feeling as the White House and DC batten down for another siege. The buses were being lined up, police all over, etc.

Saturday, May 9, 1970

The weirdest day so far. Started with E call at about 5:00 saying P was at the Lincoln Memorial talking to students. We agreed to send Krogh over, and Chapin and I got up and went in, arrived about 6:15, by which time P had moved to the Capitol. I met him when he emerged and Ziegler had also arrived, so we all went to breakfast at the Mayflower. Very weird. P completely beat and just rambling on, but obviously too tired to go to sleep. All worked out fine, he got great press credit for doing the students, and wound down a little. After return to White House, I got him to go over to EOB and talk to the soldiers who were just waking up in their sleeping bags in the 4th floor hall. P very impressed by them, but also very kindly toward the students, who were apparently all hippie types.

Finally got him to go to bed, but he couldn't sleep, so tossed around, made phone calls, then was back up again. Came over to Oval Office for a while, then over to EOB for the rest of the afternoon. Called sporadically to see how things were going, and to push on through from last night and this morning. Knows he's pooped and wants schedule cleared so he can go to Florida this next weekend for four days. He really needs it.

I am concerned about his condition. The decision, the speech, the aftermath killings, riots, press, etc.; the press conference, the student confrontation have all taken their toll, and he has had very little sleep for a long time and his judgment, temper, and mood suffer badly as a result. On the other hand he has gone into a monumental crisis, fully recognized as such by the outside, and so far has come through extremely well. But there's a long way to go and he's in no condition to weather it. He's still riding on the crisis wave, but the letdown is near at hand and will be huge.

A major test will be the Sunday press and the magazines. If we get by those, we can move with next week in pretty good shape. Then I've got to get him to spend some time with key staff and get them rolling again. If we make it, it'll be a great proof of leadership at a time that it was badly needed. If we don't, we'll have a rough couple of years of rebuilding.

Sunday, May 10, 1970

The aftermath. All quiet, White House Church. I succeeded last night in getting Hickel not to come, in order to avoid a confrontation with the P, and the press. He didn't like it, but agreed to follow my recommendation.

Several long calls from the P. He was much more relaxed, but still not unwound at all.

Thinks we're turning a corner this weekend. Remembers that in '60 and '68 we had 80 percent of the faculties against us, but 50 percent of the students for us. Thinks now the college demonstrators have overplayed their hands, evidence is the blue collar group rising up against them, and P can mobilize them.

Pondering the problem of relations with Cabinet, etc., says he can't work any harder than he does, and they have to decide whether it's better for the P to do his job or to massage them.

Called later to analyze our problem in getting over the story of the success in Cambodia. K had major briefing yesterday, but papers gave it no play. Problem starts with overriding news about the demonstration, but also comes from our failure to get enough sell in the story. P now feels he should have gotten into this in his press conference, the only way to get it out.

Monday, May 11, 1970

Buzzed me in first thing, lots of notes on follow-up. Kept me over two hours, E in and out. Reviewed trivia and a little general scheduling, discussed the Vietnam (Cambodia) story problem and some ideas about sending groups over to observe; revised plan for Governors Conference agenda; still demanding the tennis court be removed; wants to figure a way to get Hickel to leave and run for Governor of Alaska.

E got pretty direct with P when he was boring in on bad reports from kids about his Lincoln Memorial bit. E told him he was tired and not very effective. This made him mad, and it came up several times later in the day. Real trouble is, he's just totally pooped and is not up to his usual performance.

This was really in evidence at Governors Conference. He did a darn good job, but went on and on, frequently irrelevant. Still made his points, but would have done better in half as much time. It went very well and they seemed to be well impressed with us. Hard to be sure until they got out to press. P made great defense of whole concept of United States involvement, domino theory, etc.

Rogers called me afterward very concerned about P. Same reason as above. Feels we've got to keep him on short leash until he gets rested up. Unfortunately he has a dinner tonight for Sir Alec Douglas Home. Then a busy morning. But we can keep week light.

Tuesday, May 12, 1970

P in late, finally got a little sleep. As usual had a lot of stuff for follow-up, notes from the dinner last night.

Concerned about Senate strategy for Church-Cooper amendment about Cambodia *(which would demand P remove all American troops from Cambodia by July 1)*. Wants to be sure that whatever they do is not interpreted as defeat. Problem is they seem to have enough votes to carry it, although there is a pretty good possibility we can get it amended on basis of protecting American troops. Still pushing hard on getting out the Cambodia story.

Wants to try to implement Billy Graham's idea about a big pro-America rally, maybe on 4th of July.

Had a new idea about cutting off all Defense money to universities that closed down or caved in to demonstrators. Wants to make university administration go on record saying they want the Defense money, so we aren't in an apparent position of forcing it on them.

K all disturbed about some tap data about his staff, so P has decided to instruct Hoover that all this material now should come to me, not E or K. Then I have to decide who gets what.

This refers to reports from the FBI telephone wiretaps placed on certain NSC staff and other people suspected of leaking National Security classified information. This procedure, ordered by the P and implemented by Mitchell and K, was producing reports that upset K, so it was decided that I should receive the reports and only pass on to others anything that was relevant to the leak concerns.

Had our first meeting with Chancellor *(George A.)* Heard of Vanderbilt. The P let himself get snookered into appointing him as a special advisor on campus situation for 60 days. A bad choice, because he's clearly not on our side in any way, but this came out of the meeting last week with college presidents and K carried it out with no staff discussion, so we're stuck. Decided Heard's main contribution could be to set up a mechanism for assuring that academia can be heard at the White House. Will also have him involved in the review of Kent State killings, etc. Pure window dressing of a questionable nature, but it did get pretty good publicity.

Wednesday, May 13, 1970

P up early and over to EOB at 7:15 where he dictated a ton of memos, mainly to me, plus his recollections of his trip to the Lincoln Memorial Saturday. Rather remarkable document and equally remarkable cover memo.

He came over to Oval Office at 9:30, went over current trivia with me, then had J. Edgar in to discuss the new procedure for tap material, only to me. Hoover very pleased. He came on like gangbusters about public approval of P, etc. He does a great job of self-promotion. Dropped a few goodies about Kent State (later proved to be somewhat inaccurate), and then reviewed the whole conspiracy theory about campuses.

Then P met privately with Moynihan, who said he feels he has to leave. Wants to go July 1, but P got him to stay until August. Will then return to Harvard on grounds his two years *(maximum Harvard sabbatical)* will be up soon and he wants to start the fall semester. P appears more relieved than concerned to have him go, and this timing should work out pretty well because he always said he was only here for two years.

Thursday, May 14, 1970

A very busy schedule before departure for Key Biscayne at 5:00. Started at 9:30 with Laird, *(Joint Chiefs Chairman Admiral Thomas)* Moorer and K, about Cambodia. Called me in about status of fight in Senate on various amendments. Wants to be absolutely sure that however it comes out we have established a position that it doesn't hurt Administration.

On plane *(to Key Biscayne)* had K up for a while, then me, mostly in review of need to get our story out, covered a lot of specific items. In pretty good spirits, but still cranking on minute details, and not at all relaxed as he usually is on way to Florida.

This whole period of two weeks of tension and crisis, preceded by two weeks of very tough decision making has taken its toll. P won't admit it, but he is really tired, and is, as some have observed, letting himself slip back to the old ways. He's driving himself way too hard on unnecessary things, and because of this is not getting enough sleep, is uptight, etc. All this OK if he can unwind this weekend, and if nothing big comes up in the interim. *But* could be rough if a new crisis arises, because he's not ready to handle it.

The establishment press has really leaped on us and the domestic tension. They obviously wait for their chance and this has proved to be a beautiful one which they are exploiting to the fullest.

Friday, May 15, 1970
In Key Biscayne. The unwinding process is not succeeding.
P on the phone every few minutes with little things to check
up on.

Saturday, May 16, 1970
In Key Biscayne. More of the same. He just keeps grinding
away, call after call after call. He *is* sleeping late in the mornings, which helps a little, but he sure has *not* gotten his mind
off of business. I spent hours on the phone following up.

Finally in the afternoon he took off for Walker's *(cay off
the Florida coast),* after I talked him into at least staying over
until Monday.

Sunday, May 17, 1970
P in Walker's most of the day. Back late afternoon and on the
phone again. Mainly wanted a rundown on things, no major
changes.

Monday, May 18, 1970
Still at Key Biscayne. Harlow still trying to maneuver a deal
in the Senate. Not too much luck so far, but Cooper did at
least agree to consider modification. Bryce doing a great job
of pulling all the strings, etc. His real forte! P pushing hard
on getting the poll out. Also had long conversations on phone
with E and K. Trying to stay on top of and in touch with
everything so we didn't really get him away from it very much.
But the news is better, the word from around the country is
that P's support is strong, the polls are good, and maybe we'll
turn all this around soon. It's tough to keep fighting it, and
amazing how easily everyone crumbles.

In plane on way back, P had me up alone for the first hour,
then added E about Cabinet agenda for tomorrow. Then added
K, and said the three of us had to take the brunt of the heat
these past weeks and we deserved an award like the Purple
Heart, so he had devised a new award, The Blue Heart, for
those who are true blue. Then gave us each a blue cloth heart
made by Jane Lucke (Bebe's friend) and said the honor was
to be kept very confidential. He was in a good mood, relaxed,
confident, optimistic, not driving hard, but does want to spend
time this week on the economy, turning around Cambodia and
getting something going on crime. Also talked about Cabinet

changes coming soon, but after November in most cases. Says
Mitchell has to go unless he can solve the Martha problem.

Tuesday, May 19, 1970

Back to DC and the routine. A hot and heavy schedule today.
Leadership Meeting about Senate anti-Cambodia resolutions
first. All the leaders who have been out in country say support
is strong for P. Most of them want to extend the debate instead
of compromising, feeling time is on our side and that we can
always give in later if necessary. Scott still intent on maneuvering a compromise with Cooper. All agree that Democrats
are only going for political benefit of appearing to have forced
P out of Cambodia, when he's already going to get out anyway.

Then a Cabinet meeting under rather strained conditions, as
Hickel still much in the air. P did a masterful job of talking
to Hickel indirectly through the Cabinet about not trying to
affect policy by making a speech outside. A lot of discussion
about role of Cabinet under reorganization. Rogers led argument for need for discussion before decisions, fear of cutting
Cabinet out, and becoming just pro forma. Laird made strong
pitch against the line that P made hard lonely decision, this
does not build P. Good briefing on background for Cambodia
decision and progress to date.

P had me in for couple of hours at lunchtime, got into long
harangue about his revised views on PR. Now feels he was
completely wrong in his original concept about building mystique and image. Realizes this is impossible when press is
against you. Roosevelts, etc., only succeeded because they had
press with them (not sure that's true). Feels we should give
up the struggle and just present our case via P on TV. Realize
Nixon will never have good public image, so don't try. I think
he's partly right, but that's no reason not to keep trying. But
it would work a lot better if he would quit worrying about it
and just be President.

All this he says is result of lot of thought over the weekend.
Not too concerned, sort of reflective. I think he's realizing he
has been pushing all this too hard, and if he'll go back to the
original approach he'll do better. All that really counts is that
he make a few good big moves, the rest then will fade away.

Thursday, May 21, 1970

(P) wants to bring Finch into White House as counselor, put Rumsfeld in charge of OMB, move Elliot Richardson to HEW, Weinberger to budget. Do all this now, except Rumsfeld is barred constitutionally. Then wants to wait until after elections and clean out Cabinet, especially Hickel and Romney and Kennedy.

> This whole merry-go-round of proposed Cabinet changes was a constantly changing process in the P's mind as he contemplated better use of people in the various assignments. Some removals were simply to get better people for the jobs; some of the changes and rotations were to use the right people more effectively. The main force for change at the moment is Bob Finch's health, which was not good, at least partly due to the strain under which he was operating in a primarily managerial and administrative job for which his talents were not well suited.

Thinks we're still too timid on mobilizing the Silent Majority. Thinks all our people are working hard but just don't know how to do it. Feels he should probably go out into country and draw crowds and show popular enthusiasm. Really pleased by our poll and says it's remarkable with economy the way it is.

I had hard-sell meeting with my crew about launching a new all-out offensive to turn things around.

P had Rumsfeld, E and me in about how to handle the staff and Cabinet disloyalty problem. Rumsfeld made point you have to establish record of trying to work things out before you fire someone. P pretty well convinced there's no way to get real control except by cracking down hard. Wants Don Rumsfeld brought more into the inner councils.

Friday, Saturday, Sunday, May 22–24, 1970

In Los Angeles, no contact with P except a call Friday night just checking in. He went to Camp David Friday afternoon and stayed until Sunday. All pretty quiet. I gave speech at UCLA banquet Saturday night and stirred up a bit of a flap with reference to Eastern establishment media and isolation of the P. Had a good session Friday with students.

Monday, May 25, 1970

A few weekend odds and ends to catch up on, and another huge batch of P memos that he did at Camp David. Some discussion with P and E about care and handling of Cabinet. P to go to California this weekend instead of Key Biscayne, and will meet secretly there with Abrams about Cambodia, then go on TV midweek next week to announce progress report and withdrawal plan.

Buchanan has a hot new Agnew speech blasting Harriman, Vance, and Clifford, for Thursday night. P a little leery, wants to be sure it's not too rough. Also he doesn't want to louse up atmosphere before his TV deal next week.

Called all shook up about stock market drop of 21 points. Said to be sure no one gets upset or overacts, must act confident. Problem is, no one shows any sign of undue concern except him.

Tuesday, May 26, 1970

Suharto *(Manila)* arrival, meeting and dinner. Kept P busy most of the morning. Also a meeting with New York hard hats that marched for P last week. And a reception on Hill for Speaker this afternoon.

K pleased because they *(the North Vietnamese)* called Walters in Paris, and said their man would be gone two weeks. K thought they'd call off deal, but they're keeping it open, sign of real weakness.

K very disturbed about his staff problems, several leaving due to Cambodia.

Wednesday, May 27, 1970

A busy morning with Arthur Burns, then the economic group, then LBJ before the lunch for McCormick. Then tonight the stag dinner for business leaders to try to calm down the stock market which has been dropping steadily at an alarming rate. Guess it worked before it even happened because market gained 31 points, highest one-day rise in history. *Really* neurotic.

Time doing a cover story on E, K, Mitchell and me. Want interview and P reluctantly agreed, but thinks we're being naive and will be shafted, probably right.

P musing on where things would be today if we had *not* gone into Cambodia. It would have fallen, our casualties would be way up, we'd be under enormous pull-out pressure from within, and P would have badly deteriorated in world position.

Some more worrying about our internal economic unit, as P feels Quadriad had nothing to offer today, and we don't have a real strong economic leader on staff.

P spent afternoon at EOB, mainly just pondering the overall situation and getting his remarks ready for the business leaders tonight. Did call to have me turn off VP on his very tough speech for tomorrow about Harriman, Vance, Clifford. P feels this is not the time for it.

Monday, June 1, 1970

Back to DC *(from San Clemente weekend)* at 3:00. *(P)* had me up for a while on the plane. In a pretty good mood, did say though he thought he would not come out for 4th of July, can't afford to be gone ten days at that time. Good weekend. Really helps to get a change and to spread people around a little.

Lousy *Time* cover story today, on me and E and K and Mitchell.

Tuesday, June 2, 1970

Back in DC. Caldera arrival and State dinner are the only scheduled activities. P spent all afternoon at EOB working on speech.

Had me over for two hours at 5:00, general chat while he was waiting for Buchanan to finish latest draft this afternoon. I told him market only off .75 on big day, strong at end. He was delighted, since this makes a week with overall gain of 79 points, a record.

Also told him about Gallup poll for Sunday which has him *up* another 2 points. Absolutely remarkable since it was taken two weeks ago when media had us at the absolute bottom. Shows people have some sense in spite of all they see, hear, and read. P is at 59 approval, which is darn good in normal time, unbelievable now, in spite of Cambodia, the economy, the students, and the press.

All this good news got him cranking a bit, and I did it on purpose to get him up for tomorrow night. I really don't think things are nearly as bad as our press "friends" are trying to make it appear.

Wednesday, June 3, 1970

Another speech day. P spent the day at EOB getting speech ready for TV tonight. Worked a lot with K and Buchanan. Is trying new process, making them, especially Pat, do most of the writing and rewriting as he critiques. Thinks he can get more mileage from the writers by not demanding total perfection, which he can only get by doing it all himself. Feels he should be doing more speeches, and this is the only way he can.

Concerned about Wallace winning in Alabama, mainly to be sure our investment was properly used.

Feels Wallace poses problem to Democrats, forces them further left, we play center strategy right down the middle. Need to build up fact it was a pure racist victory.

Speech went very well. Many thought it his best, I think because more confident and factual, less defensive, belligerent, personal. Used film clip very effectively to display captured arms, etc. He wasn't too sold on the idea, but it worked well and he liked it, now wants to use more often.

As usual, said to hold all phone calls, then later asked if there were any, and we had about 15 racked up, he returned all of them. Loves to gab after these deals, and so we run our little system. Problem is most people don't even consider trying to call P.

Thursday, June 4, 1970

Busy day of appointments, Caldera farewell (which P wants to be the last farewell meeting on State visits); Presidential scholars (a high-school-grad group who announced their opposition to P's policy before the White House meeting); a signing of Crime Executive Order; greeting group of Iowa businessmen; a boys choir from Pennsylvania; the Prime Minister of Morocco; F. Murphy. In between a couple of vital staff sessions about saving the Penn Central Railroad, and a meeting with Cap Weinberger about his taking on top budget job.

P talked to Hoover and Mitchell after crime meeting and they told him his TV picture was bad last night. Very helpful! Talked with E and me at noon about staffing. Agreed to try for Weinberger for budget, Shultz for OMB. Had E and me meet with Shultz to open it with him, which we did, with no answer as yet.

P had Weinberger in to pitch him on the budget job, E and

I sat in. Cap a little startled, feels he hasn't finished his work at FTC *(Federal Trade Commission),* and was obviously reluctant to give up all his perquisites, but P gave him very little choice, and made it clear budget was much more important. Cap had just come back from Paris and wanted time to think it over.

Friday, June 5, 1970

Finch day. E and I met with Bob in morning, and I made pitch about need for him to move out of HEW *now,* and into White House. He was obviously ready for it, and went along completely. He felt it should be done as fast as possible, so we went to work on a successor. After considerable discussion with P, with E, Finch, and K in and out, we decided choice was between Franklin Murphy and Elliot Richardson, with the edge to Richardson because more our man, but then we love him at State, so decided to ask Murphy first. So Finch and I met with Franklin. Said he'd have to wait ten days until back from Europe to decide.

That settled it for P, and he had Rogers come over at noon met with P and me. Agreed immediately to move Richardson I had feeling he was glad to move him out. Richardson agreed and after meeting was obviously elated.

At last minute P invited E, K, and me to dinner on *Sequoia* with him and Bebe. P really pleased with the shift. Is excited by prospect of Bob's *(Finch)* value to White House staff. I *will* be a good setup and Bob will really help loosen me up and take on political and PR areas that I'm now stuck with.

One interesting problem, E asked Moynihan if he wanted HEW, and he said yes. Now have to turn him off, also Murphy

P had historic meeting this morning with intelligence chiefs FBI, CIA, NSA *(National Security Agency),* DIA *(Defense Intelligence Agency),* about internal domestic intelligence. Ordered them to set up a cooperative system, with Tom Huston

---

This was the start of what became known as the Huston Plan, a program designed to integrate all the sources for domestic intelligence under some central control to eliminate duplication and infighting. This was generated by P's complete dissatisfaction with the results of intelligence gathering and interpretation, particularly regarding the instigation and training for the wave of violent demonstrations. Tom Huston was a middle-level staffer who was assigned to coordinate and staff the work of the project.

Saturday, June 6, 1970

More personnel maneuvers. Announced Finch and Richardson. Worked pretty well. Haven't seen news coverage. P again all cranked up about staff meetings and building the inside group.

Then P had E, R and me in with Shultz to follow up on him about OMB. P gave him a *great* pitch, after which we all had lunch. Shultz called E later to say he'd take it. Now all we need is Weinberger and we're really rolling.

About economy, P pushing point our unemployment is up because we're bringing boys home. Not as high as any Kennedy year, higher than Johnson, but he was accelerating a war and sending men into it, we are building toward prosperity without war, which no Democratic President has achieved in modern times.

P off to Camp David with family and Eisenhowers, to celebrate Julie and David's graduation. Called to suggest considering Moynihan for UN. Good idea.

Monday, June 8, 1970

More people maneuvers. P had Moynihan in at end of full morning schedule, asked if he'd like to be Ambassador to UN. Pat was pleased with offer, and will consider.

After long midday meeting with E, Shultz and Cap, we put heat on Cap, and Shultz met again with him in later afternoon and he agreed to come in. Biggest hang-up was whether he could bring his chauffeur with him, we said no. I'm going to have a tough time getting these guys settled. All want to hang on to their cars, aides, etc.

Cabinet officers get a bundle of perks that are hard to give up to come to the relative rigors of White House life.

P in generally good mood, back to a fairly full schedule. Obviously pleased with new staff developments, and with Gallup, and general simmering down. Will coast along for a bit, then we'll be ready for the next crisis, but better able to cope with it with the new team on tap.

Wednesday, June 10, 1970
He had full day, breakfast with George Meany and Shultz; NSC; report from our UN fact-finding group; and pictures at his desk with 150-plus Congressional candidates. Plus the announcement *(of new Cabinet and staff positions).*

Thursday, June 11, 1970
Jordan crisis. We were supposed to go to Key Biscayne at 5:00, but crisis in Amman, with possible need to send in Marines to rescue Americans, precluded it. We waited until last minute in hopes problem would be worked out, but it still wasn't at 6:30, so we canceled. May still go tomorrow. But P says no. He needs time off and he can't use Camp David.

Started out as bad morning, as we screwed up one schedule item after another. Poor Chapin.

Sweated out Senate vote on Byrd Amendment. Met with Harlow in late afternoon and agreed they should continue the filibuster. Reviewed again the key Senate races as he dreams of gaining three seats so we can win a vote without sweating it out to the last second. Called me at home to say had lost an inlay and had to see dentist in morning. Wants to go with no press notice, etc. So I set it up.

Friday, June 12, 1970
Some loose ends this morning as schedule was clear for Key Biscayne. Back on his kick about our people's waste of time talking to people, students, etc. Thinks we do too much of this and don't get the word out so don't get any credit, which is the only real potential benefit. Wants me to talk to K and E about use of their time, feels some symbolism is good, but don't keep at it.

Lot of agonizing over whether to go to Florida, kept all on standby, and finally left at 2:00.

P pleased with reorganization results. Wants to be sure we get across the difference from Kennedy and Johnson Kitchen Cabinets. We've set up working institution as recommended for years, not just "if-come ad hoc" basis. Feels the procedure and processes vitally important.

Finch and me to dinner and *Patton* again.

Sunday, June 14, 1970
Key Biscayne, Air Force One home in evening. Long chat
about California Bicentennial party at White House. And some
ideas about Cabinet campaigning.

Tuesday, June 16, 1970
Busy morning schedule. Worked on speech at EOB first for
couple of hours, then appointments until about 1:00. Covered
some odd notes of his plus lot of schedule and information
items of mine as he was waiting for latest draft. Then went
back to EOB to work on speech.

Flap about Agnew as he blasted our appointee to Kent State
Commission. Creates awkward situation as Ziegler has to repudiate VP in effect. P concerned that VP would cut loose like
this without checking first. Actually hurts him more than anyone. And builds up the guy he attacked, a militant black from
Harvard *(Joe Rhodes)*. E in the middle as it's his boy, and he
staunchly defends the appointment.

Wednesday, June 17, 1970
Another speech day. P locked up all morning at EOB getting
ready. Wanted me to meet with VP to explain the whole incident and assure him it was *not* a rebuff, his judgment was
correct, but we can't remove Rhodes now because of the fuss.
VP really blew it by blasting publicly instead of working it
out internally.

P refuses to meet with the *(Kent State)* Commission, will
meet with Scranton but not the others. E pretty upset at all this,
since he put the whole thing together and it has backfired. VP
especially distressed with E because he feels he told John several times of his concern about the appointments to the Commission. Speech went very well, 26 minutes. Heavy afternoon
schedule, Ambassador Tosca, NSC, Fitzhugh about Defense reorganization, Riland, then out on the boat for family dinner. *(P)*
wants a boat dinner with FRESH staff tomorrow night. Anxious
to get cranking with his key staff. They all met at Camp David
today to explore approaches to the Domestic Council.

FRESH is an acronym for the latest informal internal staff
group—consisting of Finch, Rumsfeld, Ehrlichman, Shultz,

and Haldeman. These groups were formed from time to time
at P's direction or by the members themselves to deal with
specific or general problems or projects. They usually died a
natural death after their initial purpose was served.

Thursday, June 18, 1970

Busy schedule to clean up all the loose ends. Kept P going
solid all day. Ended with Ad Council reception, then took
FRESH group out on *Sequoia* for dinner. Good session on the
Sequoia as P really relaxed and established a good base with
the group.

Quite a bit on Agnew, as P revealed he has a lot more doubts
than he has expressed before. Still convinced he's a major
asset, but feels he really makes the wrong approaches sometimes. Ended up that we should discuss the problem and come
up with basic recommendation for P as to exact role of Agnew
and how to implement it, which P will then cover with him.

Got word on boat of conservative victory upset in Britain,
also from Blount of postal reform through House. Both good
news. P especially pleased about Britain. Had me ride back in
car with him, and talked about how this discredited pollsters
and press.

Friday, June 19, 1970

No schedule, so I spent most of the day with P as he had
various people in. After long discussion decided he has to sign
voting rights. Feels veto would be better politics, but runs real
danger of exploding the blacks. Doesn't feel we'll gain any
votes with blacks or young, but will hurt with our basic constituency, but still have to do it, against will of leaders.

Flap about *(Ohio Senator)* Bob Taft's refusal to attend Agnew dinner in Cleveland tomorrow. Built through the day, as
Harlow maneuvered to get pressure put on Taft. Ended with
Taft calling Harlow and refusing to go, really stupid. P really
furious about his attitude, and says he won't help him in campaign.

Juggled a bit with problem of Julie and David trip to Japan,
but got it back on track, in shortened version. P, Pat Nixon
and Bebe to Camp David for the weekend. A little peace and
quiet.

Saturday, June 20, 1970
P at Camp David. I spent most of day in staff planning sessions with E. Also Finch, and later Shultz. P called in afternoon. Raised idea of Pat Nixon to Peru instead of VP as I had suggested earlier. Later called and said she would do it, and for me to set it up. Wants to load the plane with medical supplies, etc., and make it million-dollar plane load of mercy, from people, not government.

Monday, June 22, 1970
Back to work, P saw Heard and some good college presidents this morning, plus couple of other appointments. Had afternoon clear for work on Jaycee speech.

Meeting with college presidents as usual did not produce much of any value, although as a group they were much more constructive and favorable than past ones have been. Problem is they all seem to feel the P or the government should solve the problems they have created by their own lack of leadership.

The Agnew question again. The college men raised it as they always do. An easy scapegoat. P wondering if we are all wrong, is he really polarizing the youth? Really hard to figure whether he does more harm or good. He's certainly not neutral. P then mused again that it's remarkable we have survived. Main reason is that we are in the teapot (of DC) and see only the tempest, country isn't stirred up the way we are.

Tuesday, June 23, 1970
Leadership Meeting, then miscellany through the rest of the morning.

Have Pat Nixon's Peru trip pretty well lined up.

Got everyone cranked up about CBS plan to give Democrats free time to counteract the time the P gets on TV. Will launch a battle to stop this before it becomes standard procedure.

P worked at EOB all afternoon, supposedly on speech, but no results so far.

K in for long talk, about his worries about very adverse stories about his dating Jill St. John. He thinks Rogers is planting them to try to destroy him. May be.

Wednesday, June 24, 1970
Cabinet meeting, P let Heard and his discussion go on and on.

Especially bad day for poor K. Turns out he made the mistake last night of getting P all cranked up about SALT problems. As a result P decided to see Rogers (exactly what K didn't want) and had him for breakfast without telling anyone. Meanwhile we jumped on K at staff meeting about credibility of P on Cambodia. Problem is K now argues we have to sustain Lon Nol government in order to protect our military and negotiating position. Then he backs off, so all get feeling of real insecurity. He later concluded we had kept on him in meeting in order to keep him from knowing about Rogers' breakfast.

P went into this whole problem this afternoon at EOB with me, especially about K's horrible way of handling a meeting and giving all the feeling that they have no part except to follow his orders. P worries about how to overcome this and concludes he has to meet privately with Laird and Rogers more often, and handle them himself instead of through K, but this will just get K up all the tighter, so!?

Still diddling around about Jaycee speech. Had Buchanan rework it but can't decide yet whether to read it or wing it.

Thursday, June 25, 1970
St. Louis and the Jaycees. A really great day! P highly elated, gave very good speech; used the wing-it approach and came through perfectly.

California. Beautiful, sensational weather. We went to San Clemente, all in good shape. P didn't come to the office. *(Called and)* said to think back on the day; it had been very salutary to get out into the country; gig the press a little and charge our own batteries.

Friday, June 26, 1970
P in pretty early, decided to open the publishers conference instead of just greeting them at lunch.

P wants to build up "forgotten minorities" idea, thinks Agnew could do a speech. Was impressed by Buchanan memo on this, and need to play to our new potential, labor, Catholic, blue collar, etc.

K came up with great *(Philippe)* Pétain quote as we were discussing education problem and students, "They know everything, but unfortunately they don't know anything else."

P talked to Rogers, who suggested he stop in Moscow on way from Tokyo to London, and meet Gromyko at airport. K and I opposed, mainly because it undermines our plans for Summit in fall, especially because it takes some pressure off the Russians for a conference. Rogers had already discussed this with Dobrynin. Upshot was for P to tell me to call Rogers and tell him to turn it off on basis this is not the right time for him to have a meeting.

Sunday, June 28, 1970
San Clemente. P up early to see Pat Nixon off for Peru. Then spent the day at the Residence working on briefing books. Took first stab at the Cambodia statement in early evening.

Monday, June 29, 1970
San Clemente. Some more talk about press-handling technique. Especially does *not* want K giving superlong backgrounders and wants to have absolute control over scheduling of all White House staff with press. Has been reading more books on past presidents. Concludes the whole trick in this business is to do something different and now to do it for TV coverage. Still feels we need to do more effective job of covering up the time off, but recognized real need for taking enough time off.

Tuesday, June 30, 1970
San Clemente. P in just in time for 9:30 meeting with Rogers and his Asian tour group. Then a session with Manescu, the Romanian Foreign Minister. Then stayed around for quite a while, just talking. Issued the big Cambodia report today *(including the announcement of the departure of the last American troops from Cambodia)*. Then K briefed, went for one and a half hours, way too long!

P really pleased with Buchanan's work on the report, and especially his summary of the highlights, which P now wants us to do on all statements.

Decided this week has really hit the news, and that we should now low-profile July. Makes point again that we have to follow up intensely on events that are successful. We can't assume they'll get adequate ride. He feels there has been a complete revolution in the means of affecting the public and that we must learn how to deal with it effectively. Must reorient our thinking to looking at the big picture, especially TV, not worry about columnists, not wasting our big bullets.

P met Pat Nixon at El Toro, brought her back to San Clemente, then we went up to Century Plaza for the night. He pushed again for maximum follow-up on Pat Nixon trip, and on versatility of first family. P worked most of evening, had me in from 10–11 just to chat, relaxed, went to bed.

Third Quarter: July–September

Wednesday, July 1, 1970

TV day. P locked up all day until left for studio at 6:00. Did another sensational job on TV. Asked afterward, on chopper back to San Clemente, if it really got through to ordinary guy or if details of foreign policy were over his head. I think P's command, etc., got over even if substance didn't, and the mystique is more important than the content. He felt good about it, and our quick checks confirmed overall success. He handled the commentators and questions very well, zinged Senate effectively and made all his points.

We had long FRESH meeting during day, mainly about White House staff personnel.

Thursday, July 2, 1970

San Clemente. Swearing in Hodgson, Shultz, Weinberger, Weber. Most of FRESH meeting was about VP, real question of how to define and then implement his role. P feels his role must be above the battle, maybe no candidate speaking, just push on foreign policy and overall Administration posture. Thinks VP can supplement. Use him primarily on fund-raising, get him to use a stump speech instead of always a new one, not try to make national news, build candidate. Agreed VP can't continue to appear to be an unreasonable figure, and against everything. Must go over to positive and especially avoid personal attacks. Okay to attack Congress. Problem is he has no close advisors or friends and P has not given him adequate guidance. Agreed to my idea of having Harlow travel with him.

Monday, July 6, 1970
San Clemente. Long session with P in office in morning as he had nothing to do until departure time. Another session on Air Force One en route to DC. Overall, P pleased with this California trip. We made enormous amount of news and accomplished a lot.

Wednesday, July 8, 1970
P had breakfast with key GOP leaders and staff about policy for future vetoes.

Had meeting in afternoon at EOB, about plan for VP. P made pitch to Harlow to take on responsibility *(to travel with the VP and offer him guidance)* and he's basically agreed, didn't have much choice. All agreed that he (VP) is the big gun for campaign, but must not use overblown rhetoric, personal attacks, racism, anti-youth.

A little problem today as P launched his Indian message with meeting with Taos tribe. No one mentioned the whole deal would have to be translated.

P had long session in morning with Laird and K. Laird pushing for accelerated troop withdrawals and decreased bombing and tactical air, as result of budget cuts. K fighting to maintain current levels, at least through July, to maintain pressure. P assured K he would back him.

P still keeps the main heat on me about PR follow-up, on family, himself, the program, the opposition, etc. He's right, but it's hard to stay at top trim on all these fronts all the time. Have to keep hammering away at the troops.

Thursday, July 9, 1970
Odd day, P had breakfast with Mansfield. Then hit me with a few random notes and some discussion about schedule. Then over to EOB for lunch and the afternoon. A long session with E, including review of poll data I had given him at noon. Our poll shows him down to 53, new Gallup is 55. Poll of ours shows enormous weakness of Republican Party, and shows disapproval of P on all areas of major concern except South East Asia war. P doing a lot of analyzing of this.

In late afternoon had one-and-a-half-hour meeting with Mills and Byrnes about foreign trade policy. Then a cocktail session in the Map Room to celebrate House victory against Cooper-Church. We won by 84 votes, were shooting for 100.

P tonight really cranked up about getting this sold as Administration victory and built up. Didn't have anything scheduled this afternoon, but it worked out very productively, maybe a good idea to keep more time open to use on ad hoc basis.

Friday, July 10, 1970

Cabinet meeting all morning. Supposed to be a one-subject meeting, on OMB, by Shultz. But P started it off by asking K to cover foreign policy briefly for 10–15 minutes. An hour and a quarter later Shultz finally got on. P kept adding to K's points and members had questions. Got pretty funny, especially since Shultz had been filibustered out of his part in the last three Cabinet meetings.

At one point during discussion, P asked Volpe a tough question and Volpe replied by asking if it is all right for a Cabinet officer to say "No comment." P instantly said, "It's about time." Broke 'em all up. Had a lot of follow-up items. Has decided to start wearing a flag *(in his lapel)*. P had UN dinner.

Saturday, July 11, 1970

No schedule. Had me in for two long spells in morning, with K in between short shot with Flanigan. Then off to Camp David at 2:00.

Got going again on political strategy. Especially wants to emphasize to all our key people that everything we do, all decisions and statements, must consider first their effect on November. He was very upset that he had been led to approve the IRS ruling about no tax exemption for segregated private schools, feels it will make no votes anywhere and will badly hurt private schools *both* North and South. Thinks we opened Pandora's Box, now thinks it was bad advice. Point is, for next few months the political considerations are more important than the substantive because we *have* to pick up at least three senators.

Keeps trying to figure out how to implement his idea of changing name of Republican party to Conservative party. Based on polls, there are twice as many conservatives as Republicans. Tough legal and technical problem.

No activity at Camp David after arrival.

Sunday, July 12, 1970

Camp David. No word from P during day. He did call me a couple of times in the evening, while I was at Flanigan's for dinner. Wanted to cut Peace Corps and Vista budget down far enough to decimate them, and eliminate funds for UN building expansion, and fire some people at HEW for obscenities, re: P and Tricia in their slide show last week.

Monday, July 13, 1970

Fairly light day. More emphasis on basing all scheduling and other decisions on political grounds. Especially emphasize Italians, Poles, Elks and Rotarians, eliminate Jews, blacks, youth.

About Family Assistance Plan, wants to be sure it's killed by Democrats and that we make big play for it, but don't let it pass, can't afford it.

K in to see me for his periodic depression about Rogers. This time he's found Rogers is meeting Dobrynin tomorrow, and K is absolutely convinced he's going to try to make his own Vietnam settlement, plus get a Summit meeting, and take full credit for all. K's temptation is to confront Bill and insist they have it out with P, or else one will have to leave. Thinks he can scare him out. I urged against it on grounds he might not scare out and P can't follow through, especially before elections. Actually it would be counterproductive for K, and hurt him badly with P, and solve nothing.

Tuesday, July 14, 1970

Trip day. Office session first. Upset about the McGovern, Hatfield efforts, and "Committee to End War." Dole talked to him about it last night, said they've raised a lot of money, etc. Wants us to work out a counterattack. Called Colson in and put him in charge. Made point he's more concerned about the public issue than the Senate votes. Especially wants to hit the Senators up for election. Set it up as a campaign issue.

Had me up to cabin on flight to Louisville. Mainly just to chat. Louisville great success. Good airport crowd, great street crowds in town. P up on hood, stopped car, into crowd, etc. Good for him, and especially good to stick it to press.

Had me back up on flight home. Back onto Huntley issue, about Chet's bad quotes in *Life*. He denies them to Klein. Gives us a great chance further to discredit TV newsmen and a dig at *Life* at same time.

Wednesday, July 15, 1970

Big flap about story in *Post* section that P delayed the game last night. He didn't, and is mad at charges he did.

K is building up a new head of steam about Rogers. Bill has made some startling statements about Cambodia as a non-success; encouragement of Chinese, harm done to his Middle East efforts by White House comments, etc. K still feels this is all part of a plan to do him in and to take over foreign policy by State from White House. Talked to me several times and keeps repeating his charges and complaints but has no real alternative except to fire Rogers, which isn't very likely. I agreed to try to get Haig in with P to discuss the whole problem.

Then tonight Haig called, P had called K at a party to say he'd called Rogers to congratulate him on his press conference today. K really distressed by this because Rogers apparently made things even worse at the press conference. So we have to try to simmer it all down again.

Thursday, July 16, 1970

P had no schedule today except for Prince Charles arrival and a fat cat dinner on the *Sequoia,* time was open for preparation for tomorrow's planned press conference, which was canceled until Monday or Friday next week because E and Shultz decided P had to release major statement tomorrow about policy on vetoes of excessive appropriation legislation. So I ended up spending hours in the oval and EOB offices filling in the time.

Long session with Flanigan and Colson. Covered the attack operation, especially equal time and McGovern-Hatfield. P intrigued with Colson's tactics and plans on both. Very upset because we goofed on ambassadors at Charles arrival and didn't shake hands with them. I finally settled him down by having protocol call all of them and apologize.

Friday, July 17, 1970

Again no schedule because of planned press conference, except for Heard meeting in late afternoon. Then the big ball for Prince Charlie tonight.

Decided he wants Scranton Commission to go ahead with open hearings because it keeps the student unrest issue alive through the summer and works to our advantage. Wants to be sure we get some really horrible types to testify. Then need to get our right-wing types to blast the whole thing. Gets a little involved but should work.

Strongly feels we should go on a strong overall offensive now. The economy is with us, at least for the moment, so we can really hit the prophets of doom. Hit the crisis of confidence, etc.

Tuesday, July 21, 1970
Leadership Meeting and full day of appointments. Has idea of working up "spender" rating on all the senators up for election, to hit them with blame for high prices and to make the issue about Congressional responsibility.

Flap about Bureau of Labor Statistics release of Consumer Price Index, Shultz told P it would be lowest increase since December '68, then headlines just said Cost of Living has increased again. P has always been convinced we are jobbed by Bureau of Labor Statistics staff on these, and this is most blatant example. Shultz came in furious, and totally frustrated as to what to do about it.

Wednesday, July 22, 1970
Breakfast with Bunker and Bruce, Domestic Council first meeting and Boys Nation.

Read Dent memo analyzing problem with South and issued whole series of orders about no more catering to liberals and integrationists to our political disadvantage. Agreed to meet with group of Southern leaders.

Political group reviewed Senate races and allocations of our support funds. Agreed generally on key races we'll give to. Also covered P's general ideas about use of VP and Cabinet, he's very tough on their going only where it really counts. Is determined, though, to go as far as necessary to win any that we can. He really enjoys the political talk and planning and will be hard to contain when the campaign starts.

Thursday, July 23, 1970
Loaded schedule on last day before trip. P still disturbed about Dent's memo on problems with South. Wants me to tell all staff P is a conservative, does not believe in integration, will carry out the law, nothing more. Won't do the Watts visit because won't win any Negroes and could alienate whites.

Delighted with new Gallup poll, to come out next week that

will show P at 61 percent approval, up six points from last month.

Bill Rogers called me to relay to P his meeting with Dobrynin was very satisfactory. Now just have to get Israel to accept. He was really pleased, has finally accomplished something.

P again pushing on economy. Called Shultz in this morning to put heat on him to knock down recession talk. Opposition has really flared up today on this issue. It was all ours for last couple weeks and now they're reacting but with no real substance. Problem is we have to be sure to fight back. P wants to hit them as trying to talk the country into a recession, exactly what they are doing. It's almost funny to see the orchestration, a Joe Kraft column and three different statements all break today, after two weeks of nothing. Unfortunately for them, the market went up a big chunk today.

Friday, July 24, 1970

Busiest day yet. P started with busy round of activity at White House before leaving for trip.

Was very concerned about press report that FBI said *(National)* Guard was at fault at Kent State. Called J. Edgar, who immediately blamed it on Jerris Leonard. P told Hoover to knock it down. Is really afraid we'll end up putting Administration on the side of the students and really doesn't want that.

Fargo was not too good. Very poor crowds along the streets (we had not built crowds because of his plan to walk down Main Street), crowd at meeting place was barricaded way back and we had battle with Secret Service to try to get them up closer.

Salt Lake was great. Good reception at rodeo. On plane to California, P in good shape, very tired. A really long day.

Saturday, July 25, 1970

P slept late. Unusual for first day in San Clemente. Wants to plan Europe trip to Spain, Yugoslavia, Great Britain, Netherlands, Ireland, Morocco, and probably Pope. Was thinking of late August, but I think I convinced him to wait until September, more effect on the campaign. He feels need to reinforce strength in foreign policy, as our main advantage.

Some talk of politics again. Wants to be sure our candidates tie their opponents into hippies, kids, Demos.

Back on Huntley. Important to destroy him for effect on all other commentators.

Sunday, July 26, 1970

P home all morning, ball game in afternoon. Called after the game, said he got a great reception and was spectacular game, 31 hits, 21 runs, 11 innings.

Tuesday, July 28, 1970

San Clemente. In late again. Discussion with E and me about desegregation. Has assigned me to follow up on activities of all concerned to lower the profile, make sure we are doing no more than necessary to meet what the law requires. Feels very strongly that anything we do will have adverse political effect, therefore should only do what we have to, and not brag about it.

Had me tell Mitchell not to open Southern offices and not to send his men down en masse, only when needed on a spot basis. Also set policy that we'll use no Federal troops or marshals to enforce, must be done by locals.

Thursday, July 30, 1970

Press conference. P holed up all day at Century Plaza *(Hotel)*, only a couple of calls about more material. Had me in for a little while at noon to run through random notes about schedule, etc.

Press conference went well except for power failure that cut audio in the room just before airtime. Pace was a little slow, but good show overall. He was a little concerned on chopper back that it had been too slow. Very good general reaction.

Saturday, August 1, 1970

(San Clemente) I stayed home. P in office for a while, meeting with K. Called to check in, said he was going to drive through Yorba Linda, etc., then to Chasens for dinner. He did. Created quite a flap with press because no notice. Ziegler called me in evening saying had huge crisis. Survived.

Monday, August 3, 1970

Back to DC. Big flap arose from incredible comment by P at brief press statement that *(Charles)* Manson was guilty of LA murders. *(This statement occurred before Manson's criminal convictions.)* He was trying to make point about media responsibility for glorifying criminals, but it came out wrong. We had quite a time on Air Force One trying to work out a correction. P had John Mitchell and E write up a statement (Ziegler wanted him to go on TV on arrival). Just one of those things that's hard to explain or overcome. Press overjoyed at catching him, and playing it up big as possible.

Tuesday, August 4, 1970

Back to the routine. We had major discussion at staff meeting about plans for vetoes upcoming, of whether to veto all over-appropriations, and at once, or to go selectively. Basically political question about tactics for fall campaign. Shultz exercises main leadership on these debates.

Major session with P, VP, Attorney General, Richardson, Kennedy, E, Finch, Harlow, Shultz, Garment, about Southern school desegregation. P made it absolutely clear no one is to do more than law requires. No political gain for us. Do what is necessary, low profile, don't kick South around. All appeared to agree and seemed optimistic, except VP, who felt they were glossing over the problem, especially about bureaucracy not on our side being overzealous. Others cited all the good news. VP argued pessimism.

Wednesday, August 5, 1970

Two-hour meeting with FRESH and Harlow about strategy for upcoming vetoes. Went round and round, no plan from group, although they'd been meeting on it all afternoon and we had covered in morning staff meeting. Decided to regroup tomorrow. Turns into *the* decision of the year domestically. Will have enormous and far-reaching consequences, and may be chance for the big move politically, especially now that war issue is somewhat neutralized.

Thursday, August 6, 1970

Loaded day, Deputy Prime Minister of Australia, Cabot Lodge back from Vatican, Governor of Guam, Senator Prouty, DDE stamp, Georgia Integration Committee, Posthumous Medal of Honor, Foreign Minister of Spain, capped by two hours with group of Southerners in to bitch about Administration shift to the left.

Back on veto question, wants more staff work, to try to arrive at a conclusion as to recommend specifically.

I had a tiff with K today about my involvement with Bill Rogers in his desire to stop some adverse (to State) actions about AID and international economic policy. He'd called me to see P, and I was in the middle of checking it out. K upset, but we talked it out satisfactorily. He's just obsessed with conviction Rogers is out to get him and to sabotage all our systems and our foreign policy.

Friday, August 7, 1970

Another busy day, then off to Camp David for weekend. Wants to be sure to stop Richardson and all others who are running loose on integration operations. Wants E to police it, which poses problem since E is assuming I'm doing it. Wants to be sure all know we are to move only at snail's pace.

Long afternoon session with FRESH group, except Shultz, plus Harlow about veto policy. Basically decided to let Education Bill go with statement, veto HUD and youth on Thursday, with message and big blast about Congress overspending.

Sunday, August 9, 1970

At Camp David. E and I had long talk about desegregation, etc., which brought out E's feeling that P has lost confidence in him. Says he hasn't seen P alone for a month. Feels he can't go on making domestic decisions, etc., unless he knows he's doing what P wants. I said we should confront P with whole thing and get it cleared up, so we did.

In about three-hour chat with P at Aspen, E laid his problem out quite clearly and P shot it down very well. P did lay out his concerns about liberal appointments to commissions, overreaction in South, etc., and air was pretty well cleared up.

P made some good basic points; we can't pick up support from radicalized partisans. Need to reexamine all our appointments and start to play to *our* group, without shame or concern or apology. Should feel our way, *appear* to be listening to critics, but we have now learned we have gained nothing by turning to the other side.

P has changed his mind, reached a new conclusion. Is convinced policy of sucking after left won't work, not only can't win them, can't even defuse them. Wants E to shape policies so as to move our way. P changed mind about school desegregation statement of March 24, thinks it went too far.

P main point; we must put our imprint on the men as well as the policies in this Administration, all the way through it.

Monday, August 10, 1970
Decided to go ahead with Labor Day dinner as a buffet supper, to get in all national union heads, then do military tattoo on lawn after.

P called Mitchell at ABA *(American Bar Association)* and told him to blast the 100 volunteer lawyers going into South to ride herd on integration. Said to call it gratuitous insult, harmful effects, is sending vigilantes, hit on give our citizens' committees a chance, don't let Northerners get away with pious hypocritical attitude, say they should clean up their own section first before they point the finger at another.

Wants to go out for a ride with Julie this afternoon, and Ziegler is not to be told, no press to follow.

Some talk with P and K about plans for European trip.

Tuesday, August 11, 1970
Leadership this morning with a surprise development. P had planned to let Education Bill go through without signing instead of vetoing. By end of discussion, P decided to veto, which he had wanted to do all along. So moved up HUD veto from Thursday and did both today, with statement to press this afternoon. Especially enjoyable because *Washington Post* reported on front page this morning that he would *not* veto. P knows they'll override, but he makes his big issue on spending much more clearly this way.

Had a real bunch for Congressional half hour. Afterward P very relaxed and pleased with vetoes, said, "Boy, we had the damnedest collection today. Jesus Christ what a bunch of nuts." Had Ziegler in to gloat over shock of press corps about veto.

Wednesday, August 12, 1970
Postal Bill signing at Post Office Department went pretty well.

Asked me to try to work out some kind of jobs for Julie and Tricia, both want to go to work full time, and really need something productive to do. They're in a tough spot. Also some problems about Pat Nixon news coverage. Guess last night at dinner didn't go too well. K said P wandered into his office, seemed to have no purpose, said little, but obviously had something on his mind.

Considerable discussion about P's picture. He still doesn't like the official one, so we looked at others. Wants to make a change. Reneged on plan to remove tennis court.

Big deal for the day was critical ABM Amendment vote in Senate. We won 52–47, better than we had expected.

Thursday, August 13, 1970

P delighted with news Angela Davis (UCLA Communist) had owned the guns used in San Rafael judge killing. Shows the conspiracy linkup more clearly than anything yet.

Big new word from Soviets, didn't get word from K as to what, but he's got something cooking.

Saturday, August 15, 1970

No schedule. P had me in from 9:00 to 1:00, with K for quite a while at the start, then out for a meeting with Rabin about Middle East.

Discussion with K about Soviet-China probabilities; K agrees that something big is stirring. P rather surprised to hear this.

Big plan for trip to New York next Tuesday to visit *Daily News* and have dinner, etc. Mainly to shaft the *(N.Y.) Times,* plus Pat Nixon is going up anyway for shopping.

P talked to Moynihan, who agreed to take UN post in January.

P planned to spend night on *Sequoia* with Bebe and Hobe, then added Rogers, then shifted to Camp David, so we all went up there, including E and Finch. Quiet night.

Sunday, August 16, 1970

At Camp David. Very quiet day. Monumental flap with K, who called accusing P and me of playing games with him yesterday about boat ride, etc., to cover up plan to have Rogers up to Camp David. Incredible. But he was really convinced, as, apparently, was Haig. Guess they sat there all day stewing. Really ridiculous, because we released Rogers to press as part of party, no attempt to cover it at all. Guess K is uptight about Middle East and is imagining things. He made reference to several early morning phone calls from P yesterday, with quick hangups. Very hard to figure, but has to be cleared up. He called me again at home, but I didn't quiet him much.

Monday, August 17, 1970

(P) asked me about K's reaction to weekend, and I told him about the flap, which K had continued today. *(K)* still convinced we were playing games with him. He's really very bitter and uptight, and when I totally refuted his claim, he backed off and said, "Well anyway it should make you realize how paranoid we have become because of the State Department's maneuvering." He claims Haig agrees with him.

All this really worries P because it creates doubts about K's reliability on other recommendations, and gets in the way of his doing his work. P realizes K's basically jealous of any idea not his own, and he just can't swallow the apparent early success of the Middle East plan because it is Rogers'. In fact, he's probably actually trying to make it fail for just this reason. Of all people, he has to keep his mind clean and clear, and instead he's obsessed with these weird persecution delusions.

I'll have to talk to K some more because this will prey on P's mind until something *(is)* settled, but I don't think it's curable. P said several times that K may have reached the end of his usefulness. I disagree and think instead that we have to recognize this weakness as the price we pay for his enormous assets, and it's well worth it. Probably can convince P to let me take heat on this and try to keep K from hitting him with it, which is his greatest concern, other than the impairment of K's work.

Tuesday, August 18, 1970

Day started with a bang after P's breakfast with bipartisan leaders of Senate about Geneva protocol. P had Scott in tow and had a letter from Cardinal Krol of Pittsburgh about Solicitor General's refusal to back Administration position on parochial schools, and P really hit the fan. Had E and me in, read the riot act, ordered E to get it changed or Solicitor General fired today. P said was both concerned by the politics of this but more because his policy is not being carried out.

Then got into K problem again. Wants me to let K know that we caught him on his bluff on this one, he's building up a monstrous story that does him no good.

Things picked up a little later when K popped in to an-

nounce he had word from North Vietnam that they wanted to
meet with him in Paris and their big guys would be there, a
week from Saturday. This brightened K's attitude enormously,
and may help cure the current problem. New problem arises
as K wants to go secretly, but P thinks he should go in open
because will get caught, which will be a political problem. So
I'm supposed to swing him around.

New problem with Mitchell arises from the Catholic situation, in that John clearly is not always carrying out P's orders,
but won't admit it to P, which P recognizes. John does this on
basis of judgment that it is best for P, but still makes it difficult.

Wednesday, August 19, 1970

(Senators) Baker, Bellmon, and Dole in for early morning appointment, to tell P of problem of White House staff relations
with all good guys in the Senate. (Dole says he's never even
met E.) P overreacted with all kinds of ideas for curing, along
lines of open lines from senators to E, Shultz, me, etc. Had
me in, and K, and later Shultz, to go over this, and had me
meet with them after. Trouble is, even the three of them don't
agree on either the problem, or the solution.

Thursday, August 20, 1970

Off to Mexico! P had me up for about three hours of the four-
and-a-half-hour flight. Had lots of trivia, notes, etc. He had
worked last night after the dinner. Is still concerned about K.
Had a lot of political ideas left over from last night. P would
start to work on his Mexico briefing book, then shift back to
other things, not really very excited about going to Mexico,
no real substance to the visit.

Great reception, street crowds, confetti, burros with flowers,
happy people, warm, good motorcade. Huge Mexican luncheon (small group but lot of food), adequate toasts, quite personal and warm. After lunch (5:00) substantive meeting
produced agreement about border problem, and the two Presidents went to press hotel (unscheduled) to announce it. No
evening activity, P home and to bed. We stayed on beach and
in ocean until after 8:00, then downtown for fiesta for few
minutes with E's, and K with his CBS girl producer.

Tuesday, August 25, 1970

San Clemente. Discussed domestic security problem (E and I had discussed with Mitchell yesterday). P said I should take it over because I'm only one J. Edgar Hoover trusts and will take orders from. Others, especially Mitchell, want it under Domestic Council, with a staff of intelligence types to evaluate input and order necessary projects, etc. Will do it one way or the other, in any event will drop the interagency task force approach which we've started and run into snag with FBI and Hoover. Main problem there is Tom Huston.

P in good spirits, enjoying being here, doing all his work, not pushing on anything. Great!

Friday, August 28, 1970

P talked about Real Majority and need to get that thinking over to all our people. Wants to really ram this home and make all decisions based on it. Very impressed with Buchanan memo analyzing it. Wants to hit pornography, dope, bad kids.

Pleased with idea of Moynihan trip to UN and Asia before announcing him as UN Ambassador, wants me to brace Rogers on it, and have him talk to Pat to set it all up. Talked about economy. Hard to believe it keeps improving, want to be sure we have plan for handling any drop, i.e., CPI *(Consumer Price Index)* or other bad news.

(The next week in San Clemente was a combination of catching up on open details, meetings, and planning sessions.)

Monday, September 7, 1970

Labor Day, but not much of a holiday, P in office most of the day. Discussed political campaign, especially importance of candidates taking good hard line on bombings, etc. Point of pushing opponents to the left. Doesn't want us to clean up the Obscenity Commission, because he wants the issue of their bad report.

Wants me to assemble staff to review Buchanan analysis and make it clear we have to play the line. Also a lot of political instructions for Finch, about weekly issue bulletin to all candidates, keep them on three to four solid issues.

Very anxious to develop some dramatic Administration action about hijackings, need tough shocking steps, especially guards on planes.

Labor dinner tonight, a real coup. Large group, and not the

usual White House guest types. Meany's toast was excellent, compared presidents, referred to Tricky Dick, said FDR just as tricky, and Lyndon no slouch either. P later said Meany was really rough on Bobby Kennedy during dinner conversation, also on McGovern, et al. Did dig us a little about the economy, but overall very favorable. Good army tattoo on South Lawn, with 4000 union headquarters employees. Darn good move overall. Lot of press comment, and labor guys were clearly impressed.

Tuesday, September 8, 1970
Back to work. Some critique of dinner, mainly because it ran late and he didn't get a chance to talk with the men before the entertainment.

Had long afternoon session with Rogers, Laird, Helms, Mitchell, K, and J. Edgar, mainly about hijacking. Then had trouble lining up a group for dinner on *Sequoia,* ended up with J. Edgar, Rose, and me.

Almost unbelievable conversation at dinner as J. Edgar went on and on about his friends (Clint Murchison, George Allen, Hap Flanigan, etc.) and his enemies (Bobby Kennedy, Lindsay, Mayor Washington, Pete Flanigan, etc.). He really lit into the bad guys. Also full of firm political predictions (most of them pretty far off) and detailed reports of great FBI operations. A real character out of days of yore, hard to relate to current times. Goes to race track as often as he can, never bets over $2.00, loves the fast set, but apparently just as an observer. P seems fascinated by him and ordered me to have lunch with him twice a month to keep up a close contact.

Wednesday, September 9, 1970
Long morning meeting with political operations and VP's crew for the campaign. P really in his element as he held forth, for Safire and Buchanan, on speech content, campaign strategy, etc. Came up with some darn good lines and ideas, all the stuff he'd like to say but can't. P was delighted with Pat's kickoff speech for VP, which really hits hard. Really wants to play the conservative trend and hang the opponents as left-wing radical liberals. Said to say, "Our opponents are not bad men, they are sincere, dedicated, radicals. They honestly believe in the liberal left." And force them on the defensive, to deny it,

as they did to us about Birchers in '62.

Had me over to EOB for four hours in afternoon.

Thursday, September 10, 1970

K got me at end of staff meeting to plead that Rogers be kept out of meeting with Golda Meir next week, on grounds he's most hated man in Israel and would be a disaster; K said he'd stay out too. I covered later with P and he agreed.

Lot of discussion about hijacking actions. P still pushing hard for strong positive steps, Flanigan has a plan but P rejected the statement completely because not direct enough. Wants to say "I have directed that," not "I urge that." Also wants to add embargo on countries that provide sanctuary to hijackers, but Rogers objects because that would include Egypt and would louse up peace negotiations. Have to figure out a way, P especially wants to hit Cuba on the embargo.

Friday, September 11, 1970

Morning pretty well filled with GOP leadership followed by bipartisan group about hijacking statement P released later in day, about armed guards on planes, etc.

Was especially impressed by lady during Congressional half hour who gave him a flag she had made, with 78,000 stitches and "Every stitch represents something good in America."

Very anxious to get moving on action about campus unrest. Is fully convinced this is "the" issue this year and we should be on record with positive action.

I spent good part of afternoon on huge flap with Bob Dole, who was incensed about screwup of announcement of our Kansas trip; Governor (Democrat) made it in Kansas, ahead of Dole or the University. After tracking it all back, found it was Dole's fault.

On chopper to Camp David got into reminiscing about war days, as he was thinking about inviting his old Pacific group to White House, as we did the Whittier class. Then he started telling tales of the war days, sounded just as bad as anyone else! Wants Hughes to have services make a study of his old buddies, work up a list and get them in.

Saturday, September 12, 1970

At Camp David. P slept most of the morning. Worked on speech and accumulated follow-up folders in afternoon. Then he had me over for several hours to clean up his notes. Sat in the study.

Has several plots he wants hatched. One to infiltrate the John Gardner "Common Cause" deal and needle them and try to push them to left. Feels we can benefit from a third party to the left. I'm not so sure, might push Democrats to center, better to have them go left. Next, a front that sounds like SDS to support the Democratic candidates and praise their liberal records, etc., publicize their "bad" quotes in guise of praise. Give the senators a "radiclib" rating.

Pushing again on project of building *our* establishment in press, business, education, etc. Long general talk about '72 plans and after. Agrees with my idea that we should shoot generally for replacing all key people by mid '73 and then really charge ahead to accomplish something during first half of second term, our potentially most productive period. No problems of political balance, etc., and a favorable Congress, hopefully. Fun to contemplate. In meantime should gear everything to '72, reelection and winning Congress. Not a bad approach anyway. In most cases what's good politically will be good otherwise also.

He agrees, too, with my concern about who runs '72 campaign, have to get a new RNC Chairman. (I hope Rumsfeld will take it, he's the best on the scene.)

Tuesday, September 15, 1970
Got started again this morning on basic political approach. Wants to review the list of critical votes on which we'll base the radiclib labeling; wants action about the main issue. Really upset that the Domestic Council has come up with nothing, not even his plan to withhold Defense funds.

Wednesday, September 16, 1970
Trip day. To Kansas State for Landon Lecture. Huge success, beyond all fondest hopes! Mainly because the speech was excellent, on student violence, etc., and there was a *small* group of about 25 bad guys in the audience of 15,000, and their shouts, etc., played right into P's speech. Was really great! Bulk of students really enthusiastic and anti's whipped them up even more. Another coup!

Then on to Chicago for Midwest briefing and press reception. P folded early after a hard day.

K came in to talk in Chicago after the briefing. Deeply concerned that we are pissing away all we've gained in 18 months, both with Russia and North Vietnam. And getting nothing for it.

Feels P must have a personal advisor on Middle East, not State, and recognizes it probably can't be K, but someone has to catch all the nuances.

K emphasizes he agrees 100 percent with P statements at briefing today, there's no difference on policy, just on letting Rogers run loose. K feels sure P can't take Rogers seriously on foreign policy.

In Middle East everything is stirred up, with no concept of what to do or where to go.

Thursday, September 17, 1970

K woke me at 2:00 this morning with call that war had started in Jordan, King taking on fedayeen *(Palestinian rebels were fighting King Hussein, and Syria was poised at the border)*. Possibility Israel will go in, especially if Iraq or Syria does. Afraid Rogers may panic, so K needs authority to keep things from breaking, tighten alerts, etc. Haig wants United States full alert but K feels no. K wants to take position *(that)* he notified P tonight and act on basis of P orders. We agreed no need to call P, no decisions needed because all actions are preparatory and imperative and nonvisible. K then called Rogers, Moorer, Packard, Sisco, told them he'd talked to Chicago, implied P, all OK. Rogers scared enough not to go off. Has taken all emergency measures, etc. Question of bringing P back to DC in morning, K feels may be necessary (I disagreed). Later called after WSAG meeting, all under control, no need to come back.

P had good day in Chicago.

On Air Force One talked about value of more days of off-beat stuff. Especially pleased with encounter on street this morning with group of hard hats, and with crowd at Marshall Field *(department store)* when he went in to buy ties. Wants more such chances.

Friday, September 18, 1970

Golda Meir meeting, P once again impressed with her strength and toughness. Guess it went pretty well, though he was not looking forward to it.

Lot of talk about ways to get the Kansas speech replayed on

TV prime time, even using our money. Got Colson to work on it. Networks all turned it down, even using an existing sponsor's time. Gives us good issue, but would rather have the TV.

To Camp David at 6:00, after greeting reception for Congressional staffs.

Sunday, September 20, 1970
At Camp David, K called first thing about latest in Jordan.

> On September 18, Syrian tanks crossed into Jordan. K sent a strong note to the Soviets; Rogers made a strong public statement to the Syrians. The tanks began pulling back—but K was sure it wasn't over yet.

K now worried because State wants to take to UN.

K very worried about Rogers' plans. Finds he's in New York this week and just learned Dobrynin coming back and spending two days in New York.

K wanted me to call Rogers, tell him not to see Dobrynin, K didn't want to talk to P about this, but later agreed to on my recommendation, and it worked out fine. Says P problem is his reluctance to understand that tactics turn into strategy, and you can't let things go along and then try to save them without brilliant maneuver. Feels the real stake is Nixon credibility with Soviets.

Monday, September 21, 1970
Busy day back at the White House. Lot of action last night about war in Jordan. K up most of night, called P at 3:00 and 5:00, had meeting in K's office, with P until midnight.

> Syrian tanks moved back into Jordan. K informed the Israelis we would support their air strike if necessary. P put troops and naval forces on alert in the Mediterranean.

Had a meeting at 8:30 this morning (K wanted at 7:30) of the top level, Laird, Packard, Rogers, Sisco, K, Haig with P. Decided to move with ground troops and K worked with (Israeli Prime Minister Yitzhak) Rabin. After meeting, Rogers went into K's office and K urged they work together in crises, not at each other's throats. Rogers had accused K in meeting of withholding some information from P, and Rogers repeated charge in K's office, all based on question of whether Israelis needed advance notice to provide time to mobilize forces. Rogers feels K trying to force P to rash decision. All this from K, who called me in to lay out the night's history for the record.

This whole struggle went on through the day, K and Haig dropping in to my office three or four times to report the latest. K really disturbed that Rogers will win out. I covered some of this with P in late afternoon. He had me go into K's office with him, to get updating and K started in again on Sisco (he says now Joe plays P when with P, and Rogers when with Rogers). P okayed K's plans but cut him short on complaints. Then walked over to EOB with me, talked about the problem. Said he's about come to conclusion can't tolerate any longer, either K or Rogers has to go, no other solution. Problem is he gave no clue as to which. I believe letting K go would be a disaster even though he's a lot harder to deal with than Bill, and I can't imagine P letting Bill go. He knows K is right.

Tuesday, September 22, 1970
Things back on a more even keel as Jordan seems to calm down a bit.

> The Syrian tanks withdrew again, this time for good, and Hussein's soldiers were besting the rebels.

Still pushing on daily action about crime and students. At Leaders' Meeting today he announced 1,000 additional FBI agents. Fascinated by our poll that gives him 64 percent approval, but shows 47 percent think he's not strong enough about students. Same poll shows 71 percent think college administrators are too lenient. Did agree to hold up on Defense research funds letter to colleges, on my recommendation (per Flanigan) that it could cause student demonstrators to try to force administrations to reject funds and we'd be blamed for starting it. Instead will wait until something stirs up on a campus and then use this to react to it, so it will be *their* fault not ours.

P seemed in much less preoccupied mood than yesterday.

Not as concerned about Jordan and possible consequences and K not grinding as hard about all the potential disasters. Sure is a difference in the atmosphere in the inner circle from one day to the next.

Wednesday, September 23, 1970

A huge new flap developed when Rogers called me and said K told him to send a flash cable that he believed was contrary to P's desires and he wouldn't send it without talking with P. The P was taking nap at EOB, I told Haig, and he and K hit the roof. Problem was Rogers was going against direct P order to K about wording of cable.

While we talked Rogers arrived and sneaked into EOB and was with P, so we shot over the paperwork and waited. K built up a monumental head of steam, said he'd see this through and then had to leave, couldn't take more of this, about then P had him come over.

One more down.

On September 18 we had received word that the Soviets were building a submarine base in Cienfuegos Bay, Cuba. We kept it absolutely quiet while we decided what to do, but on September 24 the word leaked out. That day P and K gave Dobrynin an ultimatum, and over the next few weeks, after many meetings and notes, the Soviets backed down and abandoned the base. Most of the material relating to this incident was deleted from my diary by the government for national security reasons.

Friday, September 25, 1970

P pretty busy all morning, alone at EOB good part of the afternoon. Decided to see Scranton Commission tomorrow and try to get it all over with fast as possible. Had me over for couple of hours at late afternoon.

Back onto the K subject. Wants Haig to keep K from always looking like there's a crisis. Best way to manage a crisis is to look like there isn't one. Keep cool, act very strong in private channels. K apparently blew one in briefing today by saying Cuba is serious.

Saturday, September 26, 1970

P received the Scranton report *(on Kent State)*, we did all our little projects to discredit it and that is now underway, after all the agonizing about how to handle it.

Big day for political discussions as P tries to get the line set and some action underway before we leave. Mainly concerned with not letting Democrats, especially presidential candidates like Ted Kennedy, Muskie, HHH, etc., get away with their obvious present attempt to move away from the left and into middle of road. He's right, our people are letting them do it and press is not nailing them.

And off to Europe tomorrow morning.

Sunday, September 27, 1970

Off on another trip. Eight-hour flight from Andrews to Ciampino Airport at Rome. Choppers into Quirinale. K met us here, from his secret talks in Paris. He felt it went well. Saw P for an hour or so tonight.

Monday, September 28, 1970

Rome. A really good day, with the highlights two unscheduled activities, which were great. Then we learned the American hostages were coming through Rome on their way home, here for fueling stop only. P met them, talked a little on the strip, then went up into plane and talked some more. Guess he did extremely well.

He extended his meeting with Pope well past the 45 minutes. He wanted to go back into city and see people before boarding chopper, in St. Peter's, so we worked out plan for him. Crowds big and very enthusiastic. Stood up on car, moved through crowd. Great!

Then chopper to *Saratoga,* for overnight. Then the Cabinet officers and staff had dinner in flag mess and started a movie. Interrupted by word that *(Egyptian President Gamal)* Nasser had died. So we had a big conference about how to handle. Agreed should issue statement from P and should cancel firepower part of tomorrow's operation. I woke P up and told him. He agreed with statement, then went back to sleep.

Then K and I got into the whole question of continuing the trip, a real problem because *(Yugoslavian President Josip)* Tito will undoubtedly go to funeral on Thursday. We finally came up with a plan that lets P visit Tito on Wednesday.

Tuesday, September 29, 1970

Sixth Fleet and Naples. So far trip working *very* well. The two big events of yesterday, hostages and motorcade, were not planned or advanced, but our crew swung right in and carried them out very well. Best test.

Wednesday, September 30, 1970

NATO and Belgrade. The airport arrival was 100% correct and protocol, *no* crowd, no cheering, etc. After usual courtesies at the Palace, P left by his own motorcade to Tomb of Unknown Soldier. Decided to try a detour into the city on the way back. Told Hughes (all by radio in car) to cut wreath ceremony as short as possible. It was scheduled for 25 minutes; we did it in 10. Then went back into city to shopping district, hit it about 6:00, and it worked perfectly. P stopped the car a couple of times, was completely engulfed by crowd, got up on hood, held a baby. As we moved slowly, crowd was *very* enthusiastic.

Tito's dinner started a half hour late, then they were even later arriving at reception, and it ran overtime, so P was over an hour late returning to Palace, after midnight—and tomorrow is a really loaded day.

Fourth Quarter: October–December

Thursday, October 1, 1970
Yugoslavia. P off this morning for his meetings with Tito. Then at noon off by plane to Zagreb. Since Tito added himself at the last minute, we had no control over the motorcade so couldn't slow down or stop.

Was really a shame because streets were jammed and people very enthusiastic, even in pouring rain. Would have been a great scene if he had stopped in the middle and they'd let the people come in. P was really disappointed when they didn't. Came back to staff section in plane on way back and talked about it. (Was trying to escape Tito for a few minutes. Had been with him all day.)

Then after strange little reception in Zagreb, had to drive to Tito's birthplace because weather too bad for choppers. A one-hour drive each way. Tito rode with P, which wasn't so bad, but two Croat leaders hopped in too, and no interpreter. Must have been a total disaster, although he didn't seem to mind. Spent quite a while in the birthplace, still pouring rain on all of us outside. Back to Belgrade for our State dinner.

P asked me to have it speeded up, and so I stayed in kitchen and supervised the whole deal, and we served a four-course dinner in exactly one hour.

Friday, October 2, 1970
Madrid. A sensational day! Miles and miles of people packed solid, band music over speakers the entire route, flags and banners over the street and on all the poles and buildings. Motorcade never stopped, per *(President Francisco)* Franco's orders, but they were sure out en masse and excited. The horse guards were great, but did block the view of the crowd.

The Moncloa Palace is a truly beautiful residence and gardens. P rattled through an afternoon schedule, then to 9:30 white-tie dinner at Royal Palace. Absolutely amazing crowds; still there when we came out at 12:15, and P went over and shook hands while they mobbed him.

Dinner was magnificent, as is the Palace. Room after room with unbelievable ceilings and furnishings—table for about 140, in hall with 15 huge crystal chandeliers.

Saturday, October 3, 1970
Ireland. Good welcome at Shannon and motorcade through Limerick and Hospital to *(businessman Jack)* Mulcahy's estate, Kilfrush. A spectacular home and setting, in opulent luxury. Good crowds full of Saturday night cheer (and beer). The crowds are boisterous and the cops really tough.

Mulcahy had dinner for P, Prime Minister, top staff, and Rogers. A six-course affair, started at 9:30, lasted until 11:00. Then over an hour of Irish entertainment, very good but very long and very late. P and Prime Minister both exhausted, so it was a little rough on all concerned.

Sunday, October 4, 1970
A nice easy day at Kilfrush.

Monday, October 5, 1970
Ireland, and home. Made the morning pilgrimage to Timahoe to visit graveyard and former *(Quaker)* meeting house site of the Milhous clan. P seemed to enjoy seeing it. They had done a good job of clearing the grass, uncovering foundations of the meeting house, locating a grave, and placing a commemorative cement tablet. P chatted with the 94-year-old man who remembered the Milhouses, and Mrs. Goodbody, the Secretary of the local Quakers, read a little speech and gave P copies of documents tying him in to the area. P gave an excellent mini-speech on peace, Quakers, Irish, Catholics, and back to peace. Very moving. Sensational little boys' band played "God Bless America" and we were off by motorcade across the countryside.

Some good crowds in the little towns. A bit scary in one as the kids surged up to his car and in between the other cars. Horribly dangerous, but no accidents. Got caught in a real downpour, but P stayed up in his open car, and he and the crowds got soaked.

Then the meetings with de Valera, Prime Minister, luncheon, etc. P car was hit by eggs on way to Dublin castle, and it splattered all over him. So P kept the car moving at good pace in spite of *very* good crowds.

Then Air Force One, and the long trip home. P spent a lot of time on his Vietnam speech for Wednesday night, had me up a number of times.

Wednesday, October 7, 1970
Speech day, nothing scheduled. Speech itself went very well. Low key and fairly fast reading, no dramatics (which bothered Frank Borman who thought it was too "meat and potatoes"). Usual aftermath of phone calls, reaction, etc. TV did pretty well on the commentary, all seems to feel it puts us on the initiative and ball is now in Hanoi's court. Doves and hawks both jumping in to acclaim the move for cease-fire. Another good stroke by P that appears to be a move to further defuse war issue, or maybe even put it on our side. General public reaction seems to be excellent.

P proposed a cease-fire in place throughout Indochina, a negotiated withdrawal of all U.S. troops, and a political settlement which reflected the existing situation in South Vietnam.

Thursday, October 15, 1970
One of those bad days operationally. Started with a flap last night about briefing folders and it carried on today. P was horrified to see a front page picture in *Post* of several thousand policemen in uniform who visited the capital about legislation against copkillers. We had known nothing about it, hence P did not receive them and we missed a great opportunity. Then we had a Crime Bill signing ceremony at Justice and had no signing pens. Then we signed a Transportation Bill at White House, and repeated the omission. By this point, P was becoming a little discouraged for good reason. Also his briefing papers were all way too long, and left out the really important points.

Lot of discussion all through the day about campaign stops.

Called tonight all cranked up because Macalester College kids gave Tricia a bad time with obscene signs. Wants Dewitt Wallace, who funds the place, to put the screws on them.

Some talk, as there is almost every day, about plans for after November, getting rid of bad guys and excess baggage. Laying groundwork for '72. Wants to divide United States into four regions with a White House political czar over each one, and move Chotiner in to run RNC under Finch.

Friday, October 16, 1970

Big excitement this afternoon as Kent State grand jury indicted 25 students and *no* National Guard. Totally refutes Scranton conclusion. P comes up with all kinds of ideas for follow-through, with candidates, etc.

Obviously P is really geared up to hit the trail, I just hope we've taken the right course because he's really committed now. If the general view that voters are really confused and seeking direction this year proves to be right, our tour may make the difference. But most of our candidates have a long way to go.

Saturday, October 17, 1970

The campaign begins. Before we set out P had me in to make sure we were not letting anyone get out of line about the Kent State grand jury report. He wants to be sure we keep that issue our way, and the report works for us ideally.

Day went very well, crowds, logistics, etc., all fine. P in good form, reworked his speech as he went along. Had some rocks thrown at Burlington, first stop, and some hecklers, so he picked up theme of need for the Silent Majority to stand up and be counted. Don't answer the rocks and obscenities in kind, use the strongest voice of all, your vote at the ballot box. *Very* effectively ties the Democrats to the student demonstrators.

A long hard day, and his voice showed it at the end, but he didn't slow down at all. Good effect with the locals, should make some real mileage. He feels he got his basic line well started. Will work on variations next week.

Monday, October 19, 1970

Off again! A full day of campaigning, from Columbus to Grand Forks to Kansas City. Big and enthusiastic crowds. Less heckling (none at Kansas City because we screened the entrants). P followed same basic lines as Saturday, building and revising as he goes. Will build hard on "one vote is worth 100 four-letter obscenities" and "it is time for the Silent Majority to stand up and be counted." These work very well. The other big crowd pleaser is about "bad youth do *not* represent this generation and will *not* be the leaders of the future." Lots of kids in the crowds and they're really fired up.

Late tonight he called Moore, Ziegler, and me in, said he had a plan to screw (Los Angeles *Times* reporter) Loory, the current number one bad guy in the press. Tomorrow on trip home put all the baddest guys on Air Force One as the pool, then at last minute P will go over and ride press plane. (Not a very good idea, but he got a kick out of thinking about it. We'll shift away from it tomorrow.) He got pretty tired by day's end, and has a sore throat, but wouldn't go to bed early.

We successfully brought off a surprise stop at Ohio State after the rally. Worked perfectly, no one knew he was coming. Just a few kids lying around the quad, then a big crowd gathered as the word spread. He had a chance to talk with them, no press except the pool cars. Good move!

This was an occasion when I forcibly overrode the Secret Service, who had absolutely refused to follow my last-minute instruction to divert the motorcade to allow an unscheduled stop at the University. Bob Taylor told me that he would not and could not permit P to make the University visit. But P had given me very specific orders that he *would* make the stop. Taylor said he would have to take his objection directly to the P, which he did, and he was overruled, much to his great, and understandable, consternation. However, both P and I felt that the spontaneity of the move would preclude any planned demonstrations or violence—and that turned out to be correct.

Tuesday, October 20, 1970

On the trail, Johnson City, Tennessee, Asheville and Ft. Wayne. Another really good day, crowds, etc., although all cities had rain. *No* hecklers even at the two outdoor stops (I think the radical leadership had told them to stop because they're playing into our hands). P was really tired by tonight and didn't really rise to the opportunity of a wildly enthusiastic crowd. Cold is bothering him.

Gag is now that P has clearly drawn the line with his attack on obscenities and advice to answer not in kind but with your vote, the good four-letter word. Now is question whether you'd rather F--- or vote.

Thursday, October 22, 1970

(Soviet Foreign Minister Andrei) Gromyko and speech preparation. P extended the Gromyko meeting to two and a half hours, and took him to EOB for private talk at the end. Got agreement on Summit, but not on announcement next week.

Concern this morning about cost of living index problem. It was the main news lead and Democrats have, of course, jumped on it to prove inflation still going. Hard to answer, although quarterly trend is down.

Still has cold and husky voice.

Friday, October 23, 1970

United Nations. Usual lousy reception, really bad for United States President to be treated that way.

He really roared through his own speech and took off like a bolt after he finished. Not a good deal for us.

Saturday, October 24, 1970

Baltimore. P had me stay at White House to compile full analysis of current status of all campaigns. He had Sato meeting, then UN dinner. I went to Camp David with Chapin and Larry and families.

Monday, October 26, 1970

(Nicolae) Ceausescu. Took up most of the morning, plus State dinner tonight.

P pretty much preoccupied with political thinking the rest of the day. Especially anxious to get good readings on all the key states, House and Senate both. Had me make calls to many of the key people, all feel they are a little ahead and will win, but narrowly. Some bad reports in the news summary and that got him started. Real problem is the economy, and as all the weeklies say today, key is whether the "social issue," crime, violence, students, etc., overrides the "pocketbook issues" or not.

P projects loss of 12–15 in House, four governors (including Florida, Ohio, Pa) and gain two or three in Senate.

Tuesday, October 27, 1970
Back on the trail to Florida. Two evening rallies Palm Beach and Miami. Went OK, nothing special.

Haig called me on plane to report Soviets turned down idea of announcing Summit this week. Say they need more time for preparation. Actually just don't want to help us in the elections. Warned against any leak, would scuttle whole plan. P not very disturbed, seemed to expect it.

Thursday, October 29, 1970
The rough one—Chicago, Rockford, Rochester, Omaha, and San Jose, with an added speech at his initiative in Chicago for the Junior League at breakfast.

San Jose turned into the real blockbuster. Very tough demonstrators shouting ''1–2–3–4–etc.'' on the way into auditorium. Tried to storm the doors after we were in, and then really hit the motorcade on the way out. We wanted some confrontation and there were no hecklers in the hall, so we stalled departure a little so they could zero in outside, and they sure did. Before getting in car, P stood up and gave the V signs, which made them mad. They threw rocks, flags, candles, etc., as we drove out, after a terrifying flying wedge of cops opened up the road. Rock hit my car, driver hit brakes, car stalled, car behind hit us, rather scary as rocks were flying, etc., but we caught up and all got out. Bus windows smashed, etc. Made a huge incident and we worked hard to crank it up, should make really major story and might be effective.

After arrival in San Clemente, P went home, then kept calling with ideas about how to push the line. Then called and asked, ''How are things at your place?'' I said fine and started to talk. He interrupted and said we're having a fire here. Laughed and said house had caught fire from his den fireplace. Told me to come on over. Place full of smoke, hoses, firemen, and water. Not too much damage. P took me in his bedroom (he was padding around the patio in pajamas, slippers, and a weird bathrobe when I arrived), said there was no problem. It was full of smoke, I could hardly breathe. He said he loved smoke and would sleep there. I talked him into the guest house. We went over there, had a beer and talked about the day. Finally to bed about 1:00.

A really weird day, especially the last parts of it. He was very tired, but in great humor. Pulled down his pajamas and showed me horrible bruise on his thigh from motorcade in Rochester.

All through the day he delighted in giving the ''V'' to the peaceniks.

Friday, October 30, 1970

Speech day. P worked most of the day on TV for tonight at Anaheim. Safire wrote a great draft of a new speech on violence. P decided not to try to use it. Used the basic speech with modifications. Was a disappointment to all of us.

Also Ronald Reagan screwed it up badly by taking way too much time, which cut even more into P. All in all it may have come out for the best, but it wasn't what we had hoped for. Reaction *was* pretty good, but most wanted a little stronger. Tomorrow will be.

Long evening of phone calls from P afterward.

Saturday, October 31, 1970

The final swing. Phoenix the big deal with the read speech about violence. Darn good. We taped it to use on TV. Good crowds all day, P *really* tired and loose after Phoenix. Rambled on and on in Las Vegas, but was back up for evening in Salt Lake City in the Tabernacle. Did a great job there, especially a short spiritual talk after the program, *very* effective.

Decided to go ahead with the national TV of Phoenix, trying to buy half-hour time, will probably have to go with 15 minutes.

Monday, November 2, 1970

TV night, and a real disaster! There was a terrible audio problem on the tape of Phoenix and we didn't know how bad it was until the first network, NBC, went on the air. We had bought all three. Complaints poured in, including to the P. After all kinds of checking we could only conclude we had laid a bomb. Also our purchase gave Muskie three quarter-hour shots *(for the Democratic reply on all three networks)*. His production was very good, but the content and delivery pretty bad. I think we really came off with a net plus, but not what it should have been. When the real facts were apparent, P was very calm and understanding, although he had been cranking pretty hard at first.

Considerable division of opinion within staff about net effect, I think most feel it was bad, some think a disaster. The hard-liners still feel it was good. But the whole mess points up the necessity of checking and rechecking on all these things. We certainly would have been better off to have done nothing, and then Muskie, too, would have done nothing.

Tuesday, November 3, 1970

(San Clemente) Election Day. P at loose ends after voting early. Sat in the office most of the day, except for a drive in afternoon. Long talks, reflecting back on election days, and how hard they are for candidates and family. He rather enjoyed being a non-candidate. Reviewed again plans for changes in Cabinet and need for posts for *some* of the candidates if they lose. Made a lot of phone calls, to candidates, finance guys etc. Reviewed final predictions. Long talk with Bill Buckley *(about his brother's Senate candidacy in New York),* and said "I don't know how you mackerel snappers look at others, but if a quiet Quaker prayer will help, you've got it. Tell Jim to go to the bar with the warm beer and relax a couple of hours after the polls close."

Then a long night of tallies. P in office, with TV, I took reports in all night. Called winners as announced. Up until about 1:00. Finally gave up, Indiana still hanging.

Wednesday, November 4, 1970

The day after. Fairly rough, since results were at best a mixed blessing. *(We had gained 2 seats in the Senate but lost 9 in the House and 11 in state legislatures.)* P obviously disappointed not to do better on Senate, although he only predicted 2 to 3. I think he had hoped for at least several more.

Driving hard to get interpretation our way, as major victory in Senate. Big loss of governors is hard to override, especially since it was a complete surprise. P very upset by stories saying it was an overall defeat. So he went before the TV cameras to set his own line. Did a *superb* job and should really help.

On flight back to DC, Pat Nixon blasted me and P about West Wing interference in social operations. Feels we override Lucy and slow down decisions, etc. Wants all control in East

Wing, so we'll try that. Patterns are well enough set now that it might work.

After we got home, he was on the phone again, as a result of the DC papers. Wants a concerted attack to get our point across. Obvious we're up against a conspiracy in the press. Feels we need an all-out plan for next couple of days, to set the line.

Thursday, November 5, 1970

And the reaction goes on. P did great job at end of Cabinet meeting putting whole thing in perspective and shooting down all of the negative press theses. Then ground away all day on other ways to combat it.

Fortunately had the Mountbatten dinner to keep him occupied tonight.

Friday, November 6, 1970

And more reaction. NSC filled most of the morning. He semicanceled Key Biscayne plan for this afternoon, holed up in EOB, calling for more statistics, called a junior staff meeting to give them the pitch, decided at the last minute to go to Key Biscayne after all.

Brooded over and over about political meeting and decided to have it tomorrow, hauling everyone down to Florida for the day. Just can't get himself away from the subject. Afraid to let down for fear he'll have left some base uncovered, and just can't stop thinking or talking about it. If tomorrow's meeting doesn't wrap it up I think I'll confront him directly.

Saturday, November 7, 1970

Key Biscayne. The big meeting. Mitchell, Finch, E, Rumsfeld, Harlow and Colson. Ran from 11:00–5:00 with no break. Sandwiches brought in, plus gallons of coffee. Accomplished a lot as P really got into gear on future planning.

Decided major personnel changes. *Cabinet:* Romney out. Rumsfeld to replace him. Hickel out. Whitaker as Under Secretary.

Hickel out. Russell to SBA. (Mitchell tell him. Don't use audit as a club to keep him quiet unless necessary, because may backfire.)

Kennedy hopefully out. Then Mitchell explore Treasury with Bob Anderson. Also have to get Walker out. (P called later, Flanigan as Under Secretary.)

Morton out of RNC, to Interior. Harlow to RNC. Sandoval out of SBA. MacGregor for White House Congressional liaison. (After considering Bush, better for him to take Under Secretary of Commerce.) Make Siciliano a judge in California. Move Chotiner to RNC as organizer. Keep Dent in White House to handle South.

Issues: Go for value-added tax and huge revenue-sharing (lump all categorical programs and grants and give to locals with no strings, $30 billion).

Lot of discussion of economy, and need especially to knock the mythology. All agreed this, in some form, must be the core of the State of the Union. Hit crisis of U.S. fiscal policy. Agreed we don't work with Congress, we go against them.

Figure Democrats' strategy will be series of major programs designed so we can't approve them.

P said will hold off Summit until serves our purpose. Will go for increases in military budget and military assistance and squeeze the Great Society programs.

Discussed need for new roles for VP, positive and constructive. Environment, health, Congressional relations, labor union relations, South, take on all presidential candidates.

We take *very* conservative civil rights line.

Good meeting, covered lot of ground and for once got something done.

Sunday, November 8, 1970

Key Biscayne. P at Walker's, went right after meeting yesterday in afternoon and completely revised the campaign analysis letter we're sending out. All 40,000 had already been mailed but we caught them at the Post Office and will revise tomorrow.

Monday, November 9, 1970

Key Biscayne. Obviously still completely absorbed with politics. Said he'd been working on organization of states for '72. Wanted to review purge list, talked about people assignments, etc.

Called to say he'd decided to go home tomorrow, move Mexican luncheon to DC. (Pat Nixon doesn't want it here.) Finally talked him out of it with support from Rogers. But that made him mad and he now says he'll go home Thursday, right after luncheon.

Tuesday, November 10, 1970

De Gaulle died last night, and P immediately decided to go to memorial service in Paris, thus ending the question of Key Biscayne stay. First instructions were no Secret Service sitting with him at service and he goes down aisle alone.

A beautiful day, and he made me come over for about four hours and sit inside going over all sorts of details, especially election results and analysis, a subject he can't escape from. Plus a *lot* of odds and ends, he's really been storing up: Mitchell to Key Biscayne for Christmas; fire Ambassador McBride (Mexico); get Moynihan UN deal settled with Rogers on trip; shift Mexican luncheon; worry about costume for Paris service; cleaning house in Administration, purge list, appoint loyalists; charge up White House staff, get some "holler guys," dump all incompetents but keep the enthusiasts; deal with Nelson Rockefeller, appoint him Secretary of State late next year (Rogers should resign after Summit), thus get Malcolm Wilson as Governor in New York, a complete loyalist; have to start on health issue, called Richardson, set up meeting tomorrow before departure; plans for social—Church, Evenings, etc., use wholly for our political purposes; discussed convention, in a state we need to win, late as possible, make it good TV; man to man operation on Democratic candidates; need to develop key publishers and editors for '72 endorsements; press conference in next couple of weeks; move now on Nixon organization in South; plus plans for all key states.

Then back at it again on the plane to DC, for two more hours (and no dinner). Basically more of the same. Turned out he had an incredible stack of little white note sheets with amazing array of trivia. Then on and on about analysis of campaign, just can't get off the subject.

Called at home, very late, to discuss French restaurants, hotels, etc., then Shriver, then on to a new analysis of election for about a half hour. Horrible!

All of this obsessive boring in on details and trivia, some mixed with reasonably important points and most focused on the political aspects of the just past Congressional elections and the forthcoming Presidential election (in two years), was a combination of clearing stacks of little stored notes that he wanted to get off of his desk, and reviewing lots of ideas that he wanted to get off of his mind. This happened every once in a while, when the pipeline of these things got so clogged up that it had to be cleared. It was a good process, because it then enabled him to drop these matters and turn to the issues at hand. But it meant an enormous amount of work for me and my staff to be sure all matters were carried out.

Wednesday, November 11, 1970

To Paris. First breakfast with Mitchell, locked him up to run '72 campaign and covered lot of other political ground.

Had me up for couple of hours on plane, almost entirely political analysis of '70 and planning for '72. Very upset to find HEW starting to push integration suits in North and ordered it stopped immediately.

After arrival at Embassy residence, had me come over from hotel, back onto another two-hour political review from 1:00 AM to 3:00 AM. Decided Bush would be better for Republican National Chairman than Harlow, more enthusiasm and better image, had me call Mitchell, who totally disagreed, so we dropped that one.

On learning he had to stay for reception tomorrow afternoon, P decided to go out to good restaurant for lunch. K talked him out of it, so we'll have luncheon at Residence. P then sulked about never gets to do anything fun that he wants to do, always has to do what's right.

Thursday, November 12, 1970

In Paris. De Gaulle service, Bruce meeting, appointment with Pompidou. Embassy luncheon, visit to Embassy personnel, Pompidou reception, chats with all the big leaders. On plane for return he had me up for several hours of political rehash (after he took a 4-hour nap).

Friday, November 13, 1970

Back in D.C. Echeverria meeting. Not much today on political. Maybe it's finally fading. P in late.

Off to Camp David, then called me in evening, but nothing

important. Had report from Mitchell about Romney, George won't leave quickly, will have to be fired. So we have to set him up on the integrated housing issue and fire him on that basis to be sure we get the credit.

Monday, November 16, 1970
Welcome to the new senators.

P pretty much getting back into gear. Hardly any talk today of campaign or results. One flap about Colson and the ads, and a *Time* story about P supposedly saying Ted Kennedy would be 1972 opponent. Both will blow over. Set up a busy week, and also next. P originally decided to have a press conference next week, but I talked him out of it, in favor of waiting until after Thanksgiving.

P impressed by a long Moynihan memo, gist of which is the lack of real intellectuals in the Administration. P agrees, and wants E et al. to recruit in this direction. As of now have no real ferment of new ideas and no real tough intellectual challenge of present ideas or programs. Main problem is most intellectuals are not on our side.

Wednesday, November 18, 1970
Things piled up and eliminated the usual clear Wednesday afternoon. Main problem was bipartisan Leaders Meeting, scheduled for first thing in morning, changed for Democrats because of caucus, shifted all over, finally set for 3:30.

P had long secret meeting with Laird, Rogers, Moorer, and K about a new secret plan, to try to rescue 90 POW's, we'll try it Saturday, I talked with Rogers first about changes in State and Moynihan to UN. He's not very responsive, sort of fuzzes it up.

P still had fair amount of free time, is now focusing more on business. Had E in and reported to us on his breakfast with Rockefeller. Report on New York politics, especially *(New York Mayor John)* Lindsay. Rockefeller can't figure out where he'll go, is lost in New York City. Then got on to economic policy and told E he was seriously considering complete change in advisors, since they failed in the one prime objective he set, to keep unemployment under 5 percent in October. Doesn't want to take *any* chance on screwing up 1972. Problem is not just advice, it's that they don't get in and fight.

Some talk again about need to build up staff morale. He

keeps trying to think of devices, i.e., circulating good columns. Not really a problem, but he thinks it is.

Thursday, November 19, 1970

A loaded one from breakfast with Mansfield to dinner with Ash Council. NSC about NATO, apparently very good meeting, P took strong stand about maintaining support. It obviously got to him because his toast at dinner turned into a 20-minute speech about need for maintaining #1 position in world strength.

Pleased with "fat cat" dinner last night. They pledged $7 million, from Stone, Mulcahy, and Scaife for '71, '72, and '73 deficit if any. Had long talk with *(lawyer Herb)* Kalmbach after and has him lined up for 50 percent of his time, handling super fat cats and special assignments.

Apparently had a good talk with *(economist)* Milton Friedman, and said after it was nice to have someone say we're doing things right. Friedman urges we stay on present economic course. Says we're in good shape if we stay with it. P still concerned about '72. Can't afford to risk a downtrend, no matter how much inflation.

Friday, November 20, 1970

The POW maneuver for Saturday was moved up to today, and all were on pins and needles awaiting outcome. Too bad, it didn't work. Turned out no prisoners were there. Still went ahead with big bombing, etc. *(extensive air strike to protect U.S. reconnaissance planes operating over North Vietnam).*

P told K he'd worked out new plan for Vietnam at 2:00 this morning. Wants to blast talks, give last chance, then pull out. Mine Haiphong (or blockade), take offensive, and announce stepped-up withdrawals at same time. Put real heat on North Vietnam.

P was really impressed with John Connally at Ash dinner last night. Wants to get hooks into him. Is convinced he can be brought over for '72.

On POW move, told K in the morning "Don't do any planning for success, it's bad luck."

P very impressed with Ash recommendation about reducing size of Executive Office. Intrigued with reducing 4000 personnel to 1500. Off to Camp David for the night.

Monday, November 23, 1970

Results of P's weekend became evident, several tapes full of miscellaneous memos, and five full tapes of a long (25 pages, single-spaced) memo to me. I had produced 6 tapes myself. So the typists were busy today. All of this primarily to analyze, summarize, and act upon the staff memos about election results and plans for future.

Lot of reaction evident from P, i.e., he canceled Florida for Thanksgiving and California for Christmas because some criticized excess travel.

Lot of reaction to North Vietnam bombing, will leave all explanations to Defense. Launched a push (PR) about the effort to spring POW's. Decided it was good counter-story to the bombings even though it failed. P had the Colonel *("Bo" Gritz)* who led the raid brought in and was *really* impressed. Went on for a half hour after about how great these guys were, told Ziegler to try to get someone in press to recognize it. Told Ziegler to treat any skeptics with utter contempt. He was as cranked up as I've ever seen him.

Tuesday, November 24, 1970

Big push this morning was to keep the push going about the POW raid. P still very much impressed by the Colonel who led the raid, gets quite emotional about their bravery, etc. Wants to really rally the people on this one. Is convinced the liberals are again on the wrong side, as in Cambodia, and wants to push his advantage.

P furious about reports from State backing off of support of North Vietnam bombing. I called Irwin *(Rogers in Canada)* to order investigation and retraction. He moved fast and they did retract.

P gave Ziegler full background of POW raid, to be sure his story is clear that it was his idea and initiative. All started by his instructions to use some imagination about POW's.

Wednesday, November 25, 1970

Big day, topped by dismissal of Hickel. Had a session with Moynihan, he wrote P yesterday to say he couldn't take UN after all. Gave whole range of reasons. So he's going back to Harvard. I told him P understood, but would want critiques and suggestions from him as he has done all along.

P decided to have award ceremony for the POW raiders

today. Put it together fast and I guess it went well. He was pleased, and felt it very good idea to honor them now. Good Congressional attendance.

P got into discussion of press this morning with K and me. Apparently reflecting on his words to Keogh yesterday. Made whole thesis that they all suffer from excess intellectual pride, totally self-centered, hence can't admit they're wrong and can't tolerate being proven so. Thus their hatred for Nixon who's proved them wrong so often. Also none has integrity, no religious quality, because of their intellectual arrogance.

P wants me to launch plan for "lib" mailings supporting Muskie to all Democratic leaders and editors in South.

An example of the "dirty tricks" concept—in this case, mailings supporting Muskie that would appear to be from a strong liberal source and thus offensive to the conservative South.

Back on press, said the intellectuals of the left are actually a new group of fascists. And Keogh (who was a former editor of Time) told him most young journalists are activists, feel they have a mission, not to report but to influence.

Tuesday, December 1, 1970

Unfortunately, the P had a large gap in his schedule, and kept me in for about four hours today. I did get all the backlog of schedule and information items cleared up. As always, got back on political analysis. He's quite concerned regarding youth, especially because of a new Harris poll. Mused over reasons and cures for the problem. Wants our own poll and a program to handle it. He saw (Massachusetts Senator Ed) Brooke and offered him the UN post, but Ed wants to stay in the Senate.

Not pleased with the Leadership Meeting, mainly because of the lack of any enthusiasm. He's obviously still very much absorbed in political and PR analysis and not really back on track about basic governmental matters. Will probably take major crisis to revive the focus, problem is that can't come in domestic area and that's where he should be getting involved. May just come in time. Basic problem is to get him interested and talking to other people on substantive matters.

This is the point at which I stopped recording these diaries in handwritten form and started to dictate them each evening at home onto tape cassettes. The reader will undoubtedly notice a substantial difference in form and a major increase in content when I started the easier process of speaking rather than writing the diaries.

Thursday, December 3, 1970

There was a flap this morning at an awards ceremony at the White House when a girl who got a bravery award made some crack to the P about how she wouldn't think he was sincere about this until he ended the war in Vietnam. This of course drove him right up the wall. He called both Hoover and Kleindienst and jumped on them, since these awards were a Justice Department project.

He got back going on the PR thing again, making the point that the story we need to get across is what kind of a man is he, rather than the pitch on the machinery. He concludes we now have the image of a PR-oriented Administration, but we've totally failed in our real PR. Also, we've missed in the foreign policy area where we had three major accomplishments: Cambodia, the Middle East, and the Vietnam speech, but we don't get across the courage, the independence, the boldness, standing alone, overruling advisors, that go into this.

After K went out, he got into a discussion of Rogers, and concluded that he may have to bite the bullet here. Wants me to put a fully documented case together and sit down with Rogers and make it clear that State has broken its pick at the White House, and point out to him step by step why. I think he's basically concluded that he's not going to be able to keep Rogers on for much longer, and he's starting to build the case for removal.

Friday, December 4, 1970

P worked most of the day on his speech for tonight and then came on up to New York at about 7:00.

Speech went very well. On the plane on the way home, the P had me up for the whole trip because he didn't want to talk with the Cabinet officers. We got into the Connally thing. It turns out that he had meeting with Connally this morning for about an hour, the last 15 minutes of which he used to make a pitch to Connally to take the Secretary of Treasury. He now wants me to call Connally and give him a further push on it. That the P wanted him to know that he feels urgently that Connally is desperately needed in this position now, and for another more important position in the future. Really he wants you here as a counselor, advisor, and friend. He feels you're the only man in the Democratic Party that could be President, and that we have to have someone in the Cabinet who is capable of being President. The P doesn't have a man in the whole shop that he respects in this way, and he's very concerned about the whole question of determining whether the United States or Russia is going to be number one. He's not interested in the idea of political purposes, either in Texas or to get a Democrat in the Cabinet. That occupied most of the trip home.

Saturday, December 5, 1970
P came in late. Spent the morning kind of cleaning up loose ends before he left for Camp David at 2:00.

He had Colson bring in the photos and file on Teddy Kennedy's activities in Paris. P seemed to be pleased with the evidence we have on this and wants Colson to follow up on getting it out.

> Colson had a private detective follow Kennedy in Paris and take photos of him with various women. Colson then leaked the photos to members of Congress and to the press. In Paris, on the eve of de Gaulle's funeral, Kennedy was seen dancing until dawn with the daughter of the former King of Italy.

I finally got Connally on the phone at about 11:00 tonight, and interestingly enough, he seems to be favorably inclined towards taking the job. He was obviously pleased that I had called, and that I felt as strongly as I did about his taking it. He made the point that he wasn't just interested in just being Secretary of Treasury or any other department, but he was very much impressed with what the P said about wanting his help on a broad basis and wanting to put him on the NSC. He has the problem of personal finances, and will have to make extensive adjustments. One of his concerns was the flak we'd get from within the Republican Party and the concern that they might waylay him at every corner. He's also concerned about the timing and whether he can divest and organize his financial things in time to meet the P's deadline of January 20. He had talked with his children tonight and with his wife, and found no negative block there. He's going to meet with his partner tomorrow.

Monday, December 7, 1970

A big day with a lot of action. Started with the P having breakfast with John Connally, as a result of which he has succeeded in getting him to take the post as Secretary of Treasury. He told me right after he came into the office, then wanted to be sure that no one else knew. I reminded him that he had discussed the possibility with E, and he said to cover John on not telling anyone. Connally had made the point to the P of the overriding importance of getting something for Bush right away, because we couldn't do anything on the Connally announcement until Bush was set. P then wanted me to talk to Rogers, and try to work Bush out for the UN, get that assignment settled right now.

The next development was a note from Bryce, saying that he wouldn't be able or willing to take the National Chairmanship, and he submitted his letter of resignation effective Wednesday. On the basis of this, the P told E and me to move on Rumsfeld, and try to convince him to take the job. We did so, and got an absolute stonewall flat "no" answer.

Considerable discussion of candidates for RNC, and it boiled down to Finch, Bush, Kleindienst, Dole, and MacGregor. Finch is ruled out because of the South. Kleindienst because he wouldn't take it and Mitchell doesn't want him to anyway. Dole because he's an incumbent senator. So we're down to Bush and MacGregor. The decision was for me to talk to MacGregor, see if I could get him to take it. We would then move Bush into the MacGregor post of Congressional liaison.

The Connally appointment and the repercussions of it will be one of the biggest things we've done and should be extremely effective in startling the media and the establishment. It will create some monumental problems with John Tower and some of the other Republicans. And we're going to have a tough time selling some of them. The RNC is another tough problem, and I think there's real doubt that MacGregor will take it, but we'll give it a try.

Tuesday, December 8, 1970

P had a relatively light day. He added a breakfast with Bill Rogers sometime late last night, which resulted in his getting in a little late. The only schedule item this morning was an hour meeting with King Hussein. We added a few quick items after that. He then has a small working dinner with Hussein tonight, and that's it.

(P) asked Henry for an answer for his press conference on a question about the Tet truce which is being pushed by Senator Jackson and backed by Rogers, much to Henry's chagrin. Henry has indicated that any such thing would be disastrous to us, in that it would permit the enemy to build up during the truce, which they're already doing, to get ready for a major drive on either Laos or Cambodia. The only way we could possibly set up a truce would be to include the stipulation that they would have to stop infiltration, and they would of course be unwilling to do this. I reached Connally this morning, having missed him last night, and passed on the P's message together with my own pleasure.

The biggest problem is to try to get this done without getting any leaks ahead of time, and obviously the thing to do is to move as fast as we can. The only problem is that we've got to get Bush settled before we can move on Connally, and that gets back to the whole parley on the National chairmanship, because we have to see what MacGregor will do.

Wednesday, December 9, 1970

Another day almost totally involved, on my part at least, with personnel maneuvers. P had no schedule except for a presentation ceremony at noon.

As we discussed things in the morning, P decided that he definitely wanted to bring Bush into the White House on a general basis. I then called Bush in, and gave him the pitch on taking a White House job. He was clearly disappointed because he had been hoping for the UN spot. Bush made such a good pitch to the P about what he'd like to do at the UN in the way of really being an advocate for the P, not only at the UN, but in the overall New York community. The P decided this was in fact a better use of Bush than having him at the

White House, and we'll go ahead and announce Bush on Friday, which will get him locked up before the Connally announcement, which is still planned for Monday. This really does work out better, because it gives Bush a more prestigious appointment and a seat in the Cabinet, which will help when the Connally blow strikes.

All of this left us with a problem as far as the National Committee's concerned, and after considerable agonizing, the decision there was to go with Dole, even though he is an incumbent senator. We'll have to find a really top-level executive director to work under him. On this basis, Harlow and I had Dole in, and raised the problems with him so that he could start thinking about solutions. We did not tell him he was the P's choice, but did say that he was very favorably regarded. It will now be up to him to get some groundswell started for himself. P had a nice chat with Harlow to say goodbye, this is Bryce's last day. Told him how we would be counting on him for help in the future, on a general basis, and wanted him to sit in the Leaders Meetings, and that we would be using him for a lot of other things. All this made Bryce very happy. In discussing ways to screw NBC, the P, thinking Nancy Dickerson is on CBS, asked me to explore the possibility of his doing a half-hour or hour nighttime special with her. It would be just a warm conversation about his personal views of the Presidency after two years in office. It would make a darn good show, the problem is apparently Nancy Dickerson's with NBC, so it wouldn't really screw them after all.

In order to get the human side of things out, he's come up with the idea of having Dick Moore, or sometimes Safire, attend all dinners and sit in on all meetings, looking for anecdotal material and general human interest stories.

P was pretty upset about the fact that 25 of the White House press corps met yesterday to try to figure how they could trap him at the press conference tomorrow night.

K was back in today, all disturbed about the Israeli situation. He thinks that the same kind of problem is building up now as he faced all last summer, when the P wouldn't consult with him on developments, as we moved closer and closer to the brink of war. His most recent evidence is the fact that the P doesn't want him to sit in the meeting with Moshe Dayan, and was going to have Rogers sit in. It's now been set up that only

Laird will be there, which somewhat pacifies K, but he's still concerned. He told me that if the situation developed into the same thing as last summer, he would definitely have to leave, that he couldn't go through that sort of operation again. This has been a frequently repeated threat, but I have a feeling he's more serious on this one than he has been on some of the others.

Thursday, December 10, 1970

Press conference day. P stayed locked up at the EOB all day, and I didn't see him for the entire day, something of a record. He didn't leave the EOB until just time to go over to the Residence and change clothes and go down for the press conference at 7:00. Went back up right after the press conference and spent the evening with the family. The press conference itself was, in most people's minds, a great success. P was particularly pleased with his answers in several areas, probably the most important one being his explanation of the need for foreign aid to Cambodia, where he explained how this was the most valuable investment we make because of its saving of American lives. He was extremely effective on this. The high point probably on most people's minds was the fact that he admitted he was wrong on the Manson comments and a couple of his others where he's prejudged trials that are in progress. He gave a brief 13-second answer, but in effect said that he was wrong in his comments on these things and he was sorry about it. Overall, was well worthwhile. It's just too bad it wasn't on later so it could reach more people.

The whole personnel process goes on and on as we try to put the puzzle together. Dole still leads in contention for the National Committee, but there are many with very deep reservations.

Friday, December 11, 1970

During the day we had several inputs from Senator Scott about his total disapproval of Dole for RNC, and he is mobilizing senators to oppose the Dole possibility.

As a result of the press conference and the press's efforts to mobilize to take on the P preceding the press conference, we have launched an all-out antipress offensive through the attack group. The press corps made a real mistake in getting together in their secret session to try to figure ways to make the press conferences tougher.

Saturday, December 12, 1970

P was in early and apparently had been up late last night dictating also, since he had five tapes for me to get started on when I came in the morning.

I used a good part of the day to cover some general meetings, one with Chapin and Larry on Connally arrangements, and another long session with Henry, on the question of whether he should stay on, since he's now got to make a decision in the next couple of days as to whether he stays or not. I told him of course he should stay, that there's no dissatisfaction, etc., but that he should talk with the P, and make his offer to go back to Harvard, etc., so they have a chance to review the thing and settle it once and for all.

Henry's main concern is that he is going to get back into the situation similar to last summer on the Middle East, where he doesn't have the P's confidence and is not involved in what's going on. I pointed out that this is bound to be a problem from time to time but that overall he is indispensable to the P, and both he and the P know it, and he's got to stay here.

Monday, December 14, 1970

John Connally day. We got cranking early and hard this morning. P had breakfast with the Connallys at 8:30 while we had our regular staff meeting, at which I could say nothing. Very awkward since Finch and Rumsfeld did not know about the coming appointment. P had his meeting with John Tower, which had been scheduled for 10:15. While he was doing that I met with Rumsfeld and Finch, gave them the word. Finch received it with considerable pleasure. Rumsfeld was totally noncommittal and looked as if he was deeply distressed.

On my way down to meet with Finch and Rumsfeld I had been handed the handwritten letter of resignation from Kennedy and also a brief handwritten note to the P which inadvertently I read and discovered that Kennedy was making a pitch to be named Ambassador at Large. I told him (P) very briefly what Kennedy said in his note, he would like to be an Ambassador at Large. P asked very quickly if Rogers knew about this and I reminded him that Rogers had suggested it to him, but it had not been discussed further. The P said fine and shot through into the Cabinet room for the Cabinet meeting.

He built up somewhat the announcement by leading gradually into what Kennedy was going to do as a follow-up and went through the UN post and other things and ruled them out and then announced that he would be taking a post as Ambassador at Large. Through this buildup, both Kennedy and I were panic-stricken because we thought the P had misunderstood and was building him up for the UN job, which he very definitely did not want. It turned out fine in the long run, however. Bill Rogers rose to the occasion beautifully and responded as if he had known all along that this is what we were going to do. The P then made his pitch on Connally and told them about that appointment.

The Congressional leaders were also present at the meeting and Tower was included. They were all pretty much stunned at the announcement.

Following the Cabinet meeting, Connally, Mrs. Connally, and Mrs. Nixon were brought into the Oval Office. Then Kennedy and Rogers were brought in from the Cabinet Room. We finalized the presentation plan. Then the group went from there directly to the Press Room, where the P made his announcement first of Kennedy's new post, then of the Connally appointment. Press corps was absolutely flabbergasted. They were all craning to see who was coming in behind the P and were totally bewildered by the parade of the P, Kennedy, Rogers, the Connallys, and Mrs. Nixon. As they figured it out, they appeared to be completely astonished. It was fun to watch because the surprise was total. For the first time we really did keep an announcement confidential until the zero hour.

Dole called me later giving me his report *(on the RNC situation)*. He says he's now got 28 senators signed up, so support is building up. The P got trapped by Mrs. Nixon into standing in the receiving line at the Congressional open house today, shaking hands with everybody although his intention was just to come in and sort of stroll through and let it go at that. Also, Mrs. Nixon called me at home tonight, very upset about her discovery that they were planning to light the Commerce, the FTC, Archives, and Justice buildings. She feels that this should not be done, that only the monuments and the White House should be lighted, and that the White House is, in fact, a monument. That it downgrades it by having the buildings done. And also that it causes a political problem because of the big effort to get people to hold down on their consumption of electricity. I don't know whether we can do anything about it at this point.

Tuesday, December 15, 1970

The P cut off the GOP Leadership Breakfast with the wives fairly promptly. We got into some more discussion of the Dole candidacy. I gave him Dole's report from last night. He thinks now we should stir up the House and try to get over half the GOP members there lined up so we can get that pretty well set, too. We had a long discussion on the subject in the staff meeting this morning. The general feeling is very strongly against Dole on the grounds that he is divisive rather than inclusive and that his appointment would be a signal that we were taking the wrong direction politically. We all tried to put the heat on Rumsfeld, but he resists very strongly. I don't think there's any chance of getting him to shift.

K came in and the discussion covered some of the general thinking about Vietnam and the P's big peace plan for next year, which K later told me he does not favor. He thinks that any pullout next year would be a serious mistake because the adverse reaction to it could set in well before the '72 elections. He favors, instead, a continued winding down and then a pullout right at the fall of '72 so that if any bad results follow they will be too late to affect the election. It seems to make sense. Overall, he seems to be in a good mood. Generally relaxed and moving with things as they come. But he hasn't really gotten to grips on the budget and the State of the Union yet. He's got the guys working, but he hasn't started to dig in. He did get underway tonight on his Christmas-tree-lighting speech and mentioned on the phone that he thought he probably would not read it but would instead do an extemporaneous deal.

Thursday, December 17, 1970

This was *(British Prime Minister)* Edward Heath day, with the usual arrival ceremonies and private meeting all morning and State dinner tonight. The afternoon was pretty much occupied with a visit to the Department of Agriculture operation in Beltsville, Maryland, and the session with Scranton.

The big flap of the day was the Army domestic intelligence

activity, which has been blown up by the TV and the press as a result of a letter of some former Army sergeant sent to Senator Ervin. The whole episode poses a major problem for us in the area of repression, which our enemies are trying to build up in that this implies we're using the Army to spy on political people. Most of the charges are not basically true and we can prove this in at least some of the cases. Also, whatever activity had been going on was stopped last June, and the files destroyed. Our key thing is to get the White House out of this, so we covered it thoroughly with Laird and instructed him to handle the entire thing in Defense. We've told Ziegler to stay off of it here.

A bit of a blow today on the new Gallup poll, which showed the P at an all-time low of 52.

Friday, December 18, 1970

Another Heath day, as the P took him to Camp David for meetings in the morning and lunch at Aspen.

He got going again in the morning on the Army spy deal. He wants to launch an all-out assault to make a bigger story out of our denial than the original story. We've got to attack the attackers on this one.

In the afternoon he had Henry in and just sort of sat and chatted, using up the idle time. He got into a discussion of the Poland uprising and the possibility that this could cause a major problem for the Soviets, especially if it keeps on going. If it stops at the point it's already reached it won't make very much difference. They also got into our operating plan in Laos where they're going to move the South Vietnamese in for a major attack operation, this time without US support, so it will be substantially different than Cambodia.

On the PR side, the P got going on the need for a two-year tabulation of all the things he's done, the people he's seen, meetings he's held, countries he's visited, states he's visited and, particularly, his meetings with minority groups, Cabinet officials, congressmen and senators, etc. He wants to do a complete log, trying to put all these statistics together primarily, of course, to shoot down once more the isolation theory and the idea that he doesn't work hard.

Also got into the Dole question on National Chairman. Dole keeps calling him to get guidance, since he's pushed the thing about as far as he can. The P's view on that still is that we ought go with Dole, but he wants to let the opposition work itself out first to be sure that we're fully covered, also to force Dole to build his own support.

Tonight was the Christmas Party for Old Friends, an "Evening at the White House" with David Frost, which turned out to be something of a frost. It was saved by the P's discovery this morning that a group of Korean children were here on a singing tour and he brought them into the party.

Saturday, December 19, 1970
The P kept himself busy this morning, which helped to give a little time to get some work done. He went out to the hospital to see Senator Russell, who probably will die in the next few days, so this was what the P considers to be his last visit with him. He was very much impressed again with how powerful a man he is and how much more impressive he is than our Northern senators. He mused quite a bit when he got back about the fact that patriotism is so much higher in the South.

During our chat he had Colson in for a while, who reported on the Teddy Kennedy question. He's getting the pictures distributed and maintaining the effort on that, also Chuck's following up on the knockdown of the press, during their poor performance at the press conference.

Henry came in for part of the time that Chuck was there to get the P's signature on a letter to Frank Church regarding the foreign aid supplement. The P blew up when he discovered that the purpose of the letter really was to let Church get off the hook on his anti-Cambodia position. The P told Henry to change the letter substantially to correct the language so as to make it absolutely clear that the P was not changing his position but that Church was changing his.

We had a long meeting with the VP, E, and Finch this morning regarding his *(VP's)* takeover of the responsibility for relations with governors, mayors and county executives. It went pretty well. VP was in a good mood, wearing a T-shirt and a sort of sweat jacket. He was obviously very anxious to take on this responsibility on a full-scale basis and seems to understand the level of activity it will require of him and wants to do it. It is astonishing how bad he is on judging staff, however.

I had a long session with our new TV guy, Mark Goode, or at least our candidate for the job, and on and off with the senior guy we now have, Bill Carruthers. I think we're putting together a good unit here. If we can now get the PR communications worked out, we'll have solved a couple of our major hangups and be able to move ahead more constructively.

Monday, December 21, 1970
With the morning clear, the P had me in for a couple of hours to go over a whole range of odds and ends.

Henry was in for a while and the P discussed a possible trip for next year. He's thinking about going to Vietnam in April or whenever we decide to make the basic end of the war announcement. His idea would be to tour around the country, build up Thieu, and so forth, and then make the announcement right afterwards. Henry argues against a commitment that early to withdraw all combat troops because he feels that if we pull them out by the end of '71, trouble can start mounting in '72 that we won't be able to deal with and which we'll have to answer for at the elections. He prefers, instead, a commitment to have them all out by the end of '72 so that we won't have to deliver finally until after the elections and therefore can keep our flanks protected. This would certainly seem to make more sense, and the P seemed to agree in general, but wants Henry to work up plans on it. He still feels he's got to make a major move in early '71 and he could make the commitment at that time that there would be no further use of draftees in Vietnam and also make the long-range troop-withdrawal commitment. Henry's argument is that this precludes, then, the necessity for periodic announcements or explanations and covers the whole thing in one swoop, as did our 150,000 announcement last year.

The P came up with an interesting idea for the Christmas program next year. Instead of having David Frost do the readings, he'll do them himself. He wants to include letters he's received and some Dickens-type Christmas readings. He's also thinking about using educational television from time to time to take an hour and answer his mail on TV, having some of the incoming letters read and then discussing them in the form of an answer to the writer.

The P is chafing at the overabundance of Christmas activity and is already outlining his regulations for next year wherein he wants much less involvement of himself in the Christmas-season stuff. Overall, though, spirits are pretty good considering the fact that he's had no time off at all, really, for weeks. Somehow we've got to convince him that he ought to get out of here once in a while, but so far we haven't succeeded. I talked to both Bebe and Billy Graham, and they said they'd work on him, but there's been no visible result to date.

We had the Cabinet/Sub Cabinet year-end briefing and reception today. Moynihan gave his valedictory address and it was superb. He came through with exactly what we wanted in terms of a charge to the troops to get out and work for our policies.

Tuesday, December 22, 1970
Another pretty busy day with a few breaks in between for discussion, especially late this afternoon.

Teddy Kennedy called this morning saying he had to talk to the P, that he had something urgent regarding prisoners of war. The P refused to talk to him, told K to return the call. Teddy refused to talk to K. Upshot was that Teddy got from the North Vietnamese a list of prisoners' names, which he made a big play with on the Senate floor. It turned out later they were the same names we already had and the whole thing was something of a cruel hoax on everyone concerned.

Henry came up with the need to meet with the P today with Al Haig and then tomorrow with Laird and Moorer because he has to use the P to force Laird and the military to go ahead with the P's plans, which they won't carry out without direct orders.

> The plans in question involved cutting the Ho Chi Minh trail in half by attacking enemy forces in Laos. Only South Vietnamese (ARVN) troops would be used, but the U.S. would supply air cover and artillery support.

He (P) had a long talk with Rogers on the phone regarding the line for his press conference tomorrow, told him to blast Teddy on the POW hoax, take a hard line on the surveillance we're conducting on Cuba, and play down Mansfield's proposal for POW exchange versus cease-fire. He also had K call Dole and have him take Teddy on mercilessly on this, which Dole will do tonight and tomorrow morning.

Wednesday, December 23, 1970

A Colson story was a major item today, as the P was determined we should try to find the source of the leak. I had a number of people spending considerable effort to try to do so. We finally tracked it down to somebody on the conservative side on the Hill who was genuinely concerned that Colson was going to be appointed National Chairman and, in order to protect Dole's franchise, was trying to destroy Colson.

John Connally called at home this evening, disturbed because he had gotten word somehow that several days after his announcement somebody in Washington ordered all of his tax returns sent up to Washington from Texas. He's very upset that someone is playing games here and wants to be sure we get on top of it, so I'll check on that. It's interesting that he would know this had been done, which shows that he's got his sources in the local IRS office. Also interesting that he reacted as strongly and quickly as he did.

Thursday, December 24, 1970

The P came up with an interesting conclusion as he was thinking through the whole youth problem. He decided there is a reverse reaction of the teenagers on their parents which results in making the parents doubt their own values. In the past, parents stood firm, the kids were always screwed up. Now the kids are still screwed up, but instead of standing firm, the parents follow their lead. He thinks this is a problem within our own staff because many of them have kids with serious problems. It is very hard for our guys to keep their balance because they're beat on by their kids, by the press, by the people they meet socially, etc. He's concluded, therefore, that the major effect of the youth revolution is its effect on parents and their guilt complexes.

He got back on the need to get out something good every day to build the staff up, to give them a lift and to counteract the constant hammering they get from press and Congress, etc. The P's point is we need poetry, excitement, and spiritual quality. We've got to find a way to get it. He then bet that all the year-end interviews would come out very pragmatic, low-key, and businesslike, analyzing where we've failed or succeeded rather than getting into the real value of the thing. He commented, while Ziegler was in the room, that Churchill's books regarding war are like Tolstoy's novels regarding war: they're great because they don't concern themselves with war, but rather with people. You end up knowing the men, the personalities, and the great forces that went behind the great wars rather than just the technical details of the battle.

The P visited the Home for the Incurables today, at our suggestion, to wish them a Merry Christmas. He refused to take any press or even let them know he was there until after he had gotten back, which drove Ziegler up the wall, but made the visit work out extremely well. I watched him for a while as he went through and he did a superb job of dealing with the kids or older people as he would hold on to an arm to keep it from waving around and then shake the hand. He talked with them in a normal conversational way, even though they couldn't talk back. When he came out, he made the comment as he got in the car, "Boy, we think we've got troubles." It's just amazing to watch him in this kind of situation because he handled it so well.

We got back to the office, sat and chatted for a little while, then finally gave up for the day and went home for Christmas Eve. We had some suggestions in through Julie that they go to a Christmas Eve service tonight and to the Children's Hospital on Saturday, I don't know whether he'll do that or not.

Friday, December 25, 1969
Christmas Day. The P stayed home until about 4:00. Then he went up to Camp David with the family. They did go to the church service last night, but didn't tell anyone, so no word is out on it. The P called about midday. He said to take five minutes off anytime during the day and enjoy Christmas.

Monday, December 28, 1970
The P had no schedule today, as is the case for the rest of the week, except a few minor functions at midday on a couple of the other days.

He had me in for about an hour in the morning, interrupting my session with Roger Ailes, at which time I was telling him we were getting a new TV consultant.

He asked me to have a talk with Haig because he's concerned as a result of his conversation with Rogers yesterday, that Rogers is aware of what Henry's doing with the Russians. While Henry thinks he's operating secretly, he's not really.

The P feels that Henry's got to open up the fact of his secret channel so that Rogers knows about it and we have some more candor in this whole thing because the problem now of playing it two ways poses a very bad situation for the P. For example, on the past trips, Tony Lake, who's now working for Muskie, was with Henry, so he knows all about them, yet Rogers doesn't know about it. There's a good chance that this will come out, which would be a very embarrassing thing. The P feels Henry's got to realize he's not a secret-type person, that the things he does do come out. He summed it up by saying the whole situation now poses a major problem for the P because Rogers knows that K's meeting with Dobrynin. Maybe the thing to do is to tell Rogers that both he and Henry have to meet with Dobrynin independently, and both of them should understand this. To do this we have to get K and Rogers together, especially as we approach the possibility of a meeting with the Russians.

I went out for about an hour, then he buzzed me back in at noon and kept me in for another two and a half hours, this time with Colson there. He got into sort of a long, rambling discussion on follow-up items: who we'll need for an attack on the Democrats; the need to develop our contact program concentrating on the top hundred people in the country spread across contributors, press, political, labor, religious, educational, etc.; then he got back onto his story of having never called a reporter or complained about a story, etc., the fact that we haven't gotten that across; the need for a spokesman that we can trust who can get on TV and talk about what the P is like.

Wednesday, December 30, 1970

P spent the morning getting his annual physical checkup. Unfortunately, we blew the plan for Tkach to brief afterwards. He did the briefing but Ron didn't really get over to him the point of getting out the line that the P needs to stop working so hard so Walter, instead, gave a pretty straight medical report. This led to great concern on the P's part. That was compounded by his discovery that we had completely failed to get out the story of his meeting with the Boys' Town group yesterday. This led the P back to the discussion last night with Connally and the fact that we don't really get out the points that we should be getting.

Then he got back onto checking on some of the odds and

ends and mentioning some of Connally's other points, one of which was that Lincoln was the great figure of the 19th century and Churchill and de Gaulle were the two great figures of the 20th century, and the big thing about all of them is their comeback from defeat, not their conduct of wars, etc. Connally feels we should very much build the comeback story.

Also, the P decided on the basis of an Alsop story in the paper today that leaked all of our plans for the State of the Union that we'd have to reevaluate the decision to drop the value-added tax idea. He thinks if we do just a small one we can get away with it. E totally disagrees. They had a long session this afternoon to discuss this.

Rose snuck in and conned the P into accepting her invitation to attend a Keogh going-away party at Blair House tonight. The P spent several hours after that, agonizing over it, and was very distressed that he had to go, but couldn't figure out how to get out of it.

Thursday, December 31, 1970

We had a flap with Teddy Kennedy, who is trying to capitalize on the decision of the Spanish government to commute the death sentences of some Basques. Teddy is going to put out the fact that he had wired the Spanish government before the decision and was wiring them his approval after the decision.

The P spent most of the afternoon over at the EOB. He told Ziegler not to let the press leave because as long as he was working they might as well too. So Ron didn't put a lid on and some of the press had to stay around. At 6:00 the P called Ron and told him to bring whatever press was left, there were only about six, over to the EOB for a drink. This apparently worked out pretty well. The P gave them about a 40-minute Q & A session standing up. It was kind of funny when they walked in—Frank Cormier, Helen Thomas, and Herb Kaplow were the only reporters—plus a couple of photographers and a radio technician. Helen Thomas, while the P was mixing the martinis in his little bar, said, "Now I know why you spend so much time at the EOB Office." The P apparently did make a number of pretty good points to these people. Ziegler was particularly amused by his statement that I and the other key members of the staff had the highest IQs of any White House staff people at least since Roosevelt, and that as a group, E, Shultz, Weinberger, and I were the most brilliant White House staff in history, intellectually. Ron, for some reason, thought that was very funny.

The P called me later at home wanting to be sure that Ziegler was getting across the importance of this little meeting with the press, the fact that he just called them over and handled it on an informal basis and the subtlety of this as a special event. Ron's working to peddle that and we'll see what we can get going.

1971

First Quarter: January–March

Friday, January 1, 1971
The P went to Camp David and E and I also came up, bringing our whole families. The P was very upset by a report in the sports section today that the Stanford football team was running around their hotel in sandals and shorts and that their quarterback had enjoyed posing for pictures with the topless dancers from San Francisco. The story was trying to make them out as being good guys because of this, and sneering at Ohio State as squares because they were wearing neckties and blazers. The P said for the first time he was going to root for the Midwest team in the Rose Bowl.

He was concerned about some press stories that hit us for not inviting Muskie to the Clean-Air-Bill signing yesterday and wants Ziegler to really use this as a case in point to hit back on this being a bum rap for us, and then shift to the point that the P has been the most gracious, nonpolitical P in history in terms of his treatment of his present, future, and past opponents. Actually, this is true in that Truman never had Hoover at the White House, Eisenhower never had Truman, Johnson and Kennedy never had Nixon, whereas Nixon has had Humphrey, Johnson, Muskie, Teddy Kennedy, and everybody to the White House on various occasions. Then we get one little incident like this and we're stabbed unfairly.

Saturday, January 2, 1971
At Camp David. The P had me over to Aspen at 2:45. I was there for three hours for just a general discussion in his study. He spent all the time inside. He hasn't been out in the snow at all, although it is beautiful here. He's obviously been doing a lot of reading, but also some general homework. He wanted

to be very sure we got the statistics on Presidential activity really worked up well and out to Congressional leaders and our own people so as to keep that story going. He thinks Ziegler ought to do a once-a-month recap on a slow news day to build up a cumulative effect and eventually get through on this point, and also the graciousness to our enemies story.

We discussed the general PR question. He's concerned about the memos we're getting out and also the danger that in getting all those memos in to him he will overreact and try to change himself as Johnson did. Also, by writing the memos there's a tendency on the part of the staff to shift responsibility to what the P should do, rather than what the staff should or is doing. He made one interesting point, which is the need to really get to work on our foreign policy PR because this is our strongest point, and, especially since the death of de Gaulle, we have a real opportunity to build the P as *the* world leader. Muskie and all the rest of them will try to move in on this field, but we must continue to dominate.

Sunday, January 3, 1971
Still at Camp David. He had a long talk with K apparently, who is very worried about Tony Lake and his defection. The P had to give Henry a big pitch trying to make the point that these people are just seeking power and that there's no reason to be disturbed about that kind of thing, it's too late to worry about it after it's happened. He pushed the line that brave men die only once, but cowards die a thousand times, and made the point that we have to keep our people from consulting their peers and that we can't keep worrying about things after they've happened. He does want me to talk to Haig about the necessity of keeping their people cranked up, that they can't just run a tough show in their staff, they have to give them some inspiration and uplift also.

Along that line he wants me to do the same thing in every morning staff meeting because he's concerned that even though we don't feel there's any staff morale problem, there is to some degree always that danger, and especially among the people that travel in the Washington social set, etc. He made the point that very few personalities are as immune, tough, and thick as he and I are to criticism and attacks. Most people don't respond in a vigorous upbeat way to these things as we do, so I have to keep working, he feels, with the other staff.

Monday, January 4, 1971

He got into a discussion of his concern about the Tony Lake situation. Henry told the P that Lake didn't leave because of Cambodia but because of disagreement on domestic policies. He's afraid that Lake could expose the whole Paris thing and would destroy the Administration internally because if this came out, Rogers would quite likely feel that he had to resign in protest to the P for having this kind of thing conducted without Rogers' knowledge. He also had a few things for California scheduling thoughts and the plan for tomorrow before we leave.

Tuesday, January 5, 1971

Day of Cabinet meeting. Our first with the new plan of having biweekly meetings at 8:00 AM lasting for just an hour. The P carried this one for an hour and a half because he's just not able to convince himself you can hold the thing to an hour and keep everybody happy. He told the Cabinet he's going to make a new troop announcement on April 15, and then launched into some views on the economy. He made the point that his kids had not been totally impressed with the TV *(a "TV conversation" with network newsmen he had done the night before)* and that they prefer the press conference, but Eddie Cox had called Tricia—the P identified him as a Harvard Law type—and said I doubt if those Harvard Law types understood any more of what I was saying about the economy last night than I did. Then he referred to Wilson as the most intellectual of all P's and said, of course, that was because of his education, or perhaps in spite of it. Then he said what Lincoln might have been if he'd gone to school, it probably would have ruined him.

He then led them into quite a discussion of the economy, which lasted about an hour. He hit the theory that there is no formula for low unemployment without war, and said that this is the one thing we are going to accomplish, and it will be a marvelous achievement. He raised the point of the possibility of further changes in the Cabinet, and said there would be no more at the P's request, that this is the team that we have here now, unless any of you decide you want to leave.

Elliot Richardson got into a discussion of how we can better influence commentators and opinion leaders to give them a better feel for the depth and range of the P's knowledge and understanding, for example, of economics. He was making the point that the people would be greatly enlightened if they could see the P in action, the way the Cabinet just had this morning.

After the Cabinet meeting the President had a series of appointments that kept him busy through the rest of the morning. We left about 12:20 for the airport and on to San Clemente.

Wednesday, January 6, 1971

The P is still in San Clemente and I'm still in Palm Springs. Mitchell told the P that I'm the only one in the White House he will deal with. The P's concerned that we've got to broaden Mitchell's viewpoint, although he agrees that we've got to put Mitchell in complete charge of political operations. But he thinks John tends to be too exclusive in some of his decisions and that we need to work on that while still giving him whole authority.

As a result of some of the reports in the paper on the Reagan inaugural, etc., the P concluded that Reagan's going to have a tough year ahead of him. He thinks he's going to have trouble as he moves into trying to solve the revenue and welfare problems, especially since he doesn't have the student issue as an overriding distracting factor.

Friday, January 8, 1971

The P's still at San Clemente. He apparently had a discussion today with Ziegler and E regarding the question of taking time off and vacations. Ziegler made the point that he's now well positioned to take time off because of the doctor's instructions and the feeling that people think he should be off more. He seems to buy this concept and may be willing to take a little more time than he has in the last couple of months.

He also raised the K problem again. Apparently Henry had talked with E this morning about the question of whether he should go back to Harvard or not, and all of his problems with Rogers. E, I guess, took it upon himself to fill the P in on all of this. The P makes the point that Henry craves the ego satisfaction of raising these questions and having people reassure him that he's in good shape and all. He also makes the point that he'd be a damn fool not to stay on.

Saturday, January 9, 1971

San Clemente. I'm still at Palm Springs. It was his birthday. I called in the morning to wish him a happy birthday. He got talked into a walk on the beach for a birthday picture by Ziegler, and it didn't come out too well, but didn't do any great harm, I guess. *(It was a stiff picture of the P walking on the beach in a windbreaker, shorts—and black wingtip shoes.)* We don't seem to be able to set up a system where we leave him alone as we've tried to do here.

Monday, January 11, 1971

San Clemente. I called Connally to follow up on his conversation with the P regarding Presidential PR, and he basically recapped the same things he had told the P, and that the P had passed on to me already. He did make the point that he had met last week with a small group of the top bankers in New York, and had taken the opportunity to devote 15 minutes of his conversation with them to just talking about the P and what kind of a man he is. In doing so he made the points that the P has the best concept of his problems than any man Connally knows, that he is isolated to a certain extent, as any P has to be, that he has allocated his time better than any man he has ever seen, that he has an extremely competent staff and delegates, more than any other P, and it's the only way a P can operate effectively; he is highly disciplined mentally and physically, knows his people, their strengths and weaknesses, and his adversaries and their strengths and weaknesses, both foreign and domestic, that he's ruthless enough to be a great P.

He also made a fascinating political point, which is that there's nothing wrong with having certain elements against us. He made this in the context of the press conference and its adversary nature, which he thinks is good. His point is that the basic political rule is to pick your enemies carefully and then hang on to them, but be sure they're always the same ones. This is something we haven't consciously or adequately done.

Wednesday, January 13, 1971

San Clemente. The big problem of the day arose between Dole and *(RNC Co-chairman)* Tom Evans, with Mitchell in the middle of it, and also Rog Morton. Dole decided he was going to make a power play to see how far he could get in establishing total control of the *(Republican National)* Committee, vs. our plan to have Evans exercise a major force there. The main flap apparently had arisen because Dole was late for an appointment in his office with Evans, and so Evans left, and this got Dole into a huff. In any event, the thing raged on through the night. Mitchell finally had Rog Morton get Dole simmered down and they put the thing together, but not until Mitchell made the point to Dole that if he didn't want to take the Chairmanship, that was fine. We'd put John Andrews in, and let it go that way.

Thursday, January 14, 1971

From San Clemente to Lincoln, Nebraska, for an address at the University, and then on to DC. The P did a very good job at the University with a serious, uplifting speech preceded by his football presentation, which went over very well. He got a good reception by the students. There was a group that attempted a "Peace Now" shoutdown at the very beginning, but they in turn were shouted down by the rest of the audience, and they never let out another peep after that.

He called me after getting home to explore whether the speech today in Nebraska was too soft-line on the students. Apparently, Henry had told him that he had been too apologetic and backed down too much. I don't think that's the case, but there obviously is a fine line to be drawn in this regard.

Friday, January 15, 1971

Back in DC. The P was very concerned early this morning about the Nebraska coverage, primarily because the *New York Times* story, by Semple, implied we had conceded we were wrong in earlier comments regarding students, etc. The P wanted to be sure that Ziegler and everyone else understood the basic rule that you don't capture people by surrendering to them. They capture you. It's extremely important that the leader never be in the position to allow the impression that he was wrong. He was quite concerned about this, but all of us, in reviewing the piece, agreed that it had really come out quite well and it didn't have the problem.

The big deal of the day today didn't involve the P, but rather K, who got into his usual tirade against State and Defense at the staff meeting this morning, and I hit back at him on the point that he had created some problems himself by the failure to notify Rogers of his last meeting with Dobrynin. That upset him. He packed up his papers and left the meeting. He came back about ten minutes later and asked Klein to leave so that he could talk to the four of us: Rumsfeld, Shultz, E, and me. He then said that he had to make his decision about going back to Harvard in the next day or so, and that if this wasn't straightened out, he was going to go back and not stay here. He was more uptight than he usually is on the subject, and this was the first time he had raised it with the group, although he's been discussing his problems with E during this past week in California, while I was away, and has John quite disturbed, although it's basically the same routine over again. As a result, John and I met with him briefly a little later in the morning and agreed that something had to be done in the way of a showdown with the P on the whole subject, but that it should not be done until after the State of the Union speech. This successfully stalls Henry past the time of his return to Harvard, which I don't think he has any intention of doing. The P has gone to Camp David for the weekend. I'm staying home.

Sunday, January 17, 1971

The P had some ideas regarding the Buchanan memo on the fact that we basically had sold out all of our Republican conservative policies in our "move to the left." I think the point is getting through to the P that our movement is somewhat to the left and he doesn't want to get too far off of his natural base. The Buchanan theory of course is to go all conservative, which would be equally bad, but we do seem to be moving too far leftward at this point.

Also he has come back into the whole PR area in making the point that nobody's doing an adequate job of selling the story of the man. I'm working up my basic memorandum on this and he wants me to review it with Connally before I send it to the P. He wants a lot more push on this area. He did make the point that we can't worry about the columnists as they take us on, because they're always going to be attacking; and he commented that he could sit on the Statue of Liberty holding an open door and they wouldn't write anything good. He made the point to me that I'm going to have to get my desk cleared because I'm going to have to handle all the political stuff for the White House and also should ride herd on the PR side, so he doesn't want me involved in the administrative stuff, which fits exactly with what I've been talking about with Butterfield et al. We're going to make some changes there, and I think it all will work out pretty well.

Monday, January 18, 1971

The P had a full morning of meetings, the principal one of which was a session with Rogers, Laird, K, Helms, and Moorer to discuss Laird's trip and the results therefrom. This principally concerned the level of troop withdrawals and the timing for same, and the plan for some new attacks in Laos and Cambodia. *(It was at this meeting that he authorized the Laos operation.)*

During the discussion with Henry and me he talked about his troop withdrawal plan and the point that Thieu had strongly urged that we not reduce the level below 200,000 prior to his *(Thieu's)* election in October or November. We would be down to 280,000 in April, so that permits us to withdraw only about 75,000, or 12,000 a month for the next six months after that. We could then, of course, announce the massive withdrawal right after the Vietnamese elections, and this is the P's present plan. All this also relates to the question of a trip to Vietnam, which I think he's still planning on doing in April, and he'll probably make the new announcement at that time and also use that as a means of bolstering the Thieu government and our confidence in them.

The other big flap today was the problem of an article in *The New York Times* regarding the decline of the State Department, which understandably had Rogers quite upset, and he succeeded in getting the P into the same frame of mind. The P's reaction was to put out a statement from him blasting the article, but a careful reading of it convinced me that it's got enough basis in fact and accuracy that it wouldn't be a good thing to do. He did have me call Rogers a couple of times to tell him that we were moving on it, trying to find out who had done it, planning a statement by Ziegler to shoot it down, etc.

In discussing this, I talked to Safire, who makes the very valid point that this whole situation is really the result of a backfire of the State Department's PR effort at the middle level, where they've been strongly selling the line that K has taken over the development of foreign policy. They've been doing this as a way to try and stab K, but as Safire had apparently predicted earlier, instead it's backfired and this one writer at least, with the *Times,* has picked up their line on a straight basis and is throwing it back at them. Safire's convinced they've been on a real campaign to chop K in the NSC and that's what really led to this. It'd be hard to convince the P and Rogers of this point, but I'm sure Safire is right.

Tuesday, January 19, 1971

Cabinet meeting this morning for three hours to cover the State of the Union presentation. E and his crew ran the show and did an excellent job of presenting our general budget plans and then reviewing the main new programs in revenue sharing, executive reorganization, health, and environment. In the middle of the Health presentation, P made the point that we should not provide full free health care because most of the time, when someone's got a pain, he'd be a hell of a lot better off not to go to the doctor, it'd just make it worse.

This afternoon Ziegler was in to get some guidelines on how to handle Cambodia. We're being accused in the press of a credibility problem again because we have stepped up air activity and they're trying to pretend that this is a change in policy. The P told Ron to hit the credibility question directly and to hit it hard. We've already clearly pointed out there would be no American ground action and no American advisors in Cambodia. We said we would assist Cambodia, and this was okayed by Congress with dollars and logistic assistance. We also said we would continue air activities, where necessary, for the purpose of inhibiting the enemy from reestablishing their sanctuaries. That was presented to Congress and was written into the legislation. The P wanted to be sure Ron hit this hard.

A little later, K was in and there was quite a discussion of *(Senator)* Muskie and the results of his *(Europe)* trip. The P obviously is not pleased with the reception Muskie was given by the Soviets and by Willy Brandt. He wants to have Muskie hit on the total irresponsibility of his statement, or his proposed statement, standstill in the disarmament talks. He should be hit on his amazing ignorance; say it's unprecedented for a senator to do this. He made the point that we've got to recognize that the Soviets will play a role in United States politics. They definitely want to get Nixon out, and will do what they can to see that it happens. K argues that they have to balance this against their fear that Nixon may win and they'll have to live with him another four years. The P says, "I'm willing to try the negotiations," and so on.

The P had a dinner in his honor given by the Cabinet at Blair House tonight, as they did last year on the anniversary.

Wednesday, January 20, 1971

The second anniversary of the Inaugural. To mark the occasion we had a meeting of about 60 top staff people. White House and OMB. E opened it with a general overview briefing of the State of the Union. The P came in at 9:30. We let the press in to cover his opening remarks, then tossed the press out and he talked for about an hour more. A very inspiring message to the troops. He kidded them along some, but also took them to the mountaintop on the tremendous importance of the first change of direction of government in the 190 years of the country's history.

He spent the day at the EOB working on the speech, alone most of the time. He had me over for one spell between drafts, primarily to get into some PR items. He particularly wanted some very strong reaction to the *Life* and *Newsweek* blasts this week. He wanted us to get across somewhere the story that *Life* had offered Tricia a cover picture and story with the understanding that she could have editorial control as they gave to the Kennedys, and so forth. Tricia refused, saying that she didn't like *Life* and the way that they handled things, and therefore would not want to be a part of such a thing.

We had a long meeting this afternoon with E, Shultz, Mitchell, and K at Henry's request to discuss in detail his problems with the State Department. He walked into the meeting with huge thick folders for each of us with all kinds of papers documenting his case on the terrible things State has been doing in the public press, and how they've been undercutting him in internal operations, and how they've disobeyed Presidential orders, cable traffic and all sorts of stuff. He did an extremely good job, for a change, of presenting his case quite unemotionally and very rationally. This made it far more effective than it usually is when he gets going. He really wrapped it up by saying he wasn't going to discuss it with the P, but was hoping we would find a way to approach it, and that the problem had to be resolved. He would not continue this method of operation. If it couldn't be resolved, he would leave; if it could be, he'd be perfectly willing to work within a new approach as long as NSC has complete control and Rogers is, as he puts it, "brought to heel."

I also had a meeting this morning with Mitchell regarding the whole political structure. He claims the P has never asked him to take on the assignment of running the campaign, so I confirmed that was, indeed, the P's intention and John agreed that he would do it. He then discussed his plans on retiring from Justice and felt that he would have to do so later this year. He could not continue as Attorney General and still run the campaign, but that didn't seem to bother him. He's ready to resign when it's necessary and says there's no problem because he can go on back to the law firm after the election and would be happy to do so.

Thursday, January 21, 1971

The P spent the whole day at the EOB, working on the speech. He reacted at first quite indifferently to news of Teddy Kennedy's defeat as majority whip in the Senate, and said he didn't think it would have the significance that the commentators would probably try to give it. He made the point that you don't kill a man who's been built up the way Teddy has, by a defeat, any more than you killed Nixon by his defeat in California. He thinks it will provide a momentary setback, but that Teddy will move ahead in spite of it, with considerable strength.

Henry came in this morning to say he had discovered that Rogers and Laird had met secretly with Alexis Johnson yesterday and had decided to send a cable to our Ambassador as an attempt to try to turn off the planned Laotian operations. Alex Johnson felt so guilty about it, he ended up calling Henry and telling him, and we put out an all-points bulletin to make sure that the cable didn't get to the P, since Rogers had said that he was not going to send the cable in through the system, but would get it cleared directly with the P. We had everything covered, but in spite of that the P got the cable. We later found out Rose Woods had taken it to him because Rogers' secretary had called her and said that they were sending this over in a sealed envelope marked "Eyes Only" and it was to be delivered directly to the P, not through any individual or department. As soon as the P opened it, he reacted exactly as he should have, and called Henry over, said the P would not approve this, and that it was up to Henry to handle it through his system. Henry took the matter to the WSAG *(Washington Special Action Group)* meeting and brought it up there.

Friday, January 22, 1971

State of the Union Day. The big flap in the morning arose when he read the morning papers and called to say, "What in the name of good God hell is going on!" because the *Times* and *Post* had both leaked all the details of the reorganization plan, which was the one really well-kept secret. The P's reaction was to decide we wouldn't give the text of the speech to the press prior to delivery. He of course backed off of it and agreed to let it out, but was very concerned about tracking down the source of the leak. He also made the point that he'd come to the tough conclusion that it's not worth telling people anymore what we're doing, especially the Cabinet, and so on; that from now on we should just wait until the day of the event so that we don't run the risk of leaks of this sort.

He called several times during the day regarding television plans for the State of the Union, and he had decided not to use makeup, etc., but backed off under Carruthers' strong recommendation that he has to use makeup because the lighting in there makes it even more necessary than their normal circumstances. Then he got up to the house and discovered Carruthers had picked narrow ties and a blue shirt. He felt he should wear a white shirt and wide ties. Again, he backed off and wore both the ties and shirt that Carruthers wanted him to. Net result was an excellent picture on TV. Reaction to the speech afterward was extremely good.

The other big problem of the day was Senator Cooper and others in the Congress who are starting to criticize the Cambodian buildup, and the P wanted me to have Rogers get to Cooper right away and convince him that this whole thing does not involve ground troops or advisors, or anything of that sort, and that it was being done only because it was necessary to interdict the enormous buildup of the sanctuaries. He felt Bill should warn Cooper that he's on a bad wicket and should not push it too far. It turned out that when I called Rogers he had already done exactly this with Cooper and he was delighted to have caught us ahead of time.

Saturday, January 23, 1971

The P got going under a pretty good head of steam today with a long meeting with Reagan at the Governor's request, mainly so Reagan could assure him that he would be heading a Nixon delegation to the convention and would not in any way allow himself to become a candidate. They also discussed welfare and the whole range of State of the Union items.

Monday, January 25, 1971

The start of Congressional follow-up week. A GOP Leadership Meeting first thing in the morning, and then meetings in the afternoon with the Senate bipartisan group and the House bipartisan group to start selling the program. The P was not too pleased with the Leadership Meeting, first of all because there was absolutely no enthusiasm. They were deadly, just sat around and whined, as they usually do. No one had charged them up. He resents having to go in and do the charging up himself, and says it's hard work, like pulling teeth, which I'm sure it must be.

Tuesday, January 26, 1971

State visit with Juan Carlos and Sophia of Spain. After the first of this week's four Congressional breakfasts. There is a State dinner tonight.

P had another one of those sessions with Moorer and K today, as a result of which he wants a meeting with Laird, Rogers, and Moorer tomorrow. Henry got me into the office, just as I was going home, to go over the general plan of what they're really up to. They're planning a major assault in Laos which, if successful, and Henry fully believes it will be, would in effect end the war because it would totally demolish the enemy's capability. The problem is that it will be a very major attack, with our troops massed heavily on the Laotian border, and the question is whether the heat generated in Congress and across the country will be worth it. Henry's point is that our action in Cambodia, etc., cleared things up so we've got no problem in '71, but could have them in '72. This new action in Laos now would set us up so we wouldn't have to worry about problems in '72, and that of course is the most important.

Henry does feel that there's one alternative, which is that we've discovered the enemy has our plan and is starting to mass their troops to counteract. By going ahead with our planning and letting them go ahead with their counterplanning, we can draw them into a monumental trap and then move in and bomb them, maybe with the same effect as going ahead with the plan. This of course would be a much more salable alternative domestically. The problem with either of these plans is that all of a sudden the Russians have come around and Henry's had a very productive meeting with Dobrynin that's resulted in their agreeing to move ahead on setting a Summit for midyear, plus a basic SALT settlement and a couple of other items that we've been after them on. The massive Laotian attack would probably abort the whole Soviet effort, and the question is whether the Summit, etc., is worth more to us or whether winding down the war is. This is the tough question that Henry's got to face now, and he asked me to think about it tonight and talk to him about it some more tomorrow.

The SALT talks had been bogged down for over a year, but now for the first time the Soviets had indicated they might be willing to talk about both defensive and offensive weapons, as we had been suggesting, instead of just defensive weapons. The Summit agreement was also a breakthrough.

Thursday, January 28, 1971

The P extended the Congressional breakfast a little longer today. Each one seems to be longer than the one before. We had a pretty light day for him otherwise. The morning was basically clear, and he spent it just chatting in general with me. He called Senator Stennis to thank him for his remarks yesterday on Cambodia in defense of the Administration. Had quite a long talk outlining his Cambodia position and making it clear that we absolutely were committed to no ground troops but to full use of air as needed to knock out the rebuilding of the sanctuaries and protect American lives.

In the late morning the P agreed to let a group of twelve college student editors come over. This was a group that was visiting the State Department for the day under Mike Collins' Public Information Program. The P greeted them in the Oval Office, then chatted with them a little there and had E give them a quick rundown on the revenue sharing and other domestic program points from the State of the Union. They were totally bored with that entire presentation and the P, unfortunately, gave them a chance to ask a question. The bearded guy immediately jumped on Cambodia and the fact that we had troops in there. First E stepped in and corrected the guy, who was using as his "facts" the CBS presentation last night, which claimed that we had men working on the ground in Cambodia. E jumped in and corrected the facts, then the P moved in and made a very clear and complete statement of our position on Cambodia. I don't think he convinced the students, but at least he covered his point with them.

He spent most of the afternoon coming back to that session because it clearly bothered him. I think that part of it may have been good because it will make him think a little about the public information aspects of the actions we're taking in Cambodia.

Along similar lines, Mitchell has come up with a recommendation that we should call a grand jury for further investigation at Kent State. Bob Taft is strongly opposed to this. The P wasn't quite sure what his view is but agreed with me that we should just let it lie where it is, that opening it doesn't do us any good. Also, J. Edgar Hoover has told him that the facts don't warrant a grand jury. He wants E to try to work this out.

Friday, January 29, 1971

Buchanan, the VP, K, and I were called into the P's office after the few morning schedule items he had, and before we departed for the Virgin Islands. The P first had Henry review the plan for the Laotian move and get all the things set on that. Henry's still not sure we're going ahead with that step, but they're working on the plan for it in any event.

He then got into the purpose of the meeting with Buchanan et al., which was that he feels the VP should go for a big play on live television to comment on the recent press coverage of Southeast Asia. He feels he should speak more in sorrow than in anger and should not be defensive about Cambodia. He should work from Bill Rogers' testimony and make the points that the press attacks are unfair, irrelevant, and inaccurate as well as conflicting, that we would think that they were writing about the previous Administration. They ignored the total difference between what we're doing and what LBJ was doing in Vietnam. Make the point that we've kept every promise we've made and cite the examples of the sanctuaries and no ground or air support in the sanctuaries. Then make the point that troops are down, casualties are down, and this can continue only if the Nixon Doctrine continues to be applied. Then make the point that the press has a vested interest in seeing us fail because they predicted that we'd fail. Everyone agreed that there is a need to soften the press in advance of the stepped-up activity next week, which will drive them right up the wall.

The only activity after we got into Virgin Islands was a call from Buchanan, who's all distressed about the TV news tonight that reported the appearance of a major buildup on the Laotian border of ARVN troops ready for attack. Apparently this arose out of Rogers' news conference and some observation of troop activity along the border. Pat felt we should rush to the P with this, but of course we didn't. The P has gone for a swim and holed up in his cottage here and appears to be very pleased with the setup so far.

Tuesday, February 2, 1971

In Washington. Day started with Prayer Breakfast, which he regards as total torture at best. This one went pretty well except that the Chief Justice, who was supposed to be the main speaker and go on for only ten minutes, took twenty-five minutes to explain word-for-word and over and over the true meaning of the 23rd Psalm.

The Cabinet met for a brief session. Rogers, just at the point of adjournment, jumped in hard on foreign policy, making some very good remarks on attacking the point that some

in Congress are trying to imply that we've violated the spirit
of the law in our Laotian buildup. Rogers made the point that
there is no such thing as "spirit of the law," the question is
the word of the law. If the words are not clear, so that one
cannot tell precisely what the law means, then you look to
the intent. In this case, Cooper-Church, the words and the intent are clear. The prohibition on use of air power was specifically removed from Cooper-Church before it was passed,
and it is absolutely clear that the intent of Congress, as well
as the word of the law, the letter of the law, is that there is
no limitation on the use of air power. The P then hit the same
point, saying that we are candid, we are honest, and we are
within the law.

The latter part of the afternoon was consumed with a long
session with the War Action group, getting final plans laid for
the next move. He's pretty well girded up for the effects of
any major move. I actually don't think there are going to be
any great problems, because I think the thing has already been
discounted by the heavy press anticipation and the people are
pretty well prepared for whatever steps we do take. There certainly doesn't seem to be any likelihood of a Cambodia-level
reaction, although I guess anything can happen.

Wednesday, February 3, 1971

The P originally had an NSC meeting scheduled for this morning but canceled it as a result of his long conversation last
night with Henry after the "Evening at the White House."
Apparently Henry had become very concerned about the TV
news reports regarding the Laos buildup, and especially about
Dan Rather reporting that the P had met with the Action Group
late yesterday afternoon, and that they were trying to persuade
him not to go ahead with plans for action. On the basis of
that, Henry felt that they probably should cancel the plans and
hold up on the Phase II operation.

The P put off a decision on it, though, until this morning
and said that he wanted the NSC meeting canceled and instead
he wanted to meet with Mitchell, Connally, and me to review
the bidding. We had that meeting at about 9:30. The P first
spent some time with Henry and then called me in before the
others arrived and reviewed the bidding on the situation to date
and what he considered the options to be. Henry's argument
was that the bureaucracy was so completely out of control that

we wouldn't be able to hold them in line if we went ahead, therefore we should do so. By this morning, however, both Henry and the P had pretty much changed their minds and swung back to feeling that we should go ahead with the operation on the basis that if the P now allowed himself to be talked out of it, in effect by the press reports which had been leaked from State and Defense, that he would lose any hope of controlling the bureaucracy. My argument was that it had some validity, but even more important was the fact that we needed the move in order to ensure our continuing safe withdrawal, and also that I feel strongly that the proposed negatives that the others offer are certainly not assured, and in my view not even probable. That is, I don't think the reaction in Congress or on the campuses, or in the press, or with the public is going to be nearly as strong or adverse as we are assuming it might be. Mitchell and Connally had pretty much the same views.

The P had me back in and discussed some more concern on how to get a hold of all this and also some concern on the PR side of it. He wanted me to work closely with Henry on that.

Fortunately, because of the earlier developments, I guess, Henry asked me to attend the WSAG meeting, and he also asked Ziegler to attend the first part of it. I tried to leave when Ziegler did, after we had discussed the basic PR plan for the Cambodian operation tonight, and for the removal of the embargo on the Laotian press coverage tomorrow. Ziegler left at that time and so did I, but Henry came up and called me back down to go over the whole scenario for the Laotian operation Sunday night. I did so and participated in all of the PR thinking. As a result of this, the P has concluded that this is probably the best way to handle this thing from now on, that is, for me to sit in all critical meetings and to force attention and consideration of Congressional and PR factors when they're making the decisions, and force them not to let that kind of decision be made by the generals and undersecretaries. I think this will probably work pretty well, and it will of course be fascinating to do, as it was to sit in the WSAG meeting today and review the whole scenario for the operation.

We had a rather interesting episode as the P's appointment with Dr. Riland came due and he proceeded to take off his clothes and go into the outer room and have us sit down and continue the discussion with him while Riland wrenched his back and went through his manipulations. Following the Riland treatment, and after he had left, the P sat in one of the chairs in his outer office with just his shorts on and pursued the conversation a little further. Then Henry and I left with the understanding that the plan was set and we would go ahead.

Thursday, February 4, 1971

A big day on the Laotian buildup. I sat in the WSAG meeting again today and will plan on doing so regularly from now on. Unfortunately, I blew it on this one because Henry got into the question of whether Rogers should do an appearance on Monday at the Senate Foreign Relations Committee, and I argued that he should because it would give us our story on television Monday night, after the Sunday-night move. Henry didn't want it done that way and was furious at my stepping in, slammed his book shut, sat and stewed at the head of the table for a few minutes, and then abruptly adjourned the meeting for a five-minute recess and then started the 40 group. I talked to him afterward about the tactic there, and he realizes that his maneuver in closing down the meeting really did more harm than my taking the position I did to begin with.

Mitchell and I had a two-hour session with the P on a number of items. First we discussed the whole question of J. Edgar Hoover and whether he should be continued. The decision was that Mitchell should go ahead with his implementation of his internal security planning operations, which Hoover opposes. This may bring about a confrontation. If it does, we'll see how we handle it from there. The P made it clear that Hoover has got to be replaced before the end of Nixon's first term because we can't run the risk of the possibility of Nixon not being reelected and of someone else appointing Hoover's successor. The problem is, we need to make this point to Hoover in such a way as to get him to resign without any big problem.

There was some discussion of the Wallace question. It appears that Wallace is interested in making a deal of some kind that will make it unnecessary for him to run for P, which he apparently does not want to do. Mitchell seemed to feel that we might still want Wallace in the race, but the P felt very strongly that under any circumstances it would be better for us to have him out and that we should try to work this out. We also got into the question of a possible deal with Mayor Daley, who has indicated that he will not do anything to oppose the P if Clem Stone agrees to stay out of the Governor's race in Illinois.

He had a talk with Bill Rogers regarding follow-up plans after the Sunday-night move, made a few agreements which will drive Henry up the wall, but I think we can work them out.

Friday, February 5, 1971

Laos continues on a pretty even keel today. There were a few flurries here and there, but the embargo's lifted and the news is out, and it doesn't seem to be creating nearly the stir that people were afraid of. I think we'll come out extremely well on it. Everything went very well at the WSAG meeting today. The P was planning on going to Camp David tonight, but the icy rain made the weather conditions bad, so he couldn't fly, and he decided he didn't want to try to drive. He will probably go up tomorrow instead.

Sunday, February 7, 1971

The P left Camp David this morning at 9:30. Henry and I flew down with him. He was in pretty good spirits on the plane. He talked a little about the press this morning, particularly the story regarding the Laos invasion, which was completely wrong in that it said the decision had now been made not to go in, and a big effort was made to point out that Nixon had gotten cold feet and the planned move into Laos had been canceled. The P feels that this article, and I'm sure that he's right, is just a forerunner of what they would have hit him with if he actually hadn't gone ahead with the Laos move. He therefore feels very good that he has gone ahead.

Monday, February 8, 1971

The day after the Laos move. Everything went OK last night, and this morning the follow-up fell into line just as it was supposed to. The P seemed in good shape as the reaction and plan generally fell together. He of course wanted to push hard on getting our side of the reaction going.

The P is very anxious that we not let the Democratic candidates look good on this issue. Muskie has moved out in opposition and he wants to be sure we keep him out on that limb and push hard to make an asset out of this. He wants to be sure we don't take a soft-handed defensive position. We should whack the opponents on patriotism, saving American lives, etc., and really go to work on it.

We got the dope on the volume of troops, food, and ammunition that's moved on the Ho Chi Minh trail. The P wants to make a strong point of the real significance of the trail so that we build up the significance of the Laotian operation and he wants to really push the strong positive points. He also had an idea of making a positive out of the antipress on the blackout or embargo, by making a point that the alarm and confusion and uncertainty that the press has been talking about was in the press, not in the people, and that obviously we wouldn't telegraph our punches to the enemy, and thank God we finally planted some alarm among them, etc. In other words, again taking the positive approach.

Later in the day we got into a huge flap regarding briefings because K and Rogers had agreed that there wouldn't be any briefings and then K let Colson et al. set up a late-afternoon briefing session for him with about 15 top conservative columnists. When he realized what he had done, he realized also that he'd have to cancel it, so we ended up with a pretty awkward situation which was unfortunate. But they did cancel the briefing and kept the commitment to Rogers.

The P got into some discussion with me about the problems of Henry's briefing tactics. He feels that he does too much of a good job of telling the people what they want to know, rather than what we want them to know. Then he also got into the point of the need for K to be more discreet regarding his glamorous young women, especially in public and especially in Washington, DC. He feels it's OK for Henry to be a swinger in New York, Florida, and California, but he should not be in Washington, and he wants us at the White House dinners not to put him next to the most glamorous gal anymore, but rather put him near some intelligent and interesting woman instead.

Tuesday, February 9, 1971

Laos is still going well, and that's led him to think back on the whole Cambodia question. He feels strongly that we've completely failed to get over the success story. Use Laos now to establish the success of Cambodia and make the public see it as such. NBC last night reported a poll they had taken that showed that people don't feel that Cambodia was successful. He thinks we've got to take the two key points: one, that casualties have been reduced 75 percent, and the other that withdrawals are not only insured but now can be stepped up. He pointed out that Colonel Cook had told him when he came back from Vietnam that everybody in Vietnam says Cambodia was the best thing we've ever done.

Today was one of those days where things get screwed up. The prime thing was a reception for the Freedom Foundation where we had full press coverage including a whole battery of TV cameras, and the P was pretty disturbed because he didn't have anything to say to them, and wasn't expecting to have press coverage, although his briefing paper, of course, said that there would be. He feels that we've got to avoid this in the future. This also arose yesterday in a related problem where he had wanted to use a TelePrompTer for recording the environment message and there wasn't a TelePrompTer set up. Our staff didn't get it worked out right. Today a similar kind of flap, regarding the Pollution-Control Council that meets tomorrow, in that he feels the environment is not an issue that's worth a damn to us. He has a very uneasy feeling about it because he thinks it works the wrong way for us, that we're catering to the left in all of this and that we shouldn't be. They're the ones that care about the environment, and that they're trying to use the environmental issue as a means of destroying the system and we're playing right into their hands.

He says that he and the family have agreed that Isabel Shelton and Judith Martin (of *The Washington Post*) both must be banned from the White House as accredited press people for social functions, and says that it's ordered as of now and must be carried out and he'll fire whoever is responsible for letting them in, if they ever get in again. This came out of several flaps, apparently. The story that Judith Martin ran on Beverly Sills' bra-strap breaking, plus the story that ran today downgrading Sevilla-Sacassa as a result of the diplomatic reception last night caused the P to put the pressure on Mrs. Nixon again to agree to keep the people out, which he says she's now agreed to do.

Wednesday, February 10, 1971
The P had his first breakfast with the Democratic members of Congress this morning. Apparently it went very well. He was particularly pleased with the story he told them, saying that he had noted there had been some reports regarding the political effect of the reforms he was proposing and he had serious doubts as to whether this would be of any political benefit to him; he said that English history showed (and he made the point that Fulbright could correct him if he was wrong on this) that those responsible for reforms in government are generally thrown out, and he cited the example of Disraeli as reported in Blake's biography, where there was a big battle between Gladstone and Disraeli and Disraeli took the reforms that Gladstone had proposed and had been fighting for and he got them through. Among them was an extended franchise, as a result of which there were a lot of new people able to vote. In the next election they voted Disraeli out of office and Gladstone in. Everybody laughed at that point. The P then pointed out that six years later the same people voted Disraeli back in and the P said, "I assure you that I don't plan to come back in six years to try again."

The big issue today was the Lockheed problem. Right after the breakfast the P called Connally into his office and had E and me come in to talk privately about how to handle the thing. The problem is that Lockheed is in serious danger of going broke as a result of the collapse of Rolls-Royce, and thus the nonavailability of engines for the Lockheed Air Bus. If Lockheed folds, it's quite probable that both TWA and Eastern will, and also Collins Radio, so the domino effect becomes horrendous. Pete Flanigan has been working on this, but the P was determined, it was obvious in our brief meeting, to put Connally in charge of it and have him handle this from here on out.

Thursday, February 11, 1971
He was pretty fully occupied this morning. He didn't come into the office before going over to the State Department to sign the Seabeds Treaty. Then, when he got back, he went full tilt through the Kennedy swearing-in in his office, the Connally swearing-in in the East Room, and a number of other meetings preparatory to departure for Key Biscayne.

The principal problem arising this morning was in relation

to the VP, who apparently called the P on the phone from California to object to the health message as it's presently contemplated. The VP feels there's some serious mistakes being made in this, and that adequate consideration hasn't been given to them, and also that he was misrepresented in the option paper going to the P. This of course created quite a flap, resulting in a session on the plane with Weinberger and Shultz to discuss the whole thing. The P felt the paper probably hadn't been adequately staffed, but his principal concern was that the VP would come to him on it, rather than working it out with the staff. He feels that we've got to keep the VP out of substantive policy development, that we cannot have him fighting the White House staff or the Cabinet, that he must not get involved in policy because he tends to zero in on one feature and jump on it rather than looking at the whole picture. He feels we need someone on our staff who has the confidence of the VP who can hold his hand, and he's decided Weinberger is the one who should do this.

Friday, February 12, 1971
At Key Biscayne. We had a discussion with Rogers and K on the whole Laotian situation. Primarily on tactics, as to the need for putting all the necessary effort in there. The P wants to be sure that we do everything that we need to do, and that we pull no punches at all. He discussed the fact that it's important for some civilian input into military planning and cited some of the earlier instances where he pushed the military to go further than they themselves had intended to go, and that it was beneficial and desirable that he had done so. He's doing that again on this one, feeling that, for instance, we should bomb the passes and perhaps some other things in order to make sure the Laotian operation works out.

We also got into a fairly lengthy discussion of the press problem as a result of an ABC film report last night purporting to show that there were American ground troops operating in Laos. They apparently had gotten some film of an American body being removed, which was wearing an ARVN uniform, and they found that very sinister. Rogers made the point that the key here is what appears on television, and that we've got to keep riding herd or we're going to get clobbered. He is of course absolutely right. Henry, on the other hand, was more concerned with the Reston column that complained that we weren't permitting the press adequate access to cover the war. Rogers' point was, that kind of complaint hurts us not at all, but the picture on television and the commentary that goes with it hurts us enormously, and that's what we've got to watch out for.

Monday, February 15, 1971

At Key Biscayne. This was by far the best day of the weekend, and, unfortunately, as soon as I got out on the beach, the P called and had me come over, and I was stuck inside the house for almost four hours going over his long list of odds and ends. He was somewhat concerned by the new Harris poll, which I reviewed with him, giving a comparison of Presidential personality standings at present versus 1968. It showed he had declined in the rating of strength and decisiveness, two basic characteristics he feels are most important for us to get over. He's still high in both of these, but has gone down over the last three years. This again indicates the job we've got to do in the personality side.

Wednesday, February 17, 1971

The P was holed up at the EOB all day, getting ready for his press conference, and had hardly any interruptions. He did call once and was particularly interested in talking about the results of a youth poll reported in the news summary today. He is intrigued that it showed that youth want stronger leadership, more close family ties, and they recognize the need for hard work to achieve success. He feels there's a real problem for us in it, in that their most admired men are JFK, Martin Luther King, and Bobby Kennedy, with Nixon coming in a poor fourth at 9 percent. He felt it was interesting that Teddy was not in this list, however. He thinks this whole study shows that the youth are a very vulnerable target for us, and that we ought to be concentrating on our opportunities to reach them.

Henry was in, agonizing over his TV problem. It appears that Klein wants somebody on for a special full hour of "Face the Nation" after the State of the World next week, and Henry of course wants to go on himself but professes to believe, as I do, that he can't. He's opposed to Laird and/or Rogers going on because he's afraid they'll louse up his report and/or take credit for it. Unfortunately there's no way of talking him out of this line of thinking, and the net result probably will be that we won't have anybody go on. We'll try to use the time for domestic policy.

Friday, February 19, 1971
He *(the P)* raised the point again of his concern about K's staff; the fact that the news today reports that one more has turned left, this time Mort Halperin going to the Common Cause staff. He wants me to work with Haig and make sure that Henry examines his staff very closely and is really set to kick out any potential traitors and not to let any others in.

This afternoon he did the Young Republicans' leadership conference gathering and apparently got a spectacular reception, and again did an excellent job, culminating in sitting at the piano and playing "God Bless America" while they all sang.

Saturday, February 20, 1971
No fixed schedule today, except a meeting with Colombo to bid him farewell, which was first thing this morning. That led, of course, to the inevitable objection to second day meetings with foreign visitors, and he had Henry in this morning and outlined some rules as to who does and doesn't get in for this kind of session from now on. Henry was delighted with the way the P had handled the meeting this morning with Colombo, and told the P so.

The news flap today was on an Arthur Burns story in the paper this morning, resulting from his testimony yesterday where he had said the problem wasn't one of money supply, but rather of confidence, thereby implying he, as Chairman *(of the Federal Reserve Board)*, didn't have confidence in the P's policies. The P was really upset about this. Arthur was trying to call him during the day, and the P said he would not take the call and, rather, had me call Arthur and tell him of his distress and make the point strongly to Arthur that he can't get away with this kind of thing. The P has the strong feeling that we've got to really put the screws onto Arthur and that he is not showing the proper gratitude or appreciation for the P's having put him where he is.

Another flap arose from the continuing effort of *(antiwar Republican Congressman Paul)* McCloskey to discuss impeachment of the P. He's not actually called for it, but he keeps talking about it. We're going to move now to get a petition going in McCloskey's district demanding his resignation and putting the heat on him since he's betrayed the trust of the Republicans who elected him.

There was the usual relaxed Saturday morning with long chats with E on some of the above and then with Colson on how his Project Muskie is coming along and some ideas on ways to carry that further ahead; also on general PR planning and thinking. The P left for Camp David to spend the night. He called a couple of times after he got up there, mainly on details of the State of the World.

Monday, February 22, 1971

I had a three-hour lunch with Rogers, ostensibly for the purpose of discussing State Department personnel, which we did go into in considerable detail. It was clear, however, that Rogers' principal concern was to try to work out the Henry K problem, and he specifically asked for ways that he could direct communications to the P directly, rather than via Henry. Basically he is sincerely trying to do what he thinks is best for the P, and of course so is Henry, but the two of them just stay on a collision course and somehow we've got to figure out how to work it out. Henry caught me later and made it clear that his dissatisfaction is again reaching a peak also, so we have a lot to do.

Wednesday, February 24, 1971

Henry was in this morning with great concern about the military situation in Laos. He will not admit publicly that anything's wrong, but he wanted the P to know that he was very much concerned that the military reports were not giving us the straight poop.

In any event, he proposed to the P that he send General Haig out to check up on the whole thing on the scene. He kept making the case over and over that military history shows that the real problem in wars is that military commanders tend to become locked into and infatuated with their basic original plans, and refuse to change them even when the situation so dictates, and that's one of the major reasons for military defeats. He's afraid that it's possible, at least, that this might be the case with Abrams at this point, and he at least wants to check it out. The P's reaction was noncommittal and pensive while Henry was in there. After Henry left, he talked about it some, and obviously was concerned and felt there might be merit to it, although he deplored Henry's constant repetition and citing of military history to try and prove his point.

The K-Rogers problem continues, and the P spent quite a little time talking about it. He keeps asking me what plans I have for dealing with it, and of course I don't have any. I think that we've got to push to some kind of confrontation to try to make both men realize they're performing childishly, and to the detriment of their country as well as themselves. But I'm not sure we can make any progress by doing that.

The P wanted me to have a meeting with some of our key political and right-wing types to try to develop a line and a plan of strategy for how to handle the Democratic attacks on the war, which are now becoming strong and very partisan. We've got an opportunity because the various Democrats have taken different positions, Muskie calling for a pullout this year, the Democratic Policy Committee calling for a pullout by 1973, Jackson taking a hard line, Harriman not going quite as far out as Muskie. The P's point is that we ought to be able to posture ourselves for maximum gain on this, and exploit the differences within the Democratic Party. The question is whether we accept or jump on the Democratic Committee's position or maybe divide and hit it both ways. There's one huge flaw in it on the basis that they want to get everything out, including the POW's, but they overlooked the problem of how we get the POW's out, and there's obviously no way we can.

Friday, February 26, 1971

The K-Rogers thing goes on today, even though the State of the World is over with, now because of the Middle East. Henry persists in rushing in to the P and telling him we're about to get into a war in the Middle East. The P asks him what he wants to do about it. He doesn't have any ideas, except that he wants to take over. Says we need a scenario, etc. This stirred up quite a bit today; Henry had several sessions with the P between his various public events, and then the P saw Rogers later in the day, and then Rogers called to say he'd received the message from the Israelis that he had been expecting. The P told him to send it over, and then told me to have it routed through Henry, and to tell Henry that's what we were doing. So I did.

Had two public events over at the Residence today: George Bush's swearing-in this morning, which went rather routinely, and the Adams portrait presentation this afternoon, in which the P did a superlative job of reciting some obscure John Quincy Adams history and reading a poem written by Adams while he was in the Congress. All this came out of Carl Sandburg's *Abraham Lincoln,* which the P had been reading and found a couple of pages on Adams, which gave him some material that none of the writers had come up with, and that none of the other speakers on the program offered, so he did very well on that one.

Saturday, February 27, 1971
He got into considerable discussion on the general PR situation, questioning whether any of what we've done in the domestic area has really done any good. Also, he's starting to take the line again that things are pretty well set, so we might as well quit trying.

He then gets immediately back to trying to figure out how to handle the Laos ground action in Vietnam, taking on the networks, how to get more going on the Hill regarding Vietnam, and a long discussion of timing of TV press conferences, as to whether they should be every two weeks, every week, or what. Ziegler was in for part of this discussion. He also made the point that when Eisenhower left office there were no American ground forces or advisors in Vietnam, and no Americans had been killed in Vietnam. Eight years later, when Nixon came in, he found there had been two hundred thousand American casualties, for over forty thousand American dead. The Democratic administrations of the sixties got us into the war. The Nixon Administration is getting us out. If the Democrats want to fight the war issue on a partisan basis, this is the way they're going to have to take it. He wants Dole to take this on and for others to follow up, softening it, of course, by saying that we have a strong level of minorities of Democrats who support the P in his efforts, and that they deserve great credit, and then cite them.

The P at 3:00 all of a sudden ordered up a helicopter for Camp David and said he wanted me to go along, so I had to rush out and take off with him.

The Connallys are up here for the weekend, so the P had them plus John E, who came up for the dinner. It was Connally's birthday and we had a birthday cake, very pleasant, light-hearted dinner chat. The P selected *Around the World in 80 Days* as the movie because the Connallys hadn't seen it and he was sure they would be delighted with it, which they basically were. He was hysterical through it; as each scene was coming up, he'd say "You're going to love this particular part, or the scenery is just great, now watch this closely," and so on. He obviously has seen it time after time and knows the whole thing practically by heart. He also got a big kick, as did Connally, out of identifying the old stars as they appear in their bit parts.

Sunday, February 28, 1971
After a late breakfast the P called me over to Aspen at 11:00 for about a three-hour session. Connally, E, and I had a meeting in Laurel for a couple of hours after that, mainly discussing the whole PR question. Connally thinks that we should portray the P as a student of the Presidency, that we should recognize his weaknesses and let those be pointed out from time to time too, but make the strong point that he understands the uses of power. That Laos, and Cambodia, for example, are demonstrations of his perceptive use of power, and that we should get other illustrations. Also, his recognition of economic power, the mobilization of the government to use this power internationally. That he recognizes that the Marshall Plan concept is a thing of the past, that the Nixon Doctrine is a policy of power, that what he's doing is far-reaching in concept, that over a long-term basis he's laying a foundation.

Monday, March 1, 1971
Des Moines trip day. P didn't come to the office. He went right from the Residence to the helicopter. The Des Moines trip went well in general, especially the appearance before the State Legislature, which was a very good move, and the P did an excellent job. The only flaw was a fairly substantial number of quite militant demonstrators at the Capitol, who then came over to the hotel for the latter part of the day. They were chanting the usual obscenity and some pretty bad signs, etc. They appeared to be pretty much college age. They threw some rocks and other things before the P came out, but didn't

create any problem with him. It'll be interesting to see how the press plays it, and I'm sure they'll give it a pretty fair buildup, but it was not really that significant.

The other big news of the day was the bombing of some office areas in the Senate side of the Capitol. There had been earlier threats from the Weathermen, and they may very well have pulled this. The demonstrations in Iowa were basically SDS, and all of it could very well be part of a general plan, leading up to their April 24 demonstration and then their May Day plan to close down Washington.

He was obviously pretty tired on the way home and still had the dinner ahead of him, so tomorrow will be probably not too good a day. He's pushing for loading things into the schedule tomorrow, which doesn't seem to me to be a very productive idea since we're still shooting for the press conference on Thursday night. We may have to shift that because of Israeli developments.

Tuesday, March 2, 1971

The P went through some various reactions to Des Moines yesterday. He had read the news summary this morning, and of course all the reports were to the effect that the reception had been chilly, and not as enthusiastic as we had hoped. He made the point that we should be sure, for Rochester on Friday, that we have a big crowd and a lot of enthusiasm.

He did want us to get more intelligence on how the students had organized and how they had gotten there, trying to find out why our intelligence had not told us about this ahead of time.

The big flap today was a speech Symington gave on the Senate floor, about Henry K and executive privilege, blasting Henry for refusing to testify and in the process really cutting Rogers on the basis that he didn't amount to anything and that all the power was in K, etc. Apparently there was also a colloquy on the House floor that was equally tough on Rogers. Bill called in regard to this, and felt we had to move on it quickly. The P talked to him on the phone and then got Ziegler in and worked out a statement, (which) Rogers actually watered down substantially from what the P was willing to say.

Then, after the day's schedule, at about 5:00, E was still in the P's EOB office, and the P called me over. The three of us had a long discussion about the whole Rogers-K problem, trying to figure out whether there's any solution. John feels that it's reached the point where it is actually insolvable, and that one or the other has probably got to go. He feels that Henry's at a point emotionally where, when one of these things hits, he's going to come charging in and quit before he actually even realizes what he's doing, and that once he does so, it will be too late, there won't be any more we can do about it. I question whether this is likely to happen but I guess it might. The P made the point several times that the price that he has to pay to K in terms of emotional drain on himself is very great.

Wednesday, March 3, 1971

The big problem is still the K-Rogers situation. *(P)* repeats again his recognition that Henry is more valuable than Rogers, and as he evaluates Rogers, he is being more realistic than he has been sometimes in the past, recognizing that Bill doesn't have nearly the loyalty that Henry does. The P made the point, for example, that if we got to the stage where somebody had to fall on a sword in order to save the P, Henry would do it, but Rogers wouldn't. I made the point that I agreed with that, but that if Henry did do it, he would do it with loud kicking and screaming and make sure the blood spurted all over the place so he got full credit for it, but he would go ahead and do it, whereas Rogers would find a way to avoid it and get someone else stuck.

Henry says he called Rogers this morning and said that the two of them should get together and make sure they have a unified front in the face of this latest attack *(by Senator Symington and the House the day before)*. Rogers told him he just didn't have time to get together. Rogers told me basically the same thing later today, and said he would get together with Henry, but didn't think there was much point in it.

Thursday, March 4, 1971

Press Conference day. The P spent the whole day over at EOB working on his briefing book, did call several times on the phone but I didn't see him at all during the day. He decided, as usual, not to use makeup, and then backed out under Carruthers' urging and agreed to go ahead and do it. He fully recognizes the importance of covering Laos adequately tonight and talked about it considerably during the day with an understanding that he's got to get the point across of why we're there and what we're trying to do. As it turned out, he did this beautifully in the press conference.

We got the results of our poll, which I gave him, showing his popularity down to 48. This bothered him a little bit, but he felt it was good for us to get this, because if not we wouldn't have learned how useless our domestic programs are. He feels we need a much more skeptical attitude regarding the importance of domestic programs, and that we must have the P seen on TV more often in the things the people are interested in. He feels that we also have to consider whether there's a possibility that maybe the people just don't like our domestic programs, and look at the way Reagan romped on welfare as being maybe a better way of going at this than we have.

He agreed to the cancellation of Rochester tomorrow after we got weather reports indicating blizzard conditions and a very difficult situation trying to get in there. That's a real break for us because there were threats of some major demonstrations by both hard hats and students, and this was a good way to get out of it.

Friday, March 5, 1971

No regular schedule today because of the plan for going to Rochester, which was canceled yesterday. The P called a mini-NSC meeting this morning on short notice, and that took up a good chunk of the morning. All in all it worked out to a darn good day of activity and gave him a chance to get some follow-up on last night. He was obviously very tired today. He apparently didn't sleep very well last night.

He was particularly charged up about a reaction to CBS's counterattack on war coverage. We should now pick an enemy and go with him, and that the networks should be it. He thinks we've got a lot to gain from doing this at this point, particularly on Cambodia and Laos coverage.

Monday, March 8, 1971

The day of our big Senior Staff Dinner with John Connally. The P started out by calling me in first thing this morning, so I missed the staff meeting. *(An)* interesting item of the day was the plan for the meeting with the ladies of the press on Mrs.

Nixon and women's roles generally.

K came in late this afternoon following up on an earlier visit by Haig regarding the problem of the State Department meeting on the Middle East. The question now is what to do about Rogers' attempt to get around the NSC system. Originally Rogers had scheduled the meeting for today in preparation for the NSC on Wednesday. Today's meeting was to discuss one segment of the situation regarding the Suez Canal *(which was still closed)*. Then today he canceled that meeting, which Henry was not going to attend, but was going to send Haig instead. Rogers set another meeting formally for tomorrow to discuss the entire Middle East *(peace)* settlement situation, prior to the NSC meeting on Wednesday with the P. Henry feels that he can't possibly attend such a meeting because if he ends up in agreement with Rogers' position, then he and Rogers will confront the P with a lack of options. Henry's standard rule always is not to take a position and to force all the options out before making a recommendation. This maneuver of Rogers' makes that impossible. Henry's view, in light of that, is that he has no option but to confirm to the P that he's going to leave in December. The P can then back him all the way, knowing in his own mind, although it would not be publicly known, that the thing will come to an end at a time certain. I don't exactly understand Henry's reasoning on this, but that's the point he takes.

Tuesday, March 9, 1971

The big thing of the day was K's decision to finally confront the P with his plan for resignation, which he actually did. The P told him, according to Henry, that he would not discuss the matter at all with him at this time, there were too many important things involved and we just couldn't even consider it, that we have to get to it later on. In the late afternoon, P had E stay after a meeting with Shultz and then called me in. After some hemming and hawing about other things, told us about Henry's situation, and we had quite a long talk, making all of us late to dinner. The upshot of which is that we didn't really come to a conclusion on how to handle it, but all of us feel that Henry's taking this action may purge him of his internal problems and make it easier to deal with him and the whole thing.

Thursday, March 11, 1971
The main feature of the day was the law speech to the American Judicial Council in Williamsburg. We choppered down
and back. The trip went pretty well, no major problems, a few
demonstrators, but we had enough of a crowd of our own
people that they didn't get any play.

K was in for a session this afternoon also after we returned.
He got into some detail on Laos, where he's concerned that
the Vietnamese now have decided to pull out as quickly as
they can because they're afraid that the North Vietnamese are
massing for a big attack and that their guys are going to get
trapped and slaughtered. Henry is most anxious that if there's
any way we can hang in for another three weeks or so, that
we do so, because they can inflict so much more damage and
buy so much more time for us down the road. The problem,
of course, is that if it's a real disaster, it'll hurt Thieu politically, and we can't afford to let that happen either. They're
sending Haig over on Sunday to check the whole thing out,
and hopefully to get the South Vietnamese to hang in for three
to four weeks. If they do, we can then time the removal of
ARVN from Laos to the P's April troop-withdrawal statement
and make it all into one big "ending-the-war" type deal. They
also got into the Middle East on Henry's concern that we
should not try to go for a comprehensive solution. We rather
should work on it bit by bit.

He thinks that we can get more done that way and that it
can be more effective in dealing with the Russians. His point,
however, is that it's got to be worked out on the basis of trust
with Israel, and that the Israelis don't trust anybody except the
P. Therefore the P will have to meet with Rabin and work it
out, and then send a letter to Mrs. Meir.

Henry and the P then got into another chapter in their running discussion of WW II German generals. The P has read
one of Churchill's histories of the war recently and has become
a great expert on the relative merits of the various German
generals, a subject which, of course, Henry dearly loves to
discuss.

The other major item today was Lockheed's problems. The
P had a meeting with Connally and has agreed with his recommendation to go ahead and try to save Lockheed. We're
giving up on Rolls-Royce and letting them collapse; we'll have
to do it all here in the United States. So the P agreed that

Connally should remain in charge of this, that Flanigan should be the White House man on it, and of course Packard at Defense. He made the point that we've got to pump in whatever money is necessary to save Lockheed, and that we can justify it on the use of Federal money because if Lockheed collapsed, we'd have as much of a loss in tax revenue as the cost would be to us of propping Lockheed up at this point. This will be a ticklish maneuver and it will be interesting to see how Connally does in running it.

Friday, March 12, 1971

David's commencement exercises from OCS *(Officers' Candidate School)* at Newport. We flew up in the morning with the family. The P delivered the address, which was extremely good. The only fly in the ointment up there was a gathering of some eight or nine hundred hard hats and Catholics who were combined in some sort of protest. The P wasn't even aware of it, but it got thoroughly covered, of course, on the TV news.

After we got to Florida, he called a couple of times, got very upset because unfortunately he saw the CBS news coverage of the Newport affair and didn't like it very well, so he wanted a lot of action taken; he wanted me to call Colson, Magruder, etc., which I did, but it was a good thing because he called later to check up on them.

Tuesday, March 16, 1971

Pretty full day from a schedule viewpoint, with the Irish Prime Minister arrival and meeting this morning plus a number of other miscellaneous appointments, Cabinet meeting this afternoon, and some other odds and ends. The P managed to stay pretty heavily involved. I sent in to the P a letter from Moynihan that got him fairly disturbed because it made the point that businessmen are very upset with the Administration and its policy of repression. That they're getting this feeling from their children, and that we don't adequately have a program for active defense on the part of businessmen who are with the Administration. He was obviously quite startled by the news of Tom Dewey's death and is planning to go to the funeral if we can work it out Saturday or late Friday. He feels that it's important for him to go, especially since he's doing the Whitney Young funeral tomorrow.

Wednesday, March 17, 1971

Whitney Young's funeral. We left fairly early. The plane loaded with black leaders and a few top staff people. The P did a superb job in his ad lib eulogy.

He spent a good bit of time this afternoon on the phone talking to various people. In talking to Safire, he became very disturbed because Bill was making the point that the P is seeing a lot more people and talking a lot more openly now as part of a PR plan to improve his image. He, of course, is very distressed that anybody would suggest this, and particularly distressed that Safire would think it was a good idea to push this kind of a line. He's terribly anxious that we not let out the idea that we're changing our PR approach, adding a lot of interviews and that sort of thing, to try and hustle things. He feels Safire needs the facts so that he isn't in the danger of building stories on a myth. Actually, Bill agrees and recognizes that we have stepped up our activity, the press knows we have, and they're going to write that we have. So we should try to turn that around to a plus rather than pretending that it doesn't exist.

The fascinating point that the P raised was the observation of the enormous uplifting effect of the Clay-Frazier fight. It had the chemistry and drama that really lifted public spirits. The P feels that people need to be caught up in a great event and taken out of their humdrum existence.

Tricia's engagement announcement and the rest of the party last night apparently went very well. Got extremely good press today, and ought to carry us with the excitement of it and so forth through the summer period. In fact, this may be one of the event-type things that the P's talking about, if we can take advantage of it properly.

Thursday, March 18, 1971

After considerable discussion and weighing of other alternatives, the P decided to drop his plan for an in-office press conference tomorrow. He felt it would undercut the Howard K. Smith interview Monday night, and makes the point that even a one-network TV deal is worth a hundred times the writing press all put together.

Henry was in for a while and reported that he had received a long proposal from Dobrynin today on the proposed Berlin settlement, which is still not in form to be satisfactory to us, but it's getting much closer apparently, and Henry thinks maybe there's something workable that can be developed from it.

> Negotiations had been going on for a year with the Soviets about ways to ease transit between East and West Berlin, and otherwise defuse the tensions of the divided city.

The full House voted on SST today and defeated it, which is something of a blow, but there's still a chance of saving it in the Senate, where it will now go.

> The P wanted the U.S. to build a Supersonic Transport plane, like the Concorde, but Federal funds were required and there was Congressional opposition.

Saturday, March 20, 1971

The P's at Camp David. He was very much interested in the report on the reaction to the VP's dinner last night with John Connally and the Cabinet. Don said that it had gone very well. It was a relaxed, friendly kind of meeting, with a knitted feeling that the Cabinet was much groupier than they have been before, and it was a very different kind of meeting from those they've had in the past. He said it started a little as a bitching session but shifted to the positive, and compared to previous gatherings, was definitely the best.

The introduction was very skillfully done by the VP, as he led into Connally's remarks. They got into quite a discussion of the election.

The P also raised the question of the need to really ride herd on the plans for Tricia's wedding and the handling of the events leading up to it. He wants to be sure that we take a hard look at everything. A lot of people will be interested in what's going on, and the P asked me to set up a system to make sure that things get in to us before decisions are made, so that we have control, ostensibly in the P's name. So we'll set that up.

Monday, March 22, 1971

The Howard K. Smith interview on ABC at 9:30 tonight. The P spent the entire day at the EOB getting ready. He didn't call me over at all during the day. The interview went extremely well on TV; staff reaction was very good. It was too late at night to get our usual round-the-country reaction wrap-ups, but we'll get those tomorrow.

Tuesday, March 23, 1971

The P had a pretty heavy schedule through the day, with the Leadership Meeting this morning, a number of groups through the day, and a small dinner tonight with Heatherington on the Voluntary Action project. At midday, while Henry and I were in, he did get into a general review of Laos. As Henry wrapped it up, it comes out as clearly not a success, but still a worthwhile operation. Both he and the P feel that they were misled by Abrams on the original evaluation of what might be accomplished, and that Abrams went ahead with his plan even though it was clear that it wasn't working. Henry feels strongly that they should have followed Westmoreland's advice and gone south to cut off the Ho Chi Minh trail instead of going in to capture Chapone, which was a visible objective but turned out to be basically a disaster. They concluded that they should pull Abrams out, but then the P made the point that this is the end of the military operations anyway, so what difference does it make.

On March 18, the ARVN began a strategic retreat from Laos, but the air support was poor, the enemy offensive was strong, and some soldiers panicked, jumping on the skids of the evacuation helicopters, and clinging there. Mediawise it was terrible.

Wednesday, March 24, 1971

The SST vote was this afternoon and we lost, in spite of the P's efforts. He obviously was discouraged by the loss and feels that it's a real mistake to have let the thing go, but we really did do all that we could do.

Thursday, March 25, 1971

The P reversed his decision on canceling the California trip on the basis of strong recommendations of all the senior staff and then agreed to go ahead in spite of the fact that the weather's bad and he's not particularly pleased with the whole thought.

He got into some further discussion on Congressional relations, particularly the need to get a group of hard-core protagonists in the House and Senate. He feels we've got significant weaknesses in this area, and we need to pull it together and start getting things organized. He feels that the staff doesn't understand that we are in a continuous campaign. That all our people do a good job of running the government, but not much of a job of selling it, and he doesn't want to dawdle along anymore on it.

He made the point in musing over general schedule planning that maybe we should just scratch all the trivia on the schedule and only do the major things. This is a trend that comes up from time to time, and I think that it's something that he does seriously consider as a possibility. His other point is that the SST failure and the lack of strong initiative to get up and accomplish things may really mean the end of the American era.

Friday, March 26, 1971

A pretty well loaded day in Washington before departing for San Clemente, starting with breakfast for Albert, Boggs, and Ford, at which the P really laid out the line on the question of Congressional resolutions limiting the P's powers as Commander in Chief or requiring a withdrawal by a date certain. He hit them very hard on this and made the point very specifically that if the Congress in any way tied his hands, and as a result of that we had to bug out of Vietnam, losing American lives, or the Thieu government fell and Vietnam went to the Communists, he would have no choice but to go directly to the people in his campaign next year, taking on the Congress and blaming them for this situation. He had a Cabinet meeting on the subject of construction industry wage problems and so forth. He then had a few remarks at a conference of religious leaders on the drug problem, which he felt did him and the cause no particular good.

After we got here *(San Clemente),* he told Henry that he

wanted him and me to come over to talk with him at the house. He was up in the study with only one light on, the fire burning and the tape player going very loudly. He turned off the tape and we sat down. P now agrees with Henry's long-held view that there is a remote possibility of a settlement on Vietnam with Hanoi, probably partly as a result of Laos. The P clearly has sort of a mystic feeling about the Laotian thing, and says so. He's not sure what it is or why, but he has the feeling that there may be more involved here than has so far met the eye.

He then got into the point that he had called us in for, which was to say that he'd been giving a lot of thought to our whole strategic situation at the present time, and specifically as it related to our schedule here in California. His decision was that there would be no press conference this week; that it doesn't serve our purpose at this time to have one. There's nothing that he wants to say, and no advantage to making any news that might come up at such a conference. In other words, the basic rule is that we should never go to the press except when we're up; we've got nothing to gain now. The only argument for a press conference is for the benefit of the press, but we should have press conferences only when it serves our purposes.

He feels that Ziegler should announce on Thursday or Friday that he will be making the troop announcement on the 7th of April, rather than waiting until the 15th, using the rationale that he's committed to making it by the 15th, and since Congress will be gone at the time, he wanted to make it at the close of this Congressional session before the recess. The mood he has is a very mystic one, and he's not highly optimistic, but certainly not down in the dumps, and has the feeling that something is happening or is about to happen.

Saturday, March 27, 1971

The P was in early in the morning, still running on Eastern Time. Decided to definitely announce the troop statement on Tuesday, so as to precede the Democratic Caucus meeting on Wednesday. He wants a plan ready for countering the opposition, because they'll say this isn't enough and we've got to make sure that the issue is clear that it's a matter of ending the war; that it shows our Vietnamization success; and that it shows the value of Laos. He wants to hit this day in and day out and make the point that the opponents are asking for an American defeat instead of peace with honor. In other words they ask for defeat with dishonor and give aid and comfort to the enemy, etc.

He choppered up today to Sam Goldwyn's house for a presentation of the Medal of Freedom to Goldwyn, which was a great idea and went very well. Goldwyn was very much touched, the P made some good remarks, and Sam, who is basically paralyzed but is able to talk a little, turned to the P (or not turned, because he can't turn), but said to the P in a low voice after he'd hung the medal on him, "I'm glad you beat those bastards in '68; they were the worst bunch of sons of bitches we ever had in there." He then said louder, and it was heard by the press, that Nixon was his favorite president, that he was a good, strong fighter with guts, but that he always fought clean. Some pretty good quotes.

The P decided to drive back rather than taking the helicopter, and I rode with him as we went from Beverly Hills down to Santa Monica and all along the beach cities before cutting back into the freeway just before Long Beach. It was a long ride, and he chatted generally about his sort of fascination with the real world, as he rarely sees it, and the fact that there are so many small businesses. He was very interested in them as he drove along the streets. He was also sort of fascinated with the large number of hippie-type people on the streets. Of course, that wasn't too surprising, considering the part of town we were in. He went right to the residence when we got back, and stayed there for the rest of the day.

Tuesday, March 30, 1971

Another day with nothing planned except the Allen Drury interview and of course the news announcement of the plan to make the troop announcement next week.

The P went home at about 6:00 and called me right after he got there. He suggested that I come over for dinner. So I went up to the study, where he had the fire going and the record player blaring. We talked for about 15 minutes before Manolo served a delicious steak dinner with fried onion rings and a beautiful cheese soufflé. He talked about his concern of Tricia and Julie using government planes for their personal trips, and came up with the idea of having the Air Force charge him the commercial airline fare when they do use such planes, which is an ideal way to get around the sticky wicket there. He came up with the idea of trying to organize the administrative assistants and secretaries on the Hill that are for us, as a counterbalance to the predominant left-wing types. That led him into a question of how we can better charge up the White House staff, and he feels that maybe we need a weekly meeting when he gives them a little pep talk. This of course will last about one week, but it does come to mind every once in a while.

I managed to get out after two hours, and I think he went on down and went to bed. He was obviously in kind of a retrospective mood, and walked out with me to the car, sort of generally chatting along the way but nothing apparently particular on his mind. Some general thoughts as of the end of March: our position, looked at objectively, would appear to be at an all-time low at the present reading. The polls show us the lowest we've been: Gallup at 50, Harris showing a drop just the other day from 43 to 41. The credibility figure is way down, the rating on handling the Vietnam War is the lowest it's been, the magazines did one of their periodic "this week Nixon's in deep trouble" sort of orgies. The Laos withdrawal effect is at its peak, or bottom. In spite of this, the general attitude of all of the staff people, and certainly of the P, as well as most of the Cabinet members, seems to be very much upbeat, positive, and optimistic.

The reason probably is best expressed by the phone conversation I had with Bill Rogers yesterday, in which he reported on a talk he had with (Chicago Daily News *Washington Bureau Chief*) Peter Lisagor earlier in the day. Lisagor had raised the question with him that he couldn't understand why he seemed so happy and optimistic, and why everybody in the White House seemed to be the same way when it appeared to Lisagor that we were in serious trouble and getting worse. Rogers answered that the reason in his mind was that we know what we're doing and where we're going, and therefore are not concerned about the outlook. On the other hand, the press and perhaps the people at this point, don't know, and won't for a little while, so they take a more pessimistic view. Rogers went on to say that when we came in here two years ago we inherited a number of monumental problems, and now we're on the road to solution. All of this may be overoptimistic, but there are all kinds of potential optimistic factors that aren't even taken into consideration in it. At the very least, it would appear that the economy has bottomed out and is gradually inching back into a sound position, and that we're going to get out of the war one way or another, and we have a pretty fair chance of getting out honorably.

Looking beyond that, there are a number of monumentally optimistic possibilities. Henry definitely feels he's got the SALT thing lined up, and that we can announce that in a couple of weeks that will lead to a Summit, and a four-power meeting after that in the fall. We know that at some point not too far off, we'll be able to announce that no more draftees will be serving in Vietnam. Henry feels, and now the P concurs, that there's a 50/50 chance at least of getting a Vietnam settlement this summer and ending the war completely. The Berlin negotiations appear to be reaching some sort of productive possibilities. The economic situation could turn out to be substantially better than we think it is at the moment. Then of course there are all sorts of unforeseen possibilities on the bright side, as well as many on the dark side that could come up.

All in all, the outlook appears to be strongly balanced in our favor, and I think all of us feel it both rationally and intuitively, and that provides the basis for the optimism that everybody seems to have. Overall, the conclusion would be that probably this week, or this period of two or three weeks, will mark the low of the first term, and also that probably the troop announcement next week will be the basic turning point from which things will start moving upward.

Wednesday, March 31, 1971

The Democratic Caucus had their vote this morning on the question of pulling troops out of Vietnam. They got a reasonably good compromise through, and on the basis of that we had long discussions about how to handle a reaction and decided that our position should be that we were very pleased that they're supporting the goal of the P to end the war and get our prisoners released as soon as possible. It did avoid stating a specific time certain, and our particular victory was that they didn't put in a date of the end of 1971. They have called for end of involvement by the end of the 92nd Congress. We've turned it basically to a positive for us, and I think it will stick pretty well that way.

Later in the day, the House voted on the draft extension,

and we almost lost our two-year proposal to a one-year amendment.

The bigger thing today was the Calley decision, which was announced yesterday (or several days ago), of guilty, and then the sentence today of life in prison. The public reaction has been enormous, and all in favor of Calley and against the conviction. The question now is what the P should or should not do in reaction to this, as public opinion continues to mount. There's a number of varying views within the staff, and we still haven't gotten it figured out.

On March 29, 1971, an Army court-martial found First Lieutenant William Calley, Jr., guilty of the murder of 22 South Vietnamese civilians in 1968. Many felt the sentence was excessive. The case became a political football for the left and for the media.

Second Quarter: April–June

Thursday, April 1, 1971

Calley dominated the day today. The P started out with a 9:00 meeting with E and me to review the general situation and his conversation on the subject last night with Connally. He makes the point that the military is not concerned really with the honor of the military service, they're concerned with the system of which they're a part. He feels that there's not enough in it for us to fight for the military. The lawyers, on the other hand, provide no political gain for us in their argument. We do have to be for orderly process, but we've got to act on the basis of what does us the most good. He feels that maybe there's a position to be taken that an act of compassion on the part of the P wouldn't be a bad thing to do at this point. He feels that we've got to move now, making the statement that the P will review this in the appeal process and will order that he (Calley) be allowed to remain in an apartment.

He feels we've got to get it raised above this case. Make the point the war is bad, so we've got to avoid more bad wars. It's got to be dealt with not on the merits of the case; there is no reasonable doubt of his technical guilt, but there is doubt regarding the motive. It gets to the question of whether this man is a criminal who should be treated like Manson, and the answer is no.

At noon he made the point that if we don't move, the support we have for withdrawal from Vietnam, etc., will evaporate or become discouraged. We've got to keep our eye on the main ball, which is to maintain our public support. He feels that the question is, we either do something Monday or we temporize for a year or two. He thinks he can indicate that he's ordered the file out to study, and that he's ordered the General to release Calley to his apartment. He then picked up the phone and called Admiral Moorer and issued the order releasing Calley from the stockade. When he hung up, he made the comment that at least a P can do something once in a while. He then said of Admiral Moorer, "That's the one place where they say, 'Yes, sir,' instead of, 'Yes, but.' "

The P agrees with my feeling that he can't be in the position of going on television Wednesday night without taking any action regarding Calley. The general public reaction has been stupendous, and we can't simply ignore it. We left it up in the air for tonight, but we'll have to make a decision first thing tomorrow morning.

Friday, April 2, 1971
This turned out to be pretty much Calley day all day, as we worked on the whole question of the approach to further action. The P wanted to be sure that we got out the details regarding his decision yesterday to release him from the stockade. He referred to the Lincoln period, and his study of that history, and his idea that the presidents have this right but it must be exercised personally.

There was about a three-hour break for a meeting on welfare with Reagan, and then back to Calley considerations again. The P decided finally, after going through all the range of options, to take precisely the action that Dick Moore had recommended at the very beginning, that is, to announce now that he will review the case before the final sentence is imposed.

He reviewed with E the basis for making the announcement on this action. Wants him to make the point that he's consulted with the Attorney General and the Secretaries of Treasury, Defense, State, and HEW, and has received a lot of advice from them and other sources. Some said he should move now to free Calley or lighten the sentence, but he decided not to because this would be a derogation of the review process and he had learned that it would take two months before the trial record was even available. Others said he should not get involved at all, some of them even objected to his action yesterday.

Public opinion runs strongly on this. The awareness level of 96 percent is the highest we've gotten on any subject in any of our polls. With this whole thing behind him, he now plans to turn to the Wednesday night speech, and has had Buchanan come out tonight to get started on that.

Saturday, April 3, 1971

The P got to working on the speech this morning, and has changed substantially the approach that Henry was originally taking. He's going to go fairly quickly through the basic-detail stuff he has to cover regarding Vietnam, Laos, and the troop withdrawal, and then get more into a general approach to the situation that we now find ourselves in regarding the war, the need for national defense, and the general public attitude toward all of this.

Even though it was Saturday, and a sensationally beautiful day, the P stayed in the office all day, going over these things with me plus reviewing periodic speech drafts with Buchanan. This should get him in shape to take tomorrow off, and we'll see what happens.

Sunday, April 4, 1971

The P apparently stayed at the house most of the day. Went down to Red Beach in the afternoon with Bebe. He only called me once, and that was just to check on the news play, with which he was already basically familiar.

Monday, April 5, 1971

San Clemente and then to DC. Bill Rogers called this morning with some thoughts on the speech. He thought the P should consider, at the end, getting away from the text and speaking directly to the people, making the point that now the time has come to withdraw and that's what we're doing. The P had good sessions with Henry and John on the plane on the way back. He had me up for just a few minutes to go over some insignificant odds and ends that he had notes left on. And now we're back to the Washington grind.

The P called me late in the evening at home. He had just read the *Washington Star* report on Congressman *(Hale)* Boggs' attack on J. Edgar Hoover, and his call for Hoover's resignation. The P wanted me to call Hoover and tell him not to respond: to be silent and let his friends respond for him. I called Hoover, and he appreciated the whole thing very much. He told me that Boggs was drunk today when he made the attack, and that he (Hoover) had talked to the Attorney General, who had issued a statement demanding that Boggs repudiate his charges and deny all the allegations. Hoover also made the point to me that he had testified two weeks ago, and had said that since 1924 there had never been a phone tap on any senator or congressman, and that even when he had people under surveillance, he had lifted the surveillance when they went onto the Capitol grounds. I reported this back to the P, and he made the point that we should also use Johnson's influence on Boggs, that we should attack Boggs on his drunkenness and try to destroy him, and that we should release the ORC *(Opinion Research Corporation)* poll that we have on Hoover. He then made the comment that we will have an interesting week, and said goodnight.

Tuesday, April 6, 1971

He had me over first thing this morning, and obviously wanted to have a long chat. But I had to leave to go to Ann's school for Fathers' Day. We did get into a few items, and it turned out that what he wanted to talk about was his concern about jittery members of the staff. He feels that this is the time that we should ruthlessly weed out all of those who will not stand strongly behind us. He made the quote that "None of the staff are here because of what they did; they're here because of what I did—and therefore there's no reason for anybody on the staff to be strong in a tough time like this." He then stated very positively, "I shall not go forward with anyone who has shown weakness in this situation. I want them all weeded out within thirty days." He said the Cabinet is a different problem, and he doesn't quite know how to deal with that.

He said it's a question of those who are so emotionally disturbed about situations and serious events, that they'll have to desert us, and we can't give them that opportunity next year. We've got to weed them out now. He made the point that he didn't think I see this as clearly as he does, but wanted me to be thinking about it in any event. I left then because I was late for the trip to Ann's school.

This afternoon he had me over again and asked how everything was. He was in kind of an introspective mood. Discussed a few of the minor logistics regarding the speech and then settled back and said he wanted to read me the speech. He made the point that he was not showing me a copy so that I would be able to say I had not seen the speech, and use that as a backup argument for not letting anyone else see it. He then read it through quite quickly. He feels it will run 18 to 20 minutes as it's now written, but it only took him 12 minutes to read it to me, even stopping to make a few notes from time to time. It comes off very well and makes the case exactly as he should. It's my view, at least, that it will be pretty successful in accomplishing what he's after. He had the OAS white-tie dinner tonight. All of the key staff were at the Finches' for dinner as a sort of farewell party before they and the Rumsfelds leave on their European trip.

Wednesday, April 7, 1971

The day of the latest Vietnam speech. The P spent the whole day at the EOB working on the speech. He had a session with Laird and Rogers at noon and then a bipartisan Leaders Meeting at 7:00 to brief them on his withdrawal announcement plans. He had me come over a couple of times for general conversation as he had his drafts finished and was sort of relaxing. At one session, while Henry was there, he said he was going to let me in on the secret part of the speech, the ad-lib closing, and he then read me, from his yellow pad, his notes for the closing. As it turned out, they were almost verbatim what he used on the speech, and he obviously had been working very hard on putting them together. They related to the Medal of Honor incident when the little boy saluted him.

The general reaction to the speech was extremely good, especially to the closing segment because of its emotional quality. There is, of course, considerable disappointment and concern because the withdrawal rate (of 100,000 troops) has not stepped up far enough, nor is there any fixed terminal date, but the sincerity, conviction, and basic emotion of the P's presentation seemed to override this with most people, and I think overall we'll end up with a very positive plus.

In the middle of the day I got the poll report from our interview on Monday and Tuesday, and it came out extremely well. The P's up from 41 to 54 in approval, so, although he had told me he didn't want to see the poll before the speech, I decided he ought to know about it and went over and gave him the results, which of course cheered him up considerably.

The Calley case popped up again this morning in the form

of a release of a letter to the P from Captain Daniel, the prosecutor, which created a substantial flap. He feels that the prosecutor must have had higher clearance in order to have made this overt move. He was also distressed that E didn't go out and answer this head-on, but John talked him out of it on the grounds that it was a one-day story, and that would only accelerate it. I'm not really sure that's the case.

Later in the afternoon we had a long general talk about Connally and staff and so on, the P's dissatisfaction with the Cabinet primarily about the fact that none of them had called him up before the speech to wish him well or anything of that sort. The reason, of course, is that he's never encouraged that kind of thing, and none of them feel they can call him up. In any event, he expressed considerable disappointment in this situation, and then got to talking about Connally and the VP, and revealed his thought that the way out of the whole deal is to have the VP resign later this year, which then gives the P the opportunity to appoint a new VP under the new law of succession. This subject to a majority approval of both houses of Congress. He would then appoint Connally, which would set him up for succession and probably would work out extremely well. He was up late tonight and on the phone to me even after I got home, three or four times, in the usual follow-up kind of activity. Even though he said he wouldn't take any calls, he did take a number of them and made several himself.

Thursday, April 8, 1971
The main effort today was speech follow-up. The reaction based on last night was overall very good and I think we accomplished what we were after and I think the P feels that way too. He did have Henry and me in early this morning, and made the point that only the two of us had stood up, and that he would never forget it. He also would never forget the fact that no one else did stand up, and he would keep that in mind as time went on. He was fairly emotional on the point and obviously feels quite strongly about this. He still has a very strong feeling that there is a lack of moral support, both in the Cabinet and in the staff, and that he has no use for weak men and that's really what we've got.

He was very pleased with the way he worked the emotional

part into the speech, and thinks that's what really made it, and of course, he's absolutely right.

Friday, April 9, 1971

We got into quite a discussion with Ziegler this morning on several PR items, particularly the Calley question as a result of the problem of the letter from the prosecutor, *(Captain)* Daniel. The P now feels that E should not have answered the questions regarding the Calley case when he announced the P's decision to review it. He feels we have to educate our people not to be responsive, and to recognize that a briefing is not for the benefit of the press.

He hit me on making sure that we don't appoint any more establishment people to any commissions, etc. He wants to go for Midwest, Southern, and Western people, and not pick up any more Eastern establishment types.

In the afternoon we went to Good Friday church services at St. John's, across from Lafayette Park. All was worked out on the basis of a last-minute run, but somehow someone got the word, and when we arrived there were a half-dozen minister types standing out in front, shouting, "Peace now!" The P went in and remained for the twenty-minute service, and then, as he went out a different door, the demonstrators had gathered there and were chanting again, this time something about Christ died to save men's lives or something. The P's reaction was of course that he would not go to Gettysburg for Easter services, since it had been announced he was going, and that would just set off more demonstrations. So we had to work out a plan for canceling that and setting up an unannounced trip to Thurmont for Easter services. Left for Williamsburg at 4:00. The P left for Camp David at 5:00 to join his family there for the Easter weekend.

Monday, April 12, 1971

Back to a regular schedule at the office. We started our new 8:15 staff meeting setup in the Roosevelt Room, and it all went reasonably well considering it was the first day. The P had me in at 9:00 and went through an hour of odds and ends that he had stacked up over the weekend. A lot of notes, mainly regarding some schedule changes.

P got into the question also of talking to Mitchell about Hoover. He feels that with the *Star* editorial calling for Hoo-

ver's resignation and the other pressures that are mounting,
that we're going to have to move on it. The P talked to Hoover
over the weekend, and he had told the P he would be happy
to resign whenever the P or the Attorney General felt that he
should. The P feels that we've got to work something out on
this, and do it fairly soon. Maybe the best idea would be to
have Hoover retire on his 77th birthday, which is January 1.
Another point on Hoover was that he got to thinking it would
be a good idea to have a Congressional letter of support of
Hoover so we can build up some strength before we let him
resign. Obviously he can't resign now under pressure, so
we've got to do something to shore him up, in order to get
him out.

Late this afternoon the P had Henry and me in, just a little
talk before he went home for dinner. He reported on his
meeting with Rogers, and Henry seemed to be pleased with
that. He then got into a general talk about China policy; all
of them very pleased because of the Ping-Pong exchange
which may be a good lead-in to our trade announcement on
Wednesday.

> We had been pursuing an opening to China through several
> channels for two years now, but this was a totally unexpected
> breakthrough: an American table tennis team competing in the
> world championship in Japan had been invited to play several
> exhibition matches in China. It was a typically subtle Chinese
> move, and would usher in the age of "Ping-Pong diplomacy."
> The Wednesday announcement was an already-planned ter-
> mination of our trade embargo with China.

The happenstance that the P met today with the Chinese
Ambassador, and also with Anna Chennault, should make the
press sit up and wonder what we're up to, and could be kind
of intriguing. Henry feels that our whole policy, and the current moves on China, will help to shake the Soviets up, as will
Brezhnev's need to make a big peace move of some kind,
which should play in our favor for a SALT agreement and a
Summit conference.

The big thing now is to make sure we get credit for all the
shifts in China policy, rather than letting them go to the State
Department, who of course had nothing to do with it, in fact

opposed every step the P took because they were afraid any moves toward China would offend Russia.

Tuesday, April 13, 1971
A reasonably busy day for the P. After a general discussion of odds and ends this morning, he got Henry in and, in comparing his problems to those of previous P's, mentioned that he had Henry up to the Lincoln Room for dinner last night and that had gotten him to thinking, as they were talking there, about the many problems that other P's had, and certainly some of them had been great. Ours were probably more substantial than anyone except Lincoln, whose problems overshadowed everyone's by a wide margin. He commented on the point that Lincoln had the cannons in the street in New York to shoot draft resisters; that he had a rebellious Cabinet; Stanton wouldn't speak to him; his wife's insanity and her two brothers killed in the Southern side of the war, etc. All of those, added up, make our situation look pretty simple. He then got into a discussion of China policy, arising partly out of Scali's recommendation that we do something to recognize the United States Ping-Pong team when it comes back from the tour in China. The thought here is that we're making some progress, but we can't start claiming any success or doing any public events such as that because it will get in the way of future progress.

E and I had a brief meeting with him on the Hoover question. John Mitchell had called E to say that Hoover has sent a memo around to the top members of the Bureau, telling them not to route their domestic intelligence information to *(Assistant Attorney General Robert)* Mardian, which is directly contrary to our orders, and also implying that, at the direct order of the P, Hoover has been doing some wiretapping and other high-level surveillance. Neither of these is true, and John wanted to check them out with the P for the Attorney General so he'll know how to approach the situation.

He had a fairly long meeting with Connally and called me right afterward, started to report it on the phone and then asked me to come over to the office. He obviously was very pleased with the talk. Connally feels the problem is that our people don't hit anybody, and that we've got to do that. He also made the point again of the failure to show personal concern, no warmth, no human qualities, and that this has to come from the little things, because you can't do it in the big appearances.

The real question posed is whether we change the P's own approach to the press conferences and interviews and so forth, to try to add emotion and warmth to them. He does feel that he can try to get some more schmaltz into the speeches; make them warm instead of brittle, make the anecdotes warm and find a way to work them in.

They discussed Agnew, and Connally feels that he can survive if he stays on his present course and doesn't go overboard. The P doesn't agree. He's told me to have a private talk with Connally regarding the Vice Presidency, and start getting him built up and ready for it. He agreed with the idea of considering moving Stans to Finance Chairman and putting a strong spokesman into the Commerce slot.

Wednesday, April 14, 1971

He got into quite a long discussion again this morning on the PR situation regarding Connally's point, which really differs from what other people are saying. He feels that the real problem, apart from what the P does, is that the Cabinet and staff don't have any passion, they don't show any commitment to the P and his policies. It has to be more than just reciting the facts, they've got to cry, be outraged, etc.

He had Henry in at midday. The China plan was discussed in some detail. We were reviewing the background of the P's initiatives on this, going clear back to his article for *Foreign Affairs,* which laid it out even before the campaign began *(this 1967 article discussed the importance of relations between the U.S. and China),* and then a number of his speeches and other actions since then. The whole Asian tour, of course, was basically focused on opening lines to China, particularly with the meetings with Yahya and Ceausescu. *(Presidents Yahya Khan of Pakistan and Ceausescu of Romania were two of our channels to China.)*

Thursday, April 15, 1971

Still bouncing on the stock market rise yesterday and the continuing rise today.

He got back on the general PR question again, the point that we've not created a mythology, that the courage, boldness, and guts hasn't come across. We haven't made the point that it's not true that everything is political. He feels that the most important factor in the first two years is guts, and that we've got to get that across. He also got into the POW wives question while Henry was there, because of Dole's report yesterday that they're pretty shaky, and that we've got to do something dramatic to keep them on track. The P told Henry to see the wives this week and to work out something with them that will buy us three months' time, because we can't afford to let them come unglued at this point, while everything else is going so well. The P met with the Prime Minister of Morocco today, who came all the way over just to tell him that the King couldn't come next week. As a result of this, the P's thinking about State visits and come up with the decision that there will be no State visits in 1972.

Saturday, April 17, 1971

The P was in early this morning because of a long series of morning meetings on foreign trade.

Apparently Pat Nixon was sick last night to the point that after examination at the White House they took her to the hospital for X rays. They had feared it might be a collapsed lung, but it turns out to be a minor pleurisy problem, and she seems to be at least resting comfortably today. The P got into a review of the ASNE last night *(his appearance at the American Society of Newspaper Editors)*. We talked about the questions and that kind of thing; his reaction was that the editors hadn't done too well on their questioning, and he was glad that the thing hadn't been on TV. He was pretty funny in commenting on the first question, in which the editor asked him if he ever woke up at 2:00 or 3:00 in the morning and what he thought about at such a time. The P had answered it saying he thought about working for peace and so on. He said this morning he wished he had answered with what he really wanted to say, which was he thought about going to the bathroom just like everybody does when he wakes up in the middle of the night.

After the morning appointments we had a long, typical Saturday-afternoon gab session. Henry was in for a good part of it, and some of the discussion was on China, in fact, most of it. Henry feels that what makes the P so formidable in his dealings with the Communists is the fact that he has turned their theory of protracted war against them, and apparently the Communists have that same feeling. He wanted to give some thought to letting the Ping-Pong team come in, just as another hypo to the fact that this was what was done. Henry's basically opposed to that, and doesn't want to overplay the China thing until we get something more going.

We had a long discussion of our long-range strategy regarding SALT and Defense and the Soviet ABM, making the point that we have to get some of these things done in order to break the back of the present establishment Democratic leadership. But that we can't do much about building a strong defense for the United States during this term because Congress won't support us. What we have to do is get reelected and then move into the defense setup at that time.

Another point that was made was that the whole China thing has given us maneuvering room with the Russians because now we're not backed against the wall. The problem now is that we've got to avoid making too much hay out of China, because they might pull the rug out from under us and we don't want to get our neck out that far. The P's concerned that we still keep the heat on the opposition; they've all joined with us on the China thing, and that, in a way, is not as good as when they opposed us, such as in Laos. Teddy Kennedy is scheduling hearings this week, and the P feels we need to get Rogers to testify up there and really hit them. He also wanted to check on whether Hubert, Teddy, or Muskie had made any statement regarding China. As far as any of us could remember, they had not.

We also talked a little about McCloskey, and I filled the P in on McCloskey's tirades and temper tantrums in Laos. It would seem that he's really not very stable or rational, and this is something we may be able to take advantage of. We're set to counteract whatever McCloskey comes up with on his TV interview tomorrow.

Monday, April 19, 1971

The main item this morning was reaction to McCloskey, who was on the Sunday television yesterday attacking us on bombings in Laos. The P told me to order State to have Sullivan take McCloskey on and knock him off. The question is whether Rogers should also do so. The point is that State's under attack on this, and it's up to them to counter it. The P does have mixed feelings on the McCloskey thing, and wants to be careful not to build him up. He points out that you must not give a demagogue too much attention. We at the White House should soar above this and not get into it.

He had a very upbeat feeling as a result of church yesterday. The Texas A & M choir came through the line, told him they were all for him, ready to go to Vietnam, etc. He makes the point that this is the audience we should speak to. He choppered down to Williamsburg for the Governors' Conference; did an excellent job on welfare reform in his talk there.

Tonight was the DAR, and that went very well, although the speech wasn't particularly outstanding. The highlight really was seeing a DAR convention, because it looked exactly like a DAR convention; they were all in their pastel formals with their official sashes across the front, and looked exactly like the little old ladies of the DAR should look. He got a good reception; gave a good upbeat speech. Everybody's in general agreement now that things are going much better and that we should take exactly that attitude on a very positive basis and not let the constant sniping bother us.

Tuesday, April 20, 1971

The P had a pretty busy day, starting with the leaders at 8:00, then agricultural editors, the Jaycee leadership, the President of the International Red Cross, a session with Shultz, session with Hardin and Lincoln on the Texas drought, meeting with the Attorney General, and a meeting with our pro-Nixon senators in the Cabinet Room. In between these, he had me in five or six times for fairly extensive sessions, adding up to 14 pages of notes. One item of concern was Bill Rogers' plans for extending his trip next week to include Israel and Egypt and a couple of other Middle East stops. This of course has Henry going right up the wall. He's opposed to the whole idea of Rogers getting into the Middle East, as always, and particularly doesn't think he should go there, but the P confirmed that he had told him he could. Henry then raised the specter of Rogers probably coming up with a proposal for going to the Soviet Union, and the P said absolutely no on that without any equivocation at all.

The next big item of the day was a rather weird, off-the-record press deal that the VP had Sunday night in Williamsburg. Apparently, after midnight he called nine press people to his suite and spent three hours in an off-the-record backgrounder with them, during which he expressed his disagree-

ment with the idea of letting down the barriers with China and
his extreme dissatisfaction with the press reporting of the Chinese Ping-Pong tour. K said that he had sent Haig to brief the
VP Friday on China. The P wants him now to get off this
wicket and say he was completely misunderstood. K had recommended that Ziegler say that the VP's expressing his personal view. But the P disagreed with that, and agreed with
Ron's recommendation that he say that the VP's authorized
him to say that there is no difference on the part of the VP
with the P's policy on China. The VP completely agrees with
the initiatives the P has taken. He says it's clear that he doesn't
understand the big picture in this whole Chinese operation,
which is, of course, the Russian game. We're using the Chinese thaw to get the Russians shook. Dobrynin will be back
later this week, and Henry will get a reading on how it's working.

Henry also raised the point of the need now to get a direct
channel to deal with the Chinese, and is thinking of the idea
of sending *(General Vernon)* Walters to Warsaw to set up the
communications. The P got again to the point that Agnew
shows qualities here that are very damaging. He wants me to
talk privately to Connally, and to move very, very slowly; but
to start getting him with it, in this area of possible Vice Presidential candidate.

The next thing to come along was the Supreme Court's
unanimous ruling on school desegregation, which is apparently
quite a milestone decision and knocks down the P's neighbor-
hood school idea and upholds busing for the purpose of desegregation. The P spent considerable time with Ron, and later
with the Attorney General, working out the precise wording
of how Ron should handle it. He obviously was very much
concerned about the decision, and feels that we've got to be
very careful in what we say. After a lot of discussion, they all
agreed that we would make the point that now that the Court
has acted, it's the law of the land and therefore it's the obligation of the local school authorities and the district courts,
which have jurisdiction in these matters, to carry out the mandate of the court. He doesn't want Ron to go any further than
that.

He then made the point that he wanted E to get Richardson
in, and ordered him that HEW is not to do anything except
what is specifically required by the law. They are not to take

the initiative, they are not to get out in front and charge. He
wants to be sure that there's an absolute order to them on
this; that they don't screw us on the court decision. He wants
to kill the idea of any philosophy of our getting credit for the
decision, or getting out in front of the court on it. We go
straight down the line, and not one step beyond the law. He
decided to have a meeting with the Attorney General and
Richardson and E in the morning to lay the law down on this

Wednesday, April 21, 1971

Another busy day for a Wednesday. Most of the morning spent
working on the desegregation business. Then a session with
the head of the Ping-Pong team that toured China. *(P)* also
greeted the 4-H Club group who were here, and was extremely
impressed with them and invited them out to look at the Rose
Garden and remarked several times, as the day went on, what
a fine group they are.

At 4:00 Mitchell and I had a two-hour meeting with him
on politics. John did a good job of stalling on any commitments by giving him a general rundown on how he's starting
to put the political organization together, but strongly making
the point that he's still just putting the players together and
that he doesn't want to get locked into anything until he's got
the whole deal thought out. The P wants us to start polling
the key states, particularly to measure the effect of how we
stand with Wallace in or out, in those states. He covered a
lot of specific items on individual people and individual states
where action needs to be taken. As we were adjourning
Mitchell used the opportunity to zing in on the E order telling
him to stop his ITT antitrust action. He got the P to wave off
on that.

The Justice Department had lost an antitrust suit against International Telephone and Telegraph, and were now appealing.
The P was not a fan of antitrust suits and ordered them to stop,
but Mitchell explained there would be personnel problems if
he did, so P withdrew his objection. As it happened, the case
was settled favorably for the government, but we would hear
a lot more about it in 1972.

Thursday, April 22, 1971

The P had three major meetings today, and had me sit in on each of them. One with Dole and Anne Armstrong, one with John Connally, and one with Bill Rogers.

In the Dole meeting, other than a general political discussion, Anne Armstrong asked the P how he answers the question of how to deal with youth, and how we should approach this problem. He made some very interesting points: we've got to give them a challenge, we can't let them escape responsibility for themselves and blame their problems on external factors. We can't let them think solely of self, any more than a nation can think solely of itself. They've got to explore the unknown. They have to do something. He diverted for a minute to say that the United States should be first in the world because we will use that position to help others and to maintain the peace, to do good, rather than to do evil, to help rather than to harm others. Back to the dealing with youth: we should be understanding of upper- and middle-class parents because they really do have great problems with their kids because they've been given so much. It's a mistake to think that the way to greatness is to make it easy to get there. For instance, the two greatest nations in the world today (other than the United States) are Japan and Germany, and they became so because they were defeated nations that had to rise up by their own bootstraps. He said we must not destroy the character of children by permissiveness—permissiveness that denies the child the opportunity to look in a mirror and finally realize that the problem is me— not my teachers, not the war, not the environment, but me. It was a fascinating insight; he got quite absorbed in it and made these points very strongly.

He also told Anne the story, as he had Henry earlier, of how his mother had to support his older brother while they were in Prescott, Arizona, and he was recovering (actually, he died) from tuberculosis; and in order to finance living over there, his mother took in three other tuberculosis patients, all of whom were also terminal cases, and nursed all of them, with Mrs. Nixon providing the full care. The two stories together made quite an impression, I think, on Anne Armstrong, and she's going to use the points in her appearances.

The meeting with Rogers this afternoon was to cover the points that needed to be covered before he took off on his trip. It went very well, and there was nothing of any great substance; I had written a memo for the P's file on the specifics. In general, Rogers made the point that he doesn't think there's going to be a war in the Middle East because there's nothing in it for Israel, no reason for Israel to start a war, and obviously no reason for the Egyptians to start one because they'd lose it.

The other big item today was the continuation of the veterans' *(Vietnam Veterans Against the War)* demonstration problem. We had a long session this morning to try to determine what to do in face of the fact that the veterans are in violation of the Supreme Court order by staying on the mall, and it's really our job to enforce that order, but the P has ordered the Attorney General not to use police and not to evict the veterans. Our decision ended up to be that we just continue negotiating and try to negotiate the issue to death. Later this afternoon the Attorney General, under pressure from Burger and the Court, went back to the District Court and asked them to dissolve the order on the grounds that there was only one more night left and it wasn't worth pursuing.

Apparently, the circuit court judge blasted us on this move, and said that the court had been put in a very bad position, which actually it has, since we asked for the order to begin with and then didn't enforce it after we got it. Which put the veterans in the position of violating the law and us in the position of not enforcing it. Fortunately, I don't think this point has come through very clearly, and it probably won't. We did move a little too fast on getting the order to begin with, though.

Friday, April 23, 1971

We got into quite a discussion of the media problem; they're really killing us because they run the veterans' demonstration every night in great detail, and we have no way to fight back. It's a tough one, and we've been trying to figure out some ways of getting back at it. One thought we're going to try is to have Rainwater of the VFW *(Veterans of Foreign Wars)* call all the network presidents and ask if they'll assure him of equal time for veterans in favor of the Administration's position on the war next week. Obviously they'll turn him down, and at least that will give us an arguing point. In the meantime we're getting pretty well chopped up.

We also got into the analysis of our quick poll last night,

which shows a drop in Presidential approval of about 3 points and a switch back to disapproval on Vietnam from our previous position of fairly strong approval. It's a hard one to figure, because since we last polled, we've had the ASNE *(American Association of Newspaper Editors)* appearance, the DAR speech, the Governors' Conference speech, all the developments in China, the good economic news of last week, and really no bad war news except the veterans' demonstration, and still we go down. The only conclusion can be that the veterans' deal, and the coverage of it, is the cause, so we've got to see if somehow we can't make the media the issue. We'll probably have to crank up the VP again and get him going on it. In any event, we've got to work out something.

The P took off by helicopter for Julie's house in Virginia Beach. He called me after he got there to check on follow-up on the above things, and also to urge that we get some mileage out of the great picture he thinks they got this afternoon of the little deaf kid in the office. He goes on to Camp David after dinner tonight with the family.

Saturday, April 24, 1971

The P is at Camp David. The day of the big peace demonstration in Washington. I was in most of the day, mainly to be on hand if anything arose on the demonstration, but nothing did. They developed a huge crowd, close to 200,000. No violence, basically a pretty non-stirred-up group. They gathered in the mall and started the march early down to the Capitol. Had the usual speeches and singing, etc., at the Capitol, and then pretty much dispersed. No problems from our viewpoint. That will probably come next week when the violent group gets started. They were smart to do this at the Capitol because the crowd looked a lot bigger there than it did last year at the monument grounds.

The P called from time to time to get updated on how it was going. He was mainly interested, of course, in seeing that it was downplayed as much as possible. He didn't seem to be particularly concerned about it. He did think we ought to try to counteract in some way the veterans' effect of last week, and particularly the failure of the media to give us any coverage while it really supercovered them.

Sunday, April 25, 1971

The P's still at Camp David; he stayed up there all day. Rogers called this morning; he leaves on his trip tomorrow. He wanted to urge that the P in his press conference this week start claiming credit in the Middle East and make the point that he sent Rogers out, in his quest for peace. He thinks this will help to overcome the view that the P isn't interested in the Middle East if he says that he asked Rogers to go even with the diplomatic risks involved. He could also point out that this is an historical trip, and that no secretary of state has ever before visited a country that we don't have diplomatic relations with. Also, he thinks it would help with Israel to show that the P is behind Rogers, because the Israelis always say, "Yes, we know what you think, Mr. Rogers, but we also know what the White House really thinks about this."

Monday, April 26, 1971

Staff meeting this morning. Got into the whole question of our position about the demonstrators, following up on our PR staff meeting yesterday afternoon. The general feeling was that the P should say something to show that he's not frightened, but also not insensitive to the demonstrators, their feeling that his absence from Washington is evidence of the fear of being here and his insensitivity to the problem. They generally felt that it got through that the demonstration is now respectable, and that we need to keep that under consideration. I discussed this later with the P, and we got into quite a discussion as to what the statement should be. The P's first inclination was to recite all the bad things that they did, after saying that he was pleased the demonstrations were peaceful on the whole, but that it's too bad they tore down the United States flags at the monument, burned the benches, stopped traffic in New Jersey, threw bottles at the police, etc. After Ron came in, we went back over that ground and decided rather to make the point that the message of the demonstrators is that they want to end the war, and there's no argument with that. The P does too. The question is ending one war and preventing others. The P's building a structure of peace so that the teenagers who are there demonstrating won't have to fight in a war. This takes long-range planning and hard decisions, and the track record of those who have shouted "peace now" in years past is not one that speaks very well for their leadership.

The general feeling was that last week's press coverage of activities is bound to have an effect, but our people are over-active, they feel that we have to do something fast, and this is the problem that LBJ became obsessed with. The important thing for us is to maintain serenity and calm. The P made the point that anyone who had been through the Hiss case wouldn't get excited about all these other things. The question now is just to see it through. You'll either win or lose, and you can't let it be personal.

While Alger Hiss was Director of the State Department Office of Special Political Affairs, he was accused of collaboration with the Communist underground—a charge he vehemently denied. Against prevailing sentiment, then-Congressman Nixon urged that the investigation be continued. On December 15, 1948, Hiss was indicted because of Nixon's perseverance. This success catapulted Nixon's political career.

We discussed various possibilities of preparedness for breaking up the blocking of the roads, which is going to be the important problem next week. The feeling is that the district police are going to be able to handle it themselves unless the numbers become really massive, in which case the National Guard will have to help. It turns out that we can use the National Guard without declaring a state of martial law, and this, of course, is something we wanted to avoid at any cost.

The next antiwar demonstration was scheduled to be an all-out effort to stop the business of Washington by blocking the roads and bridges into the city and thus preventing government workers from getting to their jobs. Our position was that it was imperative to prevent the success of this plan.

The P talked with Henry about the problem of the effect of the demonstrations on Hanoi. Henry's all concerned that they may have misinterpreted the thing and weakened our position, which of course to some degree they will, but there's no point in worrying about it. The P made the point to me that we're going to have to play the propaganda role more skillfully, and that he's only going to let Henry go to Paris once, or at the very most twice, and then we'll give up on the negotiations. He feels that if we wait more than a couple more months, we won't have anything left to negotiate anyway, except the residual force and the bombing vs. the release of POW's. The problem is that we need one more stab at negotiations, so we can't set a time certain yet. After we've taken that stab, if it doesn't work we'll just go ahead and set the time certain, and that's it.

The P also made the point in a phone call that sometimes we really dodge a bullet, and that he was sure glad this morning he didn't make a statement praising the peaceful protests, because it would have ridden right with the reports of today's activities and would have really looked bad for us.

Tuesday, April 27, 1971
The P had a pretty heavy appointment schedule today. The P had Henry and me in at one point this morning, and Henry obviously was very much depressed because the general developments had not been what he had hoped. I didn't get a full reading on what the problem was. I suspected at the time that his SALT plan had probably fallen through, and I don't know whether that's the case or not. In any event, the P made a very determined effort to try to cheer Henry up, and didn't really succeed.

We had a session with the Attorney General and Kleindienst, and (White House Counsel) John Dean and me, this morning on plans for the demonstrations. We've sorted down to a little bit more sensible approach now, and are going at it on the basis of the DC police handling all of the actual law enforcement responsibilities, with the understanding that they may not be able to get the streets cleared immediately, but we will clear them as fast as we can and bring people in at whatever time the streets actually are cleared. There wasn't much activity in the way of demonstrations today. A little flurry at Selective Service, and that was about it.

Wednesday, April 28, 1971
The P spent the day in press conference preparation supposedly, but because this gave him free time, I got caught for some long sessions, including an especially long one this morning with Henry.

The P led into his major development, which I won't cover here in specifics but only for recall. Henry reviewed the past record and read the current document.

This "major development" was the initial planning for the Nixon trip to China, which was at that time a matter of the highest possible secrecy. All of the early steps were planned and executed by Nixon and Kissinger, working through various foreign intermediaries. The "current document" was a handwritten message to Nixon from Chinese Premier Chou En-lai responding (a bit belatedly) to President Nixon's message to him of December 16 of the preceding year.

This message stated that China was willing to receive publicly in Peking a special envoy of the President of the U.S. for the purpose of direct discussions.

I did not record this specific reference in this diary because of its enormous level of secrecy at the time. On the morning after the message had been received, I sat in on a meeting with K and P and made the following notes.

Then there was a long discussion about implementation, primarily the question of selection of an emissary, with the P ruling out himself or Rogers, and then ruling out K, because that would break all the china with State. This boiled it down to David Bruce or the remote possibility of Nelson Rockefeller. This was discussed in some detail along with timing and various potential outcomes and scenarios, with no decisions made at that time. We had another session in the afternoon at the EOB, and Henry had his thoughts more in line by then, and made the point that he was the only one who really could handle this, and that the way to go at it was in effect to set it up for the P, with a secret meeting prior to that with Henry, and that's the way it was left as Henry took off late this afternoon for a week in Palm Springs. No action will be taken for a week or ten days, and then we'll start moving from there.

The P called several times concerning the question of whether or not to use a podium for the press conference; whether to eliminate the platform and put it at ground level; whether or not he would use makeup. Obviously he's spending some time on the mechanics. He also called one time in great glee because he had learned the market was up to 950 today, on 24 million shares, second-highest day in history. The upswing is really pleasing to him.

Thursday, April 29, 1971

Press conference day. The P spent the whole day at the FOE preparing. He called several times on the phone on odds and ends; then, during the session I had with him at the EOB, and again later at the Oval Office, he raised the question of the mood of the P in the press conference. Buchanan had urged that he hit it harder and express real anger regarding the demonstrators, etc. I thought he ought to stay consistent and take the same tone that he has in the past—which, as it turns out, he ended up doing. He was very pleased afterward by the way the thing had worked out. Most of the questions were on Vietnam and China; only one domestic-policy question, and that was on the school-busing decision by the Court. He particularly liked two new lines that he developed regarding foreign policy: one, in relation to China, he said that now that we've broken the ice, we have to test the water; and regarding Vietnam, it isn't a matter of peace in our time, but (referring to the teenagers) a question of peace in their times.

Friday, April 30, 1971

On Air Force One en route to Southern California, in talking with Al Haig on the plane, the P made the point that in describing Nixon you have to make the point that he's always like the iceberg, you see only the tip. You must never think that the surface is all that's going on. The real power is beneath the surface. He was discussing this in relation to Russia and China. He wanted to be sure that we got word to all our troops as well as the State Department people, and also to the Congressional leaders and so on, that everybody should keep quiet about China at this point and let things work their own way out, at least for the time being. After we arrived at Pendleton we had an excellent Marine ceremony. The P moved into the crowd afterward and got some darn good receptions from the Marines and their families. Then up to San Clemente.

Kleindienst called with a problem that Packard won't permit the use of Federal troops to handle the Washington demonstrators, unless there's a proclamation or unless he's ordered to do so, without a proclamation by the P. This gets into the factor of what level the P becomes involved. The proclamation would require the P to determine a general disorder, federalize the National Guard, and put the General in charge of the troops, which is just what we don't want to do. So we told him that the P was ordering that the troops be provided without proclamation, and that's what they're going to go ahead and do.

Saturday, May 1, 1971

He checked this morning on the demonstration plans and made the point to me that he wants a very hard line taken in Washington on Monday, and that he's going to take a hard line on the press conference, using the term ''The party's over, and it's time to draw the line.'' This concerned me, and I talked with E. It also bothered him. So John called him and talked him out of using that particular phrase. He is concerned, though, that we go hard on this. Fortunately, that's exactly what they developed in Washington, and E called me later in the day to say that their plan now is to bust the demonstrators Sunday morning, and probably move in with narcotics agents to arrest as many as they can. Thus they think we'll bust up their plans and make it hard for them to do their traffic-stopping exercise on Monday.

The P then had his press conference in the driveway of the Residence, and that seemed to go pretty well. Now he wants to go hard for picking up the phrase that he used in regard to demonstrators, which is that the right to demonstrate for peace abroad doesn't include the right to break the peace at home.

Sunday, May 2, 1971

He started the day in Palm Springs. The P did his Farm Speech thing this morning and did a tape for national radio release. He got into demonstration plans, seemed to be satisfied that they were OK. John said that they moved in hard and fast, arrested a lot of them, and that most of the rest were packing and going home, and he thought they'd really broken it up pretty well. The P was somewhat concerned that maybe we had moved too hard on the thing, and that it was a close call as to whether we should have done this or forced them to go ahead with their plans. I think we came out right.

Monday, May 3, 1971

The day of the big demonstration. It all went reasonably well; they were able to keep traffic open all day and keep the city under control, although a lot of the demonstrators were running loose. Ultimately they ended up arresting about 8,000 of them and holding them in a stockade sort of setup out at Kennedy Stadium. They finally put them in the Uline Arena to hole them up for tonight and do the processing and then releasing them after putting up bail. The P was concerned that we perhaps should let them out and let them disrupt traffic rather than keeping them locked up.

Tuesday, May 4, 1971

The P had a busy day, pretty well loaded with appointments, and I had very little time in there, which was great because I was able to get my own work completely cleared up. We had a long discussion about the effect of the demonstration yesterday, the coverage of it last night, and activities today. Everything is very low key today with hardly any tieups or vandalism this morning. A fairly large crowd did gather this afternoon and march to the Justice Department, where a couple of thousand were arrested, but no apparent violence. There's starting to be a buildup from the left and the civil liberties types now, about reacting adversely to the arrest procedure, but I think public opinion is basically with us. The P's been very pleased with the job Chief Wilson has done.

Friday, May 7, 1971

Agriculture day today. The P did a good job in the extemporaneous speech at the Agriculture Department auditorium this morning. He had a meeting with Meany this afternoon and got his commitment to help on both the SST and Lockheed. Speaking of Lockheed, there was a monumental flap late last night as Haig, and later K, called me to say that Dave Packard was furious with the Lockheed decision, which Connally announced yesterday, and that he is going to resign and blast the Administration for the position we're taking on Lockheed. Henry was pretty disturbed about it, having talked to both Packard and Laird, and felt that there was a real danger here. So I suggested that he call Connally and see if Connally couldn't get it untangled. Connally stepped right up to it.

He talked to me later in the day; he did meet with Packard. He said Packard was really upset about the whole thing; that he had paced back and forth in the office, and the only way Connally could talk to him was to get up and pace along with him. Packard said he just felt it was completely the wrong decision and that he couldn't support it. It ended up with Connally's getting Packard to agree that he wouldn't take any steps, at least at this point, and that he'd wait and see how the whole thing developed; but that he did not support the decision. Connally feels it's very clear that Packard's upset about a lot more than just the Lockheed decision, which Henry confirms because Packard has been very uptight, and Henry thinks that Packard's been looking for a way to resign for some time, anyway.

Monday, May 10, 1971

The morning was spent on our New York trip to view the new parkland. I had fairly long sessions with the P on the plane on the way up and on the way back. He is cranked up on follow-up on the SST vote in the House this week, and agreed to meet with a group that Gerry Ford would put together for a breakfast tomorrow morning in order to get it going. He got into a discussion of general tactics regarding how we approach things. Makes the point that we're going to quit meeting with the people that are against us, and playing to the issues such as consumers, environment, youth, press, business elite, intellectuals, volunteers, etc., and that he won't meet with these groups except when it's solely a question of a delaying action. He feels the battle lines are drawn now; we should play our friends all out and get only our people in. The key now is to fight the main battle, which is Vietnam, and not to be diverted to the fringes. We had our Monday-night staff dinner. Henry came late and left early and had nothing to say.

Wednesday, May 12, 1971

The usual clear Wednesday, which creates monumental problems for me as the P has nothing to do and so keeps me in there talking for hours as he did virtually all morning and for a good chunk this afternoon.

We had the SST vote in the House, and it came out in favor of restoring the SST funds. The P was delighted and made a number of calls to congressmen assuring them of our support in trying to get it through the Senate. Also, the Ways and Means Committee reported out the Welfare Reform Bill today, so it was a good day at the House of Representatives.

The big flap of the day was the proposed NATO Troop-Reduction Amendment offered by Mansfield, and the question of how to deal with it; the decision was to fight it for a defeat in the Senate. That got us into a K-Rogers tangle as K started launching all the plans for it, but the P wanted Rogers to lead the charge and talked to him about it. Rogers said he would, but in talking to K later backed away, and obviously didn't want to really take over on it. We went through a painful exercise, with Henry in the office, while the P was trying to work out a way to force Henry to get Rogers in.

Addendum from May 12. This item's added as Henry K called me after I had done the other tape, to report that in his meeting with Dobrynin today, he had gotten agreement in all of the specifics of SALT except for one minor technicality that relates to translation in the letter, as related to the wording in the press release. Henry says there's a nine out of ten chance that we'll be able to make the announcement next Thursday, and that if it gets hung up at all, it will only be hung up on this technicality, which can be worked out in two weeks. He's very pleased, and thinks he's gotten over the first hurdle in his series of negotiating plans, and now we will anxiously await the next one.

Thursday, May 13, 1971

K and I were in for a fairly long session first thing this morning, since the day had been kept clear for a possible press conference. The P got into a review of Laos and the fact that casualties were way down now; that there's been no spring offensive despite the largest matériel input ever in Vietnam, including at Tet; and that it's really remarkable proof of the effectiveness of the operation. We also got to talking about China and the whole plan for possible follow-up on the initiative. Henry's ecstatic because he's heard back from the North Vietnamese, and they want to meet with him in Paris on the 30th, so he's going ahead with that plan. He still thinks the Chinese thing's going to work out, but there's been no word, of course, from them, and won't be for a couple of weeks.

Then we got into the problem of Rogers and the SALT agreement, since that's now set and will be announced next Thursday. The problem is how to fill Rogers in ahead of time without his feeling that it's been maneuvered behind his back, which of course it has. The P's very sensitive to this, but doesn't seem to have any fixed ideas on how to deal with it.

He got into a discussion with E later in the morning, on the need to think regarding goals, rather than programs, and got into quite a session with John covering the same ground that I'd been pushing on, trying to shift the emphasis of the Domestic Council's approach. The P pointed out that we've got to personalize and conceptualize in broad visionary terms regarding goals, instead of just developing programs and legislation. He said politically the new American Revolution is a dud. The people don't care how you run the government; they only want it to cost a little less. He wants to go for water, education, narcotics, street crime, and whatever positive issues we can develop.

Sunday, May 16, 1971

He had me come over around noon for a couple of hours, pretty much just to generally get caught up. He got into the PR thing, thinking back on Buchanan's memo that we're overdoing the human interest stuff. He thinks Buchanan's wrong, and that the deal here is not to talk about the PR aspects, but we do need to get this kind of thing out. He makes the point that Kennedy was colder, more ruthless, etc., than the P is, but look at his PR. He came through as the warm, human guy sponsoring the arts, loving his family, and all that kind of stuff. Then made the point that PR is right if it emphasizes the truth. It's wrong, at least for us, if it isn't true. We should only do things that help on the PR impact.

Monday, May 17, 1971

Got into a discussion of the letter he had received from Bowling, the President of Earlham College, which he felt was very astute in its analysis of the Middle East and the Israeli attitude. He wants me to send a copy of the letter to Rogers, telling him the P found it very interesting. More importantly, he wants me to sit down with Haig and go over, on a cold-turkey basis, that this is a view of a Quaker and that we've got to realize we can't play the Jewish game. That all they're trying to do is string us along until the elections next year when they hope to replace us.

Tuesday, May 18, 1971

SALT was the big activity today, as our original plans for the Rogers, Laird, and *(chief SALT negotiator)* Gerry Smith meetings were one by one dropped and shifted because Henry didn't have the final OK from Dobrynin on the wording of the agreement and the final decision to confirm announcement on Thursday. As the day went on, Henry became more and more nervous, as did the P, because it looked as if maybe there was a snag we weren't going to get through. That all proved to be unfounded, as at 3:45 Henry burst into a meeting the P and I were having with Colson, to say that everything was all set. We talked in some double-talk so Colson wouldn't understand what we were saying for a while, and then finally Chuck left and we went into the plans for how to handle it. We'll go ahead with briefings tomorrow of Rogers, etc. The P is still extremely worried about how to tell Rogers, and went back and forth on that, frequently, on and off during the rest of the afternoon, but we locked him in for a 9:00 appointment in the morning and he's going to have to face up to it now.

There was, of course, considerable discussion as the day went on, of looking back on how the whole thing had come together. The tremendous role Henry's played in this, implementing the P's decisions in his many secret meetings with Dobrynin, which have finally progressed to the point of something that we can actually take to the people. This puts us in a marvelous position because of the general feeling on the part of many of the doves in Congress that SALT had broken down, and Muskie's plan to start holding hearings, etc. This, of course, shoots all the ground out from under them. The problem now is how to handle the announcement and follow-up on it in such a way as to tread the very fine line between making sure that the enormous significance of the step is clearly understood, but that we don't oversell it or appear to have arrived at any final decision.

There was a lot of back-and-forth discussion between Henry and the P as to who deserved the credit, etc., Henry making very clear the point that it was the P's courage in the decisions that had made it all possible, but obviously Henry feels he played a monumental role also and I guess he really did.

E reported that the SST revival was dead since Boeing had decided to fold their hand and not attempt to go for renewal, on the basis that they can't win in the renegotiation of the contract. This came as something of a blow to the P. He's especially concerned because it's obviously a slur on us, in that the House revived the thing and we weren't able to carry it through with the supplier. He's furious with Boeing, and has made it clear they'll get nothing more from this Administration as long as he is in office.

He also got into quite a long thing on the lack of leadership in the Congress, particularly in the Senate, making the point that Gerry Ford really is the only leader we've got on either side in either house. And that led into some reminiscing about the old-time greats in the Congress.

E reported that in his meeting with the President of Boeing, T. Wilson, this afternoon, Wilson got into a pitch on their new hydrofoil and John cut him off, saying that he really didn't think this Administration was going to be very interested in a new contract with the Boeing Company, at least at this time, at which Wilson got up hastily and departed.

We had a little flap with the Director of the National Institutes of Mental Health, who apparently said the other day that he thought marijuana offenses should be handled like traffic violations. This sent the P right up the wall, and he's told E to get the guy fired, which it turns out we're glad to do because he's been causing some other problems and shows some clear disloyalty. So John's moving ahead on that.

Wednesday, May 19, 1971

This was about a 99 percent SALT day, as we set the notification process in motion. Henry met with Gerry Smith for breakfast at 8:30. The P had Rogers in at 9:00, and they informed both of them. The P called me in at 10:20; also Henry was in, and reported on Rogers' reaction. The P had the feeling that there was very much of a problem, that Rogers' reaction was really almost no reaction at all, but he clearly had the feeling of wondering what was going on. While we were in talking about this and starting to lay plans for timing for tomorrow, Rogers asked me to be called out of the meeting with the P and asked me to come over to see him.

I then went over to the State Department; had about a hour with Rogers. He was clearly very upset. His basic point was, "Why didn't you tell me that you were doing this? There's no need for me to be involved, but I do have to be informed." He also made it clear that he's hurt, and raised the question of whether the P's sending him a signal. If so, he'll go. I didn't really respond to that.

He made the point that if the P doesn't trust him, he can't do his work. He was very clearly upset; he didn't buy my explanation regarding the cutting across party lines and so forth. He very clearly resents K; he asked how many meetings Henry had with Dobrynin and whether there were memos of conversation. He claims he's fully posted Henry on everything that he's done, but is not being posted by Henry. This is in direct opposition to what Henry says, and I raised that and Bill got quite distressed.

To sum it up: it was clear he was very worried about the short-term impact on his own image and hadn't yet figured out the long-term implications.

When I got back to the office he called, saying he had been thinking about it and it was clear that we should develop a party line as to how this all transpired. I then went back into the P's office and reported all of this to him, after which he had Henry come in and we discussed it some more, particularly the point of establishing the line. He said that I should make the point strongly, that our line is that this is a Presidential initiative; that we will not discuss the details of how it was accomplished, we won't let anyone describe the process. We don't want any puffing because it was a mutual thing with the Russians. The point is the P broke the deadlock and then it was implemented at the appropriate levels in the government. If Bill's asked whether he was involved he should say we won't disclose any details of the negotiation, but he can say he was informed.

The P then had me go out and call Rogers. In the meantime, Rogers had put a call in to the P, so I called Bill, filled him in on this, and then the P returned his call and had a pretty good chat with him. Right after he hung up the P heaved a deep sigh, looked out the window, and said it would be goddamn easy to run this office if you didn't have to deal with people.

Thursday, May 20, 1971

This afternoon the P had a meeting scheduled at 4:00 with Connally. Instead of having him come over, he had me call at 3:45 and say that the P was going to be tied up, but that he was sending someone else over to see Connally. Then the P went over and surprised him in his office. He had me go with him and sit in the meeting, which lasted about a hour and a half, and then the P spent a half hour wandering around the Treasury Building, meeting people and so forth. By this time a crowd had built up outside, and he stopped and chatted with them as he worked his way back across the street.

Connally and the P discussed the whole SALT thing, and were very cheerful on the reaction to that. Then the P made the point that he wants Connally to serve as the chief Administration spokesman on the economy, and that he wants to delegate all of that responsibility to Connally. Connally made a little speech about how he certainly didn't want to take on this task, and all that sort of thing, but that it was certainly clear that the P should have one single spokesman and that it had to be the Secretary of the Treasury, so he modestly allowed as how he would take it on.

Friday, May 21, 1971

The P was in at 7:20 this morning. Apparently still cranked up from the whole SALT deal. Last night he decided after dinner to drop by the Tulane University Alumni Dinner. Nobody even knew anything about it, but they finally found out where it was. The P shot out and went over. Fortunately the Army band was there; they played "Hail to the Chief," he came in, gave some apparently very good remarks and left, scoring another pretty good hit.

The P continues in a kind of bouncy and detached mood, as he was yesterday afternoon. I think basically in reaction, now that he's finally got the SALT deal settled. Bebe arrived late this afternoon, and the P was bouncing around touring him in offices, sort of like he was touring the Treasury and East Wing offices yesterday.

Saturday, May 22, 1971

This is the day of the trip to the Johnson Library. We left early in the morning and I didn't see the P at all on the plane on the way down. He had Rogers, Connally, and George Bush up

for a long talk; also Henry up for a while. The library dedication went pretty much as planned; no problems and no great
accomplishments. Johnson looked pretty horrible; he seems to
have suffered some from that stroke apparently, because he
was limping and has put on a lot of weight, but was in tremendously good spirits, of course, and the whole event must
have been very cheering to him.

The P had me up for an hour or so on the flight to Key
Biscayne. He got into the budget problem and the need to cut
down on things such as the NSF *(National Science Foundation)* grants, especially when they go for teachers' salaries; he
wants to put that kind of money into something else, where it
would do us some good, and not worry about the squeals that
it will bring from the universities. He's afraid that he's been
sucked into some things, such as that and other educational
expenditures, food stamps and other left-wing proposals that
he hasn't taken a close enough look at and he wants to be sure
we're not getting caught on any of these.

He talked about Honor America Day. The Committee hasn't
come up with anything much in the way of a proposal except
to do an outside show at the Jefferson Monument, which the
P definitely does not want to do because of the demonstrator
problem.

Monday, May 24, 1971

(Key Biscayne) The P had me come over at about 10:00. We
had set up a deal for him to meet with Miss USA at 11:00,
since when she was selected yesterday she indicated that the
person she would most like to meet was the P; said she'd like
to talk with him about various things. So we set up the opportunity and it worked out very well.

He got into some ideas on library plans, obviously arising
out of the Johnson visit. He said that LBJ had tried to amend
the Congressional regulations on USIA in order to permit their
film to be used in Presidential libraries. He hadn't gotten this
done and he wants us to move on it right now on the basis of
Johnson. He's concerned about the plans for our library; he
doesn't want to create a monument like Johnson's. He's also
worried about oral histories, and has very much of a feeling
that he does not want any oral histories made.

He got into quite a bit of discussion on domestic-policy
matters. He's very much concerned about handling of the

drug situation; wants the whole thing taken out of HEW. He makes the point that they're all on drugs there anyway, but he wants it handled in Justice. He also wants Finch and Rumsfeld to quit emoting about the drug problem, which only builds it up. We should be talking about our solutions, not about the enormity of the problem. He feels NET *(National Educational Television)* is no good; the whole thing is a bad idea, subsidized public broadcasting is wrong, even if we could influence it to cover things in the right way. So I'm supposed to try to drop it over the edge and see that it's not funded in some way.

He's also worried about the Peace Corps and thinks we're making some mistakes there. He feels we're not using our power enough on these things. That we should really look into this; put a tough guy on it who hates the left-wing press and do something about it.

Mitchell, he feels, should get onto the YAF *(Young Americans for Freedom)* deal, they've now announced they're going to back Reagan for P. He thinks Mitchell should move into that and straighten them back out because we need the group enthusiasm of the right wing.

The P spent the afternoon out boating, and I guess he's going over to the Key Biscayne Hotel for dinner. We'll be leaving tomorrow for the Alabama trip.

Tuesday, May 25, 1971

Started out in Key Biscayne, then on to Alabama for stops in Memphis and Birmingham, then on into DC. I had no contact at all with the P during the day except for a quick phone call in the morning before we left Key Biscayne, when he wanted to overrule the indication in the schedule that he would be riding in the bubble-top in the motorcade.

The bubble-top is a special Presidential limousine designed for motorcade and parade use, with a bulletproof transparent plastic bubble over the backseat that enabled the P to stand up and be seen by the street crowds, without exposing him to the danger of something thrown or shot. Nixon felt it was security overkill, and did not like using it, preferring instead the regular convertible, where he could sit or stand in the open.

We had already changed it and put him into the Secret Service follow-up convertible, so that was no problem. We had great crowds in Memphis and Birmingham, and the trip went extremely well. It should have had some pretty substantial significance in terms of Southern strategy. George Wallace was with us all day. Couldn't have been more friendly. Stayed right with the P, got in every picture with him that he could.

Wednesday, May 26, 1971
Back in the mill in Washington. Actually he had a light schedule set for today—the address to the Associated Council of the Arts. He made the point earlier this morning that he wants to put out a statement on marijuana that's really strong, as he said, one that tears the ass out of them. He also commented on the question of why all the Jews seem to be the ones that are for liberalizing the regulations on marijuana. He wants to find a way to hit hard, head-on, dramatic, do it through Congress. As a follow-up on this, he has E and Krogh *(Egil "Bud" Krogh, a lawyer on the Domestic Council staff)* going, and I think they'll probably be coming up with something pretty good.

He had Henry in for a while this morning. He then delivered himself of a whole series of fascinating Nixonisms as he discussed various international matters with Henry. In talking about the problem with India invading Pakistan *(a possibility, since tensions were high between the two countries)*, he said that they have an old saying in their country that trust is like a thin thread: once you break it, it's very hard to splice together again. He brought this up in the context of Laos, making the point that in effect we had broken our thin thread with the American people as to the winding down of the war when we moved into Laos, and that it's going to be very hard to put that together again. He made the point to Henry that all wars are close, this was also in reference to Laos and the question of, if we'd only hung on two weeks longer we would have had a success there instead of the mess that we ended up with, but he said to Henry, "You've got to realize that all wars are close. That nobody wins big in any war. . . ."

Then he got to talking about the fact that foreign policy was not doing us any real good, although we had accomplished a lot of things, and he explained that to Henry's country, the intellectuals and the social jet set, etc., we're doing an out-standing job, but in what he referred to as "my country," that is, the plain folks out in the middle of America, they don't know anything about what you're doing on SALT and all these other things, they just want things to simmer down and be quiet, and to them we have not accomplished very much. Then he got to talking about election issues, and made the ironic point that of all the major issues, the only one that is a sure thing for us is Vietnam. That all the rest are in doubt, but we know precisely what we're going to do and where we're going to be on Vietnam.

Thursday, May 27, 1971

King Faisal's visit today. The P ended up approving a full-scale arrival ceremony, and that plus the meeting and then a luncheon, followed by a private meeting with Secretary Rogers, not with Faisal, but Rogers and K to discuss the China-UN situation, used up virtually the entire day until 4:00, at which time the P met with E and Krogh to go over the narcotics situation, and then added Elliot Richardson. The P had sort of a dull session, apparently, with Faisal, who talked on and on at the arrival ceremony, again in the meeting. The P says he speaks perfect English but won't use it, so they had to go through the interpreting business on the entire conversation, which really bogged it down.

Friday, May 28, 1971

The P got into a discussion of the general political situation the first thing this morning. He wanted to track down whoever had done the attack on Julie's new teaching job to see whether there was a partisan source to it. That led him to thinking that we should put permanent tails and coverage on Teddy and Muskie and Hubert on all the personal stuff to cover the kinds of things that they hit us on in '62; personal finances, family, and so forth.

Henry's all set for his trip this weekend, and is urging the P to give him three weeks for a reply, which will still get one in before we go to Midway to meet with Thieu on the 28th. The P emphasized that all foreign policy initiatives are going to have to be completed by July 1972 because after that there will be a Democratic nominee and they'll insist that he be taken along on any trips and brought in on any discussions.

The ideal scenario still would be to get the Vietnam thing settled this summer, have a Summit this fall, and wrap up the first SALT agreement; announce a China visit and have it in March or so of next year. Whether we can pull this off or not remains to be seen.

.

Saturday, May 29, 1971

The P did his visit to West Point today, which went extremely well, and he seemed to be very pleased with it, both during and afterward. He obviously gets a tremendous kick out of chatting with the cadets and seeing the outstanding caliber of young men that we have in groups such as this. It clearly gives him a charge, and trips of this kind may be worthwhile for this reason only. Before we left the White House, he had Henry in for a final discussion before Henry's trip to Paris tomorrow, and called me in at the latter part of it, as he sort of wandered around discussing the history of World War I, some of the problems made then. He was pointing up the significance of the date March 21, which this year relates to Laos, but in 1918 related to *(Erich)* Ludendorff's big offensive, which was considered a great German victory but which turned out to be the turning point in the war and the principal German loss. He sees Laos in the same possible perspective. It turned out that at the battle of March 21, 1918, the Germans lost more of their high command and senior officers than the British did, and that result was a major setback for the German cause. He also got into a discussion on MacArthur at the Yalu, and other specific military strategy items. He clearly has been reading some military history, and enjoys discussing that kind of thing with Henry.

On the way back on Air Force One we got into a discussion of our press relations approach. I had reported to him that *(John)* Scali *(who was now working with K on press)* had called in Dan Rather to bring him to task on some factual errors he had made, and also had called in *(Hugh)* Sidey to blast him for *Time's* coverage of the Acheson group meeting, which *Time* had totally distorted. He questions whether Scali is doing the right thing. He makes the point that Ziegler's been trying to do this on factual corrections for two years and has gotten nowhere. We have to realize the press aren't interested in factual accuracy, and also that if we straighten them out on the points of factual matters, they'll hit us even worse on the judgment-type questions. His theory is different from Scali's and others in that he believes the press and TV don't change their attitude and approach unless you hurt them.

Sunday, May 30, 1971

The P's staying at Camp David. Called first thing this morning to get a general reaction to the news, which I couldn't do much on because I hadn't read the papers yet. We did get excellent TV coverage last night and good press coverage today on the West Point appearance. The P makes the point that this shows the advantage of doing something on a Saturday or Sunday, when the news is normally light. He pointed out that he'd found out from Julie that Davis had written a blistering letter to *The Washington Post* regarding their attitude toward the Southern trip, and makes the point that we should develop the idea of using a Cabinet officer or a congressman or someone else with a big name to write letters of this kind as a part of our letter-writing program. The celebrity letters of course will get a much better chance of being printed.

The P was at Camp David until about 2:00 and then returned to Washington, went right over to the OEB, and continued work on press-conference preparation. He did call on the phone at midday from Camp David.

Wednesday, June 2, 1971

He had Henry back in again at 11:00, and we were all in until about noon. During that time the P got into questioning Henry, and that led him into a discussion of the whole question of moral war. He made the point that after World War II he had visited Germany, stood on a hill, and looked around where all the terrible damage was, with hundreds of thousands of people killed. And you could certainly say that was immoral, to have killed all those people, to have bombed the areas and so forth, but the real question is, would Hitler conquering that area be more moral? Same point applies, that the North Vietnamese bombing is a tragedy, but it's even more immoral to send Americans abroad and not back them up with air power. He got quite cranked up on this whole subject, and made the point that he will not go out of Vietnam whimpering.

Tonight at home Henry called me to say he had received his letter from the Chinese and that it was even more accommodating than he had thought it would be. He was obviously quite ecstatic about the whole deal.

At midday the P had Finch in for an hour and a half on California politics. Bob reviewed his memo of recommendations. He has a main point of contention with Mitchell on the question of Ronald Reagan as honorary chairman of California. Finch thinks that this will give Reagan's people the feeling that they've got a franchise to organize the campaign.

Thursday, June 3, 1971

Henry called me in this morning to follow up on his phone call to me late last night reporting that he had got his message from the Chinese. He let me read it this morning, and it really is effusive, and I can see why Henry's so excited. They are really leaning over backward to set up a meeting, and specifically confirmed the meeting with Henry and want him to come practically immediately, which he of course can't do. He's going to have to hold it off for a month, but it looks as if we have the ball rolling in that area, and he feels that will put a lot of pressure on North Vietnam to settle with him when he meets with them secretly at the end of June. So he's extremely optimistic that we may get all of the settlements that we're working toward on all of our initiatives, and if we do that we'll really be in great shape.

Friday, June 4, 1971

The P had a pretty busy schedule. He met with the VP at his request, and it turned out he wanted to make a pitch for his going to Red China while he's on his trip to the inauguration in Korea. It was almost unbelievable, because he raised it in a way that made it awkward for the P to have to tell him that he couldn't go, and then once told, he didn't give up.

Saturday, June 5, 1971

The P went to Tulsa today. We went up to Camp David with the family, and the P arrived there late this afternoon. Called me, not realizing I was at Camp David, to cover a couple of items, on mainly the reaction to the trip. He was very pleased with it; he had followed Bill Rogers' idea of making the point that America's a great country and that we get a distorted picture in Washington, DC, and he got a very good reaction to this. He sort of laughed and said that after Oklahoma, Alabama, and Texas they'll really be talking about our Southern strategy, but he agrees that we should be playing to the areas where we're strong. He made the comment that it really warms your heart to have a group like the Tulsa University Choir, all crew-cut and not a single demonstrator there. Overall, obviously he thought the thing had gone very well. At the end of the conversation he asked me why I didn't come on up to Camp David for the weekend, and I told him we were already there, which pleased him.

Sunday, June 6, 1971
At Camp David. The P stayed all day again through the night tonight because Pat wanted to stay up there, apparently to get a little rest from the pressure of wedding planning. We had quite a long talk about Connally and the Vice Presidency, and he says he thinks it's time for me to sit down and have a frank, confidential talk with Connally about the problem. See if he thinks it can be pulled off. He feels Agnew doesn't really have it; he's not broad-gauged enough. We just can't keep him working in the South because whatever he says down there will play all over the country. Also, he's not upbeat; he doesn't give anyone a lift. It all adds up to the P's convinced that he can't do the job, and that will affect his ability to campaign. So I'm supposed to get into all this with Connally.

He also got into the public TV thing again, which has been bugging him and he's concerned that nothing's been done. His point is that it doesn't do anything for us, that supporting NET can't help us in any way, and so we need some action to do something to get the thing unfinanced, and his point is that the board doesn't make any difference, and even if we have appointed most of the board members now, they don't have much to do with day-to-day operations.

Tuesday, June 8, 1971
The P had E in with Weinberger and me first thing this morning after the Cabinet meeting to discuss a new approach to the budget. He made the point that we are not now thinking of spending in political terms. He wants us to stop helping professors and that sort of thing, and look for other areas like that, where we can cut back even though we take some lumps.

Concerning the Domestic Council, he wants them to look

for more things like the automobile safety business, where we can cut back programs that screw things up. In the environment, he wants to take some risks in order to produce some jobs. All of the decisions in the environment and the consumer areas should lean toward things that will create jobs. He makes the point that there won't be any tax legislation in time to do any good as far as stimulating the job level, so we want to look at all budget items in terms of jobs and whenever we can, put them in California. On housing, we should use whatever Administration discretion we can to subsidize housing and thus create jobs.

Late this afternoon he called Colson and me in to tell me about his meeting with NBC where he apparently really whapped the NBC top management on the basis that we ought to quit kidding ourselves and recognize that we all know their newscasters are all completely biased and anti-Administration. There is nothing that management can do about it. The P understands that and doesn't hold it against them, but he wants to be sure that we are all realistic and understand this. Apparently he played this beautifully and Colson was practically ecstatic over the effect he felt it had on the NBC people.

Wednesday, June 9, 1971

Late morning he had E and me over and got into quite a discussion on priorities. Makes the point again that out of all the things we've done, nothing comes through clearly. The Cabinet officers have established no image of themselves. E raised the point that he wants to do some polling and analysis and get out the whole question of fear. He thinks that the questions in the polls are not asked right. For instance, on crime, he thinks we have got to bring the issue back on allaying the fear of crime. That we've accomplished this; people aren't as afraid now as they were when we came in. They are not afraid about the war, they are not afraid about the crime in the streets, they are not afraid about the riots on the campuses, they are not afraid about the cities burning, etc. But they don't know why they are not so much afraid, and we have got to get that point across.

He raised the Teddy Kennedy question again, makes the point that we've got to do some long-range planning regarding him, on the basis that it may very well go his way, and if so, there will be great pressures to forget Chappaquiddick, which is, of course, his most vulnerable point, that we can't let be forgotten.

Thursday, June 10, 1971

P this morning got into a discussion of how we're going to have to make a shift, as of now, throughout our entire shop to begin a totally oriented commitment to relating everything we do to the political side, without appearing to do so. This has got to apply to everything. The question to be asked in weighing every answer is, "Does this help us politically?" He says it's OK to do a few nice things, but damn few. And even if they don't directly help us politically, if the answer is no, it doesn't help us politically, but that failure to do it looks political in the act of failing to do it, then we should do it because we have to.

Late in the afternoon he decided to take the *Sequoia* out for dinner to avoid the pre-wedding dinner parties, and at the last minute had me ask Connally and Rogers, and then he added E and Flanigan and me. At dinner, Rogers leveled an incredible blast with some pretty strong language at the whole Commerce Department. Saying that their personnel abroad were terrible, but their whole setup was very bad. This sort of shocked everybody there, and no one knew exactly how to respond to it.

Rogers also got into quite a defense of the State Department, particularly on the drug business. He's concerned that at the Monday meeting of ambassadors, on trying to stop drug production and traffic, that we be very careful not to be critical of the drug-producing countries but rather appear to be trying to work cooperatively with them. Overall, Bill did not distinguish himself at this session, and I don't think that he gained much in the eyes of the P.

Saturday, June 12, 1971

P came into the office this morning to while away the time before the wedding. In the early afternoon, he went over to the EOB and had some lunch, then after a while he called me and said he wanted to go down to the press tent and see what the setup was before the wedding.

During the morning, he kept looking out to see if it was going to rain, because that was the big problem with the question of having the wedding outside. He felt very strongly that it should be outside, and finally, by noon, when they were about to make the decision to move it inside because it was raining a little bit and looked like it was going to rain some more. Then, at my suggestion, he called Tricia and talked for a little while and bolstered her up because she wanted to keep it outside also, although Julie and Pat and everybody else was urging that they move it in. On that basis, they made the decision to go outside, and it was a good decision, even though it was touch-and-go for quite a while because it did rain on and off and the guests did get a little wet.

Anyway, from the EOB he called and said that he wanted to go down to the press tent. Ziegler and I joined him and we walked down West Executive into the Southwest Gate, across the drive, and down to the press tent. He did a walking press interview all the way and they got a lot of pretty good personal questions. The one where he got tangled up a bit was on the honeymoon. They asked where they were going and he misunderstood the question and thought they were asking if he was going, which he said he could tell them he wasn't and they said no, we're asking where they're going, he said that wherever they're going, I won't be there. Thus giving them a pretty good hint that it was Camp David.

The actual seating of the guests had to be delayed for about 45 minutes because of the rain. They held them in the South Hall. The P started getting pretty nervous; he kept calling me from upstairs, saying to hurry up and get it set up. Especially after the rain stopped, he didn't want them to waste time pulling up the plastic covering from the carpet or anything else, he just wanted to get the chairs up and the guests seated and the thing underway. As it turned out, it worked out beautifully and the whole thing was a sensational success.

On the way out of the aisle, the P and Mrs. Nixon cut out from the regular procession and went over to greet Mrs. Tkach, who was in a wheelchair and is in extremely bad shape. It was a very touching moment. As Jo and I went through the receiving line, Tricia made the point that it was Bob and Daddy who stuck with us on doing it outside and worked the whole thing out, and obviously she was very pleased that we had. The P distinguished himself during the dancing period as he very graciously danced

not only with Tricia, but then with Pat, and then Lynda Robb
and Julie, and I guess one or two others. He looked like he was
having a good time and did a superb job of it.

After the bridal couple left, the P and Mrs. Nixon went
upstairs and he called me up. He and Pat, Julie and Bebe, were
in the West Hall, talking the whole thing over, and the P asked
me for a rundown on how it had all gone. I gave him a very
enthusiastic report. The P was in great spirits.

Julie wanted to watch the thing on TV, and the P said if
you do, I'm going to have to leave, but we persuaded him to
look at it on TV, on the NBC special which came on right
at that time. He saw himself going down that aisle and made
the comment that, well at least I'm standing pretty straight.
Obviously the ladies in the family had been nagging him
about standing up straight, and he was pleased to see himself
looking pretty good. The TV was great and he realized it, so
it was a good thing he did watch it, and I think that bucked
him up, too. All in all, the whole thing was a sensational day.

Sunday, June 13, 1971

The P spent most of the day at the EOB with Bebe, while
Mrs. Nixon helped Julie pack for her departure to join David,
after a reception for the Nixon and Ryan families in the
morning at the Residence as a follow-up to the wedding. The
family then took Julie to the airport and returned to the house
for dinner.

The big deal today was a break in *The New York Times* of
the reprinting of the 40-volume Vietnam Papers, that covered
the whole McNamara operation. Haig called to tell me about
it before I had seen the *Times*. Apparently we didn't know
that the papers had been taken out and *The New York Times*
has all of them except one volume of the 40. It really blasts
McNamara and Kennedy and Johnson. He *(Haig)* feels that
it will cause terrible problems with the South Vietnamese
government. The point is that it's criminally traitorous that
the documents got to *The New York Times,* and even more
so that the *Times* is printing them. The *Times* says they plan
to print the whole series of articles. The key now is for us to
keep out of it and let the people that are affected cut each
other up on it.

These were of course the "Pentagon Papers," the 7,000-page study of American involvement in Southeast Asia from World War II to 1968 which had been commissioned by Robert McNamara while he was Secretary of Defense. It was the largest leak of classified documents in American history.

Monday, June 14, 1971

The day started up with some more follow-up on the *New York Times* story, which was discussed at the staff meeting. When the P called me in, he raised the point, too, that there's cause in this for everyone to be concerned, especially regarding foreign policy. As to staff leakage, etc., the P is especially concerned about Henry's staff. He thinks that we should get the story out on . . . at Brookings, who is the suspected villain.

The first suspect for the leakage was a former Defense Department employee who was then a Fellow at the Brookings Institution.

Just smoke Brookings out, using names, and demand that charges be brought. He also wanted me to talk to Haig about the staff situation, particularly with concern to the P's papers and how we're taking care of them.

Tuesday, June 15, 1971

The big thing today was still the *New York Times* story follow-up, as they go on running it and the whole thing builds substantively. Mitchell went ahead last night with his request of them to cease publication; they refused. So today he went for an injunction, got a temporary restraining order, and probably will be able to get an injunction. After meeting with the P this afternoon, decided to file criminal charges. So we're pretty much in the soup on the whole thing now. The real problem is to try to establish clearly that the Administration's interest here is in the violation of Top Secret classifications rather than in the release of this particular material. The problem otherwise is that we're going to be tied into it and get blamed for the same kind of deception that was practiced by the Johnson Administration.

The P dictated a memo to me this morning, issuing orders

that there is to be no contact and no interviews by any member of the White House staff with *The New York Times* unless there is express permission from the P, which he does not intend to grant. I called all the key staff members and covered them on this, and interestingly enough, they all agreed that it was the right idea. He also felt that we should launch an attack on the *Times;* that it was a reckless disclosure of secrets and shocking breach of security. The other point that he wanted us to emphasize was that this is a family quarrel of another Administration, that they're washing their dirty linen in public and that we aren't going to get into it, but we do believe in the security of secret documents and we'll have to enforce that.

Wednesday, June 16, 1971

New York Times reaction again dominated the day today, starting with the staff meeting, where we got into a discussion in the 8:00 meeting, with Shultz making the point that there are three main issues: the question of whether this should have been classified or declassified to begin with; the point that Top Secret material is published every day and the question of why this is any different from others; and the concern about how devious Defense and Foreign Affairs intelligence are. They're always playing a cat-and-mouse game, never a straight statement.

There's a real problem here of Johnson's pure deceit, for instance at his press conference where he said he was not doing exactly what he was doing. Another idea was that we should declassify all the material that can be declassified and announce now that we're going to do so. Do enough of a release so that we can't be accused of suppression. That, though, creates the problem of declassifying other documents or releasing them to the Senate on the basis of their being leaked or on any other basis.

The P got into this, on and off all during the day, wanted to be sure that we're making an all-out effort on editorials.

He feels that we do have to make the issue that the press is massively endangering our security, paint them as lawbreakers, disloyal, etc. That there's no question of right to know or how we got into Vietnam, but we must maintain the integrity of government.

As we were talking at midday today, he heard some kids

shouting out on the South Lawn and realized the 1,000 Rural Electrification Administration youth group were gathering to be addressed by Cliff Hardin and then taken on a White House tour. After pondering the whole thing, on and off for a while, he decided that he should go out and greet them, which he then did on a completely spontaneous and unannounced basis, and it was a big success. Now he feels he wants to do more of that kind of thing, which indeed he should.

Thursday, June 17, 1971

New York Times is still the major item of the day. P spent considerable time at a number of sessions with Colson, Ziegler, E, K, and various combinations of them, going over points to be made. Particularly anxious to get across that this is no skin off of our hide, this involves the Kennedy-Johnson Administrations; there are no documents from this Administration.

He asked me to tell E that he wasn't sure Mitchell should delay the grand jury. He thinks that we have to play boldly and not be afraid of the risks. Mitchell delayed it anyway; in fact, he already had when the P was talking to me.

He made the point that things were the same way in the Hiss case, that everybody will get a little jittery and want to start pulling back, but we want to fight it. This involves security.

P worked on the ideas of what he ought to say at Rochester tomorrow. His point is to speak to the policy of this Administration regarding security. We've got to enforce a law that is passed by Congress. He then mentioned to K, E, and me, that he's thinking in very big terms on this and that he may argue the case before the Supreme Court himself, to indicate the importance of it. He wants to use the line that the *Times* now says that stolen goods are fit to print. Also, he ordered Henry to get the Lodge files on the murder of Diem. Part of which is covered in the files that the *Times* has, but part of it isn't, and he thinks that we should get some of those in our possession. Apparently Lodge has the only files at this point.

Friday, June 18, 1971

Again today *The New York Times* papers is the big story.

We pretty much agreed, although Henry K was in violent

disagreement, that LBJ should go on to defend the Presidency. But then learned late this evening that Johnson had completely collapsed, was in a state of being totally unstrung, feels that the country is lost, that the P can't rule and that they're out to destroy him, etc. So that ended any participation by him.

The whole thing kept going back and forth in phone calls. E set up a meeting of the group in Washington to work on final recommendations, etc. As of late this evening, the matter was still pending consideration by the courts. There was something of a flap on the point raised by *The New York Times* that the question was now moot because *The Washington Post* had the materials, so we went into the DC court asking for an injunction against the *Post,* which was not granted and we moved immediately to the Court of Appeals. The question of whether to go into the DC court was raised by John Mitchell, calling E while we were in Rochester. John and I agreed we should go, as did Mitchell, so that was the way that was set.

First thing this morning, the P met with President *(Leopold)* Senghor of Senegal. That was supposed to be a half-hour meeting before we left for Rochester; unfortunately Senghor wasn't told that, and didn't get to the point of anything that he had planned to discuss until the meeting had been going about forty-five minutes. Also, he speaks only French, so translation was required. This, needless to say, didn't get the P off to too good a start for the day. Rochester itself went pretty well. The crowds weren't as big as we had hoped for, but then the demonstrations weren't as bad as we were afraid that they might be, either.

Saturday, June 19, 1971
At Key Biscayne. The P had me over this morning for three or four hours at the Residence; he had the door open to his study so it was extremely hot. He had his bathing suit on and a sport shirt and was smoking a cigar; I had on my coat and tie. He had called me about 8:30 in the morning, talked for a few moments on the phone, and then told me to come over. I hadn't even gotten up yet, so ended up never having any breakfast. He got into a critique on the Rochester trip, feeling that we had missed some things on the motorcade operation, etc., and he had some ideas on kinds of things that he could do in these towns when we're on the road that would make

the trips more effective. Another idea that concerned him was the stock market drop, for which he was having trouble figuring the reason.

Sunday, June 20, 1971

At Key Biscayne. The P was on the phone for a long time this morning, caught me over at the hotel at breakfast, then frequently on various ideas during the day as they came up, all regarding *The New York Times* case. He explained to me that in order to understand this whole thing, we have to understand the Hiss case. That they're very similar, although none of us really realizes it. In that case, too, the papers themselves didn't make any difference. They were old and outdated and unimportant; the key thing was that we got across the point that Hiss was a spy, a liar, and a Communist.

The question on this one is basically the same thing. These papers are not what are important in themselves, what is important is that someone stole them and that the *Times* printed them. He feels strongly that we've got to get Ellsberg nailed hard on the basis of being guilty of stealing the papers. That's the only way we're going to make the case of the press having done something bad and violated the law in publishing stolen documents.

> We now knew that the papers had been leaked by Daniel Ellsberg, a former Pentagon aide who subsequently worked at the Rand Corporation.

Monday, June 21, 1971

Still in Key Biscayne. The P went over to the Teamsters this morning on short notice, although we had tentatively worked out a plan for doing it over the last few days. He went into their executive board and constitutional committee meeting and met privately with Fitzsimmons for a few minutes beforehand. The whole thing was very cordial. He talked primarily on foreign policy, gave them a good buildup, emphasized that he was the first President since FDR to visit the Teamsters, and got a big hand for that, as he did when he said that he knew that he could always count on them for solid backing on matters of foreign policy and anything that affected the security of the nation. It was a good session and well worth taking the time.

Tuesday, June 22, 1971

The big problem currently today was the round of Senate resolutions launched by a Cook-Stevens amendment to require an end of the war in nine months. This got all hung up in a lot of parliamentary maneuvering, amendments, etc. The net result was that Cook-Stevens was amended by Stennis to put in a relatively favorable amendment for us, and then it passed on that basis. But then Mansfield offered his resolution as a substitute for it and Mansfield passed 57–42, which is a pretty strong vote and solidly against us. So we've now taken our basic defeat in the Senate on the antiwar deal.

This worried the P some, and worried Henry a great deal more. He got very cranked up about it because he really feels that this is the collapse of the country and it will mean not much chance for his negotiation in Paris this weekend, which is especially galling to him. It is contradictory on its face, because setting a deadline is totally inconsistent with a cease-fire negotiation and release of POW's. So the enemy's incentive to negotiate would be eliminated.

The *New York Times* papers question goes on. The P now wants to have Huston set up a small team under E to start rifling through all the secret documents and especially the Cuban missile crisis, etc., as well as Vietnam. And then get some newspapers to demand that it come out and also get a congressman to do so.

He got to talking on the general subject and made the point that he had a call from the *Chicago Tribune* and that they're demanding that we release and declassify World War II and Korea documents, also the Bay of Pigs and the Cuban confrontation. The P is ordering that this be done; everything that's not involved in current security.

Wednesday, June 23, 1971

The P had breakfast with Mansfield this morning and apparently he relayed to him two points. First, they went into the question of the release of the Pentagon Papers, and the P worked out a deal whereby we will turn the Papers over to Mansfield and Albert and they can figure out how to handle them. This puts the heat completely on them. It fits in with

E's strategy on the basis that they will then have to hold hearings, etc., to follow up on this, which will be an enormous problem for the Democrats to figure out how to cope with.

The P then, after leading Mansfield on, and finishing that up, indirectly led him into the question of the Mansfield amendment yesterday calling for a date certain to end the war in nine months, and the P gave him a basic ultimatum regarding the harm that the Senate did. He rather happily described this to K and me and E, who was there for it, in his office. He made the point that we are in the middle of negotiations that started May 31 and we'll know within a month whether the Senate action has ruined those negotiations. If so, the P will have to go on to the people and explain that the reason for the collapse was the action of the Senate and that Mansfield will have to take that blame. He made the point to us that if we do get to the point where we have to withdraw because the negotiations failed, he will do it with a total bombing of the North to eliminate their capability of attacking, so in order to get out, we escalate to accelerate our withdrawal.

Henry was in and out several times in the morning, as he was getting ready to leave for London for his cover-up to his move on to Paris this weekend for the negotiations. The P made the point to him that he's got to get it settled, that from here on everything is based on the domestic political outlook and he's got to realize that. He makes the point, too, that with the Mansfield resolution, now maybe we have the excuse for flushing the whole deal. We had to make that decision last year, either to stand up or to flush and we made the decision to stand up, feeling that we'd never have the chance to decide it again. But now we probably do have that chance, because of the Senate resolution, and if the negotiations fail, that may be exactly what we will do.

On the release of the material, he made the point we won't compromise codes and sources, but we are going to release other materials, and he wants to have the *Tribune* start demanding papers.

Regarding the declassification of other papers, he's determined to do everything we can to our advantage, on the assumption that we have only a year to do it, for sure. He wants to move into World War II, Korea, the Cuban Missile Crisis, the Bay of Pigs, and the murder of Trujillo. He wants me to set it up to give someone free rein in these files and put a full team on it that's absolutely trustworthy and get it all done within this next year. Also, now that we have our man in the IRS, he wants to pull the Clark Clifford file and also all the top supporters of the doves, the full list with a full field audit, and see what we can make of it on analysis.

Thursday, June 24, 1971

We took off at midday for the trip to Indiana, where the P did the dedication ceremony for the plaque, or historical marker, commemorating his mother's home. He gave an excellent little talk in the courthouse square, and the whole thing came off extremely well as a bit of rural Americana. There was a big crowd, very enthusiastic, heartland-type people. The principal of the school was the emcee, the little girl who was the chairman of the Junior Historical Society introduced the P, and at the end the band played "God Bless America" while everybody sang together. Then the P followed through on his plan to drive from there to Indianapolis, rather than taking the helicopter back. We had given no advance notice and our subterfuge worked well. We had only the press pool with us.

I rode in the car with the P. Unfortunately, it was hot as the dickens and, with the glass top and sides of his car, it got hotter and hotter inside. We kept looking for opportunities to stop on the unannounced route, and finally found one in the form of a little local newspaper office, where they had heard on the police radio ahead of time that we were driving in and had whipped up a sign on wrapping paper saying welcome Mr. President and Max. This referred to Max Friedersdorf of our staff, who was born in Jennings County and was a friend of the editor of the paper. The P stopped there and chatted with the newspaper staff for a little while. Then we drove on and saw a bunch of old ladies standing on the road, stopped to talk to them, and discovered they were from an old folks' home. There were quite a few people along the way, as the word got out by radio that we were coming. Overall, I think that it was well worthwhile doing it. But both the P and I were dripping wet and really hot by the time we got to the hotel in Indianapolis. Fortunately there was time to take a shower and get cleaned up. The Hovde dinner came out fine.

On to Chicago. Mayor Daley met us at Meigs Field and

rode in with the P to the hotel, and as the P described it later, it was a real comic opera operation. Daley is just unbelievable. He had the fireboats out, spraying red, white, and blue water, and when we arrived at the hotel, he had his Mayor Daley bagpipe band out in front playing for us. Apparently the P had a good chat with him about a number of local and national issues. Daley made the point strongly that he was with the P all the way on foreign policy, and the P was very pleased with him.

We had a flap because a couple of hours before we arrived, a man was found carrying two guns in Grant Park, along the route we would have taken to the Blackstone, where we usually stay, but didn't stay tonight. The police got into a gun battle with him and shot him eight times, killing him. That created a bit of a local stir.

Sunday, June 27, 1971

At Camp David. Meeting with John Connally. I discussed the Vice Presidency problem with him; he basically agrees that there is a problem and that either we have to change the VP's posture and attitudes and the P must give him something to do in a very clear-cut way. If he's going to keep him he has to use him, otherwise he's got to let him go. He is inclined to agree that he's more likely to be a liability than an asset, and that replacement would probably be a good idea if it could be done without creating a stir. He wasn't aware of the possibility of appointing a replacement, but seemed very much intrigued about it when I raised it. He didn't express any thoughts as to who the replacement should be. He felt that it should not be either an all-out conservative or an all-out liberal, but rather a man in the P's basic image, who will articulate the P's position well. Principally, one who will be an asset in the campaign. He said he'll give it some thought as to specific suggestions as to who it ought to be, but he didn't have any ideas offhand. Obviously, he was very interested in the whole concept of the change being made.

Monday, June 28, 1971

K was in this morning, reviewing his schedule for announcements. As of now, he expects to announce on July 15 that we will be sending Bruce to Peking in October, and that's all we'll say at that time.

The announcement is to take five minutes of prime time at 8:00 California time. The P made the comment that we're sitting now at a great watershed in history, clearly the greatest since WW II. Henry interjected that he considered it to be the greatest since the Civil War, as far as the overall effect on the nation. We then got into some discussion of who goes to Peking. Definitely, Rogers would. Then the P raised Mansfield and Scott, which both Henry and I are very much opposed to. The P made the point that Henry must get an agreement out of Chou En-lai that no Democrat is to go to China before the P goes. The question was also raised as to how we postpone the UN date.

As the day went on, we got into a monumental flap between K and the State Department as Henry discovered in *The New York Times* an article that indicated that K would be going to Peking as the P's representative sometime in '72. Henry's convinced that Rogers leaked this on purpose in an attempt to try and stop Henry as the negotiator with the Chinese, and to try to break off his relations with Dobrynin. The same story had a number of accurate reports on changes in ambassadorial assignments, which Henry feels were just put in to validate the other points.

The P told me to talk to Haig about keeping Henry calmed down, because there's nothing we can do, we just have to play out the game. He also said to order Ziegler to make the point that we have no comment on these speculative stories.

The P met with his economic group: Connally, Shultz, Flanigan, Peterson, the Council of Economic Advisors, and Hodgson. (Stans was unable to be there.) He really cut loose on them this morning. He sat all alone on his side of the Cabinet table. The rest of them lined up on the VP's side. As he started talking, a thunderstorm hit and there were loud claps of thunder outside.

President's Talk to Economic Group
He made the point that he has made a number of tough decisions regarding foreign policy in recent weeks and months. That before each of them there was a lot of opposition, from Defense, State, Joint Chiefs, etc., and that some of them had gone to the extreme of sending memoranda in after the decision was made, but before it was announced, giving the department's view on the decision. He said that it's perfectly all

right for them and others to do this, but the right way to express a dissenting view is in the form of a memo to the P, with the clear understanding that the memo is for the P. He then injected sarcastically that he'll be sure, once he's received it, that it's marked Top Secret so it will get out in all the newspapers. He said that we cannot have a debate in the press; it must be a debate inside because the P must know all the views.

He made the point that the one who goes up or down on any of these decisions is not you, it's the P. If it works, I'll give you credit; if it doesn't work, I'll keep your views a secret. Then he referred to Cambodia, and the fact that a number of people who had written memos to him on Cambodia were very happy that he had not made them public, since they were all opposed and it had turned out to be a great success.

Then he said the decisions on the economy are final, we will not have a wage price board. We will have jawboning, but his way. There will be no change in tax policy now and he doesn't want any discussion now regarding the possibility of a change in policy later. To have any confidence, there must be certainty. To have certainty, there must be one voice. So he's designating one man, the Secretary of Treasury, as the economic spokesman. He's ideally suited for this role because he doesn't leak things in advance. He said that everybody in this room will follow the line announced by the Secretary of Treasury, or on occasion by the P. He even said, "I sat in that chair as VP for eight years, and if I disagreed, by God, I always told the P, I never told the press." We have a plan, we will follow it, we have confidence in it. No guidance is to be provided to the press, off the record or any other way. If you can't follow this rule, or if you can't go along with the Administration decision, then get out.

Having said that, he got up abruptly and walked out of the room, leaving them all pretty much gaping. He had Henry and me sit in as did E. Henry was ecstatic afterward and made the comment, that was one of the great moments here.

Tuesday, June 29, 1971

Today started with the 8:00 Cabinet meeting at which the P delivered his blast to the Cabinet along the same lines that he had done with the Economic group yesterday. He was in for a half an hour, which was the total length of the meeting, and the P did all the talking. Walked in, started it, delivered his pitch, got up, and walked out. He opened with the point that this was probably the most important Cabinet meeting this year, and perhaps through next year. He had only the Cabinet members present, with a couple of undersecretaries sitting in for those who were absent, and I was the only staff member present.

President's Talk to Cabinet

He started by talking about the controversy on the Pentagon Papers, and said if we are going to have order in government, there must be a process for making decisions so we can get the best possible advice without being compromised by it being publicized. We are not talking about history, we're talking about now. Down in the government are a bunch of sons of bitches. Some of those that you've appointed may be well-intentioned sons of bitches, but there's still a problem. There are some in the Civil Service who are dedicated, but many who sit in the meetings and debriefings, etc., are out to get us. This is true of all administrations but it's worse now, and it's strange because I've been much more permissive than any other P.

We have yet to fire one of these people.

From now on, Haldeman is the lord high executioner. Don't you come whining to me when he tells you to do something. He will do it because I asked him to and you're to carry it out. The P must have the best possible advice, with the bark off, but he must not see it in the newspapers, and that isn't going to happen anymore. We've checked and found that 96 percent of the bureaucracy are against us; they're bastards who are here to screw us. We don't need to be concerned about the so-called open Administration. We're pretty open—like a sieve, everything gets out. Every day we see that one department is fighting another. Justice versus Treasury, and so on. Of course they are and they always will be, but they cannot be doing it in the press. The P will make the decisions, such as appointments to various posts. I'll make them. I'm not referring to you here, but to the people in your woodwork.

You've got to realize the press aren't interested in liking you, they're only interested in news or in screwing me. So don't fall for the line that they want something just for their guidance and background and so on. They're going to screw you with it. Regarding Presidential decisions, appointments and otherwise,

I want discipline. It's up to Haldeman to police it. We have ways to do it that will be extremely effective. When he calls, I want action. Unless we act effectively on the leaks now, it will be too late later next year. In the economic field this is a very difficult subject. The economists don't know what to do. For example, Arthur Burns has changed his mind over and over. He has memos in on all different positions. Unfortunately, he said each of them publicly before he sent the memo to the P. There are many different views now regarding the economy, taxes, and so on. A lot of papers have been presented for the historical record and it's fine for everyone to do that, but the outcome depends on success or failure. From the advisors' viewpoint, if he's wrong and we succeed, it'll be forgotten and the P will never reveal the fact that he had given the wrong advice. If the advice is right and we fail, it'll still come out that he advised the right thing and he can be a hero while we fall. So the advisor has the luxury of winning both ways. The P doesn't have that choice. He's the only one in this room who has to run for office.

Regarding the economy, I've made the decision. It'll be announced by Connally today. He's our economic spokesman. You're free to express your views only when you support the P, but the whole damn thing on the economy has already been in the papers and thus it affects the decisions. So we've created the impression on this thing and on other things, not that we're wrong or that we're right, but that we're not sure. So what does the businessman do? He decides to wait and see what we're going to do. There's only one thing worse than being wrong and that's not being sure. So we're stopping that crap today. The first time there's a leak out of this Administration regarding an inside debate, we're going to crack down on the people at the top or at the second level and they're going to go, so start looking for the scapegoat. You're all on the top and each of you have a few loyal lieutenants, but beneath you you have a whole department full of vipers and they'll strike because they want to beat us, especially next year. For example, Goldstein at the Bureau of Labor and Statistics, a left-wing radical who hates us. So the Secretary of Labor now gives the policy and political interpretations. Don't worry about not being an open administration. Civil servants weren't appointed to represent us. Regarding the economy, we can't stop the situation with the Fed. Burns can say what he pleases. I hope he'll see the wisdom someday of being helpful and restrained in what he says, or he can be independent. Period. Our decisions are there will be no wage-price controls, no wage-price board. We will call in the steel people and raise hell on both prices and wages, on specifics. We are going ahead with the depreciation allowance, but there will be no increase in exemptions, no investment tax credit. There's no point in these, because we can't get them through Congress anyway and that would just show the impotence of the Presidency. Many of you have been on one side or the other of these, or both sides. I believe we're on the right track, but there must be confidence that we know what we're doing and that we have competence in what we're doing.

Haldeman will be telling the White House staff all of this, right down to the pipsqueaks. We've got a lot of little people who love to be heroes. *(Daniel)* Ellsberg has gone out and said he's not guilty because what he did, he did for the sake of the country. Hiss and the Rosenbergs and those people all said the same thing. It's irrelevant which side Ellsberg is on, we can't have the decision made regarding what is to be released made by someone who doesn't have the responsibility. This ruins an orderly government. I get a lot of advice on PR and personality and how I've got to put on my nice-guy hat and dance at the White House, so I did it, but let me make it clear that's not my nature. We're going to go forward on Ellsberg and prosecute him.

The success or failure of the Administration depends on discipline. Absolute frankness on advice around the table here, and I'll take the responsibility, so don't hesitate, don't worry that you'll look bad, I won't tell. You'll make the record if you look good. We want a strong hard line regarding the decisions before they're made, or we can't govern, especially regarding the budget, which will be tough. Put the blame on the P, he said no, that you can't tell the press anything until it's decided. The P has the right to advice without pressure, especially pressure by leaks to bring press pressure. I want you to make this same talk to your subordinates. Haldeman has the worst job that anybody can have in the White House. I remember poor old Bedell Smith, who had to carry out a lot of tough decisions for Eisenhower. In his later years he started to drink a lot, probably to try and forget the things he had to do in his early years. He was at my house one night and he started to cry, and he said, "All my life I've just been Ike's prat boy, doing his dirty work." Well, Haldeman is my prat boy—he'll be down the throat of anyone here regarding leaks if they affect the national interest. When he talks, it's me talking, and don't think it'll do you any good to come and talk to me, because I'll be tougher than he is. That's the way it's going to be.

Then he just got up and walked out, that was the end of the meeting. It was pretty impressive, for all of them. I walked out right after he did. They seemed to be very much impressed, so I think it had its effect.

Wednesday, June 30, 1971
We had the Court decision *(on the Pentagon Papers case)* this afternoon, and that pretty much dominated the developments. The Court went 6 to 3 against us. After the NSC meeting this afternoon, the P had Laird and Mitchell into his office and called K and me in for a discussion on the Court decision and how we should handle the reaction. Laird took the view that he should supply copies of all of the Pentagon Papers to the press because they have agreed to delete the sensitive sections. Henry argued very strongly that we have to maintain the principle of the security of government, and that we should not give the papers out.

There's a general agreement that there is very definitely a conspiracy here, on these papers, and Laird alluded to some intelligence they had that he didn't get into detail on.

Third Quarter: July–September

Thursday, July 1, 1971

In discussing the Pentagon Papers question, in one of a long series of long meetings today, the P raised the point of the Hiss question again. One of the points he kept making about Alger Hiss is that his family was beyond reproach, etc. He wants E to realize that we have a great opportunity here, that this is a conspiracy. He really got going again on trying to get somebody in fast to take this whole project on, like the P took on the Hiss case, 18 hours a day, with total dedication, tracking down every lead, leaking stuff to the press. He made the point that the establishment has a new intellectual arrogance which leads them to think that they know best and that the determination regarding what the public should know should be made by them. We serve a different morality. Elected officials establish the law; the courts enforce them. Those who disobey, even if they think the laws are wrong, are immoral. If the cause is right, they say it justifies breaking the law, but that's fascism, the means justify the ends.

Friday, July 2, 1971

The P had his schedule free for the day except at midday with a bunch of open-office-hour-type things and a luncheon. He was interested in the follow-up on the conspiracy question. He wants to get Huston back on one special line of inquiry. He had some points that he wanted Colson to follow up on.

He had E and me in late this afternoon, making the point that there are two phases to this. One, that E should handle the whole declassification and protection of documents, dealing with the courts, etc., but the other is the investigation and development of the conspiracy, which requires a dirty guy to really go after it. The committee can then call up the witnesses before they're indicted and we can start hauling all those people in. This will require great preparation, and a top staff man; depends on hard work, running down everything. He thought that it was almost worth pulling E off the domestic stuff and having him do it, because he really wants to get it done.

We had a flap with Rogers that Haig called me about. He had waited until Henry was gone and then sent a memo in saying that he was going to send Sisco back to the Middle East to try to bring Israel and Egypt together into a settlement. Haig feels this would be disastrous, and asked that I help in trying to cool it somehow. I talked to the P, he agreed that we should tell Rogers that this has possibilities, but he's a little uneasy about moving now, so he wants him to hold up until we can think it through. I told Haig to go ahead and handle it that way with Rogers, which he's going to do.

The other big item of the day was the unemployment announcement down to 5.6 from 6.2 last month, the biggest one-month drop in history, and obviously a great story for us. Unfortunately, as usual, the Bureau of Labor Statistics screwed it up and said that it wasn't really important because it was due to a statistical quirk. This drove the P right up the wall tonight, and he started hounding Colson on the phone every couple of minutes, demanding that we get Goldstein fired, etc. Colson overreacted and started bouncing around in the woodwork, getting action underway and finally got around to calling me. In the meantime he had Shultz on a special airplane being brought back down for a 7:30 meeting tomorrow morning to get things started so they can give the P a plan at 8:00, when he says he'll be at his desk. I doubt that he will, but he just might out of orneriness.

Monday, July 5, 1971

At Camp David, in the morning, he phoned while I was up at the pool. Concerned about the weekend's news on the economy and says we're going to have to start playing a harder game with Arthur, and also we've really got to put the screws on the bad guy at the Bureau of Labor Statistics. He's talked to Colson, told him to get a group together regarding Vietnam, making the point that we shouldn't fall for the Democratic line that Vietnam is not going to be an issue. That we've got to make it an issue, making the point that the Democrats got us in, Nixon got us out, and then the Democrats tried to sabotage Nixon's efforts to get us out. Also, he wants E's people to get going with major accomplishments: one, crime, pointing out that we've reduced crime in the major cities, we've reduced student unrest, we're launching successfully a war on drugs, we've strengthened the Court, and we've ended the era of permissiveness. The second being the war. Third is economics. It's what happens that will count, nothing that we can say is going to make any difference.

He witnessed the certification of the Twenty-sixth Amendment, the 18-year-old vote, today. We had a group of 500 musical kids, singers and musicians—The Young Americans— who are going to make a tour of Europe starting tomorrow. They did a spectacular job. They were really enthusiastic when the P came into the East Room, and gave him a tremendous ovation. Several of the girls crying, as they were so impressed with the whole occasion. The whole group of 500 sang "The Battle Hymn of the Republic," and it was really great. Unfortunately, as usual the TV gave us virtually no coverage, and that got him stirred up later on this evening.

Tuesday, July 6, 1971

Started in Washington, with some meetings this morning. One with Mitchell and E regarding the whole conspiracy theory. The P is, of course, convinced that Ellsberg is not a lone operator, and that we've got to move on this thing. He made the point to Mitchell, that we need the cooperation from Hoover. This has to be a case that's tried in the newspapers; not the Ellsberg part, because he's already been indicted *(on June 28),* but we need to get the rest smoked out, via Congress and the press, rather than letting them get into court cases, where they pick up legal protections.

Kansas City went pretty well. Basically uneventful—the usual routine of a media briefing, etc. Nothing really worth covering there. On the plane from Kansas City to San Clemente, he had me up for a while, then had a long session with Rogers, Helms, and Haig to discuss the Middle East. He reviewed that meeting with me afterward and feels that Rogers is basically right on some of the points that he makes, particularly that we should appear to be doing something. Rogers apparently told the P that, talking to some of the editors at Kansas City, especially of the bigger papers, they felt the briefing really wasn't worthwhile. They said that it wasn't too interesting, and that the only thing that saved it was the P's participation. When we got to San Clemente, he headed for home, as did I.

Wednesday, July 7, 1971

The P got into the office at 7:00 this morning. I didn't get in until 8:30, and he called me in then and had me in there from then until nearly 1:00, which is a pretty long solid session. After I got home this afternoon, the P called while I was out sailing and left word for me to call back. When I did he made the point and was quite pleased about it, that as he said, the plot thickens. We now have a message from the Pakistanis, and the secret meeting that they set up is on, but for security reasons, they want it moved to Peking. He thinks this is very significant because they want it at the highest level, and he thinks it's possible that he'll see the old man *(Mao Tse-tung)*, as well as the guy who he originally was going to see *(Chou En-lai)*. He's concluded that he'll have to tell Rogers tomorrow. So this is highly significant and historic.

Thursday, July 8, 1971

At San Clemente. The P called me in with Haig to discuss the plan for informing Rogers of K's mission, and he got into quite a long discussion of how we would handle the notification process on next week's announcement and all that sort of thing. Henry leaves for his trip over the mountain at 3:00 our time, which is 4:00 AM in Pakistan. He goes all the way to Peking, apparently, and will be there overnight.

> This was Kissinger's famous "stomachache maneuver." He pulled out of his meetings in Pakistan on the excuse that he was suffering from a stomachache, and it was announced that he had been taken into the mountains to recuperate for a few days. Under this cover, he actually was flown to Peking to meet with Chou En-lai. This ruse was employed to maintain total secrecy regarding K's meeting with the Chinese.

The P felt very strongly that he would make the announcement on TV, without any preliminary announcement, and the only notifications being to a few of the key countries, and then only 15 minutes before air time. No press briefings in advance, no Congressional notification. He decided that he wanted Haig and me in with him when he told Rogers. He had me call Rogers at 10:15 and ask him to come over at 10:30.

The Rogers meeting really went very well in spite of the P's fear about the whole thing. The P did a superb job of picking up from my earlier information to Rogers, when I told him that there was something cooking in Pakistan, and that *(President of Pakistan)* Yahya Khan had asked for a personal Presidential emissary to pick up a high-level message. The P then said Henry had learned after he got there that they had shifted: rather than just delivering a message to him, they wanted him to come to Peking for a meeting with Chou, and that's what he's doing. Rogers took it all extremely well, and the P went on to elaborate that this all was part of the planning for a visit. Rogers, of course, would be going on the visit, as would Henry. We'd keep it at the lowest possible level as far as numbers, and all this seemed to work out pretty well.

The P obviously is really cranked up about this whole Chinese thing, and did go on and on talking about it. Rogers also was very positive and intrigued, and I would say that the meeting accomplished everything that the P had hoped for, and then some.

Friday, July 9, 1971
In Southern California. P shifted the schedule around to set the budget meetings for Friday and Saturday, and he wants Connally to sit in on all of the meetings. He got back into the whole clearance business, as he keeps doing from time to time. He made the point, too, that we don't want the Pentagon Papers to die, that we want to keep the contents of them built up, and keep that story going because it's important to us. The other item for today was Harlow's report on his conversations with the VP while they were on the trip. Bryce says that he thinks there's a three-out-of-four chance that of his own volition, the VP will withdraw from the ticket, probably in January or so, and that he has some very lucrative outside offers that he'd like to take on, and wants to take on the battle of the press from outside the government, so that thing looks as if it's pretty much lined up.

Saturday, July 10, 1971

Another day starting out early in the morning and ending around midday, as we have all this week. It's worked out great because the P's pulled out somewhere around 1:00 each day, and as soon as he does, I take off to go back to Balboa.

He made the point that when Henry gets back, he'll be the mystery man of the age, and he'll kill the whole thing if he has one word of backgrounder to any press people. So there are to be no backgrounders whatsoever. He has to quit seeing anyone from the *Times* or *Post* on any basis, including the columnists, except for Joe Alsop. One factor, of course, is that Rogers is easier to handle if K doesn't background.

The P made the point that the key to this whole story, however, is to create doubt and mystery. Never deny the "stomachache" thing in Pakistan. Say it was true, but then the other things also happened. The P then went back and sort of reminisced on the conversation that he had with Henry when the message came in. He said Henry was literally trembling when he brought the message up to the P in the Lincoln Room, and the P had ordered out a glass of brandy for each of them, and had a toast, after they read the document. We've got to keep it locked up tight. A call from Henry on the result will probably come around 4:00 or 5:00 tomorrow morning. The P told Al to notify him as soon as Henry called, and they discussed some code words to set up so that Henry would just simply say that it's on or off or postponed, because he doesn't want to risk any leak. He said to use "Eureka" if there was a success and to find out what the Greek word for failure is, to use for the opposite. Also said that when Henry lands here on Tuesday morning, he's to go direct to the P, regardless of the time.

Sunday, July 11, 1971

I didn't go into the office, and there was no contact with the P other than a phone call at 7:50 this morning, when he called, obviously quite pleased, to say that we got the message all right, that they agreed on the time for making a joint communiqué, that the meeting has been put off to spring of next year. The thing was very dramatic in that Henry had met with him for seventeen hours. The communiqué will indicate the meeting Henry had, the place that he met, and the participants. The game on this, of course, is still to play it mum, no word to anybody. The P will tell Rogers. He kind of chortled then because he had talked to Billy Graham just before talking to me, and Graham had asked him how K was feeling, that he was so concerned about his illness, and so on.

Monday, July 12, 1971

The P also had Haig meet with Rogers and tell him about Henry's activities in Paris, both past and present, so that Rogers will be completely up-to-date on all the missions that Henry's been on in the past, and the full deal on this trip. Haig was very concerned about this, and thought that it will probably permanently break it off with him with Henry, but that he would go ahead and do it anyway. I told him I didn't think it would, and that Henry would realize that this was the right thing to do.

Tuesday, July 13, 1971

Today is the day of Henry's return, and that dominated everything, of course. We got in early for Henry's helicopter arrival at 7:00. The P and I met him at the chopper and then the P took him in his golf cart over to the Residence for breakfast. They were there until after 9:00, when the P came over to the office, and I guess Henry went home. The P called me in at 10:00 and quickly reviewed Henry's findings, which basically we already knew. He made the point that our real problem now is to set up something for Rogers to say, and to find a way to finesse Vietnam on Thursday night. The problem being that with all the attention there's been on Vietnam, the public is going to expect a Vietnam announcement when the P says that he's going on the air. It's clear now that Rogers can't give the speech on China in London on Monday, so his speech should be on Vietnam. We got into handling the China question with the United Nations. We will vote in favor of admission of the People's Republic of China, but we will vote against expulsion of Taiwan. We have to figure out how we avoid double-crossing Taiwan in this. The P concluded, therefore, that he can't have a press conference until Rogers announces our China policy, and that either Rogers or Bush has to announce it. Henry was concerned that we not appear to the People's Republic of China to support a two-China policy. The P got into some reflection of how everything all turns around. Years ago he fought the battle for Chiang, and he's always taken the line that we stand by the South Koreans, and that we stand by the South Vietnamese, etc. It's ironic now that Richard Nixon is the one to lead the move in the other direction.

The Chinese visit was apparently a fascinating experience for Henry. They put him directly in a government guest house when he arrived, they told him to rest, and then the top people with whom he conferred, Chou En-lai, the Ambassador to Canada, a sort of Defense Minister–type apparently, and one or two others, plus two very good interpreters, all called on him at the guest house, and they had their talks there. The talks were abruptly recessed and the parties came and went from time to time as they tried to work things out.

Henry hung very tight on our points apparently. At least the way he tells it, and came out extremely well, in that we got the visit and the announcement set up pretty much the way we want it. It's pretty clear that the Chinese want it just as badly as we do and that makes it easier to negotiate. The general feeling of the group was that the North Vietnamese, when they find out about this, will undoubtedly be pushed even more strongly toward working out some negotiation with us, and so that enhances the hope that something will develop there.

After I got home this afternoon, the P called and raised the point that maybe it would be a good idea to take Henry out for dinner tonight. Let him unwind a little. I stalled him and checked with Haig, who was already planning to take Henry out just to block his evening; felt he was dead on his feet and would just want to go for a quick dinner and then get to bed. So I called the P back and he agreed. The P also made the point that K was obsessed with doing something with the press. My own view is that we should avoid the backgrounder with Henry. I agree with Rogers on this, but that's going to be hard to do because Henry really is determined to do it. He obviously did a superb job, and feels he did, and is really ecstatic about it; he thinks we've come off quite well.

Rogers really reacted extremely well, didn't raise any objection except to the idea of Henry backgrounding, and was most gracious in congratulating Henry on the work that he had done, both on China and on Vietnam. So I think that we're over that hurdle, although the P was very worried about it, up until this morning.

Thursday, July 15, 1971

The day of the big speech *(that the P would be going to Peking).* The P was in good spirits and completely relaxed during the day. We got into quite a little discussion on plans for the speech. He's not going to release an advance text, and we didn't inform anybody, including Ziegler or anyone else, of what the content of the speech was going to be, until we got to the TV studio.

We got into some of the problems Rogers pointed out, that we're going to appear to be letting our friends down and they will object. Also, the liberals, on the other side, will make the "Tricky Dick" claim and will complain that there was no consultation with Congress, and do everything they can to scuttle it, so we have a delicate path to tread right down the middle. Rogers urged that we have to make clear what we didn't do. That no agreements were reached, we have no secret deals, no promises, no concessions. We have to reassure them of that, and assure Congress that we will cooperate with them in making the plans. Bill's concerned because he'll be called to testify and wants to be able to cover this. He thinks that we should not use Henry's idea of saying that; because of the delicacy of the situation we will have no comment. We are changing our basic policy and we need to reassure our Pacific allies that we are not changing our policy regarding them, that we don't deal with our friends behind their backs, etc.

Then the P, as he's always done on every speech, read the final draft to me. Then a little later he called Henry in, and again read it to him. He seems to be quite satisfied that it's the way he wants it. So we headed on up by helicopter to Burbank, where we originated at the NBC studio. The speech went well. On arrival at Burbank there was quite a large crowd outside the parking lot, with a surprisingly enthusiastic reception for the P, which, of course, pleased him greatly. We then afterward drove over to Perino's for dinner, the P, E, K, Scali, Ziegler, and me. Had a delicious dinner. The P thoroughly enjoyed himself. We went through a lot of the background discussion on how it had come about, Henry telling some of his stories, which we'd already covered in some detail. The main highlight of the evening for the P was a long lecture on wine selection that he gave to Scali as he ordered up a magnum of Lafitte Rothschild 1961, which turned out to cost $250.

Even with the preparation this afternoon for the speech and

all that he had on his mind, the P called me from his house
to say that he'd been reading the San Diego paper and saw all
the discussion about the convention site and felt that we were
missing a bet by not making a big thing out of the announcement of the San Diego selection and thought we should do
something about that.

The other big thing this afternoon was a call I had from
Connally, who was furious because he had been told that we
had hired a new Treasurer of the United States and that this
had been done without consulting him. This got Connally extremely upset and he said that as a result of this and other
things, he was going to check out. In other words, resign. He
wanted to talk to me about it, but that he was fed up with this
whole thing. I called him later from the studio to try and simmer the thing down after I had checked it out, and gave him
the story on what had happened, but he didn't buy it. He said
that he just wasn't going to tolerate this kind of thing, that
obviously it's forecasting what's to come. At his press conference this morning a reporter said to him that he had word
from the White House that Connally was forced to have the
press conference. He was not a peon and was not going to
function as a slave to the White House staff, and that he knows
he's got a problem when Rogers is out here knifing him with
the P, referring to him as a "gunboat diplomat," etc. There
wasn't much I could do about it today, and I did not tell the
P and told Connally that I was not going to until tomorrow.

He called me at home after midnight to make the point that
we'll have a delicate problem with Rogers tomorrow, regarding K doing the briefing. He wanted me, in notifying Rogers
of it, to emphasize the shift of the focus to the P as K did with
the SALT briefings, and so on. So once again I get to do the
dirty work.

Friday, July 16, 1971
The main focus today was on the aftermath of the speech and
a follow-up on the Connally flap. The P had some follow-up
things. The response to the speech was surprisingly favorable
from all quarters, even the conservatives, and this leads the P
to want a poll this weekend.

We got into the Connally thing a number of times. He had
me call Connally and try to settle it, which I was not successful
in doing, and we ended up getting back to the point that the

P would have to talk with him. Connally requested 30 minutes with him on Monday. At the P's request, I asked Connally to come out here and talk over the weekend, but he didn't want to do it, so we left it that we'd meet on Monday, and the P's now decided that he wants to take Connally and me to dinner on the *Sequoia* and put it to him regarding the Vice Presidency, making the point that we made a big play on China and now we're going to make another big play. If we can't work that out, then we'll go for Secretary of State, as was discussed earlier.

Saturday, July 17, 1971
Still at San Clemente. The P was in for the morning, mainly reviewing the China announcement, going over some follow-up plans. He got into some changes in the schedule plan, as he realized that he was really pretty tired as a result of the tension of all of this, and that he hadn't had a vacation out here, even though he had taken most of the afternoons off. I made the case that he had built himself in his position up to a point now where it seemed to me he would be perfectly justified and would have no problem in announcing a two-week vacation and actually taking off in San Clemente for two full weeks in the latter part of August. He agreed with this, so we'll go ahead and schedule on that basis.

We also got into Bill Rogers' reaction. He felt the whole story on the China thing had played very well, but he said he wanted some time with the P to be sure that what he says and does is correct. He's especially concerned about how to handle the representation question in the United Nations. Needs to decide whether the P wants to make a maximum effort to save the Taiwan seat, and it's ticklish as to whether we really try this or whether we just go through the motions. If we fight, we may still lose, but if we appear to fold, the conservatives will hit us.

In terms of general commentary regarding the whole China thing, P made several wide-ranging observations. One thing, he was commenting on how stupid the Birchers are in attacking us on this, because they should see this in terms of a matter against the Russians and be delighted with it. The point to make is, what would have happened if we hadn't done this? We'd be collapsing now in Vietnam, and the Congressional resolutions on pullout would be passing; the UN issue for

China was lost anyway. He told Henry to tell the right wing not to get out on a limb on this stuff, that they've got to trust the P. Then we got to talking about Yahya's cooperation in this whole thing with Henry, particularly how funny it was that Yahya made such a point at the luncheon in Islamabad of making a fuss over Henry's so-called stomachache, and in effect ordering him to the mountain retreat, saying he would send his Deputy Foreign Minister to keep him company, and so on, making a big public fuss out of Henry's indisposition so it would be reported as such and give Henry the cover he was seeking.

He commented at some length with Henry as to the strain that he'd been through on this. You don't realize how much tension you're under in trying to keep a secret of this magnitude. He also commented that the thesis that the right wing has, that there should be no contact with the Communists, is absolutely wrong. The P has always felt that was wrong. He's always favored the need to talk. Talked about the pressure for a press conference and decided that, while he could refuse to discuss the Vietnam negotiations and the substance of China, he was better off not to even try one before the 26th, when Henry goes back for his next secret meeting in Paris with Le Duc Tho.

Monday, July 19, 1971
Today was the day of the meetings, starting with the breakfast with Mansfield. I haven't had any report on how that went. Then the bipartisan leadership meeting. The P made the point there that we need time for setting up the China meeting because it's regarding substance. It's going to take a lot of planning, which is completely different from a goodwill trip.

Bipartisan meeting was immediately followed by the Cabinet meeting, and there the P emphasized the necessity for total discipline on what we say, that without secrecy the meetings will not succeed, that we have long and torturous discussions that we've already been in, that we'll continue to be in now, and will be in after the meetings. There must be discipline through all the departments. It's essential that we don't speculate.

Rogers said, we've got to work in three areas: Congressional, our own family, and other nations. The P said that the points to underline are the questions on how it affects the

Russians—this is not directed against any country—how it affects Vietnam—we won't speculate. In the meantime, everybody's to shut his yap, except what the P says. This is not a goodwill trip, it's not cosmetics, it's not to see China, but to see the men. You have to consider the alternatives. If we were to work with the Soviet and Chinese neighbors, with little détentes here and there, such as arms control with the Soviets, it is worthless if China is outside the communications orbit. In 25 years you can't have a quarter of the people of the world isolated and have any chance of peace. The answer regarding becoming soft is that no one is less euphoric than the P, especially on the United States versus the Communists. No one can be more pragmatic in this matter, but the United States can't just stand by without trying to affect the world.

No one knew about this because it was not possible to bring it off if they did know. Even then, we were worried because we might talk in our sleep. You must exert discipline over your people. They'll be sucking around everybody in the government. Any little blip can be disastrous. We have not established trust and confidence yet. The Chinese must feel that they can talk in secrecy. Laird said we've got to maintain the other pillars of the Nixon doctrine. He's concerned that some will read in this the wrong points regarding the need for preparedness and a strong national security position. We must not have negotiation as the only pillar. The P said this is the beginning of a dialogue, and it does not change the power position in the world; we must maintain our defense posture.

These talks will take place, but nothing's changed regarding the need for defense. We will change only when the situation changes, but the Chinese are very sensitive to tone, nuance, and timing. We have to avoid building up great hopes.

The P also came into the staff meeting and practically drove Henry nuts because he said he was only going to stay in for a minute and a half, and he stayed for twenty minutes, giving his opening remarks. During the process of which, Henry got more and more nervous, and finally broke his pencil, he was so distressed. The P's key point was that this whole thing is in our vital interest and in China's, and those vital interests may in some areas coincide, but we are both consulting our own vital interests.

The Connally flap, I guess, was settled today; the P had a two-hour talk with him over at the EOB. Called me afterward, said he had a good talk, that he took him on the mountaintop, by which he meant he talked to him about the Vice Presidency. Turns out that another incident was rubbing Connally, which was the hiring of a secretary. Connally told P he had total confidence in E and total confidence in me. Said this thing just kind of built up, that he had no complaint at all regarding me. They did get into the VP thing.

The P said there's nothing I should do to follow up now, but sometime I should give him a call, tell him the P filled me in on their meeting, and if there are any more picayunish things, he should call me. It was emphasized that any problems he has substantively on domestic policy, he should talk to E, any other problems he should at all times talk to me.

Tuesday, July 20, 1971

P had a Republican Leaders Meeting this morning. Briefed them on the China thing and then had Shultz cover the economy. Apparently didn't go too well, especially the economy part. The P was really fed up with the attitude of the leaders. He told me to tell MacGregor that he's got to avoid letting these Leadership meetings becoming a crying towel. He's got to brief someone to step up and cheer a little bit. He made the point that if that had been a Democratic meeting, they would have cheered the P's initiative and been babbling all over about it. He sighed and said it's such hard work for the P to have to buck them up all the time, which I can certainly understand.

Then he had Dole and Timmons in. Dole going through the motions of getting his views on the convention site. The P immediately opened the meeting by saying any of the three sites you have in mind is acceptable to me, and the line you should use in going out to the press is to say we discussed this, that the P left it up to the Committee to decide. He really does feel it's up to the Committee. On that basis, Dole says the decision will be San Diego, although he thinks the Committee really would prefer Miami.

This afternoon, after a session with K, the P had E and me over for a talk, and made the point that he had decided to have E go with K and Bruce on the September trip to China to handle the advancing. I didn't say anything at the time, but when Henry came in and joined the meeting later, the P raised the same point again. Henry was clearly shook by it. I too think it's a very bad idea, but E is dying to go to China, and this is the one way he can get in on the act, and he maneuvered it with the P this morning. Later this evening Haig raised the question with Larry, and said K was absolutely furious about the idea. We can't have a substantive person going over to meet with them, and I think Henry will probably scuttle it, which is just as well.

The other problem on the China trip is that we're probably going to have to take some Democratic visits to China before the P gets there. The Chinese notified Henry today that it was very difficult for them to withhold permission to visit, for other political people, as they have been doing, now that our visit is arranged. I argued strongly that we should still try to talk them out of it on the grounds that they could welcome those people after the P's visit. The P, I think, is resigned to the fact that we're going to have to let them do it, but he's pushing hard to at least hold Mao in reserve and not have them meet with him. The P made the point that the Chinese have to have this trip, they initiated it. We need to maintain our bargaining position, and we don't want to do anything that cuts that down.

Made the point that we should change the name of Air Force One, immediately, to "Spirit of '76" so that it's done before the trip. Then K came in and the P raised with him the point of whether we ought to consider doing the Russian Summit first, and Henry definitely says no. Instead, we should plan on Russia in the spring, but announce it before we go to Peking; this is the way he's put it to the Russians, and he wants to hang tight on that.

K reported on his interview with Sidey, and said Sidey was very much with us all the way, but made the point that his editors are absolutely beside themselves, that it's driving them wild to think that Nixon is the one to do this, and they just think it's terrible, which is an interesting insight into *Time/Life*.

Before he had come in, and again after he left, we had quite a discussion on the VP thing. The P seeking John's and my views on what the situation is and how to deal with it. His feeling is that the Democrats need an issue, now that we've taken foreign policy away from them, and so they'll zero in on the economy as the substantive issue, and the VP is the way of cutting us. Also he got into quite a long talk about the question of succession. Making the point that he may not live through even this term, let alone a second term, because of the possibility of accident or ill-health. That raises the question of whether Agnew is somebody that we're willing to see become P. He enumerated some of his problems, that he's dogmatic, his hidebound prejudices, totally inflexible, and that he sees things in minuscule terms. We then talked about what to do to get him out, and we concluded that it's impossible for him to announce, such as in January as he apparently is willing to do according to Harlow, that he will not run, because that would open a horrible battle for the nomination. Also, Agnew himself would be immediately dead once he does that.

The P then got around to raising the Connally question with E and made the point that the only one we could put on the ticket is Connally; we couldn't afford a battle, because out of that, Reagan would clearly come up with the nomination, which would be disastrous. Conclusion then is if Agnew is not going to be on the ticket, he must get off by resignation. Given that, the sooner he resigns, the better.

Then the P told E and me that we were to talk to Connally on the VP problem. The P wants to stay one step away from it, but I should call Connally, ask him for a couple of hours of free time for John and me, and then we should just sit down and talk the problem through, see if he's got any ideas on how to approach it.

Wednesday, July 21, 1971

P had the day clear except for a scheduled meeting at 3:00 with Connally and a group of us on labor. He came in late and went right over to the EOB, had a long session with Henry, and then called me over. I used the opportunity to go through the whole scheduling folder and get all of the backlog of schedule stuff cleaned up. He agreed to do a quick trip to Iowa and Ohio. The following week he wants to go to Maine and New Hampshire. He's still planning on doing the California vacation.

We also got into some discussion of the China trip. Henry had hit him on the idea of E doing the advance and had refused to allow E to go with him, and is very much upset about E going at all. The P also thought we ought to take a really hard look on what we want to do regarding press on the trip. We talked about using San Francisco as the point of departure, stopping on Wake Island on the way over, and stopping in Alaska on the way back and going on to Washington. The P said he's going to take charge of the advance himself, especially the Secret Service and staff thing, keeping it to an absolute minimum, cutting down on the numbers; that there's no reason to mar this with a lot of extra people.

The P was horrified by a proposal K made to go on a secret trip to Hanoi after he leaves Peking on the next trip. The P's point being that Henry is now getting carried away with his secret diplomacy, and going too far.

The P first raised the point of whether we couldn't develop a program of issuing government bonds for special purpose projects as a way to get big things done, such as general research, cure for cancer, environmental questions, and so on. He says we have to find a way to do big things but without raising taxes, and this might be the way to do it. The P raised the point that Connally has a theory that it's good to have an enemy, and that one of the best we could have now is John Kenneth Galbraith, who has come out yesterday in favor of permanent government controls on the economy. The P feels that we should have a concerted effort to blast him, as the economic spokesman for the liberal wing of the Democratic Party, their chief guru. By hitting this, we can turn the control argument our way. In other words, he feels we can win this debate if we scare them enough on it.

The P added a sort of a long philosophical thing, then, making the point that the ordinary working guy makes up two-thirds of the people in this country who never went to college. In this period of our history, the leaders and the educated class are decadent. Whenever you ask for patriotic support, they all run away: the college types, the professors, the elite, etc. So he concludes the more a person is educated, he becomes brighter in the head and weaker in the spine. When you have to call on the nation to be strong on such things as drugs, crime, defense, our basic national position, the educated people and the leader class no longer has any character and you can't count on them. We can only turn for support to the noneducated people.

He says look at Meany, Fitzsimmons, and Brennan. They're shortsighted, partisan, hate Nixon politically, but they represent the constituency of uneducated people which, plus the farm heartland, are all that's left of the character of this nation. He's concerned whether the country really has the character to do what really has to be done. He cited his meetings with the group of college presidents, the new managerial business class, the science advisory group, who have absolutely no character or guts. They're all permissive, with no character. The nation's editors and reporters have no spine or guts left, so where do you go?

If you don't communicate with the labor leaders, they can go to the masses, the rank and file of labor, and say we don't care. So we've got to communicate with them. Plus they are men, not softies. So we have to find a way, intelligently, to fight them where they're wrong. Go over their heads when it's necessary, to their troops. He feels the country is in a great moral crisis, a crisis of character, and we won't get leadership from our class. When we need support on tough problems, the uneducated are the ones that are with us. So it was generally agreed that we must maintain an open public communication, regardless of how the labor leaders kick the Administration. There are many ways to get the working people with us. Jobs is the main one, but the racial issue and a lot of others can also be used. The P feels the Democrats will now have to nominate an ultraliberal, that there's no way they can avoid it. They will have trouble pulling labor in behind them, and that's our chance.

He then ended the meeting, all of that took about two hours, asked Connally and me to stay behind. He raised directly the VP question, asked me to report to Connally on my talk with Harlow about the VP's three-out-of-four-chance evaluation that he will not run for reelection. We all agreed, as the P and I had yesterday, that if he's not going to go for reelection, he's got to resign now and let the P appoint somebody. The P then made the major pitch again for the fact that somebody has to be Connally; he's the only man who can be P. The appointment has to be made on the consideration of the man may very well become P. Connally emphasized, as he said he had with the P two days ago, that he had no ambition for the job; he then went on to say that, as a matter of fact, he wasn't at all sure he could stand being VP, that it seemed like a very useless job, and he was much better off as a Cabinet officer. The P jumped on that, emphasized that depended totally on who the VP was and how he worked with the P. With the two of them and the relationship they have, the VP could be an extremely meaningful job, much more so than it's ever been in history. He would use him as an alternate P, and I'm convinced he really means that.

He didn't try to push Connally into any kind of decision, in fact very carefully avoided pushing him at all, but obviously is giving him a pretty good shove in the right direction. It was in its way quite an historic meeting, and it will be fascinating to see what comes of it. It's clear that Connally feels strongly that Agnew does have to go, and he doesn't have any suggestions as to who would be a replacement for him other than himself. He'll have a pretty strong hand to deal from now, and it may be very difficult to work with him, but it will be interesting to see.

Friday, July 23, 1971

The main activity today was the budget meeting process. I'm missing my notes right now on the morning meeting; I'll add those later on this tape, so they'll be picked up. They're quite detailed and important. I'll go on to the period after that.

Before the afternoon meeting, I reviewed with the P a new Elmo Roper poll, which shows that 64 percent of the people feel that things in this country have seriously gotten off on the wrong track, and only 23 percent feel they're going in the right direction. In asking what they feel the causes of the problems in the country today are, 47 percent say drugs, 40 percent Vietnam, 33 percent racial tensions, 31 percent people forgetting the golden rule, 30 percent the lack of strong leadership, 27 percent the economic situation. It's kind of interesting the way those stack up. The P was very intrigued by this, and came back to it a couple of times later in the day. He feels that the reason for this result is quite simple: that people are discouraged about the war, that they're mainly discouraged about the kids. Also, there's been an unmerciful beating by ministers, teachers, media, and leaders in general, saying that everything's going to hell.

This is the basis of our Presidential approval problem. The country can't approve of a president if they think things are bad. So there needs to be an Administration offensive on what's right about America.

Some of our successes such as China, Vietnam, etc., should have an enormous effect in this direction. Problem here is that if people are not satisfied, they will vote for a change in the Administration. We have to hang Congress for the status quo, blame them for the way things are and not us. Make the point that for the first time in forty years we'll have peace and jobs.

Then, after the budget meeting, he got into some follow-up on some of the items he had covered in the morning meeting. He sums up the basic budget thing by saying we've got to come in with, first of all, a lower budget; second, a tax reform with a little reduction in taxes included; and, third, a 10 percent cut in Federal employees. If we can develop that combination, we'll be in good shape. He told me to get to E and have him work out a recommendation for legislation on busing that will enable him to take direct action—a constitutional amendment, an executive order, or a law, and he wanted to get the whole PR group in to push on "the man you can trust with world leadership" question.

For the afternoon budget meeting the basic subject was domestic-policy budget, and the presentation was by E and his people. The P started by saying he wanted them to reexamine all pollution bills in terms of their current economic effect and put the brakes on where we can. On water pollution, he told them to prepare a veto message if it's over $6 billion—he'll veto it. Also, he said to expect no health proposals to be passed this year. He gave an order that there are to be no White House conferences anymore for anything—no more commissions, no more councils.

E's group then made their presentation on what they considered to be the major issues, going on the thesis that ideology is not important to the voters but issues specifically are. They came up with their main issues being jobs, taxes and inflation, crime and drugs, and then some specific issues for special areas: Veterans, Agriculture, Environment, Education, Aging, and Health. Regarding crime, it was pointed out that over half the violent crimes are committed by teenagers; that the best things we can do are code reform, gun control, and criminal rehabilitation. Next one is drugs. Basically our job is supporting the present program, along with the tougher international line. On veterans, they feel that the Vietnam veterans have been overlooked, and the key is to move more things to them. On environment, the key is to balance between environment and economy. On agriculture, the farmers feel forgotten, but we're dealing with a two-sided coin here on prices. If we get them up for the farmer, we also raise the cost of living. Education came in for quite a little discussion. They proposed the voucher plan and tax credits; discussed going for a constitutional amendment for private-education support. On aging, we have some big opportunities in terms of population concentration in Florida, Missouri, and Illinois.

The P said we have done great things, and we have great things to do. We've got to make the point on peace and prosperity. We haven't had this, without a war, for forty years. The country needs a purpose. Maybe we have to demagogue it. We've been program-oriented, now we need to be purpose-oriented.

E said we should relate all this to a keynote such as new direction. The war is over, the old programs haven't worked. We need some new directions in this country. The P made a very key point: that the liberals have let the country down, something that we can develop. The old liberals used to be for things and move positively. The new liberals are totally negative and against everything.

That's the end of the notes on the budget meeting. Obviously it was quite a session, it went on quite a long time, I think a little over three hours.

Saturday, July 24, 1971

The big stir this morning before the tax meeting was reaction to a story in *The New York Times* yesterday that was based on a leaked memo regarding SALT. The P had called E early this morning to really stir things up, told him to line up everybody that had access to the memo and get them polygraphed before the weekend was out. Cancel all their tennis games and trips to Bermuda and order them all back in, line 'em up and run 'em through the lie detector. He also got into quite a stir about some Porter leak that Henry mentioned to him, or a leak about Porter's appointment to Paris, but in checking out I found that wasn't really a valid one to be stirred up about. Brought Bud Krogh in on the whole thing, and after some discussion, managed to simmer it down because it turns out the Defense has a prime suspect on the case and will move on him and then widen it as necessary, rather than going on a broadside attack. Poor Al Haig was practically beside himself, afraid we were going to go ahead on the original basis. Apparently they had some real flaps in Defense in the old days about lie detectors, and Haig was determined to try and save us from a repetition.

The P also was pushing hard to use the polygraph ruthlessly, also to set up a system so that everybody who has access to the secret documents sign an agreement ahead of time that they will take a polygraph test. He wants to move immediately on this with State and Defense and NSC. Go to all the people, and make the point that if any document which has been in my possession is leaked, I agree to take a polygraph test as a condition of my clearance. So we got some stuff stirred up that way.

We got into quite a continuing K-E flap, starting yesterday at the staff meeting when Shultz and E jumped on me because Henry wasn't available for the Defense section of the budget meeting, and was causing them to shift all their plans around, etc. So I asked Henry to come in and join us. E then jumped on him pretty hard, on not only that, but also the intelligence thing, and the international drug problem, and the fact that Henry piles stuff up and is not available to sign off on it himself and won't let anyone else sign off on it. E says that since we have this logjam, there's nothing he can do but go around Henry to the other people. At this point Henry blew and said as long as he's here, nobody's going to go around him, and he is not going to permit anybody to sign off for him on these things. E got a little more rough on him, and that resulted in Henry saying E couldn't talk to him that way, and getting up and stalking out of the meeting. I tried to stop him on the basis that walking out wasn't going to accomplish anything either, but it was too late for that.

I talked to Henry later in the day yesterday, and told him I felt both he and John had been wrong, and that we did have to work this out. He didn't back off very much. Again, this morning we got into it a little, but Henry's now on his way to Paris for another one of the secret meetings, so there isn't much opportunity to get it worked out now. The problem still exists. I think a chunk of it, from E's viewpoint at least, results from irritation on his part towards Henry for being knocked off the China trip, which John feels is completely unreasonable.

Sunday, July 25, 1971

This is an insert of the budget meeting of Friday, July 23. I was missing the notes for the morning of the 23rd, and I'll add those in here. I walked in late, and at the time I came in, the P was doing quite a powerful lecture on the point that K has to really cut the Defense budget, but in the right ways.

Leveled some violent blasts at officers' clubs, Air Force excesses, and so forth. He told Henry to take thirty days and really shake the trees.

On a general basis, the P said never has a country spent more for less on defense than does America. Then he got to intelligence, said we've got to take the same approach there, the CIA tells me nothing I don't read three days earlier in *The New York Times*. Intelligence is a sacred cow, we've done nothing since we've been here about it. The CIA isn't worth a damn. We have to get out the symbolism, so a 25 percent across-the-board, get rid of the disloyal types. Then he told Weinberger to cut the AEC *(Atomic Energy Commission)* 25 percent in personnel, let the scientists go back to MIT and steal documents. K committed for an NSC meeting in mid-August, on the basis that they've got to hear this from the P. The P then turned to Connally and enlisted his help on all this, too. He then defined intelligence on how to spend $5 billion and learn nothing.

He wants a story that we're cutting 10 percent of the government personnel, that people will understand. So cut all civilian agencies 10 percent, Defense 5 percent, in such a way that we can announce it. Wants an example set at the White House. As Cap Weinberger was jotting all these down on a pad, he said in an aside to me, "This is the pleasantest morning I've had in years."

The P, in referring to the 25 percent cut in Intelligence, said it won't save a lot of money, but it will do a hell of a lot for my morale. That was the general thrust of that session. It shook them up quite a good deal.

Monday, July 26, 1971

Started at Camp David this morning. The P called me over at noon for a session at Aspen. He had read a report from the Michigan Survey Research Center that indicated he is not thought of as an activist president, but rather as a pacifist. That got him cranking on the need for activism, but making the point that there's a problem on the other side, that activism has negative effects in terms of the letdown that comes later. On the other side of that, we have achieved a cooling of the country, and that's the problem of a low-key Presidency.

Then he got into the need for a continuing attack on the Pentagon Papers, getting the material that we've found out, leaked out, rather than waiting and worrying about the legal cases on it. Feels that we've got to keep the Democrats fighting on the merits of the Papers, regarding the Vietnam responsibility, we need to keep the fight alive, and not be too subtle about it. They've had their round, now we have ours, not fighting the press or the *Times* but keeping the Democrats on the hook.

The Apollo shot was this morning; the P slept through it, but we put out an announcement that he had watched it with great interest.

Tuesday, July 27, 1971
The P had an extremely heavy appointment schedule today, and I spent very little time with him. Was in for a little while this morning and was talking about the need to develop a schedule for radio talks because he wants to get going on that as one of his activist areas.

K got back last night from Paris and filled me in this morning on his meetings there. He had apparently a pretty good negotiating session with the Vietnamese, and they're in agreement now on eight of the nine points. The ninth point is that they insist that we agree to overthrow the Thieu government; Henry will not accept, and told them there is probably no need for any further meetings. Le Duc Tho said there definitely was, that they would come back in four weeks with a new proposal for a political solution. Henry said he couldn't wait four weeks, it would have to be in two, they settled on a compromise of three, so he goes back again. He also met with his Chinese contact. They now are stalling a little bit, want to put off Henry's next trip until late October because of their early October Independence Day celebrations, their national holiday celebrations, which they'll be preparing for in the latter part of September. Could be a stall, but probably isn't.

Wednesday, July 28, 1971
We had a pretty good flap on Arthur Burns last night and this morning as a result of leaking some stories that the P was being advised to expand the Fed, and to bring it into the executive branch and eliminate its independence. Also that he had refused Arthur Burns' request for a huge salary increase. This got Arthur pretty upset, as it was intended that it would,

and he's now trying to find out ways to get in and around the problem for himself.

The VP returned from his 32-day around-the-world tour. The P asked Bill Rogers and some of the Cabinet people to meet him at the airport. Rogers rode in with him, the P met with him for about an hour at the White House, with a photo on arrival, as being the best way to do it. After the meeting the P was pretty discouraged because apparently he had to spend most of the time bucking the VP up because of his distress about his press coverage, which of course he had brought upon himself.

We had a stir today also because the conservative group, Bill Buckley and his troops, plus the other *Human Events* types, met on Monday and decided to issue a statement of nonsupport of the P, which they did today. We had some discussion as to how to deal with that. The P is not too concerned, although he wants answers communicated to them, but he makes the point that we don't need to worry too much about the right-wing nuts on this, we do need to be concerned about Buckley getting off the reservation, and he wanted Henry to talk to Buckley, as well as having Mitchell talk to Mahoney to make sure the Conservative Party doesn't get off the track in New York.

Thursday, July 29, 1971

The P was loaded this morning because we crammed a full day's schedule into the morning so he'd have the afternoon clear to work on his speeches for the weekend. He started his appointment schedule at 9:00 and went solidly through until darn near 2:00 without a break. I had no contact with him at that time. I did see him for a few minutes early in the morning to clear up a few odds and ends that he had from last night and again late this afternoon. After the schedule period he went over to the EOB and holed up for the afternoon to work on the speeches.

Chotiner in to see him this morning, as a result of sending a letter in saying he had to see the P personally. It was to report on the VP. Apparently Chotiner had been in Spain at the same time the VP was, and Agnew had pulled him aside and unloaded his troubles to him. He had launched into a tirade on the Domestic Council and E, and complained that they don't give him anything to do, and no responsibility, they don't ask for his advice, and pay no attention to him. Said he was annoyed by low-level people calling him. The clerks call and tell him to do things. Murray said the VP was really up-tight, that creates a problem for us because we can't have him get into a huff and go off on that basis, so P wants me to talk to Mitchell and see if we can't work out some way of handling it. Also he thinks Mitchell and I should talk to Chotiner. The P asked Murray why he hadn't brought this up with Mitchell to begin with, and Murray said Mitchell cut him off, and so I'm supposed to get that straightened out too. So the problems never end.

Friday, July 30, 1971
The VP problem dragged me in today, as the P asked me to go over and see him *(VP)* to explore the conspiracy of the White House staff that he feels is out to get him. I went over and had the meeting and the VP gave me a document which purported to conclude that John Scali was the one who was leading a high-level White House effort to try to make the case that the VP didn't know about China, and that his attitude on China and the China question was going to result in his being dropped from the ticket. I tried to smooth the thing over a little, and didn't succeed very well, so left it that I would look into it and see what we could develop on the actual facts. I talked to the P about it later and he got all cranked up.

He got to talking about domestic policy, and made the point that he feels deeply troubled that he's being sucked in too much on welfare and environment and consumerism. This all was a result of my reading to him a speech by Tom Shepherd of *Look,* who hits pretty hard on the environment and con-sumer issue particularly. The P feels that we've got to shift to a domestic approach on the things where the P feels deeply, that we have to get some sharp edges in domestic policy, and the only way to do it, the way he does in foreign policy and on crime, is to have conviction. So we have to have the P in the position where he doesn't feel uncomfortable. He now does feel uncomfortable. He feels we need to get into his speeches more of a sense of conviction, not just mouthing the stuff that we are now. Also he wants to get Shepherd in to talk to him, and consider maybe using him to edit material for the P, to get off the mushy liberalism and get someone who writes like the P thinks.

Then we took off for Canton, Ohio, where the P did the Football Hall of Fame tour and then spoke at the Hall of Fame dinner. He did a superb job, as we had expected he would, because of his unbelievable knowledge of football. He really dazzled them at the Hall of Fame, and did a darn good job in his remarks at the dinner, tying football and Chief Newman into the point that America needs to be number one, and that the way to be a good loser is to hate to lose and come back again to win. We had a big crowd at the airport, and unbelievable crowds along the streets all the way into Canton, and even all the way out and off to the motel in Akron, at 11:30 at night. There is obviously a strong groundswell of support there, because this was not a generated crowd by any means; it was people who were out to see the P on their own initiative. The P was very pleased with it, and feels we've really got something going in the heartland as a result of it.

As we pulled up to the hotel, there was a Vietcong flag in the crowd across the street. The P said to get it down. Denny Shaw and a couple of the other Secret Service guys went over and got it, and then came back to the hotel, came in and chatted with the P for a minute, told them how they'd done it, etc.

Saturday, July 31, 1971

We spent last night in Canton. This morning the P had me talk to Hodgson to get an update on the steel strike and the rail strike. Guys have been negotiating all night on both and still don't have settlements, and Hodgson seemed pretty discouraged. Thinks there's a real possibility of failure and definitely does not want the P to get involved, so we hang tight on those for now at least.

We went on up to Camp David after returning from Iowa, and I did another check on the strike situation, and it appears that we're still in a problem. The P talked to Hodgson just as we landed at the airport. He says the problem is still very difficult and problematical and he still doesn't want Presidential involvement. Then late tonight Shultz called at Camp David and said he wanted to wake the P up because we had to make a basic Presidential decision on the steel deal. The negotiators were 1 percent or 1½ percent apart, and Abel says he's as low as he'll go. The companies said to Hodgson, "Do you want us to give in?" They're trying to trap us into telling them to. We then were in the position of having to decide whether to go along with the settlement or not, and Shultz felt that we should but felt that the P should make the final decision on it, that we now have a chance to get a settlement, so we'll take a stab at it.

Sunday, August 1, 1971

At Camp David. The strike thing was the first question again this morning, and Shultz had a more optimistic report. They had negotiated on both steel and rails all night again last night. Steel postponed their strike 24 hours because they were making some progress. Shultz thinks it was done without getting us into too much of a box. It's mainly a matter now of clearing up details. Same basically applies to the rail thing. George adds it up as being the odds now favor contracts on both of them by Monday morning. Then, at 9:00 tonight, the steel people announced a settlement. So at least that one is done. Rails are still negotiating.

The P called me over to Aspen at 1:15 today, as it was pouring rain. He had called me earlier, and I was out playing tennis, so he told me to wait and come in an hour or so, but then the rain came, so I went on over. He had ordered a fire in the fireplace, although it was boiling hot outside, and when I walked in, his study was completely full of smoke and Manolo was running around with papers trying to get the fireplace to draw. Kind of incongruous in August in Washington.

He got to talking about scheduling a little bit, made the point that I've got to protect him against overscheduling a day, especially a twelve-hour day. He says the problem is that he hasn't recognized himself, the wear and tear and the emotional strain of all the problems that he has on his mind. That it's different being P and moving around the country, because the candidate only worries about the next speech, where the P's got to worry about that, plus all the decisions, and the things that are hanging fire. He feels that a P can't take as heavy a load as a candidate can, a point that I've been trying to make to him all along, but haven't really scored on.

Monday, August 2, 1971

This was a big news day, with the Lockheed vote coming out in our favor in the Senate by one vote. The P spent a lot of time before the vote, calling senators to try to line up the ones that Connally thought were winnable. The P made the pitch to him, as to all the others, that he was talking with Reagan who was really uptight about this, that if we lost the vote, it would be critical to our chances in California in '72, and that was the appeal the P made to each of them.

E met with the VP, who told him that his problem was not so much with E, as it was his concern that he was not involved in the final decision process. He thinks that under his particular circumstances, he should be handled differently than other VPs have been, and he made a plea for the P to cut him in on the decisions. The VP apparently continually came back to the point of China, and raised the question of how you'd feel if the P winked at his National Security advisor when the subject of China came up, and then says he can't get into a discussion about that, that we had some things going on, but he couldn't talk about them. He feels that the P should have confided in him.

The P had a session with E and Morgan on the Austin school busing case, and told them that they've got to get the point across that our filing an appeal does not in any way mean an endorsement of the HEW plan or any other plan for busing. The P then raised his question of a constitutional amendment. John said it's possible, but there's a better alternative in the Emergency School Aid Bill, because we can put a House amendment on regarding no use of funds for busing. The P said we should take the initiative. He thinks that we may have something so fundamental that we have to have a constitutional amendment. He agreed with John that we could hold this until next September or put it in the Republican platform in August.

He had a long session with Connally. The net of this is a huge economic breakthrough based on the international monetary situation which would provide for closing the gold window, a floating of the dollar, a wage and price freeze for six months in the United States, a reinstitution of the 7 percent investment tax credit, and the imposition of a 10 percent import tax quota. These, Connally feels, would be self-balancing measures to control the economy, both the inflationary side and on the import side, as well as to meet the international monetary situation, and get us away from being the victims of the foreign governments that are arbitrarily floating their currency and leaving us hanging.

This becomes a rather momentous decision, and it will be

interesting to see what develops. Mitchell appears to be basically in favor of it, and Connally is pushing hard for it. Shultz will put some brakes on, but I'm not sure he'll be able to be effective.

Wednesday, August 4, 1971

The P had his press conference, which totally swamped them. We pulled it with no advance notice at 11:30 this morning. The P spent the morning over at the EOB, getting ready for it. He opened with a statement on Pakistan, said he was sending Rogers to the UN to deal with it, and that shot the ground out from under any questions on that. The next several questions were on the China trip, and that led into the Soviet-Chinese question and SALT. From there to a couple of questions on Vietnam, and then they got into the economy, and the final eight questions were on the economy. He was prepared for questions on Agnew and his trip, the conservative revolt, and the whole busing problem, especially in Texas, but didn't get any on any of these.

He drove Henry right up the wall when he said that he and Gromyko had discussed the possibility of a Summit, and had agreed that it would be useful only when there was something substantive to discuss. At this point Henry practically panicked, and a few minutes later left the room. I found out later that it was to call Dobrynin and tell him of this, and explain that the P was saying it only to put the Russian visit in proper perspective versus the Chinese visit. Problem was that the contents of the Gromyko talk have up until now been secret, and it was agreed with Gromyko that they would be. Henry was also terribly disturbed because the P, on the Vietnam question, got into the point that we are very actively pursuing negotiations on Vietnam in established channels and that the record, when it comes out, will answer the critics. He really slammed them pretty hard on this, and it obviously tipped the press off to the possibility that there was something going on in the way of secret negotiations. Henry feels this is going to undercut his Paris project very seriously.

Friday, August 6, 1971

P started out with a busy morning, prior to leaving on the weekend trip. He had breakfast with Speaker Albert, then came into the office and made a few minor schedule changes. Then went over to greet the Girls Nation group in the State Dining Room. He did a superb job with them, speaking on the role of women in government, and so forth, but then emphasizing . that the real role of women is as wives and mothers, and he gave a very eloquent pitch for considering the importance of that role too, as contrasted to women's lib.

We left at about noon for the trip to New Hampshire and Maine. The P got a spectacularly good reception in Manchester, NH, in spite of the fact that Loeb (*publisher of the* Manchester Guardian) had written an anti-Nixon editorial in the paper this morning. The motorcade from Manchester airport to Nashua was spectacular, with people crowded on the road all the way. Good tour of the nursing home, and the P did a superb job afterward in his remarks on the importance of nurses. Then on to Bangor, where we had another great reception, crowd at the airport. We choppered off to Minot Island for the night.

Saturday, August 7, 1971

At Minot Island. Things were quiet until 10:30 this morning, when P called, asked where I was staying, and was surprised to learn I was on the island and suggested that I mosey up to the house here. So I went up. He was in his little sort of porch at the house with all the windows closed, and the door, although it was a beautiful day outside. He was smoking his pipe and polluting the air royally. We reviewed the reaction to yesterday. He felt that it had been extremely successful, and that led him into thinking about other trip kinds of things that we might do.

Then he launched into a long general chat. He obviously had not had anything specific in mind that he wanted to cover, so he rambled around a bit, got to the end of his rope, and said that was about it. We did cover some domestic policy items. He wants to shift more to a conservative stance. For instance, Maury Stans has told him that there's $5 to $6 billion of private industry investment that's being held up because of the environmental restrictions we've put on. P wants an objective look taken at it. His point is that we need to look at things from a conservative standpoint.

That talk lasted about an hour and a half, and that was the end of it for the day. The P spent the rest of the day just loafing on Minot Island, apparently, and everyone had another lobster dinner tonight.

Monday, August 9, 1971

(White House) P had the morning clear, unfortunately, and called me in at 8:45, and I was there for over four hours as he wandered through odds and ends with various people. He had Henry in for a good chunk of the time. Talked about the question of the Chinese trip, vis-à-vis the Soviets, and some of the media reaction, etc. Some of the negatives are starting to come in now, but none of them seem to bother him very much. On the Hirohito visit, he wants to be sure it's played just as a gesture, because of its being the first time a Japanese Emperor has landed on United States soil, this is not a State visit, it's got to be handled very delicately but put on with real style. He then got into the media study that's coming out in September and had all kinds of ideas on how we should be following up on that.

We talked a little about the plans for attending the opening of the Kennedy Center, and he bought my idea of going a second night, not attending the main concert and letting the Kennedys take the glory there. He got back on the writers again, still concerned that they don't read any books, so they don't get any background or inspiration, and he's not getting anything from them arising from the mail; still needs anecdotes, still needs heart and fire, still just dry dull statistics. Later today I learned that Connally was still in town, although we had expected him to go to Texas. He had stayed here because he didn't like the feel of the international monetary situation on Friday, and he's going to stick around through today and tomorrow morning to see what the reports are.

Tuesday, August 10, 1971

P started out the day with a little discussion with me and Henry on the Defense budget, just prior to his meeting with the Joint Chiefs of Staff on that subject. Commented on New Hampshire that the crowd sizes become irrelevant, the problem is the adjectives that are used. For instance, in reporting by the commentators on McGovern and Bayh at the Democratic meeting, they all slobbered all over them, and made their thing with 300 people sound as good as ours with 30,000. Whether we get a good crowd report doesn't matter, the question is the adjectives and the description that give people the impression of what happens.

This evening we went on a dinner cruise on the *Sequoia* with Billy Graham. The P also had Mitchell, K, E, Rumsfeld, and Dent. The P and Graham dominated the conversation, Graham reporting at considerable length on the great success of his crusade in Oakland, particularly in interesting the college youth from Berkeley.

The P went into considerable detail on his leadership decadence theory at dinner, making the point that our real problem in this country is not the youth, not the hippies, not the people that have fallen away, but rather our leadership class, the ministers (except for the Billy Graham–type fundamentalists), the college professors and other teachers (except for the old-line great teachers), the business leadership class, etc., where he feels that they have all really let down and become soft and that is where our problem lies; that we need to turn that to a position of strength. Graham agreed with him, but expanded that what this country needs from the P is a very strong challenge, rather than the government giving them everything; in other words that he should hold forth a call to the people that taxes them and requires them to sacrifice and work, such as Kennedy did rhetorically but never did substantively. He feels that, plus a recognition of the importance of the spiritual side of things and the growing interest in spirituality, would be extremely effective and popular. Graham also expanded on his firm belief that it was absolutely imperative that the P be re-elected next year, or there wouldn't be any hope for him and his movement or for the country. The P had Henry expound a little on his point of the need for our being number one and taking a firm position of leadership. The P is expanding this point quite strongly in private conversations, and I think he's probably leading to a major public statement on it at some point in time.

Wednesday, August 11, 1971

The staff meeting this morning started with a report on the busing problem in Texas. Mayor in Dallas has said he wants to meet with the P, and we got into the problem of the P's statement on busing making no sense, because the Federal Government under the court order has forced busing, and then we have come out under the P's order and are supplying no funds to do it, which lends validity to the charge that the man in the White House speaks with forked tongue.

There was a flap on the new White House Health Unit today, because Congressman Shipley and his staff were investigating it, fired some cheap shots about it being a "Roman Romper Room," etc., and this got the P quite disturbed because he thinks it's the kind of story that is going to build and keep getting thrown back at us. He went through quite a bit of agonizing over it this morning, and kept coming back to it during the day. His main concern is that we get off the idea that the P is using the Health Unit; he wants to be sure it's known that he never uses a masseur, and make the point that he fired the Johnson masseurs when he came in. We're going to try and do a job story on the House gym to get back at them, because they, of course, have a much more elaborate setup and all than we do.

Henry was in talking with the P about the Chou En-lai interview in *The New York Times,* in which Reston really took some shots at the P. As a result of this, P has ordered that Henry not see Reston at all, and that we enforce our rule throughout the place of no contact with *The New York Times* and he's not going to take them on the China trip. He feels that Reston's motive was clearly to sabotage the trip, and we've got to recognize that. Henry was in, following up on his meeting with Dobrynin last night, in which he got a confirmation of the Soviet Summit, and that led today into some schedule discussion of how we go about both the trips.

Back on the busing thing, the P told Ziegler to say that, first of all, the P's against busing period; secondly, that the Supreme Court has held that steps must be taken, and they've held that busing could be used as one of the methods of meeting their criteria. Therefore, the P will carry out the law, but he has directed that every appropriate Cabinet officer is to carry out the law, but because the Court does not require compulsory busing, they are to carry out the law wherever possible without busing, and also he's asked the Congress that no federal funds be used for busing. He's also to say that he's issued both a written and oral directive on this. Ron put this out and got into quite a flap because nobody knew there was a written directive, and the press all started asking to see copies of it.

Thursday, August 12, 1971

Connally called me today to say he was going to come back up, he was in Texas on vacation. He was going to come back up this afternoon as soon as possible, because we had a bad day in the gold market yesterday and another bad day today, and he anticipates a really bad one tomorrow. He says the uneasiness is continuing in many countries and deteriorating daily. He says there's no panic, but it is getting worse and worse, and we're losing the initiative.

> One factor in this: the British had asked for $3 billion to be converted into gold. If we gave it to them, other countries might follow suit. If we didn't, they might wonder if we had enough gold to support the dollar. In either case, it was a major crisis.

So he came on up and met with the P at 5:30 today, after which P called me while I was out to dinner to say that they had decided to go ahead on the whole move on Monday, and that we were going to pack up the key people, including Arthur Burns and the key Treasury and economic group, go to Camp David tomorrow afternoon, spend the weekend there and get it worked out, and make the announcement on Monday. We'll cover the whole thing when we do it, apparently, so it's going to be quite an earthshaking operation.

Friday, August 13, 1971

As a result of last night's decision on the economic move, today's schedule was shifted substantially. The P went ahead with his NSC meeting on Defense budget at 10:00 this morning and that lasted all morning. Then we set up a 2:30 departure for Camp David, took the Quadriad with the P, and announced there'd be a Quadriad meeting up there. Had the other people go up on a separate chopper from Anacostia so we wouldn't create an undue stir about the attendance. We went round and round on the schedule for the meeting and various arrangements of cabin locations and all that sort of thing.

> Because of the enormous worldwide economic significance of the decisions that were to be discussed, this whole Camp David

weekend was set up under conditions of total secrecy. In order to avoid any premature leaks, all of the attendees were instructed to tell their staffs and families that they were tied up for the weekend, and could not give any information as to where they were, with whom they were, or for what reason.

Right after we arrived at Camp David, we started the first meeting at the P's lounge in Aspen. It started at 3:15 and didn't end until 7:00. The P, Connally, Burns, Shultz, McCracken, Stein *(from the Council on Economic Advisors), (head of the International Economic Policy Peter) Peterson, (Treasury Undersecretary Paul) Volcker,* Safire, and E were in attendance. The P opened the meeting, after a brief updating by Volcker on gold loss problems in the market today. Agreed that we must act on the international money situation; there are many options that are now closed to us, so there's no point in reviewing those.

He made the point, then, that no calls are to be made out of here except to get information, and then you're to cover it so we don't get any leak out of here as to what's going on, leaks in the past have compromised our position. Between now and Monday, everybody here is to say nothing. If you talk to someone, you assume the responsibility.

He said there was general agreement that action is needed: first, on the international monetary situation, second, to deal with its causes—domestic inflation, fiscal problems, tax problems, and wage/price problems; third, an import tax that we would send to Congress, but make retroactive.

He turned the meeting over to Connally. Connally said it's clear that we have to move in the international field, to close the gold window, not change the price of gold, encourage the dollar to float. If we close the gold window, we'll need an import tax of 10–15 percent. This will keep foreign products out and be inflationary, so we'll need a further stimulant: we will reinstate the investment tax credit at something greater than 7 percent, such as 8 percent or 10 percent. He feels there'd be no problem with Congress, and business will react, of course, very favorably to this. There's a problem in the automobile industry, especially relating to imports; there's no reason for an excise tax on autos, so we'll repeal the excise tax on autos, with the assurance from the industry that they'll pass this through in price reductions. This he feels should affect 10 million people who will be new-car buyers this year. We'll move forward the increases in personal income tax exemptions, we'll remove all the financial controls that we've promised to remove, we'll also ask Congress to change the antitrust regulations to exempt United States industries doing business overseas, and we'll impose a wage/price freeze until January 1. Such a program will leave a clear impression that this has been analyzed in depth, not just a reaction to pressure. It will be an act of great awareness, great statesmanship, and great courage, and must be presented to the people this way.

A detailed discussion of the import tax followed.

The P said, now let's turn to the gold-window question. Arthur Burns' view is correct domestically. The argument from the other side is to take the rap now.

This got us up to 4:00, and Arthur Burns then took over for the next 15 minutes with a lecture on the whole subject. He said that Volcker and Connally may be right in their view regarding closing the gold window, but I think they're wrong. If they're right, there's still no rush to close the window. We should analyze the steps we take this weekend; these are dramatic steps, wage/price freeze, border tax, government spending cuts, tax cuts. These will not augment the budget deficit. These will electrify the world, and the flight from the dollar will cease, so we don't need to close the gold window. On the other hand, there are grave risks in closing. First, political. If we do this now, Nixon will get the blame. He'll be responsible for devaluing the dollar, for dropping gold. *Pravda* will headline this as a sign of the collapse of capitalism. It will be exploited by the politicians, hated by business and financial people.

The second risk, he felt, was economic, and that would be very hard to evaluate. Question of what will the stock exchanges do? Up or down, you can't predict. Once the dollar floats, the trade basis will change. The risk to world trade would be much greater. The profit margin in world trade, which is already very narrow, will vanish. There'll be retaliation by other countries, and ill will. The bankers feel it would follow quickly. Foreign exporters will clamor for action. We release forces that we don't need to release.

He recommends, therefore, that we take the other actions, and send Volcker abroad to explain them. Then Volcker and the Fed start negotiating on exchange rates, but without closing the window.

The P answered Burns by saying that speculators would start a run on the dollar. Burns said if that happens, you can close the window the next day, but you could try to get by without closing. The P said the argument on the other side is that the gold window action is needed for domestic opinion, and he recited the range of arguments on this. Burns says, so it all works, then how do you know? How do you know it won't collapse two months before the election? You must realize that you're taking a uniquely powerful action. Connally said, what is our main problem? The international gold situation, so we must act on it. Why do all the stuff to ourselves domestically and still stay exposed to the mercy of the world by not acting on the gold window? We can't cover our liabilities, we're broke, anyone can topple us, and he recited the headlines all over the world regarding closing of the gold window; they've already reacted to it. Burns says, well, all you're demonstrating is that this is widely expected, but for the other countries, you've taken unilateral action, contrary to their interests. Volcker said he agrees with Burns, but this is not the disaster that he thinks, except in international banking circles. What everyone would dislike is closing the window without trying promptly to negotiate. Connally makes the basic argument again, and Burns keeps rebutting.

> Further discussion followed concerning the reactions of business, labor, economists, and the media.

Connally recommends that we talk as if we have alternatives, but we don't have alternatives, we have to recognize the problem and face it. We should say that this will make us more competitive in the world. That's the purpose of doing it now, while we have a cover for it, so we should not wait a day or a week later, we should do it the same time we do wage/price and the other domestic actions. If you wait, then you are in the hands of the money changers. Burns says, you must realize you're dealing with the money changers, the central bankers of the world. They won't ask for gold if you take the other steps, and you'll solve the problem that way without having to take the drastic action. Burns says, I get reports from the central banks the world over, every day. If we take the domestic steps, they'll applaud it, and they won't hit the dollar. Connally says, they may not hit it, they'll just nibble it to death.

At this point we put the gold question aside, and the discussion focused on budget cuts and a new tax package.

The P then turned to the wage/price freeze, and asked Shultz to cover it, and then Burns to follow up on it. Shultz said 1) the wage/price freeze will have the most immediate and significant impact, 2) it works best when related to international crisis, 3) whatever device is used, it has a short effective life, 4) consider how you stop once you start (the P injected, especially if it's working), 5) how to get labor cooperation; it blows up when labor walks out. The plan is for a freeze, not to last too long, but simple, no exceptions, short so that you don't need a bureaucracy. The P expressed his concern that an economy in a straitjacket with the bureaucrats would be a disaster.

Shultz suggested a tripartite board, seven members, to set criteria, spin off the problems on the specific areas, maybe create a governmental body to refer cases to the board. The period of effectiveness for the board would also be limited. Shultz said this structure would be minimal employees, that is, about a thousand, and it should be kept small.

Burns says it could be done with less than a thousand. Burns says Shultz's ideas are remarkably similar to mine. I think we should set a freeze for only three months, the purpose is shock value and to get time for the machinery, then set up the machinery. Peterson raised the question of whether an announcement of a period of a freeze, in advance, is a good idea. Burns said, don't lose your advantage as the apostle of freedom. McCracken said, there's a problem if you announce a freeze without the duration stated, because you throw people off balance if they're caught. Shultz said, the shorter the freeze, the less pressure builds up, and thus the better chance to avoid upsetting equilibrium. Burns says, the authority expires next

May. Shultz says, no, we have two years. Peterson says, what are the P's legal sanctions; Shultz is not sure, thinks fine and jail. Burns says, you don't need enforcement, the period will end before enforcement is needed. Stein says, don't underestimate the difficulty of transition from a freeze to a board; you'll need more sophisticated rules and more power.

The P made a little speech about prosperity without war; we have to find a way to direct, stimulate, divert the American energy in peacetime to provide full capacity. The P then went into his approach to the speech, and said the way to kick it off is to start with subject A, which is peace. The United States at long last enters an era of peace. We all welcome this, but it presents enormous challenges. It's a very competitive world. Is the United States going to continue to be a great nation, number one? Don't assume that, unless we're ready to meet the challenge.

The United States looks at itself and what do we find? First, the problem of unemployment. We need to take steps to absorb the 2 million people that we've released from the defense industries. Second, as the rest of the world becomes more competitive, the international speculators attack our dollars. What can we do about it? There's nothing to be frightened about, but we're not going to allow the dollar to be destroyed, so we'll impose an import tax and tax credits to deal with the problem of jobs and keeping America competitive. Third, we have the inevitable heritages of war and inflation. We've made some progress, but not enough, so we take new actions. Freeze wages and prices. This requires that the American people give their total moral support. We talk about what can you do. The general public can support the freeze. The businessman can invest in America. The consumer can buy products.

As a side note, Burns stayed afterward to make a personal pitch against floating the dollar, and asked for a private session with the P later, which the P hedged. Arthur then left and the P kept me for a few minutes to say that he wants E and Shultz to know that he leans to Arthur's view about not going ahead with the gold window, but to do that we'll have to bring Connally along. He wanted E and Shultz to work on Connally this evening, and see if they could bring him along on this. I then left the P's residence, and we went over to Laurel and had dinner at 7:30.

At dinner, during a discussion of the need for secrecy, Bill Safire recalls that Paul Volcker made the point that the necessity for avoiding leaks was that "fortunes could be made with this information." Bill says that I, mock-serious, leaned forward and whispered loudly, "Exactly how?" which broke the tension of the moment.

Connally took complete command at the close of dinner, clanked on his glass, made the assignments, told them what rooms to go to, and they divided up into the three working units and used the three rooms of Laurel for their meetings. At 9:45 the P called me and said in view of the lateness of the hour, why don't you let the work group go on working tonight, and I'll be available anytime after 8:30 in the morning to meet with them. Nobody had any intention of meeting with him further tonight, but he seemed to think they might, so he was turning it off.

Saturday, August 14, 1971

At 4:30 this morning, I was awakened by the phone ringing. It was the P, who said he was sorry to wake me up, that he was working on his speech, and that he'd be ready to talk first thing in the morning. He wanted to see Safire first thing in the morning. He wants to put a little more zip into the speech that he's drafted, but he doesn't want any cuties from Safire. He says the major problem is the one Arthur raises, regarding the gold window, and that now he kind of thinks it may be good to go ahead with it.

That conversation ended at about 4:40. He called again at 8:40 and said he'd stayed up rather than going to bed after he talked to me earlier, and had finished his notes on the dictating machine and sent them to Rose.

He wants Safire to know that the form and structure of his notes should be followed. He knows the outline is right. He likes the gutsy rhetoric, and he wants to keep that feeling. Safire is to show it to no one except for the technical points. He doesn't want to get people into the rhetoric. Then he had a great line for Safire: "Don't make it brutal and beautiful, rather, brutal and effective."

Said he had gotten up about 3:00 last night and worked on the speech and then called me and then did the dictating. He had come out with the tapes to get them to Rose and was looking for someone, came down by the pool and saw a chief coming out of the sauna, and said, "Good morning, chief," and the chief said, "Yes, ma'am. I mean, yes, sir!" The P was quite amused by that; he said he scared the hell out of him.

During the morning, Connally had been meeting with his separate groups, and he assembled everybody at lunch at 12:30, sort of got the reports together, formed four groups to meet with the P starting at 2:30: first on budget, second on wage/price, third on taxes, especially import, and finally the mop-up crew to cover the overall aspects from yesterday's meeting. He pointed out that the decisions yet to be made were the gold window, capital controls, and the antitrust amendments. The groups started their sessions at 2:30. I stayed up by the pool working, and didn't go down to Aspen until about 4:00.

The P then kicked all of us out except the Quadriad, and settled down to a discussion with them of whether to close the gold window. By that time he had decided to do so, and the point was to sell Arthur, so that he would go along with it. At 6:00, the meetings ended, and the P called me over, he was down by the pool, smoking his pipe. He told me to talk to them tonight regarding the information process, who calls whom, the briefings, etc. This was a brief meeting, and I went back over to Laurel for dinner. The P called me at 7:15, said we could set up a picture of the group at 10:00 or 10:30 tomorrow morning.

I ran staff the review on follow-up, the discussion getting our spokesman on the air afterward, notifying the key publications to hold their front pages, the press briefings ahead of TV, the basic assignments, and so forth. We got the basic plan worked out on that. Then E, Weinberger, and I went over to Aspen at 9:00.

We walked in and the living room was empty, the P was down in his study with the lights off and the fire going in the fireplace, even though it was a hot night out. He was in one of his sort of mystic moods and, after telling us to sit down and informing Cap that this is where he made all his big cogitations, he said what really matters here is the same thing as did with Roosevelt, the second Roosevelt, we need to raise the spirit of the country, that will be the thrust of the rhetoric of the speech. We're at a time where we're ending a period where we were saying that government should do everything. Now all of this will fall unless people respond. We've got to change the spirit, and then the economy could take off like hell. You must have a goal greater than self, either a nation or a person, or you can't be great. Let America never accept being second best—we must try to be what it is within our power to be.

> The P delivered the speech about the economic moves on television Sunday. Most of the response was favorable—though not all.

Sunday, August 15, 1971
The working group started again at breakfast this morning. Got things wrapped up pretty well, then went over to Laurel for posed pictures with the P. He was in pretty bouncy shape and set up the various shots that he wanted. He decided not to go back with the group, he wants them to go on ahead. He got into considerable discussion on various arrangements and details regarding the speech and the follow-up.

We had staff meetings this afternoon, a good briefing by Connally, and then I went over the logistic plan, both with my operating unit and then with a full staff unit. I think we have everybody tracking extremely well. The P stayed out of touch until time to go on the air; he called me right after he went off. Seemed to feel pretty good about it. He said he was trying to get some emotional lift into it, he especially liked his line regarding what the guy had written in 1775 about America having seen its best days.

Monday, August 16, 1971
Today started with the Cabinet meeting, although the P had me in for a few minutes ahead of time, generally reviewing the things from last night. He made the point that we should release the picture of the Quadriad as the men that made the decision. At the Cabinet meeting, the P opened, then went into some of the details of the meetings at Camp David—what a marvelous team effort it was—and that he will always be grateful for it. He referred to how helpful Arthur was in the

process and said that he needed strong support from everyone in the Cabinet.

He decided at the last minute to shoot over to the State Department and open the sub-Cabinet briefing that E had set up. So he did that, then came back to the EOB, changed his clothes, and went out to Burning Tree to play golf with Bill Rogers. Had me ride out with him to Burning Tree. We had a ridiculous motorcade going out there with a huge police escort, which was really horrible, and they drove right into the club grounds and up in front of the caddie house, which was very embarrassing, and then it was topped off by *(UPI correspondent)* Helen Thomas getting out of the car and standing there watching him, when the press car wasn't even supposed to come in and no women are allowed at Burning Tree.

Wednesday, August 18, 1971

Got going this morning (on the plane out to Illinois) on the speechwriting problems. He wants Price to go back and look at his various extemporaneous speeches to see the way the P does these things. He talks in gutsy terms, and he wants his stuff to be closer to Harry Truman than to Harding. He doesn't want beautiful prose, he wants memorable prose, not trick phrases, because they're too contrived. He says the speechwriters have good ideas, but they don't get them in the right style, and therefore he has to shift them to his style, and that he shouldn't be required to do.

The Illinois visit went very well, with huge crowds in Springfield, along the motorcade routes in front of the Capitol, and at the State Fair. The P gave an outstanding extemporaneous talk at the old Capitol on the occasion of signing the bill to set up the Lincoln birthplace as an historical site. He was completely mobbed by the crowds at the fair, all of the reaction was positive, and there's again a strong feeling that you can't help but get from this, that things are a lot better in the country than they were.

In Idaho he also had an exceptionally good reception at the airport before we helicoptered up to the Grand Tetons to spend the night. He came up with the line on our counterattack that we ought to tie Meany to Muskie, and talk about the Meany-Muskie partisanship, which would hurt both of them, upset both of them, probably cause them to deny it, which would create even more problems.

The TV tonight was very good on our coverage of all of the trip stuff. We got a lot of mileage out of it, except for one bad shot by Daniel Schorr, who kicked us on the fact that we haven't done anything about aid to parochial schools; we were just talking about it. The P had a beautiful cabin overlooking the lake. He called me over before dinner for a brief review of the day, and then, I presume, folded up early.

Thursday, August 19, 1971
We started out early with the P calling me over while he had some trout for breakfast. We had trout last night for dinner and again for breakfast, too. He was talking about really moving on this Schorr deal, on the basis of, it's typical of what the media did during the campaign, where they kill us on something we do that does us some good, by saying that we haven't really done anything about it, we're just talking about it.

We went on the boat tour of the lake. The scenery was beautiful, but the timing and logistics didn't work out too well, and the P wasn't very happy with it. We cruised across the lake for about a half an hour, then visited a little village near a campsite, then went back to the P's cabin, left a little later, and headed for Dallas.

Labor problems continue to build, as our group met this morning with the AF of L Council. Earlier on the "Today" show, Connally was asked, as his first question, what we were doing on the problem of labor, and Connally cracked that he always thought M and M was a candy, but now he understood what it really stood for, which was Meany and Muskie.

Dallas went reasonably well. We helicoptered right from the airport to the stadium and back, so we had no crowd situation anywhere, and to avoid any demonstrations on the busing problem. We landed on time in California, and the P headed for San Clemente by helicopter and I came home.

On the plane to California he got into a discussion with E and me on the follow-up strategy on labor. He feels that we should drive the wedge in, to try and separate one union from another on the basis of their support and also to separate the bad union leaders from the rank and file. He's now expanded his M and M, the Meany-Muskie thing, to the three M's: Meany, Muskie, McGovern. He makes the point that we've got to make a virtue out of necessity: if the labor people are against us, we might as well take them on, and we might as well try to get some mileage out of doing it. We landed on time at 6:00 in California, and the P headed for San Clemente by helicopter and I came home.

Tuesday, August 24, 1971

(San Clemente) P came in just before 10:00 this morning. He had a 10:00 appointment with Ambassador Porter, which he didn't realize he had. He came in wearing a sport shirt with no tie. So he shifted the Porter appointment, chatted with me, changed his clothes, met with Porter, then with John Mitchell. Mitchell reported on his dinner with the Reagans, at which there was a great deal of carping about a lot of trivia, mainly from Nancy Reagan. They're concerned because there's a conservative meeting in Houston that's basically a conservative rebellion, especially regarding national defense, and P got upset about that, said the conservatives are aiming at the wrong target, they should be hitting the Congress, not the P, that we need to posture in the public mind that we are for national defense. We're getting a bad rap on that.

The P returned a call to Mayor Daley, who wanted to discuss the Northern Ireland Catholic problem with him, and at the same time Daley told the P that he had made another statement urging labor not to play politics on the economic deal and to support the P.

Henry was in, discussing the problem of the Vietnam election again, which does pose a serious problem. The P is strongly toying now with releasing the fact of our secret negotiations, blowing the channel, and forcing them to deal with us publicly, and then attacking the Senate opponents, saying they forced us to abandon our secret negotiations, and so on. K also got back on the line of what a real heartbreak the whole war situation is because we really won the war, and if we just had one more dry season, the opponents would break their backs. This, of course, is the same line he's used for the last two years, over and over, and I guess what all of Johnson's advisors used with him, to keep the thing escalating. I'm sure they really believed it at the time, but it's amazing how it sounds like a broken record.

In the forthcoming election in South Vietnam, Thieu was running for President against Nguyen Ky and General Minh. The

Communists had strongly suggested the U.S. drop its support of Thieu or the negotiations would be seriously jeopardized. As it happened, Thieu found a way to disqualify Ky, Minh pulled out, and Thieu went on to win.

The P took off, called me late in the afternoon to report that the oil slick from a leaking naval ship had fouled his beach, so he can't use it.

Monday, August 30, 1971

San Clemente. The P got into some odds and ends, he spattered out a few ideas on poll questions as the day went along. He wanted to see whether they show that people support Ralph Nader, and thus get into the advisability of taking Nader on. He has a feeling that Nader probably has some strong public support, and we should not take him on, even though we certainly should not agree with him. Also he wanted to get some feel of whether the people like the idea of the P going out to the country, and also among those who do not approve of the P, as to why they don't.

He discussed Pat Nixon's schedule some, wants to be sure that we're working up some schedule activities for her, and he talked a little about fundraising in general. He wants me to talk to Kalmbach, because he's concerned that out of Kalmbach's list of contributors, where he's raising $10 million, that $8 million is coming from money we already had, such as Mulcahy, Stone, etc., and that we need to set a deal that broadens the base, getting some key people in New York, Palm Beach, and Chicago, to hit the elites there. He wants to be sure we don't have a money problem, so that we can do every little thing that we want to do.

He was pretty distressed when he discovered today that Henry K had ordered the P's barber down to San Clemente for a haircut, and that got him to questioning Henry's use of helicopters to get around in Southern California, also. He put in pretty much a full day at the office, finally left in midafternoon.

Wednesday, September 1, 1971

I didn't go into the office. The P did call several times and I spent most of the day on the phone. Someone told Rose Woods to take in to him a letter that had been sent to him by Rose

Kennedy, complaining that he wasn't attending the opening of Kennedy Center. That got the P concerned that he should be going, so we went back and forth on that. Then he called out of the blue, said he wanted to invoke the Taft-Hartley on the dock strikes out here, and for me to get it set up. I still can't figure out what prompted that, but I talked to Shultz, who said this wouldn't be a good idea, and urged that we not do anything until after Labor Day. I called the P back and he agreed to hold up on it although he really wanted to give them an 8-hour ultimatum.

Friday, September 3, 1971

P came in late this morning. He was only in the office for about a half hour before departure. He left a little after 11:30 for Ohio, then Chicago, then Washington. Chapin called this evening to report on the trip. Said all had gone well. Chicago crowd was tremendous and very enthusiastic, and he feels we came out in good shape.

Tuesday, September 7, 1971

We're all back in Washington now. The P was in the office first thing, had a two-hour meeting with the Committee on International Economic Policy, and then spent the rest of the day supposedly getting ready for the Thursday address to Congress. Most of it was spent haranguing me on schedule changes that he wants made. Pat Nixon decided she didn't want to go to California before the Alaska trip, instead wants to go direct to Anchorage; so the P's changing the schedule to go out to Detroit on Thursday of that week, and just go out and back, and then go directly to Anchorage. Then as the day went on, he kept calling with various changes on that, finally ending up with the idea of spending Saturday night in Seattle, going on up to Anchorage Sunday, back to Portland for Sunday night, and then back to Washington on Monday. A further complication is that Mrs. Nixon has to be back, she thinks, for the Mamie Eisenhower salute Monday night, so it's really pretty royally screwed up, thanks to her.

He had Colson in today, mainly to go over some general follow-up. He wants to be sure he's attacking Muskie on the basis that he's panicked because of his slump in the polls, that's what brought about his ridiculous tax proposal. Also, he thinks someone needs to keep hitting Meany on the basis that

The author, with his ever-ready camera, filming a Presidential motorcade. Besides a written record of the Administration, the author also kept an extensive filmed record.

In China, during the historic trip. The author with Chou En-lai; William Rogers and Henry Kissinger in the background.

The day of the Pentagon Papers leak with Ehrlichman aboard the Presidential yacht, *Sequoia*.

Alexander Butterfield and Dwight Chapin at the South Portico of the White House.

In the final days of the 1968 Presidential campaign, the author and candidate Nixon discuss strategy.
(UPI/Bettmann)

The author with Rosemary Woods, Nixon's secretary, on Inauguration Day, 1969.

With Henry Kissinger aboard Air Force One.

Everyone close to the President was assigned code names by the Secret Service. Here is Wisdom (John Ehrlichman), Wood Cutter (Kissinger) and Welcome (the author).

The President, in a favorite chair in his study in the private quarters of the White House. *(Burt Glinn/Magnum)*

The President, heading for the White House from the Executive Office Building, with a Secret Service agent and the author. *(UPI/Bettmann)*

A view from the Oval Office, looking into the Rose Garden, as the President and author walk. *(Black Star)*

The author in his post–White House years.

The author and his wife, Jo, with their grandchildren at home.

Attorney General John Mitchell with his wife, Martha. *(UPI/Bettmann)*

The President in Key Biscayne meeting with John Mitchell, Robert Finch, and the author. *(UPI/Bettman)*

John Connally, one of Nixon's closest allies, with George Shultz and Elliot Richardson. *(Sygma)*

Vice-President Spiro Agnew, a constant concern for the President. *(Black Star)*

he's a great American, but it's sad that he's out of step. He asked me to talk to Mitchell about Hoover, P wants a plan because he thinks now is the time to get him to step down. I did so, and Mitchell agreed, and thinks we should move ahead on that as quickly as possible.

Wednesday, September 8, 1971

P had the day clear to work on the Congressional speech for tomorrow, had me over at 10:00 this morning during a break on speech drafts, to go over schedule plans in detail, particularly the Northwest trip.

He raised the question with me of his concern on Henry's delusions of grandeur as a peacemaker, in that he keeps hitting the P on the idea of his going to Hanoi secretly to try and settle Vietnam. The P doesn't want him to do it, first, because he doesn't think it'll work, and second, because he doesn't think it can be kept a secret. He's concerned that it would be a disaster to do it and fail, the risk is too great, and also there's no use meeting with Pham Van Dong anyway, the P doesn't feel. He wants me to have Haig tout Henry off of this. He feels Henry doesn't realize that the Communist method of working is to keep talking and to screw you behind your back while you're doing it. To them, talking is a tactic to win, not to work out an agreement, whereas Henry keeps trying to work out an agreement with them.

He wants to be sure that Colson and his crew blast Muskie on his busing statement, not for avoiding taking a position. He doesn't want to leave them on an "I don't know where he stands" hook. He wants to hit him for holding the wrong position, which is, that he is for busing. They want to get the antibusing people to take him on with this.

Thursday, September 9, 1971

P was fascinated this morning to get a report on the Kennedy Center opening of the Mass last night. I described the program, and Bernstein's performance, and after asking a few questions and making a few comments, he paused a minute, this was over the phone, and then said, "I just want to ask you one favor. If I'm assassinated, I want you to have them play 'Dante's Inferno' and have Lawrence Welk produce it," which was really pretty funny.

He did a superb job on the speech to Congress, and all the

reactions were very good, especially on his presentation and delivery. He called right afterward on the phone and said, "Well, it was a damn dull subject, but that's as good as it could be said," and then a comment that he feels we need a speech doctor to go through and write in cheer lines, like FDR had, after the speech is written, which is what the P now has to do.

We had a little flap after his meeting with Connally. Connally was concerned about a memo he received, signed by the P, telling him he couldn't go over 20 percent in the Japanese negotiations on the yen. The P felt we should never do a thing like this without checking with Connally first, and he was upset with Alex and me and so on for putting this on. We tracked it down, discovered it was a K proposal, so he called Henry in. Henry pointed out that the directive said just the opposite of what Connally implied. In the first place, the P hadn't signed it, Henry had, secondly, it had been designed for the purpose of putting the responsibility into Connally's area and keeping the other people out of it. K had read it to Volcker in a meeting and then sent it over to Connally's office, asking if there was any problem, before he sent the memo. So we're back to the problem of internal dissension in Treasury, which I think is fairly substantial.

Tonight was the symphony concert opening at Kennedy Center. The P went, handled it very well, called me after the concert at home. Said he would have chosen a different program, thought the orchestra was quite good, but that Dorati was trying to show off by doing the Stravinsky thing, that Stern was wasted on a Mozart chamber music piece, and the great chorus was wasted with an odd Schumann composition, so the only quote he put out was that the orchestra sounded beautiful and the acoustics were great. He again expressed his pleasure at not having to go to the Mass the night before.

Friday, September 10, 1971

We had quite a little discussion this afternoon on the whole philosophical question of what kind of press coverage we want in China, the basic point being whether we push for putting in a ground station so they can do live coverage and transmit film directly from Peking. Ziegler of course arguing for this, as is Scali and the others, but the P, Henry, and I all have the basic feeling that we should permit the minimum amount of coverage possible within China, and that this will give us much better coverage and maintain the aura of mystery, etc. Nothing much settled on that.

Monday, September 13, 1971

Cabinet meeting first thing this morning. Bill Rogers opened by congratulating Mrs. Nixon on her TV last night *(an interview on ABC)*. All the Cabinet wives were present, and gave her a huge ovation. Shultz then filled in on the background of the economic program, emphasizing that things were good and getting better, but our move was to consolidate it, rather than turn it around. The P, at the end of the Shultz presentation, made the point that there was a big question of dealing with state and local government pay as well as Federal pay. He caused a laugh by commenting that this is an area where there certainly has been no increase in productivity.

The P turned the meeting over to Connally, asking him to cover the domestic tax thing primarily, not to put too much emphasis on the international, because most of us won't understand it. Connally said that's OK, because I can't explain it anyway.

The P then said that we need to have no illusions regarding the superiority of our economy, that the impressive thing about the Communist leaders is their total absolute conviction that they're going to win, and their determination to do everything to win. The point is, if they with their totally inferior, oppressive system could have such dedication, we, with all we have, should have at least as much. So as you go out, speak up, talk strongly for our system, what it is, what it's done for the world. If you don't, I'll have you back to have some of that fish.

After the Cabinet meeting he called Governor Rockefeller to tell him he backed him to the hilt on his move on busting up the prison strike in Attica, New York. He assured him he was right not to grant amnesty, and that the P was behind him all the way. It turns out there were seven guard hostages killed, and 32 prisoners, all black. The P made the point again to Rockefeller that we can't tolerate this kind of anarchy, and that he was solidly behind him in his move on it.

This afternoon he got into a little harangue on IRS investigations, saying that he had been told by Billy Graham that the IRS is currently investigating him. Fortunately, Connally was there when Graham said it, so Connally got the notes on it, and was very surprised, but it is a problem. The P wants now to be sure that we get the names of the big Democratic contributors and get them investigated. Also the Democratic celebrities and so forth.

Tuesday, September 14, 1971

Henry got back from Paris last night and reported to the P. Came in, saw me this morning, went over the plans. The North Vietnamese have closed off the negotiations in effect because of the screwup on Thieu's election, at least that's Henry's view, and he in turn has basically turned off the talks. He now wants to go to Moscow and work the same kind of a deal there, or at least make the record for it, so that when we do the pullout in January, we'll have that as a final wrapup attempt to settle by negotiation. His logic is that if we're going to pull out anyway, we might as well try to get all the mileage out of it that we can.

Apparently his meeting with the Chinese went pretty well. They were horrified, however, at his information that the press corps traveling with us would be a minimum of 150 people. He didn't even raise the question of the ground station, which would take another 100 people. I'm convinced, incidentally, from a memo I got from Scali, that we should try to press for the ground station if we can possibly get it, so that we can have live coverage of our morning activities in Peking. The Chinese did not go along with Henry's plan to announce his trip and the date of the P's trip on September 21; instead they want to wait until October to announce Henry's trip. They want to wait until after Henry's trip to announce the date of the P's trip so they'll have some substantive reason for Henry's making the trip. I don't see any problem with this, and I don't think Henry does either, so we'll probably go ahead on that basis.

The P called me at home tonight and said that in his long talk with Henry this afternoon, Henry had brought up the fact that *(James)* Reston *(of* The New York Times) was in to see him, or that Henry had talked to Reston, and he had asked for an interview with the P. Henry was actually raising this with the P. It's completely incredible, because several weeks ago, in the P's office, Reston's stories came out and the P then made the point loud, clear, and solidly to Henry that under no circumstances would he see Reston at any time, ever, and that

Henry was not to see him at all, that we knew he would be coming around trying to get an interview when he got back to Washington, but that he was to be flatly turned down. Then next thing we know, Henry's back and is talking with him. So I've got to hit him on that tomorrow.

Thursday, September 16, 1971

MacGregor reported at the staff meeting this morning that he had heard from Mel Laird that Senator Hollings told Tom Moorer that at a meeting of Democratic senators, Mansfield made the point that the Draft Bill was a straight-line, 1972 political issue, that any senators up for reelection who failed to support the Mansfield position would not receive funds in '72. Also the question involved here was who brought the war to an end, and that they must fight to make sure it's the Democrats in Congress, rather than the Republican President. This, needless to say, stirred us up a bit, and we got some things cranking during the day to get that story out. As a result, the thing backfired and late tonight MacGregor called me to say that UPI was running a story attributing the whole report to Safire. We had used Safire to leak it and one of his sources had pulled the pin on him, so the word was out. I told him not to worry about it, actually I think it works out pretty well, we got the story on the wire instead of just leaked into one paper.

He *(the P)* was very discouraged that his long meeting with Mansfield had apparently accomplished nothing in the way of getting any cooperation from him, which, of course, is the usual situation when Mansfield's playing the partisan role. He made the point that he wanted Colson and me to get together this afternoon and develop a plan for an offensive against the partisan obstructionists, putting that label on the Senate Democrats.

The press conference went very well. He had a chance to answer most of the questions he wanted to cover. He did a great job on the Draft Bill, which was the first question, saying that if they tabled it, it would be one of the most irresponsible acts on the part of the Senate that he could think of, that it would jeopardize our peace initiatives, that a vote against the draft seriously jeopardizes United States interests around the world, and would make the United States the second-strongest nation in the world.

In Vietnam, he hit very hard on the question of cutting off aid to Thieu, and pointed out that of the 91 nations that we provide aid to, only 32 have elected leaders in the sense that we would call a democratic election, so we would have to cut off aid to two-thirds of the countries if we followed that theory.

Some good questions on China and he zapped Reston pretty hard by saying nothing appeared in the Reston piece in the *Times,* that Chou En-lai hadn't told K in much greater detail already. I had a staff dinner on the *Sequoia* for all our key staff and their wives, which came off very well.

Friday, September 17, 1971

P had the bowling champions in this morning, and after greeting them in the Oval Office, took them over to his bowling alley at the EOB for a press photo. He put on his shoes and rolled his first ball, which went into the gutter, to everyone's amusement. Then he moved to the other lane, rolled another ball, and scored a strike, which is now being billed as "Nixon's latest comeback."

He got going again on the need for human, warm-type follow-up, and said he had spent a lot of time last night with the astronauts' kids. They had all kissed him good-bye, etc. and the astronauts themselves were totally captivated by this.

Henry was in this morning about Vietnam. The P told him he thought it was important to give them a hard shot now to create in them the fear that the P may do more. So he ordered Henry to get a bombing attack going over the weekend. Said to handle it on a low-key basis from a PR standpoint, that it's protective reaction and dealing with their violation of our understanding about crossing the DMZ. He feels that it's very important to make broadly the point that he did in the press conference yesterday, that the way we got into Vietnam was the overthrow of Diem, and the way to get out is not by throwing out Thieu. Henry came in later to report that they had the attack deal worked out and would go ahead with it on Monday as an all-out blast at the DMZ. The military want to take five to ten days of bombing, but we can't do that.

E was in on a couple points, in the process of which the P agreed to meet with J. Edgar Hoover tomorrow to seek his resignation. The big news today came from a call I had this morning from the Attorney General, saying that at 3:00 this afternoon, Justice Black would be sending a letter to the P telling him he would resign at the pleasure of the P. The Attorney General wants guidance from the P on what he wants to do on a replacement appointment. Feels that we've got to really think it through carefully and establish our position on it. The P said to consider Arlen Spector as a Jewish seat. He would look with favor still on William French Smith in California. It turns out that Harlan is meeting with the Chief Justice this afternoon, and he probably will resign, too, because of a serious health problem. The P later also talked to the Chief Justice, and was sort of musing about the fact that we'll have two court seats to fill. He wrote handwritten letters to both Harlan and Black this afternoon while I was in his office.

Saturday, September 18, 1971

P met with the Attorney General this morning for quite a long time. At the latter part of it he called E, and then later Colson and me, in. That led to some discussion of the Pentagon Papers. The P making a point that everyone had said this was going to tear the Democrats up, but this is only going to work out if we keep it grinding.

On another front, we could also move to open Bay of Pigs and Cuban Missile Crisis, and we can do those right away without waiting for the Vietnamese election. The question is how to open it up. We need to maybe put our guy on TV, such as our CIA guy. We should take the next two weeks to develop a scenario. The P ordered E to have the full Diem story on his desk by the end of next week. Also, the total Bay of Pigs story. Also told me to get Huston back to finish the bombing halt story.

The P and I left for Camp David. The P asked me to set it up to have Hoover in for breakfast at 8:30 Monday morning. He's going to give him the word on his departure at that time, apparently. Mitchell called me at Camp David to let me know that the P had also raised the point of making Hoover a counselor to the P, Mitchell thinks he got that turned off, but he was just warning me. I didn't hear anything from the P at Camp David, except a brief phone call while Jo and I were out playing tennis and the P asked if we were watching the football game on TV and I said no, I was playing tennis. He said UCLA was doing pretty well. They were ahead of Texas, 7 to 0, but that I ought to get them not to televise the rooting section, because they were a pretty ratty-looking bunch.

Sunday, September 19, 1971

At Camp David. The P called me over at noon. He was in his
study, with the fire going in the fireplace. There was a thick
fog or low cloud outside. There had been very heavy rain this
morning. He talked a little about Vietnam and the point that
he was sorry that we hadn't been able to actually end the war
directly, but made the point that there really was no way to
end it—it was doomed always just to trickle out the way it is,
and that's now become clear.

He told me to talk to the Attorney General about the Agnew
issue again. It would be good to indicate his confidence in
Agnew and say that if Agnew so desires, he intends to keep
him on the ticket. He recalled the damage that was done to
Eisenhower in '56 by his hesitation on keeping Nixon. It raised
hell with the Nixon friends and the conservatives, made Eisenhower look bad, as these people pounded on it. The P's
view is that Agnew is a liability, although we can't prove it,
and the only way we could check this is to run a tandem trial
heat process, but he still thinks he should indicate his support,
whether or not he intends to drop him later, and he thinks also,
it's a good way to get the P out of the black VP question,
which is sure to arise. The advantages of backing Agnew now
would be that it totally mutes the press on the question and it
pulls the rug out from under the extreme right.

Monday, September 20, 1971

Mitchell called this morning to say the Chief Justice had called
him to report that the other Court resignation is forthcoming.
It can be delayed if we want to, but we should weigh the
question of when the impact does us the most good. In any
event, we can't hold it for very long. Mitchell's inclination is
to think we should face up to it and put the two vacancies
together and put them both out in the open, which I certainly
agreed with and recommended to the P. He concurred, so he
called Mitchell and asked him to try to get the resignation in
to him right away. Puts the P in the unique opportunity of
appointing two justices at once, which will give him his four
on the court and darn near control of it.

At the end of the day, he got around to reporting to me on
his very much off-the-record breakfast meeting with J. Edgar
Hoover. Said that it's "no go" at this time. Hoover didn't take
the bait, apparently, and is going to stay on as a political mat-

ter. He feels it's much better for the P for him to do so. He will then pull out at any point in the future when the P feels that it would be politically necessary. He claims he is fully dedicated to the P's reelection, wants to do whatever he can to ensure it, but feels that his departure at this time would be counterproductive in that regard.

Saturday, September 25, 1971

The big item today, as we left for our Western trip, was the question of the Pacific Coast dock strike negotiations. The P had me up during the flight out to Montana. He wanted me to make it clear to Shultz that his desire was to use the Taft-Hartley Injunction process, and he discounts Shultz's argument against that, which is that it doesn't meet the requirements, because he says Labor always says that a strike doesn't meet the Taft-Hartley requirements, and that actually the P can decide on that.

We had good stop in Montana. The main story out of that being that the load of cement that the P and Mansfield were supposed to dump at Libbey Dam didn't work right, and so the photographers got a great picture of the two of them and the Congressmen straining to pull the rope.

The Portland session was a Q & A, which went very well. A good range of questions and good pacing. The P opened it with an announcement that he had met with Bridges and Flynn, which he did just before the media briefing, and that they had agreed to go ahead with negotiations, try to get the thing settled in the next week.

We had a fairly substantial group of demonstrators. Not very many in number, but very noisy, outside the P's room in the hotel, which created a problem from 5:00, after the media briefing, until about 7:00, when we finally had the Secret Service invoke the Federal law and move them out, which they did without incident. Worked out fine, but it was fairly rough up to that point because they really were making a lot of noise and were driving the P right up the wall.

He had me into the room at the hotel in the evening and was talking about the Supreme Court appointment and his feeling that he really should go for a woman judge, if we can get a good, tough conservative. He thinks this is the opportunity to score on that point, that we would make tremendous political mileage in that while many people would be opposed to it, nobody would vote against him because of it. On the other hand, a lot of people who were in favor of it would change their votes to Nixon because of such an appointment.

Sunday, September 26, 1971

We left Oregon early this morning, but the P was up even earlier. Made a lot of phone calls before we got underway, including a call to the Attorney General on the idea of a woman judge. He said the Attorney General wasn't very happy about it, but he is going to work on it some. Washington went very well. He gave a good talk at the Hanford Atomic Energy site, making the point that we can't consult our fears.

We had a good stop in Alaska. The Japanese Emperor visit went almost perfectly, as far as our operations were concerned. The Emperor himself was a little shaky as he stumbled coming down the stairs off his plane. Had to have his hat pulled out of his hand by the chamberlain as a clue that it was time for him to read his speech, and then he had a terrible time getting it out of his pocket and was a little ludicrous in the way he held it up and read it. No substance to the visit, but great ceremony and certainly well worthwhile.

The Hickel reception preceding the Emperor's arrival went very well, with a good, friendly greeting outside. Hickel did succeed in trapping us into listening to a couple of Burl Ives songs, including one that sounded like it was going to turn into a horrible peace song, but I think Ives left off the last verse and it came out all right. Then Hickel caught the P on the way out and trapped him in his den for a ten-minute talk, which the P later told me was fairly satisfactory. He will support him next year, but feels he should wait a while before he comes out with an open endorsement and should start building the groundwork first.

Monday, September 27, 1971

Not much sleep last night because of the time change between Washington and Alaska, and then a long plane ride to Washington. The P took a nap on part of it. When we got back into Washington, we had to go to the Mamie Eisenhower birthday party, and that was another disaster, with Ray Bolger going on and on. Finally the Marine Band leader had to just interrupt him with "Ruffles and Flourishes" in order to get the P in, and the P had to take over at the close, after the Happy Birthday singing and the cake cutting, to bring the program to an end by giving his little remarks, which Bolger had forgotten to call on him for.

Tuesday, September 28, 1971

The big debate this morning was whether or not to go to Justice Hugo Black's funeral today. Mitchell, E, Dick Moore, Garment, etc., all urged that he should go, that it would be very helpful in the current climate regarding the Court and his relationship to the Court in showing respect for it, and would counter the charge of a political attitude toward the Court. Very much against his better judgment and mine, the P did, at the last minute, decide to go, on the basis of no press and no advance notice. It turned out to be the wrong decision, as the Unitarian minister who gave the eulogy gave a very political talk about why Black disliked strict constructionists on the Court. It was directed pretty bluntly at the P and Mitchell, was very inappropriate, and the P was quite distressed that he had gone.

He talked some today about his reaction to the Secret Service, coming off the Alaska trip, where we did have a problem in the motorcade because they thought there was a group of demonstrators that were going to rush the P, so they wouldn't let him stand up in the car, and also they held the crowd way back at the curbs, which they're not supposed to do, so we missed an opportunity for some great crowd shots and a great crowd story. He now wants the Secret Service ordered to change some of these things and he told me to stay on top of it to be sure it's played right.

As far as the Justice Black funeral, he said he wanted the staff to know clearly that he went under duress, that he feels it was a mistake, that he was throwing his pearls before swine, that this was the result of the same kind of thinking that got him to fire Hershey, to go to a black church on election day, and to meet with college presidents. He obviously wasn't very happy with it. Henry came up with a big problem on the China trip. Rogers is opposed to his going, and he talked to the P about that. Rogers' argument being that Henry should send a lower-level person and that he was worried that it would louse up the UN debate because that comes at the same time. Henry, of course, has to go because we're committed to the Chinese. He and the P discussed that on the basis of my talking to

Rogers and trying to get him straightened out on it. It will be one of those continuing agony type things.

Thursday, September 30, 1971

Staff meeting this morning. Shultz was particularly concerned because we're moving to an extensive control system and that the planners are working on the assumptions that the P has implied in his speeches. The Cost of Living Council is developing plans without authoritative guidance and the papers that they produce will be Stein's, without any guidance, and they'll need Presidential input before they're finalized. He's also concerned that the P doesn't understand what Laird's doing regarding the Defense budget. As a result of this, we squeezed in a meeting with Shultz in the middle of a fantastically loaded schedule today.

We had quite a discussion in the plane on the way down about how to handle the notification to Rogers of Henry's China trip. The P said that it was up to me to notify Rogers and that I should do it by mixing it with the Soviet trip and the fact that we can't change the signals now, after the meeting with Gromyko, but he says that I should wait until Sunday to call Rogers so that it's too late to do anything about it.

Fourth Quarter: October–December

Saturday, October 2, 1971

Late last night we got rumors that Poff was considering withdrawing, and that was confirmed this morning. He made it irrevocable. Told Kleindienst to call off the ABA consideration of his nomination, and he drafted a statement hitting the controversy on civil rights and saying it would be divisive and not in the best interest of the country, the Court, or his family to stay in.

The P says that he's going to go for a real right-winger now, that is stronger than Poff on civil rights. The worst thing he could do is go to the left. He wants to get someone worse than Poff and really stick it to the opposition now.

> Richard Harding Poff was a Republican congressman from Virginia, and eventually became a Justice of the Supreme Court of Virginia.

On the Court, he came up with the idea of *(Robert)* Byrd of West Virginia because he was a former KKK'er, he's elected by the Democrats as Whip, he's a self-made lawyer, he's more reactionary than Wallace, and he's about 53. The P left this afternoon for Grand Cay for the night.

Tuesday, October 5, 1971

The P had me in first thing this morning for some general schedule notes. The more odd among them being that, in spite of all his sarcastic comments about tennis and the people that are interested in tennis, he now wants to stage a special tennis match at the White House courts; putting up bleachers, setting up linesmen, etc., having Billie Jean King and Stan Smith and some of the top stars play. This springs out of his phone call to Billie Jean King yesterday, when she became the first woman to win $100,000. He also decided he ought to have one "Evening at the White House" this season, and we should have Lawrence Welk star in it.

He then met with Safire for a while to go over what he wants to cover in the *(Phase II economic)* speech. Gave him some pretty good guidelines, on the basis that he wants to refer to the fact that the freeze has been enormously successful due to the cooperation and support of the American people, and then that we're going to follow on with the continued program. He doesn't want much detail on how it works, but we will have a Pay Board and a Price Board.

Our goal will be to reduce inflation to 2 percent or 3 percent. This will be great benefit to every American. There may be selfish interests that oppose it, but he will count on the cooperation of the people. This is the way to provide more jobs, new prosperity. Says the handling of profits is very ticklish. This is the time not to assume that prices always must go up. The consumer should get some of the break on productivity, too, so let's have some price reductions. He wants more poetry than prose. Upbeat confidence, reassured; things are going well.

Wednesday, October 6, 1971

We started out today with another series of K-Rogers flaps. Henry came rocketing through the halls first thing this morning with a *Christian Science Monitor* story that indicated Rogers had saved the China trip by his remarks over the weekend, and that he had forced the Chinese to react, which was why we had been able to make the announcement of Henry's trip yesterday. A little later, he bounced up with a *New York Times* editorial that, in effect, said the same thing, so he's practically beside himself, again with probably some reason.

The P spent the whole day at the EOB getting his speech ready for TV tomorrow night. Had me over several times. He raised the point of "summitry." He was thinking about the Russian announcement next week, making the point that he basically doesn't believe in Summit meetings unless they're going to produce something, but these two meetings are necessary and they're different, and the P is superbly and ideally qualified to handle these meetings because: first, he knows the men on the other side; second, he knows the subject, third, he has unprecedented experience, and fourth, he is a tough, realistic negotiator, but conciliatory and subtle.

Monday, October 11, 1971
The P spent the day at the EOB, getting ready for the press conference tomorrow. He did come over for a couple of hours at midday to meet with the Italian Foreign Minister and to receive an award from the Sons of Italy.

The P had me in and we spent quite a little time on overall schedule review and also got into the China question and prep for the staff meeting we were having this afternoon on the subject. He is very strongly in favor of the ground station and having maximum TV coverage available, in spite of Henry's objections to all of that. He raised the question of Mrs. Nixon going, thinking it might be a good idea because of the TV coverage she'd get, but if she does, it would have to be understood that she would be the only woman going. Not Mrs. Rogers or any other wives.

We then had our staff meeting this afternoon. Henry was furious because I had included Scali in the meeting, so he at first didn't come and then did come and sat and sulked and objected to our discussion of the ground station ad nauseam, and left. So I finished up the meeting with Scali, Ziegler, Chapin, and Hughes, then had Henry and Al Haig come back in and we went over the whole thing, worked it out quite satisfactorily. He's agreed on a press corps of 150, including the ground station personnel, and basically bought our minimum level overall approach, which I think will work out pretty well if we can get it from the Chinese. Henry's concern on all this is that we not make a circus out of it, and that we not appear to be staging the whole thing for the benefit of domestic TV, which would cause people to react adversely, not only in China, but in the rest of the world. He's obviously got some merit to his point, and it's pretty hard to argue it, except that from our viewpoint, and the P concurs in this, we need maximum coverage in order to get the benefit from it, especially in the short term. Henry is very much of the view that we should only be concerned with the long term, which, of course, is not realistic.

Tuesday, October 12, 1971

Press conference today to make the Soviet Summit announcement. The P stayed holed up at the EOB all morning. Came
over at noon for the press conference in the press room with
film coverage, but not live. He opened the conference with the
announcement of the Russian Summit, reading the joint communiqué and then took questions.

He was up pretty tight during the morning getting ready for
it, and evidenced that by his reaction to the story yesterday,
"killing the Byrd to the Supreme Court" story from the weekend. He was very upset and wanted to be sure that the Byrd
story still rode. He had a chance to cover that at the press
conference and did it with a vengeance.

He felt strongly that after the press conference we should
really go to work playing the "Man of Peace" issue all the
time, move all the other issues to a lower level and really build
that one up, because it's our issue and we have to use it.

Wednesday, October 13, 1971

As he reviewed the schedules for this morning, he looked with
considerable disfavor on the discovery that he had to do a
diplomatic credential ceremony this afternoon and said he
wanted to skip those from now on, and as much other stuff of
that kind as possible, so we cut the ceremonies down to eliminate the 5-minute talk. The P simply received the credentials
and ushered the Ambassador to the door. That gave him a little
guilty feeling, and later in the day he came up with the plan
of having each ambassador bring his family to watch the ceremony, but still eliminate the 5-minute talk. So we'll try that
in the future. He was very anxious to try and work out the
opportunity to go to Dean Acheson's funeral, but we can't do
it. He did call Mrs. Acheson and gave her a military aide, etc.

We had quite a long discussion this morning about China
plans. He said that Henry's book, that he went over with him
last night, is brilliant, but the P now wants a brief memo that
tells, first, what are our goals, and, second, what will the Chinese want that we have to resist. He wants the book boiled
down to its essentials, to come directly to the point, and cut
out the BS on historical processes and everything and get it
buttoned down. I covered this with Haig, who immediately
told Henry, who was in Chicago today. Henry called me back
for clarification, being somewhat upset by the critique.

Thursday, October 14, 1971

The P had no schedule today. It was set aside for unscheduled meetings with Connally, K, etc., getting ready for Henry's trip and following up on economic policy. Later this afternoon the P had Henry and me over to the EOB for a discussion of the China trip. He went into the whole question of Pat Nixon's going, making the point that people contact is more important than meetings, in terms of public reaction here, and that Mrs. Nixon would be one way to get some good people pictures, so he wants Henry to raise the Pat Nixon question. If she goes, then the P doesn't have to go out into the people. If not, he will have to. If she goes, she goes solely as a prop. No Mrs. Rogers along or anything like that. Later, Henry summed it up that at some point he would discuss this with Chou alone, making the point of the enormous interest in America in Chinese people, and so on, that Mrs. Nixon would be going to Russia, but that we recognize the problem and we want them to be honest with us. This is an opportunity to convey the human side of the Chinese to the American people. K is to feel his reaction and not press it on him.

The P said at the beginning of the meeting, he wanted his schedule cut to three days and to stay in one city only, just Peking. He then expanded that to four and then agreed to move it to five and to consider doing one other city for one day, maybe on the way out. Hopefully, not overnight, unless the Chinese want it, and will give us publicity and get us on TV and it will mean a big public reception. He points out that on TV the American President received by a million Chinese is worth a hundred times the effect of the communiqué, and that we're not to miss an opportunity for the Chinese to give a good welcome. There must be masses of Chinese people somewhere, and we must have some chance for pictures with the people. Henry is to try to find some way to get color into the trip. He should point out to them the receptions the P received in Yugoslavia and Romania. He says sightseeing, no. Great Wall, no. People, yes.

Friday, October 15, 1971

The P discussed with me his problem on the Supreme Court. Mitchell was in this morning to see him, having told me last night that he had to talk to the P this morning for a few minutes on a Court problem. It turns out that *(Warren)* Burger has told

Mitchell that he will resign if the P doesn't appoint distinguished judges to the Court, and he doesn't feel the current list meets that qualification. The P's view is, if that's his feeling, let him resign, that he will not cater to Burger's demands on this kind of a thing and the P feels quite strongly about it on the grounds that Burger would never have even been considered for the Court, let alone Chief Justice, except by Nixon.

He then had Henry in for final guidance discussion on the China trip before he leaves tomorrow. He made the point that he doesn't want to go to any of the other cities just to see the leaders there, that the point of going to other cities would be to get out to the people.

K argues that the Chinese have a different attitude toward foreigners and they will not respect the kind of approach that the P traditionally would take. The P still argues that he wants to let the people contact be the message that gets through. Henry says it's tough to raise the question of creating crowds, but he'll make the point in a complicated way, which probably means he won't make it at all, but we'll see what happens.

Saturday, October 16, 1971
The P was at Camp David, presumably all day, and apparently watched the World Series this afternoon. He did call at 4:30 about the World Series, and said, ''I think I'll give up this business and start predicting baseball games.'' He had predicted the outcome of this game, as he had the third game, very much against the general prognostications.

Monday, October 18, 1971
Henry is in Hawaii on his way to China, and the P raised some concerns, particularly about a George Sherman story in the *Star* last week that implied that Henry was dominating the making of all foreign policy. The P was quite concerned about it, first because it's not true, particularly the China initiative for instance, was not Henry's. Second, that it would drive Rogers up the wall. Third, it creates the impression that the P's doing all this for cynical reasons and that he doesn't know anything about what he's doing, and fourth, he thinks this results from the way Henry does his briefings and that it creates a problem. In any event, he wanted me to talk to Haig and try to get that worked out.

The P also reraised the public broadcasting thing again. He's fairly upset at the inability of our people to get control of any of it, and feels that we've got to find a way, somehow, to avoid letting them stockpile all the anti-Nixon newscasters and subsidize them. We have Malek working with Colson and Flanigan to try and get at this. The problem is, we don't have working control of the board and there's virtually no other way that we can take any effective action. This evening was the opening of the Eisenhower Theater at the Kennedy Center. The P attended. It was a good opening, I guess, but rather a dull play: Ibsen's *A Doll's House.*

Tuesday, October 19, 1971

Back into the Court again. He met again this morning with John Mitchell. He's now thinking of some different approaches and is not telling anybody what he's really up to, but he's forcing Mitchell to reevaluate. He's decided now that if the ABA gives *(California Supreme Court Associate)* Mildred Lilley a good rating, he'll go with her. If they don't he'll drop her and blame them for it, so he wins either way. He seems to be intrigued with Howard Baker as a possibility, which was a suggestion that came in from Len Garment, and that I passed on to him yesterday when I was making my pitch for looking for some more distinction.

Wednesday, October 20, 1971

The P started the day this morning by calling Malek and me in to ask whether any of our recent high-level women appointees are lawyers, and if so, how many years they have practiced and so on. This obviously relating to his decision on the two Supreme Court appointments.

The P made several allusions during the day to the plans for nominations, but never said anything specific and made the point that he wasn't going to tell anybody this time, which apparently also includes me.

The P then called me again to say that he needed a fast writer to help on his text for tomorrow night, so should enlist Safire. Said he wouldn't tell him tonight who the nominees would be, get started on that tomorrow. He seems to be pretty pleased about the nominations. I think he's going for people who have not been on the list of six that was submitted to the ABA, and probably who have not been speculated much about. My own guess would be that it would be the fellow from

Virginia who is the former head of the American Bar Association (I can't remember his name) *(it was Lewis Powell)* and Howard Baker, although I think it might well be one of those two plus Mulligan from New York. The theory on the woman is that the ABA is not going to approve her, and therefore he'll let her pass and blame them for it.

We talked also a little about China plans, and the P wanted me to be sure to have Haig remind Henry that the P must see Chou En-lai and Mao alone. Separately. Without K, because he has done this with all other heads of state. He wants at least one meeting with each of them, with only interpreters present, and these are to be in addition to all other meetings. We must have them on some occasion. He makes the point that not only do we need to do it because of the other countries, but so as to make it clear that Henry isn't manipulating the entire operation, but rather, the P is clearly in command.

Thursday, October 21, 1971

The whole thing today was the Supreme Court announcement. The P went over to EOB first thing this morning, spent the whole day over there, except for a couple of midday appointments in the Oval Office. He made quite a point of not telling me or anyone else who the nominees were, except Dick Moore. Then he had me working with Dick Moore to get things organized over at Justice and, of course, Moore assumed that I knew and spilled the beans to me. Turns out that they were set on Powell, the guy from Virginia who I expected, and thought they were set on Howard Baker as the second seat, but apparently, at some point toward the last minute last night or this morning, the P decided to go with Rehnquist instead of Baker, and they shifted over, even though Baker had been made the offer and they were waiting for his response at 9:00 this morning when he was supposed to have it in. He didn't call until about 9:30, at which time he said he would accept. By then the P had decided to go the other way.

The P was very firm on making the notifications late this afternoon or this evening.

The P decided not to have anybody work with him on the speech, and he wrote it himself. He came out several times during the day with the need to make the point of a stacked jury at the ABA, that there were no women on the selection board. He wanted them hit hard on the fact that we learned from inside the ABA that they considered Mildred Lillie the best-qualified woman that we could have submitted, but then they voted 11–1 against her on being qualified for the Court. He also wanted to hit hard on the point that the ABA does not have veto power; that the Constitution requires the advice and consent of the Senate, but does not require the consent of the Bar Association.

He was shocked at Willy Brandt's announcement yesterday as the Nobel Peace Prize winner. Made the point today that we've got to watch out now that *Time,* in order to needle us, may go for K as the Man of the Year, which would be very bad, so we should try to swing that around a different way.

The P did a superb job on the announcement, which ran 15 minutes. Reaction was very good overall, especially to Powell, because everybody considers him outstanding. Most of the people we checked with were not familiar with Rehnquist, but said he sounded good on his qualifications. I talked to the P a couple hours after the broadcast and said I thought he had scored another 10-strike, and he said, "Well, probably so, except for my wife, but boy is she mad." Apparently Mrs. Nixon really hit him on his failure to appoint a woman, because she felt she had a commitment that he would do so and didn't buy the argument of the Bar turning her down. So that apparently was the only really sour note.

Saturday, Sunday, and Monday, October 23, 24, and 25, 1971

The P spent the weekend at Camp David. I had no contact with him at all through the entire weekend, while I was down in Florida at Disney World. Apparently things went well up here. The big blow was late Monday night, when we had the UN vote expelling Taiwan. That'll create quite a stir, I'm sure, tomorrow.

Tuesday, October 26, 1971

The main action today was on the UN vote. Reagan had been very upset last night and tried to reach the P after midnight and the P returned the call this morning. Reagan feels that the P should go on TV and make a big thing that we won't abide by any UN votes in the future, etc. The P explained to him why we couldn't do that and that apparently didn't calm him down much. Rogers called Reagan later and thought he had made some headway, saying we're going to sleep on the whole thing and see how it works out, but then Reagan saw Rogers on TV later, saying that we weren't going to suspend funding of the UN because of the vote, and that got Reagan all upset again. He talked to the Attorney General after that and said that he thinks we've at least got to call Bush down for a consultation. Goldwater was in Tucson last night and said there was quite an uprising over the news, and also a problem at the Republican luncheon today. That he thinks that now that we're pulling in our horns on foreign aid and the currency reform and all that sort of thing, that the little nations are now flaunting their independence.

The P called me at home later this evening and said that he had his talk with Henry, who was back from China, and that Henry had called Reagan as I asked him to do, and will also call Buckley. The P makes the point that we need to keep the right wing on track. The plan is to keep Bush down here two or three days, which will shake them up a little at the UN and, in some way, we'll say we're disgusted by their performance. He feels that, beyond that, there's nothing we can do about it. We just have to ride it through. We have to see if K can keep Reagan in line and try to do so with Buckley also, and we've just got to keep Reagan from jumping off the reservation. He does want to make it clear to the conservatives that the P fought the China battle as hard as he could, and the right wing should understand that, and that the point is that we mustn't be defensive with them. They've got to face up to the fact that we have common enemies and that the people they should be after are the UN, not the P.

Wednesday, October 27, 1971

The P had his breakfast with Rogers and K this morning to let Henry fill Rogers in on the China trip.

Henry is convinced that Rogers pushed the UN vote for Monday night so as to downgrade Henry's trip and give Henry's trip the blame for the Taiwan loss. The P's point is the problem is not Taiwan, it's the UN, and he's concerned that the Democrats are going to seize upon this as the reason to blame us for the defeat, that we put on too much pressure because of the China trip. Apparently Rogers accused K of being too soft on his dealings with the Chinese. The P said he definitely decided he would travel in a Chinese plane in China so we could work out the trip to Hangchow with Chou En-lai accompanying us. Chou will not travel in an American plane.

The P also told Henry to call Ronald Reagan today and try to get him straightened out. He then had Ziegler in and we talked about UN funding. He told Ziegler to back Rogers' statement. He should refer to the glee displayed at the UN would have a detrimental effect on the United States people in the Congress. Said the P does want to get into a position on this, saying the conduct was a disgusting spectacle. The delegates of many countries the United States supports were gleeful and all. That the UN was very seriously impaired in terms of support from among American people and the American Congress. Ron picked up that line and used it today and it had quite a big play.

Monday, November 1, 1971

George Shultz came up with a theory at the staff meeting this morning, and reexpanded it at our dinner meeting this evening, that there are a lot of deep currents beginning to flow now, that we have cut a lot of our basic moorings and we don't know exactly where we're headed. For instance, there's opposition building to a controlled economy, or the idea of one, and to the loss of foreign aid and to the China seat. He thinks we should lay out all these and look at them as a tableau and consider the whole picture, not just the pieces. He thinks the P has unleashed a lot of new forces, so that every little nuance now becomes important, and we must be very careful regarding their reaction. Thus it's a very difficult time and delicate time. He comments that the P tends more than anyone to play the whole mosaic, while the others play the specific little items with which they're personally concerned.

He (the P) got into quite a few discussions of personnel today. For instance, the problem of the Attorney General and whether we can let him leave to run the campaign. He talked about the problem of Kleindienst succeeding, feeling that we can't get him confirmed, so maybe the thing to do is leave Mitchell at Justice, and have Kleindienst come out and run the campaign under Mitchell's guidance. Or leave them both at Justice and let Mitchell run the campaign from there, or maybe have Mitchell take a leave of absence, or as a final alternative, have someone else run the campaign. He discussed Elliot Richardson and made the point that he would be an outstanding

Chief Justice, and that since he's now got the two conservatives set for the Court he would be willing to go to a middle-of-the-road guy, and if anything should happen to Burger, he wants to keep Richardson in mind, because he thinks he would be a towering, historic Chief Justice. He also got into the Hoover question. The P feels we have to delay the removal now. The P's feeling is that we just let it go and announce sometime next year that Hoover will be resigning after the election and after his successor has qualified. That will put the heat on for Nixon's reelection to make sure he's the one that appoints the successor.

We had a meeting this afternoon with the Attorney General and Shultz regarding the Hoffa question. Mitchell raised the point that the time has probably come for the P to exercise executive clemency. He suggests burying this in the Christmas list in a batch of 250 or so. The P was trying to get at the point of how you position it. The question is what our political benefit is, and what is in the balance. The inevitable charge will be that this is done for political support. The line the P would use is that he's met the normal requirements for release and there should not be discrimination against him because he's a labor leader.

Wednesday, November 3, 1971
The P spent the day at the EOB office with no set schedule. He had me over there virtually all morning, with K, E, and Ziegler in and out during the session. He spent the first part of the day following up on yesterday's local election results. Primarily calling the winners, including Rizzo in Philadelphia, who apparently, although a Democrat, is totally for the P and in effect told him so. The P told all of them that we want to work with them, and that E would be in touch with them to set up the ways of doing so. He wants to be sure that we pound home the fact that the mayor races prove our political strategy, that the place for us is not with the Jews and the Negroes, but with the white ethnics and that we have to go after the Catholic thing.

Thursday, November 4, 1971
The main event of the day was Mrs. Gandhi's visit. The P was particularly pleased with his welcoming speech, and hoped that we'd get some people to pick it up, make the point of his

ability to do these without any notes, with great simplicity, eloquence and brevity. He wanted to see if we could get a column on it. He had a good line, making the point that our commissions are not bound by a treaty because we have a special relationship that doesn't require a treaty. He made the point that we need to get the whole story of his toasts and arrival statements out at some point.

Overall he's in kind of a strange mood. I think mainly because he's sort of in between things here, waiting for the next shoe to drop. Also he's very much concerned about Henry's attitude and mood, and as a result of that asked Henry to go to Florida with him. He's also got Mitchell coming down for a political meeting on Monday. His whole approach is one of sort of bouncing around on loose ends at the moment.

Friday, November 5, 1971

Called me in at 7:45 this morning. He was in the office early, even though he had the Gandhi State Dinner last night.

We had a long Cabinet meeting this morning. The P opened it to launch the subject of politics, and said this was the 25th anniversary of the day he was elected to Congress the first time, November 5, 1946. He made the point that the men around the table had worked for three years and contributed enormously to the Administration and the country, especially on the domestic side, and they may wonder what recognition they've gotten. The foreign policy initiatives have gotten some acclaim. Some domestic initiatives also deserve it but they don't get it. On the domestic front, generally, this Administration, as far as people are concerned, is dull, gray, unimaginative, and status quo. This is not the fault of the people around the table; it's that everything is relative. We are responsible button-down people, we don't demagogue, and we're naive to think that we'll get credit for doing a good job. There is some need to change policy and attitude; the Cabinet is very positive, honest, responsible, but already the drumfire has begun. The Democrats don't have to be positive or responsible. We have to understand that in order to make news you have to hit somebody, not in an unfair or irresponsible way.

(After P left, John Scali said) The most important thing you can do is become zealous defenders of Nixon. Articulate advocates, reacting to the partisan political attacks and recognizing the necessity of defending one man. Nixon sits there day

after day, listening to the tirades against him, and he can't reply personally. You must respond automatically, without a signal from the White House, to these charges. It's necessary that each of you learn how to wrap up the points that you want to make in 30 seconds or less. This can be done on any subject, but you have to decide what is the key point, write it in simple language. The way to do it is to start with a subject, then a predicate, then end it and lower your voice so you know it's the end. It's essential to a film editor for you to do this, and on that basis he'll give you the free time you're after.

He made the point also that from December 10 until the time of the new Congress you have a unique opportunity to dominate the news, and we should have news conferences with Cabinet officers every day. He said he was impressed with the number of problems that end up on the P's desk. You all have many problems that you solve alone in your departments, but your tough ones all end up here, on the back of one man. He wanted to be P; he's not complaining. Then he told the story of the farmer whose cow went dry. He tried all the remedies and the vet couldn't cure her, so he got in a headshrinker who went in and spent two hours with the cow alone in the barn. All of a sudden there was a terrible roar and out came a tidal wave of milk. The farmer asked the headshrinker how he had done it. The headshrinker said, how long have you had this cow? He said eight years, giving a record crop of milk all those years, and the headshrinker said, well, during all that time that you were sitting there squeezing that cow's tits did it ever occur to you to say I love you? He then said to the Cabinet officers, keep in mind that farmer.

He says the single most important thing you can do is play an important role in the reelection. You must use the talents of your department better than you have. Advocate and defend this man. The history books will write Richard Nixon in large letters. Your name will be there with his if you measure up to the challenge and make it possible to reelect this great P.

Thursday, November 11, 1971
The P worked at the Residence this morning. He told *Time* to come over and meet with Earl Butz, the new Secretary of Agriculture nominee that he announced this afternoon. He then went to Arlington Cemetery to place a wreath at the Tomb of the Unknown Soldier on the occasion of the 50th anniversary

of the placement there of the unknown soldier. There was a nonspeaking ceremony. Very impressive and came off very well. He then spent the rest of the day at the EOB in preparation for the press conference tomorrow, except for the Butz announcement at 4:00 this afternoon. He had Henry and me over to discuss the European trip plans. We've got a problem now of a place to meet with the French because Pompidou won't come to French Guyana and doesn't want to come anywhere in the Western Hemisphere.

We elected that Henry would try and work it out with Pompidou, see what we could develop. That got into a discussion of the international economic situation. K kept raising the point that we have to settle the European economic situation. The P told him to talk with Shultz. He also told him to drop the Burns line regarding return to the gold standard and so on, but Henry argues against Connally's strategy because he thinks that we're linking structural problems with special interests and that this makes a mistake. He feels that Connally is like all Texans, and is just basically antiforeigner. He argues that we should state what we want to the other nations and then start negotiating on the basis of an established strategy. The P told Henry to see Connally immediately when he gets back, and to get into this with him. See if he can't get him lined up.

Henry thinks that Laird has sabotaged us as usual on the troop withdrawal announcement for tomorrow by leaking a stronger position than the P is actually going to take. He also thinks that Rogers has declared total war on him and is maneuvering to sabotage him on all fronts except Vietnam, which is an area that Rogers isn't interested in. He's convinced that they're moving on Middle East, India, Pakistan, and other areas without our knowledge and it's driving him right up the wall. Probably some merit to it, but there's no way I can evaluate that. The P called at 5:30 to say he didn't want any more phone calls, but both Rogers and Laird were trying to reach him and obviously just wanted to get in their views on the record before the group announcement thing, so he said to tell them he was tied up in a crisis on the Pay Board and wouldn't be able to talk with them this evening.

Friday, November 12, 1971

The P spent all morning preparing for his Vietnam announcement press conference this afternoon, and didn't seem to have any particular problems in getting ready. He did a superb job at the press conference. I think it was probably one of the best ones he's ever had. He used the pressroom and was on film for the entire conference, opening with the Vietnam announcement *(of 45,000 troops to be withdrawn by February 1, 1972)* and then taking questions for half an hour.

Also in the press conference, they asked if he would consider amnesty for the draft dodgers who had gone to Canada and he answered with a simple no. In talking about it afterward, said that the line there is that serving in Vietnam is a difficult problem for young Americans, but 2.5 million chose to serve and 45,000 of those who chose to serve died for their country. On the other hand, a few hundred chose to desert their country, and they have to live with their choice.

Saturday, November 13, 1971

The P called me over to Dogwood at 10:30 for a couple of hours of general discussion, starting with plans for Mrs. Nixon's trip to Africa. The P had a lot of ideas on how to structure the trip mechanics, such as how to set the plane up. A little later Mrs. Nixon and Julie joined us and agreed with the basic plans. Julie suggested we try to sell the coverage to one network on an exclusive basis and wants Ziegler to explore that. The P said Mrs. Nixon should have a talk with the President in each country where she goes, and he said he wanted to have her entire delegation in to meet with him before they leave. He also got into some discussion on the plan we have for a TV day in the White House and he had a lot of good ideas on it, improved on most of ours. He wants to be sure we bring the dog in. We got into quite a thing late in the afternoon because he discovered that Julie didn't have adequate preparation material for her trip. He wants me now to put *(speechwriter John)* Andrews on it, and get some really good Q&A things worked out for her and some talking points on Administration programs and achievements, the kind of points that we want her to get across such as we would give a Cabinet officer.

Tuesday, November 16, 1971

Henry was in quite a stir this morning because of the story in *The New York Times* that obviously had been leaked by Defense, giving the figures on ultimate troop withdrawal numbers and strategy regarding residual force. We got into quite a discussion of it with the P and it was decided I should call Laird and hit him on this. Which I did, not getting to him until quite a bit later in the day. Laird finessed the whole thing, blaming it on all sorts of other people and ranting and raving about how he's really clamping down on the Joint Chiefs, etc.

The P decided this noon to break the ice with Peterson on Commerce and tried to call him to get him in to tell him. Peterson was out to lunch with Schweitzer, of the IMF, which made the P a little bit upset. He later got him in at 3:30 this afternoon with Shultz, E, and me, and did an absolutely terrible job of telling him he had decided he was going to move to Commerce. He didn't even offer the job to him or give him the chance to discuss it. He just said that's what we've decided and didn't even do that in a very enthusiastic fashion, but I guess Peterson swallowed it all right.

A lot of discussion during the day on whether or not to do the AFL Convention. The P's gut reaction this morning was not to, because he feels we can't let Meany have it both ways. He's been kicking us around, especially on foreign policy, and the P doesn't feel we should go down. Colson on the other hand feels very strongly that we should. That the atmosphere is not wrong. A lot of the delegates support the P and he could score a smash hit, and that he shouldn't let Meany scare him off.

Wednesday, November 17, 1971

Staff meeting started out this morning with the AFL question, whether the P should go down to the convention. E has now shifted to being conditionally in favor if it is made unmistakably clear that the P has not sold out to Labor in the past. In other words, rewrite the history of what is believed, but do it in the presence of Labor. Shultz also votes to go. They both feel there should be a maximum buildup on the "Daniel into the Lions' Den" thesis. The question then came up with the P, who basically had the feeling he should not go. That it's a question of throwing pearls before swine and he just doesn't think we should. Also he reviewed Cook's first draft of the speech, or actually the fifth draft, and he has totally the wrong idea because it's the kind of speech the P really wants to give, whereas his plan was to have a written speech that was basically the dull routine standard speech that they would be expecting, and he would then not deliver that, but he would say that he stands behind it and speak extemporaneously. Also it praised Meany to the skies, which is, of course, ridiculous.

The thing then went on through the day in some doubt, but he decided he'd make up his mind at 7:00 tonight whether to go or not, and if he decided to go he would leave at 9:00 tonight, go on down to Florida so he would be ready to speak at noon tomorrow. At 7:00 he said he would go. He told me to go ahead and get it set up. We had that preworked out with Shultz, and it was then his task to call Meany and confirm it. It took him an hour and a half to reach Meany. In the meantime we had run out of time, really, as far as leaving tonight, but at 8:30 Shultz finally did get Meany, and Meany, in effect, said the P can go to hell. That tomorrow was his day at the convention and he wasn't about to let the P come in and up-stage him, and he put it really on the basis that the schedule was all set and he couldn't change it. He did say he could speak at 4:00 tomorrow or at any time he wanted to on Friday. Our recommendation then was that he speak at 10:30 Friday morning, and after some discussion the P agreed. Colson and Shultz were pretty furious with Meany's attitude and were practically tempted not to go. Felt that we shouldn't let him get away with this kind of approach to the P, but actually, when you get down to it, it was really pretty logical and un-derstandable that he would take that position.

We had some discussion during the day today on the Pe-terson problem. He told me to tell Shultz to take Peterson totally out of the play on international financial policy. This arising from Connally's feeling that we're speaking with too many voices. He said that Peterson is to quit talking to people such as Schweitzer, who he had lunch with today. He's to have no more external talk, especially to foreigners. This is to be done under the assumption that Shultz, McCracken, and Pe-terson are all told to have no more discussion with foreigners, but actually the one he's after is Peterson. He got into this after the whole thing of asking Peterson yesterday to take the Secretary of Commerce. All of us, incidentally, agreed that was about the most graceless exercise we had ever seen. Really on both the P and Peterson's part.

Thursday, November 18, 1971
We had another round on the AFL question this morning, since Shultz was due to call Meany, and I wanted to check with the

P first to be sure he was still on track regarding making the trip. He was a little annoyed because he felt that we ought to get a commitment out of Meany that they wouldn't walk out on the Pay Board before we agreed that the P would go, which, of course, we can't do. He ended up agreeing to go, however, and Shultz called Meany this morning and confirmed 10:30 tomorrow, and we went ahead and announced it.

Today was the day of big Congressional problems. We have another batch of antiwar amendments in both the House and Senate, and the campaign spending thing has become a serious problem since the Democrats have put in a one dollar checkoff on tax allocation, which would be the worst possible thing that could happen to us because it would automatically raise $20 million for each party, which we don't need, but the Democrats would be saved by it.

We flew down to Key Biscayne this evening. The P worked in his cabin all the way down and didn't have me up at all, which sets a new record.

Friday, November 19, 1971

The day started in Key Biscayne with the AFL speech. The P looked pretty tired when he got on the helicopter and all of us felt he had probably not slept much, been up most of the night working on the speech. He used the whole ride over on the helicopter to work on his notes again. The whole deal in the hall was somewhat incredible. He walked in without any announcement, Meany had canceled the band. Refused our advance man's suggestion that they announce the P before he came in the hall. Had him sit in the second row on the platform. We learned later he had tried to get the executive committee to not sit on the platform with him, and he had instructed the people not to do any kind of response, positive or negative. They did stand and applaud when the P came in and again when he left, and interrupted the speech a couple of times with applause because they really couldn't help it, but overall they followed their rules pretty effectively. The speech was a real masterpiece. He followed his plan of saying he had distributed the text to the press and he stood by it, but he was going to throw it away and speak to them straight from the shoulder, the way they like to hear it. The text of the speech is well worth studying in the style of going back and forth that he used, and it was quite effective. They managed to avoid any reaction in the hall to the extent they could.

When we got back to the hotel he called to say that he had forgotten to mention that it was important that we should have Moore and Scali follow up on this and he hoped they were there. They weren't, and he felt that was quite a mistake and obviously was a little pushed out of shape on that. Made the strong point to me of the need to get the whole drama of the moment over, that it's not a spot news story. The real point is the color and drama of his moving into this hostile situation and so on. I got Colson and our crew on the phone up north. There was then considerable telephoning from then until departure time. With the P coming up with more reactions, ideas, things that ought to be followed up, and I was lashing the Colson crew to get things moving, but there isn't an awful lot they can do except get some of these background items about Meany's rude treatment out.

The networks tonight gave us what appeared to be pretty bad coverage, in the sense they emphasized the hostile reaction. They did play our points on the rude treatment and the specifics about no band, no announcement, and so forth, and they made a big thing out of the fact of the P shifting at the last minute and returning to Washington instead of staying at Key Biscayne.

Saturday, November 20, 1971

The P was in to the office early this morning and cranking away again on AFL reaction. He was pretty distressed with *The New York Times* coverage, which was all he had seen. We gave him the report on the networks and that didn't seem to help very much. He still feels we missed the point. The point is that we have to override the cool reception story and change it to a "labor is rude to a courageous president" story.

One break that all of us felt was monumentally valuable to us is that the executive board raised Meany's pay from $70,000 to $90,000 and we had a lot of discussion on how to handle and whether to take advantage of that. We need a clear attack by the P. He also made the point that we should be sure that someone gets pictures of Meany at the racetrack, playing golf, and getting in and out of his limousine down there. We should set them up as the "bloated barons of labor."

He called later in the afternoon to comment on the UCLA football game, saying the Bruins were really holding on and playing in a spirited way. That SC was really loaded with talent. Game ended up a tie. He said he'd been looking at the telegrams *(supporting P against Meany)* and was really quite excited about them. Read me quite a few of them and they really are strong and emotional. So he thinks we've really got something going now, which is exactly the point I'd been trying to make from right after the speech yesterday on. He feels now that we've come to three conclusions. First, that we can't make peace with the labor unions. Second, that the Pay Board must be tough and not back down to them, and third, that it'll be very hard to make the Hoffa move right now, under these circumstances.

Monday, November 22, 1971

Henry burst in at noon to say that the radio and TV reports that India has attacked Pakistan. He has no confirmation. By 9:00 tonight he still didn't have any confirmation. Our vast intelligence network doesn't seem to be able to tell us when a couple of major nations are at war, which is a little alarming, to say the least.

> East Pakistan was in rebellion against Pakistan, and India had taken advantage of it by attacking East Pakistan. What was especially worrisome was that India had become aligned with the Soviets, and Pakistan with the Chinese. The situation was very volatile. The P expressed his displeasure very strongly to both India and the Soviets.

Tuesday, November 23, 1971

The question came up this morning at staff meeting on the tax-bill strategy. The principal concern Shultz has is that the bill is going to be managed by the Treasury when it goes into conference. Connally will be gone, which means it's up to Treasury staff, and he's very concerned that they won't handle it in the P's interest.

The P decided this afternoon to go out to a Redskins practice without any announcement, but at the last minute had me go along. He went out and spent about 20 minutes there. Did a great job and really jazzed them up. It should be good for some excellent coverage and great photos. They gave him a big cheer as he came out on the field. He completely befuddled them with his tremendous knowledge of football, as he went through all of the comments he had to make about each of the individual guys, etc.

Wednesday, November 24, 1971

The P had a super solid schedule of meetings today as a result of restacking the schedule to set up for early departure, although it was all to no avail because he then postponed the departure until 5:00 so he could have a second meeting with Connally this afternoon. All of this mainly on budget, domestic and foreign policy, with E and K in on parts of the meetings. He agreed to move on Taft-Hartley on the dock strikes in the East Coast and Gulf ports and told Shultz to put that into motion.

On the plane out to California this evening the P had me in. He had talked to Colson on the phone and was concerned because we had tentatively decided to go ahead with the Federal pay increase. The real question is the psychological effect of the P agreeing to raise pay, and the detrimental effect on holding the line against pay increases. This being a bad time to do something like this. We now have the letter in hand confirming his selection as *Time* Man of the Year, so he's agreed to do an interview with *Time* but wants to make it as late as possible so that it'll be as timely as it can be.

Thursday, Friday, Saturday, November 25, 26, 27, 1971

We've been in California. I've been over in Palm Springs for the entire weekend and have had no contact at all with the P.

On Friday night I was called at 11:00 by the VP who said they had a problem on the golf game tomorrow because there was something going between Hope and Sinatra. Paul Keyes had gotten into the problem of who rides in the cart with the P. Keyes had told Hope that the P wanted Sinatra to ride with him and that this apparently had Hope's nose out of joint. In any event I told the VP that I had nothing to do with setting it up. Rose Woods had handled it all for the P and that he should call Rose, which he agreed he would do in the middle of the night.

Sunday, November 28, 1971

No contact again today until we were on Air Force One back to Washington. The P had me up just for a short time during the flight, mainly to cover some schedule items. We're setting the Trudeau visit and he wants to give a dinner for him, stag, with a certain amount of show, primarily for the NBC TV, since that's the day we're having the "Day in the Life of the President" coverage. He raised the problem of Frank Sinatra and Bob Hope. Apparently there was a flap, and they got into a sticky thing on how to handle that at Palm Springs.

Monday, November 29, 1971

Back in Washington. He had an 8:30 meeting this morning with E, MacGregor, Timmons, and the Attorney General regarding the campaign checkoff problem and as a result they decided not to meet with the Congressional leaders, but rather have MacGregor do a press conference at noon and put out the word that we probably will veto. He had Ziegler and MacGregor in afterward to get a report on it, apparently it went pretty well. The P then said why don't we screw the networks? Why don't we put in a plan to provide for free TV time for Presidential candidates and take the revenue out of the networks and give us a counter ploy? So MacGregor is going to work on developing that.

As to the Federal pay raise, Congress passed it at 5.5 percent effective January 1, so our view didn't make any difference. It passed by the Senate, 70–1 or something like that.

Monday, December 6, 1971

This is the P's NBC "Day in the Life of the President" for TV, and he really came on like gangbusters. They started the Congressional leadership breakfast meeting 15 minutes early at 7:45 and the P went full tilt, without a pause, from there through about 7:00 PM, when he finally went over to the Residence to get ready for dinner. Then the dinner started at 8:00 and went through to 10:30, when he went upstairs for his interview with Chancellor, which ended a little before 11:00. All in all it was quite a tour de force. He had the TV cameras in the office much longer than we'd expected them to be, and so they got considerably more coverage than they had planned or we had planned to give them, which is of course all to the good. His attitude was a little snappy at the start of the day, but it picked up considerably, and when he had me in at 9:30 for the staff period, he was cranking under full steam. He was talking to Bush on the telephone at the UN telling him to hit hard on our India-Pakistan position and making that very clear. Then he moved to set up a meeting on India-Pakistan with Rogers, Connally, Laird, Moorer, etc., which had not been on the schedule for the day, so that filled in the noon hour and ended up with no break at all at midday.

John Chancellor and the NBC people were ecstatic with the way the whole day went, particularly with the amount of time the P was letting the crew stay in his office. Apparently he was putting on the same kind of performance right on through the day. He had the Trudeau meeting at 4:00 for two hours and then the Trudeau dinner tonight.

At the dinner tonight, the P decided to launch into calling on people to make little talks, and he closed it with his "300 boys dying in Vietnam three years ago" talk before he finally broke the dinner up and headed upstairs for his wrapup interview with Chancellor. All in all it should be a fantastically good show for TV and obviously was well worth doing, although I'm sure it really took a lot out of him.

At the staff meeting this morning, Shultz reported that a good friend of his has seen Meany in the hospital and gave him a pretty good report on the true situation. Apparently Meany is in a coronary emergency section. He did have a serious heart attack. He's feeling good now, but he's still in very serious shape. The doctors say maybe he can be out in six to eight weeks but they aren't allowing him to read the papers or see TV, and O'Connell thinks he's pretty well through as far as any active leadership is concerned. He also says that the labor people generally think Nixon is going to win and we therefore should be dealing with the international presidents, since some of them, at least, want to cooperate with us, especially with the thought that we might win.

Tuesday, December 7, 1971

Main question today was a monumental K flap. He came in at midday and told me that, as he had warned me some time ago, if we got to a substantive impasse where State actually screwed something up on a substantive basis and he felt he couldn't deal with it that he would resign. He has now reached that point.

He says that he would like, therefore, to wait until Congress leaves and then announce that he'll be resigning next year at around June, before the political campaign. He's rationalized some thought that this would all fit together and work out fine. Obviously he wants to get the drama of the resignation, plus the benefit of staying on through China, and then get out before the heat of the political campaign. I talked to him a little bit about it without making any attempt to dissuade him, and then, because the P recognized there was a problem by the way Henry was talking with him, I filled him in on what Henry had said, and he was, of course, considerably concerned about it, but felt we should take a hard line with Henry and not back down to him. I talked to Henry again later in the afternoon. He came bouncing in before his backgrounder and I tried to push to see what the problem is. The trigger was Rogers' talk at the dinner last night, which wasn't helpful as far as India-Pakistan was concerned, and mainly it's an ego problem with Henry resenting Rogers being called on, both last night and yesterday afternoon, when they were doing the TV filming. He says now that this indicates, as do other State actions, that they're not going to help in carrying out the plans. He points out that he can bring off the other things alone.

I talked later this afternoon with the P about the whole thing again. He feels, as do I now, that there's more to this than just India-Pakistan, and that there may be personal problem with K or maybe it is really just the hangup over the dinner last night. In any event, I talked again with Henry and played it a little brutally with him this time by saying that if he was going to announce his resignation in December, he should resign in December. He couldn't just announce it and then hang on, and he said, oh no, he couldn't do that because he couldn't leave the P alone to go to China, and I said you couldn't go to China with him, having announced your resignation, that would put him in a much worse position. So I think I've given him something to think about and we'll see what develops. I'll try to spend some time with him tomorrow and get a better reading.

Thursday, December 9, 1971
Henry has a note from the Soviets on Pakistan regarding a possible cease-fire agreement, and it looks as if things aren't all lost, as he thought they were yesterday. The P told him to develop a game plan as to where it was we want to end up

and what we want to accomplish, and then to work that out.
Henry then made an urgent pitch that the P see the Soviet
Agriculture Minister who was here today, because he's a
strong personal friend of Brezhnev's and has a message from
Brezhnev and also the P can give him a message back, laying
it out very sternly.

> We had received information that India was planning to attack
> West Pakistan as well. Yahya Khan had realized he could no
> longer defend East Pakistan and had accepted the UN call for
> a cease-fire. India had not, however. The P authorized a task
> force of 8 ships to the Bay of Bengal, and sent another message
> to Brezhnev. Then we waited for a reply.

Henry also said, as Haig confirmed, that the P will have to
meet with the WSAG *(Washington Special Action Group)* this
afternoon because they're in open rebellion against Henry and
the P's position, but that will depend on what position they've
decided on at their noon meeting regarding a game plan. The
P agreed to do this as he's sort of going along with Henry
now and trying to get any problems resolved.

Haig came in to see me on this whole question. He agrees
basically with the general conclusions that the P and I had
come up with yesterday, that is, Henry is physically tired, that
he does realize he's at fault in the failure in India-Pakistan to
date and doesn't like that feeling. Also Haig points out that
Henry basically is bored. He's just tired of fighting the bureaucracy on all of these things, but Al shares my belief that
Henry isn't about to quit, no matter what kind of threats he
makes, even though this time he says he's deadly serious and
claims he's going ahead with it. The P is resigned to our taking
a hard line on this, and if Henry quits he'll just have to quit.
I personally think that's the only position he can take and that
there's no great danger in it, because I don't think Henry has
any intention of walking out before China, and the P won't let
him make any announcement or intention to do it if he wants
to go to China.

The P again went round and round in trying to analyze the
problem. Henry's ego, his way of working, etc. It's very hard
to pin down what specifically is wrong and I believe Haig's
right, as are we, in our analysis that it's a combination of a

number of these factors, but I think my position with Henry of hitting him very hard on the fact that if he's going to announce he's leaving, then he's got to leave, whether it's now or next June or whatever. He can't announce now and then leave later because it would leave him as a lame duck with no power influence or ability. Also I pushed him on the point that if things are in such a bureaucratic mess, he obviously can't leave. He's got to get things untangled first and then leave. He can't just walk out leaving the P sitting with a disaster. He seemed to be in a much better mood today and I think as action is starting now, he's developing a plan and getting into carrying things out, that he's much better.

On an unrelated matter the P apparently met with the Attorney General yesterday and agreed to pardon Hoffa.

Friday, December 10, 1971

Shultz raised the problem today of the Defense budget. He's concerned that K hasn't closed the deal with Laird on the budget as it's supposed to be, and Laird is pushing for an $82 billion budget and Shultz is convinced that Defense can't spend over $74 billion, no matter what they do. In any event, he feels he's being pretty much dealt out of the action on this, and is unable to get to Henry, who is supposed to be handling it.

We had a big flap today on the plan for Julie's Christmas TV special. She decided not to do it apparently because Pat Nixon told Julie it wasn't a good thing to do. We rattled through it on and off during the day. The P felt strongly Julie should do it. Especially since we've gotten into the flap with CBS yesterday on the blackmail question of whether they would even do the Julie show unless the P agreed to do the one-on-one. We then agreed to do the one-on-one, and now Julie's talking about cutting out of her show. I finally got to Julie at the end of the day, when she got back from North Carolina, and told her what the situation was. She agreed to take one more stab at it with her mother, and Rose called a little later in the evening to say that Julie had done a superb job. Had Mrs. Nixon sold on it and they were going ahead with it.

K was in with the P this morning on the Pakistan question. K says Pakistan will be all over by Sunday, and that the P turned it around yesterday afternoon in his hard line with the WSAG group. The P pushed Henry hard on following up more

on protesting the Indian strafing of our planes and Indian
bombing of the orphanage and all that sort of thing. He thinks
our PR apparatus on foreign policy is lousy, and that we're
not getting the kind of mileage out of these various incidents
that we should, and would, if someone were riding hard on
them and following up.

The tax bill signing became a big issue today as we went
round and round on the signing statement, and the P did end
up signing it, feeling that we'd get some substantial mileage
out of it. The P was supposed to have a half-hour interview
with Jerry Schecter of *Time* this afternoon, regarding the Man
of the Year cover, and he extended it to an hour and ended
up by saying he'd take him up to Camp David tomorrow to
look things over up there if he'd like to do it. At 8:00 he called
me at home to say he was going to drive up to Camp David
at 8:30, and he seemed to be very pleased with the whole day
and the way everything had gone.

Sunday, December 12, 1971

The P did his bit with the CBS TV people for the Christmas
tree thing this morning. Apparently felt he did extremely well
on it, because on the plane to the Azores this afternoon *(to
meet Pompidou regarding international financial conditions)*
he called me up to say he wanted to make some effort to get
more coverage on the show than was originally planned, and
to try to get CBS to use his particular commentary as a separate piece. Apparently he went into quite a thing on the meaning of Christmas, the background of Christmas, and relating it
to peace with the point that in spite of the teachings of Christ
all the wars we've had since Christ have been basically involving Christians, and that maybe we're arriving at a new
stage now where Christians will be able to avoid war instead
of getting into them.

On the flight K discovered the P wanted Rogers to do a
press briefing tomorrow in the Azores after the morning meeting. He thinks that will ruin the whole Pakistan effort because
Rogers will say the wrong thing and blow it. That was bad
enough, and then the P ended up having Rogers do a briefing
of the press on the plane and that had Henry really up the wall,
but apparently it worked out fine and caused no trouble at all.
Henry was in and out of the P's cabin as were Rogers, Connally, Dave Kennedy, etc. It was a fairly difficult five-hour

flight since he felt he had to be involved with all of them. He seemed to be very relaxed and not really put upon at all, however. The arrival went according to plan and we're settled down at the Air Force base in the Azores.

Monday, December 13, 1971

The schedule on meetings for today went pretty well. The P got a good reception, very enthusiastic pleasant crowds in the streets in the town where the meetings are. After we choppered over from the Air Force base, he met Pompidou in the garden and went in according to the plan. Henry said to me during the photo session that he thought he'd step out of the meeting and wait for the P to call him in, and I said he shouldn't push his luck, he should just go in and settle down. As it turns out I was right, because the entire morning meeting went through its full course of two and a half hours and the P never did call Henry in, so he sat in a little room outside stewing. He wouldn't go into the Rogers meeting because he wanted Rogers to think he was in with the two presidents, and that backfired when the Rogers meeting finally ended and Bill came out and went into the room where Henry was, and thus discovered that Henry was not in with the P.

Tuesday, December 14, 1971

This day started pretty early. In that half hour after midnight last night, when the P returned from the Pompidou dinner and after I had gone to bed and gone to sleep, he asked me to come over, so I had to get up and get dressed. He decided to try to figure out return plans so that he could probably go to Florida tomorrow. Put the other people on the other plane, as he was planning to do anyway so that he wouldn't have to ride with them, but he does want Henry to go with him so that he can have a chance to talk with him and also get him calmed down. He feels that he's had quite a problem keeping Henry on track through this whole session and wants to sort of wrap it up with him on the plane on the way back. I talked to Henry and to Chapin after that talk about 1:00 this morning and got things reasonably well on track for setting up for the P to go to Florida, although Henry's still reluctant because he feels it'll be a bad signal in his maneuverings with the India-Pakistan situation and that it would be better for the P to go back to Washington.

Then at 4:20 this morning the P called me again. He had

been up all the time listening to the Redskins/Rams football game on Armed Forces radio and he was calling to tell me that first of all he'd decided he'll go to Washington tomorrow definitely. That we should leave the Cabinet guys on the P plane so that he has a chance to chat with them on the way back. Then he said incidentally the Redskins beat the Rams, 38–24. They had an 80,000 capacity crowd. He was all excited about the whole thing. I could hardly believe it, since I didn't even know they were playing. I guess it was a big victory. He tried to reach George Allen by satellite telephone, but wasn't able to get to him. Then at 8:15 he had me over again before he left for the final Pompidou meeting, so that he could go up to Camp David as soon as he got back to Washington and spend the rest of the week there until it was time to go to New York on Saturday.

He says K's still trying to find out whether we've got a deal or not on India-Pakistan and that he won't know for a few more hours. He's going to have a long talk with K on his attitude and all. He feels that he's been a problem on this whole exercise and he doesn't want to have to keep putting up with that.

Henry, by midday, was in good shape because he had the Pakistan deal put together and he now feels he's got that solved.

On the way back P said that he thought he'd probably go to Florida tomorrow, since the Pakistan thing is pretty well settled and Henry feels he's no longer required to stay in Washington. After he got back to the house, he decided not to go to Camp David tonight. He went up to the solarium and watched the taped replay of the Rams-Redskin game.

Wednesday, December 15, 1971

At the staff meeting this morning K got into the India-Pakistan question. Made the point that we need a maximum attack on the Hill against India, and felt that we needed to get a Congressional meeting cranked up with Connally, to try to get this kind of reaction going. Things are really on track and he's practically ecstatic. He thinks that the deal has been made with the Russians and that it's primarily his maneuvering that has backed them down. There was some discussion about the threat in his backgrounder that we would call off the Soviet summit, which CBS made a big thing about.

> The Soviets so far had replied only with vague assurance that
> India would not attack Pakistan. On the plane from the Azores,
> K had hinted to reporters that P might call off the Soviet Sum-
> mit if they didn't restrain India.

The P told Ziegler to cool that on the grounds that the issue
hasn't reached that point and that it might later if the Russians
don't act to stop the cannibalizing there. Henry argued that his
Summit threat was good because it showed that the P is now
in this. So when we get the settlement, which we are going to
get, the P will get the credit for it, and he thinks that what he
did, while he didn't intend to put that line out, it does work
to our long-range benefit.

Thursday, December 16, 1971
The P called at 11:30 and said the Indians have declared a
cease-fire in West Pakistan. Haig called me to say Rogers was
sensing a PR coup in this whole thing and trying to get into
it and get on top of it, but we should keep it for the P. The
only other development during the day were the progress reports from MacGregor on the Congress. He was very pleased
because he got a House up and down vote on the Mansfield
Amendment and it was defeated 130 to 101.

Tuesday, December 21, 1971
E called, said that he and the Attorney General had to meet
with the P and me immediately upon our return tonight, which
we did. It turned out that in their investigation of the Jack
Anderson leaks, they had uncovered the fact that a yeoman in
the NSC shop, assigned to liaison with the Joint Chiefs, was
the almost certain source of not only the leaks, but also the
absconding of information from Henry's and Haig's and other
people's briefcases, which were turned over to the Joint Chiefs
of Staff. The P was quite shocked, naturally, by the whole
situation and agreed that very strong action had to be taken,
but very carefully, since we don't want to blow up the whole
relationship with the Joint Chiefs of Staff. Apparently they had
set up this system for getting the information to them. The
question is, who at the Joint Chiefs was aware of it?
In any event, Mitchell is going to proceed on the basis of
having Henry tell the Admiral that works for him now that he

can go ahead and answer questions. The Admiral has refused to answer some of the key questions on the grounds that his personal relationship with K precludes it. In the meantime they've sort of semisuspended the yeoman and figure that they don't want to prosecute because that would just accelerate the situation. So it's a tough one to figure out.

> The previous week, columnist Jack Anderson had printed ver-batim transcripts from the WSAG meetings on India-Pakistan, revealing K and P's pressure to "tilt" toward Pakistan despite official neutrality. It had created an uproar in the press, and during our investigation we discovered that a Navy yeoman on the NSC staff had actually been copying classified documents and passing them to his superiors in the Pentagon.

Wednesday, December 22, 1971

We had a long session this afternoon with the Attorney General, John E, and David Young on the NSC security leak problem, which was quite interesting because they have now tracked the thing all the way through. It turns out that Admiral . . . was taking the material that the yeoman was stealing from Henry's briefcase and the burnbags and all other sources, sorting it out, and transmitting the pertinent things directly to Admiral Moorer. This creates a highly sensitive situation, since it's directly tied to the fact that the yeoman was also transmitting the India-Pakistan stuff to Jack Anderson, who was running it in the columns. So we have a clear breach of security that's actionable. Although the yeoman hasn't admitted it, his polygraph makes it clear that he did it, plus all the other circumstantial evidence. The P said that E and I should get together with Henry and move on the thing with him, and the P was particularly concerned because Henry and Haig had not raised it with him, although it was such a clear security problem. He can't figure out why they didn't do this when they do know at least some of the particulars. Laird apparently is trying to shut it off completely, and there will undoubtedly be a monumental hush-up all the way around on it.

We had a meeting with the Attorney General on general politics, particularly the problem of working out Stans' move to RNC finance, but the P agreed we should meet his conditions and get him moved over there.

Thursday, December 23, 1971

I had a long talk with Scali at his request this afternoon. He is deeply emotionally upset, partly as a result of bruised ego problems, because he isn't being brought in to the degree that he wants to be in and thought he would be, but the real problem is that he's convinced that Henry has practically taken leave of his senses. That he's lying to the press, lying to the Secretary, and worst of all lying to the P, particularly on India-Pakistan. He thinks there's going to be a substantial problem for Henry with the press because a number of them realize he's lied to them and are out to get him, and that Rogers also realizes this. He has confronted Scali with the fact and John just doesn't know how to cope with it. On the other hand, Henry had talked to me, saying that he suspected Scali was leaking. There is a valid problem here, and one we're going to have to figure out how to deal with. I told Scali I'd work with him on it, but that I needed some time to figure it out and that I probably would have to wait until a time when I could spend considerable time on it directly with the P, which is what I intend to try to do.

Rogers had a press conference and Henry called me tonight because he says Rogers has shot us down on two principal issues. First, saying that there was no danger of cancellation of the Russian Summit, which Henry was using as a threat, and second, saying there was no agreement to defend Pakistan, which the P had told Henry to get out that there was, to show off Kennedy's involvement in Pakistan. So the thing seems to get more tense and less solvable all the time.

Friday, December 24, 1971

I didn't go in the office today as it was a holiday. The P was in a good part of the day, bouncing around, touching base with people. He called in the afternoon to say we were still dealing with the K problem. Basically it's Rogers in India-Pakistan. The P made the point to me that there's going to come a time when K's going to have to shape up and start worrying about the P instead of worrying about himself, and he feels that K should now stay out of the line of fire and avoid backgrounders and the press, and that we should let Scali know that we'll get him out front at the proper time. I covered with the P my talk with Scali yesterday, in which John expressed his view that Henry had really become so obsessed with all this stuff that he was irrational and thus doing some real harm. The P didn't seem unduly concerned about that and I don't think gives it too much credence, but does feel that we've got to find a way to deal with the K-Scali problem. So that was it, other than wishing me a Merry Christmas and then he called me late tonight after The Julie Show to ask how it had gone. I gave him the details on it. So he had something to talk to Julie about. Overall it was a darn good half-hour program and we came off extremely well, I think, which is what I told him.

Monday, December 27, 1971

The P is in Key Biscayne. I stayed in Washington today and then went down to Key Biscayne this evening. We had a problem of the *(Vietnam)* Veterans Against the War Demonstration. They occupied the Statue of Liberty today and E decided to send the park police in to bust them out at 5:30, then the court didn't uphold the injunction, so we weren't able to knock them out after all. The P called this afternoon from Key Biscayne. He said he made an enormous number of phone calls over Christmas. The best one of the bunch was to the Redskins when they lost because no one expected him to do it. He's worried about K, who's got the flu, and he wants me to try to help keep him in bed and out of the line of fire. That'll be good for him to get some time off.

Thursday, December 30, 1971

The P had me over this morning for a couple of hours, general discussion, scheduling. Sort of odds and ends. He confirmed the plans for the First Lady on Africa and wants to go ahead with some scheduling himself in California. We changed the Japanese schedule to drop the Annenberg golf game since the Japanese don't want to do that. Instead the P will give a luncheon at his house.

Late this afternoon Henry came over to talk to me. He says he's going through a period of very deep thinking and serious evaluation as to what his position is and how he's going to go at things. He feels that the P has lost confidence in him and that he's being maneuvered by the P in the same way the P maneuvers Rogers and others, and this worries him. He wanted to talk through the whole problem with me. I told him I didn't feel there was any question of loss of confidence. That there was a problem on the P's part in knowing how to deal with the personal battle between K and Rogers and that would always exist as long as the battle existed. He seemed very uptight. He admitted that he was egotistical and nervous and all that, but also said that he felt he was a great value to the P and that he wouldn't tolerate the kind of battle he'd been fighting. That maybe he would just move to a very low-key position and do the best he could there, but he then tossed in the thing of his being essential to the China trip and so on. I didn't say much. I let him talk through his concerns at this point, as apparently he and E did on Christmas evening. I told him that I felt we ought to talk about it some more out in San Clemente when we had more time and that's what we'll do.

Friday, December 31, 1971

The P called on the phone before we left Key Biscayne. Was concerned about the phone list we had turned in because he still wants the top contributors on it and also he wants a breakdown list for each of the nine major states showing the ten most important people on a power basis in those states.

He got into some schedule questions as to when Hubert and the others are announcing and whether we can shift our New Hampshire date around. He's obviously trying to work out the Vietnam announcement schedule. He wanted to see if we could change our dates so that he could readjust his plans. In answer to Rather's question as to whether the P would like to meet with him before the broadcast (of a one-on-one interview), the P said to tell him no, that he feels it's important for the credibility of the thing to be able to say that they didn't talk before the program. Of course Rather is free to ask anything he wants, and that both of them have an interest in making the program as good as possible. He said to be sure to be very cordial with Rather when I gave him this answer.

1972

First Quarter: January–March

Saturday, January 1, 1972

K called from New York all disturbed because he felt someone had been getting to the P on Vietnam. He said that the P seems to feel, in conversations Henry's had with him, that he's under terrible pressure on Vietnam. He therefore wants to give an all-out speech prior to Congress returning. K thinks this is a mistake because it'll just focus Congress on Vietnam rather than letting them wallow around for a while undirected. He thinks we shouldn't worry about the Congressional resolutions that are coming up and that we should do our Vietnam announcement at the latest date possible.

Henry's concerned that the P's looking for a way to bug out and he thinks that would be a disaster now. His instinct is that the North Vietnamese are ready to give, so we'd be totally wrong to show any nervousness. If we do the peace plan early in January, it'll spur the opponents to tear it to pieces. We need to do it as late as possible but before they have another rallying point. He didn't want me to talk to the P about this but obviously just wanted to talk it over with me to review his concern.

Sunday, January 2, 1972

I talked to the P a couple of times on the phone today, namely on minor details. He was concerned about a report in Buchanan's news summary that told about the Daniel Schorr story last night *(on CBS),* saying that Connally and the P were having a falling-out. The P said he wanted to see Connally for dinner Wednesday evening in California and suggested I give Connally a call to make sure everything is OK there. I did so and Connally couldn't have been more cheerful. I asked him if he thought we had suffered from the North Vietnam bombing this last week and he said not at all, that the story only lasted a couple of days and in ten days from now no one will remember we did it.

Monday, January 3, 1972

The P called me in at 8:00 in the morning. He was up early and obviously hadn't had much sleep because of the reaction of the TV last night *(the Rather interview),* and he was pretty antsy. He kept me in until about 9:00 and then we both went into the morning staff meeting. He talked with them about the press mainly. Said that the staff had done a remarkable job last year. He referred to Rather in his interview and made the point that in spite of all we had done, Rather sort of piled it all up to what has to be done this year.

Later in the afternoon the P and I met with the Attorney General for what was supposed to be an hour meeting and ended up going for about two hours. The Attorney General had breakfast with Henry this morning, so he had the latest batch of Henry's input, although I had met with Henry also during the day today. Henry boiled it down to the point that he's got to have his demands met. First of all, that Rogers has to understand that any attack on K by the State Department or any of its people is a direct attack on the P. Second, that all cables and communications out of State must be cleared at the White House first. Third, that there is to be no communication between State and the Soviets without prior knowledge of the White House and without a memcon afterward summarizing everything that was discussed. Henry feels these are probably impossible demands and therefore he'll have to leave, but he won't do so until after the Russian trip. In discussing this the P understood Henry's view. I went further than the Attorney General and told the P about Henry's further view that the P had lost confidence in him and that the evidence, at least to Henry, was the fact that the P was constantly trying to butter him up and keep him happy and was not really getting into the nitty-gritty of foreign policy anymore. Henry sees this as a slippage in his own standing and that probably is what worries him more than anything else. That, plus the fact that he knows he made the mistake in India-Pakistan and doesn't know how to cope with it. In any event the P agreed that we should put the ultimatum to Rogers and agreed with my recommendation that Mitchell and I do it as soon as we get back from San Clemente. Then Mitchell and I are to meet with Henry as soon as he gets back, later in the week, next week, to lay out to him the fact that he's got to get in line too. I don't know whether it'll work but I don't see any other solution at this point.

On the discussion about the plan for the Vietnam announcement, the P now decided to go on the basic announcement of troop withdrawal on the 13th and will do that on a pretty low-key basis. Probably just going to the pressroom in the afternoon, and giving the three-month figure of another 70,000 troops out. Then he'll wait until the 18th, the day Congress comes back, and at noon announce that he'll address the nation that evening in a major foreign policy statement. Then the plan will be to go on TV, review all of our peace overtures and then publicly make the offer that we have already secretly made to the North Vietnamese. This he figures will be a major blockbuster on the Vietnam thing and that it'll be especially effective because the first announcement will suck all the peaceniks out and the second move will chop them all off. The bombing reaction has done some of that already.

Wednesday, January 5, 1972
The Anderson papers *(on India/Pakistan)* are now back again as a big flap. E and I had a long session with Henry this morning and then some more discussion with the P. Henry's staff got him all cranked up on the basis that the story in *The Washington Post* had totally destroyed Henry's credibility and there was nothing left for him to do but quit. He, of course, soaked that up. We jumped on him pretty hard on the point that he couldn't go out to the press and defend himself and his credibility, which was one alternative he had decided to take, and that we needed to determine whether there was a credibility problem. Henry was full of the usual charges of nobody on the staff defends him, but I don't think he really believes that much anymore. He just tosses it out. The P talked to him later and told him the same thing. He told him not to do anything now and not to talk to the press. So we've probably got it pretty well bottled up for the moment.

Thursday, January 6, 1972
Sato arrived on schedule and everything went according to plan. Seemed to be very well done. The P spent the afternoon and evening with him.

Friday, January 7, 1972
Ross Perot called today, ostensibly to endorse Bill Clements for Undersecretary of Defense, but really because he wanted to make a pitch to me to talk with the P. He made the point that he's never had a personal relationship with the P. He's never asked his opinion on anything, on the economy, or Wall Street, and so on, even though he talks to lots of other people, and since Ross is willing to take risks on the P's behalf he should be able to put in some input. He said he does have ample contact with all the other candidates but the one he really supports is the P and he would like to feel he had a relationship with him too. This is actually a little farfetched because Perot, of course, has reneged on almost everything he's promised to do for us but I told him I'd see what we could work out.

Saturday, January 8, 1972
Shultz called this morning, on the F-111 question. The problem being whether to continue it another year; if we shut it down then we'll close out in the fall of '72 just before the election, it will cost $160 million in fiscal '73, plus $20 million in '72, to continue it. The Air Force doesn't want the plane and doesn't want to continue it, but Laird says Defense won't make the decision, that this is a White House political matter. I checked it with the P, he of course said they should go ahead with it.

Monday, January 10, 1972
The dominating factor today was K again. Starting with a call this morning to me. He said he had talked to Laird on the troop announcement, and Laird was dragging his feet, saying the P couldn't go as high a number as he had planned, but he would review it and confirm it this afternoon. He also said Laird was raving about all the papers that the Joint Chiefs got from us legally, and the big problem we had on that.

He then got into his general basic problem again, saying that now he can't brief anymore because of terrible coverage he got in the magazines this week, and his credibility was destroyed, and so on. He abruptly at one point said he didn't choose to discuss it any further, and hung up on me. He apparently immediately called the Attorney General, because I tried to. It was busy, then I got to him a few minutes later, he said he had been talking to Henry also.

I filled the P in on these problems this afternoon over the EOB, and he picked up the phone, called Laird, and then told him he's going to have to go for the 70,000 troop withdrawal, that they'll announce it Thursday morning, and he wanted Laird to go out to the press with the P. Henry had reported this to me earlier, saying as usual we're following our policy of rewarding traitors.

P in pondering the whole thing also wondered about the question of how big an issue K is in the public mind, or whether this is something that we're worried about internally. I talked to K a little later, and he said that the latest thing today, now, is that there are rumors all around that he's resigning, and he said the real question that they ask is why is a Presidential assistant under attack with no word of support from his boss? He says we may be beyond the point where anything can be done, that there's clearly a major campaign working on the combination of leaks and briefings. The whole thing is a complete disaster.

Tuesday, January 11, 1972

P didn't call me in till 11:30 this morning. He came in late and worked alone for quite a while. Raised the question of our meeting of Attorney General with Rogers, then me. The P has every confidence in Rogers, but the State Department leaks like a sieve. Said we should tell him we will keep Rogers posted on China, but not down to the bowels of the State Department. Point out that Rogers has got to be ruthless and selfless. Let Rogers know how much handling the P has got to do.

Armed with this advice, we set up the meeting. Made the points that the P suggested, and said we have got to work out a means of dealing with all of this. Rogers said the basic problem he has is that he simply doesn't trust Henry, that Henry has lied to him, saying he was lying under orders, and that's the only time. Bill feels, therefore, that when he gets instructions from Henry or any kind of information, that he's got to question it, and that sets up a very difficult working relationship. He also said that he's got to have a direct line of communication with the P, so that when he does question something or wants to raise a caution or something, he can do it directly to the P without going through Henry. Next he and

I agreed that he can use me as his conduit to the P directly, and Rogers thought that was fine. Then we agreed we had to set up a method so that Rogers would keep us posted on all the meetings he has with the Soviets or the Israelis, etc. Rogers agreed that he would, if K would notify Rogers about all of his meetings, unless the P tells him not to notify. The basic principle to apply is whatever one of the three knows on foreign policy, all three should, between K, Rogers, and the P.

P called me at home to see how the meeting had gone. He said we do have to find a way to bring Rogers in on the China things, we should tell Haig to find a way to present it without giving in to the sensitive parts of it. He said that Mitchell and I should now meet with Haig and K together.

He said he had been thinking about the campaign, what he would do in the last two weeks was six huge night rallies in the Astrodome and such places, to show huge crowds and great support, but now he's thinking maybe that isn't the best approach. He thinks maybe we need to poll the question that Hallett raises on Muskie's image of a strong, thoughtful man versus Nixon as pure cosmetics. He said he might want to consider the possibility of a joint appearance with Muskie, I don't know why in the world he would do so. About youth, we have to find a way so that they're not all against us. We need some action on the bomb Muskie crew, especially Agnew, he's got nothing to gain in fighting the press anymore, but he should brutally attack Muskie, leaving Hubert and Teddy alone for now, since Muskie's way out in front.

Wednesday, January 12, 1972
The P, after going back and forth a couple times, decided to come down from Camp David and be here to work on whatever Ray *(Price)* came up with, and get his appointments out of the way this afternoon and then to go back up to Camp David tomorrow afternoon after Mrs. Nixon's tea. This evening he called in a big stir about Mrs. Nixon's tea, which was with the Russian Minister of Culture, saying he wanted to invite the whole Russian ballet company. Then he called back again and said he wanted to be sure that all of them are going to get pictures of Tricia backstage after the performance. He's really anxious to make a big public thing out of his cultural tie with the Russians. He made the point that since we're hitting them so hard on the substantive stuff, it's important for

us to be very friendly and open to them, and the soft stuff such as the cultural thing.

Thursday, January 13, 1972

I had a meeting with the VP today to work out campaign relationships. He says he trusts only me at the White House and wants to deal directly with me on any orders he gets from the P. He also has an idea to come up with new legislation for our Top Secret classification, that will be declared only by the P, and not subject to question as to substance, so that we'll have a way to convict people who leak stuff.

Friday, January 14, 1972

P's at Camp David. We had some bad economic news today, the GNP figures revised downwards will be out, also the wholesale price index is up eight-tenths, which means the '72 deficit projection will be way up. We had announced in September it would be about $28 billion, now it turns out it's going to be over $35 billion, which will be a tough one to live with.

This morning Attorney General and I had our meeting with Henry and with Al Haig as a follow-up to our meeting with Bill Rogers in an attempt to try and solve that problem. Henry said, "Tell me what your proposition is, and I'll do it, I'm not here to strike a treaty with the P." Every time when we tried to tell him, he'd interrupt again. He made a lot of sort of random points.

K says he's caught in a dilemma with the P, because the P doesn't want details on any of the matters, so K does them, and that creates an endless battle with the State Department, and then when the things blow up, the P wants to go through the whole thing and find out what happened and get in the middle of it.

When it was all over, we ended up not having accomplished a great deal, but at least we didn't lose any ground, I don't think.

Saturday, January 15, 1972

K called this morning, and he's now concluded that he can't leave the government now because of the country and the P. He said he's sent Rogers an order that all communications have to be cleared with him. He wants me to back up the directive, and also make the point to Rogers that he's got to deal with K, and he's got to have advance notice on any meetings that they set up.

P called at noon, made the comment about poor old Ashbrook and McCloskey, up there trekking through the snows of New Hampshire *(conservative Representative John Ashbrook and liberal Representative Paul McCloskey were opposing P in the New Hampshire primary)*, reflected on the real problem of the Democrats, which is, where do they get their dough? He can't understand how any of them can get enough money to campaign at all, considering the deficit the party has.

Sunday, January 16, 1972
The P called at noon to see how things were going. He was amused by the Howard Hughes story in the paper today referring to the Nixon loan, said he had never met Howard Hughes, that he had talked to him once on the phone about sending a 707 to Russia.

Rogers called later this afternoon, first, to say that Muskie did pretty well on TV, that the reporters went after him hard but he came out very well on it. He kept his cool as they interrupted him, and so on. What he was really calling about was the memo from K. Said I have a peremptory memo from Henry and I won't take it. I have orders from the P and I'm following those.

Monday, January 17, 1972
There's a building story again on the reopening of the Howard Hughes loan. P said we should get out the facts, as we did in '62, point out that the loan was repaid by the transfer of property, but don't let the impression of guilt build up, as responded to in '62, and there's nothing to it now. Figures maybe we should have Klein handle it, and we discussed the possibility with Ziegler later in the morning.

He had a fairly long session with Henry in there, during which he sent Manolo over to the house to bring his H. G. Wells book over, and he skimmed through it and found a devastating quote about the military mind and the fact that it is, by definition, mediocre because nobody with any real intellectual talent would submit himself to the military career. He also said that, of course, Wells has the feeling that the solution to all problems is education for everyone, and that's a terrible idea, especially for women, says the P.

P then had me lay out the Buchanan thesis that maybe the "professional President" is the wrong political posture and that rather we should be a "fighting President" and find someone or something to do battle with. Connally said until after the trips, or at least until after China, the P should take on no enemy, but at the right time, he has to come out as a fighter, and he has to have an enemy. P said both parties have had it, that is, Eisenhower told him once in this office after the '56 elections, damn the Republican Party, what we need is a new party. P thinks maybe we should form that party after this next election, and he cites the growth of the Independents versus Republicans and Democrats. Then says to Connally he needs good advice as to what is the right posture to take. Connally says the reason the polls aren't greater at this point is people don't think they know Nixon, so they don't go all out for him regardless of what the consequences are. They don't know how to judge Nixon. Kennedy had them mesmerized in that regard. Connally says that if the natural enemy shows at any time, we should grab it, but it would be better to wait until after the conventions. If we do anything now, we should take on our Republican opponents, but it's better not to have a fight now.

P went back to his earlier point and says how do you get people to know the P? Connally says you have to change your way of doing things. Like once a week you should pick a group and meet with them. Maybe have a stag dinner here of 100 people. Mend fences with the hurt folks that we've let down. Should have them for dinner and have a real hair-down session, tell 'em you need their help, and ask 'em how they think you're doing. P said that's fine for the leaders, but how do you break through to the masses? Connally said by becoming a fighter. P asked if he meant using more press conferences, and Connally said no, that won't do it, although you should have one of those a month, but you need to be strongly for and/or against something. You need to do it fairly soon, to start preparing. Something that touches the lives of people, like taxes or the bureaucracy. He says all people think the P's doing an excellent job, but no one loves him, fears him, or hates him, and he needs to have all three. The good "professional" president doesn't appeal to the motivating emotions.

Tuesday, January 18, 1972

P called at 6:45 to say Safire had done a fine job on the Vietnam speech, it improved on the P's outline, got it done on time, and he was really pleased. He says he's finished with the State of the Union and he'll get a final copy from Ray at noon tomorrow. I talked to Price this morning about the Connally and Buchanan political strategy. Ray feels that none of that indicated any change in the State of the Union, that they're right about the need for an enemy, but it should be later, but if you heat up too much too soon, people will get sick of it. Says the State of the Union isn't a fighting speech now, it plays against the political mood today, and he thinks it's a good posture to be in. He thinks that Connally's thesis is partly valid and partly not, but in any event feels the combative mood set now would be bad. 'Cause it can't be maintained for eight months. That we should build our credibility now for an attack later. Our weakness is our credibility and political image and just general suspicion of government and other institutions, so the time for attack, crisis, battle, etc., is further down the road.

Wednesday, January 19, 1972

During the staff meeting this morning, Shultz and E and I got into a discussion of the whole Connally situation, with George basically raising the issue. Looking at it realistically, we're moving to a position of Connally functioning as Deputy President for International Economic Affairs, he already is Deputy President for Domestic Economic Affairs. Still he is also the Secretary of the Treasury, with vast responsibilities which he is not carrying out, and he's the Chairman of the Cost of Living Council.

It's hard for anyone else to do anything. Connally has no staff and no time to do it. So in effect Shultz now reports to Connally not the P. Shultz says he realized yesterday in the meeting with the P how disconnected he has become from the P. Question is, are Shultz's orders now to report to Connally? The problem is Connally doesn't have the depth, breadth, or ultimate responsibility. Also, he has a strong interest in having no strength in the White House, therefore, he won't deal with anything that builds the White House. He goes off on his own. They feel the P needs some people in the White House who are his own people, who know what's going on, for example, Shultz knows nothing about what's now going on in international trade. Connally has the ball, he doesn't consult, he operates.

We reconvened a little later in the morning to resume the discussion, after Shultz was again available. Made the point that the question really is how the P sees the White House staff at this point. He has to come to grips with the way he's setting up Connally. He says Nixon is a much deeper, more subtle man than Connally, has values, Connally doesn't. Connally has much less judgment. We are all Nixon men, not Connally men. I had the thought as we were talking about this, that the P really is putting himself hostage to Connally, unnecessarily, as he's also done with Rogers, also unnecessarily.

I had an opportunity a little later in the morning to get into all of this with the P, which I did, reviewing basically all the points that E and Shultz had covered with me. P was very thoughtful about it and seemed to appreciate this.

He then said, after thinking a bit, that he'd like to talk to me in a different dimension and he said he hadn't intended to tell me this, and he had not told anyone else, and was not going to tell anyone else, but that he had a very difficult time with Connally in California. That the night they had dinner at the P's house, Connally told him he had spent his time in Texas going off on a horse, thinking through his future, and he had concluded that he had completed what he had come here for, the job that was needed, and he would be, therefore, leaving at the end of January. This he had talked over very firmly with Nellie, and there was a firm decision. P really had to go to work on him, apparently, to make the point that this was not in the best interests at this time. P's feeling is that we can't afford to let him go now, that we've got to pay the price that's necessary to keep him, so he really is, in a sense, a hostage to him as I had suspected earlier today.

Thursday, January 20, 1972

P spent the morning over at the EOB, called a couple of times prior to State of the Union time. Was concerned that we not let the staff get depressed by setbacks, that we should just remember that something else will be the headlines next week. We find out it's important to remember the great capacity of MacGregor and Colson, who were both fighters and realists, and know the importance of not getting down in the mouth. State of the Union went well, and he had MacGregor, Colson, and me in afterward to analyze reaction. We all agreed that he accomplished exactly what he was after and that it was the best possible way to have done it. He does want to be sure our Congressional types follow up with a very rough, positive attack.

We had a dinner for the Cabinet, particularly in honor of Stans and Hardin tonight, and Price, Harlow, and Pat Moynihan each gave very good clever little talks. Stans gave an excellent, fairly serious talk about the P and then the P gave an outstanding talk about the accomplishments of the Administration to date and the fact that we're now about to start the fourth quarter, which is when the decision will be made as to who wins the game. Text of his remarks should be in the file with reference. It was extremely impressive and had many of the people in tears, or very near it, and was, it seemed to me, almost completely ad lib. Obviously he had done some prep for it, but it was one of those that was not polished in the way that his prepared remarks are, so must have been developed pretty much as he was delivering it. After the dinner we left for Key Biscayne, arriving there about 2:00 in the morning.

Friday, January 21, 1972

At Key Biscayne. P called at 10:00 this morning just to check to see how things are going. Said he had gone for an early swim. This afternoon he went over to Walker's *(Cay, in Florida)* and I heard no more from him.

Sunday, January 23, 1972

P stayed over at Walker's last night. Got back today, was interested in comparing the press reports on the Vietnam war with the press reporting of WW II. I had made the point to him that there was nothing about Vietnam until you got to the Third Section today, because the news was good news, so they buried it. He was thinking back to WW II when they really played up big the good news and played down the bad. Just the opposite of now.

He had a directive that Henry wanted sent to Rogers about the planes to Israel and the Israel-Egypt negotiations. P decided that I should handle the directive rather than Mitchell in order to keep it out of politics. He wants Rogers to know that he expects him to play it politically, that we can't have the American Jews bitching about the plane deliveries. We can't push Israel too hard and have a confrontation, so he's to keep Sisco slowed down. I'm to say that he's doing the plane paragraph in the memo, for the record, so that he can tell his Jewish friends that it's been ordered. We must not let this issue hurt us politically.

Monday, January 24, 1972

Budget message day. P also released a statement calling on Congress to set a ceiling, which stirred things up a bit. He met with Rizzo, the Mayor of Philadelphia, who was in to see E, and P had John bring him in. Rizzo flatly informed the P he would back him, would announce at any time he wanted him to, and felt he could deliver Pennsylvania, so this was good news. P told him not to announce now, they'll just pull the Democrats along for the time being, wait till after their convention, and then come out for Nixon, which is the plan.

E came up with a startling thing as a result of K's breakfast with Laird this morning, which I guess was over the weekend. Laird told Henry that the White House had asked for his security jacket, but Laird assured him that he would protect him and not send it over to us. Very curious. Nobody at the White House has asked for it and in any event, we wouldn't ask Laird, he doesn't have it.

Tuesday, January 25, 1972

P was in the office this morning, spent quite a little time in just general conversation, since he had the speech pretty well wrapped up for tonight. He was concerned about a news summary report about a Sidey column (*in* Time), saying that the P had too much access to TV and other facilities, which made it hard for the other candidates. P's reaction was that we ought to explore the question of whether Sidey ever deplored Nixon's problem for the eight years while he was out of office, when he traveled around the world alone with his briefcase, got no coverage, a lot less than even Scoop Jackson gets now. Did Sidey at that time complain about Kennedy dominating news? Did he argue for equal time for the Republicans? It's kind of curious to explore the double standard.

K was in for quite a while, we talked about the speech for tonight, making the point that we've got to realize that the press is going to kick us on Vietnam, not because they think we're wrong in what we're doing on this, but because they know we're right, and are furious because we're the ones who are doing it, the same way they did on Cambodia, and to an extent on China.

We reviewed also the question of probability that North Vietnam will create a real crisis in the process of this. One of the reports said that while the P's in China, they might very well move to cut Vietnam in half and create a super crisis that we would have trouble dealing with. Henry made the point that this was quite possible and we have to figure that could happen. Also, we've got to prepare a plan for our approach if the Viet Cong or North Vietnam turn down our peace offer, and we've got to go on the basis that we stick solidly with the position and don't waver at all. Attack our opponents and keep the heat on for consideration of our proposal. We have to establish the point that the P has done exactly what he said he would, and try to get this across somehow.

We had quite a thing with Laird about a *Washington Post* story this morning that quoted Pentagon officials and officers, in quite vehement criticism of the White House's orders of bombing raids on North Vietnam. P told me to hit Laird on this, saying we want to know who put it out, and establish the facts that the Joint Chiefs are the ones who wanted the five days, where the P originally ordered a three-day bombing. The article said the White House insisted on five, which was not true, the Joint Chiefs did. Also, it said that the White House had screwed up the target selection, whereas the White House had approved all of the targets from the Joint Chiefs. Also told me to call Moorer and make the point that the P has been standing up for the Joint Chiefs and it's up to Tom to find out who did this, or we'll have to skewer the Chiefs from the White House.

I made both calls, got Laird midday, and Moorer this evening after he got back from a trip. Laird immediately joined me in complete indignation about the whole thing, said it was just terrible, and they'd checked it out, and that the *Post* reporter had gotten his stuff from military officers on the Joint Staff. He's just going to try and work something out. Then when I got to Moorer, he said that they had checked it carefully and it was nobody on the Joint Chiefs, must have been somewhere else, so as usual they're all denying it and we get nowhere.

We set up a series of K briefings this afternoon. Fortunately, the first one was a staff meeting, and it didn't go well at all, because Henry started with a long reiteration of his negotiations and made the thing sound like a dismal defeat rather than a strong, positive move. It was lucky it was the staff, because he got considerable questions and criticism, as a result of which we regrouped for an hour and worked out a totally different approach, which he then used with a State and Defense group, and hopefully with the press.

The speech itself went very well, and P did an excellent job in his method as well as content of presentation. The phone reaction afterward was as good as any we've ever had, and I think we've probably scored at least a minor coup, maybe even a major one in terms of public opinion and reaction.

Editor's Note: The speech revealed the secret negotiations K had been having with the North Vietnamese, and the details of the latest peace plan. It linked a withdrawal with a POW exchange, a cease-fire, and new presidential elections in South Vietnam. The dramatic disclosure was meant to break the deadlock.

Wednesday, January 26, 1972

We spent some time this morning on speech reaction. He's very concerned that we don't assume that the reaction's going to get across and that we realize we have to ride it. He was not pleased with the *Post* and *Times* headlines saying reaction had been mixed, although basically they were as accurate as could be hoped for. We're moving to get out the positive response. All the analysis indicates the speech scored extremely well, and now it is just a matter of working the follow-up, the thoughtful people and so on. He was very distressed by the VP's performance at the Leadership Meeting, because he apparently was critical of some of the facets of the announcement, and said so in the wrong way at the wrong time. P talked to Bill Rogers about this later in the day, and Rogers agreed it was a problem, but nobody seems to know what to do about it.

Thursday, January 27, 1972

Back to some more speech follow-up today. The P's furious with the *Washington Post* editorial, wants Henry to write a letter to the *Post* rebutting it. Also, said he's taking the *Post* off the China trip, and that Ron is not to come simpering and arguing about it. They deliberately screwed us, and we're going to have to get back at them. Ziegler's not to tell any press people they're going until the P reviews the China list again.

Friday, January 28, 1972

P stayed at Camp David last night, came down this morning in time for schedule today. He did a bunch of memos last night at Camp David, a long one to E outlining his decision on how to handle his integration/segregation issue. He's decided to take the hard line against integration, and wanted me to get the line out on Vietnam that the critics are now "consciously aiding and abetting the enemy" as contrasted to prior to the announcement, when they were just echoing the enemy line unconsciously.

P and I met this afternoon with the Attorney General on the overall political plan, particularly the specifics of his departure. It was agreed the announcement would be made the 16th, effective March 1, and that the P at the same time would announce that he was sending the Kleindienst and Pat Gray nominations up for Attorney General and Deputy, respectively.

The other question discussed was whether Mitchell could go into the law firm, which he wants to do. Everybody else has felt that he should not, but he talked the P into his viewpoint on the basis that we're going to get criticized anyway, and it won't be any worse if he's in the firm than if he's not. I don't think that's right, but that was the decision.

I did a nearly two-hour interview today with Barbara Walters for the "Today" show, the whole thing in my office for use next week. I'll probably really bust things open because I used the conscious "aiding and abetting the enemy" line in answer to one of her questions, and I'm sure it will create quite a stir when it comes out.

Saturday, January 29, 1972

The big news today was the flap over the Wallace dinner last night, one of the girls pulled out a "Stop the Killing" sign from her dress and read a speech about ending the war, which thoroughly shocked everybody there. P was talking about it this morning, felt that it really hadn't done us any harm, although Mrs. Nixon was pretty disturbed about it.

We got into quite a discussion this morning on the Connally problem. He's apparently home sick with the flu. P wants to be sure that we don't let the White House staff throw their weight on him. Wants me to have Alex go overboard on Connally, that is, getting him to Camp David and all the other perks, have him use the Eagle any time he goes. Wants the Attorney General to go over and talk with him about once a week on politics, put his feet up and chat. Get his advice. Don't try to use him, just chat with him. Wants to be sure K keeps in touch with him. Wants E to watch him like a hawk, not just get sign-offs from him, but go over things with him and get his judgment. If Connally's not for it, then the P won't do it. Wants me to make the point that the P's concerned about how hard he's working.

Sunday, January 30, 1972

P called this afternoon to get some information on Laird's performance on one of the talk shows today, so he could call and congratulate him. Called me later to say that the operator called and said that Don Nixon was calling, and he didn't want to talk to him, of course, so I told him, of course. I'd have E handle it. E called me later to say that the reason Don was calling was to say he was going to be having an interview with Jack Anderson tomorrow, just wanted to check in to see if there was anything particular he should cover. Rather fortunate he had it turned off.

Monday, January 31, 1972

Rogers called this morning, on the China trip planning, said that Henry was having the State people over for planning meetings and Bill would like to be included in these and feels that the P should get himself involved. I raised this in a meeting later in the day with the P while K was there, and Henry was horrified at the thought, but P said to call Rogers back and tell him that he knows how the P abhors bull sessions and that he learns much better from the written word, so he would like them to get their papers in first, let the P have time to study them, then he'll meet with the group, and ask his questions and so forth, but he'd like their papers in before this weekend. Henry was delighted with that solution.

Attorney General called today about the Howard Hughes problem. He's gotten a report from the United States Attorney in New York, who has a draft of the Noah Dietrich book, that indicates that Hughes apparently contributed, or made a gift of, $195,000 to Nixon, after the '60 election, and said it could be considered a belated campaign contribution. Mitchell's concerned that we get the background on that. Wants me to talk to Rose on that and see what we can find out, which I will do. P got into the whole Connally problem this morning, he wanted me to call Nellie and see if Connally would like to go to Florida and stay at the P's house for a while to recover from his cold. Also, he wants me to sit down and talk to Connally and say that the P says, because he's carrying such a burden and the P considers him the indispensable man, that I'm to see that his path is as easy as possible within the White House staff. We also talked a little about the idea of getting Connally to head up the Democrats for Nixon, using that as a campaign role for him.

The Don Nixon problem arose again as E reported to the P on the Anderson thing *(Jack Anderson interview)* and we had some discussion on how to handle Don, and agreed that it's got to be done through *(Nixon's lawyer Herb)* Kalmbach.

Tuesday, February 1, 1972

E reported this morning that the latest with Don Nixon is he's now learned that the story Jack Anderson has on him is that there's a development in San Clemente in which Don Nixon has an interest. It has some Federal funds in it, and also that Don's involved in some sort of land deal in the Bahamas. That's the latest horror story from there.

P did a good job at the prayer breakfast this morning, and had Billy Graham into the office afterward for an hour and a half. There was considerable discussion of the terrible problem arising from the total Jewish domination of the media, and agreement that this was something that would have to be dealt with.

Wednesday, February 2, 1972

P was somewhat disturbed with the Bob Semple piece in *The New York Times* on describing his day yesterday because it concentrates on his seeing Boy Scouts, football players, and Republican governors. Makes it appear that he does nothing of substance, and he thinks we've overreacted in trying to get out the personal interest stuff. I think basically he's right.

The big thing today was Muskie's speech, he was supposed to give an environment speech to a churchwomen's group, and at the last minute changed it to what he billed as a major foreign policy address and used it as a platform to blast the P on Vietnam. We spent considerable time working on the approach to answering him. The feeling is that we need to take him on pretty hard. The P wrote a memo covering some of the points he felt ought to be covered. We ended up having some senators hit him today and Rogers is going to go at him hard tomorrow if Scali's successful in getting him to do so. This will be a good chance to smoke Rogers out also on whether he really will do this.

Thursday, February 3, 1972

After breakfast we had a long discussion with K on how to handle Muskie, and as a result I put the heat on Colson and Scali, had a strategy session with them, got a number of things going, and Colson and Scali did a good job of getting Rogers programmed, and he got really cranked up, went beyond where I think he intended to go, at noon today at his press conference, really blasted Muskie for jeopardizing the peace, and so on. It was a very good, strong attack, and because it came from Rogers, it created quite a major stir.

P went on to Key Biscayne tonight after the reception for the drug-abuse athletes. I'll go on down tomorrow per his instructions although I had hoped to be able to stay home this weekend.

Friday, February 4, 1972

Talked to Colson after I got to Key Biscayne just to get a report on the day's activities. He says Rogers needed a lot of propping up, that he was really shook by the Scotty Reston column today (*in* The New York Times), which took Rogers on as being "un-Secretary-of-Statesmanlike." They're working the columnists, Stewart Alsop's going to bomb Muskie in *Newsweek*. Brock's doing a tough speech on Monday, Scott kicked Muskie hard on the floor today. Jackson took him on. Things look pretty good.

Saturday, February 5, 1972

P had me come over about three hours today and wandered through a number of things. When I arrived, he was just taking a phone call from Henry in which he had a long discussion about the Vietnam military plans that he wants. He told Henry that he wants some nonroutine approaches rather than the usual military thinking. For example, a 48-hour stand-down all over Vietnam, and then a 48-hour total-force attack against one area. For instance, hit everything there is in the B3 area. In talking about this, he referred to the historical battles of various wars, and what ought to be done.

He got into the question of campaign strategy as to whether we should consider more appearances out in the country to counteract the adverse media. Thinks that maybe our campaigning in the country will be indispensable to combat the standard coverage that we get on the media side. Then he wanted us to go back over '61–'69 and make the record as to when the networks provided equal time or fairness to Republicans other than State of the Union. The record will show, I'm sure, that they provided none.

He got back to the idea of moving back into the country, and said he veers away from Price's concept of serenely soaring above the battle.

Monday, February 7, 1972

Feature of the day today was my blast on the Vietnam critics, which appeared this morning on the "Today" show. Escalated gradually during the day to the point where it ended up being the lead story on all three TV network news channels tonight. Mansfield has blasted me, Scott's defended me, and the thing has turned into quite a donnybrook. Ziegler was concerned about how to handle it, but seems to have come out all right in trying to sort of semi-waffle it, in the middle, between repudiating me and escalating the attack.

P made a point late this afternoon when I was over at the EOB, of getting a chance to tell me not to worry about the whole thing. That it would blow away and it was his very thoughtful way of trying to make sure I wasn't worried about it, which basically I wasn't.

We had a session with E and Rose in part of it, about the Don Nixon problem this morning. That's come back up now, because Don's now demanded that he see the P, this week, and he's going to go see Anderson also. It was agreed that we cannot allow Don to see Anderson under any circumstances. Then John reported that the Attorney General said that Don

Nixon should see Anderson, but then he reversed it and said he would turn it off. P made the point that he has to save himself as the big gun for the big problems, therefore, he can't even know what's going on with the Don Nixon calls.

Later in the day, E discovered that Don had already talked to an Anderson reporter who he thought was just a personal friend of Johnny Meyers from the Howard Hughes organization. So it spilled the whole bundle of stuff to him, which Anderson has and is going to run in a series of three columns starting later this week. Don now knows this and that's why he feels he has to see Anderson.

Tuesday, February 8, 1972

P started with a combined Cabinet/Leadership Breakfast this morning, which I did not attend, but which apparently went very well. We had spent some time yesterday making sure that it was programmed to be a very upbeat session to get people off on the right foot before the Lincoln recess, rather than a bitch session of any kind. Rogers did a very good job, apparently a superlative job, of building up the P's role as the man of peace. Connally did a great windup on the P himself, as well as the economy, but the star of the day I guess was Hugh Scott, who really got into good form and did a very good job on making the whole pitch, defending the P against his critics, etc. Scott also went out before the press, along with Gerry Ford, afterward, and of course got hit with the Haldeman "Today" show question, but handled it very well.

Everybody's basically taking an approach that they're not repudiating me in any way, although nobody is going as far as I did, or saying that they specifically agree with my precise point.

We had considerable discussion on and off during the day on the whole Vietnam question, as stirred up by my speech, as the reaction starts building up. P feels that the Democrats really have a problem on Vietnam, because they've got to decide where to put themselves. The point now that we've got to make is that they're postponing the peace.

Wednesday, February 9, 1972

By now, my "Today" show thing has really escalated into a super-confrontation type of thing. P is dealing with it very well. He makes the point that Muskie's now trying to hit him

on the basis that his call for silencing critics doesn't make
sense because he attacked Vietnam in '66 and '65. P makes
the point that Muskie can't get away with that, because Nixon
didn't attack anybody in '68. He also can't get away with the
point that I didn't qualify my statement in trying to say that I
was speaking for the P.

The P taped his State of the World announcement today and
in the speech wrote in a paragraph of his own that basically
answers the attack on me. P says he woke up at 3:00 in the
morning and dictated this section, which is a strong defense,
really, of my position. P made the point that I stand behind
my people when they make a mistake.

He had me call Bebe to suggest that he talk to George Wallace's cousin, and point out that he has a real opportunity in
Florida for Wallace, so that he's not just a one-issue man, that
Muskie has opened himself up now, and Wallace can say that
he didn't criticize Johnson, just as Nixon didn't in '68. He can
take Muskie on for undercutting the P, and the chances of
peace, and calling for surrender and so on.

After Ziegler's briefing and the talk this morning, P concluded that we're in a good position now. He told Ziegler to
whack the staff for hitting me. Got into some other items on
making sure we have some of our blacks in the Secret Service,
the stewards, and so forth, on the trip.

E, Mitchell, and I met with Don and Ed Nixon to go over
the Don Nixon problems, had a rather rough two-hour meeting
that at least opened Mitchell's eyes to the real problem we've
got with Don. He just has no realization of the position he's
in, or the super care that he's got to exercise. He's clearly not
badly motivated in any way, he's just not smart enough to
exercise this super caution that he should exercise. Ed Nixon,
while playing an adversarial role in the meeting, got E afterward and said he'd work with us to handle it, that we'd gone
at it just right.

Thursday, February 10, 1972

P feels that our whole Haldeman flap gave the State of the
World some visibility, and that was probably a good thing. He
got back onto the subject tonight on the plane going back to
Key Biscayne, and made the point that it's imperative that
everyone follow the line that he took in the press conference
today, which was really very good in that he made it clear he

wasn't questioning the patriotism or sincerity of any of the candidates, but that he was a vigorous critic of the policies that got us into Vietnam, and the actions that contributed to the assassination of Diem and the conduct of the war. Once he became a candidate and the peace talks began, he said that as a man seeking the Presidency, he would say nothing that would in any way jeopardize the peace talks, and that's the position he feels a candidate should take.

Press conference overall went very well, it was an in-office deal, and the press was more than usually surly, partly because it's been so long since they've had a press conference. Jim Deacon, after the "Thank you, Mr. President," asked if they could have more questions, and came in with a couple of snarling ones, but the transcript on the press conference is fairly interesting.

Rogers was very concerned this morning before the press conference because President Thieu had attacked him on the basis that he'd said that we'd be flexible on the question of when Thieu should step down before a Vietnamese election. Rogers obviously did have a blooper there, but wanted the P to stand behind him. Actually the P couldn't strongly stand behind him, but he did handle the question in such a way that Rogers could have no dissatisfaction. As a result of that, the P filed out of the press conference, we came out in very good shape on Vietnam and on Thieu.

Friday, February 11, 1972

P had me come over early this morning about 9:00. Wanted to get into the basic line for our people to use, mainly that we've got to be careful that the Democrats don't succeed in making the point that they're more for peace than we are. The answer there is that they're prolonging the war and hurting the peace. The answer with Muskie is, who has the best credentials? Those who stood silently by while we were getting into the war and the deaths were going up? Those who were part of the group that got us in, or those who were getting us out? Who are you going to trust, the one who stood by silently while we were getting in, and now criticizes the peace, or the one who said he would get us out and is doing so? Somehow, in other words, we've got to get over that we're more for peace than they are.

Monday, February 14, 1972

The Attorney General stopped by this morning to give me his letter of resignation and talk a little about the procedure for handling it. We'll announce it tomorrow, effective March 1. P dictated to me a little later some thoughts on what to put in the official letter of acceptance. Then he's going to write a handwritten personal letter to him, not for release.

K was in at midday. Henry got into a discussion with the P on his latest report in Paris. He's ecstatic because *(General Vernon)* Walters called to say that the North Vietnamese had called him and had been the most pleasant they've ever been, said they wanted to invite Henry for a luncheon meeting on March 17, exactly thirty days after the day we leave for China. Henry was particularly ecstatic because they said it would be for lunch. They have never had any American official for any meal before in all of Henry's meetings with them, although they ran from 10:00 in the morning to 4:00 in the afternoon. He thinks this is a significant time. Xuan Thuy and Le Duc Tho will both be there, and so he thinks at the very least this will insure no major offensive, as we've been fearing. Quite possibly it may even lead to a breakthrough in opening the peace talks on a serious basis, which would be a spectacular break—actually, the fact of not having an offensive is spectacular in itself.

He and the P then got into quite a discussion on the whole question of these dealings, plus dealing with the Chinese, and P questioned Henry pretty strongly on the whole point of why he thought there was any real significance to this, that it wasn't just a North Vietnamese ploy. Henry feels there has to be some element of seriousness this time.

They then had some discussion also about their technique of dealing with the Chinese, and how they're going to go about that, and P emphasized that he's going to take a very strong position all the way through on that. Henry's afraid, I think, that the P's going to take too strong a position, though he wants to be sure that he does all the necessary philosophizing and everything with the Chinese and doesn't just charge in on a hard-line, fixed position. P feels that the progress that we've made with the North Vietnamese can be attributed in no small degree to the heavy attack we've laid on the peace critics here at home, and that would include my attack last week as well as the others. He felt that had we not done that, they would have figured we were back in a weak position. By fighting back hard instead of just being kicked around by our critics, it was clear that we meant business on the peace proposal, and so there's a real chance that will buy us the relief from the offensive. Also, he thinks our current heavy bombing of South Vietnam must have had an effect, as well as moving the three carriers into position and that sort of thing. Henry feels the same way and thinks that it all adds up to very positive situation for us at this point.

Tuesday, February 15, 1972

P seems to be gradually moving into getting some grasp on the China trip details and planning, but still not very much, and this has got Henry somewhat concerned because he feels that he's really going to need to focus on it. I pointed out to him that he's got six solid days to work on it, that he need not be too concerned that the P's got to take some time on these things to get into gear, but once he does, he'll really plow into it.

In the meantime he's trying to get his sleep caught up and get himself in a good physical condition for the whole trip, which is a darn good thing for him to do.

Wednesday, February 16, 1972

P spent most of the day, till 3:30, at Camp David, working on his China briefing. Called several times just to check in and to review plans for departure and for the Hawaii and Guam stops, mainly the question of whether he had to speak, which he does not want to do on arrival, but will have a brief comment on departure for each place. He got down here, met with E and Kleindienst, and got his hair cut, did Dr. Riland, etc., to get ready to go. He had me in for a little while, just on a general wrap-up of odds and ends before departure, cleaning up a few ambassadorial appointments, etc.

Thursday, February 17, 1972—China trip

The departure ceremonies and the takeoff from Andrews all went very well, with no problems. P seemed to be in great spirits on the chopper going over to Andrews, as he too felt the whole thing had gone well. Leadership meeting had been very positive and upbeat. He received a standing ovation, and everybody, even including Fulbright, had wished him well on the trip, so things seem to be off to an auspicious start. We saw a little bit of the TV coverage after we got on the plane, because they had the set on the table in the staff room, and it appeared that coverage has been extremely good, according to those who had watched it, by getting out to the plane early. It was kind of an odd feeling because they covered the actual takeoff of the "Spirit of '76" and we were on the plane watching the TV covering the takeoff, which was sort of fascinating.

Called me up at 11:10 and kept me up till 2:10, so I had three solid hours in the cabin with him, starting about a half hour after takeoff. P emphasized the need for close discipline on the press during the week, that no one is to talk to the press unless we decide to do so, that we've got to create the impression that this is a very tough bargaining session, not all peaches and cream. He then raises a subtle point that someone can make, but not us, which was that the last visitor the Chinese had who came from Camp David was Khrushchev, and that wasn't a good experience—we hope this one will be different.

The Hawaii arrival got a little botched up, since there was a huge crowd at the airport, and the P felt he had to go to the fence, although it was agreed he wasn't going to. He did, but very briefly. The P was obviously in great spirits as a result of the departure activities and all, and seemed to Henry to be doing his homework and in very good form also.

Friday, February 18, 1972

In Hawaii. The day dawned dark and cold, and stayed pretty cloudy all day with a fair amount of rain, and a very cold, very strong wind. P called me over at 10:00 this morning. He discussed some of his tactics for handling the meetings, and the techniques he's going to use. He says Henry's urging him to do it Henry's way, which is to get into the long, drawn-out historical and philosophical discussions with Chou, which the P is not inclined to do. Henry is also urging him to start in the plenary session with reading a written statement, which the P also is not inclined to do, and intends to follow his own technique on this rather than Henry's advice.

Saturday, February 19, 1972

In Hawaii. P had me over at 10:00 this morning. We got into some domestic questions on the busing thing, the Poverty Bill, the dock strike, and equal employment opportunity. Talked to

E while I was with the P and covered some of those points with him. P also mentioned that he wanted me to go out and buy a large supply of Chinese mementos for him, in varying price ranges, to give to people when he gets back, so I'll do that when we get to China.

Sunday, February 20, and Monday, February 21, 1972

In Guam in the morning, and then on to China. Losing a day in the process, so it's now Monday, the 21st.

This morning in Guam I talked with Hodgson, on the dock strike, and he said that the thing is settled, that the P should sign the bill in China. We left it that the P would sign it tonight after the banquet, which would be at midday Monday in Washington.

On the way to Shanghai from Guam, the P called me up. He's very concerned that the whole operation at the Peking airport be handled flawlessly since that will be the key picture of the whole trip. He doesn't want anything to be blown on it, so I had to work on getting every detail of that set out exactly right, so there are no dangers of slipup.

We arrived in Peking and went through the airport ceremony just as the original plan had been laid out, and we didn't have any untoward circumstances. The P greeted Chou exactly as planned, went through the ceremonies, got in the car, drove rapidly in from the airport through the town and out to the guest house, with virtually no public attention at all. It appeared as we drove through the streets, particularly in the downtown area, that people had actually been kept away from the motorcade route, because as you looked down the side streets, you could see quite a large gathering of people one block away, being held off by a barrier. There were some pedestrians and bicycle riders, etc., on the main streets that we drove on, but they studiously paid no attention to us, and it almost appeared that they had been put there for the purpose of ignoring us. It's hard to imagine that a motorcade the size of ours could whip through town without creating any attention at all; it also appeared that the people on the barricades had gathered there to see what was going on, but weren't permitted to do so.

We arrived at the Residence and were escorted into a reception room, where Chou En-lai greeted us, then we all sat down in a horseshoe, with the P and Chou at the couch at the

head, the rest of us ranged down the two sides. Had tea, cookies, etc., and the P and Chou engaged in a fairly extended
conversation while the rest of us sat quietly and listened. It
was mainly an exchange of general humor, no real substantive
points, some chitchat about the advance party, the original
early arrangements, and that sort of thing. Both seemed to be
very friendly, but noncommittal. They didn't get off of the
trivial ground at all during that session.

The P called me up to his room as soon as we got in, or as
soon as the tea party broke up, and just wanted to review
things in general. We talked a little about getting out the line
that we weren't concerned at all about the lack of people in
the streets and so forth. The P wanted to be sure that we got
that line out, that this was exactly what we'd expected, and
point out the significance of other things, such as Chou En-lai
being at the airport, their playing "The Star-Spangled Banner," and that sort of thing. A little later I got a phone report
from Mort Allen on the news coverage and it turned out that
the networks handled it exactly the way the P wanted, there
was no need for us to put out any further line.

I left the P around 2:00, then came down and had a chat
with Henry, who was concerned and wanted me to talk to the
P about the problem of the P making quips about him at the
little tea gathering here at the guest house with Chou. Chou
paid several compliments to Henry, about his good work in
setting up this meeting and so forth. Then the P made some
quips about it, saying which one of our advance people did
the job, which had Henry disturbed that it would put him down
in the eyes of the Chinese. He wanted me to talk to the P
about that. During this time Henry was kind of wandering
around with nothing much to do until his meeting with Chou
at 3:00.

At about 2:30, or maybe a little bit before, apparently Chou
En-lai appeared at the guest house, unannounced, got a hold
of Henry, and said that Chairman Mao would like to see the
P, if he would come over. Henry rushed upstairs, told the P,
he slapped on his coat, the two of them went out, grabbed Bob
Taylor, on the way, and took off for Mao's Residence unbe-
knownst to anybody else. Taylor came into Chapin's schedule
planning meeting and said this is what they're going to do. He
was very concerned about it, but that he was under orders to
tell no one, and that they were not to tell Ziegler or make any

public thing out of it until they got back. So Dwight came
right down and told me. We debated how to handle the thing
for a while, called Ziegler, and had him come over. I told him.
We spent a very long hour and a half trying to figure out what
the various contingencies were, since we had no idea when
they'd be back, or what would happen in the meantime. The
press was on its way over to the Great Hall of the People to
set up for coverage of the arrival of the P for the plenary
session with Chou, which was scheduled for 4:30 now, then
postponed. The networks were planning to cover the arrival
live, and the press pool was on its way over here to the guest
house to cover the P's departure. Since we couldn't announce
any of this, we didn't exactly know how to handle it. We
debated it back and forth as to what to do. Also speculated on
all the wild range of possibilities that you have when you're
sitting in a Chinese guest house with Red Army troops guard-
ing you outside, and you kind of wonder if the P's taken off
alone with no staff, no security, except one agent, no doctor,
etc., but the worries generally turned out to be unfounded since
the P returned shortly after 4:00, and they delayed the departure for the plenary session another half hour. We just kept
the press waiting, saying the thing had been postponed.

In the meantime, of course, Bill Rogers had called me and
was very concerned about the delay of the meeting, so I just
had to stall him for a while. I went up to see the P at 4:45,
just before he left for the plenary session, and he approved my
suggestion that I call Rogers and tell him that the P had met
with Mao. I caught K on the way in, and we worked out a
plan for announcing the meeting, because Mao had agreed that
it could be announced jointly by us and the Chinese.

It's kind of funny: when I had called Ziegler in here to begin
with, I sat him down in my room and told him not to go up
the wall when he knew we had to be prepared for surprises,
and that he should just be calm, but I wanted him to know
that the P at that moment had left here, and was over meeting
with Chairman Mao at his Residence. Ron was holding a tangerine in his hand, took a bite of it, getting about half the
tangerine in one bite, peel and all. He was, to say the least, a
little startled.

Anyway, the P called me up and told me he had been over
to see Mao. Obviously, he was very impressed with the whole
thing, but didn't get into any details at that time. He said that

to explain it to Bill on the basis that the reason that the meetings were delayed was that Chou came by unexpectedly, and asked the P and K to go over for a private meeting with the Chairman prior to the plenary session. Henry is now working out the plan for release, which the P discussed with Chou in the car on the way back.

K came in 40 minutes later. I was still up chatting with the P, he was just back from his meeting with Chou. They had agreed on the release and so forth. Then the P read his toast to Henry, also. Henry made a couple of suggestions on some deletions of things he felt would be offensive to the American right wing, and with which I completely agreed. Then it was time to leave for the plenary session, so I gave the corrections to Rose just as we were going out, then rode over to make sure the session got started right. P mused a little bit more, just before he left, on how impressive the Mao meeting was, but again didn't get into any detail.

After he came back from the plenary session, we had to get dressed quickly for the dinner. I was up there for a little while, working out some minor details with them on that. Then we left for the dinner, which worked out fine. Very good Chinese meal. We went through the whole handshaking business on arrival at the Great Hall, and down some receiving lines. Up a spectacular grand staircase to the banquet hall area. The toasts went extremely well. It's a little awkward at the Chinese dinners, because they have a glass of wine, a glass of Mao Tai, and a glass of orange juice at the table, and your Chinese hosts keep drinking to your health in Mao Tai, and you're supposed to respond, which is not too bad until they call *ganbei,* which means "bottoms up." At that point you're supposed to empty your glass, which I explained to them I couldn't do for religious reasons, but I did finally get away with it, although it was a little difficult making it stick, and they kept trying. They obviously delight in going all out on the toasting bit.

The Chou En-lai toast was very good, and after the toast he came down and made the rounds of all the official party tables, individually toasting each American at all those tables. The main toast he gave was in the middle of the dinner, and the P's was between several of the latter courses. P followed the same pattern that Chou had in toasting the individual Chinese at the official party tables, which took a lot longer, since there were about eight Chinese to two or three Americans at each of the tables. P did a superb job, he's really impressive. As he completed his toast and they completed the Chinese translation, the band, which was also superb, the Red Army band, struck up "America the Beautiful." It was quite an emotional moment. The P then made the rounds, and he was really charged up. He moved very forcefully, took a firm stand in front of the individual, looked him squarely in the eye, raised his glass and clinked the other person's, took a quick sip, then he raised his glass again and gave a little staccato bow to the individual, and then he turned, marched to the next individual, and repeated the performance. It was really quite spectacular, as "America the Beautiful" was playing in the background.

Then the dinner concluded, the P and most of the rest of us in the American party moved through the hall to the other side, to thank the band for their performance. They had played "Turkey in the Straw," and an "American March," and "Home on the Range" as well as "America the Beautiful" and our National Anthem at the beginning of the dinner. It was very impressive and quite overwhelming, even to the cynical members of the press corps, apparently. We then came back to the Residence, and the P had Henry in for quite a while. I had got undressed and was just ready to go to bed, when he had Henry tell me to come up and we sat and talked for about an hour. He was sort of just looking back over what was obviously a rather overwhelming day. I was able to give him a report on the general press coverage, which had been extremely good, and he was very pleased with that.

He got to talking some about his meeting with Mao, which obviously was quite an experience for him. He said Mao was basically in pretty good shape, although he had trouble walking. His mind is very sharp, has a very good sense of humor, and he felt they had a very good first session. He was particularly impressed by the fact that at one point Mao reached over, talking, and grabbed the P's hand and held it for more than a minute while he made his point. P felt that was rather significant, and was especially pleased that the Chinese film cameras had managed to cover it. The Chinese had agreed to make the film and their still photos available to us for release, which Ron got later tonight and put out. So we should get some great coverage as a result of that.

P finally decided to fold up for the day after we reviewed the schedule for the week again, and that's the end of a very memorable day in American history.

Tuesday, February 22, 1972

P called me up at 9:00 this morning. We reviewed the news summary, and he was extremely pleased with the reaction. The shift in coverage has been very good. While they responsibly reported the low-key arrival ceremonies yesterday, they're shifting to almost euphoric reporting of the banquet and the Mao meeting, both of which had enormous significance, which interestingly enough was realized by the networks and the wires and thoroughly reported. The network coverage of four hours, live, of the banquet period was apparently very impressive and they got all the facts the P wanted, such as his use of chopsticks, his toast, Chou's toast, the P's glass-clinking, etc. So that came off very well.

P made the point to me that after his toast, when he went down to clink Chou's glass, Chou said to him that he had the band play ''America the Beautiful'' because the P had it played at his Inaugural, and he assumed it was one of his favorite songs. He then said here is a toast to your next Inaugural, which is obviously very significant.

In the tea party meeting at the arrival at the guest house yesterday, Chou had made some comments regarding the P's need to stand for election, as contrasted to the situation in this country, where they don't have to do that. There was some light quipping about the difference in the two political processes. Also, at the opening of the plenary session yesterday evening, Chou made the point that the P's party was very young, he said our men here are all quite old, your people are all very young, and he specifically referred to Chapin in that context.

This morning at 9:45, Henry joined us and again reviewed the press reaction and his general plans for his meeting with the counterpart guy this morning, to get his agenda prepared for this afternoon. P and Henry both in very good spirits, feel they're off to an excellent start, but all of the indications so far are extremely significant, particularly the Mao meeting, and Chou's attitude, and so we're doing well so far.

The afternoon session went as scheduled from 2:00 to 6:00, and apparently went very well. I went out shopping. Fascinating session as we went into the bank to exchange our money, and went through the whole involved process of the operation of the Chinese bank, with one girl at the first desk behind the counter, who took our order, had us sign the form, then handed the form to the next lady, the lady at the next desk, who fanned out the money and counted six hundred dollars in almost un-believable quick time. Then they ran some calculations on the abacus, and counted the money again, then handed it across to a man at another desk, who counted it again, looked all the papers over, and stamped it three or four times, then the girl at the first desk handed them to me, insisted that I count them again. The total honesty is astonishing, there's just complete determination not to cheat anybody.

We had dinner at the guest house, apparently a standard Chinese dinner, then went to the evening ballet performance, which was quite an experience. We drove to the Great Hall of the People in a motorcade and were ushered right up to the entrance to the theater, where we went into a little room and sat down, that is, the top members of the official party sat down for tea and refreshments, after going through the hand-shaking process. Then we went into the theater, which was quite a small one, with the usual applause from the gathered group. We applauded back, took our seats, and comfortable easy chairs with tea tables in front of us, and tea on the table, and watched the first three acts of the ballet "The Red De-tachment of Women." We went back out to the lounge room for tea at intermission, then back in for the rest of the ballet and then home. The ballet itself was just as we had been led to believe, a complete propaganda operation, extremely well done. Music was very good, a modernized form of traditional Chinese music. As was the ballet, a modernized form of tra-ditional Chinese ballet. The interpreter seated behind me ex-plained the ideological aspects of the ballet all the way through, and wanted to be sure I understood all the points. In fact all of the Chinese kept asking all of us if we were under-standing the point that was being made, but it was a rather odd sight to see the P clapping at the end for this kind of thing, which would have been horrifying at home, but it all seems to fit together somehow, here.

He had me up to the room afterward, and obviously was very much impressed by the performance and by the music.

Wednesday, February 23, 1972

When I woke up this morning, it was snowing, and it snowed all day. There was a white ground cover, which makes the usually totally brown Peking much more attractive. P again had no schedule in the morning, and worked here at the house. For the afternoon session today, the P invited Chou to come to the guest house, so the session was held here, from 2:00 to 6:00. Once again, I went shopping for that entire period, in at times, a driving snowstorm.

Tonight at the guest house, we had a delicious American dinner, which was very thoughtful of our hosts. We had a fish course, delicious fried fish, and then a steak, little fillet sort of, with green beans, carrots, and fried potatoes, and ice cream and a pastry for dessert. After dinner we went to the gymnasium for the athletic exhibition, which also was very good. Again, we gathered for tea outside first, then we marched in while the 20,000 people in attendance clapped and we returned the applause. Again, we were seated at an area where the counter was in front of us, with the teapots on it, and also we towels, which were changed three or four times during the performance. The P seemed to enjoy the whole thing thoroughly, as did Chou. Fascinating in the preperformance sessions, the way Chou is so relaxed and a great master of small talk, as he greets each guest and has various comments on a personal basis for each one, or for most of them. Any that he hasn't shaken hands with before we get into the room, he leaps up and comes across the room to greet, as he did with me this evening, and it's really very impressive.

The impression from the gym show was one of total control, the hall was packed, every seat was filled. They were filled by sections, with the big section filled with an Army group in green uniforms, another section for an Army group with blue uniforms, other sections for people in civilian clothes, a section for athletes in red sweat suits, another for athletes in blue sweat suits, etc. Also, they had a lighting system that enabled them to turn on sections of overhead lights for the television cameras, and as each section was lighted from time to time, the people in it would all automatically start cheering for the camera. The regimentation is enormous. The athletes themselves march in with a big strut and swinging arms, stand at attention and face the Premier before they start their particular event.

After returning from the gym, late this evening, we learned

that Chou had decided to give a Peking duck dinner for the official party at the Great Hall of the People tomorrow night, to which the P also was invited, which creates problems, since P was counting on tomorrow night as his one night off with no event and no dinner, but he'll undoubtedly have to accept, there's no real way to get around it.

One building issue is the problem of Rogers. He called me today to say that he was concerned about the news reports as they were building at home, which pointed out that he wasn't involved in any of the important meetings, and was being kept out of things. He was obviously uptight about being left out of the meeting with Mao on Monday, and made the point that if there's any other meeting with Mao, he wants to be sure that he is included. He also was carping about the fact that Henry had two NSC people in the Chou meeting with the P, while there were no State Department people there. Later today, Henry charged in, furious, because he'd learned that Rogers had raised, with the Foreign Minister, the question of their participating in writing the communiqué, and the Foreign Minister had said no, that Prime Minister Chou had assigned it to Dr. Kissinger, and Mr. Chiao. So it put Rogers in a rather embarrassing position. This is a problem that's going to continue, I think, on a similar basis. Scali got me before we went to the gym, and complained that his talents weren't being adequately used, and that we ought to be consulting with him on press problems, and that sort of thing. So we have a problem there, too.

Thursday, February 24, 1972

This morning we were up early to go out to the Wall. The snow had stopped, but was still on the ground, which resulted in a longer driving time to get out to the Wall, but didn't really create any problem. As a matter of fact, it worked out fine. There was no wind, and it was warm and sunny at the Wall, so we had a beautiful visit there, and at the Ming tombs. After we finished the Wall visit, we had to stop at the little house at the bottom to have tea, which we all sat around and did. Chou did not go out, but the Vice-Premier did, as well as the Foreign Minister. Then we went to the Ming tombs, and went into a little house there, where they served a fantastic lunch. Although it was supposed to be just a snack, they had all kinds of meats, pastries, etc. Most of the pastries done in the shape of little animals of various kinds, and the girls just kept passing one after another, topped off with a delicious sort of chocolate jelly roll sponge cake.

The Wall and the tombs were basically as expected. It was funny, on the way into the tombs, the park area surrounding them, they had staged groups of people playing cards, children doing jump rope, a family eating, so that photographers had ample material as they walked along.

After the dinner tonight, the P had me up for a little time killing. Got into the question of tomorrow's schedule and wants to cut the tour of the Forbidden City down as much as he can, and wanted to try to eliminate all the handshaking and glass clinking at the dinner tomorrow night, but at that point Henry came in and felt that was a mistake, that it was the Chinese way, so we probably will. Also, we're going to have a plenary session tomorrow, to bring the Foreign Minister types in.

He got into a discussion with Henry on the communiqué. They're still having a terrible problem on ironing out the Taiwan question, and Henry is meeting with this guy tomorrow night at midnight to try to work something out. We ended up agreeing to do the communiqué release on Sunday night, in spite of the disadvantages of that from the viewpoint of delaying it for our newsmen, who are becoming rather restless. We had a discussion of that situation, and the P and Henry both feel there's really nothing we can do about it, except sweat it out at this point, figuring that the communiqué will cure it when the time comes. They talked about the general attitude here. Henry feels that everything's going very well, and that we're going to come up with a good communiqué, but the P made the point that we just may have to end up with no communiqué at all, if we can't get Taiwan worked out, and we may not be able to work it out. Henry agreed it was a possibility, but didn't think it would happen, because they've committed to a communiqué.

Friday, February 25, 1972

P called me up at about 7:30 this morning, was upset about the toast for tonight because the research group had given 800 words instead of the 200 that he wanted, and hit the point that the hardest work is editing, and what they should do is take one idea and develop it. He then went through the ''Oh, I'll have to do it all myself" routine, and apparently proceeded to do so, since he's dictated the toasts down that he's going to give. He also debated whether to read it or not, depending on what Chou's going to do, but ended up deciding that he would read it. At that point Henry came in and there was some discussion about the communiqué, main problem being the paragraph on Taiwan.

P commented that it was fascinating the way Chou picks up colloquialisms and jumps on each one of them that is raised, and he obviously was sort of fascinated with that. He made the point, as Henry was talking about the fact that he'd have to go through this thing all night tonight again, that you two are young, and don't need sleep. He said that he had a really tough time sleeping and he really did look tired this morning, not really as sharp as he has the past mornings. He's also in kind of a strange mood, as he discussed all these things and sort of brooded over the problems he was dealing with, the lack of understanding of him by the press and others that are here.

After this morning's session, the P had the visit to the Forbidden City, which worked out pretty well. Then Henry reported that Chou had just come over here to meet with him, but they had postponed this afternoon's 3:00 meeting to 4:00, and that Chou had instructed Chiao to work out the communiqué with Henry. They were going to meet at 2:30 and try to get it done before the 4:00 meeting, at least the one tough paragraph. They still have a few sections on trade that Henry says they can easily finish up tonight.

The P's attitude was much more positive than it had been this morning, and we reviewed some of the domestic news as well as the coverage of the trip, and then, I think, took a break for some rest before the 4:00 meeting. The afternoon session today kept getting delayed more and more as Henry kept working on trying to get his communiqué thing worked out. Having originally been set for 3:00, then moved to 4:00, then moved to 4:30, it ended up starting at 5:50. P had me up at about 4:30 to 5:30, just killing time, waiting for it to start, and he was just sitting there on an alert basis, waiting to go to the meeting whenever Henry finished his thing and they were ready to meet. So it's kind of a long wait for him.

He's particularly upset now because Henry's told him that Rogers has come in with a rewording of the communiqué that revises even the State Department wording, and he's submitted his material, saying that we must not go any further than what he's said. The whole thing re-raises the basic Rogers problem. He mused over how to handle it, and I told him that the only possible way is that the P's going to have to sit down and talk with him, and just flatly explain to him how the thing's going to work, and make him understand it. I think that will work, but the problem is getting the P to do it, and I'm not at all sure that he will.

The dinner went well tonight, and both the P's and Chou's toasts were very good. The P did end up reading his, and it's good he did because it came over better. Chou made a strong commitment to Chinese-American friendship and Henry felt that was significant, especially in the way he phrased it. Before dinner, P called Rogers, Henry and me over while we were waiting for the picture-taking session, and told Rogers that there would be a plenary session at the airport tomorrow at Chou's request, and Bill didn't seem to spark much to that. He obviously was in pretty bad spirits. Then Rogers raised the question about another meeting with Mao, and the P said he didn't think there was going to be one, and was sort of leading Henry on. Henry took the bait in the wrong direction and told Rogers the reason was that Mao wasn't well, which we're not supposed to say anything about.

Later tonight, after the dinner, P had Henry and me up in his room, and told Henry he was concerned about having told Rogers about Mao, and to say that I should go see him and get that straightened out, that he's not to say anything to anybody about it. So then the P spent quite a little time agonizing about how to get Rogers in line on the communiqué, etc.

Henry left to go down for another meeting on the Taiwan section, came back up about a half an hour later, with a victory. He has the statement basically the way we had ended up wanting it, so the P approved it, Henry's now got that locked, which means we will almost certainly have a communiqué by tomorrow, which seems in good shape. We talked about the question of another Mao meeting and agreed, as I told Henry earlier, that there was no need for one from our viewpoint.

Saturday, February 26, 1972
P called me in at 7:30 this morning to do some general talking. He had awakened at 5:00 and then called Henry to see how

the communiqué was going, and Henry apparently locked it up at 3:00 this morning, with nothing left now but word changes. It was agreed that the P would see Rogers at Hang Chow, and go into details with him there, so that he won't know that it's an accomplished fact and that it's up to him to go along with it and support it.

Editor's Note: The communiqué stated the differences between China and the U.S. on Vietnam, Korea, Japan, and Taiwan. However, the U.S. acknowledged that Taiwan was part of China, and expected the "Chinese themselves" to settle matters peacefully. The communiqué also provided that neither nation would seek to dominate Asia and would oppose the efforts of other nations to do so.

Sunday, February 27, 1972

P started early again this morning in the Hang Chow guest house and asked me to come in early, but I went ahead and had breakfast first, and then went down to his room. By the time I got there, Ziegler was already there and he was just reviewing some of the general news coverage. I gave him the report I had just gotten about Muskie, which was rather fascinating regarding his breaking down in New Hampshire. *(There were reports that Muskie had wept during an outdoors news conference.)* He was intrigued with that, but we couldn't get into it much because it was time for him to leave for the airport.

(In Shanghai) things sort of started moving. Rogers is saying that the communiqué is going to pose a lot of big problems even though last night Henry fought over the points Rogers wanted, and got all of them except the things on Taiwan. Rogers arrived at the suite, and said he wanted to see the P. The P originally first said, tell him I'm asleep or something, then he agreed to see him, and had him come in. Rogers made the point that he wasn't trying to undercut the communiqué, that he would support it, but Rogers did want it understood that there were, in his mind, some real problems. He enumerated some of those and the P spoke in great detail about each of those points, and obviously was far more familiar with them than Bill, and was able to answer his objections, although I'm sure not to Rogers' satisfaction. Then P clearly hit Bill hard,

and said he expected him to instruct his bureaucracy to stay behind us 100 percent and support it fully, which Bill said he would do. P played it pretty coolly, and I think Bill got the message.

P had me get Ziegler in to give a report on all the press we're having on the communiqué, which Henry had briefed on this afternoon. All Ron had were the early wire reports, which are treating it on a pretty straight basis, not overly enthusiastic. Then the P had me get Henry in, he was obviously dead on his feet, but the P was determined to talk, and we went on till after 2:00. P sort of recapping problems and triumphs of the whole visit, the fact of the great accomplishment, the real breakthrough, the lack of understanding of what really has been done, but the fact will come out eventually. His admiration for Henry's accomplishments and the whole thing, with Henry sitting on the couch just itching to get out to go to bed, which I tried to bring about several times, but the P made the point that Chou En-lai stays up all night, so will he.

He ordered some Mao Tai and had several of those, which he had also done at dinner, and had at least half a dozen before and during lunch today. He did finally let us go out on his terrace and take a look at Shanghai at night, and then excused us. Obviously, he was feeling the historic nature of the occasion, and just couldn't bring himself to fold up, but we did finally manage to do so.

Monday, February 28, 1972
On the plane the P had Henry and me in for quite a long time several times during the flight, working out plans for the K background to the press. Then he told me to make a note of the fact that K has worked hard and I'm to call Rebozo and have him give Henry all of his phone numbers of girls that are not over thirty.

When we got to Anchorage, P wasn't able to go to sleep, so had me over at his house for a couple hours, and we went through all of the same things again. He was obviously trying to unwind, and we just spent quite a long time talking before he finally folded up.

Monday, February 28, 1972
(*A second February 28—we crossed the dateline.*) P had me over early this morning before departure since he didn't sleep

much during the night. He said he had gotten up at 5:00 and gone down, sat in the living room for a couple hours, then gone back to bed at 7:00, got up at 8:00, that's when he had me over at about 8:30. He reviewed again the need for following up with the conservatives. He's very concerned, because on the flight from Shanghai to Anchorage, we got the newspaper report of the *Post*'s coverage, which was pretty negative and made a big point of the sellout of Taiwan, which had him concerned. As we got later reports and ones that came in this morning, it became clear that the general press was not playing it that way, and that we were really in very good shape, but it was hard to convince him of that at that point, and he was afraid we were dealing with a bad story and we'll have to move hard and fast on it to avoid getting really clobbered.

The arrival in Washington was extremely good, and the P did a great job on his arrival remarks, even though there's quite a hassle getting them done on the plane. We also discovered that Buchanan was very negative on the whole thing. Henry spent some time trying to give him some background so he could swing his position around, but it didn't apparently do any good, since Pat stayed negative and Rose joined with him.

So that's the end of February 28, and the end of the China trip.

Tuesday, February 29, 1972

P started this morning with the Leadership Meeting, and had me in a little time just to talk on general approach to things. After the Leadership Meeting, which ran about an hour overtime, he had a Cabinet meeting. Made the point that the more deeply you believe in something, the more softly you can talk about it. He was referring both to himself and Chou as following the same tactic in meetings. He said the most important thing out of the China trip was that there's a profound new relationship between the PRC and the United States. They both agreed not to resort to the threat of force or the use of force in international relations and in relations with each other, and they agreed that no nation should dominate Asia. This is the heart of the communiqué. There is now a new relationship at this time. We support the proposition of peaceful settlement of international disputes and disputes between ourselves. The question is whether we can learn to live with our differences, or whether we'll die for them. He said that in their evaluation of us, the thing that impresses them is not our wealth, but our power, and more importantly our purpose. They see our material emphasis as a weakness. They look for strength of character, willingness to sacrifice, to fail, to believe. He emphasized the continuity of the China trip as it evolves from the Nixon doctrine. After the Cabinet meeting, he had Henry and me in to evaluate both meetings, and was absolutely horrified by Rogers, handling of both the Cabinet meeting and even more so the Leaders' Meeting.

Wednesday, March 1, 1972

More China follow-up this morning and also P had chat with Connally and Shultz and so forth to get things cleaned up before he leaves for Key Biscayne. He wants to get notes off to Nelson Rockefeller and the other key people who have supported the China trip, wanted Rose to call all of the families and tell them gifts are coming to them. Wanted K to get hold of Buckley this afternoon if he could. Wanted Butterfield to offer Camp David to Connally for the weekend. On the plane to Key Biscayne, he wanted to be sure we sent a bottle of Mao Tai to Abplanalp, saying, "Try this for starting your fire." Wants to have the phone cable turned off, take things easy.

Thursday, March 2, 1972

In Key Biscayne. P had me over first thing this morning for about four hours. Henry came in for the second half of it. He feels Henry isn't getting across on the PR standpoint on the P's handling of the situations in China. He says the main thing for us in China is the P's position as a big-league operator. He's done it for years. The unusual world statesman capability, the personal qualities of the man. He wants to refer to this as a classic battle between a couple of heavyweights, each with his own style.

Buchanan called me this afternoon to say that he had thought the whole thing over and decided he had to resign and would like to come down Friday evening and meet on the courier plane with the P to tell him he was leaving and why. I jumped on him pretty hard on the basis that he had no right to interrupt the P's brief time off with something like this, and also that he basically had no right to resign at all. He feels he's got to be his own man, but he can't support the communiqué, and that if he can't then he has no business staying on the staff. He seems to overlook the fact that his leaving would create a major stir and shatter a lot of the confidence that's now developing in the China trip, but I don't know whether I'll be able to persuade him of that. I discussed that whole thing with K and E at dinner tonight, and we all agreed that we've got to find some way to avoid Buchanan's leaving. That he just doesn't have the right to do it, and he's got to swallow his pride and problems, and find a way to live with it.

Sunday, March 5, 1972

We got into the Buchanan resignation problem. The P says that he won't talk to Pat, that he thinks he should go to work for Mitchell. He's afraid he'll poison the well at the White House if we keep him there. He could write bombshells for attack purposes at the campaign organization. P's basic inclination is to let him go rather than try to keep him around. He just doesn't think it's a good idea to keep him on the staff and that we should at least get him off the news summary, because he doesn't want to have any excess negativism. He then, however, started talking about the arguments to use on Buchanan, the fact that his successor hasn't yet been trained, that if he goes, he's got to keep quiet. It would be the height of disloyalty for him to attack the P at this point. He has no right or business to talk about the communiqué, and they should point out that the P never said Chinese Communism was good. He should look at the subtlety of the comments.

Monday, March 6, 1972

Big item today, starting the staff meeting and going through the day, is the ITT case and Kleindienst.

Editor's Note: Jack Anderson was claiming that a lobbyist named Dita Beard had written a memo boasting that the ITT settlement had been influenced by an ITT contribution to the Republican convention. The charge was not true—the contribution had nothing to do with the settlement, and in fact had been made to the city of San Diego, so the city could bid on the convention (ITT's Sheraton division was opening a new hotel there, and it was thought to be a good promotion). Kleindienst, who was up for Attorney General, had been in charge of the case, and called for new Senate hearings to clear his name—this gave the Democrats on the Committee a chance to make political hay. Beard would later testify that the memo was a forgery, but the damage had been done. For the White House it was a public relations disaster.

We all agreed we need someone to manage the whole project, that at this point we don't have anybody really on top of it. P was concerned about what's at the root of all this, where did this story start, who leaked the memo, who was it written to, and so forth. We don't seem to have the answers on any of that. He wants to be sure that Colson keeps a low profile on this, that there are no statements from the White House, that we refer everything to the Justice Department. He felt that we should try to get a good statement from Justice by the Attorney General about the case, before the Thursday press conference, so the P can stand on it and that it can be elevated to the Presidential level. Wants to get it all set beforehand, in other words.

He had Rose in, and she reminded us that Dita Beard, the gal who wrote the memo that started all this (and he talked to Jack Anderson), is the tough, profane character who was Ted Rogers' secretary in the '60 campaign. *(Rogers was the P's press advisor then.)* E talked to Mitchell, and he said that he would not make a statement, didn't feel he should, before he testified. Suggested instead that the P should simply respond, saying that he was glad that Kleindienst wanted to clear this whole thing up, and had asked for the special hearing. As long as we've got the thing and are paying for it, we might as well get some credit for it.

First thing this morning the P talked to me about Buchanan. Wanted me to tell him that the P understands completely what his problem is and that we'll work it out, but we'd like to make the date April 1, so that we have time to get things in order. Then on my own, I should say that I feel he should work in the campaign, that there's a wide-open spot as director of the answer desk. P feels there's a problem with the attitude in the entire staff, in putting their personal prejudices above the common good here. I then talked to Buchanan and I opened with the P's view but then Buchanan said he had thought the whole thing through, that he had now realized that he had expressed his view to me, to K, Rogers, Haig, and through me, to the P, and that there was no need for him to express it any more publicly than that and that he would do the cause more good by being inside than being outside, and therefore he decided he should stay on. When I reported this back to the P, it was clear that he wasn't particularly pleased that Buchanan was staying. At that point, he was pretty well ready for Pat to go on his way.

Later in the day, E asked him how he thought New Hampshire was going to come out, and his prediction was that Muskie would get 54 percent, because he'd pick up some rank-and-file sympathy, and get a little more than the polls say he will. McGovern will get 22 percent, and not do as well as the polls say. On our side, he said he'll get 65 to 68 percent, McCloskey 20 to 22 percent, Ashbrook about 10 percent.

Tuesday, March 7, 1972

We got into the Rogers problem, with the P trying to figure out how we ought to approach that. He had me sit in the Rogers meeting this afternoon, and Bill made a pitch for the need to solve the problem of his apparent downgrading and the press coverage thereof. His solution was for the P to announce that Rogers was in charge of the planning for the Russian trip. The P finessed that, as he should have, and made it pretty clear to Rogers that he wasn't about to be put in charge of the trip.

Wednesday, March 8, 1972

Last night the P called several times after I had gone to bed to check on New Hampshire results, and some more discussion on it this morning. Generally he was satisfied with both the results *(as it turned out, Muskie beat McGovern by only 46 to 37 percent)* and the way they were played, but concerned about making sure we followed up on it.

The ITT thing is still a building story, very discouraging because all of the press goes the wrong way. We haven't been able to make the point that this is not a contribution to the National Committee or to Nixon, that it's to San Diego. P felt Dole should make a speech and hit a hard counterattack, disclosing who contributed to the Republican host committee, and then calling on the Democrats to do likewise. In other words, attack the attackers, saying they're playing politics with us, trying to smear an innocent man, and that sort of thing.

I got a recommendation from E and Colson that the P cancel

his press conference idea for tomorrow, because there's no way he can adequately handle the ITT question. So, I went over and told him this and he agreed to drop it. Thinks that maybe we should give the money back to ITT or Sheraton, with a real blast by the mayor of San Diego, saying this is a smear job, that we've always refused the $400,000, and knock down that the P had any knowledge of the money at all.

He was concerned that we don't seem to have any dirt to throw back at the Democrats. We've got to find a way to turn around the PR on this, because we're getting screwed unfairly.

Thursday, March 9, 1972

At the staff meeting this morning, Shultz came up with an interesting point, that he's been analyzing Connally, and feels that he has a totally different point of view about his basic approach to politics. Whereas we feel that we should meet each problem as it's shown in the polls, and worry about how the statistics play and so forth, he thinks it's a mistake to worry about the bits and pieces, that we overreact and worry too much. When things are going your way, you should just let them go, not work on each little thing, that we're too antsy. We should brush the other guys off and not worry about them. He's very concerned about our overreaction, thinks we need more of a feeling of stability and confidence. It's an interesting point. My answer to it being, that he's a Democrat and always has been in Democratic politics where they can do that, because the press is with them. We can't afford that luxury.

The big thing today was the ITT deal again. I had a staff session where we tried to work on how to turn the thing into some positive PR. I called Mitchell to check out the statement that was attributed to him in the testimony today that the P had told him to get the case settled. He said that this statement had previously been in the Anderson column and in the press. The facts are that Mitchell has only seen Dita Beard once in his life. Mitchell never said anything like this to her, and he'll categorically deny it. Mitchell also said there's something fishy on the Dita Beard memo, that she's a drinking buddy of Anderson's secretary, and it may be that there's something involved there, also in the fact that Anderson won't show the memo to anybody.

Kleindienst called me at home tonight on the whole thing, said that the press and TV are not accurately reporting the positive testimony, they're only covering the sensational stuff today. Mitchell told Kleindienst to call me, suggested using the White House resources, first, to set up a task force over the weekend to review the testimony versus the newspaper accounts; second, the VP take it on; third, a general attack by any friendly press, Congress, government and community people we can get. He says tonight *(Senators John) Tunney, (Gary) Hart,* and Kennedy asked *(Senator James) Eastland (the chairman of the Senate Judiciary Committee)* to get the SEC inside-trading charges against ITT and let them romp through those, which we very definitely don't want them to do. He thinks it's clear now that the Anderson charge has been repudiated, and they're now after bigger game, and for this reason he sort of regrets his request for the hearing, especially since it's gone this far, but no one had ever anticipated the press and TV would come up with such unfair reporting. He thinks that the fact that *(Anderson colleague Brit)* Hume injected the P into it on hearsay shows the serious basis that they're working on.

Friday, March 10, 1972
Main thing today was ITT follow-up. First thing this morning, P was concerned that we hit on the fact that we're taking indirect testimony, that it's not admissible, especially when it's fourth-removed, as was the charge that the P was involved in this. Colson later in the day got all excited because Hume was asked for the notes again this morning, and he said he had already given them to Kennedy, so now Cook's going to call for an end of the hearings, and go to executive session, charging the committee's being used. The theory Colson has now is that we can get Dita Beard to disavow the memorandum, which would shoot down the whole case, but what she did today was just a statement by her lawyer, where she did shoot down the point that there was any connection between any antitrust settlement and the convention contribution, but she let the memorandum on the record without disavowing it. As of now, the thing stands that way, and they're still trying to figure out how to turn it around to our benefit somehow.

Sunday, March 12, 1972
P's at Camp David all day. Phoned once this afternoon and said on ITT that we've got to give a lot of credit to the Colson

group, and all of the people I had working, that they really have done a pretty good job of getting the story going our way. Made the point that the ITT stock went down after the settlement, so it couldn't have been too great a settlement.

Was concerned because Colson said he was doing his best to keep the staff morale up, which was a stupid thing to dump on the P. Also wanted to raise the question with Mitchell whether we could put out some lists of contributors just for primaries, so we don't let a fire build up on this, but instead just get it out of the way.

Then the P got into the design of the new Laurel cabin at Camp David, which he had been over to look at. He thinks there should be an office there, wants to take a small lounge and make it a Presidential office, with a desk, and flags, and so on, so he can use it for meetings if he needs to, such as a meeting of head of state or something of that sort.

Monday, March 13, 1972

P asked me to talk to Mitchell today about disclosure of campaign contributors, and I did raise it with John, he said we'd have a substantial problem if we did that, because the money was raised on the basis that we would not report it. He thinks we should just say that we'll follow the statutes, and we should just straight-arm it, saying we're complying with the law. Our answer would be that the P's not involved, this is a private committee for his reelection. He thinks it will all go away April 7 when we start reporting. We'll include all the dollars we've collected then, and since we've had a mass mailing, we should have a large number of people, which we can also mention, although we won't give them names. P felt that we should work up a statement for Stans on the contributions, using the line that we will report everything according to the law, that we have absolutely nothing to hide, that we are setting up the machinery now for reporting, mention that the P's not doing any campaigning now in the primary campaigns.

Tuesday, March 14, 1972

On ITT, we didn't get much progress today, the committee went into executive session this morning, and then had Mitchell on this afternoon. I don't have much of a reading as to how he did. The committee failed to come up with a subgroup to go out and interview Dita Beard even. *(Beard was in a Denver hospital and consequently could not come to Washington.)* So we're pretty much stalled on dead center even though they had a day of activity on it.

P had me raise the question with E of whether now is the time to surface the Pentagon Papers on Kennedy and Vietnam in a more vicious way, and get some of that going as we counterfire, so we're doing something on our own initiative instead of just reacting to the Democrats.

Florida returns in the early run show the P doing much better than expected, also Wallace doing better, and Muskie doing very badly, all of which is excellent news for us. In addition to the fact that the anti-busing thing carried 75 to 25.

Wednesday, March 15, 1972

The P called late this morning, said he could see why Colson and the rest get so discouraged about ITT, the way the papers play it, that he had read the papers pretty carefully this morning, and saw what a problem we had. Even then, though, he didn't notice the caption of the *New York Times* photo, where they said Mitchell was talking with Marion of ITT, when actually he was talking to Bob Mardian, the assistant Attorney General.

Thursday, March 16, 1972

We had quite a little staff discussion on the whole ITT follow-up. The staff reports there's very little Congressional mail on this, and no interest out in the country, so we should be careful about overreacting.

Everybody now is convinced that the memo is a phony, the typing analyst says that it was typed in January, not in June; they also had Dita Beard's testimony in hand that it's not authentic, she didn't type it, it's not her signature, she's never seen it, and she told Anderson that. All the ITT people say they've never seen the memo, and the secretary who typed the original memo can now come forward and say that this is not the one she typed. There is a problem on getting the senators out there to talk to Beard on Monday because their doctor's having second thoughts on it. P this afternoon said he wasn't too worried about the ITT thing, didn't want to get too much overreaction to it.

The other problem today was a memo from Bill Rogers to me, saying that he was going to take charge of the Russian trip and start coordinating the departments, which had Henry pretty disturbed. I raised it with the P when he was just chatting with me, and he said I should just level with him on it, that the P's taken many trips, he's always in charge of his own trips, and following that practice, the P will be in personal charge and will not delegate that to anyone. So I am writing Bill a memo in response to take care of that.

Friday, March 17, 1972
On the ITT question, Colson reports that we've gotten a bad break and the senators aren't going to go to Denver because of the possibility of a vote in the Senate, so I pushed hard for his trying to get a sworn statement from her and trying to get that out, which he said he would do. Later in the day it turned out that the Dita Beard statement was taken and released, and that's thrown some doubt into the whole thing.

On ITT, the P wanted Buchanan and Colson to get their people going on some good solid editorial columns about the double standard about Congressional hearings. Press saying that during the Nixon era and then the McCarthy era, when they were investigating Communists, the committee was constantly attacked for their failure to follow the rules of court and taking evidence, that where are those attacks now, that when the P of the United States is slandered, or the Attorney General, or a business leader, no one raises his fists, but when a Communist spy does it, they all scream. Thinks we can really work something up on that. They had the Pat Nixon birthday party tonight. P apparently stayed for an hour and then went over the EOB and hid until they went to the movie and then came back and went to his room.

Monday, March 20, 1972
We got into some political follow-up. He's concerned that we've let China dissipate as an issue because we didn't exploit it, that we have to be blatant about these and we need something to build them up, our strong suit is foreign affairs, and we need to figure out how to play it.

Also, got to thinking that we should move all the political operations, primarily Colson, out of the White House, and into Mitchell's operation. The White House has the aspect of appearing to use the super power of government, and that we've got to get Colson less visible because he offends people and rides too hard.

On the plane going up to New York for the drug trip, he came up with the idea of a club for the group that made the trip called the "New China Hands," in contrast to the "Old China Hands." The idea of the symbol being the handshake, and the point being made that the old hands knew everything about China, but yet knew nothing, whereas the new China hands know nothing about China, yet know everything. With Nixon as president, Pat Nixon as chairman.

Wednesday, March 22, 1972

The big item today was the AFL-CIO walkout on the Pay Board, which they did at about noon. Shultz and his crew met all afternoon then they all went to the P's at about 5:00 to report on it. This was a meeting with Connally, Shultz, Rumsfeld, Stein, Colson, E, and me. Shultz reported that *(Teamster head Frank)* Fitzsimmons was going to stay on, but *(UAW head Leonard)* Woodcock would probably go off, and that the public members had a press conference this afternoon, shooting down Meany's allegations about the failure of the Pay Board. And on the consumer price index, even though food is up badly, the areas that are under the control mechanism are okay, so we actually come out pretty well.

Monday, March 27, 1972

Today started with a call from Connally saying Perot called him saying that he had to see the P because he had a report from one of his agents in Hanoi, saying that there might be a breakthrough on the sick and wounded and that Perot would not go through normal channels to discuss it. He'd bring it up only with the P. I knew the P wouldn't see him, I tried to figure a way out, finally raised it with the P, he suggested that we have Dick Walters handle it on the basis that he's handling all the top secret things in the bureaucracy and that Perot should deal with him. So we're going to take a stab at that.

ITT is back up big today and mainly on the supposed question of the White House call to ITT. It has obviously bothered the P and he had me call Finch and Klein to see if they had made such a phone call, which both of them said they had not.

Anyway, we've got a problem. Also need to check into where we can get Eastland to close down the hearing. The P wants to be sure the committee report is a written report so we have something to use for the campaign.

Re-raised the questions this morning, getting into the whole point of Kleindienst's confirmation tactics *(as Attorney General).* Since the day went on, it became more clear to the P especially that Kleindienst wasn't going to be confirmed and that the thing has to do with a grandstand play to close it off. If possible, force the thing to a vote, which would be the best thing, even if he was turned down, because then he'd be rejected and we could use that as an issue. If we can't get a vote, then we pretty much concluded that we'd have Kleindienst issue an effective ultimatum saying that he had asked for these hearings, they had been turned into a farce and that the only way he could see to bring some sanity back to the thing was to announce that he was not going to continue past April 15th if they hadn't voted him up or down by then. He would ask the P to withdraw his nomination.

He had a meeting with Morton about the Alaska pipeline and was concerned that the idea of running it through Canada was not good because we're losing jobs in Alaska, and even though Alaska's unimportant, it's going to sound bad here. The thing of it being good internationally is useless to us and the environmental pluses are questionable, at the least. Jobs are more important than either one of those. So the question is whether it's worth breaking it off in Alaska now or should we just screw around with it until after the election.

Tuesday, March 28, 1972

K returned last night. Was in this morning to discuss the Russian trip and some plans for that.

ITT was a big item with the P this morning. He felt that he probably should pull the plug on Kleindienst. The P is convinced that he can't be confirmed now and that somehow we've got to cut our losses. We haven't been handling the case well all along and there's no point in struggling along with it any further. The best thing of course would be to confirm Kleindienst but not at the price of 30 more days of hearings. The other thing is to sacrifice Kleindienst in a blaze of glory.

Wednesday, March 29, 1972

Dick Walters met yesterday with Perot, at our request, to avoid Perot meeting with the P. Apparently, he's got a deal where the North Vietnamese will release 30 sick and wounded prisoners in return for a million dollars from us. Henry's concerned that we work out some way of handling the ransom so that we get credit for it rather than Perot. Henry's apparently had feelers on the same thing from other sources also.

K was in talking about the Russian trip and the problems of whether we stay at the Kremlin or not, how many days we stay and all that sort of thing. The P also raised the point of whether he ought to speak to the Russian people on television as Eisenhower did.

The big thing today again is ITT. The P had me call Kleindienst over. We met over at the library and lit a fire and brought some coffee down and Kleindienst came, scared to death. Made the point that there will be an executive session next Thursday, and they'll close the hearings. He's convinced that Eastland is able to do that as there are only three votes against him on the committee, whereas MacGregor and Colson seem to think he'll have a problem on a close vote in the committee to close the hearings. He said then it'll go to a filibuster on the Senate floor after a delay for final minority reports, etc. Thinks the filibuster will die after a while, that we have ample votes to confirm Kleindienst. He went round and round on that.

P called me later before I got home, when I returned the call he asked me to wait just a minute, that he had just gotten out of the shower and went out to get a bathrobe. Said he thought the Kleindienst meeting had gone well and been productive and he has changed his view that we should dump Kleindienst, thinks that we should ride him out as he recommends. Said we've got to remember that we shouldn't get so close to these things that we panic, which I must say, he was closer to doing than the rest of us. Kleindienst sees no chance of losing the vote in the committee where our people thought it was going to be a close vote. The P was impressed by Kleindienst feeling that we should get the White House out of the San Diego convention planning. He told me to get that done. He wants to look into the possibility of moving the convention, maybe to Miami, but he thinks it's probably too far along to do that.

Thursday, March 30, 1972
During the morning while we were talking and K was in, he
was handed a note indicating that the North Vietnamese have
attacked South Vietnam. The attack that we've been concerned
about and waiting for.

It was the beginning of a full-scale invasion of the South.

Second Quarter: April–June

Tuesday, April 4, 1972

Got into several political discussions, the P's concerned that we've got to get moving on the attack, that we should have someone attacking Muskie as a defeatist, because he's saying that we shouldn't react to the Vietnam attack by the enemy. We shouldn't let him build that line about just getting out of Vietnam. That shows no concern for the POW's or protection for the 70,000 GI's that are there. He made the point that the P has the responsibility for these people and that our continued withdrawal can only go on if South Vietnam is able to hold.

The Vietnam action goes on today. P has moved in quite strongly according to Henry and is taking control. He really banged Moorer around yesterday on the Air Force's inability to get moving. Problem is they keep saying that the weather is such that they can't bomb. The P's massing a huge attack force, Naval ships for gunning from the sea, tremendous number of additional bombers, and he's going to start using B-52's for the first time to bomb North Vietnam as soon as the weather clears. He'll base the bombing on the violation of the DMZ and move in hard. He feels that this will give us a fairly good chance of negotiations, which he has never really felt we've had up to now, but thinks they're doing this as a desperation move and then will go to negotiate. Henry has the same view.

Wednesday, April 5, 1972

Everybody was highly pleased with the Wisconsin primary results, with McGovern winning by such a wide margin, which thoroughly screws up the Democrats one more time. The P wanted to be sure that we get people to follow up on the line, that Kennedy is now the obvious Democrat candidate. He liked my idea of waiting a few days and then having Connally give Teddy Secret Service protection on the basis that there's general agreement that he's going to be the candidate.

We got into more discussion on the convention plans, the P now wants a daily report on the plan to move the convention. He's concerned that we should make the point that a crisis is developing on the question of whether the convention will be ready.

P called a meeting with Tricia, Julie, David, and Ed, together with Dave Parker and me, to discuss their scheduling. It was a little awkward and didn't really cover much, except their problems on getting the right kind of stuff from our speechwriters in terms of anecdotes, stories, examples, etc. The P expounded some of his theories on what they ought to be covering, but really didn't accomplish much of anything.

Rogers called me saying he wanted to see the P, that he had nothing important, a few things he could cover, but he thinks he should see him for appearance's sake, so that it looks like everybody's steadfast on the Vietnam move and all. He then said he is troubled some, first with the South Vietnamese still showing the world a fight, and that we'd better be sure there's no stories on this. Secondly, that we not lose a lot of American pilots and thus get more POW's. He said he had canceled his press conference for this week but if things turn for the better over there he would reschedule it.

Thursday, April 6, 1972

The P had me stay in when Henry brought General Vogt in to discuss his show. The background of this is that in a briefing the other day, Vogt mentioned to Henry that he was terribly distressed with the way the military and particularly the Air Force were handling the Vietnam situation, particularly their failure to carry out the Presidential orders and an even worse failure to come up with any ideas of their own on how things ought to be handled. Vogt made the comment to K that he would like to give up his 4th star that he was about to get for going over to NATO and be assigned to Vietnam and get the thing straightened out. As a result of this, K suggested exactly that to the P and he bought the idea. Vogt is being transferred to Vietnam, although he's still getting his 4th star and he's going to go out there this weekend.

The P was very upset with the military, he expected Vogt to step in and take it over. He then made quite a dramatic point of the fact that this may very well be the last battle that will be fought by the United States Air Force, since this kind of war probably will never happen again, and that it would be a tragic thing if this great service would end its active battle participation in a disgraceful operation that this Vietnam offensive is turning out to be. Problem being, of course, that the Air Force is relying on weather problems as an excuse for not moving in on the attacks that the P has ordered. Vogt said he understood what the P was saying loud and clear and that he'd move in and get it solved. The P told him to bypass Abrams, that he did not have confidence in Abrams, that he'd been a great commander in WW II but that Vogt was to get things done. If he had any problems he was to let the P know, not just let the thing simmer.

Vogt then raised the point that his hand would be greatly strengthened if he were made Deputy Commander out there instead of just Air Commander and the P said that is to be done and ordered Henry to get it done. It was quite a dramatic meeting and I think undoubtedly had a dramatic effect on General Vogt.

The ITT hearings were the other big items today. The problem there is the failure in the committee to work the thing out right. We were planning on getting a compromise, but that failed and now it's put off until tomorrow.

Friday, April 7, 1972

The P had me over at the house for three hours today during a beautiful sunshiny morning. On ITT, tried to determine strategy. The P thought that I should call Mitchell and make the point that what's important here is not confirming the Attorney General, that it's ending the hearings. I should level with him and make the point that there's too much in the record to risk having it come out. The P believes the Republicans should boycott the hearings. He had some other ideas for sort of PR follow-up on ITT, such as getting the story out of the number of people that we see at the White House who have special interests and that there's nothing wrong with doing that, it's a part of our job.

The other thing we got into in depth was the San Diego Convention question. The P's feeling that the move just won't wash. People will say it's because ITT didn't come through with the money. He suggested a compromise, inviting all the campaign leaders to San Clemente for a meeting after the convention. This is if we move the convention to Miami, make it a campaign planning session with all the governors, candidates and so on, with big TV coverage. He's concerned about Reagan's attitude if we were to move out of San Diego and feels that we need a very real reason to move because we can't fake a move like this. He thinks we ought to get some other PR judgment on it.

Saturday, April 8, 1972

P called me over at 11:00 and kept me there until 1:30 on another beautiful sunny morning, so I never did get outside today because I had to leave at 2:30 for Washington.

The P had me call Bowie Kuhn, the Baseball Commissioner, to suggest that the P and the VP step in to help on the owner/player negotiation. Kuhn said that there's a lot under the surface and they're moving to a good zone, there's some chance of a tentative agreement this weekend, and he appreciated the P's offer but he didn't think they should do anything about it now.

Monday, April 10, 1972

This afternoon the P talked with me for quite a while about Vietnam, going into the background and so on. He feels very strongly that we've got to make an all-out effort now, and that it really is a do-or-die proposition. The North Vietnamese have committed all of their resources to the current attack and the South Vietnamese have pretty much committed all of theirs to the defense. We're doing virtually everything we can do, short of putting American troops in, which we won't do. The P has moved the bombing activity up to a very high level and intends to maintain it there, and do everything else he can with naval action and so forth to give the South Vietnamese a chance to win this one. It's apparent that we have the potential at least to break the North Vietnamese back, but the question is whether or not the South Vietnamese will be able to hold. If they can, the P comes out in extremely good shape, because it would be almost inevitable that we'd move immediately from this attack to the conference table within the next few months, and that we might get something settled by summer.

Wednesday, April 12, 1972

P had E and me in for a couple of hours this morning, rambling through a lot of odds and ends. He got into sort of curious blast at the speechwriters. He had written a long memo last night to K, E, and me about the problems of our speechwriters, and he asked me for a copy of it and read most of it to E and me and went into quite a blast on the whole speechwriting problem—the fact that the P had to change the Canadian Parliament speech in the sixth draft, that there weren't any examples, and so on. K came in to report on Vietnam and said the Russians are really falling all over us and that they had a glowing meeting with Butz.

> *Editor's Note:* Secretary of Agriculture Earl Butz was in Moscow to discuss trade agreements. The White House was naturally apprehensive that the increased activity in Vietnam would endanger the Soviet Summit, but this now seemed less of a danger.

P told Mitchell we now have Teddy and Hubert out on a limb on it, that Dole and all of those should attack them for undercutting the Commander in Chief and risking our men. Should make sure that people know they're out on that side. We should go all out to win in the North, that's the P's strategy, while we have the public opinion at least somewhat toned down. He says the Russians are now really shaking and we're making some real headway if we can keep it up for a while.

Thursday, April 13, 1972

P stayed up at Camp David last night and didn't come down until a little after noon today. I slept in and got to the office late and when I arrived at 10:00, there were urgent messages from E and Shultz and I learned that there had been a big flap with Connally regarding the plan for a Troika plus a Council of Economic Advisors meeting this afternoon. Turns out that our PR planning group had decided it would be a good idea to bring Johnny Walters in to get a little publicity on the IRS efforts on overwithholding, and they'd gone ahead and contacted Walters, who had then gone and contacted Connally before Parker got to Connally to clear it. As a result of this, Connally blew his stack, called all of us in and raised all kinds of hell and said he wanted to see the P. I called John as soon as I got the facts on the matter, tried to explain it all to him, he was very upset, made the point strongly to me that that was the last straw, he'd had it and he was through. I went through the old rationale about how he couldn't do this and all that but he at least says that he feels there's clearly a conspiracy or at least a series of actions against him by the White House staff, and he named K with some meeting he had on Chile; E, Shultz, Stein especially, Flanigan, and that there's just too much participation by other people, that everybody calls his people and issues orders to Treasury and so on. He wants to run the Department himself, he will not take orders from the White House staff, their judgment's not as good as his, he's got a good track record in Treasury and obviously some of our people don't think so and he's not going to stay around and fight them, he's going to get out. He was firmer and madder than he's been before. It obviously concerned P a great deal. I argued strongly that we shouldn't do anything further but rather let Connally float over the weekend and then see what we do on Monday, which the P agreed to, but I think he felt it would have been better to take some action to try and solve the thing.

P reviewed the Canadian Parliament speech with him. Henry asked that he cut out the sentence about the fact that nations that supply arms to other nations bear the responsibility for what those other nations do with the arms. Henry reported that Rogers is talking to Laird about the B-52 strikes. We're backing into a position so that they can bounce both ways. If the opinion goes against us, they can say they were against it; if it works out satisfactorily, they can say that they had been right with it all along. Sort of a typical maneuver. The P ordered some additional strikes and pushed Henry hard for developing some other even stronger action in the next few days in terms of bombing action, blockading, etc. The P and Henry agreed that they should drop the press conference for next week because as of now Henry is going to go to Moscow secretly on Monday night to meet with them on Vietnam, at their request prior to his meeting on the 24th in Paris, so that changes the picture some.

After Henry left there was some discussion as to how Rogers should be informed on this, and we agreed that K should do it, or K and I together give him the whole story on the trip, telling him that Brezhnev sent a message to the P asking K to come to Moscow before he went to Paris and explaining that this is what Henry's doing, it has bearing on the trip, etc.

Henry's canceled his Japanese trip, said he will be around this weekend, then he'll head for Moscow midweek next week. We took off for Canada at 5:00, arrived for the standard arrival ceremony, and then into the guest house and a white-tie dinner.

Friday, April 14, 1972

In Canada, the P was involved all morning in the general sessions. He had me over in the late afternoon for a short time—follow-up on reactions to the visit so far, a little concerned about the demonstrators, and he wanted to check on domestic stuff—ITT, San Diego Convention moves, that sort of thing. The evening event was a concert followed by supposedly a very brief handshaker, then the P was to leave. But Trudeau sandbagged him into staying for a buffet supper, seated at a table with a place card, and kept him there for an hour. P handled it pretty well, and I blew up at the Canadians. We finally got him moved out.

Saturday, April 15, 1972

In Canada this morning for the signing of the Great Lakes Treaty, then returned to Washington, getting in about noon, then I came on home.

Henry told me on the plane that there'd been a problem in that the North Vietnamese now want to put off the April 24 talk and the question is whether he can go to Moscow or not. His inclination is to go anyway, and then just come back. He doesn't feel he can go to Moscow in May when the Paris talk will be, because it's too close to the P's trip. He spent quite a little time on the plane with the P on that subject.

P called me at 2:00 after I got home, said that they had worked out Henry's problems and that he would probably still go ahead with the Moscow trip. Also Henry had been very upset this morning because Abrams had sent a cable warning of the grave dangers of the far North bombings that the P had ordered, which almost precluded the possibility of doing them because if anything went wrong, Abrams could say they were done against his professional advice and all. The P said on the phone they're going ahead with the strike tonight and that he's seriously considering putting on a blockade later this week. So he emphasized again the importance of a good solid PR run on the reasons for this.

Sunday, April 16, 1972

The P called at about 12:30 and I asked how church was. Said, "Well, it's always good for the soul to take an hour off once in a while." He commented that the B-52 strikes were exceptionally effective, the best ever in the war. That the Pentagon was jumping up and down. We really left a good calling card. Now he's knocking off the bombing while Henry takes his trip. We'll see what they do from there. He says Rogers is prepared to take a hard line in his testimony on Monday to attack the attackers. He commented that Humphrey was really absurd in his idea of turning it to the UN Security Council, overlooking the fact that Russia and China are both on the Council and will veto it.

Monday, April 17, 1972

Staff meeting this morning. P is very disturbed about a *New York Times* quote saying that, Hooray fellas, that's the end of Moscow. Says we should hit the critics for hitting at the wrong target. They should direct their fire at the Communist forces in North Vietnam invading, rather than against the P, who's trying to stop this invasion. Regarding any limits on attack activity, the P will do what is necessary. The bombing will stop when they withdraw across the demilitarized zone. Regarding negotiations, we should look them cold in their eyes.

Tuesday, April 18, 1972

I had a long meeting with Connally this afternoon, over two hours, covering the resignation question. He's obviously determined that he's got to go. He admitted that a lot of the problem he has with the White House staff is his fault and the way he works. He wants to control everything that affects him, he will not allow others to make decisions for him and especially he will not allow staff people whose judgment isn't as good as his to do so. He assured me that he would leave on a very sound political basis, he has no intention of supporting any of the Democrats, and in fact suggested that he could, after the convention or the primaries, perhaps surface as the Chairman of the Democrats for Nixon or something of that sort. I'm convinced after the discussion that it's better for him to go. At some point he's going to blow up and walk out mad, which would be highly undesirable. If he leaves and stays solid politically and is willing to spend time counseling and speaking for the P, as he says he is, he perhaps could do more than he can at Treasury, so we may be gaining rather than losing on the whole thing. He completely agreed with my suggestion that Shultz be his replacement. We're going to go ahead on that basis, as far as he's concerned. We had a good talk. I think he is leaving for a combination of reasons rather than any single thing. The staff problem is one factor, but it's obvious he's concerned about his health, he thinks his blood pressure is up and he's doing a lot of doctor checking. He really wants to get back to Texas—he's concerned about his ranch and financial interests. I just don't think he likes Washington very well. I reported all this to the P and he asked me to meet with Connally again tomorrow to work out the details. Then the P will meet with him on Thursday.

The P went out tonight on the *Sequoia* all alone. It's a beautiful spring evening for the first time and I guess he couldn't resist the lure.

Wednesday, April 19, 1972
We got deeply into the K trip question, because I raised the point this morning that I didn't think the Camp David cover was satisfactory and I urged some other alternatives, such as our going to Florida and saying K is at Camp David or something, but the P doesn't want to go to Florida and we ended up with Camp David. The problem then was how to notify Rogers. We spent considerable time during the day on that. Ended up deciding that Haig and I should tell him first thing tomorrow morning, but then I recommended that we do it tonight after having dinner with the P on the *Sequoia*.

The P agreed, so I went out to Rogers' house at 9:00 and gave him the basic line that we had heard from Brezhnev in a secret message that he wanted to meet with the P's representative for a secret talk on Vietnam in Moscow and that Henry was on his way. He took it extremely well, we didn't have any problem at all with him, which was kind of a surprise. So that worked out probably better than we expected.

The *Sequoia* dinner with Haig was partly a report on Vietnam and partly the P blasting the press and our enemies in Vietnam. Haig told us about how reporters had been working on the young soldiers, saying they won't take you in helicopters because they're going to land you in a mined area and they're afraid they're going to blow up their helicopters. They don't care what happens to you, but they do worry about their helicopters. So they're sending you up in buses. That's when the officers had to talk the guys into going because they were starting to more or less mutiny and he referred to them as you "press bastards," you're the ones that caused all this. The P wants Agnew to use that in his speech on Friday.

Haig seems to feel things are going quite well in Vietnam. The P's air attacks, particularly the bombing of Haiphong and Hanoi, were tremendous morale boosters, both for the Vietnamese and for our troops that were involved.

On the Kleindienst hearings, we stalled most of the day but they finally put Gleason on. He was on the stand for three hours but didn't say anything very harmful, so all of the worry was for naught. Tomorrow is Flanigan and then they wrap it up theoretically at least.

Thursday, April 20, 1972

The P had a long meeting with Connally this morning, and I didn't talk to him after that because he went from there into another meeting and I left for Camp David on the K cover-up mission.

The P had dictated a long memo to K, which was his main concern this morning. He had Rose retype it and then we sent it as a cable to Henry in Moscow, providing guidance to him on the negotiations. Henry apparently plans to make a long philosophical opening statement and lead into a lot of items of background, the P's philosophy and so on. The P, in his memo, ordered him to move directly to Vietnam and insist that they get the Vietnam discussion completed before they move to anything else, such as matters relating to the Summit. He wrote quite a long memorandum, which he read most of to me. Henry isn't going to like it, because it doesn't follow his style, but he may still go ahead and do it the way the P told him to.

Friday, April 21, 1972

He called E and me over at noon for a three-hour meeting at Camp David. Obviously he had nothing particular on his mind. He got into a general political discussion following Colson's theory of McGovern's being a real possibility for the nomination. Either he or Teddy Kennedy as the far-left candidate. The P says this would not cause him to move to the center, as many suggest, because we can't compromise principle. We would rather make it possible for the people in the Senate to move to the P, since the alternative would be the far left. He talked to John about working on the Democratic platform when it's adopted, costing it out and hitting them on all the things that would have to be done as a result of that.

Then we got into K's point on the liberal establishment, that we can end the war and do everything else that they ask and they'll still be against us, not because of the Hiss case and that kind of thing, but because Nixon's not one of them and won't pay attention to them. He thinks we made the mistake in the first two years of talking to all the liberals and so forth where there's no hope of winning or changing them. We have to go to the new establishment and work along that line. The only way we can fight the whole press problem, he feels, is through the Colson operation, the nutcutters, forcing our news and in a brutal vicious attack on the opposition. You have to figure that 90–10 are against us, so we have to be 90–10 better in what we put out. It's harder to shape up the TV, but we can have a big effect on local TV. We have to get the station owners and managers aware, make them realize what their news people are doing.

Saturday, April 22, 1972

Still at Camp David. Cold, rainy, heavy cloud layer day. P called me over at Aspen about 11:30 for about three hours. He had a fire going in his study and got into the question on details of the Russian trip. He gave me a lot of instructions for Chapin on taking some very firm positions on the things that we want to do, such as using our car, using our plane, going to Leningrad on Saturday, not on Sunday. The P's convinced that the Soviets are pushing for Sunday in order to avoid the P's getting a good crowd there. I covered that by cable with Chapin.

The main area of concern was K's trip and the general Vietnam situation and plans for the TV follow-up next week. He's concerned about the effect of K's trip, whether the people in this country will think he's there because the Russians are pressing us and that this is a sign of weakness or not. He feels that we can't show any overt weakness and he called Haig several times during the meeting. Each time he emphasized the importance of maintaining our bombing and other attack levels.

Part of our problem here is K's unbelievable ego, in that he's really pushing to have the P announce his Moscow trip and make a big thing out of it. Also apparently he hasn't followed instructions from the P as to what he's to be negotiating. He's spending his time on the Soviet Summit agenda rather than on getting Vietnam settled. The P was clearly disturbed by the information he had received on Henry last night. He waited all day and into the evening for a message today, and then at the last hour it still hadn't come. It now appears that Henry won't come back until Monday, because he was determined to have a three-day meeting and he's managed to do it.

I asked him at the meeting about the Connally situation, he said Connally had agreed to do his withdrawal in sort of two steps: first, when he resigns, he would say that he has no plans for any political activity, that the P has his personal support and that of his wife. Second, he would wait till after the Democratic Convention and then come out, blast the Democrats, and announce that he was heading up the Democrats for Nixon. The P said that he thought he was the only man who could be P, and that led us back to a discussion we had started with E yesterday on the restructuring of the two-party system, the feeling being that the P and Connally, after the election, could move to build a new party, the Independent Conservative Party, or something of that sort, that would bring in a coalition of Southern Democrats and other conservative Democrats, along with the middle-road to conservative Republicans. Problem would be to work it out so that we included Rockefeller and Reagan on the Republican spectrum, and picked up as many of the Democrats as we could. By structuring it right, we could develop a new majority party. Under a new name. Get control of the Congress without an election, simply by the realignment, and make a truly historic change in the entire American political structure. This intrigues the P, and Connally, and it's obviously the only way Connally has any future, since he's never going to be nominated by the Democratic Party, and by leaving now he loses much of the chance of ever being nominated by the Republican Party. If we formed a coalition, with the two of them being the strong men, he clearly would emerge as the candidate for the new party, in '76, and the P would strongly back him in that.

Sunday, April 23, 1972

We're still at Camp David. At least it's a nice day today, so there's a chance to play some tennis. P has now found that he can't go back down to Washington until late tomorrow night because K will be coming back getting here probably somewhere between 10:00 and midnight. P was concerned about the news of the battle coverage today because the situation is more stable rather than less, but you don't get that from the news, and he feels that we're not getting our PR and our story out. Henry is very effective on the prospects for the Summit, and makes the point which, of course, drives the P up the wall, that Brezhnev has spent more time with him than he has with any other foreign visitor. P's problem is he just doesn't agree that just the trip itself will have a big effect. K justifies it as cooling the domestic furor here, and sending huge shock waves to Hanoi, but the point is we've sent the shock waves to Hanoi for months, that's typical K gobbledygook, and we don't have a domestic furor here, at least to the degree that we have to worry about getting it back. P's worried about the effect, in this country, especially amongst the hawks and our supporters, of his going back to talks in Paris. Makes the point that I've got to watch the situation concerning the day-to-day PR, that we've got to have something positive about South Vietnam. We should keep pushing the invasion line. I talked to Haig a little later, and he was very concerned about the way we're bludgeoning K. He says Henry's not getting snookered over there, and that we shouldn't imply it to him. He thinks the P's putting too much heat on Henry and he thinks Henry will overreact. The P's point is that our real problem is that the Soviets want the Summit, but they won't help us in Vietnam in order to get it. Which leaves us on a bad wicket, in that we will be meeting with them during a Soviet-supported invasion of South Vietnam.

The P in analyzing all this feels that we're trapped, and his concern is obviously very deep. Then we got into his real major concern, that Henry must be controlled about any briefing of press or senators or anyone else, on the basis that there's nothing in it for us to do any briefings on the Summit, that we've got to keep the whole focus on Vietnam, and the problem is, Henry doesn't have anything on Vietnam. P then said he's not discouraged, we just have to wait. We're on a sticky wicket at the moment about dealing with the Russians while they're supplying North Vietnam. When Haig arrived, we went back through it again. It was sort of an eerie session because we sat over at Birch cabin, the P had a big fire going, it was cold and overcast outside and while we were in there there was a tremendous amount of thunder and lightning, and a heavy rain. The P had the lights on fairly dim and it was quite a picturesque setting. P made the point of the need for positive news Monday, Tuesday, and Wednesday. Haig said he had talked to Laird, but one of our problems is that the ARVN don't allow the press in, so the press write bad stories, but Defense and MACV is going to put out the positive. Haig's going to follow up with this with Laird, Hank, and Omora.

P then made the point that we're going to have a very rough story on Tuesday, and a very tough day to ride through on why we're going back to the conference table at the time that the Russians are pushing this invasion. The way this can be answered and the only way it will be answered is by the P giving a tough speech on Wednesday night, but we've still got to ride for 30 hours. P again raised the point that K can't brief the press, that we have to play the mystery line. P seemed to feel better as we ended the Haig meeting. He called me about 9:45, said there are two things that we have to have in mind. We've got to convince Henry to be absolutely mum, which will be awfully hard but essential. The success or failure of Henry's trip is involved. The way to make it pay off is to create a mystery now. The key here is K himself. We've got to convince him that he is to not say a word about the Summit. No reflections about Brezhnev's personality, etc.

The other subject he got into earlier today was the question of staffing the new Administration. He tried a contingency plan regarding the Cabinet and top agencies. He wants to be ready on November 7 to move rapidly. He'll call in the whole Cabinet in some way and have them all submit their resignations. We've got to be hard on our friends as well as the others, and only keep those who really can cut it. Then on new staffing we've got to start on the basis of total loyalty, secondly look for youth, people in their thirties and forties, and third, self-lessness. People that are willing to get in and work without having to be babied like the ones we have now. We've got to concentrate on building the new establishment, which is his whole mission at this point.

Monday, April 24, 1972

At Camp David. The big item of the day was K's return. P had me over at 10:30 this morning for a couple hours. Talked about the plan for notification of people before the announcement of K's Moscow trip. He concluded that Henry did mean to claim the SALT deal now, rather than waiting till the Summit, although Haig had said earlier that that's not what Henry had in mind, and the P feels we've got to drive K off at this point, that we shouldn't claim anything until we get to the Summit, and the breakthrough should be tied to the P's meeting, not K's.

Rogers called, concerned that we be very sensitive about his participation in the conversations, and to be sure to include him in the meetings. He'd be glad to do anything we want him to do to help. He thinks that there are some signs that the other side is hurting badly, and that we're in better shape than the press makes it appear. He does feel, however, that the Russians are doing to the P just what they did to LBJ, on the standstill cease-fire, that we shouldn't fall for that.

Henry finally arrived about 8:30, and he and Haig and I met with the P over at Birch. The P had us gather first, and had me call and have him come over. He unfortunately had not zipped up his fly, so during the entire conversation it was noticeably open. We discussed the scenario for tomorrow, the plan for notification of the good guy congressmen at 5:30. P backed down on the K briefing. He agreed that Henry could do one to steer the direction on how the talks were arranged and how they went, but no substance or content is to be disclosed. Also he backed down on the SALT thing and agreed that we would make the announcement. The meeting went pretty well, although it was pretty tense at the beginning, the P was all primed to really whack Henry, but backed off when he actually got there. Henry obviously was very tense. Haig had called me earlier to say that Henry had sent some extremely bad cables because he felt we had not backed him, and he was very distressed that he had been sabotaged and undercut. He greeted me very frostily, but the P broke that pretty quickly as the meeting started. We all came out in good spirits. P and Henry walked together over to the helipad and talked in loud voices all the way down, while Ed Cox sat listening avidly.

Tuesday, April 25, 1972

Back to Washington, the P spent the whole day at the EOB. Had me over several times, starting at 9:00 with K and Haig discussing the approach to the speech Wednesday night. He had Johnny Andrews and Winston Lord come in, told them that he was going to make the speech tomorrow night at 10:00, on TV, ten minutes about Vietnam. He wanted Andrews to follow the P's outline carefully: don't deviate from the rhythm, the phrases, or the order. Said the P will work in a couple of vignettes himself at the end, so you ignore the fact that there's no conclusion.

Then he outlined how the speech should go: that I'm reporting on the situation in Vietnam, the role the United States will play, the efforts for peace by negotiation, review the situation when we took office, what we've done, the troops, the casualties, etc. The most forthcoming peace offers, and describe those generally. No Mickey Mouse stuff about being too accurate on that. Their answer was a massive buildup, the P showed restraint, then the Easter massive invasion. Then he wants him to get the actual number of men who actually invaded South Vietnam. South Vietnam resisted, the United States posture was, no ground forces but heavy air strikes, now report from General Abrams the general air strikes have been essential. The ARVN are fighting. We can expect another month of hard battles, with some losses. His estimate is that the South Vietnamese will be able to contain the invasion. What am I doing as P? First, I will continue the troop withdrawal with 20,000 to be accomplished before the 1st of July. Second, I'm directing Porter to go back to the negotiating table in Paris. Third, I'll continue the air and naval attack on North Vietnam. Then review why we had to do the bombing, to protect American forces, to prevent a Communist bloodbath. K recommended that he add some threats there. The P said that he would put that in his conclusion, not leave it up to these people *(referring to the speechwriters).* He said the conclusion would be damn frightening. He said we must have the point that this is an invasion, and that our bombing will continue in the North until the North stops the invasion. There is no privileged sanctuary in North Vietnam as long as Communists invade the South. He emphasized never to say "the other side," always to use "the enemy," "Communist," "invaders." Lord and Andrews left.

The P then got into a tremendous blast at the military strategy in the central highlands, making the point that any simpleton knows that they should not have allowed themselves to be driven back across that area, that when you have minimum troops occupying unwanted territory, facing a superior force attacking them, they shouldn't allow themselves to be driven back. They should pull back to a grouping point, draw the enemy in, then encircle them and cut them off. Haig said the problem is that Thieu can't write off people in the territory, so he can't just give ground away that way. K said they will run out of steam by the end of this week, P kept lashing and lashing on what did they hit and so on. He has a Congressional dinner tonight, which is good timing, and then he will be getting ready for the speech tomorrow and down to Florida tomorrow night right after the speech.

Wednesday, April 26, 1972

Spent the day at the EOB getting ready for the TV speech tonight on Vietnam. P had me over several times, going over just odds and ends on the speech. He doesn't want to release an advance copy, because he wants the congressmen to hear the speech rather than read it. He's obviously concerned about the rhetoric he's using at the opening, and I guess more particularly at the closing. He did read that to me later on during the day. He then agreed to release the text because of the argument of the press guys that we needed it in order to get adequate coverage in the morning papers.

Speech went very well, and our early reaction has been excellent. We left right afterward for Key Biscayne. He wanted to be sure that Colson hit hard the point that the attacks by the Democrats in the Senate and the House and the Presidential candidates will jeopardize the negotiations and undercut the P, and that they, therefore, must accept the responsibility if the peace efforts fail. He wants to take them on for supporting the Communists, and really go right up to the "aid and comfort to the enemy" line. He's ordered Henry to hit Hanoi again this weekend. He asked him how many B-52's we had in the Vietnam area. Henry said 130, so the P wrote down on a card that he was ordering 130 B-52 raids. Henry afterward said,

"What can I do? I can't possibly send 130 up." When we arrived at Homestead, he found out that there are two squadrons based there that were leaving the next day for Vietnam. He thought he might go over and see them off tomorrow.

Saturday, April 29, 1972

P went over to Walker's yesterday afternoon. He phoned this morning about the briefing book and this afternoon called me over at 2:30 for a couple hours and ruined the one short period of good sunshine, as he has every day since we've been here. He made the point that the most effective way now for us to build McGovern is to get out some fake polls showing him doing well in trial heats.

> This was a political maneuver to build up a weak opponent. The logic behind it was that the best way to assure that we could win was to pick our opponent, to the extent possible. We were much happier with McGovern than other possible foes.

Thinks we need to take Hubert on about all his switching of position. We need to knock him down and build McGovern up.

He talked to Henry while I was over there, gave him some more instructions on his Paris negotiations and took a very firm line that Henry is to turn down any attempt by them to delay. He's to get some positive and affirmative action while he's there, or we cut loose. He also told him to announce a thousand sorties a day and wants it for American public opinion, give it to Ziegler and Scali and put it out in Saigon. On the SALT meeting on Monday, he wants to have Rogers, Laird, and Moore all there, with Laird primed ahead of time to agree, then that only the P will go out to the press to make the announcement. There will be a photo opportunity of the group in the meeting. He got into some discussion with Henry on some obvious negotiations Henry's been having with Dobrynin about the airplane and Russia and that sort of thing.

Sunday, April 30, 1972

Start out in Key Biscayne, left at 1:30 for Texas. The Connally dinner tonight went pretty well. The P did an hour of Q & A and gave way too long answers, particularly the first question on Vietnam, where he went for 15 minutes and then had a number of other questions on Vietnam where he again took quite a little time. I think it probably impressed the guests, but it wasn't nearly as strong a performance as he's able to do. Connally was effusive in his praise of the P's courage and performance.

Monday, May 1, 1972

In Texas this morning, the P called from Connally's house, wanted to review last night a little bit. Felt that maybe the talk would have been better than the Q & A, and wants to follow up on doing a big outdoor barbecue right after the convention, which Connally suggested.

At 6:00 this evening, after a long session on SALT and some meetings with Henry, the P had me in. Henry then came in, said that everything was settled on the Russia trip logistically that we wanted, except they still insist that we use their airplane which the P says to give in on. Henry then read the report from Abrams which in effect says that Quangtri is lost, the battle for Hué begins, and K makes the point that if we lose Hué it'll be a real setback, although Quangtri is not so much so. Abrams' report goes on to say that it's quite possible that South Vietnam has lost the will to fight or to hang together and the whole thing may well be lost. Henry hedged around before getting to that part of the Abrams report, but the P kept telling him to get to the point of the summary. Henry finally did. Then the P took the report, read it himself, and we spent quite a little time just talking over the various questions of how the Vietnamese have fallen apart. Henry making the point that the pattern seems to be that they can hold for about a month, and then they fold up. We've now passed the month, and they're following the pattern and folding.

P made the point very strongly to Henry that his instructions in Paris remain the same, he's not to give anything, and that we're perfectly willing to sacrifice the Summit if necessary, but under no circumstances will the P go to the Summit while we're in trouble in Vietnam. He makes the strong point that we will go ahead with the hard strikes the latter part of the week if Henry doesn't get positive action in Paris tomorrow.

He then brooded a bit about it and said if the whole thing collapses, then all we can do is go to a blockade and demand our POW's back, and Henry agreed with that. Then the P said, but then we're defeated, and Henry said, "Yes, that's right, and then we'll have to tighten our belts." The P sort of laughed. He's obviously facing the very real possibility now that we have had it in Vietnam, and that he's going to have to deal with that situation instead of one of acceleration. Both he and Henry agree that regardless of what happens now, we'll be finished with the war by August. Either we will have broken them or they will have broken us, and the fighting will be over. There still seems to be some possibility of negotiation or a cease-fire because it's quite possible, maybe even probable, that the North Vietnamese are hurting even worse than the South Vietnamese, and that both sides may be ready to fold.

Tuesday, May 2, 1972

Kleindienst called me at 9:15 this morning to say that J. Edgar Hoover had died in his sleep during the night, raised the question of how we wanted to announce it, and what our plans were on succession. I immediately went over to the EOB, where the P was, and told him. He said definitely he wanted to announce it, talked about successors to a certain degree, but was more concerned with trying to get some Vietnam things worked out with Henry, following up on the Paris Summit report from last night. Since Henry had gotten no results they're very concerned about how to handle the whole Vietnam situation.

Editor's Note: K had flown over again to meet with the North Vietnamese, only to find the Communists to be unbelievably arrogant and insulting. K was very discouraged.

In any event, I spent quite a little time during the morning on the FBI thing. We bounced around with E and Dick Moore the whole question of how to handle it. P kept calling over, felt that we ought to have *(Clyde)* Tolson function as Acting Director because he can be trusted and the P knows him. Everybody else turned that down because he's too old. Had some other suggestions.

Then Kleindienst called with the details. The maid had found Hoover lying on the floor by his bed at 8:30 this morning. Problem was that she then called his secretary, Miss

Gandy, and she called Hoover's doctor. He went over immediately, said it was a natural death between 2:00 and 3:00 AM, probably a heart attack, but he hasn't called the coroner because we don't want anybody to know till we're ready to make the announcement. So we delayed the coroner till we got the announcement plan worked out, and ended up having Kleindienst announce it. Then the P went out to our pressroom and made a brief statement. P wanted to have him buried in Arlington Cemetery with a big ceremony and all, but it turns out that National Presbyterian is his church, Austin's his minister, and that's where he wants to be, so the P said he'd do the eulogy. He finally came down on, first of all, definitely not appointing a new Director but rather an Acting Director through the election, and everybody agreed that it should be Pat Gray. So that is the plan and it will be announced tomorrow.

We then got into the problem of the Summit, the P feeling that because of the Paris problem Henry got into yesterday and Henry's recommendation now, which is that we cancel the Summit, that we've got to at least consider doing so. He asked me to run a poll to determine what the reaction will be if the P should cancel the Summit on the basis of the continuing Communist invasion of South Vietnam supported by massive Soviet aid and military equipment.

Wednesday, May 3, 1972

Principal discussion today was again on the Summit cancellation. The P was tied up all morning with Leadership Meeting, the briefing by Moorer, some other things of that sort. He had me over first thing in the morning to set those up, to make the point that he wanted to postpone Annapolis for a week and keep the weekend clear, because if he does cancel the Summit, he's going to do it Monday night, on TV. Then he makes the point of whether there's a real question of what we get out of canceling the Summit, and whether that's the key to winning the war, and that's what he's got to weigh.

Later in the morning he was going over the thing again and made the point that the loss of the Summit would result in a massive Soviet propaganda war worldwide, and that the costs there are too high to pay for the short-term gain that we get for taking the positive action.

Then later in the afternoon I talked to Henry. He made the

point that there's no choice on the Summit, that we have to drop it, or else the Russians will, but we can't both bomb the North and have the Summit. That's Henry's strong feeling, and he feels it's essential that we bomb the North, now that we've told the Russians that we're going to take a hard line with them and with the Vietnamese if we don't get any action in Paris, and we haven't gotten any action.

The real question is how can we have a Summit meeting and be drinking toasts to Brezhnev while Soviet tanks are crumbling Hué. How can you have the P signing agreements for trade, arms, toasting peace and friendship and all that? It would be a very bad picture, and will display great weakness after the warning. On the other side, canceling the Summit is going to shatter the Nixon foreign policy; people don't like to see the government helpless. P came up with the line that going to the Soviet Union in the cause of peace while they're waging war would not serve the cause of peace. K makes the point that we have too weak a hand to go to Russia now, but on the other side the people want hope, not just blood, sweat, and tears all the time. So P told me to make the strongest case for going ahead, and to talk to Henry about it. He'll make no decision till Monday, and make the speech Monday night. My argument was that we should go ahead and bomb and see what happens. That we don't have to cancel the Summit, we can take the chance that they won't cancel it even if we do bomb. Then we have the best of both worlds. Henry's argument is, that creates a terrible problem for us because the worst possible thing would be for the Russians to cancel the Summit, blaming it on the Nixon bombings, which would make it look like we had really blown the chances for world peace.

I had quite a long anguished talk with Henry, who is obviously deeply disturbed by this. He makes the point that we have done a number of things wrong and he feels that he handled the Moscow meeting and the Paris meeting wrong, in the sense that he didn't leave any flexibility. He put the issue to them solidly as the P told him to, and they didn't back down, so now we're in a bad spot. He feels that because of that, we can't back down now, but it will leave the P in such a position of weakness that he wouldn't be able to govern even if he survived it. P feels on the other hand, that he can very well lose the election by what comes out of this and that it therefore becomes of vital importance.

In any event, he decided not to make any decision today and continue to ponder the thing. It turns out that Henry has sent a very strong letter from the P to Brezhnev, and there should be a reply on that tomorrow or the next day, and that will show the Russian attitude, which will be another factor in deciding what we do. The other thing was our poll results last night showed that 60 percent of the people feel that the P should go ahead with the Summit in spite of the invasion of Vietnam. In other words, there's strong popular demand here for the Summit, and that makes it even harder to figure out how to cancel it.

Thursday, May 4, 1972

Hoover funeral this morning. P did the eulogy and did an extremely good job. Rest of the day was devoted to the debate over the point of the Summit cancellation.

P called me in first thing this morning and said he had just gone over things with Haig. He's concerned about the public information operation in Vietnam, feels we have to ride Laird harder on watching the news reports, that they're letting incorrect things get out and not correcting them. Then he said he wanted K and me to see Connally, give him a cold-turkey briefing on the Summit situation, get his judgment, and says the other possibility for conferring would be Mitchell. In any event I called Connally from his office and set up an appointment for right after the funeral, and then the P said he had added an extra ingredient in the whole thing that he had thought of last night, which is that if we cancel the Summit, we go for all the marbles, including a blockade. He deplored again the problem of the military being so completely unimaginative. He said that I should try to get Connally to stay till June 1, that he can't leave in the middle of the Soviet flap, and the war will also be in better shape by then. He's concerned that if we cancel the Soviet thing we'll dash the hopes that we've created in the minds of people by the Soviet trip, that we'll get a very big bang against us with the Democrats on the warpath with Soviet support. He wanted to meet with Henry and me at 3:00 and go over the thing, so we went over to the EOB then and P made the point that he had made up his mind, that he can't lose the war, that the only real mistakes he had made in his Administration were the times when he had not followed his own instincts. On the EC-121 situation with North Korea, he knew we should move in and hit all their air bases but he let himself be talked out of it because Rogers and Laird both threatened to quit if he went ahead with it.

Started on 3:00 meeting with Henry. The P reviewed the point that mistakes were made, that he didn't follow his instincts, namely on Cambodia. We should have gone ahead and bombed the North at the time, although we didn't. If we had moved on that kind of move then, we wouldn't have these problems now. Same with Laos, that although Henry did basically follow his instincts on this thing, it worked as well as it could have. He said that he had been thinking it over, and that he'd decided that we can't lose the war. We're going to hit hard and we're going to move in. The Summit is not important in this context, and that going to the Summit and paying the price of losing in Vietnam would not be satisfactory.

He put it very toughly to Henry. He said he'd made up his mind, didn't want to get into a discussion about it, didn't want to be talked out of it. Henry kept trying to interrupt, but the P went on very strongly in this vein. He obviously sensed something of the drama of the moment and he was pushing his position very hard. When Henry finally did get to talk, he said that he too had been thinking about it, that the objectives that he came up with were the same as the P's. He agreed that we couldn't lose the war and that we had to do something. His difference, however, was that we should not move ahead with the bombing, as the P thought we should, but rather should first move to blockade Haiphong. The point being that bombing was what they were expecting and it's better to do the unexpected, first of all. Second, the blockade would in some ways be a less aggressive move than the bombing, although it would be a stronger signal to them and would do us more good. Henry's opposed to just a symbolic bombing, he feels that if we bomb we should do it totally, and that it would be better to blockade first and then on a continuing basis. Also by blockading it gives us a little more time to keep the bombers in the South, where the military wants them during the current tough action.

The more the P thought about it, the more he liked Henry's ideas as long as it was followed up with continued bombing, so that became his conclusion.

He then had Connally and Haig come over and join the meeting. After an hour and a half with that group we added

Moorer, and the P very strongly put the thing to Moorer. This was his decision, that it was to be discussed with no one, especially not the Secretaries or anybody at State, or anybody over in Vietnam. Moorer was to put the blockade plan together, get everything ready to pull it into motion so that it would take effect Tuesday morning. He hit Moorer on this is a chance to save the military's honor and to save the country. Moorer said he could do it; he also suggested that there ought to be some offensive action on the part of the South Vietnamese and it was agreed they would try to mobilize enough troops, 2,000 or 3,000 for an amphibious landing north of the DMZ by South Vietnamese using all our support and troop capability.

K had to leave for dinner. The P talked a few minutes more and then Moorer and Haig left and we kind of wrapped it up with Connally. Then the P talked with me a bit about the whole thing, feeling that he's done the right thing, that we justify the blockade as a means of keeping lethal weapons from the hands of murderers and international outlaws. I think he feels good that he's made a decision and that he feels it's the right one. He also feels that it's quite a dramatic step, because it is a basic decision to go all out to win the war now, under, of course, totally different circumstances than Johnson was faced with, because we've got all our troops out. We've made the peace overtures and we've made the China trip and laid a lot of other groundwork that should make it possible for us to do this.

My feeling is that the public reaction is not going to be so great on the blockade, even though it is a big move, because it's not aggressive, but the bombing that goes with it will, over a period of time, scare some people up. Some question as to what the *quid pro quo* will be on this, probably something to the effect that the blockade will stay on until there's a cease-fire, all POWs released. When that takes place, we'll lift the blockade and we'll remove all of our troops from South Vietnam within some time period.

Connally was absolutely astounded at the P's description of the problems he'd gone through and the other things, especially the lack of support and the lack of loyalty on the part of Laird and Rogers. I think he can't even understand why the P would even keep them around and thinks it's a sign of weakness that he hadn't fired them long ago and that he doesn't fire them now. He also strongly feels that he should pull Abrams back. The P backed off on that and I think rightly so.

Friday, May 5, 1972

In staff meeting this morning, we had a discussion of the Congressional situation regarding Vietnam. Apparently the doves now want to put their whole effort to curtail the P's powers, put the whole bill back regarding Vietnam funds. They don't want to be responsible for the defeats in the battlefields, which it looks like may be happening, or a cancellation of the Summit, which they are afraid might develop. The idea would be to recommit it to the Committee and bring it out on June 1. Our hawks want to do that, too, because they think we can probably play it as a victory.

We had a session with Henry and the P first thing this morning and Henry was very concerned because Rather had reported last night that the White House was speculating about a blockade. He's afraid that there's a leak here. I don't think that's it at all, I think a blockade is just one of the obvious escalation moves that the speculators are speculating on.

The P decided to leave at 4:00 this afternoon for Camp David. Told me to talk to John Andrews and have him plan to come at noon tomorrow. Explain to him that the P was going to give a speech regarding a decision that he may not agree with, but he should understand he's solely there for the purpose of implementing the P's ideas. He's not to raise questions regarding substance, because it's already decided. I told John this and he said he had no problem with that at all. We had some discussion of Congressional briefings for the speech. He's decided to go Monday night. He wants me to check the Monday TV schedule. He made the point that the Democrats are running a mortal risk because the enemies' refusal to negotiate is due to the House and Senate doves giving them encouragement, and encouraging them even in North Vietnam to continue their offensive. These people, who got us in, now are doing their utmost to see that we lose the war. Pretty tough position. The P did leave this afternoon for Camp David, and will stay there for the weekend working on the speech. I went on to Williamsburg with the family as planned.

Sunday, May 7, 1972

I went on up to Camp David from Williamsburg by chopper this morning. Henry was analyzing things, says he thinks the

Soviets will definitely cancel the Summit. There's no question but that they will launch a venomous attack on Nixon on the basis that he sabotaged the last chance for peace in the world. We had considerable discussion about follow-up and planning on the speech. The P wanted me to spend a lot of time on the use of K and his time. He thought that Henry should have a press conference on Tuesday and then Laird should have one on Wednesday.

The P had me over again at 6:00 to Aspen. Said he thought we ought to do a poll and have it ready to put out so that we could show support. Discussed the NSC meeting, getting the POW wives organized, disciplining the bureaucracy, and alerting the Cabinet that there's a major decision. In the midst of all that discussion he told me that he wanted to have Walter Annenberg donate a swimming pool to Blair House so the P has a place there to go swimming.

Monday, May 8, 1972

The P came down from Camp David last night after seeing a movie. He had an NSC meeting that went virtually all morning, from 9:00 until 12:00 and then went over to the EOB. Called Henry over. At 2:00 exactly the P said, "Well, it's 2:00, the time's up. We go." Henry was a little dismayed at that point and started arguing some more, but the P said, "Nope, the decision is made, no further discussion," and from then on I think he felt very solid on the thing and moved on that basis.

The speech went very well. I think we'll develop substantial support. At the Cabinet meeting the P explained the background, said that as far as the speculation on the Summit was concerned, we were aware of the worst there. An American P couldn't be in Moscow while the Soviet guns and tanks were in Hué and we should say we're prepared to go forward and negotiate or to continue with the Summit. The responsibility now is with the Russians. This decision wasn't easy, you can never be sure. The case for bombing, or doing nothing at all, all had to be weighed, but this is the best course at this time. To defend our interests, to get the POW's and to put an end to the war.

The VP said you can depend on all the Cabinet to support this, we're all aware of your strength over the three years, you've given careful notice ahead of all your actions, the Soviet part of your speech was extremely well phrased. The P said he wrote every word of that himself. He said the ball's now on their side of the net. Rogers said there's nothing really we can add to what you said. In all the departments we've got to get the word to our people that everybody should have a staff meeting in the morning. Tell them the chips are down, that it's easy to support when things are going well but we need to support now and there'll be all hell to pay if you don't. He said he was going to do that with his department and to tell the other Cabinet members that they should do likewise with theirs. Elliot Richardson said we've seen you a number of times on TV talking to the nation. I've never seen you more resolute or strong, or reflective, exceedingly thoughtful. There's a real possibility that the people will respond with support because of your leadership. The people want to respect and support. Rogers said that's a good line for all of us to take to our people.

The P then said, this HAS to work. We've crossed the Rubicon. It started with foolish gradual escalation by LBJ; this is cleaner and more defensible. We deny the enemy the sources to wage war. We have a definite, precise goal, to cut off the sources for making aggressive war. We should all reflect the same confidence, calm. We've done the right thing. We'll stick to the course. No weak men on the team.

Then after the Cabinet meeting he had me come over to the EOB, where we had some dinner and had Henry in. We reviewed some of the comments and Henry went out. Then he told me to talk to Connally on the basis that if the Summit's canceled, he has to stay a couple of weeks. If the Summit's on, he can go ahead and go.

We went through the switchboard being jammed, all the telegrams and that sort of thing. At 10:45 the P called Meany and asked for his support. The P closed by saying that there'll be a time when we'll all be together again. We got some good, very positive reactions, and I think we're in good shape on the response to the speech.

Tuesday, May 9, 1972

Main effort here was speech follow-up. I had all the troops in last night and then again this morning. Told them that we were setting up a little internal planning unit, that we're going to drive hard to maximize public response and laid out assignments.

Henry had his press conference this morning and did, in my view, a pretty bad job. He spent the first twenty minutes reviewing all the negotiations and going on *ad nauseam* about the background and everything. Then finally, did get into the questions and did a pretty good job there, getting most of our line across. Still no reaction from the Soviets, we're kind of sweating that one out.

Wednesday, May 10, 1972

He had Colson and K in today. Raised some points on followup, told me to get to General Walters and tell him to work independently on Vietnam propaganda, get stories in the South regarding the problems in the North, and stories in the North regarding the decimation of the regiments and lack of food and everything in the South.

Colson left and then Henry reported to us on his meeting with Dobrynin. He had told me earlier that he had to see him at 3:00. He was quite excited but it turned out that all Dobrynin had was a protest on the ship we sunk *(accidentally in Haiphong Harbor)* rather than any answer from the Russians on their reaction, particularly regarding the Summit.

Thursday, May 11, 1972

Still going on reaction, got some pretty good positive stuff. He was thinking of having a press conference tomorrow on the response from the Soviets. We did have a message back from them that was much milder than was expected. They protested the blockade but didn't demand any action in any kind of way that concerned our people.

The general feeling now, even on Henry's part, is that the Summit is going to be on rather than off, and so there's a level of optimism on that part. The general attack is going well, the P's mood seems to be very good, although he's tired. He left at about 4:30 after the Rogers meeting for Camp David with Bebe.

Friday, May 12, 1972

The problem at the staff meeting this morning was raised on the news that Defense put out last night that they're getting ready to go for supplemental appropriations in '72 and '73 because of the increased cost of Vietnam. Strong feeling in the staff meeting was that we should not allow them to do this.

Also had a problem with Defense saying that the blockade wasn't going to work and that we'd be faced with interdiction problems. This was on the news too. So we have to tighten up on them and watch what they're doing.

Haig gave a briefing at the staff meeting. He did a superb job of explaining the background, making the point that on Vietnamization we've always cut corners out there to meet the political problems at home, and that the current situation is not a failure of Vietnamization, it's a challenge of it. In January the P made a basic decision against General Abrams' recommendation not to wipe out the North Vietnamese buildup above the DMZ. He did this because of the public reaction at home and because there had been no attack on their part to provide us with open provocation. Then he engaged at that time in a monumental diplomacy effort, which of course didn't work. Then came the North Vietnamese invasion across the DMZ. Haig points out that there are two fundamental changes in the concept of Vietnamization. First, the DMZ restriction was violated, as with the '68 understandings. Secondly there was a change from guerrilla warfare to traditional war, which was not perceived by our planners. This has been marked by first, increased antiaircraft; second, long-range artillery on a massive basis; third, intensified density of armored tanks primarily. This created problems since we had cut everything to the bone anyway on the basis of our original concept. Also, the density of our helicopters is severely cut, so they don't have the aerial-supply or troop mobility that they had before. This was not a knee-jerk action on the part of the P to save United States honor. It was the action of a world leader who has developed a worldwide concept in a way that it's tied to his ability to function.

The P called first thing in the morning. He's up at Camp David for the weekend. He was saying that K was worried because his meeting with the Senate doves had been called off, and that he had been depressed about the news coverage, especially regarding the Summit. The P told him to relax, that a cancellation of the Summit cuts both ways and that it won't hurt us. I talked to Henry later and he said the P couldn't be more wrong—he wasn't the least depressed. The P also said Haig thinks that Monday was the turning point in the war, that the use of air power has changed the whole situation.

There was a lot of concern during the day about speculation

on the Soviet Summit and the P and Henry both pushed very hard to have everybody kept quiet on any kind of speculation. Henry met with Dobrynin in the afternoon, and the discussion was so strongly substantive that both Henry and the P both believe now that there's no chance of the Summit being canceled. They even got to the question of the exchange of gifts. The Soviets want to give the P a hydrofoil to play with in Key Biscayne and in return want a hot sports car from us. The P called me a couple of times, emphasizing the need to get everybody to keep quiet on speculations, since there had been some optimistic stories in the press this afternoon.

Monday, May 15, 1972

The P had a pretty busy schedule today but had me in first thing in the morning. He had written a lot of memos over the weekend, wanted to do some powerful discussion on trip plans. He's concerned about operational confusion around him, with too many aides and Secret Service and so on. Wants to cut way down on the people on the P's plane, etc. I warned him about the probable small reception in Poland, and he wants Radio Free Europe to build that up.

This afternoon we got the report that George Wallace was shot. I waited a while to try and get some information, finally went in a little after 5:00 and interrupted the P's meeting with Don Kendall and had him come into the Oval Office. I informed the P that we had the report that he had been shot. The P looked very annoyed at being told this and said, "Is he killed?" and I said, "No." I gave him a brief description of what, at that time, appeared to be the injuries and he said "OK" and went back into the meeting.

As the afternoon wore on, though, the thing built up steam. He asked to have Connally over and we discussed what he ought to do. It was agreed that he should put out a statement, which we did. That he should put Secret Service protection on Teddy Kennedy and Shirley Chisholm (*a black congresswoman who was also running for the Democratic nomination*), which he told Connally to do, and that he should go ahead and appear at the Blue Room dedication ceremonies, although he should not stay for the receiving line. He did this and it worked out extremely well because it gave him a chance to make a statement on television about Wallace, without having to set up a special occasion to do it.

He then hauled me over to the EOB and called Colson in a little later. Had us have dinner with him there and spent quite a little time going over it and trying to get reports on what actually had happened. He was very distressed with the FBI and the Secret Service for not being on top of things and knowing what was going on. We moved E in and he told Gray, who was Acting Director of the FBI, that he was holding the Bureau responsible for the safety of the prisoner they'd captured. We pushed Kleindienst, Pat Gray, and all the rest of them on a basis of trying to make sure that they understood that the question here was not on the legalities or specifics, it was one of trying to get the right posture set before the press immediately leaped on exactly the wrong thing and started making a big point of how the guy was a right-wing radical.

We got pretty good control of it finally and left at 8:15 to go to a Motion Picture Association movie. E and I came back to the White House at about 11:00, worked there until 12:00, getting updated and filling the P in on Wallace's condition and the status of the FBI interrogatory. Then we gave him a report about midnight and went on home. The battle between the FBI and Secret Service got going right at the beginning with jurisdictional disputes and then with each blaming the other for any of the mistakes that have been made. So we're back to the same old thing in that area.

Tuesday, May 16, 1972
The P had me in at 8:00, first thing this morning. Said he wanted to see E, Colson, and me right after the staff meeting. Wanted to be sure that his Secret Service is not increased at all. Doesn't want to allow a climate of fear to be created. He asked me to think of something he could do to go out today, maybe just go for a walk, or something. I suggested he go over to the Treasury after the Connally announcement. That would give him a chance to talk to the people in line waiting to get into the White House, which he agreed to do. He did, and it worked out great.

He feels that from a political standpoint this now assures Hubert's nomination, and he talked about that a little. At 8:45 we came in after the staff meeting. The Wallace prognosis is pretty grim. He probably can't be back on the campaign or anything in the way of normal work for at least three months and there's a good chance that he'll be partially paralyzed, permanently. The P feels this gives Hubert a tremendous boost with Wallace not nibbling him on the right anymore. Now he can move all the way to the left. He told E to do something fast today on the handgun thing, such as a ten-year automatic jail sentence for concealed weapons.

Cabinet meeting with the Connally announcement went pretty well. The P opened by giving a report on Wallace, on the outlook, and then describing the steps he had taken on Secret Service protection for Teddy and Chisholm. On Connally, he said that he had come in on December 14 with the understanding that he'd be here a year, and then because we were in the middle of the international monetary situation in December, he agreed to stay until the present time. Now the economy is moving and since we have the success of our inflation fight, we agreed that mid-May is the time to announce his departure. He'll stay until his successor is confirmed. Kleindienst then broke the room up by saying, "Good luck."

Wednesday, May 17, 1972
The P is still at Camp David. Called 10:15 this morning and then a couple of times right when we were playing tennis this afternoon. He said he told K to read the riot act to the writers on the Moscow speech; that he wants it cut to 1800 words. He definitely wants to take Andrews. He's going to read all his toasts or statements, and he wants them written for that purpose and not longer than 250 words. He called later to say he wanted it cut to 200 words maximum, 150 words preferable.

Thursday, May 18, 1972
The P's still at Camp David preparing for the Russian trip. Connally called me this morning. I talked to him a little about Wallace, he doesn't think Wallace can run as VP on the Democratic ticket. Hubert can't take him, because Wallace is stronger than Hubert, and third party's out of the question because he's come so far in the Democratic Party now that he'd have no reason to go over and diminish his stature. Connally feels that if he's smart, and he thinks he is, that he'll go through the Democratic Convention and then say that he can't take the platform or McGovern or whoever the nominee is so the best thing to do is elect Nixon. He would want to claim that he helped make a P, and this puts him in a good position.

Saturday, May 20, 1972–Soviet trip

Departure from Washington and flight to Salzburg. He had me
in a little after midnight when we got to the castle at Salzburg,
to report that he had talked to Rose and she was upset about
her accommodations, and the general situation which is the
usual thing on the first night on a trip.

Got into some discussion on how to handle Rogers, said I
should handle him tomorrow, that the P will see him on the
plane on the way to Moscow, and we should tell him about
the announcements and how we're spacing them through the
week. We got into some discussion of the demonstrators, who
were here in Salzburg. He was a little disturbed by it, but the
news play doesn't seem to be too bad.

Monday, May 22, 1972

(This is recorded in the P's car, sitting in the yard of the Kremlin outside the quarters where the P and our staff are staying.
It's now Wednesday afternoon, and I'll cover the period up to
this time.)

Started the day in Salzburg. Nothing eventful except the big
crowd on the motorcade route out and at the airport in Salzburg when we left, and a good flight into Moscow. The arrival
was proper and correct, as the news reported. It was as much
as we expected, but certainly no more than we either expected
or hoped for. The first surprise was the same kind of one we
had in China. As soon as we got into the Kremlin and settled
down, P was whisked off to meet with Brezhnev in his office.
Had about a two-hour meeting there, thus delaying the start of
dinner, which worked out very well, especially since it was
only the two of them. K did not sit in, so it didn't create the
problems that the Mao meeting did in China. Dinner went very
well, toasts were mediocre. No unusual problems.

At about 11:30, the P called me in to his room after he got
back from the dinner, sort of reviewed the day, especially the
meeting with Brezhnev, and the way it was set up. We have
already found horrendous problems on the motorcade's access
to the Kremlin and all that sort of thing. Our press didn't get
to the Brezhnev thing to get a photo, for instance. We had a
terrible time getting them into the dinner, and the right place
at the right time. The Soviets are not cooperative in these areas,
and apparently not at all understanding of the problem we have
in dealing with our press.

Tuesday, May 23, 1972

P was up at 4:30 this morning, went for a walk in the Kremlin. Got back around 5:30 and went back to bed and slept till about 9:00, I guess. He then went to a first plenary session. *(Rogers heard that Henry would be working on the communiqué and)* of course went up the wall. He had Henry and me in when we got back to his quarters, and he and Henry had dinner. I'd already eaten, but sat at the dining room table with them while we reviewed the whole thing.

The dinner went on till about 12:30, after which we all went to bed. The problems of logistics and operations seem to be working out a little better. We got Ziegler into the plenary session, and we're getting our press a little better posted. They seem to be in pretty good spirits. Problem now is our own staff, who are being kept out of everything, but that's inevitable.

Wednesday, May 24, 1972

P had me in this morning before the first head-to-head meeting. He and Henry feel pretty good because they think they got SALT pretty well wrapped up last night. It's now developed, as people think about it, that we're going to have a hell of a problem with the conservatives at home, and P's pushing hard for the Joint Chiefs, Defense people and other military to work on selling the hawks.

It turned out that at the morning session, Brezhnev brought in Gromyko and Kosygin and some others, so the P immediately added Rogers, and in the process gave Rogers responsibility for handling European Security Conference dealings, also the whole commercial thing. Henry's now afraid that everything he's put together is going to fall apart, and that we have a real problem on that. He told the P so, but not very clearly, not nearly as strenuously as he had told me. Actually, I think it's a pretty good solution, because it'll keep Rogers busy and satisfied, and it's the only way that realistically they're going to keep him out of getting into the communiqué-drafting business.

Henry's working hard, as he always does. He seems to be pretty uptight. He's working well with me, but is very brusque with others. P is in good shape, quite relaxed, taking things as they go. We did the Unknown Soldier this morning, and hoped to get in to the people, but we couldn't because the Soviets have it locked up so tight that there was no way for the P to get it loose. So we just gave up on it. Mrs. Nixon's having somewhat the same problem on her tours, but we've talked to the Soviet police and hope that some of this at least will be remedied.

After that, P had me in at 5:30 before the signing ceremony to go over some odds and ends on plans for the dinner. He wants Carver to be sure and play the Soviet anthem first, and he was concerned about his pancake batter for makeup and use on the TV Sunday night.

Then he went over to the signing ceremony and immediately afterward Brezhnev and he started down the hall with our advance party meeting them, and we thought they were going across to go into the Residence and down to get in his car when all of a sudden the P and Brezhnev disappeared down a corridor, zipped into an elevator, shot downstairs, came out into the driveway, popped into Brezhnev's car, and roared off, with Duncan *(Secret Service man)* just barely catching up. K had been waiting over at the Residence, planning to ride with the P out to the dacha to get a chance to talk with him, and the motorcade had left without him, K missed the whole thing and was, of course, furious, but got in the P's car and shot on out. They didn't get back until well after midnight.

Thursday, May 25, 1972

P had me in at 10:30 this morning and was reviewing last night. He said that he had been very tough on Vietnam and that this was the first time K had seen him operate like this. They had some problems on SALT as well, but most of the discussion was on Vietnam. He said they had been whisked away, went out on a boat ride as soon as they got to the dacha, and then went in and had talks. We didn't have dinner until 11:00.

Later, Henry came in and he told Henry to give me a report on the thing last night. Henry said that the P had been very tough and did a magnificent job, and that he was very, very cold after they blasted us on Vietnam, and he just sat there and let them run out their strength, and had done it superbly.

We spent a lot of time sitting around at noon, because the meeting that was supposed to be at 11:00 kept getting delayed. Henry then came in at 12:45, after we'd been there for an hour and a half or so in the P's room, to say that the schedule's now been set for 2:00 meeting on economics, and a 5:00 signing without the P there, and then Henry has to meet at 5:15 on SALT again. They're still fighting that one out.

Friday, May 26, 1972

Still struggling with SALT. At 11:00 Henry came in and said that they're developing their answer on SALT now, and he's to go get it. The Politburo's been meeting since 7:00 this morning on it, and there'd be no session this morning, it would be this afternoon on the Middle East, and the first question is whether Rogers should be there, because Gromyko will be, but they don't want Rogers there if anything's to be decided. So there was some discussion about that. Dobrynin then burst in and confirmed the schedule, and Henry and Dobrynin left. So the P was then stuck with four hours to kill.

Then at 11:30 K burst in again, to say he had just come back from the meeting Dobrynin had taken him off to. (*The Politburo had agreed on the final terms*) and they want to sign it today at 7:00 or 8:00. (*The schedule was later pushed back to 11:00.*) Then Ziegler called with the disastrous problem that the Soviets had released the commercial agreement which wasn't supposed to be put out till tomorrow, so Ron had to scurry and hold a briefing on that, which created something of a flap, but no real problem.

Shoved the dinner along as fast as possible, and ended up getting it over by just a little after 10:30, so the P wasn't in too bad shape in getting back for the signing ceremony, and it was held just a few minutes after 11:00, with everybody getting a great feeling of the historic nature of the occasion.

The problem, however, was Ziegler caught me on the way into the signing, said we had real trouble because things had gone astray at the presigning briefing, with K and Gerry Smith. Turns out that Smith came into the briefing, sort of took over from K and blew the answers on several of the items, creating totally the wrong impression, and had K right up the wall as a result. I got over to K during the signing ceremony, and under great strain convinced him, sort of, that he ought to go back and do another briefing after the signing. Klein would make sure that Gerry Smith was kept out of the way, and that Henry had the podium to himself.

After the signing, while we were waiting for Henry to go over, I spent about 45 minutes pacing up and down the halls of our quarters, trying to calm Henry down, as he was cursing Rogers and Smith. He had learned that Rogers had ordered Smith and *(negotiator Paul)* Nitze to stay on Henry's heels at all times, and under no circumstances allow Henry to have a press conference of any kind out of their presence. So that's why Smith had come into the thing. The more Henry and I talked, the more it became apparent to me that the problem was more psychological than real. In other words, Henry was upset because it hadn't gone the way he wanted it to go, but it really hadn't gone as badly as he was envisioning it in his own mind.

As we were waiting, the P called Henry and asked him to come in. This is about midnight. Henry reviewed the thing in more livid detail for the P. The P told me to call Bill Rogers and tell him that Ziegler was outraged by Smith's conduct at the briefing, that he was an utter disaster, that you're to shut him up; he's to do no more briefings without the express permission of the P or he's fired. I said, "You know, what good will that accomplish." The P said, "I guess you're right, it won't accomplish anything, so forget it." He brooded for a few minutes, picked up the phone himself, asked for Rogers, said, "I'll call him," and hung it up. Then he said, when he calls back, you take it, and tell him what I just said. So I did.

In any event I talked to Rogers, who was quite surprised by the whole thing, but did make the point to him that only Henry was to do the briefing, and that's the way it was to go.

So that night, as far as I was concerned, ended at about 1:00 or a little after. I went back to bed. P went to bed, but said Henry is to wake him up when he got back, which was, apparently, at about 2:00, and fill him in on how the briefing went. Apparently it went extremely well, so things got back on the track later on.

Editor's Note: The SALT treaty itself was historic—an ABM treaty on defensive weapons and an Interim Offensive Agreement establishing a temporary freeze on the numbers of ICBM's and submarine-launched missiles on each side.

Saturday, May 27, 1972

This was our trip to Leningrad. The crowds in Leningrad were huge, but they were totally restrained by the police, one or two blocks back from the motorcade. It was absolutely an eerie feeling to drive through the main part of the city with absolutely no one on the street except police and soldiers. A guard at the doorway to every apartment, the gate to every courtyard, with people all kept inside, behind the gates. On the cross streets, they were kept at least one, sometimes two blocks away, often with the streets blocked with a couple of dump trucks or buses so that there was no chance of people getting across, but always with huge numbers of troops. Still, great crowds of people at all these places, and actually along the main boulevard, but kept way, way back behind ropes and troops. They responded very warmly when we waved to them, although they didn't seem to wave of their own accord. It was obvious that they wanted to see us, and were not going to be given that opportunity by the Russians.

At the Tomb of the Unknown Soldier, we had a very impressive and solemn ceremony. The P was quite impressed by the mass graves, 20,000 people in each of them, and the fact that there are half a million Leningraders buried in that cemetery. He was very touched by the story of a twelve-year-old girl, Tania, who kept a diary that's in the little pavilion there, and he told Ron and me about it afterward at the guest house. Later used it in his toast at the luncheon and later on in the day said that he wanted Ray to use it in the speech tomorrow night on Soviet TV.

Editor's Note: The diary recounts how Tania slowly lost all of her family in the war, and eventually she too was killed.

We got into some discussion of the return speech, went over E's idea of going into sort of a campaign kickoff speech. The P thought that was ridiculous, and of course he couldn't get into that kind of thing, and totally rejected the idea. On the plane back to Moscow, he and I rode alone in the private compartment on the Russian plane, and discussed some of these things some more, and also the general political approach that it's not domestic issues that we should spend our time on, that's their issue, not ours. We should concentrate on the international, which is where we make the gains.

Sunday, May 28, 1972

We went to church first thing this morning. It went reasonably
well, although the Russians, as usual, had all the crowds out
of the way, and nobody saw us except the people in the church.
They had replaced a lot of the normal old folks who attend
the church with Russian KGB types, but it was still a good
event and well worth doing. It'll get good coverage back
home, I'm sure.

I got back and talked to Colson to get a reading on United
States reaction. He says that Friday night the SALT deal had
enormous impact, that the public before hadn't realized what
it would be, and now there's a great new realization that's
especially effective with the swing category type people. He
said that's the main thing that's come through, first is the overwhelming importance of the SALT agreement, second is the
very businesslike approach to the whole Summit, and the third
is Pat Nixon and her performance. He feels we won't get the
full impact on this for a week or more.

P gave his speech this evening at 8:30 to the people of the
Soviet Union, and it went very well, although we had a flap
at the last minute because the Soviets wouldn't let our 16mm
camera in, so we have no film coverage of it, only the video
tape. The reaction afterward was that everybody thought it was
great, even E thought it was so good that we ought to try to
get it replayed in prime time—thought the picture was great,
great setting, another historic event, big buildup, and so on. P
especially was anxious to get the Tania segment replayed because he thinks that's the most important part. He worked on
some follow-up plans along that line. I think we're in good
shape.

Monday, May 29, 1972

P had me in at 8:45 this morning, discussing the return speech.
K burst in to say that the Brezhnev meeting was set for
10:00. K and Gromyko had met last night up until 1:30, going
over Vietnam, and Henry thinks they made some progress. P
had me in at 12:30, and I was astonished to find him smoking
a Russian cigarette. He was obviously very pleased.

An uneventful departure from Moscow, except that the Soviet plane had one engine that wouldn't function, so after we
were all aboard and settled down, we had to get up and move
to the backup plane, which was incredibly embarrassing to the

Soviets. Then Kosygin and Podgorny came aboard. They had
brought the Air Marshal in charge of all civil aviation in to
see the P in his cabin, and said we will do with him whatever
you want. P said you should promote him. Then they looked
horrified. P said, oh, yes, because he was smart enough to stop
the plane before we got in the air and had a problem.

> *Editor's Note:* This answer by the P was a masterful stroke.
> This situation shows very graphically the difference in our cul-
> tures. The Soviets expected the P to possibly suggest some
> form of punishment, but he very wisely turned it around in
> such a way as to make the pilot feel good.

It was funny to watch the Russian TV, because they were
covering the thing live but cut it off as soon as the plane
problem started.

In Kiev, we had great crowds on arrival but they were kept
back several blocks, and so it was hard for them to see the P,
but they waved and hollered anyway.

Tuesday, May 30, 1972

Nothing special in Kiev this morning. P went through a lot of
trivia on the plane with me on the way to Iran. It was great
to get back on Air Force One, where we could really settle
down and talk. The arrival in Tehran was great, with huge
crowds and very friendly. Dinner was OK, I guess, but I had
a terrible seat, so I couldn't see any of it. The highlight was
the fact that there wasn't enough light for the P to see his text
for the toast, because of the TV lights, so he had to discard
the text and wing it, which didn't make him very happy. The
palace where he's staying and the guest house where we're
staying are lovely, and a great contrast to the Russian facilities.

Wednesday, May 31, 1972

The big problem this morning was some bombings in Iran
which resulted in the P coming down to his car to go to the
Shah's tomb. I got in with him and we waited for a few
minutes before taking off in the motorcade. Bob Taylor called
me out of the car to say that a bomb had just gone off right
at the tomb, and they felt the P should not go. The P said to
check with the Shah and see what he thought, and that he

would do whatever the Shah wanted. I had Chapin chec
through the Shah's administrative guy and it was clear that h
wanted us to go, although he left it that the P should do wha
he wanted. We talked that over, taking nearly 45 minutes, an
decided to go, even though we were by that time very late
Everything worked out fine, but we had the Secret Servic
pretty scared during the process.

The trip to Poland was uneventful. Arrival there was not a
big as we thought it might be, but very big crowds on th
streets, and they surprisingly allowed them up pretty close
They didn't get quite as emotional as they apparently had i
'59, but they were friendly, wanted to wave, and we did a
extremely effective job of running the motorcade up to th
tomb and then having the P move to his own car, taking leav
of the Prime Minister and drawing the crowd to him as h
stood up in the car.

He got out and was completely engulfed by Poles. The
started shouting "Neek-son, Neek-son, Neek-son," and the
they sang their song about may you live a hundred years.
all got quite emotional and was extremely impressive. Problen
here was the arrival statement at the airport. Our interprete
supplied by State, was apparently no good, as a number of th
Poles told me, so we made a change and used the Polish in
terpreter for the dinner, and we'll use him for the rest of th
activities here.

P got into some discussion about midnight, when he had m
in after the dinner, on the speech. Made the point that h
wanted me to check out how we happen to have a girl flut
player in the Peace Corps playing in the orchestra in Iran fc
the dinner music. He felt this was a ridiculous use of Peac
Corps funds. He made the point that in the car this morning
as we were driving to the Shah's tomb, that we probably ha
too much staff on the trip, with which I agreed, and he sai
the trouble is, when you have too many spear carriers along
you find that every time you turn around, they're sticking yo
in the ass with a spear.

Thursday, June 1, 1972

On the plane to Washington, the P spent most of the tim
working on the speech and trying to take a nap. He had Henr
and me in a couple of times. Sort of reviewing the whole tri
what a great job the advance men had done, what a great jo

K had done, the lot of hard work that was involved, how tired he was and how tired he knew Henry was, that sort of thing.

We got back, with the helicopter, drove that to Congress, and he made his speech in very good shape, although I was concerned because he was so tired that he might have trouble. Didn't turn out that way at all. He called me at home after the speech, and said he didn't know whether it was worth it or not. He's had the feeling all along that the speech was dangerously anticlimactic, and that we probably should have just finished the trip and let it go at that, but the first reaction would indicate that he's wrong, that the speech itself has had a great effect, and was very well worth doing.

He has decided to go to Florida tomorrow, which is a good thing, he's much better off down there than he would be at Camp David. He is extremely tired. He feels that he can't do anything on the domestic side because his judgment wouldn't be any good, and if there are any decisions to be made, E should go ahead and make them.

End of the Soviet trip

Friday, June 2, 1972
Had the Leadership Meeting this morning. Then the P took off for Key Biscayne. I didn't go. He called this afternoon to say that it was bad weather down there, but the base commander had several thousand people out with flags, signs, and cheering. Much stronger reaction than after China, and he feels that the Russian trip goes to the heart of what people are worried about and therefore creates a greater reaction than China's more superficial effect.

Wednesday, June 7, 1972
At Camp David. The P called me over at 10:30 this morning. He wanted to talk about the California primary results. (*McGovern won by 5.4 percent over Humphrey.*) He wants Buchanan to write a McGovern speech making the point that he's a sincere dedicated radical. He's concerned that we not let him get back on track as a reasonable man. We've got to lock him into his far-left positions. McGovern said he'd go to Hanoi and settle Vietnam in 90 days by saying it doesn't take 90 days to surrender.

Friday, June 9, 1972

E was up today. He had the meeting with the P at 11:00. It's a beautiful sunny day. We went over to meet the P at Birch. He had a fire going in the fireplace, which was sort of incredible. We need savage attack lines against the McGovern positions. Get McGovern tied as an extremist. Don't give any ground regarding the fact that he's changed his position.

The P then made the point that the difference between a conservative radical and a liberal radical is that the conservative is consistent. That's why he's conservative. Whereas the liberal will change in order to win. The conservative would rather lose and maintain his principles. The liberal would rather win and then try to bring his principles into effect. People around McGovern know what power is and they want it at any cost, so they'll change their positions to get it. We have to emphasize looking at his record. That it speaks louder than his words. His ADA voting record and so on. He's guilty by association by bringing in *(left-wing liberals)* Abbie Hoffman, Jerry Rubin, Angela Davis. We should get a maximum number of pictures of rowdy people around McGovern, while we go for the all-out-square America.

We then got the report from Colson on the Muskie press conference, where he did not withdraw in favor of McGovern, which is good news for us. Abruptly at about 7:15 this evening the P called me and said he was going home. How fast could we get up his helicopter, and he whipped out at 8:00. So I drove on home a little later.

Monday, June 12, 1972

The P had me in this morning. He wants Dent to go out and see Wallace, also Strom Thurmond to be sure we have approval in maintaining contact with him. Then call Lukash *(the P's physician)* to get a report on Wallace's current condition, and there's the question of our needing to find out what Wallace wants. See if we can make a deal with him.

Mitchell told me that he and the P discussed the Connally question. Mitchell reported on his luncheon with Connally before Connally went on his trip, at which time he asked him directly if he wanted to be VP. Connally said no, that he is interested in being P, but it's clear that he didn't see the VP as the route to that. Mitchell's view is that he wants to be Secretary of State and move from there. He did commit to changing parties and asked Mitchell when he ought to do it. Mitchell said after the election, which Connally agreed to. Mitchell feels we should go on our basis that we have to therefore assume that Agnew is the candidate, but we should work on a deal with him and make sure we've got things split up right without letting him develop a high price for taking the job.

Wednesday, June 14, 1972

The P got into a discussion this morning of his concern about the management of the campaign committee. He had been talking to Colson, who had pumped him full of what a bad job we're doing. He also was concerned about the contributors problem. The fact that they're hitting us on not releasing our list. He wants us to have our major contributors make a minor contribution now so that they get their names listed so people won't attack us for not having the names on there.

Sunday, June 18, 1972

At Key Biscayne. The P is still over at Walker's this morning. I talked to him over the phone. I reported to him on Shultz's meeting with Meany yesterday, which came out to be pretty interesting. Meany had called him, wanting to meet with him, and so they had a game of golf during which Meany told him under no circumstances could he possibly support McGovern. That he was working to try and get Humphrey the nomination still, but if that failed he could not support McGovern. The big flap over the weekend has been news reported to me last night, then followed up with further information today, that a group of five people had been caught breaking into the Democratic headquarters *(at the Watergate)*. Actually to plant bugs and photograph material.

It turns out that there was a direct connection *(with CRP),* and Ehrlichman was very concerned about the whole thing. I talked to Magruder this morning, at Ehrlichman's suggestion, because he was afraid the statement that Mitchell was about to release was not a good one from our viewpoint. Magruder said that we plan to release the statement as soon as the fact that the Committee is involved is uncovered, which it now has been. It says that we've just learned that someone identified as an employee of the Committee was one of those arrested *(James McCord, Jr., CRP's security coordinator).* He runs a private security agency and was employed to install the system of security at the headquarters. He has a number of clients. He's not operating on our behalf or with our consent. We have our own security problems, not as dramatic as this but of a serious nature to us. We don't know if they're related but there's no place for this in a campaign. We would not permit or condone such a thing.

The real problem here is whether anything is traceable to Gordon Liddy *(formerly with the White House plumbers unit, and then with CRP)*. He *(Liddy)* says no, but Magruder is not too confident of that. They were thinking of getting Mardian back to Washington (Mitchell, Mardian, Magruder, and LaRue are out in California) to keep an eye on Liddy. *(Mardian was formerly Assistant Attorney General in charge of internal security, now one of Mitchell's assistants at CRP. LaRue was CRP Deputy Director.)*

They think that McCord, our security guy, will be okay, but he's concerned about Liddy because of his lack of judgment and reliability. He's also concerned that two or three others are implicated. Apparently there's some cash and Magruder thought it was the DNC's, but it turns out it was ours.

I talked to Ehrlichman after that and he thinks the statement is OK and we should get it out. I talked to Colson to tell him to keep quiet. It turned out that one of the people *(implicated)* was on our payroll until April 1. A guy named Howard Hunt, who was the guy Colson was using on some of his Pentagon Papers and other research type stuff. Colson agreed to stay out of it and I think maybe he really will. I don't think he is actually involved, so that helps. So far the P is not aware of all this, unless he read something in the paper, but he didn't mention it to me.

With this first reference to the break-in, it's important to make two points. The first is, as the Watergate story unfolds, it has been left virtually uncut in the book. The full text of my diaries has been edited down by approximately 60%, but because Watergate is of such historical interest, it has been left to stand on its own. The important fact to note is that although uncut, the material on Watergate is minimal, as it was not a major concern until April 1973, the month of my resignation.

The second point is one of clarification. Much has been writ-

ten about the cover-up that brought down the Presidency.
Because history is more art than science, it is remembered
now only as it was chronicled then; this unfortunately is not
always as it actually happened. We never set out to construct
a planned, conscious cover-up operation. We reacted to Watergate just as we had to the Pentagon Papers, ITT, and the
Laos/Cambodia operations. We were highly sensitive to any
negative PR, and our natural reaction was to contain, or minimize, any potential political damage. Our attempts at containment became linked to other acts within the Administration
and were eventually labeled "the Watergate cover-up."

Monday, June 19, 1972

The P came back from Walker's yesterday afternoon and decided to stay over last night. Then this morning at dawn it
wasn't bright and clear so he decided to stay in until 7:30 this
evening. He reported that he had a long talk with Billy Graham. Graham has a line to Wallace through Mrs. Wallace, who
has become a Christian. Billy will talk to Wallace whenever
we want him to. The P feels our strategy must be to keep
Wallace in the Democratic Party and Billy can help us on that.
So immediately after the Democratic Convention, I'm supposed to call Graham and Graham should put the pressure on
Wallace to decide whether he's going to be used as a spoiler,
which would surely elect McGovern. Main key for us is to
keep this a two-way race. We talked to Mitchell about who's
going to talk to Wallace and how we're going to handle what
his price is.

Tuesday, June 20, 1972

We got back into the Democratic break-in again. I told the P
about it on the plane last night. He was somewhat interested.
The more he thought about it, it obviously bothered him more,
because he raised it in considerable detail today. I had a long
meeting with Ehrlichman and Mitchell. We added Kleindienst
for a little while and John Dean for quite a while. The conclusion was that we've got to hope the FBI doesn't go beyond
what's necessary in developing evidence and that we can keep
a lid on that, as well as keeping all the characters involved
from getting carried away with any unnecessary testimony.

The P was concerned about what our counterattack is, our

PR offensive to top this. He felt we have to hit the opposition with their activities. Also put out the point that the libertarians have created public callousness. Do they justify this kind of thing less than stealing the Pentagon Papers, or the Anderson files, and so on. He feels we should be on the attack for diversion, and not just take it lying down. He raised it again several times during the day, and it obviously is bothering him. He had Colson over to talk about it, and then later called me a couple of times on various specifics. He called at home tonight, saying that he wanted to change the plan for his press conference and have it on Thursday instead of tomorrow, so that it won't look like he's reacting to the Democratic break-in thing.

Wednesday, June 21, 1972

Staff meeting this morning was mainly on economics and the Congressional outlook. The Price Commission meets today, and there's some concern they may take some action on food prices. Consumer price index out today. Some concern about the Mansfield Amendment.

The bugging deal at the Democratic headquarters is still the main issue of the day. The P is somewhat concerned about it. Had Colson in this morning, presumably to cheer him up, but got into strategy on it, which was exactly what I don't want to do with Colson.

Colson apparently told the P that Bebe has been involved (*according to a report*) by Jack Anderson. He knows the Cubans or something like that (*3 of the 5 arrested at the Watergate were Cuban*). The P wanted me to check that out. And his main concern, of course, is that we make sure we keep the White House out of it.

He thinks Dole ought to attack (*DNC Chairman Larry*) O'Brien for his malicious libeling and guilt by association of the White House and the P.

Mitchell and Ehrlichman and I talked about the whole thing again this morning, and Ehrlichman comes up with the possible scenario of moving the guilt level up to Liddy. Having him confess and going from there. The problem is apparently we can't pull that off because Liddy doesn't have the authority to come up with the amount of money that was involved and that's now known under the campaign spending act requirements. So it would have to go up to Magruder in order to reach a responsible point. And that they, I'm sure, won't want to do.

The P got into concern about the campaign organizations citing an old rule which the P believes in strongly, that a campaign team must be lean in their conduct. They must think of themselves as the candidate. Avoid ostentatious appearance in terms of hotel suites, booze, and fancy restaurants and all because it just gives the opposition ammunition about us being the party of the fat cats and it's also hard to justify to our contributors and volunteers. He thinks this has to be handled very toughly with all the campaign staff. Mitchell should tighten up the organization so it doesn't look fat. Then he felt we needed a counterattack on McGovern's huge spending program. He also thinks every time we have a leak in our organization we should charge that we're being bugged. Even if you plant one and discover it.

Thursday, June 22, 1972

The Democratic headquarters break-in case took some good bounces today. The main one being that we got Judge Richey to handle the civil case. *(The DNC had filed a $1 million suit against the CRP.)* He's an Eisenhower judge. The Democrats made a mistake in their pleading because they made it impossible to have a Democratic judge, because they filed a suit on behalf of all Democrats so any Democratic judge would be a party to the suit. We've also learned that they can't trace the currency *(which the break-in people had been carrying)* and that they have no case on Hunt, and no warrant for him. So we seem to be in pretty good shape. They're going to continue to crank up the Cuban operation, leave Liddy out of the line of fire and get the FBI situation straightened out. So at the moment, at least, that looks to be in good shape.

Friday, June 23, 1972

Henry got back this afternoon *(from China)*. Met with the P and Rogers for a while and then went on up to Camp David with the P for dinner and spending the night tonight, and then he comes back down tomorrow to do a press briefing tomorrow morning.

The Democratic headquarters break-in has gone the other way now. Apparently Dean feels the investigation is out of control. *(FBI Acting Director Pat)* Gray doesn't know what to do in controlling the Bureau. They traced some of the money to one of our contributors and also the thing that came out of the Mexican bank. They'll know who the depositors are on that today. *(Campaign money from CRP had been channeled through Mexico to Bernard Barker, one of the break-in crew.)* Apparently, an informant also came in the Miami office, saying that he had a photographer friend who was developing films for Barker, including pictures of the Democratic National Committee letterhead. They feel the whole thing is at the brink right now. And it'll either open it all up or be closed. The FBI is convinced it's the CIA that's doing this, and Gray's looking for a way out of the investigation. So we talked to Walters and had that worked out.

Editor's Note: CIA Deputy Director Vernon Walters was to call Gray and tell him to stay out of it because it involved the CIA. That would give Gray the excuse to stop.

Sunday, June 25, 1972

At Camp David. The P called me over at noon for about two hours. The P got into some political stuff. He's analyzing the McGovern thing. They now are using three devices to change their image. First, the platform to get him off the hook. Second, the acceptance speech, which he'll go very moderate on, and third, the turn to the right by the VP candidate selection. That's going to be a tough one to do, but it's possible that he'll succeed in it.

We were talking about Wallace and maybe he ought to go out and see Wallace this week. At least give him a phone call. He wants to be sure we provide him with a plane to go to the convention without any fanfare, any obligation on Wallace's part.

Got into the Martha Mitchell problem. Apparently she called Helen Thomas *(of UPI)* the other night and said if John didn't get his ass out of politics she was going to kick him out of the house, but her phones were then pulled out either by her or someone in her room. She's demanded that they be reinstated, and the phone company has delayed on it, and she's now threatened to the phone man that if they don't get her phones in, she's going to blow the whole Republican deal, whatever that means.

Monday, June 26, 1972

The P is all cranked up about his baseball all-time-great story *(which the AP had asked him to write)*. Wants Ziegler to figure out how to handle this Nixon byline. He apparently dictated it yesterday at Camp David, and has figured out a super all-time team. One prewar, one postwar, one for the National League, one for the American League.

He got into a number of political things today. His principal concern throughout the day was the Martha Mitchell question. John Mitchell called me this morning and said he was going to go up to New York to get her and try and work out the problem. The P feels that John's got to close her down somehow or lock her up. But he can't just leave her speaking out like this. It's going to create a major national problem. He seems more concerned about that than about the Watergate caper. The problems on Watergate continue to multiply as John Dean runs into more and more FBI leads that he has to figure out ways to cope with.

Tuesday, June 27, 1972

P got back into the need to line up Democrats, thinks that we're not under tight enough control on that. That we should be lining up not only their Congressional and other VIP's, but all the education, labor, religious, and so forth leaders that we can. That it has to be done now before the McGovern cleanup operations start after the convention.

He made the point that the theory is that the American people are like helpless children yearning for leadership, someone to tell them what to do, and therefore you have to keep doing something in order to satisfy this yearning. This is the current theory pretty much.

K came in and he acted all excited that Dobrynin had come in to tell him that the Soviets are sending a man over to negotiate the grain deal. At quite a substantial level and that we can move on whenever we want to. The P said he wants to hold it to settle right after the Democratic convention, and we also said we can start the plenary session as he's worked it out, in Paris and Vietnam on the 13th, the secret session the following week, and that he has no concern about being able to keep the plenary thing going for several weeks, although the P was afraid it would blow right then. The P got into quite a thing about his baseball piece he's written for the AP, the all-time great teams. He dictated it Sunday afternoon and he's spending an incredible amount of time today on the whole thing. Working out all the little details of which relief pitcher the American League prewar should be on, and all that sort of stuff. Kind of fascinating and not just a little amusing.

He talked to Billy Graham, and Billy was calling to offer to help between John and Martha Mitchell on their problem and he's concerned about the publicity about Martha saying that John's in dirty politics. He thinks we need to do something to cope with that.

Wednesday, June 28, 1972

The P holed up today to work on the press-conference preparation for tomorrow night. He did have Colson and me in at noon for a general political discussion. He got going on the analysis of the '60 campaign again, and particularly hitting that Ted Kennedy quote today, that Nixon was way ahead of Kennedy in '60 and then fell behind, which he thinks should be shot down because it's not true. Wants to be sure we put a lid on stories of how well-computerized we are, and we should stop anyone from speculating on the P role in the campaign. Made the point that the Presidency has to come first. We need to build up the volunteers, the youth and so forth. Tell the pros to work and not be seen. Had some discussion on the Billy Graham thing. He's very concerned about letting the view get across that McGovern is the religious leader in the campaign because he is a former preacher and the son of a preacher.

Talked some with the P about the Mitchell situation. He's come to the conclusion, as have I, that Mitchell's got to pull out of the campaign and that we'd better put someone else in. I talked about this with Ehrlichman and Higby some today. And our general agreement is that *(former GOP Congressman Clark)* MacGregor is the one to do it. Interestingly enough, the P has come up with the same view. So he told me to pursue it with Mitchell and see what I could work out. I couldn't get to John today, although he has left with Martha and has come back to Washington. So I'll get him tomorrow morning.

The P called me from Camp David after he went up there late this afternoon to work on his press conference. Mrs. Nixon was all upset about some newspaper story that we've hired a girl to handle the daughters and Pat Nixon's scheduling. Some more of the same old stuff, where she resents anything implied that she has to have any help.

Thursday, June 29, 1972

The P stayed at Camp David until midafternoon, then came down. He had me come over right after he got back to give him a report on the Mitchell situation. I had a long talk with John just before that, and fortunately he's come up also with the conclusion that he's got to leave, and he made the big pitch to me as to why, giving me the whole background story on Martha. She felt Pat Nixon had snubbed her at the Duke alumni reception, and then very definitely she had snubbed her at the celebrities reception in California last weekend or the weekend before last. After that, John left without telling her about the Watergate caper. She discovered that in the papers or on TV, blew her stack, got drunk, told her FBI agent and John's secretary, who were staying at the Newporter with her, that her husband had every Democrat in Washington bugged, and then decided she'd call a reporter and tell him. The FBI agent got concerned at that and called John in Washington and got Fred LaRue, who said if she starts to do that, pull her phone out. So the FBI guy took his key, went up to her room, unlocked the door, went in and pulled her phone out. She then had a monumental tantrum. Started throwing things at him, demolishing the room. They locked her in. She busted the window with her hand, cut herself badly. They had to get a doctor, who had to throw her on the bed and give her a shot in order to subdue her.

Mitchell then sent some friends of theirs out from New York to get her back. They took her to the Westchester Country Club. The press got in to her there. She gave her story out. Her whole pitch is that she's absolutely serious about leaving John if he won't leave the campaign. He feels she's suicidal as well as a little cracked, plus drinking very heavily, and that there's nothing he can do to cure it. He's afraid she'll jump off the balcony at the Watergate. So he's got to quit. He'll stay on as a consultant and help us with the campaign, but will move to New York and pull out. That solved my having to raise the thing, I let it go in this instance and it worked out very well.

McGovern had a bad day today. He lost most of the California delegation on a credentials committee ruling and blew his stack, which looked pretty bad on TV. Then he's been widely picked up with his quote, that begging is better than bombing, that he'd be happy to go beg Hanoi to release the prisoners.

The P had a press conference tonight on TV. Went very well. He let it run 45 minutes. Got a lot of good questions. Some pretty bad ones. He was in better form in a sense because he wasn't so completely programmed. More relaxed, some good quips, no nervousness.

Friday, June 30, 1972

The P had a pretty full morning, although he had me in for quite a while before his first appointment. I missed the staff meeting as a result. He just wanted to chat about the action of the press conference and his general approach to the Mitchell meeting later today.

At noon he had Colson and me in. Said he had given the Cost of Living Council a lecture on press relations, which grew out of my discussion with him on Scali's memo feeling that we should move away from White House and Presidential attack on the press, except for factual accuracy. He made the point that they are ideologically against us, but we make a mistake when we react personally rather than on the issues, which is the mistake Agnew and Reagan made. He wants us to change our strategy on that, which we'll do. He then told the Lincoln story about the problem Lincoln had with his Cabinet. He fired one of the Cabinet members, then a friend said they're all so bad, why didn't you fire them all? Lincoln said that reminded him of the story of the farmer who caught nine skunks, put them in a pen, killed one of them and the stench was so bad he let the others go.

We got into the Mitchell thing at lunch today. The P had John and me over at the EOB. Lunch was served on the table in his conference room and while John and I had crab soufflé, the P ate his pineapple and cottage cheese salad. We agreed that it should be worked out. Covered some of the details of announcement procedure and then adjourned to try to work out a statement. The P met at 5:00 with MacGregor and told him he wanted him to take on the campaign manager job. We went into some of the details with him and think we have the whole thing set.

There's some new problems on the Watergate caper. Leading us to a probable decision that the way to deal with this now is to put all of them together, tie it all into Liddy's lap and let him take the heat for it, which is actually where it belongs anyway.

Third Quarter: July–September

From this point in time until the election on November 8, my days were spent increasingly on the reelection campaign. The diaries certainly reflect this. There continued to be many other duties to perform, most of which were delegated to others. It is both a blessing and a curse to campaign as the incumbent. You will certainly see in this section the importance we put on staying in office, and though it may look as if we played rough in this pursuit, we were no rougher than many other candidates, Republican or Democrat.

Sunday, July 2, 1972
(San Clemente) The P called just to check in, go over the Sunday news. Thought things had played very well, and seemed to be very relaxed.

Thursday, July 6, 1972
We had our MacGregor meetings today starting at about 10:40 with MacGregor, Malek, Timmons, and E. The P questioned Magruder as Chief of Staff *(of CRP)* and MacGregor assured him that's not his role. That will be Malek's role. Tell MacGregor to get the Colson operation under control but let people think they're running it. We should maintain a low visibility at the Democratic convention. No truth squad or anything of that sort. MacGregor should concentrate on the big plays, and he said that very few make the move onto the national scene effectively because they think parochially. We should give word to all speakers that they should not hit McGovern this week during the Democratic Convention. That

pretty well wrapped up the MacGregor meeting.

The P and I then met for a couple of hours with E afterward. Got into the Watergate caper problem. Walters apparently has finked out and spilled the beans to Pat Gray, which complicates the issue substantially.

Editor's Note: Walters had met with Gray, but told him the CIA had no interest in Watergate. Also, that he thought people in the White House or CRP were covering something up, with which Gray agreed. The President had told him to go ahead with his investigation:

Saturday–Sunday, July 8 and 9, 1972
Had no contact with the P. He took the weekend off and so did I.

Monday, July 10, 1972
He called in the morning on some odds and ends, and then again late this evening at the end of the Democratic convention on TV. Making the point that it was just hard for him to believe that the Democratic Party was actually nominating McGovern, but obviously they are.

Tuesday, July 11, 1972
Billy Graham called to give me the names of all his Christian youth types. He's very enthusiastic and thinks we have a very good group to work with us. He also feels we have a good chance on the blacks by splitting them and getting the religious blacks who are scared of the criminal elements and so on to come over to our side. He thinks we're in good shape with the Jews.

Later this evening the P called asking about some details on the convention. How we are handling ours, and so on. He says that we have the candidate we want now as our opponent, but if they take Teddy as the VP then we'll have to change our tactics a little. Quite a little laboring and thought about Teddy. He asked me to do some checking to see whether anybody agreed with the possibility that Teddy was going to take the VP, but all our people, all our analysis, says that he will not. The P felt we should still put out a prediction that he was going to, so that we could shoot it down as a cynical move if he does do it. We decided not to do this, because there doesn't seem to be any possibility really of his taking it.

Thursday, July 13, 1972

I started with the P at 9:00 this morning on our general political discussion. He wants to review the plans for our convention. Feels that immediately after the convention he should not appear to coast and therefore should not come to California, but rather go back to Washington and get right into going on things. The P is concerned with Rose. She feels that the P should shake hands with all the delegates at the convention. Which he's not about to do. She's making the point that we don't have the enthusiastic intelligent young people that McGovern has and so on. He's concerned about campaign material. Wants a report on what we're doing on the bumper strips and buttons and all of that. K came in and we had some discussion of the briefing of McGovern and finally agreed that K should do the first briefing. Henry feels strongly that he should do it so that he can cover the kinds of things that we want to be sure McGovern gets and doesn't get. Then after that we would like Haig and Dick Helms to handle the follow-up briefings.

Connally arrived this afternoon. We had our Connally dinner tonight. Just the three of us at the Residence. We were planning to watch the acceptance speech, but the convention got screwed up. It was delayed so late that we went home and then watched it after we got home (*it was nearly 3:00 AM EST before McGovern gave his acceptance speech*). Connally is obviously very tired. Obviously interested in and willing to take on hitting up the Democrats, but concerned about getting that involved and is very much worried how he can get the time to do it in the next few weeks, especially in getting all the details set up.

It looked as if we were going to lose the sale. So I suggested that we put Colson full time on this for the time being. Let him work under Connally. Get it set up for him and then let Connally replace him with his man when he's ready to. Connally bought that, and on that basis I think we'll put the thing together at our meeting tomorrow.

After we got home late tonight, the P called after each of the major speeches, the Eagleton speech, Kennedy speech and

McGovern speech at the convention. He felt that Eagleton was
not good. Didn't come over well on TV, although he basically
looks pretty good. *(Senator Thomas Eagleton of Missouri had
been picked as the VP nominee.)* He felt McGovern did exactly
what he thought he would do in trying to pacify his party but
not terribly effectively, and agreed with me and I think everyone agreed that Teddy Kennedy completely upstaged both of
them and the contrast was quite remarkable.

Friday, July 14, 1972
Connally, K, and the P met for a couple of hours this morning and then Connally, the P, and I got together again over
at the P's Residence in the study, and it worked out pretty
well. Connally thinks McGovern's going to scare the country
on the whole leadership question and that we should set up
the contrast just by being a leader. He discussed Wallace, and
it was agreed that we've got to make the Wallace move, and
that Connally should go see him, but Connally needs to know
where the ball is now and wants to talk with Mitchell about
it first. Colson should go to Texas and meet with Connally
to get the basic plans worked out and then we'd go ahead
from there. Then we talked about the Wallace question.
Mitchell reported that Wallace backers had been having fist-
fights in Miami. That we got the story that they wanted to go
with the third party, on TV, and that this is what we wanted.
Mitchell thinks this is a phony story, but feels that we need
to move on the basis of it being possibly true. We've got to
get Billy Graham to explore it, and I talked with Graham,
who agreed that he would help turn Wallace off and he thinks
that it would be a disaster for Wallace to go on a third-party
ticket.

Tuesday, July 18, 1972
The P had Colson up for part of the flight and got into the
Wallace question with him. Colson's got a lot of input which
indicates that some of Wallace's key people want $750,000 to
keep their staff on through the election. That if we'll do that,
they'll come out for Nixon. Wallace won't, but some of his
people will, and the whole organization will work for us. So
now we've got to figure out whose deal is for real and how
to handle it.

John Dean called while we were en route home and said he

had to meet with Ehrlichman and me immediately, so we waited on the plane and met with him for about an hour at the airport. He had been keeping us posted on his very real problems in the Watergate caper business. Flew out to California one day and met with the two of us. The problem now is that there is no way we can turn off the investigation and it's leading into the channels that we don't want it in. There's no way to avoid that. As of now, Dean feels that they are going to move on Magruder and that the only thing we can do is to have him take the rap that they'll hit him with. And he feels that I've got to talk to him and convince him that this is what he should do. I'm not at all sure that's the way to handle it, that I can do it. But Ehrlichman called me at home later and confirmed that he thought we should do that, although he'd adjourned the Dean meeting after it became clear that he couldn't read exactly what my reaction was on it. This is a real powder keg, I guess, and John's sitting on top of it. John Dean is trying to keep the lid on, but is not at all sanguine as to his ability to continue to do so.

Wednesday, July 19, 1972

The P got into an analysis of McGovern. Says that there's a conclusion we've all missed. That McGovern's shift to his moderate position will be allowed by the press and by his people, because the radicals on the left want power, while the radicals on the right want consciousness. The liberals are destructive of the establishment. The right wants to conserve the good things. The left will never let McGovern compromise on power, that is control of the party, but they will let him compromise to get power. The goal is power by any means. The press, or antiestablishment, don't believe in the P, so they will do all they can to get one of theirs in. So our whole goal must be to keep McGovern hard on the left.

Connally called to say the most important man to all of us in this Democratic thing is Marvin Watson, who's entirely with us all the way. Has all the files and so forth but as the Executive Vice President of Occidental *(Petroleum)* now, we don't want to hurt him professionally. Armand Hammer *(head of Occidental)* wants to see the P regarding his Russian deal, so Connally talked to him. Told him we have to have Watson. Hammer said if the P asks and really wants him, he'll work it out, and the P will see Hammer tomorrow.

Watergate thing flared up again today with a problem on *(CRP scheduling director)* Bart Porter's testimony *(before the grand jury)* which will start the implicating of Magruder *(i.e., that he authorized money for Liddy)*. He decided to go ahead with that. Mitchell and John Dean have spent a lot of time working out the details and apparently think they have something developed that will work out all right *(to keep any implication off Mitchell)*.

Thursday, July 20, 1972

The P and I met with Armand Hammer today. Ostensibly for him to report to the P on his trip to Russia and his big oil deal with the Soviets but actually for us to ask Hammer to let us have Marvin Watson to run the Democrats for Nixon for Connally. Hammer is hysterical, came in with an envelope full of art books and his own story of Russia. Told us all about his background in Russia, and everything, which was really quite fascinating, but he's obviously completely entranced with himself, and not much of anything else. When we asked him about Watson, he did agree to let him come.

Billy Graham called to say he had talked to the Governor yesterday after the operation and that he would say that there's almost no chance of Wallace's running. Wallace asked whether he would take more votes from the P, and Graham said he would take at least 75 percent. Wallace said he would never turn one hand to help McGovern and that he doesn't have the physical strength to run and that he's 99 percent sure he won't do it, but he won't close the door completely. He did say Eagleton's coming to see him on Monday, and he asked Graham to come and see him and asked him in the meantime to pray for him and indicated that he's concerned because his abscess won't heal.

Watergate situation came up today. The P feels that we shouldn't wait for the ax to fall on Magruder; if he's going to get it, he should get out first. He also liked the idea of exploring the possibility of immunity for Magruder.

He got into some general political strategy. He thinks that we should use some nonpolitical committees that are already meeting to take on McGovern. E's got to stay on top of all the domestic issues and be sure to cover them on a political basis. We should use Laird and Rogers heavily in foreign policy, political matters. Someone should keep saying that the

Democrats have written off the South. We should use Father
MacLaughlin with Catholic groups in the campaign. We
should be doing a better job of organizing Wall Street. He
wants to fight the Nixon smear program. To hit them before
they hit us. Agreed to have breakfast with Meany Monday or
Tuesday or whatever worked out for the meeting.

The P and I went for dinner on the *Sequoia*. The P had me
up to the Lincoln Sitting Room with him afterward and chatted
generally a bit. The main point was that he wants MacGregor
and Dole to get out some good stories about the strength of
our organization and big things we're doing.

Monday, July 24, 1972

The P got into a lot of little political odds and ends today. He
wants to get going on a campaign song. Wants to know who
the orchestra is for the convention. At an early time he thinks
we have to knock down the idea of coasting. So we've got to
say he's working hard.

He wants to be sure all Wallace contacts are now handled
through Connally, and he called LBJ at Connally's request
today. There's a memo in the file on that. Apparently it went
very well and Johnson will encourage his people to support us
behind the scenes. Although he will not come out himself, of
course.

He's still a little concerned about the Watergate thing but
not pushing hard on that. We ought to set up a political-
advisory board. He's concerned that we double-check Colson
on all names used for endorsements to be sure that they have
really backed us.

Tuesday, July 25, 1972

Mainly a political day. The P had a couple of public events
scheduled which he got some good mileage out of, but spent
all the intervening time in political discussion. He got into a
discussion on how to handle Agnew. He feels we must not
build him up in terms of where he goes and so forth. That we
should put him in the South, the small states. No important
duties. He feels he shouldn't have played tennis Saturday
morning. He should have prepared for his press conference
instead.

K came in and we were discussing the need to answer Eagleton on his attack that we're keeping the troops in Vietnam

until the last minute and then pulling them out just before the election. K makes the point that this assumes we can program Moscow, Peking, and Hanoi, and thus shows a total lack of understanding of foreign policy, shocking inexperience, and ignorance. Plus the moral issue. The suggestion that any P will delay the war's end is vilification of the worst sort and destroys national unity. We should get someone to try and take Eagleton on with this.

The Eagleton item today was his announcement that he had been in the hospital three times for mental illness *(depression)* and we were all flabbergasted about that. The P, Buchanan, K, Ziegler, and I all agreed it would mean that Eagleton will have to be dropped from the ticket, and the concern is that he might be replaced by Kennedy, which would be bad for us. We're actually better off with Eagleton than anyone else, so are not anxious to have him dropped off. In any event, it creates a monumental problem for them. The P obviously is fascinated by the development as he can't help but be.

Connally called this afternoon to report on his meeting with Wallace. He said that Wallace would not make any categorical statement about not running but he did say he would not do anything to help McGovern and he's almost certain he will not go with the third party and he will not go with the American Party. Connally told him he knew that he didn't want anything, but Connally wanted the decision on what Wallace is going to do because a number of the Wallace people Connally wants to hire and he didn't want to do it without Wallace's concurrence. Wallace told him to wait until after the American Party convention on August 3 before he moved on that. Wallace said, I'm sure I won't run but there are one or two chances in a million that lightning might strike. Wallace said he doesn't want anything, although some of his people may want money. Connally said he would talk only on the basis of his personal friendship and former Governorship not on money, but he does know that all campaigns have a deficit and he's always available to talk about that area. Connally says he's obviously a sick man, and that Cornelia said he'd be two or three weeks in the hospital on therapy, and then they're taking a therapist home with them for a year. John was convinced that this is the most significant day in the campaign because Wallace is not going to run.

Wednesday, July 26, 1972

The Eagleton story was the big deal today. The P had me follow up with Dole and MacGregor to order them not to discuss this at all, even with their intimates or staffs, and we had quite a bit of discussion as the day went on about the significance and what was going to happen. There's still total disagreement as to what the effect's going to be and nobody really can measure it. Eagleton and McGovern seem to be playing it about as totally wrong as they possibly could.

We got word that Wallace is going to announce at noon today, that he would not attend the American Independent Party convention, and that on Saturday, he will announce that he won't be a candidate, and will not run, etc.

Thursday, July 27, 1972

Eagleton was the big item again today, as the debate rages on with whether he can stay on the ticket or will have to get off. Lots of rumors about other offenses, and all that sort of thing. All the strategy meetings bogged down into long speculation about what they're going to do.

We had a political dinner on the *Sequoia* with Mitchell, Harlow, MacGregor, and me, with the P, which turned into basically a bull session on some of the strategy things and a chance to let MacGregor cover in general what he's doing. Those sessions aren't really very productive because the P just kind of likes to BS and we never seem to get much done.

Friday, July 28, 1972

Senator Ellender died last night, which we learned upon arriving back at the White House from the *Sequoia*. The P discussed this morning the funeral plans. He apparently talked with Mansfield last night and as a result of this, Mansfield recommended that it would be very good for the P politically to go to the funeral, and the P decided to do so. Wants to take the key Senate people and the House guys from Louisiana, since it gives him a chance to talk.

The Eagleton problem is still the big story of the day, with no new developments today. Eagleton is saying that he is more sure than ever that he'll stay on the ticket, and there are rumors back and forth as to what really is happening in the McGovern camp. I don't think anybody really knows. The P played golf this afternoon with George Meany and then went off to Camp David for the evening.

Saturday, July 29, 1972

The P's at Camp David. I stayed home. He called a couple of times in the morning to report on his golf game with Meany. Said there's a real hatred there toward McGovern, and absolutely no chance of his endorsing. Nobody could help, if they take Eagleton off the ticket, except Teddy Kennedy, and even there, it wouldn't make any real difference. The P feels that the other side has now a serious problem that we hadn't anticipated, because dropping Eagleton in light of the poll makes the move both unpopular and weak because he's not standing by his man. This is a mixed bag for us, because McGovern could be hurt by dropping him, so keeping him on is not necessarily to our advantage. Eagleton's strong public support could give him more leverage in trying to stay on. The P, if he were in this position, would keep him on, unless he could get Kennedy, to avoid getting the campaign bogged down for two or three weeks, not because of the merits. The natural desire of the press to help McGovern would swing behind him.

Sunday, July 30, 1972

The P's still at Camp David. He had called Wallace on the phone, had a long talk with him, and with his wife. Mrs. Wallace made a big point about how she often says how much she admires Mrs. Nixon and the girls. He talked to Wallace about his travel plans and said he wouldn't come to Alabama unless Wallace felt it was a good idea. Wallace said he would love to have him, that he's got lots of friends down here. Wants me to get the film *Sunrise at Campobello* and have our man take it down and show it to Wallace as a way of giving him a big lift.

We got into the Eagleton thing again. Connally feels that they're setting the stage to drop Eagleton. The P said survival is the first law of politics and of life, and that they have to move on the basis of that. In light of this, he's concerned about the line we should take, which is that we're sorry for Eagleton, but that McGovern has handled this cynically and destroyed a human being.

Monday, July 31, 1972

We left first thing this morning for Louisiana for Ellender's funeral. The trip went very well. The P got a great reception. Lots of crowds on the streets. Governor met him and said he was for him. Senator Eastland told him that he'd carry every county in Miss. The Sheriff said he'd clean up in Louisiana, as did the police chief, etc. He had plenty of time on the plane to chat with the Louisiana Congressional delegation and pick up some political points there. Had quite a discussion with me on general political and convention plans. He's concerned about California, where he thinks we have our major problems. First, the economy; second, Reagan; third, the fact that it's youth-oriented. Got into some problems of who goes to the convention, especially regarding the Pat Nixon staff. Also, the family's obviously pressuring him to get out and shake hands with the delegates and all.

(He) is anxious to get MacGregor's staff meetings and so on started and get people fired up. Also that we ought to hit the auto manufacturers, to get them to hire people now. They're making enormous profits out of enormous sales, but instead of hiring new people they're running a lot of overtime, which doesn't help on unemployment. When we got back, we had an economic political meeting with Shultz, Stein, Weinberger, E, and Colson to discuss the basis economic issues on the basis that the experts know we're in great shape but the people don't. The problems are on inflation, particularly food prices, tax reform, unemployment, and the general area of expansion of the economy.

This evening McGovern and Eagleton had their meeting. Came out of it, and at about 9:45 had a press conference that was carried on CBS radio. McGovern announced that while he was satisfied that Eagleton's health was great and he consistently supported Eagleton, they had made a joint decision. Health was not a factor, but the public debate of it was diverting attention again from the national issues and that the paramount need for the Democrats was unity and a full discussion of the issues. McGovern said that he will consider the Vice Presidential choice very carefully, has no one in mind at this point. He won't discuss the Vice Presidency tomorrow night. He's requested free time on all three networks at 9:00 tomorrow night. He says he'll discuss the campaign to date at that time. Which should be an impossibility. At that point I called the P to report to him and missed a good chunk of the press conference.

Tuesday, August 1, 1972

The big question today was whether McGovern was going to get free time on TV tonight. It went back and forth on it and the net result was that he didn't get the time. He made his Eagleton announcement last night, and then was going to try to get the time tonight anyway. The networks wised up to it and canceled the time. Most of them furious because he's trying to con them. Also, apparently, his staff was very rough, at least on NBC, and he hasn't helped his network relations a bit by this maneuver.

Connally called to say that Marvin Watson had told him that Ed McCormick in Boston had told him that *(Boston Mayor)* Kevin White had called to say that McGovern had called him last night and said that it would be Larry O'Brien for VP. That this was something that Kennedy was pushing for, and that's why they're putting it together that way.

Also, I spent most of the afternoon reviewing the Wolper documentary films and was not very impressed with what I saw, considering the amount of money, time, and effort that's been invested in them. I may review the whole thing again tomorrow, because I'm afraid we sort of missed the boat there, although we'll see what develops. The P is going to be furious when he sees them, because he's given so much time and he knows how much film they've been shooting, and what comes out looks like a rather inadequate newsreel hodgepodge.

Wednesday, August 2, 1972

The P had no schedule today. Spent time on odds and ends. He talked to me first thing this morning about the Pat Nixon film. Wanted to set up a plan for her to review it, which we did. The P warned Rose and Tricia to sit in with her and rave about it, so that we'd get approval. They ran it at 5:00 today, and it came off extremely well, so we're in good shape on that.

Thursday, August 3, 1972

The P had E in this morning to discuss the basic problem of domestic intelligence, the need for our moving on IRS and

Justice to get some action on tax and other matters involving people supporting the opposition. Also, he has some concerns about some appointments in the education area, and made the comment to E that he's 1000 percent against the educational establishment, then said, "If I may quote someone else," referring to McGovern, who said he was 1000 percent behind Eagleton just before he fired him.

On political strategy, he makes the point that the martyrdom theory is now reversed. That is, we were concerned originally that we not hit McGovern too hard, so as not to martyr him. Now, he thinks that theory is reversed, that McGovern is under attack, he's shown he's mortal, that he has feet of clay, that he's a non-sympathetic character at the moment, and when a man has fallen in battle, the thing to do is hit him again while he's down to keep him down.

Friday, August 4, 1972
The Democratic VP question keeps coming up. The P got into quite a discussion with Ziegler on the whole Kennedy story about his involvement with Amanda Burden up in New York.

Another tie-up was the Andreas statement. Dwayne Andreas has agreed to come up with a public statement saying that he was the one who gave the $25,000 that they're trying to track down in connection with the Watergate caper. So we're trying to work something out on that. The P left this afternoon for Assateague with Mitchell, Bebe, and Abplanalp to spend the weekend. Just as he left, I conceived the idea of going to California, hopped on a plane, and we roared out.

Editor's Note: Over the weekend, after turndowns from several prominent Democrats, McGovern announced his new VP choice—Sargent Shriver, former head of the Peace Corps and brother-in-law of Teddy Kennedy.

Sunday, August 6, 1972
The P was in Assateague most of the day, then came into Washington. I'm still in California. He called this afternoon from Washington, said that he thought the beach weekend was good for John M; it was a good relief for him as well as for

the P. A problem because Martha wants to go to the convention and they've got to figure out how to deal with that. The P feels that we've got to be sure that all our speakers' talks have a proper balance of anti-McGovern material plus pro-Nixon. On the next two weeks, he says that we should do anything we can that's really newsworthy and positive. We should really crank up the revenue sharing ceremony and get the maximum mileage out of that. We're scheduling a Cabinet meeting at Camp David Tuesday night and he wants to give them plenty of time for their briefing and to ask questions. That was about it.

Wednesday, August 9, 1972

Still at Camp David. The P and I stayed over, as did E and K, but they left first thing this morning. The P had me over by the Aspen pool this morning for a general political discussion.

We got the report on Connally's announcement of the Democrats for Nixon, which was done via press conference because he refused to take advantage of the equal time opportunity we had, so didn't get on TV, which is a real tragedy, but that's the way he wanted it, so that's the way it was done. Unfortunately, we have to handle him that way to survive.

The VP called concerned about a problem with Sinatra and the Democrats. Sinatra was miffed that the VP didn't call him, instead of Connally, but he's aboard now. Rogers called to say he had talked to Meany about the platform, is hopeful to get some labor concerns mentioned in our platform. The P called me over at 5:30 and he was swimming in the pool, but kind of floated around for a half an hour and covered some odds and ends, and he wants to be sure we have a Jew in the convention program, wants Chapin to talk to Colson about Italians, Catholics, Poles, Labor, our big breakthrough areas of the ethnics. He wants that bowling alley built into the Residence, he wants to buy a house in Georgetown with a pool so he can get some exercise. Wants K to be sure we have a good Israeli plank in the platform and that he reviews all foreign policy planks. Wants Colson to get a mailer out fast to 100,000 Democrats with the Connally announcement.

Friday, August 11, 1972

Got into a flap today on the question of the détente with the press, because Bob Semple wrote a story in *The New York*

Times that makes the whole point that we made a calculated decision and issued orders to stop jumping on the press, etc., which is obviously counterproductive. So the P got concerned about handling this subtly and making sure that we still continue our attack on the press and particularly eroding their credibility.

The other big thing today was Romney. The P met with him this morning and George submitted his resignation, complained about Ken Cole and E and the advance notice to the press, all of which came out in the paper later. He agreed that he'd work in the campaign, but he wanted to get out. After the convention he can come out to California and announce that he's leaving. He apparently complained about the Domestic Council, that his views are never listened to, that no one important ever goes to the meetings, and all that. The usual Cabinet vs. staff complaints. P's view is to let Romney go, he's too negative now. E's view is to let it simmer till after the convention and see what happens. He privately thinks that Romney won't actually go when the time comes for a showdown.

Sunday, August 13, 1972

Still at Camp David. Lot of Romney flap in the papers this morning, P feels there's no need to react to it. Talked to me on the phone, wanted to see if I had heard anything from John Mitchell, and wants me to be sure to make the point to him that we're relying on him for New York, New Jersey, and Reagan, and we have to know if he's not going to be able to do it. Wanted to be sure that Agnew stays on an attack on McGovern, not on Shriver, that he should ignore Shriver totally. McGovern and Shriver were both on TV talk shows today, and Shriver did rather badly and McGovern did pretty well overall. P called me at home tonight to discuss the plan for this week. He's obviously cranking into gear to get started on writing his speech, and was trying to clear up all the loose ends before he does so. We have a heavy schedule of nuts and bolts for tomorrow morning. He wants to get away by 1:00, and get up to Camp David to go to work on the speech. Wanted me to make the point with the staff now that the P will have to button down and not get involved in anything, says he doesn't need any secretary until Wednesday, but to tell Rose to plan to come up to be available

Thursday morning through the weekend. Says he probably won't want Ray, he'll work by himself or maybe with someone else other than Ray because he's too slow. Says he wants me to review the news summary, he doesn't want to read it, and about 5:00 give him a call with a rundown. He wants a report on what's going on with the campaign generally, and then anything that might relate to the speech, and eliminate trivia. He does need to know what the folks are thinking and hearing about, though. He thinks it's better not to break or be distracted during the day, but at 5:00 to take a break and get the rundown then.

Raised the point that Ehrlichman's got to understand that the O'Brien follow-up and the attack on high-level Democrats is much more important than the platform, they come first. Wants the Watergate thing discussed, thinks Ehrlichman's plan which we talked about yesterday at Camp David is probably the best. The thought there was that we would have Mac-Gregor come out and give the full background story right at the time of the P's meeting with (Japanese Prime Minister) Tanaka, so as to be overridden, and then hope that settles our side of it prior to the issuing of indictments in mid-September.

Then he got back to the question of whether we have an adequate operation getting a list of McGovern supporters and contributors and running checks on them and see if there are any vulnerable connections: left-wing or mob connections, and that sort of thing. He thinks we should be doing this with all of McGovern's top contributors.

Monday, August 14, 1972

Back in Washington for a heavy schedule today before returning to Camp David for more work on the speech. P met first with Connally at 9:00 this morning, got into a number of things on ideas for the campaign. Need to spend the night at Connally's when he does the Democrats for Nixon at his ranch. Agrees that we should get Billy Graham to talk to Lyndon Johnson and urge him to be cool to MacGregor when he comes to see him next week, thinking that Johnson's friends won't understand if he puts his arm around him. About the strategy on debate: first make the point that the P doesn't intend to debate, especially because of the way McGovern is distorting things. Second, hang the whole thing on the national interest, just as LBJ decided to do.

Into the question of Watergate. P made the point that we should wait until the indictment. The question was raised whether we should wait until the indictment or whether we should prepare in advance. We must make a case for the Re-election Committee on how it conducted its own investigation, so when the grand jury indicts, it will cover the noninvolvement of others. First, we should leak out now about our investigation. Second, while the P's in Hawaii, MacGregor should put out a statement describing the results of the investigation. Forget the legal question, deal with the political PR, get our line out in our way. If we can absolve all the top officials, then we should put it at the lowest common denominator. The funds were misused, the culprits have left, no one else was involved. But we must be sure of our facts from the grand jury and we must know what Justice's going to seek out of the grand jury. Be sure of those facts.

P then met with Moynihan, who's writing an article for *The New York Times Magazine,* and wanted to get a view of the P's look at his second four years. P expanded quite completely for Pat on this, made the point of the coherent philosophy, tying in foreign policy, economic policy, and domestic policy. He should say that there is a new philosophy and a new way. Make the point that the FDR coalition was made up because they wanted to win, but they didn't belong together, they were drawn together by their fears. First the economy and then the war. Our new coalition will be held together, not by fears but by common hopes and a shared philosophy. Not total agreement, but a recognition for the need for civility, different ways to approach government goals. In other words, we will form a national coalition that shares common views regarding what the country ought to be, at home and abroad. We have to find coherent policies, not to suit the new left or the new liberals, but closer to the 19th century liberals. Internationalism without imperialism. Change that works. Constructive. We'll build, not destroy, based on the old values. We have to find a way to get the pragmatists and the idealists together. Moynihan was ecstatic with all this material, and got quite responsive and excited with the P's views, and should come up with a pretty good article.

On the POW offer from Ramsey Clark *(Clark had returned from Hanoi supposedly with a POW release offer),* we should refer to the fact that McGovern came back with the same deal from Paris. It turned out to be phony, now Ramsey's is also a phony. We got into quite a thing with Colson and Haig on this, and the point that Haig doesn't want to push too hard, because at the proper time, K will pull the rug out from the whole thing. We must stay away from it until we know what he has. The problem is that Clark may have a legitimate POW offer. So everyone backed off today and laid low, which was probably just as well.

Wednesday, August 16, 1972

At Camp David. P's concerned about the convention reapportionment problems but thinks we're wise in following the E plan of staying out of the battle ourselves, and he's going to do so, too. Had a report from John Dean on the Watergate business, says that things went okay with Magruder, at an informal thing last night and then with the grand jury today. He was about two and a half hours, came off okay with no surprise questions or any new evidence. They focused on me, apparently, in trying to get Jeb to tie me into the case somehow today, although last night they focused on Colson. John thinks that things are under reasonably good control there.

Got into big flap with the P on Pat Nixon's being set up for a TV interview with Maraya MacLaughlin at CBS, and apparently really got a bad deal out of it, in that she was getting a lot of rough, loaded questions. As a result of this, the P wants Ziegler to put someone on Mrs. Nixon to cover her at the convention. Get Barbara Walters and Virginia Shroeder of ABC and NBC out to her and be sure that CBS is cut out. Then he also said that he was going to have to stay at the hotel in Miami, that he couldn't stay over at Key Biscayne, because MacLaughlin in the interview made a big thing of Mrs. Nixon's being separated from the P all the time. So he told me to work something out on that. I knew the big pitch was talking him out of it, and then talked to Julie, and she agreed to try and straighten it out, and called later to say that she probably had.

Thursday, August 17, 1972

Had a long talk with Billy Graham and a report on his weekend with Lyndon Johnson. Billy says he helped Johnson modify his endorsement to make it as cool as possible, says that he's selling his TV station, Johnson is, to the *LA Times* later this week. Secondly, he's giving his home and all to the park system. Third, he advises the P to ignore McGovern. He says he should go out and identify with people, to ball games, factories, and so on. He thinks the McGovern people will defeat themselves. He feels very strongly anti-McGovern. Says the P should not do too much campaigning, stay above it, as Johnson did with Goldwater. He's very grateful regarding the treatment by Nixon for him, especially of his two daughters.

Billy Graham's a little concerned about Vietnam, and about the bugging thing. He doesn't think bugging is going to hurt us. Lyndon Johnson laughed about it, said it won't hurt a bit.

Regarding the acceptance speech, Billy feels that it should not be like four years ago, because he's now P. He doesn't need the flamboyance of the challenger. What will appeal is a high road, illuminate the accomplishments, look to the future, what can be done. Have a foundation to build a new world, and a new America, and we're just now able to do it. He says that P must talk to the workers of the campaign. Get into the issue that never mention McGovern by name. Hit the socialistic welfare state versus America where you can start at the bottom and work to the top. The only way the McGovern plan would work is under a dictatorship. Said the speech should not be long, and it should always be as P of the United States. He feels McGovern's getting more desperate and contradictory every day, that we should let him stew in his own problems. The P liked the negative view of comparing Nixon's position versus McGovern's. He thinks that makes the new coalition for the purpose of defeating McGovern, instead of accomplishing what our goals are. There should be uplift, not attack, and then talk about how to do it. We should start on strongly affirmative basis, with the goals we seek. Also, he thinks that McGovern's tactics are an attack on the institutions of this country, not on the Administration. The issue is not the incumbent versus the challenger, but the view of the nation and its institutions. One is an uncharted sea with an unknown navigator, so the conflict is between McGovern and all we hold dear, not between two men contending for the Presidency.

Had a scare today on the Jewry situation, because the Russians are going to charge duty to Jews leaving Russia, and that's created a big flap in this country. Rogers is all stirred

up about it. I'm supposed to keep Rogers from seeing Dobrynin on it tomorrow, which I think I've successfully done.

Friday, August 18, 1972

We had a 90 minute flap with the VP regarding his seconding
speeches, because he finally decided yesterday to have Dr.
Joyce Brothers, the psychologist, be one of the seconders, and
they went ahead and asked her. This obviously would be a
disaster, in that it would look like he got his own psychiatrist
to prove he isn't nuts like Eagleton is. After going around on
it, I called him back, told him he couldn't do it, he said he
wanted to check it with P, I did, the P agreed, called him back
again, said that is the decision, he agreed to go along with it,
although it would be very difficult for him, since he has to
now turn her off.

Mitchell called, very concerned because MacGregor was
putting out some stuff on the Watergate thing in self-defense.
John's very concerned because what he's putting out is not
the line, and it undercuts our legal posture, and so on. He
wanted me to call MacGregor, tell him he's got to use the line
of "no comment" because individual rights are involved.
We'll have a statement at the appropriate time and then scare
him into the fact that he may blow the lawsuit and some of
the individuals concerned if he doesn't stay with the line. He's
anticipating before we know the facts. Mitchell's concerned
because at the convention Clark will be all over the television,
and it's imperative to keep this down until after the convention.

Sunday, August 20, 1972

Camp David. P had me over to Aspen at 9:30 this morning.
He was surprised by our big lead in the West. Feels we should
watch for distortion of poll data, such as the Gallup story in
the *Post*. Mentioned that he nearly broke his ankle last night
when he took a walk with Henry and stepped into a manhole
or something here at Camp David and twisted his ankle. He
was limping this morning. K came in, we had a discussion
about his activities at the convention. Agreed that he should
do as much social stuff as he wants, that he should take interviews in the box only on an informal basis, should not schedule any formal interviews. He should do the youth caucuses,
but not for television.

P asked me to have Rogers and Price take a stab at the conclusions to the speech, he wanted the Bible thing from Andrews, particularly regarding children and peace, wanted Price to work on a short conclusion with uplift and emotional impact, very personal, with dedication to peace and a better life for the people. They turned it in, but they didn't know what the President wanted, and they didn't really accomplish much. He had me over twice and went through reviews of segments of the speech, still trying to work on the conclusion. He had Ziegler, K, and me for dinner at Aspen. Then at 9:15 he had me back over at Aspen, read through some of what he was working on. I made some suggestions. Still on the conclusion, primarily. At 10:30 he called me again, and he thinks it'll work now, and he wants to review it with me. I met him in the office at Laurel, and he skimmed through the whole speech. It is a tough and political speech. I think it's right but it's hard to tell.

Monday, August 21, 1972

Camp David. Connally woke me up this morning to report on Lyndon Johnson's feelings. He had talked to Johnson, he's mad as hell, furious about the whole McGovern approach to things. He told McGovern that he'll meet with him for one hour, that there's to be no press and no pictures. Then McGovern will have a press conference afterward.

The P wanted me up to the Aspen pool at noon, said he wanted me to check with Mrs. Eisenhower and see if she's at the farm, if he could drop in to see her after the tribute to Eisenhower at the Convention today. She was delighted to do it, so we set it up on that basis. Had a very good visit with her, had to sit around and wait for quite a while because Ron didn't have the press there. Would have made a good story. She did a superb job in the film at the convention. P got into some further questions he needs on speech statistics. He wants to use a figure of what their platform will cost, say it will increase taxes over 50 percent and add over $80 million to the welfare rolls. P reviewed his speech with me, he keeps going over it, trying to assure himself that he's on the right track. He's still not really convinced that he is, but he's pretty well past the point of no return now.

Tuesday, August 22, 1972

Started in Washington and then in Florida this afternoon. P went into a discussion of his reaction to the documentary that was on TV last night *(the Pat Nixon film at the convention)*, which he watched. He felt that the problem was that it lacked an architect and thus lacked a theme, covered too many subjects. We needed an editor of ours who was not just technically good, but personally committed to get heart into it.

Billy Graham called to report a 45-minute conversation he had with Lyndon Johnson reporting on his meeting with McGovern today. Johnson said the press are mad, but they weren't allowed in. Johnson told McGovern how he felt, and that McGovern could share these thoughts with anyone he wanted to. He said he would not campaign for him, and that it was McGovern's sole reason for coming to see him, was to get him to campaign. He cited all the good things the P's done for him, says that McGovern is associating with amateurs, that he ought to shake up his staff, and he ought to stand up and say what a wonderful place America is. He told Shriver that he didn't know what he was talking about on Vietnam *(Shriver had claimed that both Nixon and Johnson had "blown" peace opportunities in Paris),* he had the documents to prove it, and he handed them to Shriver and told him to read them. He also told McGovern that he has letters in the library, and that he should go read them, regarding Vietnam. Straighten him out on his misconceptions. He said Connally's the most important man in Texas, and you should hope and pray that he won't make a speech against you, because that'll be the end of it. He told him to get with the old pros, and get themselves away from the amateurs they were working with, that it's probably too late, that they should do this in any event. He made it clear to Graham that he would be happy to see Nixon if he wants to come and visit him. On the plane to Key Biscayne, the P got into his planning on the other speeches, the balance of this week, the weekend speech, the school speech, San Diego and San Clemente arrivals, and so on.

We did the youth rally at the Marine Stadium tonight, and it was a sensationally good idea, and worked out extremely well. P handled it perfectly. Came in through the back of the crowd, got a tremendous reception and great enthusiasm, gave a good talk, and everybody who saw it on television was just ecstatic, so I think we scored maybe the major coup of the week or maybe even the campaign with that appearance. P was very pleased with it afterward, and we had a chat at the house after we got back. He sees the value of picking up some of these things, and I think we can get him to do more.

Wednesday, August 23, 1972

At Key Biscayne. P spent the day working on the speech. Got into the details of arrangements, he wants to do his makeup in the trailer, be sure there's no commotion. He wants to be at the hall before the VP is introduced, he went through the details on how he wants the onstage procedure, that is, the VP to come up and then Mrs. Nixon up and then the family up. He doesn't want anything with the two families together, and he wants to be sure the VP understands no hands-over-head type shots.

Went into the details of getting the family over to Key Biscayne, how we'll work all that out, making sure that the crowd on the floor of the convention gets up to the podium. Lot of minor details on general arrangements of that sort, and the plan for the handshaker after the speech, after convention hall. That all worked out fine, the speech went over reasonably well, it wasn't one of his great speeches by any means, but it accomplished what he was after, I think in laying out the issues. Had me over to the house afterward to sort of talk about the whole thing. Seemed to be in good spirits and went to bed reasonably early.

Thursday, August 24, 1972

Big flap on speech problems, particularly on the Michigan school speech. The P decided to give the speech extemporaneously. As it turned out, that was a real coup because it turned out to be sensational. He gave a marvelous speech on calling some of his schoolteachers *(and telling them)* what they had meant to him, taking the line that kids should never give up, always try again, and so on. We put out a busing statement that worked well on the news, so we got the busing point across even though we weren't allowed to use it in the speech. Came out fine, but it was only by luck rather than the version that came out. The P did a good job; the rest of us pretty much blew the thing. He wants more tight material, and we've got to keep pushing on that. On the plane, he talked to me about the speechwriting problem. He feels that the mood of the country is upbeat, good news, not ugly, a good feel, not contentious, and that our speeches have to fit the mood of the audience and the country. Got into some schedule ideas for the future, after San Clemente arrival this evening, which incidentally was sensational, with a huge crowd. He thinks now that he should go out and touch up the country once a week. Wants to go over the whole schedule thing with me tomorrow, as well as speechwriting problems.

Sunday, August 27, 1972

San Clemente. He got into quite a little on scheduling. The point on the Eisenhower theory that once you start, you should go all out, the momentum theory, and he wonders if we should be doing that now or if we should hold off and still do that in the last few weeks. He feels there is some dramatics involved in getting out later, in that it would take some of the foam out of that by going out earlier. We should think in terms of winning states, not national results. We should get a lot of events stockpiled for the P to look at, that are not too way-out or patently oddball. We should avoid the dog-and-pony shows of E's. We should figure what we want to do, what states to hit, where we have pluses. He'd like to take a look at these things, to plan in advance, but keep it closely held, and keep the opposition off balance. On McGovern attacks, he wanted to be sure that Kleindienst puts out the violations of the spending act on their side, that we have to get some stuff out on the McGovern fund-raising. E's got to follow up on O'Brien, where that money went, so forth. We need someone at Treasury who will talk politically and take the attack on all this.

Editor's Note: Howard Hughes was paying O'Brien's lobbying firm a large yearly retainer, and the President had ordered an IRS audit to see if O'Brien had slipped up with taxes.

Connally was on one of the TV shows today and did a darn good job. There were some good cracks at McGovern. VP also was on, and did a very calm, reasoned thing, especially good on the media, and both of those came out very well.

This evening was the celebrity reception at the Residence,

which went very well. We had an extremely good turnout of the top stars, and a fascinating combination of Jack Benny, Frank Sinatra, Jimmy Durante, John Wayne, etc., plus a lot of the young ones. He was very pleased with it, and I think it was worthwhile.

Tuesday, August 29, 1972

P had his press conference today. Went very well. He had 15 questions, 8 of them political, 4 on Vietnam, 2 a sort of a combination Vietnam/political. One on foreign policy and none on domestic policy.

E and I met with him to take care of the overriding problem of E's attempt to move into campaign management, which they're resisting, and succeeded in doing so in the meeting. They've now got E back out of it. We also settled on a basic strategy for the time being on the release of the investigation internally of the Watergate caper. The Gallup poll is out today, with Nixon up 64/30, the highest we've ever been. Then the P raised the point of the need to have our people have confidence in our campaign. The P shouldn't have people on our staff who think they're the candidate, and keep telling the P what he ought to do. He can't get out of character, and only the candidate can feel the campaign. People should not assume that the P is unaware of the problems. So he wants them to unload on me by memo so that I can then funnel it to the P in an orderly way.

Wednesday, August 30, 1972

P had me in this morning for a series of miscellaneous follow-up items. He was concerned about the schedule for Hawaii. He didn't think we'd allowed enough time for the receiving line at Clare Luce's, wants to be sure that we sent certificates to all the medal winners at the Olympics. Wanted to be sure that the convention people were told what a great job they did; the Gallup poll shows the credit they deserve. Wants to be sure Haig doesn't let Henry's desire for a settlement prevail; that's the one way we can lose the election. We have to stand firm on Vietnam and not get soft. Hawaiian arrival was OK, not too big a crowd, but a great introduction by Governor Burns, who has indicated to E that he will have to stay a Democrat publicly but that he's voting for the P. Then good reception at Clare Luce's, and we got the receiving line done in exactly the time he had scheduled, so that problem was overcome. He says he talked to Stans and Colson on the phone to cheer them up after their deposition with the grand jury, and so on.

On the way to Hawaii *(to meet with the Japanese),* he made the point that we should use the line "The tactics of the desperate man" to hit McGovern.

Friday, September 1, 1972

In Hawaii. P had me in this morning before he started his second run of meetings with the Japanese to discuss some general strategy things. The only significant things were to be sure that we totally ignore Mrs. McGovern, and that Mrs. Nixon never comment on anything that Mrs. McGovern has said. She should always handle it as a "No comment." Got our poll today, and it confirms Gallup and Harris as far as the 35-point spread is concerned. It also gives us some good information on solid intention to vote for Nixon, etc., which is very encouraging, since we have a solid base at 47 against McGovern's 16, and it seems hard by any way of analyzing the polls to find a way that we can lose.

P had me up on the plane to go over the Vietnam part of the poll with Henry, and we had the meeting with Admiral McCain, Bill Rogers, and Henry. P had me up for most of that. McCain was most strongly outspoken in his commendation of the P's handling of Vietnam, and especially the mining of Haiphong and the interdiction bombing. He is obviously a great Nixon fan. He did a great job at the return ceremonies this afternoon before we left Hawaii in praising the P's Vietnam actions.

Tuesday, September 5, 1972

In the office at San Clemente this morning, big problem was the Olympic disaster where the Arab guerrillas captured a group of Jewish hostages. We had a lot of checking back and forth as to strategy. P moved with a statement of horror and joined with Israel in urging the games be suspended. The story went on as the day developed with a lot of conflicting reports. Remarkable coverage by ABC live on television by satellite. The day ended up with the discovery that they had all been killed. The P talked to Rabin and called me at 11:30 tonight at home, said that he wanted to have a meeting with Haig and

Rogers in the morning and K at 8:30. P said that we should
see how it develops tomorrow, that there may be a great sense
of outrage and sympathy, and he may have to take some action, such as going to the memorial service. He made the point
that any international event that overrides McGovern's whining and carping helps us in the long haul.

Wednesday, September 6, 1972

P met with Rogers and K first thing this morning on the Israeli
hostage question. Wants Rogers to take the matter to the UN.
P's fortunately off the idea of going to the services, but is
talking about going to church at the time of the funeral without
any prior announcement. Connally makes a good pitch on tax
reform, that when McGovern talks about it, we shouldn't talk
about a new program, we should hit the specifics of what
we've done. We've taken 9.5 million people off the tax rolls
at the low-income level, we've reduced personal income taxes
$19.5 billion, we've reduced the excise tax which is paid by
individuals by $3.5. We've raised corporation taxes $4.5. We
will reduce the property tax. There were two reform bills in
'69-'71 that were the most sweeping tax reform in this century, since the income tax started. We should hit McGovern's
tax proposals as old proposals that were submitted to Lyndon
Johnson, and he thought they were so bad that he wouldn't
even send them to Congress. Connally then had his Democratic
crew in. P met all of them. They were quite an impressive
group.

Friday, September 8, 1972

P had me in first thing in the morning just to review some
odds and ends on the schedule. E should move on the
O'Brien-Hughes money now, force him to divulge his other
clients, that kind of thing. Connally had raised the other day
the point that we could probably get Gene McCarthy to endorse the P publicly if we could get him a seat on the PBL
board, or the FCC. I discussed that we have the Johnson seat
coming up on the FCC in June of next year and we can commit that to him, and then try to accelerate it. P wants to be
sure that Edward Bennett Williams and all the other lawyers
of that sort in Washington, Democrats who haven't joined us,
that we should make a list of all these people, lobbyists and
lawyers, and after the election cut them out forever. Cut Wil-

liams completely, and the Redskins, and then build up our own lawyers. I suggested that this is the ideal job for Colson after the election. P basically agreed. Also wants to get individual reporters and publishers, and establish a black list there, and move on it. He wants a study made by Buchanan and Allen on the 20 most vicious, influential DC reporters and television people, and make a list for each of them of the things they would like to forget they said. He met with Stans this afternoon to try and cheer him up, since there was concern that he was depressed, also agreed that he'd see Hugh Sloan *(the CRP treasurer)*.

Monday, September 11, 1972

P had me in first thing this morning for a full morning schedule. Mainly concerned about the Watergate, wanting to know what the grand jury's schedule was, what our thorough game plan is, our PR plan on how to handle the whole thing, the need to take the offensive, develop a line, and so forth.

He also wanted to get E off his tail on the O'Brien matter, he feels John's too busy to look into it, and is having one of his minions handle it. Therefore it's not getting done, and he thinks it's extremely important.

In the political meeting, we got into the Watergate thing in considerable detail and had John Dean in. It appears that the leak the Democrats are building their case on now is Baldwin, the former FBI agent hired by McCord to handle Martha Mitchell, and was the guy monitoring the bugs at Howard Johnson's *(across the street from the Watergate)*. Feeling is that he's been immunized by the prosecutors, and that because he has the Democratic lawyer and leans that way anyway, that he's spilled the beans to them. They expect to get indictments on Friday, the government case will go to court, be assigned in a week or two, and if it's expedited, it will still take long enough to file motions and so forth, that it's very unlikely that it will be tried before the elections.

P has a virus, apparently, today, and was doing a lot of coughing and eating a lot of Coricidin and feeling somewhat sorry for himself. This afternoon, he had me in to run through a lot of odds and ends for a couple hours on scheduling White House functions, says Mrs. Nixon has now agreed on Filipinos versus blacks, and we can probably move to have Ron Jackson take over management of the Residence after the election, and shift away from all black waiters. Then he called me at home tonight to say he was looking over the girls' schedules and feels we're not handling it right; they're wasting their time doing service clubs and universities, and wanted me to look into changing that. He made a call today to Chris Schenkel of ABC at the Olympics, told him what a great job they were doing covering the games, especially emphasizing the patriotism and playing up the positive points in that area. Worried Ziegler some because he did criticize the refereeing and hit the United States Olympic Committee for trying to defend the guys that didn't stand at attention during the "Star-Spangled Banner" and then were kicked out by the International Olympic Committee.

Tuesday, September 12, 1972

Started the day with the joint breakfast meeting with the Cabinet and GOP leadership. Kleindienst spoke on the Watergate, said the indictments would be coming down Friday, that the data on the investigation would be put out to obviate the whitewash, and only the people who were indicted were involved, no one in the White House or CRP.

He had Colson and me in for a long session later this morning. On general politics, following up the breakfast meeting. He says he's changed his view on Shriver, that instead of ignoring him, we should be making him a liability and start cracking him by lower-level people. (In a meeting with Colson) P wonders about getting F. Lee Bailey in as associate counsel in the Watergate lawsuits to try and stir up some publicity. Wants to get American flags on all of our people and on the bumper strips, get the flags out to wear on the lapel. We got into a discussion of the idea of a Kleindienst special review board; wants me to talk to him about that. That is, to overcome the whitewash charges on the Watergate investigation. Had some ideas on redoing the White House after the election, the family dining room, redoing his bedroom, so forth. On the helicopter to Camp David, got into a schedule discussion. Toying with follow-up things from the RNC reception, maybe do the new airport in Kansas City. Wants to do a couple of small towns, wants a study listing all the cities that he's never visited of over 100,000. Wants to use visuals for the VP's foreign policy speech. Likes the idea of trying a new approach to motorcades, putting the VIP cars in front of the P, and had a lot of general talk about that sort of thing. After we got to Camp David he had Pat McKee *(a White House secretary)* and me come over for dinner, and we continued the schedule discussion primarily. Left early.

Wednesday, September 13, 1972

Tonight he had Mitchell, MacGregor, and Connally up for dinner and a general political planning session. Spent quite a little time on the Watergate. He agreed that the commission idea was no good, we'll go just with the press conference by Peterson of Justice with a follow-up by MacGregor.

On advertising, he okayed the present plan to start the anti-McGovern commercials next week.

Thursday, September 14, 1972

Back into schedule plans again today, and odds and ends that he thinks needs to be done. Likes the idea of Camp David on Tuesday night, and the staff planning meeting on Wednesday night for dinner. Got some input from Rizzo and Rockefeller, both of whom he met with today. Had some ideas on Rizzo, wants to motorcade the heart of Philadelphia, not the suburbs. Rockefeller, in the other direction, wants to do Westchester, Nassau, instead of the city. Agreed that he'd do a TV documentary as a wrap-up with about 8 minutes at the end for the P. Wants the Astrodome to be a one-hour television variety show with the P doing 15 minutes at the end. Wants to try a motorcade across Illinois and Ohio for the small-town thing. Do a Polish group in Buffalo.

Friday, September 15, 1972

We reviewed some minor schedule things. He ended up in the afternoon with not much to do, sat around and talked about the campaign in general. Then called John Dean in for a report on the Watergate indictments, which came out today *(the five men arrested, plus Hunt and Liddy).* Wondered if we should put out the fact that Johnson bugged us in '68, told me to ask Connally about that, then withdrew the idea. Wants to be sure we put the screws on Congress to turn off the *(Wright)* Patman hearings *(on CRP finances),* where they're trying to get Stans up to testify, and then got into quite a long talk with Dean about the need to get control of such things as the IRS and to be sure that we force all resignations right after the election.

Saturday, September 16, 1972

P was very concerned this morning about a Rather story on CBS that was based on two leaked CIA documents, and wanted me to check that out. I had Dave Young run a complete check. P is going to hang on to the list, so that we can move on those people at the appropriate time. He doesn't want any FBI check made on it, just a list of those who had access to the CIA documents, so we have a basis on which to move.

Henry was in to report further, he had covered his whole trip results with the P last night, but went into some details today. Henry feels that he's got things well in hand with the Soviets, he also thinks there may be a possibility on Vietnam. Apparently Le Duc Tho was pretty outgoing in their Paris meeting, and said, "Do you really want to bring this to an end now?" Henry said, "Yes," and he said, "Okay, should we do it by October 15?" and Henry said, "That'd be fine." Le Duc Tho came across the table, shook hands with him, and said, "We have finally agreed on one thing, we will end the war on October 15."

Had a long talk yesterday with Billy Graham, he feels things are very good, that he felt a couple weeks ago that we were behind in California, but he now feels we're pulling ahead there. Thinks we're going to have to give up almost totally on the black vote. We only have a few friends in that area. Kennedy coming into the campaign and Shriver on the ticket make the difference. He also is concerned that the radical youth are really working for McGovern, for example they were doing a very heavy registration effort in San Francisco. He doesn't think we'll win as big as it looks now, but thinks we're in good shape. Says the bugging isn't hurting us at all, it's too clouded, people think the Democrats placed it themselves, and that they've overplayed it. He thinks that the P is finally succeeding in creating an Eisenhower father image for himself, there's no one else, and he should stay above partisanship. Thinks we're still all on the positive side on the Jewish question. No problems regarding the Soviet Jews, expects to win Florida 70 percent, and told me about Johnny Carson, trying to figure out how he can help the P, and Graham telling him the way to do it is be a little biased in his favor from now on, like he has been biased against him.

P got into a talk about Disraeli and the analysis that Gladstone ended up as an exhausted volcano after his enormous reform programs, and the British people come to times when they don't want to be improved, and that we in this country may be at this stage. He's doing a lot of talking about the approach to policy for the second term, in that context. That not only do we clear out our enemies and build our own establishment, that we clear out the bad programs and so on, too.

He reviewed our latest poll results in the key states, and they're overwhelmingly favorable, and it makes the point that we probably should make a quiet decision now to move money out of some of the key states and into West Virginia, Minnesota, Massachusetts, and Rhode Island, which are the only doubtful ones, and see if we can't pick up all 50. So we are going to work on that. P left midafternoon for Camp David.

Sunday, September 17, 1972

P at Camp David, then came down for the Italian festival in Maryland. I went over to watch that; went very well. He came in by chopper, went through the crowd, gave a good little pro-Italian talk and left. Very good way to use an hour on a Sunday afternoon. I had no other contact.

Monday, September 18, 1972

Staff meeting this morning covered a number of current details. The Soviet grain deal continues to be a problem as Agriculture screws up the line that they're putting out each day a little bit worse. K came in for the first time in a long time, and that stirred up a lot of questions to him on Vietnam and other items; a long discussion of the Soviet Jew problem. Some concern about the long-range problem of the appearance of the Soviet advantage in the trade deal. Some discussion of veto strategy. There are three bills up that are candidates for vetoes.

P got into considerable detail on family scheduling. He

thinks the girls and Mrs. Nixon should not do any more press conferences or talk shows because the questioners are becoming too strident and rough, and the press is much rougher this year than they were in '68 because they realize the family is so effective. So he thinks and I agree that they should just go into nice areas and be nice, and not do any more Q & A's. Even though they handle it well, it doesn't develop a story that we want.

Wednesday, September 20, 1972

There is the question of Burundi, where he has just learned that 200,000 people have been killed by the government in order to maintain control, they're killing off all the intellectuals, apparently, or intelligent people. He makes the point that we ought to have a contingency plan to deal with this kind of thing, if they should capture a UN guy or something of this sort. He wants to be sure we make a big thing out of the fact there were no casualties in Vietnam last week.

Later today he had E and Weinberger up to Camp David for a general meeting. First, extensive discussion of veto strategy and the plans for the balance of this Congressional session. Then, a discussion of policy postelection. Feels that we've got to recognize what our mandate is. It's not toward a more liberal domestic policy. That we've had enough social programs: forced integration, education, housing, and so on. This is contrary to what the establishment thinks. They and the Congress think that the country want this stuff. He referred then to the Disraeli point of Gladstone being an exhausted volcano, with all his reforms, and the point that the people do not want to be improved. The huge social programs have been tried. They don't work. People don't want more on welfare. They don't want to help the working poor, and our mood has to be harder on this, not softer. People will say that the mandate means to go forward with all our revolutionary programs, but the P feels, totally different from Reagan, that the huge colossus of government is a mess. The people running it are incompetent and won't change, and the American people don't want to support it. We can't just allow the country to grow like Topsy. We have to do something, but we have to move toward slimming down rather than fattening up the Federal Government. He wants a review of the list of things to drop, but he wants to add to it. In the White House, he wants to drop the Science Advisor, Committee for International Economic Policy, the Advisory Boards, whatever can be done within the law to cut our own shop down. Most of the programs he wants to drop are in HEW, the higher-education subsidy, and that kind of thing. Make it clear to the NEA that they supported McGovern and they're not welcome anymore at the White House. In the health field, we should do much less. We should hit some of the sacred cows, like the Cotton program at Agriculture. On welfare, we have to support HR 1 until the election. Afterward, we should not send it back to Congress. He points out that we shouldn't assume that a great Administration is one that does new things. Maybe it's one that gets rid of old things. We should not make it Reagan-like. Not obtuse and antipeople. We should make it for people. Get government off their backs. Say as little as possible during the campaign so we have the fewest promises to have to keep, and so that we have an ability to interpret our mandate our way.

If we win, we don't intend to coast in the second term. In the first year, we've got to really do something about the government. Something that the P really believes in. Tear the State Department to pieces, and Defense. Don't just preside over the huge morass. Also, the Treasury bureaucracy is bad and so is Justice. We need a study on the VP's office in a ruthless way. Eliminate all the surplus staff and committees. Then he raised the question of who's doing the CIA study. Feels Helms has got to go. Some discussion on the problem of intelligence, reorganization, and the real problem, of course, is Defense and Congress. Wants to tell all hands that everybody should resign November 8, but no one should plan on a vacation. That the period of November 7 to December 7 should be the most intensive month ever. We should have a total cutoff of the press during that period and have some intensive Camp David sessions and really get the thing hammered together. Also, K should know there are to be no foreign leaders after the election until after the Inaugural. We should tell them that now.

Thursday, September 21, 1972
The P had a fairly full day of appointments and odds and ends. Got into some discussion on postelection ideas. On Supreme Court appointments, they're to be all conservative. The next

one is to be a Catholic, the best ethnic we can get, or the Fordham Dean. Then we need a woman. He's not concerned about Jews on either the Cabinet or the Court, any of the courts, but will keep Stein and K. As a guideline, we should work for Catholics, Labor, Ethnic, Democrats. Not blacks, not Jews. No Democrat is to be appointed to anything unless he supported the P. In other words, it's only our Democrats that are to be considered at all.

Rogers called to report that he had talked to Teddy Kennedy. There was concern before his call that Kennedy was calling to say he was going to go to Stockholm or Paris to pick up the POW families and to avoid their doing a military debriefing, and so on, but Rogers called after his meeting with Teddy, and Teddy had come to him as head of the refugee committee and said that he wanted to send a group to North Vietnam of doctors, nutrition experts, and so on, to see what's needed to rehabilitate North Vietnam after the war. He says he won't do it until after the election because it would be considered political otherwise. He'll make no statement on it before the election, but he has talked to some individual people. That he was telling Bill this just for his information, not asking for his support on it or anything like that. Bill mentioned to him that he guessed he'd be hitting the stump pretty soon, and Teddy laughed and said I'm awfully busy. I have a lot of work that we ought to do here and I'd sure like to avoid it if I can.

Friday, September 22, 1972
Brief meeting in the office this morning with Colson on schedule and quick planning items before we departed for Texas.

The Texas events were great. Laredo, we had a spectacular crowd in the streets for the motorcade, almost no anti-people, and almost all Mexican-Americans, very enthusiastic, a lot of "four-more-years" shouting, and good pro-Nixon signs and pro-Nixon reaction. Rio Grande High School worked out fine. It was small and run-down, but a good color-type thing, especially with the P pulling the impromptu idea of playing "Happy Birthday" on the piano for Congressman de la Garza, who had flown in with us. We had a little flap on the question of the Selection Committee paying for the plane fare with a Democratic congressman and senator aboard, but we'll work that out. The Connally dinner went very well. Good crowd. I don't think as many as he'd expected, because there were a lot of empty seats around the tables, but still a big crowd. Connally did a superb introduction to the P with all kinds of super praise, and that should be very effective. We got a lot of polls today. Colson reported the new Harris poll, which will show 59/31, a drop from the 63/29 that we were last time, or a 28-point spread instead of 34. He says the drop is mostly blacks and the under-30 voters.

Tuesday, September 26, 1972

Billy Graham reported today that he thinks thus far we're doing everything just right in the campaign, although he's nervous about the P being exposed as he was in the Laredo motorcade.

We got through New York and went to the Statue of Liberty exercise OK, except there were six demonstrators right down in front who shouted into the microphone and were carried over the same PA system as the P, which caused him to react, I thought adversely at the time. Although it came off pretty well on TV as he asked the cameras to note the other thousands who were listening as well as the six who were heckling.

Dinner went well. The P gave a good speech and we got good reaction to it. Bringing the kids in really helped and added a good level of enthusiasm. The P had me in for a while after the dinner to talk things over, unwind. He had a tough schedule here with the Democrats, Nixon leaders, and Jewish leaders, but all came off pretty well. He is concerned about how we develop a sense of mission in the campaign so that we don't just back into the victory and thus look as if we didn't win the election but merely took it by default. He thinks that's why we need radio speeches and maybe he should also do a press conference at some point.

He did call Tricia, or she called him, late in the evening, after the dinner, to say how well she thought they'd gone. She was at the Washington dinner. Then they got into campaigning plans, and she's going to be in the South. He told her to endorse McClellan in Arkansas, and Eastland in Mississippi, and say that she supported their reelection because they were such strong supporters of her father. That will create quite a stir if she actually does it, I think.

Wednesday, September 27, 1972

We flew from New York this morning, out to San Francisco for the luncheon there and then on to Los Angeles. The trip went OK. The demonstration threat in San Francisco didn't materialize in any great sense, mainly because the police held them all off, although there was some trashing and stirring up. We arrived at the Palace Hotel, though, under huge heavy guard with men with guns stationed all over aimed at the windows, looking down and all that. It was really like the good old days of demonstrations.

The Los Angeles demonstration was considerably larger, out in front of the Century Plaza, but much less violent. They did shout all through the evening. Once again our kids came through extremely well. We had a lot of enthusiasm at the Bay Area Rapid Transit in Oakland, in the Hall at the Palace in San Francisco, and in the Century Plaza when we arrived in Los Angeles. The highlight of the day was Rabbi Magnan's benediction at the dinner, when he prayed for four more years for the P in an all-out political endorsement. It got the audience to applaud. The P again had me in after the dinner, this time for a couple of hours, just general talk on campaign strategy.

Thursday, September 28, 1972

The P did the cancer meeting this morning and then we returned to Washington. A lot of time to talk on the plane. He reacted rather adversely to the *New York Times* endorsement, not surprisingly, that is, their endorsement of McGovern. He wants the *Times* now totally cut off as an enemy, which we all agree we ought to do. Talked a little about the grain deal and how to handle that.

K got back from Paris last evening and I talked to him on the phone, told him the P would call him if he wanted him to. Henry said no need to, that he couldn't talk on the phone, but he did have to meet with him when he got back to Washington, so we set up dinner on the *Sequoia* tonight. K, Haig, and I with the P. Henry went through his whole status as of now, and he is convinced that the North Vietnamese do want to settle and Henry has a proposal that he wants to go back with next week, when he's committed to go back for a three-day meeting. He thinks we can move to an announcement of the settlement sometime between the 20th and 30th of October, which would take effect with the cease-fire in place and a start of the release of prisoners in November.

(There was) considerable discussion, as the P had gone into the meeting prepared to tell Henry that he couldn't make a deal. He feels strongly that, as far as the election's concerned, we're much better off to maintain the present position. The part of Henry's argument that carries some weight, though, is how to deal with Vietnam after the election, and the clear point that we can't just sustain our present course forever, that we've got to go for a break and that the break preelection may be more likely than a break afterward, and that this is the honorable settlement that we sought, does not involve selling out South Vietnam to the Communists, and therefore is satisfactory to us and we should follow it. It was left that that's what we'd do, after the P did considerable questioning of K and Haig as to how they would go about dealing with Thieu. Nobody feels that there's much more than about an even chance of Thieu going along with it.

We're in the ironic position of wanting to continue the talks as long as possible if we're not going to settle, but wanting to complete them as soon as possible if we do, because the closer the settlement comes to the election, now, the more it'll look like a political ploy, which it is in no way, but it will be hard to sell that if we have to announce the settlement just before the election. Even so, it's worth doing as long as it doesn't involve the fact or appearance of a sellout, and they feel that can be avoided.

It was interesting to see Henry turn the P around on this, on the grounds of the problem of how to deal with this after the election. Since the P's approach to it was based on his thought that Henry was trying to get a settlement before the election for the value to us politically, which the P feels is negative rather than positive.

Saturday, September 30, 1972

The P was in early this morning. Spent some time before the SALT signing and then again afterward going over a lot of miscellaneous political things. K was in for a while about the Gromyko meeting and the planning for how to get the P together with Gromyko alone. We worked out an elaborate plan involving returning from Camp David Monday night after the dinner and then a separate meeting on Tuesday morning with

just the P and Gromyko. Then after we got it all worked out,
Henry called this evening to say that Gromyko would be
crushed if he didn't spend the night overnight at Camp David,
so we have to shift it back to that, which the P agreed to.
The P will meet with him privately before the dinner on Monday.

Fourth Quarter: October– December

Tuesday, October 3, 1972
The P came down from Camp David this morning with Gromyko for the SALT signing ceremony. Went very well, was very impressive to everybody there. Ziegler said that Sidey came in and talked to him after the SALT ceremony. He won't vote for McGovern. He feels he's flipped his cork on the basis of his UPI editors thing yesterday, where he hit the P as the most corrupt Administration in history. Phil Potter also came in, said that McGovern is incredible, that he disagrees violently with his remarks. Did comment that the press is rumbling about not having any access to the P and gave Ziegler a tip that McGovern and his Food for Peace thing had heavy shipments of grain abroad in '60 and '62, and that we ought to look into this. He'd like to write it up if we can dig up anything.

Wednesday, October 4, 1972
We were at Camp David all day. The P holed up working on the press conference preparations. He did have me over at noon for a while, reported that he'd returned Walter Cronkite's call. Cronkite had called yesterday, saying that he wanted to have a personal conversation with the P. Turned out that what he's after is to get the P to do an hour interview on CBS.

We had a big flap with Henry last night and carrying on today. He's in a complete tantrum that the P should not have a press conference because he's sure to give the wrong answers on Vietnam and blow the whole negotiation right as Henry is about to go into the crucial final stage. Henry actually believes still, even though Thieu has completely refused to go along with anything Haig has proposed, that we still have a 50–50

623

chance of pulling something off with the North Vietnamese
this weekend and he's scared to death that the P will louse it
up. Actually, I think he'll use anything that comes up as an
excuse if the thing blows, so it works out pretty well for him.
The P doesn't feel that there's any chance of settling, and that
probably it's not desirable anyway because any possible interpretation of a sellout would hurt us more than it helps us.

One interesting thing: I decided to drive down, as I always
do. The P wasn't going to leave Camp David until 9:30. He
called at 7:25, five minutes before I was to leave, to say that
if I needed to get home early, he'd be glad to reschedule his
departure so I could ride down on the helicopter. I said that
I'd intended to drive anyway, but it was very thoughtful of
him to show that concern.

Thursday, October 5, 1972

Press conference this morning went extremely well. One of
the best he's done in the office. After the press conference he
had a whole bunch in, Colson, MacGregor, Scali, E, and Ziegler, for sort of a general analysis and discussion. In the middle
of this, E comes up with a problem on synthetic natural gas.
The P gave him an instant answer, said go ahead and do what
you want to do, but call Connally first on the decision. We
had some discussion on the merits of a TV press conference
vs. in-office, and the question of one in DC vs. going out into
the country somewhere. Nothing really came out of that. He
had Colson and me over to the EOB a little later. Got into the
general political thing, says there's only really 4 issues, then
proceeded to enumerate 6 or 7. Those being amnesty, marijuana, welfare, tax increase, Communist government imposed
on South Vietnam, and reduction of defenses.

Monday, October 9, 1972

A big question this morning arising from a Top Secret cable
from Henry saying that there was some progress at the session
in Paris, but it was imperative to have Rogers avoid any reference to Vietnam in his press conference. I talked that over
with the P, who's agreed that I should tell Rogers there is some
movement, so we have to play things the other way now and
he should say he will not comment on anything at all. Rogers
then came back with the point that he would only repeat what
the P said about the negotiations being in a sensitive stage and

might add the point that he is certain that this is no time for talk about throwing in the towel. He said he could do nothing, refer only to the P or bring in the latter point. I raised that with the P and he felt that on balance, Rogers should cancel the press conference. That there's too much at stake at the moment.

Tuesday, October 10, 1972

Had the Cabinet Leadership breakfast meeting this morning. E did a pitch on issues state by state, with MacGregor giving an overview of the political situation. It was deadly dull, as any such thing would be. The P interjected from time to time as they were going through their poll results and so on. First he emphasized the turnaround of the blue-collar suburbs, that's there's confidence in the country, morality, economy's up, and especially of the great cities of the North. About a tax and escalated rhetoric, we should stay right where we are, more in sorrow than in anger. Hit hard on the issues, stay on the facts—defense, cut welfare and so on. It will get rougher toward the last. Don't react in kind. Don't have both sides getting personal. About the most-corrupt-Administration charge—Watergate, grain deals, etc.—*(he said)* not one instance in four years has there been any personal corruption of the Cabinet appointees or the White House. We have the strictest rules we've ever had. We should have confidence. This is an honest Administration. We will not go down on the charge of corruption.

K had me called out of the meeting on a phone call from Paris. Said that he just discovered there was a communication breakdown yesterday and that we hadn't gotten a cable from him reporting on the status of negotiations. He said there is a cable coming now, that I must understand that the situation is very complex, but they know what they're doing. We should get everybody to keep quiet and keep everybody steady. He said they were going into a meeting in about a half an hour, that if the appropriate point is reached they will leave tonight, late, getting in about 2:00 or 3:00 in the morning. Otherwise they'll stay over. He couldn't tell me a lot more than that right now.

After the Cabinet breakfast the P told Ziegler to quit trying to pander to those who are philosophically against us. Any generous move toward them only shows weakness from their viewpoint. He says the press liberals hate our guts. Not personally, but because they hate our beliefs, so we should not make any nice, personal gesture to an ideological enemy, because they misinterpret it. On the *Post*'s Watergate story today, Ziegler should just stonewall it. That the P is concerned about whether there is a leak in Colson's office somewhere that's causing this, and he came back to that several times during the day, wanting it checked out. He poured it out directly to Colson, who said absolutely not, but naturally that's what he would say.

The *Post* had reported that Donald Segretti had been hired by the CRP to conduct "a massive campaign of political spying and sabotage," including forging letters, leaking false items, and dumping schedules.

Wednesday, October 11, 1972

At Camp David. The P called me over at 11:30. Went through a whole bunch of miscellaneous things. He wants E to try and get the Congress out Saturday at any cost. Also, we should go ahead on the IBM antitrust action but try to make something out of it so we can get credit for attacking business. He's rewritten the letters of endorsement to congressmen and covered those. Likes the idea of Clawson hitting the double standard of the press as far as the sabotage/espionage charges are concerned. They're attacking us for all the things that happened, that we apparently did, but they don't take the other side on for the far worse things that they've been doing. Decided to go Sunday on radio from Camp David because he wants to stay Saturday in Washington until Congress goes out. Without telling anybody, he plans to go up to the Hill for the adjournment celebration. Then wants to keep Monday free and stay up at Camp David. He's intrigued with setting up a postelection study on the Olympic Games. Is concerned about how we're going to cut Agnew's staff after the election. He's concerned about the quality of liquor at the White House. Wants to get started on his phone calls to Senatorial and House candidates.

Called in the afternoon to suggest that Colson try to get Wallace to hit McGovern on his Vietnam sellout. Then got into some discussion on the need for a really superb one-hour documentary on Nixon's travels and so forth, to be done after the election.

Thursday, October 12, 1972

Decided he'd like to do an hour TV in Chicago after the motorcade, but would be with 4 or 5 press people from the Chicago press, so this would take the place of a press conference. I suggested we stay overnight in Chicago, do this the next day, then go to Denver late in the afternoon, which would really work out better. Atlanta worked out very well. We had a huge crowd, great confetti and color and so forth, but it just somehow didn't have the spark of super enthusiasm that you sometimes get.

Henry and Haig got back from Paris and had dinner with the P at 7:00. I went home from the airport, got a call at home saying the P wanted me at the dinner, so I drove back into the White House. We met at 6:45 at the EOB office. Colson was there at the time, and the P went over some odds and ends with Chuck, then K and Haig arrived and Colson left. We sat in the inner office, and as soon as Colson went out the door, K opened by saying, Well, you've got three for three, Mr. P *(meaning China, the Soviet Union, and now a Vietnam settlement).* The P was sitting over in his easy chair. K, Henry, and I were sitting at the table. The P was a little incredulous at first, and sort of queried Henry a bit. Henry started to outline the agreement from his secret red folder. Made the point overall that we got a much better deal by far than we had expected. The net effect is that it leaves Thieu in office. We get a stand-in-place cease-fire on October 30 or 31. They have to agree to work together to set up a Council of National Concord and reconciliation, but any action by this council has to be by unanimous vote, so it can't effectively hurt Thieu any. The cease-fire would be followed by a complete withdrawal of troops within 60 days and a return of the POW's in 60 days. We'd have everything done by the end of the year.

He then said that one of the agreements is that we provide an economic aid program to North Vietnam. The P interjected at that point, said this is the most significant thing of all because it's a collapse of Communist principle. They've always refused to accept that kind of aid because it admits the failure of their system. This gives us the leverage on them. China refused any discussion of it, and so on.

The P kept interrupting Henry all through the discussion. He obviously was all cranked up and wasn't listening to the details. He commented on the problems leading up to this agreement, the significance of China, the bombing and mining and his usual litany, kidding Henry some, referring to Haig a great deal and asking if he really was satisfied with the deal, because he had been basically opposed to it last week, because he thought we were screwing Thieu. Now he thinks it's OK, but he is concerned about whether we can sell Thieu on it. I asked him after the meeting, though, whether he honestly felt it was a good deal, and he says he does think it is. Henry kept trying to plow through his folder and all the details and the P kept interrupting. The plan will be for Henry to go to Paris next Tuesday, then to Saigon, then see Thieu. He'll spend three days there, then up to Hanoi, then back to Saigon to report to Thieu and then back to here and we make the deal. The P interjected that Haig must go with you. Henry said no, that we need him here to deal with the bureaucracy and so on. The P said well, someone's got to go. He suggested me. I felt I should not. K said no, it would raise too much anticipation. If it were known that I was going, and also I'm needed here to hold things down.

We then went into dinner in the outer office. The P told Manolo to bring the good wine, his '57 Lafite-Rothschild, or whatever it is, to be served to everyone. Usually it's just served to the P and the rest of us have some California Beaulieu Vineyard stuff. The discussion continued along the same line. Then the P toasted us all. The decision was to handle Rogers at breakfast tomorrow, and that I'm to be there. Tell him that we had a significant breakthrough on the military side, but that K has to go back to Paris next week to try to finish up the political part of it. If he gets it worked out, he'll then go to Saigon to go over it with Thieu. We won't tell him about Hanoi or the fact that the whole schedule is set now, with the P making the announcement on October 26 for the October 30 cease-fire. K wants to be sure there's no responsibilities assigned to Rogers because he'll try to parlay them at the State Department. Instead, let Henry line up Bill Sullivan, he's Henry's man and he'll take Sullivan with him. Also, he wants to handle Alex Johnson. Playing to the idea that the future of the Foreign Service depends on Johnson's cooperation on this with the P. The ultimate payoff for Rogers is that he gets to go to Paris to sign the cease-fire with the Vietnamese Foreign Minister on October 30 and that takes effect when they sign it. We went around the details some more. The real basic problem boils down to the question of whether Thieu can be sold on it. The P is obviously really cranked up with the whole thing. K reported on the very high emotional level of the talks and the fact that at the end of the 14 hours of talks yesterday that Le Duc Tho remarked that the two of them had been negotiating on this for four years now. They had some very tough times, but now we both accept the same thing, which was to make peace and today we have made peace. Haig feels that the reason they're doing this is that they've basically given up, they have no more hope and they're now going to try and establish friendship with us, which is what they say they want just like our China relationship. Overall, it boils down to a super-historic night if it all holds together, and Henry is now convinced it will. He thinks that he's really got the deal. So we'll see.

Friday, October 13, 1972

Started the day with the Rogers-K breakfast. Haig and I sat in. The P and Henry gave Rogers the general plan we agreed on last night, which covered the fact that Henry had the details of the military settlement worked out but is still hung up on the political settlement and wouldn't have that till after he goes back to Paris on Tuesday. If it is worked out, he would then go to Saigon and work it out with Thieu.

Rogers walked into the trap by saying that he didn't think we should accept any settlement that overthrew Thieu. He indicated that we should of course leap at any settlement that didn't overthrow Thieu, no matter how it was worked out, so he's now positioned to have to back the actual settlement enthusiastically, since it's better than anything he thinks possible at the moment.

The P had Henry up to the Lincoln Room after breakfast, called me in mainly for a discussion of schedule plans, but both he and Henry felt that they had the ground pretty well laid out with Rogers. Henry then went on during the day to meet with Alex Johnson as Rogers agreed he could, and with Bill Sullivan. Sullivan's nitpicking some of the details, but Henry thinks that can be worked out, and things are pretty well on track. Both the P and Henry are realizing in the cold gray light of dawn today that they still have a plan that can fall apart, mainly the problem of getting Thieu on board, but also the problem that the North Vietnamese might not buy what Le Duc Tho comes back to them with. So it's still problematical, although Henry's convinced that he's got it settled, that it will work out and that we can talk Thieu into it. I would think he could, because the settlement he's got is the best Thieu is ever going to get and, unlike '68, when Thieu screwed Johnson, he had Nixon as an alternative. Now he has McGovern as an alternative, which would be a disaster for him, even worse than the worst possible thing that Nixon could do to him.

On the schedule, the P's obsessed today with going to Pennsylvania. Wants to go to Pittsburgh at noon for a motorcade, plus we can get a good crowd in the late afternoon. Make it a mid-Atlantic meeting with West Virginia, MD, Delaware, Pennsylvania, and New Jersey. Then do the boilermakers' ball early in the evening and leave. We got into the point that we have to do Philadelphia because Rizzo's expecting it. Also that we can't do Pittsburgh because McGovern's there the day of the boilermakers' ball, so he told me to call Rizzo and talk him out of a visit there. I did that and Rizzo isn't about to be talked out of it. He's determined that the P should be there. He gave me a big pitch on how great everything was, that he had all the ward leaders in today. They're almost all on his payroll. He told them that the P either wins in their areas or they're to look for another job. Came up with a lot of ideas for things that the P might do in Philadelphia but insisted he's got to come. So we're probably trapped on that. We'll work something out as time goes on with Rizzo. The P also got into some postelection plans. He's now decided he ought to spend a week in Key Biscayne before settling down at Camp David to put the new Administration together. I think that's probably a good idea.

We got into a long discussion on the espionage charge, because it now turns out the *Post* has Chapin involved in it as a way to bring in the White House, so we spent a lot of time late this afternoon and evening trying to work out a way of answering that, which is a little hard to do because we don't even have the *Post*'s story, but I think we'll develop something that'll work for the time being at least.

Editor's Note: The Washington Post reported that Segretti had been hired by Dwight Chapin—thereby tying Watergate into the White House.

Saturday, October 14, 1972

The P had Ray Price and John E in at noon to review the whole radio speech. He made the point to Ray that these speeches need 3 or 4 quotable lines, but they are to philosophize a bit. They should be nonpartisan, nonpolitical, and nonnegative as possible. Uplifting, like the Atlanta line, where we direct attention to the hopes and dreams that unite us rather than the hates and fears that divide us.

The P shifted into his regular spiel on the thing that people don't love each other and we're not all the same and we can't approach things on that basis. The whole secret and the philosophy that we have is based on the fact that we live in an explosive world. There are differences between people.

Then he went into his anti-college-education spiel and back to the point that people are different. So are nations. The secret of the American experiment is that they learned that the things that unite us are more important than the things that divide us. He then got into his feeling for the South, that because of going to school there he had a close feeling and they resent always being put down by the Northerners. Makes the point that union leaders are like the South. They want to abide by the law and they respect the Presidency. He then said the theme to development is in regard to the heartland. Our New American Majority appeals across the board for the same reasons to people. The basic American values. A strong United States patriotism, strong moral and spiritual values. Antipermissiveness. They are turned off on welfare because it's wrong and because they are anti-elitist, plus they have selfish motives. They are Americans to the core. The Southerners are more so than the rest of the United States, because they are not poisoned by the elite universities and the media, but we're also high in Polish, Italian, mountain areas, farm states. Weak in the suburbia/big cities because here the people are soft. The analysts miss the point that the "movement" has had it. The people that are for permissiveness, anti–United States, and so forth. That square America is coming back and that we didn't just gather a bunch of haters. The real issue is patriotism, morality, religion. Not the material issues of taxes and prices. If those were the issue, the people would be for McGovern rather than for us.

Henry called about the Vietnam negotiations. He's concerned about whether he's handling the settlement right and then he raised an alternate scenario in which he would get the process dragged on a little with new demands. He'd still go through the whole schedule, but not sign the final agreement till November 15. The problem is, we'd have to stop bombing from the time of his trip until the election. I told him my concern there was trying to carry the period between the trip and the election, with all the speculation and so forth. He says if we get Thieu enthusiastic with this, then it's OK and we can go ahead. If Thieu turns it down, he feels we would have been better to have been hung up on a North Vietnamese negotiating point than on letting them know that we're hung up on trying to keep Thieu in. I said I didn't think any of this delay was possible if he went on to Hanoi, but he basically refuses to consider canceling it. Feels he's got to go through the whole route, in any event. On that basis I felt it was impossible to make any change in the scenario as it's now laid out.

Sunday, October 15, 1972

K's concerns continued as he called this morning. He says he's now persuaded that we shouldn't stall, as he proposed last night, but that maybe he should go to Saigon and come back to Washington if there's a problem with Thieu, and then the following week go through the whole run again, which would save Thieu's face and would provide an intermediate step of a one-week delay before we drop the thing. Also would have some political advantages, he feels. We've used these time schedules to get the changes fast and he's concerned about anything that gets in the way of them.

P called me over first thing this morning. He had read *The Washington Post,* which has the major front page story on Dwight Chapin being the director of the Segretti espionage activity. When I came in, he was talking to Ehrlichman *(on the phone)* regarding the Chapin story and made the point of the shocking double standard of the *Post* and the *Times.* Never say a word against the dirtiest campaign ever waged against a P, name-calling, bombing headquarters, etc. The P made the point to me when he hung up that the difference between him and Johnson sure showed up and that's that he's always backed up his staff. He thinks we ought to raise hell with the *L.A. Times* if they pick up the story. He thinks I should call Otis *(Chandler, the publisher)* and point out to him that when he was under attack in his oil deal, the P told all of us "hands off." He's especially concerned about *(P's lawyer)* Kalmbach and how he handles this and how he explains what funds he was using. He feels it needs to be tied to the Committee and Liddy rather than the other thing. There's a problem with the story regarding the lawyer for the P putting up the money. We need to be sure to tie the money to the Committee. He feels strongly, too, that we can't surface Segretti, although that was one of the things we were considering Friday.

Henry called again later this evening after I got home and said he's worried now that if he goes to Hanoi it'll look like we've given in to Jane Fonda and Ramsey Clark. We could avoid this by using option B. Going to Paris and then announcing after that on the second round. He's worried about the question of whether this appears to be the P crawling. I assured him I didn't think it was, but he phoned again, this time to ask me to help out, to sit on Rogers during this week. Apparently Rogers had Haig and Sutherland out to his house tonight, made the point that he has to take charge now and get all these things worked out. Henry's concerned that if Rogers thinks it's succeeding, he'll rush to get in on it. He's not really too concerned about it though. Henry feels now the more he thinks about it that the more it seems that we're pulling off a miracle and that we should go ahead with it if we possibly can.

Monday, October 16, 1972

The main discussion this morning was on the *Washington Post* attack, both yesterday and today on the Chapin story. The P makes the point that the main thing they're trying to do is tie in the P and say he didn't tell the truth, that no one in the White House was involved in Watergate. He feels there's no problem regarding the little games and stuff. The real question that concerns him is how Ziegler deals with the Kalmbach involvement. Thinks he ought to hit it with some sarcasm, saying he's surprised you haven't brought Pat Nixon in, too. She's also a graduate of Southern Cal, and so is OJ Simpson. Thinks Ron should hit that the issues being evaded because

the opposition press obviously feels that it doesn't have a good
case on the issues. On the P view, he's spoken out against
violence, he's given orders that are to be carried out, that there
is to be no violence or disruption of rallies. If you've noticed,
there has been none. Our opponent has not said anything about
the hecklers and violence, and so on, on us. First, we cannot
condone what was done. Second, we must separate it from
Watergate. The whole purpose of this from their viewpoint, he
thinks, is that it's the last burp of the Eastern establishment.
The only thing he's basically concerned about is to be sure we
don't lie and be sure we don't condone any bad activity. Make
the point that we're running a high-road campaign, no name
calling, we're hitting hard on the issues. The President is the
victim of the dirtiest campaign ever conducted against a President of the United States. They should start using the line of
the Eastern establishment press, make the point that they're
strangely silent on all this stuff against us. Also the point that
the *Post* and the *Times* praise spies when they're related to the
Anderson papers, the Pentagon Papers, the India-Pakistan matter. Because of their double standard, they don't seem to be
concerned with spying when it doesn't involve the security of
the country.

He had Ehrlichman in later today, suggested that Segretti
sue the *Post* for libel and give the *Star* a statement on it. Made
the interesting point that after the election we will have awesome power with no discipline, that is, there won't be another
election coming up to discipline us, and we've got to do our
planning on that basis.

He did the POW wives at the last minute this morning. We
ran it in because we had no story to counter the espionage/
sabotage story, so I went in and talked him into going over at
the last minute to do the POW wives. He had a great reception,
gave one of the best talks he's given.

Tuesday, October 17, 1972

Haig was in first thing this morning with a report from Henry
who says the talks are going well and he feels that he should
go on to Saigon, so he will tonight. We got into some discussions about Henry's attitude, along the same lines that Haig
had expressed to me yesterday. He shares the P's view that
Henry is strongly motivated in all this by a desire for personally being the one to finally bring about the final peace settle-

ment. Al feels this poses a major problem in that it's causing him to push harder for a settlement and to accept a less favorable thing than he might if he didn't have this push. He thinks that my talk with him about a successor for Haig in the second term is very helpful, in that it gave him some reassurance that he would be around in the second term, and that therefore the pressure for him to get this settled before the election was lightened and his willingness to talk it over with Haig was greatly increased. Haig urges that while Henry is gone we give every possible evidence to him that we can of total support so that he won't feel that he has to prove anything. He agrees that under no circumstances can he go to the third stop unless the whole thing is fully settled, but he's not at all convinced that Henry fully shares this view.

The P spoke this morning to a group of foreign labor leaders. Felt afterward that he'd given a very thoughtful analysis of the relationship between labor and government and the history of free labor in the United States and that no one would notice it, that he wouldn't get any mileage out of it.

Monday, October 23, 1972

P had a few odds and ends to cover on the plane going up to New York today. They were on the details for handling the trips, and some more of the same on the plane on the way back. The New York motorcade went very well. The P did feel that we needed more signs along the route to cover up the anti-signs, although there weren't very many of them. He feels that we should make an asset of the demonstrators. The Rockefeller stop worked out pretty well, the Governor had E and me join Mrs. Nixon, the David Rockefellers, and Bob Douglas for dinner, which was very nice. Nelson was obviously quite overwhelmed by the fact that the P was stopping at his house. The P didn't join us for dinner, but did come in at the end for coffee, and this Nelson obviously greatly appreciated; he made quite a point of having champagne brought in, and having a toast to the P, as the first President of the United States to stay at the house.

Tuesday, October 24, 1972

The more I get to thinking about it, the more the P is concerned about motorcade security. I told him about the report of someone's being picked up with a shotgun, and he made the point that we should be concerned somewhat with the danger. Mc-Govern haters are dangerous-type people, especially as they get backed into a corner in desperation, and this raises a question of whether or not it's wise to do any more motorcading. In Chicago, he wants to make a very short run, and then we got into quite a discussion of the cancellation of Ohio. He was making it for reasons of the war, security, health, and so on. This is the first time that I've seen the P concerned about security, but I think that he's now feeling that since we've got the win pretty well locked up anyway, there's no point in running an unnecessary and undue risk.

He raised the question again why we don't have somebody file a lawsuit to knock down the Watergate story, without getting into specific denials, but just a general suit by one of the injured parties.

We had our regular local strategy meeting this afternoon for a couple of hours, with Connally, E, MacGregor, Colson, and Mitchell. Connally opened making the point about the peace negotiations, hoping that there wouldn't be anything before the election. It would hurt us because it would look expedient. The P explained that negotiations are in the benefit stage, and we have to deal with them as they come. Connally then said that it's important that it appears that the P is in charge, that it's not K who is running this.

Wednesday, October 25, 1972

The *Post* story on me broke this morning and was the major story for today.

Editor's Note: The Washington Post claimed that CRP treasurer Hugh Sloan had given testimony to the grand jury that Haldeman had approved a large sum of money for campaign sabotage. However, Sloan had never given such testimony.

We had gotten into it yesterday evening, since they had inquired about it, and we knew that the story would probably break, and it did. Today's the day McGovern does his big speech on corruption, so they obviously will use that as the buildup. There was a lot of discussion during the day about the effect and what should be done.

Ziegler did a strong counterattack on the *Post* at his briefing.

this morning, and that will ride as the main answer with a good strong denial, also Hugh Sloan and others have handled denials. The P didn't seem overly worried about it, although he did raise it some. Let's see what develops from there.

The P got into some questions on speech schedules. He wants to get going on the foreign policy one, using the material from his San Francisco speech, but building up the point of massive retaliation being outdated in discussing the fate of small nations. We went over the timing of the various radio speeches. He also wants a radio spot on Amnesty; he feels we're not getting enough on that. Feels that Ziegler or someone should hit the *Post* on yellow journalism, that we should keep a hard attack going on McGovern, on Vietnam, and then in the middle of all that he raised the point that he wants a little press facility built up at Camp David for use as a briefing room, and a small press lounge set up.

Thursday, October 26, 1972

K called me at the 3:00 this morning to say that the North Vietnamese had gone public on the peace proposal and he was in a state of very great concern at that time. He called again at 7:00 and had simmered down considerably as I thought he would, as he found their thing didn't really look as bad as he was afraid that it was going to.

Editor's Note: K had been having considerable difficulty getting Thieu to accept the agreement, and the North Vietnamese had broadcast the plan to put pressure on Thieu and the U.S. K responded with a press briefing.

The peace move was featured in the papers, and on TV tonight after K's briefing today. The P wanted a quick poll made to see what the public reaction was to the peace plan as it stands, mainly the question of whether he should order a bombing halt, while we're negotiating, or if he should continue the bombing. He made the point that we've got to attack McGovern on his peace-by-surrender forum, and all the Vietnam-related issues, abandoning the POW's and so forth. He makes the point that only great events can change things in the campaign now, and Vietnam is the only great event happening. We've got to be sure that if it changes anything, it changes it our way. He emphasized the need in the last two weeks to keep down the jitters with the staff and said he ought to get all the surrogates in on Saturday and have Henry brief them. He told me to work with Haig on the PR on this. All that matters now is what the press says, that it's a political battle of the first magnitude. K plays an enormous and important part now and we've got to watch every development and make the most of each of them. The question that concerns him is whether it appears we're playing politics with Vietnam. He emphasized the need for Henry to see the good press people and then came up with the idea that he ought to have a press conference before the election, maybe do it on the plane, with an expanded pool on the way out.

Ziegler felt that he was very disturbed when Ron reported to him on K's briefing. Ron wrote up that the P felt that we were getting the wrong twist on this, and that K was getting the play. The announcement had been blown, where the P had hoped that he could go before the nation and make the announcement. Now it had been made by the North Vietnamese and briefed by Henry, which kind of pulled the P out of it. He was uptight when he talked with me about the K thing, but on the basis that Henry hadn't gotten our points over, the anti-McGovern points. So the P wants that followed up, making the point primarily, our peace with honor versus his peace by surrender. I said that I thought this break by the North Vietnamese would turn out to be the best lucky break of the campaign for us because it takes the corruption stuff off the front pages, totally wipes out any other news.

Friday, October 27, 1972

Had a long talk with Billy Graham. He thinks Watergate is penetrating a little bit, but the peace initiative throws it into the back pages, that McGovern himself is the major factor, that we're not in danger anywhere. Said that anytime he wanted, he would be most happy to make a statement on my behalf, or Dwight's, on our character and so forth. That we shouldn't let them get away with the whole thing. He too is worried about the security factor of the P getting too much exposure. Feels that if North Vietnam blows the peace deal it will be a real problem, and then summed up again that we need to see more of the P in the last 10 days. More publicly, that is.

Saturday, October 28, 1972

The P had a strong reaction to CBS's special report on the Watergate last night. Says, "That finishes them." He means he's ready to write CBS off.

K was concerned about his briefing the surrogates and thought that Rogers should do it instead. Thinks that we need to make the point that the P has achieved his goals in the settlement: the return of POW's, the cease-fire, and no Communist government, versus McGovern who would leave the POW's there, pull a unilateral withdrawal and disarm the South Vietnamese, and provide a Communist takeover. We should make the point that we've been working on this all down the line, and that there's no concern with the election, our concern is to get it nailed down.

P told Henry to use *The New York Times* as his outlet, and to totally cut out *The Washington Post*. He feels that the opposition strategy is to try to mar our victory, they know that they can't defeat us, so they're trying to make the victory as unimportant as possible by hanging the Vietnam thing in on a negative basis, by trying to hammer us down on the Watergate stuff. He feels that we have to be cold-blooded regarding those who have tried to crucify us on the politics, playing politics with peace. Henry says the problem now is with Thieu, his going public. The P thought that maybe he ought to have a meeting with Thieu. Henry says no, but to send a Presidential letter so they'll work on that basis. The big problem now is for the next ten days to keep the thing from blowing up either on the North or the South. So that we don't have an adverse reaction set in prior to the election.

We did the Ohio, Michigan trip today. The motorcade went very well. We didn't get very good press on it on the TV tonight, but we had great crowds, great enthusiasm, and it should have been extremely effective in Ohio. The Michigan stop also was a huge crowd at the airport, even on 24 hours' notice. So it was a good campaigning day.

Sunday, October 29, 1972

We had to go into the surrogates' briefing. The P was going to open for five minutes, but talked for half an hour. Made the point that in the final week, with all the rumors that will be coming, we must be confident, positive, not defensive. We're building a foundation for a lasting peace. He referred to the trips to Peking and Moscow, that was getting to the heart of the problem with peace, that we refused to let Vietnam obscure the big picture, especially in a historic year of 1972, where we've really developed a chance for peace for a generation. He got to the point that they may wonder whether the campaign was worth it. Then he talked about the beautiful people who sit on the beach here, and play on the tennis courts in Newport, and Palm Beach, and said that you're the lucky people. They aren't. He said that he feels that it's true of a person, that he's never his true self, his complete self, unless he's engaged in a great enterprise, and that we all played a part in such an enterprise. Then he said, I'm a tough anti-Communist, but I'm not anti-Chinese, anti-Russian, or anti-Polish.

E hit two issues, corruption and vetoes. On corruption, he said he should use every question as an opportunity to talk about our issues, the problem with the number of charges with no evidence, and it's hard to prove a negative. If we deal with the charges on the same plane as they've been made, you'll lose. We must move the answer to what you want to say. He used Chapin as an example. The fact is that his duties at the time he was supposed to be running the sabotage thing were to put together the Chinese and Russian trips. He made three trips to China, spent hours in that situation room, etc. He referred to the Godfrey Sperling (*Christian Science Monitor*) article, saying that the issue is not significant, because the public is unwilling to impute liability to the P on the basis of the charges offered. So you should move from the Chapin question, and his great responsibility for these trips, and then move to a discussion of the trips and foreign policy.

He referred to the *Post* article on me, and to take that as a case study; the sources were based on two reports and both of them have been denied. Also, he hit the point that the P is obliged by the Congress now to analyze 132 bills, which is 20 percent of their two years' work, while in this period he also has to run a political campaign and work out the war's ending. Which is all a good answer to the hiding in the White House.

Al Haig hit the Vietnam agreement, the specific points. Bill Rogers then emphasized the P's overall accomplishments, that peace is the overriding issue, but it's like good health, you don't talk about it unless you don't have it. Overall, the world is more peaceful, we came into office with two and a half wars going, Vietnam, Nigeria, and the Middle East. Now there's a cease-fire in the Middle East, we've ended the war in Africa, there are no casualties in Vietnam, and withdrawing from there and from other areas. Also, conditions are much more peaceful in the United States. The campuses, streets, and so forth. We should emphasize that Nixon is the world leader in the positive peace, and recognized as such throughout the world.

Monday, October 30, 1972

One major item today is the continuing debate on how to counterattack on the whole espionage business. The P still thinks we should consider a libel suit, using the Colson route of saying the *Post* and Edward Bennett Williams told malicious lies involving the White House tied to the Watergate. Also, Ehrlichman feels we should exploit the *Post*'s submission of guilt, but is concerned about the Colson libel suit because it will inevitably lead to his having to leave the White House after the election. He feels that the P will be forced to clean up.

The P thinks that we should go ahead on the white paper to the editors, give them the specific answers on all of the Watergate items, and that maybe E should use *US News* in next week's issue to get the whole story on record, get it established somewhere. He's afraid that it will leave a blotch on us, after the election, if we don't get the word out and all the questions answered now.

Later today, E called and said that he, Stans, Dean, and Moore had worked out a possible settlement of the Common Cause case, which is to go to trial tomorrow. So that we would disclose 5 million of our pre-April 7 gifts under court order, and this would avoid their going to trial until after the first of the year, and would keep Sloan off the stand. They feel it's a good way to cut our losses, so they're going ahead to try to work that out.

The other big item today was the whole Vietnam question, and how we deal with the attack on McGovern, and the threat of the North Vietnamese blowup. The original plan was for Rogers to hit McGovern today at a press conference about his point that he would reserve the right to renegotiate any deal that we make.

E feels that the key to Rogers' doing this is that the P be precisely positioned tomorrow in Chicago, because he would have to say some things at the regional meeting, and that K is doing a talking paper that he will discuss with the P on this.

E feels that K talks as if it's a virtual certainty that this will blow up tomorrow. The P got back to considerable discussion of what he thinks a blowup would do. Makes the point that Rogers should go ahead today, but the problem is that we had no choice, once North Vietnam was on track, we couldn't turn it off, or slow it down. He called me a little later on the phone, said he had talked to K and that they expect a message at 2:00 or 3:00, that E was overreacting, that K says that first they may agree to talk, second, they may just postpone the talks, third, they may possibly blow up, but K thinks that the third is not likely, but if it does happen that we should just take the offensive. He now feels that Rogers should not go out today until we get the message from North Vietnam. It's okay for Agnew to take on McGovern now, as hard as hell, but we have to wait until we get the message before Rogers can go out. He then cautions that we must not get jittery and hysterical. We've got to handle this with poise, that we're going through the birth pains of an agreement.

I talked to K, and he says that North Vietnam is preparing a blow for us this week. First, that they might not show up on Thursday because the negotiations are completed. Second, they might agree to meet. Third, they'd say we cheated them, so they're breaking the whole thing off. If the latter happens, he thinks we should just brazen it through. He later told the P he was concerned that we would take a murderous beating because he did get the message from North Vietnam and they simply said that they were taking the whole thing under serious consideration and would get back to us later. Henry feels that we must go on the offensive if they do blow. Publish all that we've offered. Make the point that we didn't meet with them to sign, because first, Saigon reports they're seizing territory and the threat of a bloodbath. Second, Pham Van Dong claimed this was a coalition government, which we agreed it was not. Third, we never agreed to leave all their troops in the South, and we've been watching for a unilateral withdrawal, which they were supposed to do as evidence of good faith. Then we should make the point that if in good faith we can settle, we will, but that we will not let ourselves be stampeded into doing this just for the election. He also says that the liberal press is very vulnerable in any effort to attack us, because now they've moved to the right of us, and they're complaining that we're letting good old Thieu down.

Henry feels that he should step out again, and brief the press, that it should not be elevated to the Presidential level. We should just say that the first item was to end the war. We've made major progress. If the P goes on TV Thursday night he should open by saying the first thing in looking at the future is to end the war. That we've made major progress, and then describe the situation as it stands on Thursday night. Say we're committed to a generation of peace, and we pledge that we will get peace with honor in Vietnam. He feels that the first five minutes on the talk should be on Vietnam in any event, in a strong manly way, and the P later agreed, and said that we should go to the full half hour, if we need extra time.

We then went over the poll that we had done over the weekend, which shows a drop in the trial heat, and evidence that it's not because of Vietnam, but because the corruption thing is starting to get through some.

Wednesday, November 1, 1972

The P spent a lot of time today with Ray Price, working over the various speeches. They've developed a good one on health that he's going to do on Friday and then foreign policy on Saturday, and he's polished up the TV speech. He's decided not to use the easy chair, but rather will sit behind a desk setting, but in the library with the books back of him so that it looks like a library. He also wants to get the maximum TV coverage that we can out of it, and he agreed right this afternoon to tape it rather than doing it live, and we would do it as a "sudden-death" tape, just leaving the flubs in and so on. We reviewed the general situation in our polls standing etc., and he seems to feel now that we're in good shape.

Thursday, November 2, 1972

The P spent the whole day over the EOB, getting ready for his TV speech tonight and getting other speeches worked out. He had me over after the taping this afternoon; he was disturbed because there were too many people in the room, they had to do three starts before they got a good tape, one of the cameras conked out, there were sound problems, etc. So he's not too happy about that. He also got into the general schedule for the balance of the campaign, questioning again whether he ought to hit another stop or two, and deciding on the speeches. He was concerned about the health speech, as he started reviewing it, because it appeared to be saying he was for compulsory health insurance, which he is not. So he called E and me and read the speech and did some further checking on it.

Friday, November 3, 1972

We had the three airport rallies today. Chicago didn't go very well, there were a lot of hecklers and the P got into the thing on the plane afterward. It's the organized harassment and vulgarity that's deliberate, it's a conspiracy to deny free speech even to the P of the United States. He thinks Ziegler ought to get this out as obviously a planned campaign of disruption and obscenity.

Tulsa went better, but there was some of it there, too. The problem there is the Assistant Attorney General, who insisted that they not throw the bad people out, so the P wants him tracked down and some action taken on him.

The Rhode Island run had a lot of hecklers, and we had PA problems during the day also, so the P got into the need for getting all the PA's checked out for tomorrow. He raised the point also on the plane, the need for Watergate follow-up to be worked out, so that we have a complete plan right after the election and can move on that. Wants to know who's in charge, and how that's being handled. I talked to Ehrlichman about it. He and John Dean are supposedly on top of it.

Saturday, November 4, 1972

McGovern hit us hard last night on Vietnam and accused the P of lying, deceit, and so forth, and insists that he *(the P)* debate him if he disagrees. Quite a lot of discussion on how to handle this attack, including the possibility of K's briefing the pool on background on the plane, or the P's saying something in his remarks today.

The rallies went well today. North Carolina was a real happening, with a huge crowd breaking across the ramp. New Mexico went normally well, and Southern California was spectacular, a stadium-type bleacher setup at the end of the runway.

Monday, November 6, 1972

He did his TV taping today, and it was pretty funny. They had trouble getting started, and got pretty well into the first take and they had to cut because of a fly's moving around. The P made some pretty funny cracks. As they tried to get rid of the fly, he said they'll never get it with a swatter. Then he said, "If you've got a fly, you've got a fly, let's go ahead." They finally got two pretty good takes, and we'll go ahead with them on that basis.

I talked to Connally, he thinks that we're in great shape. That they've gotten meaner on all of us, and that he has no problem readings at all. There is very little apathy and there will be a very heavy vote all over the United States. The only thing is, that minds are made up, and that's why they don't show interest now. The only problem is the majority has never been done before, and it's hard to believe that we can approach it. He figured that it will come out about 58–42. It's hard to believe that it can be bigger than that.

It's ironic, in terms of the whole North Vietnam situation at this point, that McGovern has cut loose on these last couple nights with his complete all-out blast of the P on Vietnam, making the point primarily that we have no deal and that there isn't going to be any peace. Then, Saturday, we got the word from North Vietnam that we had a date set, the 13th, or whatever other date that K wanted to confirm, for next meeting, so we knew that we had the thing ready to go, but couldn't say anything about it, so we had to let McGovern kick us around.

Tuesday, November 7, 1972

On the plane going back to Washington, we got into a review of personnel and Cabinet staff. I raised the point with him, in this conversation, because it seemed to be the right time, that I thought he ought to seriously consider letting E and me resign, and get a complete new posture as far as the close-in White House staff is concerned. He obviously has to keep Henry for a while because of the ongoing foreign policy activities, but I made the case that he would be better off changing John and me. He didn't buy it, and I rather suspected that he wouldn't. But it was a good idea to have raised it. I made the point that both of us are tarnished, not just with the campaign scandal question, but more importantly, the problems of isolation of the P, riding roughshod on Congress, and on the press, and so on, and that he could clean a lot of that up by changing us. He made the point that, from his side some of us were essential to stay on, and that John and I would be in that category. He wouldn't be able to function with new people in those jobs, where he can in some others, and therefore it's worth paying the price of the negatives, which he said he had thought about, and recognized the validity of the points that I was making.

We got back to the White House, and all the staff were out to greet the P on the steps, it was quite a cheery thing after a long flight across the country. The P went right to the Residence to have dinner with the family, and we got set for the election-night processing. Unfortunately we totally over-organized on data-processing and totally underorganized for just getting the simple returns in a form that we can get to the P quickly and understandably.

One of the first losers of the evening was Louie Nunn of Kentucky and the P couldn't believe it. The P then said, this was early in the evening, that we would have to postpone the departure tomorrow for Key Biscayne because he had a funny thing happen at dinner tonight. An old bridge that he had, had fallen out, and he had lost a tooth. He was going to have to go to the dentist at 9:00 tomorrow morning and then again at 1:00 to get the bridge replaced. As he called me from the Residence, I worked in my office, I could hear his "Victory at Sea" record playing loudly in the background. He was amazed at the losses in Maine, and some of those, and de-lighted with Bartlett picking up Oklahoma.

Was mainly interested in how the Presidential thing was going, which was sensational. He had Colson and me come over to the EOB about 1:30, where he had gone about mid-night, and, at that time, he called Hubert, returning Hubert's call, and they had a long chat regarding Hubert's attitude to-ward the P and national security, etc., versus McGovern's. It appeared to be quite a friendly conversation. He was con-cerned about how we answer the question of losing the House and Senate, was particularly interested in an analysis of Cali-fornia, and the background there, but we couldn't find any-body. They were all out celebrating, so we had a terrible time trying to get through.

Along about 2:00 in the morning, maybe it was 2:30, he suggested that he ought to have some bacon and eggs, so he ordered them up from the White House Mess, and the three of us ate bacon and eggs, and they finally brought us some toast and some milk. After that, we chatted a little bit about the general reaction of the returns and then went on to bed. I didn't get home and in bed until 4:00 this morning.

Wednesday, November 8, 1972

The P was in early this morning, I didn't get in till later, he was poring over the vote analysis.

Editor's Note: The President ended up with 60.7 percent versus McGovern's 37.5 percent. It was the second-largest-percentage of the popular vote in two-party history, next to Johnson/Goldwater in 1964.

The P and I went into the staff meeting. He opened by saying, last night he had gotten a lot more sleep than he was accustomed to getting in his elections. That there were to be no vacations, we need to get the organization set in place for the next term, concentrate on the budget, reorganizing the staff, and departments. We intend to very significantly reorganize the White House staff, and he will discuss that later with the people concerned. At the moment he wants them to know that he's very proud of his staff. They're accused of a lot of things. Maybe a frequent accusation is that they are efficient, and to that we should plead guilty. They are also loyal, and they've gotten a lot done and we will continue to have problems with the Congress, but we have more influence now because of the majority. Everyone will have suggestions on how to improve his own office, there are no sacred cows, we should tear up the pea patch in the organization of the Cabinet and the agencies and so on. As far as your plans are concerned, we'll meet you individually, we'll come out after thorough discussion and try to develop the best place for everybody. After the Eisenhower midterm victory we didn't change things enough. Maybe a P shouldn't serve more than four years, but I'm not ready to raise that question yet. Then he went into his Disraeli story about the exhausted volcano. He said that didn't apply to individuals, but it does apply to the entity, and it's the responsibility of the leader to be sure we don't fall into that situation. We can't climb to the top and look down into the embers, we've got to still shoot some sparks, vitality, and strength, and that we get some of that from new people, both in the Cabinet and here in the staff. This is not a case where we say goodbye and start all over. We do say thank you, we want your views, want to know what you like to do. Whatever you decide, these are the members of the first team. Needless to say, the staff was ecstatic.

I stayed on after the P left and covered the details of how we're handling the transition period, while he went and opened the Cabinet meeting. He spoke to the Cabinet for about an hour, and again I went in after he had left, and followed up on the details of getting them all to submit their resignations, and ordering departmental meetings, etc., to work out the follow-up on that.

On the plane to Florida this afternoon, the P got into the whole media reaction. He wants Ziegler to put a total embargo on *Times* and *Newsweek,* there's to be no background to Sidey regarding election night or anything else at any time. He wants total discipline on the press, they're to be used as enemies, not played for help. Wants the story out that a private poll in the White House press showed that 80 out of 89 supported McGovern. Told me to tell Henry that it's OK to talk to Evans and Novak, but not to the other people. He made the point that most second terms have been disastrous and that someone should write this, because he's determined that his won't be. He wants to get a leak out, that we'll have a major shakeup at State and Defense. The TV had a big crowd at Homestead, and another one at Key Biscayne when the chopper landed, and that ended the "Day After."

Friday, November 10, 1972
The P had me over at 11:30 again for a couple of hours for another general discussion. He talked with MacGregor and asked him to send in recommendations on the people for the National Committee and other jobs. He wants a manifesto on the dirtiest campaign in history against a P; they shout him down, violent disruption, and so on. Wants to be sure Rogers puts a freeze on the *Post* and *Times* and CBS. No conversation at all until the Vietnam negotiations are over. It's unconscionable that they would leak the letter to Thieu.

On the Secret Service, he says the family doesn't want them; since the law doesn't require it, they will only have full coverage on public events, but to not follow them in and out on personal errands or with friends. They are to work this individually as to what Julie and Tricia and the P want for everything, except in public places. He says that we need to find a Pole or an Italian Catholic for the Court, preferably a Democrat, also for other courts. We then got into the whole personnel thing again, and he seemed quite pleased with the approach that we're taking on the Cabinet.

He called later this evening, furious by a Navy episode where Zumwalt had heralded on the blacks that refused to sail on the *Constellation.* He's told Henry to have all the men court-martialed and give them dishonorable discharges. Zumwalt, instead, gave them active shore stations with Coca-Colas and ice cream. You can't have a service without discipline, and he wanted E to tell Zumwalt that the P was terribly displeased; he said you know he's a McNamara man.

Saturday, November 11, 1972
The P had me over again for the usual midday two hours. Again pretty much general discussion. Got into political strategy and expounded on his views on Teddy Kennedy. He thinks that Teddy and his people will have to do some figuring and decide that they don't want to take us on. They will want to handle their fight within the Democratic Party and win that, but not get in a fight with us. He thinks that might lead to their not doing the Congressional investigation, etc. This was based on the basic Machiavellian theory that if you strike a king, you must kill him, and that he can't kill us, therefore he won't strike. He also got into the election follow-up. He wants to be sure the IRS covers all major Democratic contributors and all backers of the new senators.

Ehrlichman and I had a long session with Dean on the Segretti thing, going over the details of everything he did, what he said, and so on. It turns out that we don't have any real problem, I don't think, on it. Some of the actions were questionable, but none of them was serious. And, it's clear that he was operating without direction, although he did maintain some contact with Chapin as he went along. But he did not have a direct reporting responsibility or relationship there.

Monday, November 13, 1972
On the chopper up to Camp David, the P feels that we need an analysis of the Republican vote, and the Republican Party turnout. Because we had a net loss of one governor and a net loss of four state legislators, which is the Republican Party at the lower levels, and is a hell of a drag. He wants to check to see if we really made the effort to get all the Republicans out,

or did we rely too much on Dole and the National Committee. With only a 55 percent turnout, we should have won a big Republican vote, there must have been a weak Republican effort. We should examine this ruthlessly, no excuses.

Tuesday, November 14, 1972

Camp David. The P had E and me over at 10:00 this morning for a long session at Aspen, we went over the whole basic plan of how we're going to set things up, and the P bought the concept. We discussed the VP, and he wanted me to talk to him and explain that we have a tough thing to do here, that he must cut, that we cut all the way across including his staff. He feels that we need to keep our leverage over him, so we shouldn't break it off with him now, but we do not further his interests politically for '76. We don't want him to have the appearance of being the heir apparent, we also don't want to appear to push him down. We should pitch the Bicentennial for him as a great opportunity. The summary then is that Agnew is not the ideal choice, but he may be the best of a bad lot.

Wants me to talk to Rogers, make the point that the P is closest to him, but feels that anyone who's been in for 4 years should go like Romney, Volpe, and Laird. It would be bad if you stayed and they didn't. It's best for you to finish in a blaze of glory with the Vietnam peace signing, and then you take the lead and move out.

Wednesday, November 15, 1972

Camp David. Met with the VP this morning. We started out by reviewing the campaign, and then got into the Vietnam situation summary, and he explained to the VP what our status was there and negotiations that he thinks Henry is going to be able to wrap up on this last trip. He went into some discussion of the letter he wrote to Thieu, and the position he's taking on a very hard-line basis, that Thieu has got to go along with us now, that if he doesn't, we won't have Congressional support to back him up later. The VP started talking about the problems that he has in his role, particularly in intergovernmental relations. The P interrupted and said, well, under our reorganization plans, this whole intergovernmental relations thing should be in OMB or HUD, and our reorganization gets into this, which I'm going to have E and Haldeman go over it with you after our meeting. He said the VP should be dealing with important things instead, that he and the P shouldn't have to take the heat on these intergovernmental matters. They should stay out of solving their troubles, that he should stay on the highest level. The best big new thing would be the Bicentennial, a major public event of the Administration, involving all 50 states and all foreign countries. Jimmy Roosevelt is going to be our Ambassador abroad on this, and the VP could pick that up. This he should take on as a major responsibility, get it on the tracks, it's an opportunity to get high-powered people, rather than just a mediocre staff, and he talked about enlisting our New American Majority as the focal point for the Bicentennial. The VP raised the question of Indian Affairs, said he's very interested in that, the P said that he thinks it's a loser and the VP should not be tied to a loser. The VP then said that he had reservations about the Bicentennial, and that he wants a chance to do selected tasks in the foreign field, K-type missions in the foreign area. The P agreed that he should not just do goodwill trips and funerals, but that he shouldn't worry about this. We'll handle it, setting him up for some single-shot negotiations, and foreign economic things. The P makes the point that what makes the VP important is what he does on the big play, not the number of jobs he has. John and I then met with him over at Laurel, and went through the reorganization thing, which he was in basic agreement with. He got again into the staff and made the point that he was scared of the Bicentennial, because he thinks that it could be disastrous, you can't satisfy people, and it would lead only to trouble.

Later in the day the P got into the Colson problem. He said that he really should leave now for our interests, and he doesn't really fit now, under the reorganization, in the White House, and therefore we should go another round with him. We really need him out now and not later. The question was whether to have him as our RNC counsel or instead have a member of his firm and not him. He said that I should talk to Colson and say that I'm talking without the P's knowledge regarding Dean, E, and so forth, the inevitable problems with the Hunt trial, the P can't let you go into fire, we can't be sure what will come out. On the positive side, you're needed outside now, Finch, Klein, etc. are leaving and pulling out completely, you're going for a specific purpose, and you will have a continual relation. The Clark Clifford role. The problem is that your position inside will erode, you will have no great goal to pursue, like the election. The P needs you on the outside where you are free to set up a campaign firm, as well as a law firm. Now is the time to pick up the clients, law, and PR, and we just don't have the job inside. The P is determined to get politics out of the White House, so you become the man. You've got to go into the P and say that you thought it through, this is what he should do, you reached the conclusion. Be a big man.

I had a talk with K this evening. He's concerned about some of the appointments and all, wanted to be sure that we wouldn't put Connally into Defense or State without letting him know ahead of time. He said he has some concerns about who Richardson might bring with him to State, and says the bureaucracy is really churning about what's happening. It's good for now, but the problem is that if it goes too long, that is, beyond Thanksgiving, it will turn on us. He also says Connally has put out the story that he's been offered State, and Henry is concerned about how to handle that if it's done.

Thursday, November 16, 1972

Camp David. The P met with Connally this morning. I flew up with John (E) on the helicopter, and did not sit in the meeting, which lasted about two hours. The P had me in afterward and gave me quite a detailed report. He says that Connally has concluded that there's no hope for him in the Democratic Party. He feels that if he could get the Democratic nomination he could run and beat Agnew, as a Democrat, but that he could also run as a Republican and beat Kennedy, and he thinks that it's inevitable that Kennedy would get the nomination. He also therefore decided to change parties and become a Republican. The question is a matter of timing, and what he does beyond that. The P discussed the possibility of an Administration role with him, and the two apparently agreed that it would not be wise for Connally to come in. He doesn't want Secretary of Defense in any event, feels he couldn't take State as long as K is there. He doesn't want to do that anyway because he has a lot of opportunity to make money this year, and wants to spend his time doing that. The P encouraged him to change parties quickly, which would send up a lot of signals and establish him clearly as a candidate for '76 and get some of the people rolling that might be able to be helpful to him. Apparently a satisfactory meeting for both people, at least the P thought so.

Had a meeting with Rogers this afternoon and got into the separation. It didn't work out very well, in that Rogers obviously was shocked to be told that he was to leave. He didn't say much more than that to me, except that he thought it was a bad way to handle it. When he got to the P, he made a brief pitch about his concern on the appearance of his being fired, that it creates bad and unnecessary public opinion. He made the point that loyalty goes both ways, and people expect the P to be loyal with the people who work so hard for him. He referred to the press reports about needing some reorganization of foreign policy without him there and so on. Said that the P should have consulted him first, and then decided. We then discussed the organization of State if Rogers were to stay, and he basically made a pitch to stay on to June 1, so that he can clean up things that he was doing and not look like K had forced him out. He made the point that there's a lot of Vietnam work to be done, and follow-up after the agreement. The P was quite impressed by that point, because he agreed that it was a problem. He pitched strongly that it's bad to look as if we've hatched a plot and here it is.

P told me I've got to tell K, this is after the meeting, that we're not going to face the Rogers thing yet. Also, wanted to talk to Connally and told him there's the problem with Vietnam, so Rogers is going to stay on a while. So we'll start making the changes underneath, but for Connally's own information we have a clear understanding with Bill, as to a departure.

Friday, November 17, 1972

Camp David. Dole had called yesterday. He assumes that he is going to stay on as *(Republican National Committee)* Chairman. I told him I'd meet with him next week, I'm going to have to work out a shift on the chairmanship. Will talk to John Mitchell about trying to get him to do it.

P keeps coming up with the point that we should think in terms of K's leaving. He gets caught up in the principle of it and he doesn't think that we should keep him on for very long after we get Vietnam settled. I talked to K after he met the P today. Regarding our conversation this morning with Rogers, I told him that he was going to stay on for a short time. He thinks this is unworkable for the Administration and our foreign policy. Our problem is not the Foreign Service, it's the Secretary, and he operates independently of the White House. The Department is torn between their loyalty to the Secretary versus the White House. Henry thought it's a disaster for the second term and he's affronted that it was done without discussion from him. He wants me to have no doubt regarding his feeling. He's certainly discussed it with Al, and he says it won't work either. As a long-term proposition—we'll have to think it over very carefully. In other words, he's threatening. Obviously, keeping him may drive K out. He dropped a number of veiled threats to that effect. He *(Rogers)* says if one has to carry a burden, one shouldn't have it dumped on one's shoulders. I should have no illusions regarding his feelings— he's very serious about it. He says he has to know exactly what the P expects him to do. He's not just somebody you can move around. This is a courtesy that has not been extended to him. He has hesitations regarding staying. I tried to calm him down, make all the obvious points about what we're doing, it'll all work out, etc., but I don't think I satisfied him very much.

The P kept calling me in the afternoon and through meetings later in the day and into the evening on the line I should use in talking with Rogers. He says I should have a clear understanding that he's to leave on June 1.

Saturday, November 18, 1972

I drove down from Camp David first thing this morning and went right to Rogers' house for my meeting with him. We spent a lot of time in sort of general chitchat review of election results and basic transition approach. Rogers is concerned because he feels the P's harsh way of going at the transition is hurting the opportunity for him to create a more friendly image generally in the country and thinks that we should have, for instance, waited a week before the Cabinet meeting to ask for resignations, rather than moving so hard so fast, etc. I then got into my pitch on how we structure the State Department. I made the points the P told me to, that it was unfortunate he had the impression of being fired and that the P thought he was leaving. We had no real problems with the rest of the Cabinet, they're all figured out, so you're the only problem. The P doesn't want to hurt you, but he's been through four rough years, between you and K, so from now on, things have to be through the system. The problems have been partly K's fault, but we must have a clear understanding of the June 1 date with no further discussion, and, of course, no one else should know. He totally agreed to all of these. He said there is a problem with his working with the staffing system because K lies to him and there's no way to deal with him, and he's particularly concerned with how to deal with Haig's replacement because Haig has been the key to getting along. He does trust Haig. He feels that his successor needs to be set up so that he does have someone to deal with other than Henry, which is impossible. He also made the point in that connection he must be sure that Haig goes with Henry to Saigon if he goes, because Thieu doesn't trust or like Henry. He does trust Haig.

P mentioned at noon that K was having problems with Thieu. He's gotten a new cable and apparently Thieu is causing trouble again. The P told him to just go ahead and get the best deal we can and then let Thieu paddle his own canoe. Then when the P called in the evening, he said K has now read the message and it wasn't nearly as bad as he thought, so it was another crisis that Henry was stirring up.

K called me this evening, before his departure for Paris tomorrow, to report that Peter Lisagor has an article regarding an interview Henry did with an Italian journalist woman, some of it very bad, such as the reason he's so popular is because Americans like cowboys and things like that. It'll appear in the *Star* tomorrow, and Henry was very much concerned about it. He said he thought he was just joking when he talked with her, and also that she was supposed to submit the interview for proof before she submitted it, but she didn't do it. So he's been shafted, which is not unusual.

Sunday, November 19, 1972

P kept calling today while I was supposed to be home and not involved. He said he was going to give me the day with the family but I ended up with seven pages of notes. Henry's saying that regarding China he did it alone. P had some very strong reaction. He obviously is extremely displeased by it, in particular all the stuff Henry kept coming up with. He later in the day told me I should let Henry know that obviously the EOB and the Oval Office and the Lincoln Room have all been recorded for protection, so the P has a complete record of all of your conversations, which, of course, you can carry when you write your book. *(A reference to the taping system installed in the White House in early 1971)* It's not the witticisms and all that he's concerned about in the story, it's the substance. It's detrimental in the highest degree. He made the point to Henry that he doesn't make the decisions, and when they are made, that he wavers the most. The P, I should tell him, has written the total China story for his own file.

P got into the Dole/RNC question, because of Dole saying he was going to stay and so on. He wants me to move on this to get some others to put the heat on Dole, someone from the RNC and Congress. Mitchell should build the fire on this so that we don't take the heat, stir up some people in the key states, get some young congressmen and senators to speak out, saying we need a change, etc.

Last thing he called about today was the *Life* cover picture, which he finally caught up with. Figures it's obviously a deliberate attempt to gibe us, which I think is probably right. Asked if it had occurred to me to have letter and calls made to *Life* regarding the lousy cover, and I said no. He said it has occurred now.

Monday, November 20, 1972

P had me over first thing this morning. He's decided to go up to New York with the family after Thanksgiving here at Camp David, to do Christmas shopping, go to the theater, visit Tricia's new home in Brooklyn, etc. I think he's just getting a little stir crazy and wants to get out, which is probably a good idea, from a general appearance anyway. They've also decided to go to California for Christmas and have Bebe come up the day after, and he came up with the idea of trying to have Pat Nixon named as the Grand Marshal for the Rose Parade this year. He's very depressed with the K interview, which gave away the moral ground in Vietnam, plus praising Le Duc Tho and knocking Thieu, which was bad. He wants to set up a situation for social engagement with General and Mrs. Haig as a cover and then he wants to talk to Haig candidly. He wants me to knock off K's going to China before the Inaugural, which Henry wants to do. He wants to be sure that I get from K's office all the memoranda from and to the P and get them into the P's files, especially all of his handwritten stuff, the originals, physically move it into the P's files now.

He had quite a series of meetings today. I sat in on several of them. Richardson was no problem. He was ecstatic at being offered the Defense Department post, which I discussed with him before he went to see the P. He was genuinely surprised, but clearly pleased to be selected. The P made quite a point of Elliot's ability to deal with Henry, and his understanding of him, as being one of the major pluses. He met with Helms with no preliminary meeting. P told him he was going to make a change *(at CIA),* gave him a good buildup first. Offered him an ambassadorship. They talked about specific ambassadorships. Helms lobbied for Iran, P responded very favorably and agreed to hold Iran open until Helms decides whether he wants it or not. He urged him to take it. Helms pushed Colby and Messinas for the CIA head. P said there's a question of whether to promote from within or whether to go outside for the new Director. It was basically a friendly meeting although Helms was a little surprised and obviously disappointed to be moving out after 25 years, but there didn't seem to be any problem.

Henry called from Paris to say that the press found out about their meeting place, so there'll be a lot of pictures and stories because they followed the Vietnamese there and were there when Henry arrived. He's prepared to move the meetings to the city, but the Vietnamese haven't agreed as yet, so he's sending a report that things are going about as expected, no worse, maybe a little better. They're tough but not unmanageable. They're going to meet again tomorrow afternoon. They're studying the proposals and we should say nothing. He would call again tomorrow, and that was about it.

E got a call from Bush, who met with the P earlier, and the P pitched him on the RNC. Bush said that he would do it, if that's what the P wants.

It was a long, full day, covered some pretty good ground, got a few things established, and no major problems except apparently Rumsfeld, who had his meeting with the P after a pre-meeting with E, where he agreed that he should go on out to Illinois and run for the Senate, but then when he got in the meeting with the P, he said no, that just wouldn't do, that he had to have an Administration job for a year, which was a complete shock to the P and E, and typical Rumsfeld, rather slimy maneuver.

Tuesday, November 21, 1972

P had me over first thing this morning. He got on to the Dole problem first thing, wants Ford and Scott to go to work on trying to get Dole to step down. The item came up a couple of times again as the day went on, especially since it appeared as the day went on that Bush was more likely to take the National Chairmanship. He ended up at the end of the day agreeing that he would take it. So we now have our replacement set. As a result, the P thought that Mitchell should call Dole, tell him that we've got to have a full-time chairman. The P does want him to step down, and when he comes to see the P, he should ask to be released. Should recommend to the P that he get a full-time man, and for Dole to say that he ought to step out while he's on top.

K problems came up a number of times in conversations during the day. P thought Henry ought to forget about the fetish of secret meetings. He's worried about Henry observing the freeze on *Time* and *Life,* and said that if *Time* has a Man of the Year this year and doesn't give it to Nixon, it'll probably go to K, which would really create a problem. I'm going to have to handle it. P really feels he should leave by midyear.

Next meeting I had was with Schlesinger. P made him the pitch on wanting him to consider CIA, asked him how he would go about it. Schlesinger had some ideas, agreed with the P's view that it needed to be changed. That Helms is a captive of the Georgetown set, at least to a degree, and that it is time for a change. He obviously wants the CIA job and is perfectly willing to leave the AEC. Next one was Bill Casey, the P made him the pitch for, ultimately, Deputy Secretary of State, but first Undersecretary. P said for Administration, but Casey got him shifted over to Economic Affairs, which is really better because it gives him more stroke. Casey is obviously delighted, totally agrees with the P's assessment of the State Department bureaucracy. Asked some of the right questions, but understands the problem and is willing to work with that for the interim period, and is delighted at the opportunity to get in and clean out the deadwood. I think that one's going to work out extremely well.

Henry called from Paris to report on the talks. The main thing he had to tell me was that they had another five-hour session and that they had built TV towers outside their meeting place so the cameras could see into the courtyard and they're getting pictures of him. He says they're getting pretty tough on substance. There's a cable coming later.

We had a long session tonight after dinner on personnel for remaining Cabinet posts and a complete rundown on under-secretaries and agency heads. Things are starting to fall together reasonably.

Wednesday, November 22, 1972

P had E and me over at 8:30 this morning for a two-hour meeting before he started his regular schedule. Went through a huge load of miscellaneous personnel things. K question came up in several contexts. Wanted me to call Haig in Paris and get Henry to quit posing for pictures, smiling with Le Duc Tho, and dictated a wire to K, a cable he wanted me to send, saying the P is very disappointed in the lack of progress in the negotiations to date, under the circumstances, unless the other side shows the same willingness to be reasonable that we are showing, I am directing you to discontinue the talks and we shall then have to resume military activities until the other side is ready to negotiate. They must be disabused of the idea they seem to have that we have no other choice but to settle on their terms. You should inform them directly, without equiv-ocation, that we do have another choice, and if they were sur-prised that I would take the strong action I did prior to Moscow Summit, and prior to the election they will find that now with the election behind us, I will take whatever action I consider necessary to protect United States interests. Henry called me on the phone from Paris to report they had another four-hour session, still in a very tough phase, may break through to-morrow.

After all the meetings, P had a chat with E and me. Got into some detail on the whole Watergate thing. Had John spell out the situation for him, and it's obvious that he's still concerned about that, and is pushing John to get a plan wrapped up as quickly as possible, and to him.

Thursday, November 23, 1972

P called late this evening, following up Henry's cable, wanted to know who he could talk with to send a cable back to Henry. I told him Colonel Kennedy, and Kennedy called me a few minutes later, a little concerned about the cable because it in effect tells Henry to make a settlement regardless of what the

South Vietnamese think, and that had Kennedy somewhat worried, but he's going ahead with it.

Friday, November 24, 1972

K woke me up at 7:00 this morning, on the day I had hoped to be able to sleep a little late, and go into the office late, to say that they had a meeting in Paris this morning. Very private, just the four of them: K, Haig, Le Duc Tho, and Xuan Thuy, Henry laid out our position in a private way and that we can't make the decision until the meeting tomorrow as to follow the P's instructions to break things off. The P should go ahead and go to New York. There's nothing for him to do at this point. Henry's sending a message regarding today's meeting. Essentially we'll know tomorrow what the situation is.

P then got into the whole Watergate Segretti question, making the point that while all of our discussions relate to the legalities, the main thing involved here is to protect the Presidency. We need a clear, simple statement, early, in the form of a Dean report to the P, saying that I have checked and found that there is no present member of the White House staff involved. I have also found that neither Stans nor Mitchell is involved, if that's possible. He thinks we ought to try to clear Stans and Mitchell, at least Stans, as far as the Campaign Committee goes.

Regarding Segretti, he says there has to be a flat categorical statement that I've investigated pursuant to your instructions, and then name names and answer the implications—regarding Haldeman, he didn't do anything; regarding Colson, he didn't do anything; Chapin did receive information but didn't direct the activities and so on. He makes the point that we should not harm any of the other individuals if we can possibly help it. Then Ziegler should say, there's the statement and we stand on it.

He feels we can't just let it "hang out," as Ehrlichman puts it, and hope it's clear to people. Dean has to draw the conclusion specifically that the White House was not involved. Have to say that Mr. Chapin recruited Segretti for the job to conduct campaign activities, but there's no evidence that he directed his activities. Before this is done, Chapin and Strachan should both be out of the White House. That gets to the problem of what we do with Chapin and Strachan, which concerns the P greatly. He's very determined that we not do anything that's harmful in any way to Dwight especially, but feels that we can't keep him in the White House. Says Ehrlichman shouldn't think in legal terms. What we need is a clear-cut categorical statement from Dean, saying this man was not involved, that one was, and so on.

P left for New York at midday, and E and I had a long meeting with Dean on the whole Watergate thing. Decided we'd have to follow the full-disclosure route on Segretti, and that we can't do anything much on Watergate because of the court case.

Saturday, November 25, 1972
The day started with another wakeup call from Henry at 7:00 this morning from Paris, saying that they had another private meeting. No full-scale session, that he's going to come home, but they will announce resumption for December 4. He says the other alternative was impossible, that we'd have a total public blowup with Saigon, that would be following the P's instructions to settle and ram it down Saigon's throat. He said we couldn't do that at this point. He said Thieu's emissary is still coming to see the P, and Henry will go on to New York, arriving about 9:00 or 9:30 tonight, stay at the Waldorf, and meet with the P when he gets in. He is very disturbed, because the other side leaked a story that was very unhelpful and he thinks we must not get into that.

Sunday, November 26, 1972
Henry mercifully delayed his wakeup call today until about 10:30, but that's because he's back in New York now. He called in, said that things in Paris are in pretty good shape. The problem with North Vietnam is that all the journalists in Paris have convinced them that the P has to settle now, so the North Vietnamese gave K an ultimatum on Wednesday. K hit them back on Friday, then broke off talks after their leak to the *Post*. They were terrified regarding the breakoff. Henry says the main thing now is to keep the P pumped up to sound tough with the South Vietnamese until we get over that hurdle. He thinks this could be worked out and that we brutalize them now rather than while he was there. Then we've made the record as trying to work with him and force them to take the settlement. Says we have two problems: first, an ultimatum to South Vietnam so that they're aboard—the P must be brutal

to Duc, the emissary, he can't talk gently to him. Secondly, an ultimatum to the North Vietnamese that this is it, period. He thinks we can put it in motion, get it all set for a Presidential speech to the nation by the 20th of December.

Monday, November 27, 1972

Back at Camp David. Talked with Mitchell first thing this morning about Dole. He said he is bitter because he got no credit at the election night celebration, and that he resents Mitchell because of the campaign structure he has set up. He's sure though that he will do what the P wants, but what he wants to do is stay on a year as chairman. All our RNC people want a full-time professional chairman. There's very little support for Dole staying on.

I took a call from John Dean, who wanted to report on his meeting with Chapin. He said it went fairly well and that he'd deflected it basically from me. He knew he was a lightning rod and that it would be rougher for Chapin and for the P if he's onboard when it all hits. He should leave in order to defuse the issue. Go out now with his head up, and untarnished. This apparently came as a shock to Dwight. Dick Moore then talked to him and said to get out now for his own career sake. He's having lunch with Moore to discuss that. Dwight said he was interested in the media business, the networks. He was not interested in the Universal opportunity. Dean thinks that Dwight has the hope that I'll say no, he should stay, but Dean told him his recommendation was to go. John also said regarding Strachan, he gave him a list of the open posts, and the one he wants is General Counsel to USIA, which we are going to go ahead and offer him. He said on the cash, the only way to handle that is to turn it back to the Committee, which is where it belongs anyway.

Had a meeting with K, explained the whole reorganization setup, and tried to reassure him on the State Department and related problems. He's convinced that Rogers staying on is a ploy of some kind by the P, either to hold the post for Connally until he's ready to take it, or to force Henry out, or to just leave Rogers in and go ahead coasting the way we are. I don't believe I was very successful in changing his view on this, but I tried. K and I then met with the P. They reviewed the Vietnam negotiating situation and made the point that there must be a total freeze on all comment on Vietnam from any source.

P made it very clear that the thing has to be settled one way or the other this time, that we have to handle South Vietnam on an all-out basis this week, either they go along or else we go ahead without them. This of course is hard for Henry to swallow because he wants to work out the negotiation, but the P was very firm on it and didn't let him up.

Then P called me a little later to be sure I'd leaned hard on K on the press contact thing. The P had just called him and he thought someone was in the room with Henry at the time. He could tell from the way Henry was talking that he was doing it for the record. I did hit Henry hard on the Italian lady interview. He really cried on it, on the basis that he was totally mortified and had done a terrible thing, knew it, and couldn't have bothered him more than anybody. He went on and on about this. It obviously does bother him, but he'll obviously go right ahead and have the interviews anyway. I don't think there's any way to stop that.

Tuesday, November 28, 1972

Camp David. P called me earlier at 7:30 this morning, wanted to go through a lot of miscellaneous things, particularly on White House staff. Had a meeting with Dole today, which was absolutely incredible. P made his whole pitch on all the reasons why Dole should leave now, why it would be better for him and everything, and Dole said well, if I came up here for the hanging, I at least want to say a word in my own defense. Then he went into a long harangue about his own position, that he said he was staying and he therefore has to stay, that he feels it will ruin him in Kansas if it looks like he's kicked out, is totally oblivious to any suggestion that by handling it right, he can avoid it looking like he's kicked out. Said he would have a problem raising money for his campaign if he were kicked out, and the P committed $300,000 in a special fund-raising effort for him. Committed a three-week trip to Europe or Asia for him in the late summer. Then at the end the P did mention George Bush as a possibility for the job, and Dole agreed that he would be great.

John Dean called, said Chapin appears to accept his fate. He thinks that I concur and that he's rethought his general stance and has asked Miller for Miller's advice. Miller's still rocky on it, went over the potential list of things last night. Dean is cool on his recommendations, and there are no new problems when they testify to Justice. I had my meeting with Chapin this afternoon, which was a pretty horrible experience. I had to go through the whole thing with him. He basically does understand, I think, although it's very, very tough on him, and said that he couldn't face leaving, but would probably be able to do it. He's got a lot of ideas on job opportunities and so forth, and I think once he gets moving on it, he'll find that actually it's a good move for him. He wouldn't have been as well off to stay in as he will be to get out.

Wednesday, November 29, 1972

P told me to tell Dole that we got Bush, and that Dole should come up to Camp David next Wednesday to finalize it with the P. He should take the initiative, that he should go ahead and talk to Bush, but the P has told Bush that he's his choice, and that's set. The sooner we can get the word out and name the thing publicly, the better.

Got into the K problem a little. I met with Al Haig at the P's request and told him that we had to get things under control. Al said he understood perfectly, he was very concerned. Henry, in his view, is on an up-and-down cycle all the time, and he has bottomed out on his down cycle now and is coming back up, but was in absolutely terrible shape in Paris last week.

Al feels that Henry needs a very good, long vacation and that we should be sure he gets it. He thinks the trip this week will go all right and that the deal is locked now, so there's no problem with Henry's going. Said he understood completely the problem of the Italian woman's article, and that Henry understands it too.

Apparently the meeting with the South Vietnamese envoy didn't go very well. The P spent a long time with him, about two and a half hours. The net result was the P softened a little bit, which was bad. They're going to have to meet tomorrow to try to clean that up, but the South Vietnamese, after the meeting, came back and told Henry to tell the P they would probably have to go it alone and that we should just go in, make a settlement to get our prisoners back, and stop fighting as far as we're concerned, and let the Vietnamese go on fighting it out. They don't seem to understand that our Congress won't continue to supply them if they take that route, and that they have to go along with us on a settlement, a point which

Henry would like to get across to them, and the P in the meeting tomorrow.

Friday, December 1, 1972

Colson, E, and I started a meeting on the organization of the Colson office and relations with his outside law firm, etc. The P called and said he had just gotten a study from Buchanan about ambassadors abroad, that 55 percent are from Ivy League schools of those we had appointed. Then said to have E and Colson come over and he wanted to have a meeting with us. So we went over at 10:30 and were there for several hours. He got into the Ivy League thing and saying that our problem is we're just appointing people we know and all the people we know are Ivy League, so therefore from now on we appoint no more Ivy League people.

We then got into a general discussion of the "Connally for President" idea, and the point that he is the only one that any of us would want to see succeed the P. He's got to run as a Republican and he's got to make the move now.

The "Connally for President" discussion led to a general discussion of forming a new party. E raising the idea that this is our only chance, in the next 60 days or so, and that we should give some thought to it on the basis that you use the Republican Party as a base, but add to it the New Majority. Use Connally as the focal point candidate, but that the P has to take the lead. The P was intrigued with this as a possibility, recognizing that you can never really go with the P's party into a majority and that the only hope probably is to do a new party. The question is whether it can be done and whether we really want to make the effort. I suspect nothing will come of it, but it was an interesting discussion, and as E said when we left, it's a good way to get the meeting to break up, which it finally did.

Sunday, December 3, 1972

The P had me over at midday. He started with quite a long report and discussion on K and Vietnam. He talked to Henry a little earlier to give him his final instructions before he left, and was still thinking about all that. He came up with the idea that Henry can't be the one to go to Saigon and work out the deal, and so he'd lobbed out to Henry, first the suggestion that Connally do it, which absolutely horrified Henry. Then he

moved from there to the suggestion of the VP, which Henry
thought was a great stroke, as he naturally would, because he
feels it keeps Connally out of it. The P's point, though, is that
because Thieu doesn't trust Henry, we've got to send someone
else to sell the deal to him. Apparently the VP is sold enough
on him, and the fact that Congress won't back any continuation
of the war, or any continuation of support of Thieu, so he's
the great one to go do that. The P also made the point that
Henry can't go to Hanoi if Saigon doesn't go along with the
deal. If we end up cutting a deal just with North Vietnamese,
that wipes out Henry's Hanoi trip, which he told Henry, much
to Henry's great concern.

Then he got into the PR thing and the need to get across
the "Nixon the Man" story, that he needs someone with him
at all times that feels the color, someone who's very sensitive
on that sort of thing, that we need to get the extra dimension
beyond the professional president concept. He got back into
the new-party idea and thought we ought to pursue it. He suggested that Connally come over tomorrow, if he could, to discuss this. I checked with Connally, and he can't, but he'll come
up on Tuesday and meet with the P in Washington. He got
into his need for improvements at the White House. He wants
to have a whirlpool and sauna and a one-lane bowling alley
put in with a shower and so on, in the basement, so he can
use it without having to go over to the EOB. Later he called
to say he'd been discussing it with Bebe and Bob Abplanalp
and they'd like to pay for it.

Monday, December 4, 1972

Started at Key Biscayne. K called with his report from Paris.
Said he was sending a message, but they had held a two-and-
a-half-hour private session. He just presented his position and
will get an answer this afternoon on it. They agreed to meet
tomorrow at a place we furnish. He says it's exactly on track
the way he and the P discussed. Then, after we got back to
Washington, and home tonight, the P called me to say he had
just talked to Colonel Kennedy, who had received a report
from Henry that things had been very tough in the afternoon
session and that they're going to have to break off the talks.
*(Tho was being very intransigent, and even backing off on
items already agreed upon.)* The P will have to go on TV and
rally the American people. The P told Kennedy to tell K to

stay on the hard line, that this was not a viable option and that the P has a very uneasy feeling about going on TV at this point. He doesn't think K is in touch with reality; says it's better to state it in a practical manner and just do it without going on TV to rally the people. We don't have to decide until tomorrow, so we can wait and see what happens, but we should say we haven't completed negotiations and go ahead with more bombing. Going on TV unnecessarily escalates the public reaction. It's too bad we don't have a direct line to Haig to get a feeling from him, but Henry's got to realize that we can't repeat history; we can't go on and do it again. They're going to meet tomorrow at 3:00 and we'll get a report then.

Tuesday, December 5, 1972

In Washington. The P had me over first thing this morning. In fact, he called me at home. I wasn't planning to go in until late, but I hurried up to go in. We had a problem because some of the Cabinet announcements leaked, and he wanted them canceled, although he simmered down on that. The problem was the *Post* got the story, which was especially galling.

Then got into the Vietnam problem and wanted to discuss it in some detail. The question of whether he should go on TV or not. He had K's cable, which pushed hard on his going on again. Also he got word that today's meeting had been canceled. They were going to meet tomorrow.

This led to a discussion later in the day with Colson on the same subject. He had Colson read the cable and discussed it. Chuck felt as I do and as the P does, that he should not go on. You can't rally the people again, and so on. TV's not the answer. If there's any alternative, we should low-key it as much as possible as being an interruption, not a breakdown or a breakoff. K has to take the heat, not the P, but he should not do it in despair or frustration. He should make the point that they have backed off. So then the P told me to send a message to K to tell North Vietnam tomorrow, first, that it's his belief now, that in view of the fact that North Vietnam reneging on the October 26 agreement, and their intransigence, that the P will be able to get funds from Congress to continue military action and military and economic support for South Vietnam. Also, we should avoid a dramatic breakoff by us, and should treat it as a case where we reached an impasse at this time, and each side has gone back for consultation. We'll resume when it appears productive to resume. I should cover all these points in the message. We must not assume that the gun is there to be fired. Henry's got to be turned off on dealing with this, so that he won't take the position when he gets in the meeting with North Vietnamese and lock the P into it. The P called me later and said that I should add to the cable a thing that says, "Incidentally, the P and all of us here feel that any discussion of your resignation is totally out of order." K is overdramatizing that whole thing.

Had a long session with Connally and the whole question of the new party and Connally's going for the Presidency, and it's clear that Connally is ready to run, but not totally convinced that we can do it by building a new party. The third-party route just isn't workable, and there's no point in trying it. He does feel that we could do something in the way of reestablishing the Republican Party in a different way, with a new name, such as the Republican Independent Party. It would clearly put a new cast on it, but not lose the base that we have now, which Connally feels is indispensable. He debated whether he would change parties, and came to no conclusion on that. Connally's feeling, however, is that he shouldn't change things when they are going well, and that we're in a pretty good position now, we ought to leave it that way.

Wednesday, December 6, 1972

At Camp David. The whole day today was virtually taken up with the K-Vietnam negotiation problems. The P called me over first thing this morning when I arrived to get into the question. He thinks I should get a cable to K, making the point that at the present time we don't need public support. We just need to act and let the actions speak louder than words. Our main goal must be to play this as low-key as possible and to ignore Hanoi's intransigence.

Later in the afternoon we got the cable from K giving the report on the meetings, basically that they are almost totally sure of failure. The P went through a long discussion, really agony, on the decision that K poses for him, which is whether to make one last offer in the hope that they'll take it, or to go the other way and pull out. K lays out the options on it. The P said I should get E's view on whether we should wait six months for the POW's, which is what would happen if we pull out and start bombing. Henry thinks that within six months we'd be able to make a deal with them to get our POW's. Or to take the other option, which is to put one more peace proposal in and to try to keep it going, and not put it on a take-it-or-leave-it basis. The P said that (this was about 6:00) to meet again about 8:30 with E. I went over the whole thing with John. He made the point first that any agreement's better than no agreement, and we're in a stronger position to try to deal with the North than to try to deal with the South. Also he feels that if there's no agreement, it would be a monumental blow to America's Vietnam policy, but the P should not go on TV; he should not personify that failure. He should jettison K instead, and let K do the briefing.

The P had E and me over at 8:15 and we met in the Aspen living room, by the fire with the lights low on a cold night, and the P was slumped down in his chair and sort of went through the whole thing with John. John feels we have to try the finesse before going with our big gun, the P, the finesse being to try to maintain the appearance, at least, that the negotiations are continuing. He's concerned regarding the height of expectations in the country. The P said his view is that we have to get K out of the meetings for a while, to take a look at himself, and that's the key need at this point. Both of K's options really lead to the same conclusion, which is that we start bombing now. One way, we get the POW's now, and the other way we get them in July, but Congress might pull the string on us. The main thing is to get K back here and decide here, not through the channels across the Atlantic. He feels K's approach now is not very rational. At that point he had Colonel Kennedy come in. The P read Kennedy's draft of instructions to K and then read aloud his own draft, which is much longer and more on the basis of continuing the talks. He said we have to recognize that the North Vietnamese are evaluating K personally, too. They think he has more authority than he does, and they think he has no choice but to make a deal because of what he said. The P told Kennedy to send both messages, Kennedy's as the official instructions, the P's to give the flavor and background. Kennedy expressed his concern regarding the total break with Thieu and thus his collapse, which would mean a waste of ten years, and he is worried about the effect that would have on the American psyche. The P answered that you come to a point where you have to weigh the cost. If we've made the total effort, we can do no more.

Kennedy's concerned about how we may be perceived over the long haul over time. What will the effect be regarding our relations in the world?

There was a long period then in the meeting, with a more or less silent review of the messages, with slight changes in phrases and that sort of thing. Then the P said that K is in his India/Pakistan mood, with the feeling that all is lost, but nothing is ever totally lost. We need to get Henry here and talk to him, have him talk to the P at length, to review the options carefully. The P just feels the bombing-to-submission idea won't work. The goal of just saving the POW's is not enough and we can't guarantee Congressional support for eight months. Kennedy then left to send the messages to Henry, going by chopper back down to the office.

The other things that arose during the session were Harry Truman's imminent death and the P's ideas on a message regarding that. The moon shot's been delayed due to a mechanical problem, and Dole should go out and talk to the press tomorrow.

Thursday, December 7, 1972

At Camp David. We started off the day with the Dole problem. I called him this morning to confirm his appointment with the P today, make sure he was ready to make his announcement. Then he indicated to me that there had been a lot of press stuff out indicating he was being forced out, and that he didn't think that was right. He wasn't going to go along with it, and didn't know whether he was ready to move ahead on his resignation or not. Then tonight, Colson called to report that Dole had called him saying he had decided he was the only friend he had at the White House, and then launched into a ten-minute tirade against me, followed by a statement that he was being forced out and screwed in the press. He wasn't going to stand for it.

I was over at 5:00 and he had E join us. Discussing some personnel items, and then Manolo brought in K's cable, which the P read and then reviewed the highlights with us. He apparently had made a little progress, but not very much, although he now realizes we should move for agreement. He still put the two choices to the P, though, after laying out all the pitfalls involved in each, especially the negotiating route. The P feels K's choice is the bombing option, but it won't work unless the P goes on TV, and, as he sees it, that's not in the cards. K always prefers the big-action play against all odds and winning it. The P said I do, too, if you win it. K wants to push the P into taking a course of action that K warned against. The P went into quite a lot of psychological reaction to K, and E did, likewise. E felt that deep down K would like to get out of it now and lay it on the P. That K wants subconsciously to flee rather than fight, but he'd deny that and say he's recommending fight, but actually he's fleeing from the complex and that he doesn't know the right way. The P is convinced that if K came back without an agreement, he would resign. When he returns, I've got to get him firmly on board, to see it through all the way, no hangdog position, we can't let him drop the word that he wanted to hang tough and the P forced him to make the best deal that he could. He said to give Henry a terse reply. There has been movement in to-day's meeting, and should go on. Then Henry should plan to return to Camp David so he can have a full day with the P and with Haig.

These were his instructions when the phone call came in from Henry and I took it while the P went out for a swim. Henry was calling from Paris, said he hadn't heard from me for a few days and so he was just calling to check in with me. Then immediately he said, basically, I wanted you to know that I'm in favor of going ahead, but I did want to warn you about the implications involved. Then I said, well, you're clearly making some progress in the negotiations and it looks better, doesn't it? And he said, yes, we're slowly getting there, and if we all know what we're getting into, it's the right thing to do, but it's not the millennium. It will be a better agreement than October would have been. We still have the option, though, of going the other way, and he wants us to know that then we can do it by putting the heat and the blame on the others, as he spelled out in his message. At the latter part of the conversation, the P came bouncing in from the pool, wav-ing, and said, do you need me? And I said no as I continued the conversation, so he went on into his room to get dressed.

(After considerable further discussions) the P dictated a ca-ble which I wrote in longhand, then rewrote in longhand and sent over for typing. I brought it back, read it to the P and he approved it, and I had it sent down as the cable to K telling him to take the second option *(for negotiation),* but to view it

as a fixed decision with no further debate. The P felt very relieved and figured he's made the decision now and can live with it and he then obviously felt relaxed. He had John and me stay for dinner, and after we left we had the four Secretaries come over and watch a movie with us.

Friday, December 8, 1972

Got into the Dole thing and I explained to him what the problem was with Dole's blast at me in his conversation with Colson and we moved to get Harlow and Mitchell to work it out, which they succeeded in doing by midday, but by then we had a sleet storm up at Camp David, and there was no point in trying to get Dole up. So we didn't.

Got back into the Watergate/Segretti thing, wanted to be sure that he gets his Dean report. He thinks Dean ought to talk to the press rather than Ziegler, to give the summary on it. Wants to have a meeting on that subject the first of the week.

The K thing turned out to be a four-and-a-half-hour meeting today and a plan for another meeting tomorrow. With the possibility of sending Haig back tomorrow night after the meeting's over.

The P got into his White House Health Unit thing again. He wants the thing set up for the family. The bowling alley, sauna, tub and dressing room. Then he had Julie come in and we talked about her plans, first with the family's Christmas plans and then the idea of her taking an East Wing staff job, which would be superb. The key to that is getting David *(Eisenhower)* out of the Navy now, and setting it up so that he can run for the Goodling seat in Pennsylvania. So I'm going to try to work that out, so we can get Julie in.

Sunday, December 10, 1972

The P came down from Camp David first thing this morning. He went into the EOB office and had me come in at 10:00. He got into the need for Harry Dent to take on three projects. One, to get Eddie Nixon to run for Congress in Washington State. Two, to pick a district for Ed Cox *(Tricia's husband)* to run in from New York, and third, to check immediately on the Goodling seat for David. Then also we need to work out a job for David, tied into the Bicentennial or something of that sort. He definitely wants Julie and David to live in Washington. He wants to be sure they put through no special deal for David.

It's got to be tied in to a normal group somehow. Then he got into where they should live. He'd like to get them into the White House on the third floor, which they're going to fix up, but they'd prefer to get a house, so he said they could get one with a swimming pool so Mrs. Nixon and he could get out of the White House from time to time and get over there for a swim. I'm sure that would be better for Julie and David than the problem of living in the White House.

On Safire's book, he wanted to be sure Bill understood that he can't come in and psychoanalyze the P as to what he really thinks and that sort of stuff. He'd rather him just write about him, not as if he were him. The publisher also can't be Doubleday. It has to be someone who supported us.

He had Haig in about noon, and Al reports that everything's set on the negotiations except one problem, which is the DMZ. Yesterday it bogged down on that after getting everything else cleared up, and so we closed with a compromise offer, which Al says Thieu won't be able to accept. The P made the point strongly to Al that the problem is that we pushed so hard on the settlement before the election that that put us in a bad spot. We're still trying to dig out from that. Haig agreed. Haig is very much concerned about maintaining the cease-fire. He feels we want to be prepared to react hard if they violate it, and he's sure they will. That means bombing the North. The P then took a very strong position on violations. It should be clear that it will not be on a tit-for-tat basis. It'll be all-out, regardless of potential civilian casualties, if we have a provocation. He told Al to tell Henry that, to use in his negotiating, and also have the VP be prepared to make that point. The P raised the question of the VP doing the Thieu deal, or whether the P should do it. Haig said the P should not do it, should not meet with him until the whole thing is absolutely locked. The P made the point that the VP must know this is not a negotiating mission. He is to convince Thieu as the leader of the hawks that there will be no support for him unless he goes along.

Monday, December 11, 1972

The P had Dole in first thing this morning. I had talked to Bush ahead of time and worked out the arrangement with him as to how we'd handle the announcement. He agreed that Dole should go out after the meeting and cover the whole thing, but say that Bush still has important work at the UN and that we'd have to do the shift after the General Assembly. The meeting went reasonably well. Bob came in and sort of wandered through a lot of chitchat for a while and then the P finally eased into the deal. They agreed that Bush would stay on through the session and Dole would stay at the RNC for the January meeting and Ziegler should shoot down the nonsense that Dole was pushed out. That basically covered the Dole meeting.

Got into the Watergate thing. Feels he doesn't want to leave an aura around the White House that there are a lot of bad guys there and the P doesn't care. Says the theory of "Just be quiet and it'll all go away" won't work. We need something to be said. Otherwise how can the P handle it at his first press conference? We should try just a very brief statement, but we must get something to get it out of the way. At least something that Segretti had nothing to do with Watergate. And he feels a good offense is the best defense in this kind of thing. He went through it all with E and said that the view now is that the P is trying to hide something or protect someone, and that we've got to go for the smallest statement we can make but we do have to make some statement.

I called Connally to get his reaction. He said he was mad as hell at *(new DNC Chairman Robert)* Strauss about his TV thing yesterday. He had called him and told him his remarks were ill-advised. He had gone out of his way to take a cut at Connally and said he had read him out of the party and made the point apparently that it was a sin to have voted against McGovern, and that if that's so, they ought to select new moral standards. He said he was pretty rough and that Strauss was quite disturbed. He says Strauss' election won't change a thing. He doesn't know what his deals are that he made to get the post, but in any event, the liberals will try to crucify him, that he brings no strength to the party, he's just a manager. He can't bring the South in. Wallace is the leader of the Democratic South. For that reason, we should move in somewhat to let them have a place to go, but they'll need a compelling motivation. They can't go to avoid a nebulous third party. Theoretically, they'd do it in a minute, but they don't know how to do it practically. It'll take a move—either a positive move by the Republicans or a negative move by the Democrats. We'll have to wait and see.

Tuesday, December 12, 1972

The P had me over to talk about the Julie job. Apparently Julie had talked with him last night and she can't now take that job, so he wanted me to consider what she could do over here. She's good for the P, well organized, thinks up things, and handles a lot of little things. It's good to have her around, so he wants to see what she can do at the White House. She could schedule events, getting people to cooperate and all that. She should do something where she handles people. I talked to Julie later, and she agreed that the real place for her is in the East Wing job. She talked to Ron and he agreed, too, so we're going to try to get that back on the track.

I had a call from Billy Graham today, to say he's back from his trip and wanted to report that everyone in all the countries he visited were elated at the P's election. The Shah of Iran said that we've saved civilization for at least four more years.

Wednesday, December 13, 1972

Ziegler moved in on the Julie deal today. The P told him to call Pat Nixon and meet with her and Julie this afternoon and try to get it settled, which Ron did and it worked out very well. Agreed that we'll be doing it on the basis of Julie being an assistant to the First Lady and putting a press assistant in also, Ron, in an hour and a half session, sold it completely to them, so we've now got that on track.

The P was very disturbed by the Scotty Reston story today on Vietnam, which he feels had to come from K. The P said it was totally baffling to Haig as to why Henry would have done it. Haig called while I was in the office this morning and said Henry would be home late tonight, that he was very touchy in his phone conversation that they've obviously had a rough time on the settlement.

Thursday, December 14, 1972

Henry was back. Spent most of the morning with the P and apparently the talks have broken off for now, so there won't be anything developing on that in the immediate future. The P's going to have to move to step up the bombing and hope that we can get a political settlement.

K came in to talk with me this morning about his personal problems. Wants to have a long meeting later, which we never got around to today. Got into the press thing, and it was really kind of hysterical, because he flatly told me that he had not talked with John Osborne and did not understand why the P and others were disturbed about the Osborne story, and didn't understand why we didn't trust him when he says he doesn't talk to these people. Then I read him the direct quotes in the story, and after hemming and hawing a bit, he said, well, I talked with him on the phone but I didn't meet with him.

Friday, December 15, 1972

The P's foot is still bothering him. He said this morning he had taken his bandage off and he felt that he probably had a splinter or broken bone. It doesn't hurt when he stands on it or when he's sitting, but does hurt when he walks. He's limping very badly, and is concerned about any events that require him to do any major walking. He refuses to see a doctor or do anything about it. He says wearing a shoe is just as good as having a splint and he doesn't want to make a big fuss about it.

Then we got into the whole question of K's briefing. He had Ziegler in first thing this morning, said that they should go ahead on the K briefing at 11:30, but that there should be no extravaganza over in the White House. It should just be in the pressroom.

Editor's Note: Negotiations were going nowhere, and the President had decided it was time for strong action. He authorized B-52 raids up North and the reseeding of Haiphong Harbor.

Then Ziegler should plan to do the bombing and mining briefing on Saturday, and making the point that these are just precautionary measures in the face of a North Vietnamese buildup. The P has stated that bombing and mining would continue until we get our minimum conditions of POW's and cease-fire, and he says that the point is that bombing for a couple of weeks would put us in a good position.

Ron raised the point of the *Time* magazine Man of the Year. The P said K is not to see them under any circumstances, that I'm to order him to do no interviews, social, return calls, or anything to *Time,* and he told me to call the White House operators to turn those calls off to Henry, which, of course, I can't do. He's written a long memo to K, which he was having typed up while Ron and I were meeting with him about guidance on the thing. He had Ron and Henry and me in a little later in the morning and Henry had convinced him he should not have his press conference today because of some statements by the North Vietnamese and other general developments. The original plan was to have a press conference today, then start the military actions tomorrow, and the massive bombing on Sunday, but then Le Duc Tho said this morning that they'd agreed not to comment on the talks and that he remains optimistic, so Henry thinks we have an alternate course of letting it ride today and then K going on tomorrow. Start the minor action on Sunday and the massive action on Monday. One problem with following the original scenario would be that we would be bombing while Le Duc Tho was in Peking, which would cause a heavier reaction.

The P then read his entire memo, which must have been four or five pages. Then he told K he wants to make the P appear to be the tough guy all the way through. That we should set it up today for K to go tomorrow. The P said I would rather bomb on Monday, unless you think we really need to do it on Sunday. He didn't like the idea of having a Sunday church service while he was bombing. K said he feels better than he has in weeks, because now we're in control of things again instead of being in the position of the rabbit with two snakes, having one on each side. The P got back to discussing what Henry ought to do. He said to be nonspecific on the details and he did a lot on building up of his spirit and all. The P was obviously trying to maneuver Henry into the right frame of mind on how to approach the whole thing.

After they left, the P made the point that he was very concerned about Henry's mood, and said, well, he's happy now, because we're going back to the bombing, but that's the wrong approach. He wanted to be sure that Henry had a very hard briefing before he goes out to the press tomorrow because his press things have been disasters. He must try to be effective rather than being brilliant. He then got into the point he's been making quite frequently the last few days, that we've got to get hold of the government. He keeps saying he has the feeling that the government is out of control, that the people we have don't know what to say and don't know how to say it, so we aren't getting our points across.

Had a long meeting with Stans on his whole campaign thing. He reports that on the financing deal, we spent $47.5 million, but we had budgeted $43 million. He thinks there's another million, maybe at the most, in backup bills. He says he collected $51 million, so he's got something like $2.5 or $3 million in coverage, and he's concerned about what to do with it. Thinks he should transfer it to a cleanup fund before December 31, use what's needed to pay for litigation, contingent liabilities on taxes if we have to pay them, and some refunds to some noisy contributors who were upset about appointments.

Saturday, December 16, 1972

I spent all morning in a personnel meeting, keeping the P stalled. Didn't get in to see him till later in the afternoon. I raised the point of Anne Armstrong as counselor and the P bought it. Worked up a way to go at it, and I tried to reach Anne to tell her, she wasn't available by phone. We decided we wanted to leak it to the press for the Sunday papers, to the *Star,* and called Ziegler to tell him to do that. I still couldn't get Anne. The time got to 4:30, which is the latest one could leak it, so we went ahead and leaked it without telling Anne. Then I did get her on the phone, told her. She was a little flabbergasted. I didn't get her till 5:30, and by that time, I told her she'd have to be at the Cabinet dinner tonight, and that really threw her, too, because she only had two hours to notify her family, get organized, and get to the dinner, then I alerted the P. He decided he wanted her on his right and wanted her to give a toast at the dinner, which she did do. The Cabinet dinner went off very well. A little bit rambling, as the P got up and gave a little talk about the importance of Cabinet people. Then had me give a toast to the VP and considered him as symbolic of the entire Cabinet. Then had Bill Rogers toast Mamie Eisenhower and Pat Nixon, the First Ladies. Bill very graciously also toasted Julie as the symbol of the coming together of those two families. Then he announced Anne Armstrong's appointment, told them it was a big secret until Monday, and had Anne respond with a toast to the P. She did a very good job, working in the idea that this is the period when we salute the Prince of Peace and stating that those of us who are closest to, and work most directly with the P, have a chance to gather with him at this time and to drink a toast to the man who has done the most for peace in our history. A potential awkwardness didn't seem to develop, at least there were no real problems at the dinner, although it wasn't any great smashing success, I don't think.

Monday, December 18, 1972

The P was up at Camp David all morning. He came down at noon and then he came over. He is concerned about K and his reaction to the bombing thing and all that, because Henry feels we're at another crisis point now and is going through his usual reactions on that. Later in the afternoon, he had Henry and me come over, and he went through a long discussion of the whole rationale, how we got where we are and what the current situation is, how we should be dealing with it. Mostly an exercise on the P's part to try to buck Henry up, because he feels he is overreacting to the press and so forth as a result of his concern on the whole bombing deal. The P made the point that we've been around this track before. We have a lot of friends in the country and we shouldn't be too worried. The key is that we all must show confidence. He also thinks we're in a good position because we're starting the bombing just a week before Christmas. He's very concerned about any second-guessing. K's covered everyone and they all were for it, so he doesn't think we'll have any real problem there. He wants two or three B-52's today and the P asked Henry whether the Air Force wants to pull back now. Henry says no, that we're doing the right thing, and the P says it's funny how these things work out. That we could have stalled this a few weeks but it's much better to be going at it now. Henry makes the point that the P's best course is brutal unpredictability.

Wednesday, December 20, 1972

The P had his physical this morning, apparently everything went well, except that they did confirm that he had splintered a bone in his foot, so he was right on that problem. Later he said with some glee that Haig has now joined the club, that he got kicked in the teeth by Thieu, was kept waiting five hours, and that Thieu demands total withdrawal of all North Vietnamese troops, so that we have to go out on January 3 for a separate deal if we can get it. We lost three more B-52's today. The P is obviously very concerned about the reaction on the B-52's. The military apparently anticipated three losses for every 100 planes in raids, but we're running somewhat higher than that. He says, however, that we must not knock it off, and K agrees.

The P kept coming back to the B-52 loss problem, saying we can't back off, but will we get three losses every time? If so, it's going to be very tough to take. Thieu has ended up ignoring the P's letters and stating his own demands, such as getting the troops out. The P says that, in effect, he wants us to go out alone. So we have to figure how we can without sinking South Vietnam. The real question is whether Hanoi will settle bilaterally without forcing us to cut aid to South Vietnam. They can gamble that Congress will throw out the aid anyway. If we go bilaterally there will be no cease-fire, but we would argue that South Vietnam is now in a position where they can stand on their own feet. K, over and over in the meeting, really blasted Thieu as a complete SOB. Says that he still may be just doing this to make a record, and then planning to cave at the end, but the main thing is to finish the thing as best we can. The P says it's better not to get a negative agreement, that we should go for a separate deal, which I argued against. The question still is whether to go bilateral or to negotiate it. If Hanoi accepts the January 3 meeting, we should meet, settle, and put it to Thieu. In other words, the P is now shifting to my view. We should now treat Thieu with total silence, not give him another chance. The P then sort of summed it up, that as gloomy as it looks at this point, something still may happen. Truman's death is still imminent, and may affect the P's travel plans, although nothing specific was said on that.

The P left for Key Biscayne for Christmas.

Friday, December 22, 1972
I had no contact with the P today. He's still in Key Biscayne. Ziegler did call in the evening to say that he had a long session with the P and he's very upset because he's sort of feeling that he was left out alone, nobody worrying about things. He was disturbed by a wire story covering the number of people who were having to give up Christmas with their families in order to service the P while he's in Florida. As a result of this, the

P saying that he'll probably return to Washington on Christmas evening, which would be bad news.

Saturday, December 23, through Tuesday, December 26, 1972

The P was in Key Biscayne. I was in Washington and had no contact. Made a major point out of not calling me or interrupting me in any way during my so-called vacation period.

1973

First Quarter: January–March

Wednesday, December 27, 1972, through Tuesday, January 2, 1973

Again no contact. The P was in Washington, having come back up on the evening of the 26th from Key Biscayne, and spending some time in DC and Camp David. I left for Palm Springs on the 26th and was there through this entire period. Had no contact with the P during that entire time. Other than that the period was relatively uneventful.

Wednesday, January 3, 1973

Back at work. The P had me in at 11:00 for about three hours on just a general recap on where things were. The P wants Conger to check on other possible Presidential desks for the Oval Office and says he's gotten some expert to agree to do some redecorating at the Oval Office, apparently somebody that Mrs. Nixon has been using at the Residence, that may work out. He's at least getting rid of the Boehm Birds *(decorative birds that always bothered the President)* on the shelves. He's concerned about David's Congressional seat, and wants to be sure that we're getting that set up, had a lot of ideas on the news summary, to leave out the magazines and local Washington papers, emphasize the positive rather than drawing so much on negative things. He said he'd have a reception for the National Committee after the Inaugural, wants to hold up on the diplomatic reception until Vietnam is settled. Was pleased with the Senate resolution today on Vietnam, wants the House to go for the same resolution. Met with Henry last night, and again today, and will meet with him on Saturday extensively on Vietnam before he leaves Sunday for the new talks.

683

As a general comment, it's clear to me that he still hasn't clearly focused on getting down to work on the second term, he's using the Inaugural as an excuse for not scheduling things, but he's not working on the Inaugural. I think until he gets Vietnam settled, everything else is going to pretty much stay in the background, and there won't be much concentration on anything.

Thursday, January 4, 1973

The P had Ziegler and me in first thing this morning, reviewing plans for Ziegler's briefing. Told Ron, on Vietnam to say there's no further comment from the White House because there are sensitive negotiations under way. Some analysis of Vietnam and of Congress. He can't figure why they all keep the pressure on for an explanation of why he's doing the bombing. I must say I agree, the reason seems to be obvious and I can't conceive of any intelligent person who doesn't clearly understand why he's bombing. Therefore, the question and arguments are obviously political or academic.

I had a long talk with Henry late in the afternoon, he seemed to be in good shape, feels he's got a good chance of bringing up negotiations, and overall seems to be at least reasonably optimistic.

The P still is concerned about dealing with the reaction, and the press and the Congress. That they're obsessed with negative stuff with Vietnam and are going to play it no matter what we do, and all he can do is ride it out. If we get the settlement, to comment now won't matter; if we don't get it we'll have far greater problems to deal with than what we now have.

Sunday, January 7, 1973

I got to Camp David at 10:00 and met with the P for four hours at Birch and it broke up at 2:00 and I went on back home while he stayed up till later in the afternoon. His primary concern was the whole attack and PR operation, which he feels is now dismantled and that we have nothing to work with. He now feels that we face a partisan situation right from the beginning of Congress, as evidenced by their approach on Vietnam, whereas we thought we would have a better relationship, at least at the start, because of the landslide election victory. The problem, he feels, is that we breathed a sigh of relief after the campaign and then sat down at Camp David to start reorganizing the government. Now we're paying the price. Therefore we have to have a new attack organization directed at the top.

The P also got into some discussion of his K concerns again. Made the point that Haig has got to fill his scorecard in completely and totally level with him on the K problem, so he knows how to go out on this. Then he raised his concern about the K papers, and all the P's papers on national security that K is holding, including Henry's phone calls, and conversation memos and cables and so on, which he wants to be sure we get ahold of and stay on top of as much as possible. He thinks that I need to get a deputy for myself, with maturity and presence, who can act in my place. That I have to clear time on the new establishment, with the Republicans, the financial people, and so forth. Which ones are the real leaders, and how do we build them up? He keeps talking about when I get more free *(time),* these are the things I ought to be doing. He wants me to develop a plan for this, and also to get the candidate search going quickly.

We had some discussion about Watergate, and I filled him in on all the coverage in the paper today, and the fact that it's building up. He feels that our people should take the Fifth Amendment rather than getting trapped into testifying.

Monday, January 8, 1973

In the staff meeting this morning we discussed the wage-price announcement plans. I had a phone conversation with Connally, mainly to just check in with him. He says that he was very concerned about the newspaper campaign regarding the brawl about Congress, not just Vietnam but on the overall thing. For example on the "Today" show this morning, Bob Byrd *(Senator)* said he hadn't seen the P since last year, and he thinks that the whole attack, overall, is the most vicious thing he's ever seen and it will foreclose a lot of our options in a lot of areas, and the P should therefore call for Congress to reorganize themselves, put them on the defensive instead of the P. We should not be mean, but we should toss it back at them. He says he'll probably be up this week, and then he went through some specific people and appointment items.

John Dean called to report on the Watergate trials, says that if we can prove in any way by hard evidence that our plane was bugged in '68, he thinks that we could use that as a basis to say we're going to force Congress to go back and investigate '68 as well as '72, and thus turn them off.

He says Hunt's going to take a guilty plea on three counts after *(Assistant U.S. Attorney for District of Columbia Earl)* Silbert's opening statement. He'll say that no higher-ups were involved, the rest of them will go to trial. That Rothblatt, the attorney for the Cubans, is a wild man, and he wants to go to trial. Liddy wants to go trial, because he's hoping for an error in catching things up on a lot of procedures and all, and John thinks that this is better because Liddy won't take the stand, and it will be good to have him do it. McCord will testify, but he has no firsthand knowledge. All the Cubans will sit mute, and even if they're immunized afterward they'll take a contempt charge rather than talk. There's great concern on their part that the commitments to them won't be honored, and there's a problem with funds that LaRue is supposed to be working on. John is going to assemble a Congressional strategy group of himself, Johnson, Moore, and Colson because he thinks that we may have some of our own cards to play. That we should start looking at the Hill guys' vulnerabilities and see if we can't turn off the Hill effort before it gets started, which he thinks is important to do.

Tuesday, January 9, 1973
K called on the phone, reporting, that we would be receiving a message in an hour or so. The main reason for his call was to wish the P a happy birthday, and that some of what he had been hoping for may be coming to pass. There will be a proposed schedule coming to us tomorrow and that we must keep the lid on. The cable should be confined to the P only. Tell no one else now. Then he said he mainly wanted to wish the P a happy birthday and express my gratitude to him for letting me serve. A little later, his report came, was very good news, he says they got the breakthrough, and unless the Vietnamese back down, we're in very good shape. The P had Colonel Kennedy in, said regarding K's message, it's to go to no one else except Haig. Then he decided it shouldn't go to Haig either, so he wouldn't have to tell Abrams or anyone. To Rogers he should just say that it's still tough going, it's too early to tell what's happening. The same with Laird.

The P said they should keep talking tomorrow, that there's nothing conclusive. Ziegler is to play very cool, no indication of optimism. The P said that he's not overly optimistic, that Henry is probably overevaluating it again. Kennedy, on the other hand, thinks this is it. The P's concern is that the North Vietnamese will back down the hill tomorrow. The P says the only thing that he disagrees with K on is the massive problem in Saigon. He says he doesn't think it's like it was there now. Kennedy also says he's much more hopeful that we can pull it off with Saigon. Talked about the fact that Haig should plan to go on Sunday, or as soon as possible, but we should not tell him the news today, so that he won't have to lie over there. Overall, it's super good news, and the P told Kennedy to send Henry a cable saying this was the best birthday present he's had in sixty years.

The P had a series of meetings at his initiative today. First Malek, told Fred to feel free to say the P wants this or that when you're working. He made the point that you're a good manager and judge of managers but more important than ability is loyalty. The government must act when we speak, therefore it is better to have a dumb loyalist than a bright neuter. For IRS, a loyal Jew would be good. It must be a loyalist.

Dean reported that everybody except Liddy either has, or will, be negotiating pleas of guilty, this is including McCord. Hunt has already settled on a negotiation for a guilty plea on three counts, the others have vague assurance regarding equal treatment and so on. Silbert has a problem with the judge accepting the pleas, but after the opening statement the jury and panel will take the plea and the judge will ask if there are any higher-ups and Hunt will say no. Liddy still has a desire to go to trial because it puts him in better shape, and he wants to go for a pardon. Colson made the deal with *(Hunt's lawyer)* Bittman regarding Hunt, this led to the deals with the other parties, so there is no involvement from the White House, it's all indirect.

He thinks that we can probably also work Liddy, but maybe we shouldn't. They'll take contempt if they're granted immunity, and that may bump the Congress too. He wants Mitchell to talk to *(former Assistant Director of the FBI Cartha)* De Loach to see what he can get out of him on the LBJ thing, because if he can get that cranked up, LBJ could turn off the whole Congressional investigation.

The P left early to go for a drive with Bebe out to see Julie's new house, and then for his surprise birthday party tonight.

Wednesday, January 10, 1973

We got Henry's cable regarding scheduling, and the P said that I should send Henry a cable saying to leave open the possibility of Haig's trip to the friendly Asian capitals, as well as to Saigon rather than Henry's going to Hanoi. Then the P realized that I was right in saying that we'd have a real problem in getting Henry stirred up on something like that, and shouldn't get into it. A little later I had a phone call from Henry and he said that he was sending a new scheduling approach that he thought the P would like because it solves some of the problems. When his cable came in, it turned out it does, because he's worked out a deal now where he would return to Paris to sign the agreement, rather than going to Hanoi. Then would go to Hanoi in early February to work out peace settlement arrangements rather than to sign the agreement, which would solve the problem of Saigon's objection to signing the agreement in Hanoi, and also the P's objection, plus closing down the time frame and all that.

The P had Haig come over to go over the cable and the situation, and then he had quite a discussion on it. The real point is that the P feels that he has to announce the settlement to the Americans before K initials it, otherwise there is no point in his announcing, because it's just covering something that is already done. He told Haig to get a message back to Henry saying that the new scenario was infinitely preferable to the old routine of his going to Hanoi and that we should go ahead trying to work it out with the North Vietnamese. We would like the cease-fire as soon as possible, not to drag it on.

Thursday, January 11, 1973

On the Watergate question, he wanted me to talk to Mitchell and have him find out from De Loach if the guy who did the bugging on us in '68 is still at the FBI, and then Gray should nail him with a lie detector and get it settled, which would give us the evidence we need. He also thinks I ought to move with George Christian *(LBJ's former Press Secretary, now working with Democrats for Nixon),* get LBJ to use his influence to turn off the Hill investigation with Califano, Hubert, and so on. Later in the day, he decided that wasn't such a good idea, and told me not to do it, which I fortunately hadn't done.

Henry phoned this morning from Paris and said that there would be a cable coming in a couple of hours. He got 80 percent of what the P asked for in his cable, or at least it would be doable, and it would be consistent with what Henry had said, along the lines of what we want, and that we had gotten 100 percent on substance. He seemed pretty pleased. The cable came in later, it turned out he basically had gotten everything we want, and he'll do the signing in Paris rather than Hanoi, which is the key thing. Set the date for the 23rd with the announcement, after Haig gets back from South Vietnam, if we get Thieu to go along.

The VP requested a meeting with the P today, came in with an incredible proposal. He thought that something ought to be done to divert public attention from Vietnam and the attacks we're getting in on it. He suggested that he take a trip to Egypt to visit Sadat, and see if he could try and untangle something on the Middle East. The P was obviously so astonished he didn't know quite how to answer the thing at first, but then made the point that the likelihood of anything good coming out of such a trip was almost zero, and that it would be very unwise for the VP to take the risk of being rebuffed at that high level. Then admitted, really, what the VP was after was a way to rebuild his own image, and that he's being attacked because the one substantive thing that he had was the intergovernmental relations and that had been taken away from him, so he had nothing really of importance to do.

Friday, January 12, 1973

Henry called me from Paris about noon, said they had another six-hour meeting today and that it continues the trend that he will definitely be back here tomorrow. He'll have two options regarding the announcement and that we can decide that next week. He says that we've got a PR problem, which he'll put in a cable, that will be tough to handle and that he needs an answer tonight. We got that a little later, and it turned out that he agreed to let the North Vietnamese have their photographer take a picture of the group for "historic purposes." Now it develops that they want to release the picture, and Henry's asking how to handle it, suggesting that maybe he should get a Western journalist and let them take a picture too, and release the whole thing. We went back to him on the basis that he should get only the USIA in, and that they should take a picture only for the historical record, with the understanding that none of the pictures can be released by either side until after the agreement has been signed and announced. Doubt if he'll stick with that, but at least we'll try.

On the plane to Key Biscayne, the P made the point that if we get a settlement, we should get every commentator, columnist, and so on that has hit us and really badger them on an all-out basis. He feels also that we have got to send a pressman with Henry on the final trips to avoid things like the picture problem arriving, thinks we can move the 18th announcement to the 19th as long as he isn't doing anything, and that we should split the Cabinet and Leaders Meetings to Wednesday and Thursday instead of Monday and Tuesday of the following week, so that he'll keep time clear for preparation for his Tuesday-night television. He'll probably have the Cabinet and Leaders in on Tuesday for the announcement. Ziegler came in during the flight to report that ABC had a report that we had an agreement and that K would be coming home tomorrow. It was agreed that we would say no comment on spec stories and when K returns that he'll be meeting with the P. We got into the problem with the line for the congressmen, because Kennedy has to brief Scott and Ford tomorrow for the "Meet the Press" thing on Sunday, posing an additional problem.

The P also got back on the Watergate thing today, making the point that I should talk to Connally about the Johnson bugging process to get his judgment as to how to handle it. He wonders if we shouldn't just have Andreas go in and scare Hubert. The problem in going at LBJ is how he'd react, and we need to find out from De Loach who did it, and then run a lie detector on him. I talked to Mitchell on the phone on this subject and he said De Loach had told him that he was up to date on the thing because he had a call from Texas. A *Star* reporter was making an inquiry in the last week or so, and LBJ got very hot and called Deke, and said to him that if the Nixon people are going to play with this, that he would release *(deleted material—national security)*, saying that our side was asking that certain things be done. By our side, I assume he means the Nixon campaign organization. De Loach took this as a direct threat from Johnson. He says he'll bring his file in Monday for Mitchell to review. As he recalls it, bugging was requested on the planes, but was turned down, and all they did was check the phone calls, and put a tap on the Dragon Lady *(Mrs. Anna Chennault)*. Mitchell also said he was meeting with O'Brien today, and will make reference to this whole thing in that meeting and see what he can smoke out.

Saturday, January 13, 1973

The P had me over this morning for three or four hours going through a lot of miscellaneous things. Got into the media relation question, said that I should talk to Price about his view as to what we did wrong three years ago regarding the media. He went through a whole bunch of miscellaneous personal items. Wants to be sure on Sinatra and Sammy Davis that the P wants an evening at the White House for each of them. Wants to be sure Rose is making notes on all the personal things and also that Bebe is dictating tapes on the personal vignettes on the P, what happens at Walker's Cay, and all that for the P's tape record. Wants to be sure we have a superb executive director for the Bicentennial that has lots of imagination. Wants to get in the 75 Democratic congressmen and 11 senators who stood with us on Vietnam for a cocktail to express his appreciation for standing with us during this difficult period. Wanted to read a copy of Farley's book on Kennedy and the Rossiter book on the Presidency, which I sent over to him later. Wanted to check out burial opportunities at Yorba Linda, as well as Rose Hills. I don't know how that came in from left field.

I had a report this afternoon from Dean on the Watergate. Apparently there is going to be a *(Seymour)* Hersh story in *The New York Times* saying that the Cubans told them that they're all on salary, that there's a $900,000 fund at the Reelection Committee for them, and that they dropped bugs all over town. The chain of command went from Barker to Hunt to Liddy to Colson to Mitchell. *(Director of Public Affairs, CRP, DeVan)* Shumway and Colson and Mitchell have all given flat denials on this. The Cubans have sent a letter to dismiss Rothblatt, and he was dismissed because they want to plead guilty. McCord is off the reservation now, he had a meeting last night, he thinks he can get him back on, but he has a plan regarding calls he made in September and October. He thinks he can get a tainted evidence thing on it, because the calls were bugged by the government. He's playing a blackmail game where if I (McCord) fall, all fall, but he has no hard evidence. That won't be settled for a while, but Dean thinks he can settle it. Apparently McCord was distressed at the judge's severity. The Cubans plead on Monday.

Editor's Note: Judge John Sirica was noted for his severe sentences, and McCord was threatening to talk rather than go to jail for a long time.

The main thing today was, of course, Vietnam. The P said he wanted to see K alone first when he gets back tonight, and that his chopper should be brought directly to the P's pad, and the P will see him, if he's awake, and will pound into him that he must not talk to the press and that we're going to do all possible to be sure that people think that nothing happened in Paris. In other words we need to mislead them.

He talked to Ziegler about how to deal with the press, and that the speculation has led to universal optimism and pessimism both. The P's concern with K tomorrow, and with Ziegler, is that we have to have a plan on the PR side that we can ride with through the week, so we can control K.

Sunday, January 14, 1973
The P called me at 9:00, said to come over as soon as I could. I got over at the house about 9:40. The P was sitting in the living room with a fire going in the fireplace, said that he had read the Farley book or a good part of it, and he thinks that all of our key assistants should read it because it makes a good point on the need for dissenting views, and he's concerned that we don't handle that adequately. Farley makes the point that we do a good job in our Administration through the NSC, which Kennedy did not do, but he also thinks that someone ought to talk to Farley and make the point to him the differences between our bureaucracy and the British, that he'd be good to write the story on the reorganization. He then got into some discussion of schedule for handling the Vietnam thing. K and Haig arrived. There was some discussion on the wording on the bombing-stop announcement, and then on the Thieu letter wording. The P strengthened the wording that K had drafted. Apparently he reviewed it last night, by saying in ef-

fect that I have approved every section and so forth. He wants to take out the offer to meet with Thieu, let Haig use that as a bargaining point in discussion, but not put it in the letter. His strategy there is to keep the whole approach with Thieu on our terms, and we don't want to appear to be begging, especially on the record. The P made the point that Haig must take a very hard line on Thieu, that he's here only as a messenger, not to negotiate, that the P has been totally in charge of all of this, and he will go ahead regardless of what Thieu does. The only diplomacy that Haig should exercise is to trick Thieu, if it looks like he's not going with us in regard to shooting his mouth off before the Inaugural. He's got to work out some way to stop him from doing that. If he takes on K or the agreement, he takes on the P personally and he's got to understand that.

K should tell Rogers that there is to be no testimony to anyone, that K will do nothing regarding press, Congress, and so forth. The P warned that the silence is going to be very difficult because everybody—press, Congress, and so on—will be screaming, but it's good because it builds the deal. Henry then said absolutely no purpose is served by saying one word. The P then made a long comparison of this whole thing to a poker game and told us of the time he once had a royal flush in a five-card-stud game, with the ace in the hole, and then on the next four cards up he drew the king and the queen, then the jack, then ten of diamonds. Another guy had a full house, the P played his hand as if he had nothing, in order to keep the other people in the game, and thus built up the stake. He said we're sitting on a royal flush now, but we won't get a big pot unless we're mum. The time to bluff is when you have nothing, the time to keep quiet is when you have the cards.

Henry then reviewed the whole schedule. On Monday we suspend the bombing. On Tuesday they meet at 9:30, initial at 12:30, leave at 2:15. K is on the plane by 3:00 and airborne, and then we request TV time and announce the meeting with the leaders and Cabinet. TV announcement is at 10:00 our time that night. The P told K to write two versions of the television speech of 700 maximum word length, one with Thieu going along, the other without Thieu. Then Wednesday we publish the text, there is a K briefing with the press on TV, the diplomatic activities, setting up the signing and so on. Thursday we cancel the peace talks, Friday Rogers goes to Paris, Saturday is the signing ceremony in Paris, two different ceremonies, one in morning and one in afternoon, and at midnight Saturday night, Greenwich Mean Time, which is 6:00 our time, the cease-fire goes into effect. Sunday the control commission arrives in South Vietnam and meets. The P said the line the opposition will put out is that Congress forced the "mad bomber" to stop the mining and bombing, and as a result of his stopping, we were able to get the settlement. The objective here is the honor of this country, and a country without honor has no authority. We then walked out and had some general conversation, and that ended the meeting four hours after it started.

After I dictated the report for Sunday, I had dinner with K, which I scheduled in order to keep him from going out to dinner and getting caught in the public down here. So we ate in his villa, had a three-hour chat alone, which was quite productive, went through the whole history story and status on Vietnam, which he likes to reiterate. Henry really wanted, however, to get into a long discussion regarding the question of the P's confidence in him. He's concerned that the stories that he keeps reading may be partly or totally true, that is that the P has lost confidence in him. I told him that there wasn't any problem with the P having confidence with him substantively, but the P does get concerned about the whole business of Henry's talking to the left-wing set, and the campuses and the media, etc. It's not because he's influenced by, or influences, the left wing, but rather it gives them status to have that contact with K, and that's to our disadvantage, and that's what bothers the P on that subject. He basically understands, and is compulsively unable to do anything about it.

Monday, January 15, 1973

The P had me over at noon for a brief meeting, he mainly wanted to get into some attack follow-ups on some things on Vietnam. In the midst of this he was interrupted with a phone call to Don Shula, the Miami Dolphins coach, to congratulate him on winning the Super Bowl yesterday.

Tuesday, January 16, 1973

The P had me over at noon today, later than usual because he's apparently getting to work on the Inaugural address now. I have the responsibility, he feels, to get Haig to brief all the communications staff, to get a lot of people out selling our line, and that we should do this Tuesday afternoon while K is flying back from Paris. Then he called on the phone this afternoon and made the point that he had read the Rossiter book, which he thought had a fascinating point regarding Eisenhower, which is that in terms of great leadership it is better perhaps to have half the people like what we do and the other half hate him than it is to have the great center who likes him and only a small fringe on either side who worship him and hate him.

Wednesday, January 17, 1973

For the first time since we've been here I didn't have to go over at all today. The P called at noon to check on how things were going, mainly to be sure the staff mood is up and that we're doing everything we can to keep everybody cranked up and upbeat, especially as people are starting to come into town for the Inaugural. We must put on a good morale-builder approach for them.

Thursday, January 18, 1973

The P got me on the way back from Key Biscayne on some general schedule discussion on the plane. He's trying to get his time cleared now that he's getting back to handle the Vietnam stuff after the long Inaugural and wants to keep everything as clear as he can. He then got into some discussion on Vietnam and the settlement, and more importantly, the Thieu problem, which he's still sweating out, because he hasn't heard from Haig yet. The question now is whether Thieu will go along. He's refused to give Haig an answer, at least at this point, so we have to wait for Haig to go back there on Saturday. The P feels that's a pretty cheap shot on Thieu's part, and that he should give us an answer before the Inaugural, so that the P will know, and that's the least we could reasonably expect from him. But apparently we're not going to get it.

Saturday, January 20, 1973

I had no contact with the P today. This was the Inaugural and the Parade and the Balls. He did superbly well at all of them, and I'm sure considers the whole thing a success. It ran flawlessly except for the inevitable overcrowding at the

Balls, but the P did a good job in his presentation at each of them, and did dance as he had planned to do, so that all worked out well.

Monday, January 22, 1973

Big question today was planning the Vietnam settlement. Henry had left this morning for Paris, and the P told Ziegler to get a leak out to the *Post* and to Dan Rather that the initialing will be on Friday, so that we can throw them off-balance. Then he got into a lot of miscellaneous Inaugural follow-up. He had a problem with his Inaugural address, because when he got what was supposed to be the final draft Friday evening, he discovered a sentence was missing. He called Rose and she said she had told the girls to proof it, but she couldn't do anything about it now, that she was late for a party. Then he tried to reach Ray and he was already at the Kennedy Center, so he had Manolo go down and get the press copy, and the sentence was missing from that, too. The P couldn't find Ziegler to check with him, so he dropped the sentence, but it must have been rather a discouraging sequence for him, not to be able to find anybody to take care of the problem. A little later, while we were meeting with Ray Price on the Vietnam speech, we got word that President Lyndon Johnson had probably died. I had a note from Larry saying that he'd been taken to the hospital seriously ill, then a follow-up note saying that the Secret Service thought he was dead, when they found him. Tkach couldn't get any confirmation, until finally Lady Bird called an hour and 15 or 20 minutes after our first notice and officially informed the P. We had been informed just a few minutes before that by Tkach finally, that he was dead, but that they had tried to revive him on the plane and that they couldn't get Mrs. Johnson to notify her and they didn't want to put any word out until she had been told. I then talked to Tom Johnson, at the P's request, to set up all the arrangements for any help we could provide to them.

Tuesday, January 23, 1973

Got word from Henry first thing this morning that he had initialed the Vietnam agreement and that was set (*Thieu had finally capitulated a few days before*), so we had sessions on planning of the speech for tonight. There's still the question of Haig's briefing our PR staff, which he feels he shouldn't do because it'll drive Henry up the wall. We shifted the briefings all around because of the Johnson funeral plans, so that Henry is going to do everything on Wednesday morning.

We had the Cabinet meeting at 8:45. The P opened by saying that this was basically a pro forma meeting. We're doing it for the purpose of the eyes of the world and the nation so that they will think that we have consulted with the Cabinet, but we can't really get into anything now because we can't release the agreement until tomorrow. Then he read the official statement that he will read on TV tonight, said all our conditions have been completely met. The P said the GVN and Thieu are totally onboard and will issue statements to that effect. There will be heavy fighting between now and the cease-fire (on the 27th), and after the cease-fire there will be inevitable violations, which is why the supervisory body is so important. He said we have a cease-fire for Vietnam, possibly in Laos and Cambodia. We have peace with honor, the POW's are back, the supervised cease-fire, and the right of South Vietnam to determine their own future. It's been long, painful, and difficult for all of us. This is not Johnson's war, or Kennedy's war. They did start it and they did handle it badly, but the United States was involved. We have now achieved our goals—peace for Vietnam, the right of the South Vietnamese to determine their future without an imposed Communist government. The fact that we have stood firm as a country was responsible and has had a decisive effect on the world. If the United States did not prove to be responsible in Vietnam, if this had ended in defeat and surrender, the Chinese and the Russians would have no interest in talking to us. Europe wouldn't consider us as a reliable ally, in spite of their bitching about the war. We must understand, for the United States to keep the peace and save freedom, we have to be responsible, and that's what this peace is about. It was not a Republican achievement. He has as much contempt for the Republicans who would cut and run as he does for the Democrats. Thank God for those who stood with us, like the hard hats. He got fairly emotional at the end, but did a darn good job at the Cabinet meeting, although he worried Henry a little about some of the areas he went into.

The speech itself was also very good, and reaction afterward indicated that it will take a few days before we see how the tone really sets in. In any event it's been a rather historic day.

Wednesday, January 24, 1973

Got into the LBJ plans again today, when Tom Johnson called me several times from Air Force One. They were en route to Washington from Texas, wanting to get the schedule worked out. Plans for Mrs. Johnson to stay in the Rotunda after the service to greet people and the plans for meeting the diplomats at Blair House and having a buffet supper, and so on. The services all went very well and according to schedule although a little late. Then Tom called me at home tonight, wanting to change from using the DC-9 hospital plane to go direct to the ranch when they go back tomorrow. He wants to use Air Force One and go to the Air Force base because the weather's bad in Austin.

At the Cabinet meeting, which was 45 minutes late starting because of the delay in the LBJ funeral operation, the P opened by explaining the calendar date we were giving all of them and talked about when you reach the age of 60 your days are numbered, and he started citing the ages of all the various P's when they died, many of them under 60, and that we need to make every day count. Then he said on the budget that he sat through so many of these budget meetings, that they're the most boring, depressing exercises in the world, and so on, but that you have to do it. He made the point that government spending is a lousy issue. People are for spending. However, raising taxes is a good issue. That is, being against it. Being for a balanced budget is an impossible issue.

Saturday, January 27, 1973

At Key Biscayne. The P reviewed some of the editorials that we sent him. He feels that they still miss the point. K, at Congress, didn't make the point regarding the character of the man, how he toughed it through. We should quit worrying about defending the agreement; it either works or it doesn't, and it doesn't matter, but K just can't go through the details. Why not say that without the P's courage we couldn't have had this? The basic line here is the character, the lonely man in the White House, with little support from government, active opposition from the Senate and some House members, overwhelming opposition from media and opinion leaders, in-

cluding religious, education, and business, but strong support
from labor. The P alone held on and pulled it out. K is very
popular, got good applause, including from our opponents,
and a standing and prolonged ovation at the House, but he
didn't make our points. So the P makes the point, the missing
link now is the "Profile in Courage." We've analyzed the
editorials and it's not coming through. The briefing failed on
this point. He only had the P in the last briefing three times,
where when things were bad, he had him in 14 times. Henry
kept saying we'd kill the critics, and we haven't done this at
all. He's feeding the separation idea by his failure to build
the P. Can you imagine Sorensen, Schlesinger, McNamara, or
Rusk handling things this way with Kennedy? The rift between Henry and the P is not created by leaks. It's fed by
Henry's own nuances, because the press want to think there's
a rift. We have to have Henry build the P. He comments in
the Farley book that what the Kennedy people did with the
failures for Kennedy, we've got to do at least as well with
the successes.

The P attended the peace service at 7:00 at the Key Biscayne
church tonight, which went very well.

Monday, January 29, 1973
Got into a PR follow-up and so on this afternoon when he
came back from Walker's, where he'd been last night. He
wants Henry and me to see Teddy White before he finishes
his book, wants to follow up with the wife of Lt. Colonel
Nolde, the last man to be killed in Vietnam. He has to be sure
that no one talks to Sidey. He's very distressed with *Time,*
especially since they did the Marlon Brando cover on Inauguration Week instead of covering the Inaugural as the cover
story. He says he wants no more State visits this year. He's
concerned about getting a master schedule for State visits, visits in the United States, evenings at the White House, all the
general activities. He wants to develop a policy toward press
and media, not just going on the P's hunches.

Monday, February 5, 1973
The P had a good meeting with *(Director of White House
Office of Telecommunications)* Tom Whitehead and Colson on
the whole TV thing. He urged Whitehead to be controversial
and to be heard. They told him they're moving all public af-

fairs out of public TV to keep the government out of propaganda. Whitehead feels that the best course is to kill the Corporation of Public Broadcasting by defending it. The first step is to get rid of public affairs programming, feed their own internal quarrels. The P said he'd get the staff this week, told Whitehead not to do anything without staffing. That there are a lot of yellow-livered people around here. That when we get in this fight, everyone should shut up, no sniping or bitching afterward.

Tuesday, February 6, 1973

We got into quite a long question and discussion of Henry's whole situation, making the point that he's made all the big plays now and he's trying to look for ways to maintain the momentum, which is essentially impossible. There is no way to duplicate the year that has just been completed. That's what Henry is in effect trying to do, although he may not realize it. He feels he's running down and getting bored, and for that matter, so is the P. There's a real letdown and psychological depression after the type of accomplishments that they've had. Henry's obviously not interested in taking the time to work out the details of the agreement, etc., which must be done, but doesn't really interest him at this point. So we've got to watch this as he completes his trip and comes back. Especially he is reluctant to move into the Middle East, which the P feels has got to be settled now.

Wednesday, February 7, 1973

Ziegler came in while E was there to get some guidance on the briefing, on the principal question of the Ervin investigation and how to approach that, saying that we welcome a nonpartisan investigation. The P had some broader ideas on that, but cut back on them fortunately. On the Watergate question overall, Ron is still trying to make the point that we have nothing to add to what's already been said. On the question of executive privilege, he will stand by the detailed statement on the subject the P will be putting out a little later, as he had promised.

Editor's Note: By now, Senator Sam Ervin of North Carolina had been chosen to lead a Senate probe into 1972 campaign practices. There were those in the Administration who believed that the separation of power between the President and Congress prevented Congress from having the authority to call upon the President's personal aides to testify involuntarily. The issues of the President's rights vis-à-vis Congress and the Judiciary were referred to as "executive privilege."

Thursday, February 8, 1973

The day started with the Cabinet breakfast. *(After several remarks on the budget, economy, politics and foreign affairs)*, the P referred to the barrage that they've all been under with the Hill hearings and said that the P and Rogers had some rough moments, and went back to the November '69 demonstrators and all that made things look bad until the hard hats marched in our favor. We've had moments of discouragement in the foreign field, as we're working on the China thing, Soviet, Middle East, Jordan, Vietnam—the Senate pulled the rug out from under us on Vietnam time after time. Those most for peace are the ones who prolonged the war, but look at Mrs. Nolde, the wife of the Colonel who was the last man to die in Vietnam. She came to Washington for the funeral with her five children, some brothers and sisters, the whole family, and after the funeral service the P had them come in, and Mrs. Nolde told him that in Nolde's last letter to the family before he was killed, he said that he'd like to take the family to Washington and take them on a tour of the Congress and the White House, so they have set that up. He said they were a typical American family, and that she had conducted herself and walked in with the First Lady. Then the kids, the 17-year-old boy, who had a ragged beard and mustache, and long hair, the type that CBS would pick out—and they did, in the hopes that he'd make a negative statement—prepared a statement on why his father died, which was superb, and he had a big American flag in his lapel. He said he was proud of his dad. He fought for peace. Then the 16-year-old daughter, blonde, blue-eyed, looked up at the P and said just, "Could I kiss you?" At this point, there was a long silence, and I had been making notes, looked up and the P was just standing there. He started to say something and couldn't say it, paused for quite a bit longer, more silence, and then sort of said under his voice, "I guess that's what it's all about.'' Then he paused a minute, turned around and walked out of the State dining room, while everybody sat in silence for a moment, then rose and applauded for quite a long time. It was a highly emotional and highly dramatic moment. One of the more unforgettable ones of the time we've been here, and everybody was very much overwhelmed emotionally by it.

I had no further contact with the P until we got on the plane to California. Then he got into the Nobel Prize. He said, ''Don't discuss this with anyone else, but we've got to cover the question of how to handle the Nobel Peace Prize. It's a bad situation to be nominated and not get it. Maybe there should be a letter to Miller, who is nominating him, saying the P feels he should not be honored for doing his duty, and that we can separate from Teddy Roosevelt because he was involved in two other countries. It was something outside his normal duty as P. He wants a report on the Nobel Prize—who's on the committee, what's the process, can the P withdraw his name, and so on. He also wanted a review of the Gallup figures. Wants Kendall to call De Loach in on the FBI '68 bugging thing and tell him that if the FBI finds anything that you didn't tell us about, you're going to be fired. Wants Buchanan to prepare for the P the sharpest, briefest thing he can regarding the most vicious thing said by the media in the last month. He'd like a copy of that out tomorrow. He explored some questions on Watergate and the Ervin hearing, and we arrived in San Clemente to stay here for about 10 days.

Friday, February 9, 1973

The P was in fairly early, spent quite a little time by himself in the office, then had me in at 9:30 for about three hours. We reviewed the news summary with him and he was very pleased with Rogers' blast at the antiwar people, etc., when he appeared before the House Committee yesterday, so he had me call Rogers. The book of *(the P's)* Presidential papers from 1970 was left on his desk. He apparently spent quite a little time looking through it this morning and was intrigued with a lot of the things he found. He wants to be sure that E reads the Farley book because he feels the Kennedy approach was right regarding strategy and that you've got to talk about an issue that people are interested in, or create one. He feels that Price's introduction to the book is excellent, that it should be edited and revised so that wherever the P spoke extemporaneously, it says so, that he spoke without text or notes. He wants to get this to Safire for his book, and wants Safire to also review some of the really good pieces, such as the Wyeth toast, the 1970 prayer breakfast remarks, and the remarks on the occasion of McCormick's ceremony in the Caucus Room. He wants him to do a section in his book on extemporaneous speeches, especially the point that the P never read any of the toasts at the White House and none outside except when he had to by agreement in other countries. Also, he's never read an arrival statement.

He got into Watergate strategy. He wants to get our people to put out that foreign or Communist money came in in support of the demonstrations in the campaign, tie all the '72 demonstrations to McGovern and thus the Democrats as part of the peace movement. Broaden the investigation to include the peace movement and its leaders, McGovern and Teddy Kennedy. To what extent they were responsible for the demonstrations that led to the violence and disruption. We ran a clean campaign compared to their campaign of libel and slander, such as against Rebozo, etc. Maybe let Evans and Novak put it out and then we'll be asked about it. Can say that we knew that the P ordered that it not be used under any circumstances. He thinks we should play a hard game on this whole thing regarding the Ervin investigation. Get our investigators going and so on. Also he wants to be sure we order Gray to move on the FBI investigation, investigating those in the Bureau who tapped Nixon. We should itemize all the disruptions such as the Century Plaza in San Francisco, the burnings, the Statue of Liberty, etc.

He wants me to get King Timahoe out to his original breeder and have him bred after we get back.

Saturday, February 10, 1973

San Clemente. We had Dean and Moore out for an extended session on the Watergate strategy question and made a little progress in laying out an operating plan there. The main concern was the need to draw Kleindienst into the case and to keep him in the post through the duration of the hearings and to be a buffer and to take heat where necessary in the Department for things the P needs done. We're regrouping again tomorrow on the same subject.

Sunday, February 11, 1973

San Clemente. I had no contact with the P. Didn't go into the office today. He spent a good part of the day in a follow-up on our Watergate meeting from yesterday, with Dean, E, and Moore. Basically covered the same ground as was covered in my notes. Decided to go ahead on several tacks, to move Maury Stans out front by submitting him for a confirmation post, if the P will agree to it, and put Buchanan in as the observer/commentator on the Hearings. Several other items of that kind. General agreement on the strategy that we should keep the outward appearance of total cooperation but our objective internally should be maximum obstruction and containment, so as not to let the thing run away with us.

Monday, February 12, 1973

The P had a call this morning while he was in his morning series of meetings from one of the POW officers who arrived in the Philippines last night, expressing his support of the P and his desire on the part of him and all the other men to meet the P and thank him personally. The P is very much moved by the whole POW situation. They did a superb job last night getting off the plane, as it was covered on TV, and then this call this morning was further evidence. As a follow-up to that, he said he wants to send orchids to all the wives as the men arrive back, and wants to have a thing at the White House as soon as they're all back here so that he can meet all of them, and then have a dinner for them and their wives in the evening.

The P, on the plane coming back to Washington, made the point that he was concerned about the appointments in the Labor Department, and asked for a general rundown on the Watergate thing, and seemed to be in agreement with our overall approach as covered on the weekend. Although he feels Clawson should be the reporter type instead of Buchanan, because Buchanan's too close to the P, so he would tilt strongly the other way.

The return today was hastily called last night about dinner-time, and we have yet to determine what the cause was, since the plan was to stay in California all week.

Tuesday, February 13, 1973

The P had a very involved schedule today, with some farewell calls and so on, and so he didn't have me over until 4:15. At that time he got into a number of personnel items. He says now he's inclining to go along with Gray at the FBI and to get Sullivan in under him. He thinks he'd like to bring Colonel Reisner in as the military assistant to the P. He's got the POW that called the P yesterday. In the midst of the discussion he called John Ford, the movie director, to tell him he wants to give him a Medal of Freedom, to set up something on that. He was very disturbed by the comment Senator Curtis made about the admen in the White House being the reason that the Republicans lost the election, because they didn't understand the Middle America situation. He talked about the Bicentennial; he's concerned on that. He needs a status report; wants to be sure we've got a good person in charge. He raises the question of Frank Borman again. We talked about amnesty some, he still feels strongly on that but thinks we should get some readings before we get way out on it. Asked for some brief items on Watergate.

Wednesday, February 14, 1973

The P got into a POW follow-up first thing this morning, making the point that some of our idea staff should have thought of the two key things that he came up with that have been most effective: the idea of the corsage to each of the POW wives, which has worked extremely well with pictures in the paper, on TV, etc., and the idea of raising the flag to full staff when they return, which also has had a very positive effect. He wanted to be sure that we were in touch with Ross Perot; have him involved in some way since he's been so interested in the whole POW project. Then he got into a long critique on speechwriting in connection with his speech today on the State of the Union message on the environment. He made the point that he'd done some editing and wanted the writers to review it for consideration for the future. They should look at the clarification that he's made, and the style changes. For example, you don't need transitions in speeches—you have to put it the way people talk, so we need an editor that goes

through and does this. You should never say, "I want to conclude by saying," you just spell out the points. You never start
a good sentence with "but" because that rules it out as a
quote. The quotes they select still don't make it; they're not
quotable lines, they're colorful language. For example, his line
that you need a "fair shake for American products in the
world" is the kind of thing he's looking for.

Thursday, February 15, 1973

The P got me first thing this morning on the plans for K's
return. Ziegler had apparently announced that Henry was giving press conference, because Henry and his people told him
to. So the P was disturbed because he feels that he has to make
the first statement on the aid to North Vietnam question. He
was also concerned about the fact that Henry didn't submit the
communiqué to him before he put it out, the joint communiqué
to the North Vietnamese, and he was wondering about that. I
hadn't seen it either, which I had also found surprising. He
feels there's a real problem with the K news conference on
return, he got Scowcroft in to talk about it, making the point
that we have the toughest sale we ever had on the aid to North
Vietnam and that the P has to do it.

Later in the day he told me to send a wire to Henry saying
that the P would have a press conference on Thursday morning
to do an overview on the situation; that K should plan on a
briefing on Friday.

He got into the POW question again. He wants to be sure
we have some recognition of them, such as a Presidential Citation, a ribbon with a star for each year, or something like
that. He wanted to discuss this at noon today when he went
over to the Pentagon for lunch, and raised it with Scowcroft
to cover. He also raised the question of the Presidential letter
to the families of MIA's expressing concern with their problem. He's worried about the POW's coming back and telling
of the torture that they had, and all that sort of thing, which
will make the aid to North Vietnam especially difficult.

He went through some concern about the reaction he had to
George Bush's report yesterday. He senses that he's discouraged regarding all the horrors that he keeps running into in the
State Committees and National Committee, and then in sitting
down with the congressmen in the cloakroom. He feels that I
should tell him he shouldn't submit himself to too much

grousing and bitching of that kind; he should stay above the congressmen, don't get down to their level. It's not fair or productive to him to submit to all the negatives. Instead he should invite them to his ground and meet with them in his place for lunch and that kind of thing.

Also wanted me to talk to Moore and Bill Rogers, and a few others, about what they think on the Nobel Prize matter. He needs an answer to the question in time for his press conference, in case anything comes up. His inclination is still not to accept it, but thinks we ought to check their views on it.

Friday, February 16, 1973

The P had a Cabinet meeting today. The VP gave the report on his trip. He did a pretty good job, taking about a half-hour to paint the overall picture. Regarding Thieu, he said he's in good shape, positive, would win with an 85 percent vote on an election held today, a much better position than his image in the United States shows, and the VP urged him to try and improve his image in the United States. The P then said we have to recognize that political leaders have strong isolationist feelings to deal with. That we must not pander to that. Nothing would be more harmful than to allow an economic confrontation to become so violent as to deteriorate the political and military situation. The P directed all this to the whole question of how United States companies can be encouraged to develop foreign trade. We're the only nation in the free world now that looks outward, while two major nations in the Communist world do this. The P made the point that our desire is not to build a productionist wall, it's a free flow of trade of investment, but we must not jeopardize American jobs and business. So we need the right of the P to go in and bargain so that we get a fair shake abroad for American products and American labor. An assistance program for Vietnam will be to serve United States interests, to create a peace that can last a while. It's not a question of reparations or humanitarian interests; the motivation is the same as after World War II: help our enemies because it's better to do that than to leave them as Communist targets.

Monday, February 19, 1973

The P's still in Key Biscayne. Again, no contact. He went to the AFL-CIO executive council this morning, and then to the

Jackie Gleason golf tournament afterward, all apparently in the driving rain.

Tuesday, February 20, 1973

The P came up to South Carolina at noon today, where K met him, and then back to DC. The South Carolina visit went very well. Good crowds at the airport and along the streets, very enthusiastic, and it was a good move as far as getting some public acclaim for the peace move. John and I had a long meeting this evening with John Dean, on the whole Watergate question. Dean is very concerned, especially about the financial-support aspects. But doesn't know how to handle his concern, and feels that we've got to get Mitchell into it and get some help from him.

K said that it was absolutely amazing in Hanoi how remarkably precise the American bombing had been. There's virtually no destruction in the city of Hanoi of anything but military targets, the railroad yard is completely wiped out, the airports are completely wiped out, but all the other buildings and facilities still stand. Large storage areas have been demolished, but virtually nothing adjacent to them. Henry feels that it is a really remarkable tribute to the bombing operation, and a total repudiation of the attacks on the P for his so-called carpet bombing etc.

Wednesday, February 21, 1973

The P was pretty well occupied all morning with his own efforts at schedule planning with Ziegler, K, etc. He had me in at 1:00, covered an amazing array and range of subjects. His first concern was the meeting he had with Rex Scott about the colors in the bowling alley, and he's concerned about the costs there, and says any excess cost must be by contribution. Only that which is actually a part of House operations can be charged that way. Wants Bebe and Annenberg to raise the money and I'm to handle it myself, working with Bebe. Another problem was the storage space for tables and chairs at the White House, and all sorts of odds and ends.

Thursday, February 22, 1973

The P wasn't free much today, had me in only once at 2:30, and that for just some miscellaneous odds and ends. Wants to work out plans on the "Evenings at the White House," was concerned about Watergate in general, and that was about it. There was a Leadership Meeting this morning, bipartisan for breakfast, and the VP called me afterward, asking why he was excluded. He was very distressed and more or less hung up on me. The reason being of course that it was a breakfast meeting, which the P has had frequently, and has never included the VP, so there was nothing unusual about it at all. Continuing his plan of public exposure and goodwill, the P went to the theater tonight to see *Irene*.

Friday, February 23, 1973

The P met with the Energy group this morning, and then left right afterward with E for Camp David. Took John *(E)* with him because he wanted to discuss the Watergate in some detail. He's concerned about what's coming up and feels that since John is not involved he can consult with him on it. I think he's particularly concerned about the possibility of my getting hauled in. Dean is also concerned, so we've got everybody worrying at this point.

Sunday, February 25, 1973

The P came down for White House Church this morning, called me about 2:30 just to chat in general. Said he talked to E about the *Time* magazine thing on FBI leaks, taps on Brandon and Safire, and said that he had talked to E and agreed that everything should be handled by Dean and Kleindienst on the Watergate, that E and I should stay out of it, not let it divert us.

Wednesday, February 28, 1973

The P had me in today, and is obviously giving a lot of thought to schedule, says that the problem now is that we don't have a plan. The best thing is to have meetings that are regular, otherwise the people that he has to see take more of his time. That will apply to Cabinet, White House staff and Congressional types. So he diddled around on which days to do what. He got into the subject of the book *Kennedy's 13 Mistakes,* which he's read and found fascinating, made the point that Kennedy blew practically everything and still got credit for it. Late this afternoon he had the weekly meeting with Shultz, Ash, E, and me, the first half hour of which was consumed with the discussion of the governors' meeting today, and our guy reporting on the discussion on the governors' attitudes, and the P's comments on how to deal with them. Considerable discussion in that context of the budget, revenue sharing, the need to keep selling that, the problems and so forth. He then got into his general philosophical discussion, said that the problem is that we're good managers and we do things because they're right, so we appear to be cold and efficient. People measure compassion by passion for spending, and we don't have it. So we have to do like Bobby Kennedy, say you care about the poor folk, say we want to do things. As a subtheme for making our substantive case, we have to make the case for the passionate approach, the question is not cutting, it's a question of how much we increase. Symbolism is the area where we're weak. We can't get it across because we're not as comfortable as Democrats. Then he got into the subject of the poison in the upper classes, the loss of faith in the country—they hate the country, the country is corrupt and prejudiced, the whole McGovern argument thing. He then started questioning, particularly Shultz and Ash, debating whether the whole battle with the Congress and all is worth it. We're getting into a bloody battle, and if you do that you must have the assurance that first, you're right, and second, that if you weren't fighting the battle on this ground, it would be on something else, which was Ash's answer to it. He was trying to get them to waver, and I think both of them held their ground pretty well. I think he felt better as a result of the meeting, he did drag it on for quite a while—this whole area of discussion and his soliloquies are his favorite subjects—before he took off for the barbershop and the governors' dinner tonight.

Thursday, March 1, 1973

I did my *Newsweek* interview and it went reasonably well. They asked nothing about the Watergate or any of that sort of thing. They claim they're doing a straight cover story on me, so maybe it won't be as bad as we were afraid it would be. Mitchell called and said that Hal Bruno at *Newsweek* talked to him, and he thinks it's going to be a favorable piece too, but they do keep coming back to the Barbara Walters interview and keep trying to make me out as a superconservative type.

The POW problem was solved today, as the Communists folded and agreed to release the men within the next 48 hours, so the P's hanging tight on that paid off. Now we'll go back to the Paris conferences.

The Golda Meir visit is going without any major incident apparently. The P had a long session with her this morning and then dinner with her tonight. The big problem with that is the Indian uprising. They have laid siege to some area, and are holding hostages. The P was only mildly interested in it.

Friday, March 2, 1973

The P had his press conference today, did a good job, took twenty questions in a little over half an hour, less than half of them on Vietnam. Quite a few on Watergate, and Pat Gray.

Editor's Note: The Senate had begun confirmation hearings on Pat Gray as Director of the FBI. Dean's refusal to testify at them brought the hearings to a halt.

He talked some about the probable Connally switch. The P feels that we should be getting our ducks in a row to take advantage of that and that we're not doing that. Which is right.

Sunday, March 4, 1973

The P had his "Evening at the White House" with Sammy Davis last night, which went okay. He had breakfast with Davis this morning, at least that was the plan, and then left right at 12:00 for Camp David, where he's planning to stay tonight and tomorrow.

Monday, March 5, 1973

The P came down from Camp David early today for no announced reason. Called me in at noon and was concerned about the reaction to the "Evening at the White House." He felt that we should have invited the music critics because of the lousy social reporting, and got into his whole thing of how we don't get any credit for what we're doing.

Then called Ziegler and said he was concerned about the reporters covering the "Evening" and entertainment, that he must never invite Sally Quinn (*of the* Post). She violated the rules and attacked the guests at the church service. He wants Julie to use Ziegler to control the press over on the East Wing. He knows who to let in and that sort of thing.

Got into Colson, wants to be sure that he understands as soon as he gets back, that Dean is handling Watergate.

Tuesday, March 6, 1973

The P had a very heavy day, scheduled from 8:30 to 6:00 and then first of the two "fat cat" dinners tonight. He did have me in at 6:00 for a short time, and we reacted to today, making the point that it was useless because all of the events were spinning wheels. He went over the schedule and made the point that none of the things really needed to be done, nor did any of them really advance the ball for us in any way.

E reported earlier on the P's Leadership Meeting this morning. This was just with *(Senator Hugh)* Scott and *(Gerald)* Ford, and we knew that Scott intended to come in and complain about things on the Hill and suggest that the P have a series of meetings up there with the Republican senators. Scott started off doing exactly that, and said the mood was very bad, and whined on and on, for two or three minutes. The P just let him go, then he stepped in and used a lot of apparently pretty strong profanity, and said that the senators are nothing but a bunch of asses. We never get anything from them, there's nothing that does any good, no matter what we do for them. We bring them down and give them cookies, and treat them nice socially in order to cover the things that we need to do, but we can't count on them for any vote, and never have been able to.

Wednesday, March 7, 1973

The P had me in earlier this morning for quite a long while. He reviewed the stag dinner last night, was confirmed about some way of identifying people when they're introduced. Stans apparently did a good job. He pointed out the need to do this at other parties, which we don't get done. I suggested the idea of giving people identification cards to hand out to the introducing aides, which he thinks is a good idea, so we're going to try that. He was disturbed that we have the Navy singers for tonight, had the Army last night, and he thinks that they are much better. He went into schedule review this afternoon, on plans for going out to the country and meeting with the Congress and so on. He wants E to put special attention on developing a good agenda for the Leaders Meeting. He wanted me to call Reisner and Denton, the two POW leaders, and get a reading from them on when the P should have a POW event, and also tell him that the P would like to chat with them off the record sometime when they can be in Washington. He commented that the VFW award kids who came in just looked terrible. He felt that they were probably barefooted, were wearing jeans and awful-looking clothes, and he doesn't think we should allow that.

On the stag dinners, he thinks they're good for "pro" groups and that we should do more of them because they're much easier for him than a mixed dinner. Getting into the schedule, he wants to have a formal arrival ceremony for Thieu at El Toro and then have him stay at San Clemente, no ceremonies at the compound. He said to schedule this Friday until 4:30, then he'll go to Camp David, and he can see someone up there on Saturday morning. He has to come back down Sunday morning for the church service. He talked some about the Kennedy 13 Great Mistakes book, wants me to find Malcolm Smith, find out what he really did and what happened on the book.

We covered a number of the other schedule items and philosophy, then he had to leave to get ready for the dinner. The dinner tonight, which I attended, went very well. The P gave a good wrap-up talk on the overall world situation and ended by reading the Denton letter, which of course overwhelmed everybody. He had done the same thing last night. The evening was extremely effective and very impressive to those who were there.

Thursday, March 8, 1973

The P had a superloaded schedule today, starting with breakfast with Senators McClellan and Young.

At the P's request I called two POW leaders, Captain Denton and Colonel Reisner, to get their reading on when to have the POW event, and also to check out whether they would be able come in and see the President. Denton said he would be ecstatic to see the P. He's obviously completely overwhelmed by the thought. Colonel Reisner was less overcome by the whole thing, but had somewhat the same view, although he thought maybe the show ought to be sooner then the June 14 we're figuring on, because Ross Perot and others are suggesting reunions of various kinds and this should be done first. He too was obviously most anxious to come and talk to the P. Also talked to Malcolm Smith, the author of the Kennedy 13

Mistakes book, tracked him down at his home in Long Island. He said that he couldn't get the book published, so he did it himself, ran some ads, and got a pretty big response, then did get a publisher to agree to handle bookstore distribution, but about that point Robert Kennedy was assassinated, so he pulled the thing off the market. He says he has 2500 copies and is going to send me a dozen of them.

I told him that I talked to Connally at the dinner Wednesday night and that he is going to switch, and the P wanted to be sure he did his press conference in Washington rather than in Texas. Connally said he plans to do it just as a straight press conference rather than trying to work any other kind of gimmick into it.

Friday, March 9, 1973

Started out today with a long Cabinet meeting. The point of the meeting was to make the pitch to start the Presidential spokesman program, of their getting out and selling the budget-battle program. The P opened and turned it over to E, who dropped his papers as he stepped to the podium and after getting all that together gave his pitch. The P interrupted frequently, made the point that we need a massive effort over a long period, and that Congress will change their minds because of public pressure if we keep it up. The P said always express great respect for Congress. Kleindienst interrupted and said, is that an order, sir, and laughed. The P said that he should say that the members of Congress want to do what is right, and that we've got to convince them to support this budget. This is not an austerity budget, it doubles the domestic spending versus four years ago. For instance, the higher-education lobby, they're not fighting about the money they get. They're fighting because we're going to change the plan and give the money to the students rather than the institutions, and the institutions don't want the students to have the freedom of choice. In all this though we must show compassion, but don't debate who's more compassionate. The greater compassion we can show is by not raising taxes and prices. The person inflation kills is the poor, not the rich, everybody is affected by prices. We're doing the greatest divestiture of power any government in Washington has ever asked Congress for, the problem is that they don't want the power in the local areas. The whole philosophy is to get rid of the middleman, get rid of committee action and model cities, even though there are some good facets to them, because overall they haven't panned out, cut them out so that we'll have dollars to help the poor directly, and cut out those that are in the business of helping the poor.

Made the point that we're doing well in the world peace, United States leadership and so on, now is a critical time not to blow it with bad budget that destroys economic power. The P said to add an item in all your speeches, the point of law enforcement. Take a very hard line. We have to move in this area. Step up penalties on drugs and so on. We can't cure crime, because there are always bad people, but we can take strong steps to fight it.

K burst in to announce that Chou En-lai just cabled in a telegram to release a CIA prisoner they've been holding for years. We made an appeal Wednesday on the basis of the man's mother being critically ill, and we got a response today that he's being released on Monday. They're also releasing the other two prisoners on Thursday.

Monday, March 12, 1973
The P had Henry and me in this morning to talk about ambassadors. He wants to plan a Latin American trip to three countries this fall. He also wants a 10-day trip to Africa, three countries, Nigeria, Congo, and Ethiopia. He wants to do Europe in the fall.

He got into the news analysis sheet, that Buchanan and Allen had worked up, and was concerned because it's practically all bad news except for the POW's, which we had no control over. That was the one good thing. He thinks they should point out the positives, too, that this is dwelling too much on problems instead of opportunities, and this ruins the team spirit setup. He questions whether E's value isn't greater at thinking and creating rather than doing, and whether we don't need him working in this area. He raised the point that he wanted me to have Dent get a candidate fielded and going against Sam Ervin, to give him some trouble in his district, to slow him down a little on his Watergate activities.

Tuesday, March 13, 1973
The P went into the Watergate question this morning, wanted to know if we had any polls on apparent reaction as to whom

it affects, analyzed by voter breakdowns and all, which we don't have. He thought it'd be a good idea to get that. Also he had a meeting with John Dean for a long time at midday on the Watergate thing, primarily at my instigation. I wanted Dean to raise with him the plan he discussed with me about having Bill Sullivan *(Hoover's former aide)* go ahead with the testimony he'd like to give to the Senate committee on what the FBI did under past Administrations, which would pop the bubble of our supposed political corruption of the pristine Bureau.

Later in the day he had Ehrlichman and Ziegler in and gave Ziegler some guidance on Watergate. The P said that he should say, in answer to any questions, that there's been complete White House cooperation in all the investigations up to now, and there will be with the Senate committee, but there will not be appearances by White House staff people. Sworn statements answering any questions they may have will be provided. But Ziegler should start with the point of complete cooperation and furnishing information. He should refer to this as different from the usual way of doing this. For example, Truman, in the Hiss case, issued an executive order ordering no cooperation at all from any executive branch agency with the Senate committee. We will provide sworn statements, which is a major step forward.

Thursday, March 15, 1973

Discussion at the staff meeting this morning was about the Hill's counterstrategy on our budget plan. They now plan to agree to a budget ceiling. They want to cut defense and then take the money that's left and spend it on social programs, which we've got to figure out a counterstrategy for.

The P had his press conference this morning, and over half of it was devoted to Watergate questions. He got into quite a discussion with me this afternoon about that, and his concern, which he's expressed continually, although tries to stay away from it with me, that we're in a bad position on Watergate. He keeps working with Dean every day on trying to develop ways of finding some statement that we can put out that shows that we're not just covering it up.

Friday, March 16, 1973

The P got into the POW question this morning. He wants to meet with Flynn, the Senior Officer of the POW's, who's now back. He wants to see him as soon as possible and right after that announce the May 24 dinner. Got into some discussion of POW gifts, decided he wants to give each of them cuff links, each of the wives pins, each of the kids a bow pin for the girls and tie clips for the boys, plus an ashtray or something like that for their homes, plus a unit citation type of thing and a framed copy for each POW. He wants a full plan worked out on that. I talked to Bob Hope and the date's OK with him, he's supposed to call me back on whether Les Brown will be available and then we'll go ahead.

He got into quite a thing on Watergate again, and the strategies. Concerned about the appearance of the P covering up and feels that we've got to try to work out of that position by releasing the Segretti data, or something. He also got into staff assignments. Feels that Shultz is spread way too thin, he's the senior man on labor, Russian trade, economic policy, Treasury items, monetary policy, energy, and so forth. He thinks we've got to get Ash more active on the management side, that E's role has got to be more as an advocate.

Saturday, March 17, 1973

Got into some schedule discussion this morning, a normal Saturday of time-killing. He's now decided he wants to meet with the Congressional leaders, the full GOP Leadership group every two weeks. Same program with the Cabinet, meet with the full Cabinet regularly every two weeks, basically as a domestic-council meeting, then, in between, do Cost of Living Council, CEA, NSC, and so on.

He had a long talk with Haig, and said that he had confirmed that K had accused Haig of being disloyal to him in December and had really blown at him, which disturbed Al considerably, and the P sort of reviewed the K problems. Reraised the point that he had even hit me on parking his airplane in the wrong place, which he did the day he came back from one of the peace talks, or his Hanoi trip, or something. He arrived just after the P and was furious because he didn't get any press coverage on his return arrival, blaming me for parking his plane in such a way that the press couldn't cover him.

Tonight was the Merle Haggard "Evening at the White House." The P came out looking a trifle ridiculous, wearing a huge green bow tie, which he had borrowed from Freddy the elevator operator, and was obviously in good spirits. The "Evening" was pretty much a flop because the audience obviously had no appreciation for country/western music and there wasn't much rapport, except when Haggard did his "Okie from Muskogee" and "Fighting Side of Me" numbers which everybody responded to very favorably, of course.

Monday, March 19, 1973

Got into the Ervin questions with Ziegler because Ervin was on TV yesterday saying he would have White House staff people who refused to testify arrested. And try to force the issue that way. The P told Ron he thought it was too early to draw the sword on Ervin's political circus. Instead he should reiterate the P's position regarding a separation of powers. But emphasize that this is not a case of refusal to cooperate or to furnish information, as Presidents in the past have done. Ours is a policy of complete cooperation. Ron should go on the attack regarding our total cooperation. Hit the *(point that)* sensational statements regarding forcing White House aides have obscured the central fact that we have cooperated and will continue to. On ITT, told Ron to say "no comment." He feels we need someone like Ron on top of the PR to really keep working full time in getting our digs in.

He feels from his talk with Haig last week that the problem now is that K's trying to cover his left flank and is a little confused on all these things. Wants me to talk to Safire and get our story out on Vietnam. Point out the truth regarding K panicking on Cambodia, Laos, and Pakistan while the P always had to buck him up. Show him K's frenetic messages from Paris and tell him that side of the story. Also build Haig as the unsung hero, like a rock in all of this. He obviously doesn't have any particular purpose driving him at the moment and he's sort of bouncing around covering all these loose areas. Partly trying to decide whether to do his State of the Union as an address to Congress, an address to the nation, on nighttime TV, or just to go for the evening press conference. No decision made on that. He was going to work on it this afternoon, but called Rose and me over on the schedule stuff instead. Hopefully he will get to that decision in the next couple of days.

Tuesday, March 20, 1973

The P had the Republican Leadership Meeting this morning and had me in right afterward. He raised a point that when he was talking with Teddy White the question of withholding came up, and the P made the point to Teddy that LBJ withheld twice as much as we have and that he was astonished. So maybe we have to attack the press regarding the fact that they never say anything about LBJ impounding two times as much as we do. Maybe Agnew should take up the cudgel on this.

He then got into quite a discussion of K, which rose out of the decision that he's trying to make right now regarding the question of bombing the Laos panhandle *(in retaliation for the violation of the cease-fire accords by North Vietnam)*. He feels that it's rather odd that K isn't here at a time we have to make this decision, and says that Haig intimated the same thing. The question is how much of a risk there is with the POW's if we go ahead with it, and he has to make the decision in the next couple of days. He wanted me to call K tomorrow and raise the questions with him. If there is any risk to the POW's, then we shouldn't take it. Why can't we wait and do it after they're out? He told me to stay positive on it. Then the P mentioned the possibility of the bombing, and I raised the point that if there's any risk that we should delay. The P makes the point that this is the only possible retaliation move we've got. We can't go back to bombing the North as Henry has suggested. So we've really got to give this careful consideration. In this discussion, it developed that the P didn't know that Henry was taking off to Mexico for a week's vacation, and he was obviously very miffed that Henry pulled this. I thought, of course, that it had been worked out between the two of them, but the P claims he knew nothing about it and thought Henry was taking his vacation at the end of our California trip by staying out there.

He then got into a long thing with me on Watergate, raising the various possibilities. He feels strongly that we've got to say something to get ourselves away from looking like we're completely on the defensive and on a cover-up basis. If we, who are protected by executive privilege, are going to volunteer to send written statements—which in effect we have, or the P has for us—we might as well do the statements now and get them publicized and get our answers out. The problem is that Dean feels this runs too many leads out, but the answer to that is it's going to happen anyway. Also the leads that run out don't really come from the testimony of those of us who have immunity, so we ought to take the initiative and get our stories out ahead of time. At least I think so, and that was the P's feeling. He wanted me to explore that some with Dean and Moore. He's spent hours with them and is obviously very concerned about the impact of the Watergate thing now, and this is really the first time he has been. I think maybe Dean's gotten through to him that there could be some White House staff involvement and therefore problems in this whole thing.

Editor's Note: Among other things, Dean had reported to the P that Haldeman's former aide, Gordon Strachan, may have known about the bugging, at least after the fact. That he himself had sat in Mitchell's office listening to Liddy's intelligence-gathering schemes (which he thought had all been rejected). That Magruder might have pressured Liddy on the break-in. That both Hunt and Liddy had done work for Ehrlichman—such as breaking into the office of Daniel Ellsberg's psychiatrist during the Pentagon Papers incident.

Wednesday, March 21, 1973

The P had his usual Wednesday clear except for a few ceremonial items at midday. And spent most of the day on Watergate, which he's becoming more and more involved in, and I guess concerned about, as time goes on. He had a long session with Ehrlichman first thing this morning, then had John Dean at 10:00 for a couple of hours. Had Dean give him a complete rundown on all the facts, which he had told him last night he wanted him to be prepared to do. I had told John to do exactly that, cover all the facts in considerable detail, so the P would actually know precisely what the situation was.

Then he called me in at the end of the Dean meeting. We had some general discussion about options and alternatives. Ehrlichman's intrigued with the possibility, which he raised yesterday, of convening a grand jury and having all of us go up there and file our statements under oath and getting that done. The P also became somewhat interested in that, especially after talking with Dean. But has some concerns about it.

The P felt that the time had come that Dean and Ehrlichman and I should all sit down with Mitchell, and that Dean should give us the same total fill-in on the facts as he had given the P today, and we should then try to come to some conclusions. He called me back in at 3:00 and went over some of his thoughts again before Dean, Ehrlichman and I met at 3:30. At that point the P felt that we needed basically to determine, first of all, what to do right now about the Hunt threat. He's asking for money, and says he'll blow the E story and Bud Krogh thing if we don't pay him off now, or they don't. And the question is to evaluate the whole thing and determine a course of action. We now have a different situation than we did during the election. We've got to figure all the problems and possibilities. For example, the Krogh problem on where he is. Maybe it can be solved by national security considerations or we can get him immunity, and there's a question of Sullivan's memo and whether to use it.

Editor's Note: On March 21 Dean reported to P that Magruder actually knew a lot about the bugging, and that Colson might also have been involved. That Herb Kalmbach had provided funds for the defendants' attorneys' fees. And, most disturbing, that Hunt had just demanded $122,000 more or he would talk about the things he had done for Ehrlichman and Krogh, including the Ellsberg break-in.

He thinks, on thinking it over, that the grand jury is appealing at least at first blush because it's an opportunity for all the White House to be questioned on a sworn basis with no cover-up. We'd precede it by a general statement that would be based on, or take off from, the statement by the judge at the sentencing on Friday. Then we're following up now the court has proceeded and then have Dean put out a general disclaimer. He feels we need something, and unless it's necessary to tough it through we shouldn't. However, if it involves criminal prosecution of the top people then that would be worse than having to tough it out. But if we do tough it out it means living with it which is going to be very tough, very difficult.

He feels the critical thing is regarding Ehrlichman and Krogh vs. Hunt. The question is, can we let Hunt go? Also he thinks I ought to talk to Colson and see what would happen as far as he's concerned if Hunt blows. He suggested also if we do the grand jury, we should invite the press to testify, not subpoena them but they should be invited. Not on their sources or their files but on any facts that they have. The advantages of this, of course, the grand jury approach, is that it covers all the ground under oath, provides the answer about going to the Senate. How else can we show that the P is trying to get the facts and avoid anything falling on us? That becomes the basic problem, and the question is whether to go one way or the other, or just ride it through on the containment theory that Dean's been pursuing up to now. Generally, you come out that the latter is really the only, actual possible, course, but it's not a very good one.

The P then had Ehrlichman, Dean, and me in at 5:15 for another hour or so and reviewed our afternoon discussion, which comes down that Ehrlichman doesn't think the Dean approach to the grand jury is satisfactory because Dean bases it on going for immunity before the people testify, which E doesn't think is a salable approach. So we talked for quite a while and came out about the same as we went in. We'll meet with Mitchell tomorrow morning and see if we can advance it there. Dean, after the meeting, made one point that maybe we should just draw the wagons up around the White House and let things fall where they may outside; which, of course, is the tempting choice, since there is no complicity within the White House, and we'd come out in good shape on that. But the problem is what happens to Mitchell, Magruder, etc., on the outside.

Thursday, March 22, 1973

The P had several schedule items today, but in between spent the whole time on Watergate again. Had me in at 9:00 this morning before the 10:00 meeting I scheduled with Mitchell which was postponed to 11:00. So I spent two hours with the P. He was concerned about the Gray testimony, which keeps getting out of hand, and asked who's programming Gray, since the White House isn't. I pointed out that he told us not to, that he had talked to Gray himself and then had said Kleindienst was to be programming him, which is what we were relying on. So beyond that I didn't know. He didn't regard that as a very satisfactory answer, but that's where the situation is at the moment.

He also said that Colson talked to him on the phone last night and reported that *(Senator Howard)* Baker's administrative assistant had come to Colson, and said that Baker said that he was feeling hurt because he wants to help but doesn't feel that he has anyone to talk to, and Colson suggested he should be the one. Baker said, for example, that he didn't know about the executive privilege statement before it came out and had caught him unawares and so on. Baker, of course, in talking to the P, had said he didn't want to talk to anyone else at the White House. That he wanted to have Kleindienst be his contact, which the P set up. Apparently, that's not working. So the P raised the question what's Kleindienst doing with Baker and all? What's Kleindienst doing in guidance to Gray? And he feels somebody's got to get to Kleindienst and tell him he's got to pick it up because the White House has to stay out of it. He then said to go ahead with the Mitchell meeting and he'd meet with us all at 1:30.

The whole group thought I ought to talk to Colson, find out what he promised Hunt and he wondered about *(Attorney Lawrence)* Walsh as special prosecutor if we decide to go that route. We had our long session, went through the whole facts and options. The question series again and didn't really come up with anything new except that Mitchell made the point strongly that the only real problem the P has is invoking executive privilege, which does put him in the position of appearing to cover up. John's argument therefore that the solution to the problem at the moment at least lies in getting out of the executive privilege wicket somehow, and we spent some time discussing that coming down on the side of at least considering going to the committee with the proposal that the White House people will waive executive privilege and come up, if we can testify in executive session without TV and so on, and if it's limited to relevant questions. Then we went back to meet with the P. We got into this and he believed that it was probably a pretty good approach and that's where we left it. We also felt that there should be a Dean report to the P, which Dean has pretty much completed on Segretti and can do over the weekend on Watergate, and that it should be given by the P to the committee and probably publicly released. So we're working on that possibility now.

In the midst of all that, we come up with a new problem with Gray, who was in questioning today. Got trapped into admitting or saying to Senator Byrd that he was probably right in his assumption that Dean had lied when he said he didn't tell the FBI he didn't know whether Hunt had an office in the White House. Of course the fact was they didn't ask him that, they asked him if they could see Hunt's office, and he said he didn't know that and would have to check. So Gray has sort of screwed us again.

Friday, March 23, 1973

I came down to Key Biscayne this morning and the P called me over to the house at 1:15. Had me there until 6:30 going over primarily Watergate. He said that he wanted me to check Colson on the point that Dean raised about clemency and how that was handled with Hunt. What specifically did Colson say to Hunt on this subject. He feels that we need to make our move now rather than just wait, but Kleindienst should do something this afternoon because of what's been said. Perhaps the grand jury is directed to call all concerned. He wanted me to talk to Dean and find out if Strachan testified at the trial, with the idea of being concerned about his possible perjury. Also whether Kleindienst has contacted Baker and Ervin, as the P told him to in the office the other day, in the phone call. The P feels he doesn't like just sitting here. The P is expected to do something and he thinks he should. We should get Kleindienst going, finding out what's up as far as Sirica is concerned. Also get Moore's judgment, Mitchell's. Have Dean ask Kleindienst.

He then had me go in the other room and call Colson on the phone and find out what his deal was with Hunt. I talked to Chuck, and he said that through Hunt's attorney he had indicated that he felt that Hunt had already been adequately punished, and that he, Chuck, would go to bat for him. Hunt's attorney said to Chuck that Hunt doesn't want to go to jail. He hopes he'll be out before the end of the year. Colson said I can't answer that and I won't try. He says he phrased it very carefully. First, that I know what Hunt's concerns are. Secondly, I'm Hunt's friend and I will do all I can. Specifically, he limited it to his desire to help Hunt. What was said and the impression on what he actually said vs. what the impression gained on the other side might differ, though,

Chuck admits. He said that they may have reason to believe that he told them he has reason to believe that his opinion would be respected by others. But he made no mention of having discussed this with the P or anybody else. He says he's had no dealing with McCord, doesn't know him, had no dealing with Liddy.

Then I hit him at the P's request on the telephone call. Specifically, whether he had, in the phone call he made to Magruder from his office while Hunt and Liddy were with him, did he mention the P or anybody else pushing him on getting anything done? He says that the story on that was—actually, Chuck was a little surprised that I knew about the phone call at first—and said that he didn't think Magruder remembered the call and that he was not doing anything to recall it. But he said Hunt and Liddy dropped by his office late one afternoon or early evening and said that Liddy was setting up an intelligence operation, and Hunt would work with him. But that they can't talk to anyone to present their ideas and that's why they've come to see Chuck. Chuck said they shouldn't talk to him, they should be talking to somebody over at CRP. They said they had tried, but nobody would listen to them, and so Chuck called Magruder. Told him that these guys had this plan and that he didn't know whether they want to do anything about it, but they should at least listen to it. And that's his story of the phone call.

He says he wrote a memo after the Watergate, putting down everything he could remember, and he said in it that Hunt and Liddy had come by late in the day regarding intelligence and counterintelligence. He had said to them, don't tell me. Liddy had said no one would talk to them and Colson called Jeb. Told him to listen to them. He gave this memo to Dean and Dean gave it back to him. Said not to show it to anyone, because Jeb doesn't remember the call and it would be damaging.

He said he has made no representation regarding any clemency to Hunt, but Bittman might extend what he did say. Although Bittman would not disagree with Colson's report as to what he'd actually said, but might say that he was logically interpreting more to it than what was actually said. He has a tape of Hunt's call to him later, where Hunt said that he was very sorry that Chuck had become involved in all this, because he, Hunt, knew that Chuck had no knowledge of it and he was sorry his name had been brought up.

Regarding the grand jury, he thinks that's OK as far as he's concerned, but we should hold our executive privilege. The problem with the grand jury is that there are no safeguards and they can go on a wild fishing expedition. He says he doesn't know enough facts to make a judgment. That we should get someone else in to represent the P and his interest. Like Walsh or J. Lee Rankin or Tom Clark as outside special counsel regarding executive privilege, etc.

The P also then had me call John Mitchell and get a reading from him on what McCord was likely to say. This was, of course, all stirred up because this morning McCord's letter to Sirica came out, in which he said he had a lot more information that he could provide and so on.

Editor's Note: Before the sentencing, McCord had given Sirica a letter which said he had been offered clemency in return for silence, and that perjury had been committed at the trial.

Mitchell said he hadn't the foggiest idea what McCord was likely to say, and that in any event most of it would be hearsay, since he didn't have any direct involvement in anything. Says McCord was head of security and was a private investigator for CRP right from the beginning. He's certain that Jeb and so on had no dealings with him. That Liddy probably got him into the Watergate thing, but none of our people knew he was in it. He knows nothing except what people would have told him. Sloan and Liddy were buddies, so Sloan could have talked to him about it. I discussed with Mitchell what his views are on what the P ought to do in context of all this. He said we already have a grand jury. The question is what are the options. Anything the P does gives the McCord development credence. So he should hunker down. The judicial process is still running its course. The rights of defendants are involved and so on. The ball is in the judge's court and that's where we should leave it.

We should probably hold up on releasing Dean's report to the P, although Dean should go ahead and write it so we have it put together. We should do nothing until there's more information available. That's nothing overt at least.

He then had me call Dick Moore to get his view, and he

said, first of all we can't react to a prisoner's statement, so we should do nothing in response to the McCord thing. The question is what Justice should do. Right now they're saying no comment. But shouldn't they have some kind of reaction? Or should they say they'll await information from Sirica? He feels that the surrounding climate is such that we can't step up and talk big on this now. We've got to be careful. But on the question of cover-up, there's a danger of using government power, including executive privilege, because of the appearance of cover-up. We should appear to come forward, ideally, we should not wait to be dragged out. The P should say I'm going to get to the bottom of this and he should get an outside lawyer to advise him. The P can't just sit for very long. But he should not just react to the McCord letter. He should consider going for a new special prosecutor and a new grand jury. This one apparently didn't cover the entire case. But we should recognize that going to the grand jury is a monumental step, because we don't know where it leads—such as the area of how these people got their money and so forth.

He says we've been successful so far on our day-to-day strategy. We probably can't play the McCord thing this way. We're now on a new level of concern. That is, with the first charge of perjury and so on. And even if he's lying, there's the question of what others might now do as things start unraveling.

I then talked to Dean. He said that Kleindienst doesn't have a position on this as of now as to what Justice ought to do. The problem is that McCord will be dealing with hearsay and innuendo. That in analyzing it, one possibility is that what he has to say may be very limited just to a few specifics with little firsthand knowledge. Probably a lot of hearsay, such as from the Cubans, Liddy, and Hunt. On the other hand, he may be able to do a lot of damage with information that's more than hearsay. For example, his apparent defense of Sloan in his letter bothers Dean, and he thinks the perjury thing is probably Jeb or Porter or *(White House aide Robert)* Odle. He feels we should not overreact, we should watch and wait. McCord's greatest danger is post–June 17. He's hit on Dean's greatest concern, which is obstruction. The problem is that we're one step behind now, and from a strategic viewpoint we should question whether we should try to jump ahead.

I reported on these various conversations to the P. At that

point, Ziegler came in to the meeting, and the P called Klein-dienst, told him that he felt Justice should put out a statement saying that they will welcome any evidence that McCord turns up and will of course follow through on it in the appropriate way. He told me to call Bill Rogers and get his advice on the whole thing and fill him in on some of these background things. See what he thinks about the idea of going to the grand jury.

On a different subject, he injected the question of whether to do the appearance before Congress or a speech on TV next week. He feels that Watergate is subject A now and there's no use hitting on something else. So we don't gain anything by making a big thing out of the other subject. On Kleindienst, he made the point that on Gray we should stick by him and see what happens. That actually we will withdraw and send up *(Chief of Police Metro Department, Washington)* Jerry Wilson. Wanted me to tell Dean to be sure that he and Kleindienst don't offer anything to Ervin if they meet with him. The plan now is to hard-line the Senate regarding executive privilege and go for sending all of the White House people to the grand jury instead. There was a lot of other sort of general discussion of options and so on. And the meeting ended at that point at about 6:30.

Saturday, March 24, 1973

I made the phone call to Rogers at the P's request, to raise the question with him, first, of where he feels we now stand in the public eye, and, second, what his advice is on our general Watergate approach. I covered the background with him and so on. He said he felt that until recently we looked all right, that this whole thing hadn't had much impact, but in the last couple of weeks it was starting to look like a cover-up. That was not widespread yet, but it could develop. First, that we have the matter of Gray focusing attention on the FBI, which is unfortunate because it appears not to be beyond reproach now, and also the position he's taken with Dean puts a cloud over the institution. Especially the McCord statement, where he says he doesn't trust the FBI or Justice. Second, the Klein-dienst problem will be revived, on the theory that you can't trust Justice and the development of the idea that Kleindienst was close to Mitchell, and Mitchell's name now is recurring in the subject. Third, the judge, who appears now to be a man of integrity, fighting everybody. So it's no longer a political battle. Before, it was the Democrats fighting us, so it was political, but now it's the judge and the forces of righteousness, and that concept will gradually sink into the public mind. Fourth, there's the continuing possibility, actually certainty, of judicial and Congressional investigations, which will keep the public interested. Especially since there's not much else in the news now.

An accumulation of all these things, especially the McCord letter, brings the thing into a new focus. The McCord letter is very significant just in itself, regardless of what it does or doesn't develop. Also you have the added danger that the press is just gloating over this whole thing, obviously, as Roger Mudd *(of CBS)* showed on TV last night. He felt that the executive privilege question wasn't much of a problem. But it's starting to become one. The thing is it makes sense and the public accepts it if it's related to communications between the P and his advisors. But it's very tough to hang on executive privilege in other areas and the blanket exercise just doesn't wash. Fundamental problem regarding the grand jury is now the suspicion is cast on the Justice Department and the FBI. So you might have to appoint a special prosecutor. But that would be a real slap to the Attorney General. As long as there's a cloud on the FBI, everything else is clouded, because there's no pillar of integrity to rely on. If Gray goes down the drain, we should get someone else in, like a Federal judge, that everyone will trust, but that's too late for the immediate problem. Also the Kleindienst problem because of his closeness to Mitchell.

Sending the White House assistants to the grand jury would relieve the pressure about refusing to send them to the Hill. He thinks there is validity to the idea, basically Ziegler's, that we should not allow the senior White House staff to go to the Senate because that might be just the hypo that's needed to really throw this thing over. The point being that it would be a complete circus and would be very hard for us to have to live with. He thinks we should go very slow on the idea of bringing in special counsel. That it's a bad idea, he has a very negative viewpoint on it, because it would be construed as if the P is in a jam and he has to hire a lawyer, but it is important, he thinks, to get a special prosecutor. Someone like Walsh, because of the suspicions that are raised. You don't want to appear that the P is worried about his position. The right impression is that the P wants to be sure there's no cloud over the White House or over Justice.

Maybe we should have the Attorney General retain special counsel, since he's the P's lawyer. That's his job. Maybe Kleindienst should bring *(Solicitor General Erwin)* Griswold in for this purpose. The main issue is still there, though. Do you reverse your field and turn over everything to the prosecutors and let the chips fall where they may, or do you still want to keep some control? If you try to retain control, it's very difficult, because it's hard to stop the thing from unwinding. We're thinking about people for the special job. Walsh would be much better than Rankin. He's had a lot more experience, great integrity, but once you turn him loose, you could never pull him off.

You could consider him first as a special prosecutor before the grand jury. But that breaks the china that you can't put back together. Second, as counsel to the Attorney General regarding executive privilege. Third, as counsel to the P on a quiet basis, which would be very hard to do. He feels we have some time and we shouldn't rush. We can take the first step of Walsh talking privately to the P, but you'd almost have to decide first whether to A) stay where we are and hunker down or B) change position radically. Have an independent prosecutor and go all-out. Whoever is hurt, gets hurt. The in-between position, to say we're pretty clean, but we've got to hold back a little, is not tenable. We couldn't bring someone else in without his becoming part of it, unless you hire a lawyer and do what he says. If you do bring one in, you should make him a special assistant to the Attorney General. You'd have to clearly define what for, in the public sense. That is, he's to deal with the question of executive privilege and the court cases regarding that. Then in that capacity he can be used by the P for general advice. He feels that using anyone else as the P's lawyer undercuts the Attorney General totally and we shouldn't do that.

The P had me check with Dean on the phone to get a progress report, and he says that Colson's concerned about the phone call to Magruder and our overreacting to that. He, Dean, is going over all the options, reviewing them. He's holed up at Camp David. He thinks that one alternative would be for the P to direct Dean to go to the grand jury and tell everything, and then let them decide if they want anyone else. The problem is that we've been bailing out everybody else and it's gotten out of hand and compounded the problem. Now we have to protect ourselves. The problem is that Dean, as they pointed out in the case, Dean was everywhere. He feels that his testimony before the grand jury won't hurt anyone in the White House. He thinks the only problem for the White House is post–June 17. We did things to hold it down before the election that are right on the border. If Dean is immunized when he goes to the grand jury, then those things will go no further. But then he'd have to be canned if they came out of the grand jury's secret coverage.

Dean says that he's devoted to Mitchell and has great loyalty to him, but he has a higher loyalty to the P than to Mitchell, and he's concerned about his own ass, so he thinks he ought to go for informal immunity and try to get this cleared up at the grand jury.

The P also wanted me to call Rogers on the phone this afternoon while I was over there, and I tried, but he was out playing golf, as one would expect him to be on a Saturday afternoon when the weather is beautiful in Washington.

The P got into a discussion of the FBI. Wondered about Walsh as head of the FBI or Jerry Wilson. The problem is that Walsh was involved as ITT's lawyer and that would be a problem in appointing him to the FBI. Told me to tell Ehrlichman that we now have to bite the Gray bullet fast and we should move on it this week. Wants me to move with Rogers on getting him as the inside advisor. Give him the whole story. Use him instead of Walsh or someone like that. Also discuss with him the question of Dean's going to the grand jury and whether he ought to go before the sentencing this week. Said to tell Ehrlichman that he's decided Gray has to go and that Ehrlichman should talk to him. That we can't get the votes, and that even if we did he still wouldn't have confidence, and for political reasons he's been irreparably damaged. So we should appoint Jerry Wilson. The P won't go the Kleindienst, Mitchell route regarding their reluctance on Wilson. He has the best crime-cutting record in America.

The P raised the question of whether Dean should suspend himself as counsel if he does go to the grand jury. Also we need a statement for Dean to cover in a briefing with the Cabinet and leaders to assure them that the P and the White House are not involved. And that we're doing all we can to cooperate.

We have to say that the P is not involved, nor is the White House staff, and that we're vigorously following up. He also wanted to pursue the question of the tactics on releasing the Segretti statement.

I did later get hold of Rogers this evening. He said he doesn't know Jerry Wilson, so he can't give a view on that. His thought would be for the FBI that we should get a young Federal judge who's had prosecutor experience. He thinks it's very important for us not to let the FBI go downhill.

Regarding getting Rogers into it, he agrees that he's probably the one that should do it. But initially at least, it should just be between Rogers and the P. Then he could decide on maybe bringing me or someone else in. But it has to be very closely held. On the idea of reassuring the Cabinet or briefing them, he thinks that's not good, at least now. And on the leaders, he thinks it's a very bad idea. The point being that we can't answer all their questions and it doesn't do any good to tell them everything is OK and then hold back some things. The real problem on this is what's been done after the event, not the Watergate event itself. That, we don't really have any problem with, but we do have a problem on why it's been covered up. I talked to Dean on the phone and his candidate for the FBI is Bill Webster, a former U.S. Attorney who's now in the district court in St. Louis. He agrees with Rogers' idea of getting Federal judge.

Sunday, March 25, 1973

Talked to Dean on the phone this morning. He sees signs of the domino theory coming in. For instance, Hunt had dealings with the Cubans, Dean didn't. LaRue may have, so some of them may spill. He thinks McCord will name *(former NYC policeman, White House undercover agent, and investigator John)* Caulfield because he leaned on him for some help. He wrote Caulfield a letter and Caulfield met with him on some technical points on his defense. He'll probably hit Jeb regarding perjury. Dean thinks we should take action before Thursday when McCord will meet with Judge Sirica. Such as the action of Dean going to the grand jury. He thinks that if we try to fight it, we'll eventually lose. He's back to his cancer theory, that we've got to cut the thing out. Cut out the cancer now and deal with it. He says Colson thinks we should fight it, but he doesn't know the whole picture. He denies any knowledge of Watergate. The question of who McCord names will not be made public on Thursday so we don't have a problem with that. Dean has no knowledge of what Mitchell knows or did, nor does he really on Jeb. Also he doesn't know the full extent of Gordon Strachan's knowledge. He thinks that we ought to check out the legality of Gray continuing as acting director of the FBI if we withdraw his name from nomination.

The P called me over at 10:00 this morning. Had me there for a couple of hours. Has decided that he is going to hold up the TV thing until Wednesday night because we won't know for sure on Vietnam until then.

Thought that I should have Dean get a clear picture of what Colson's views are. What approach does he think we should take? Is he opposed to waiving privilege at the grand jury? Wanted to explore what if McCord names Magruder on Thursday, or Colson, or Haldeman. We have to respond that those people will be appearing before the grand jury. But do we take executive privilege? The thing is we want to see that our names are clear. The alternative would be to put out a sworn statement, but that isn't really very satisfactory.

He wanted me to check with Dean to see if he had ever talked to the Cubans or if he knew who met with them at the Arlington Towers regarding clemency. Also felt that we need an answer ready for Thursday on McCord. Raised the question on Kleindienst, whether anybody could talk to Weicker, who's making a lot of talk about how he's going to name higher names and all (*maverick Republican Senator Lowell Weicker was on the Ervin Committee*). Feels that Kleindienst should check as to who the names are, and if he's got anything, we should go after that we've seen what you said. He later called Kleindienst himself and told him he ought to check this out with Weicker.

Wanted me to check with Bill Rogers on the Bill Webster suggestion for the FBI that John Dean raised. He thinks that sounds like a good idea. He thinks I ought to talk to Ehrlichman, Dean, and Rogers about the FBI and the question of leaving Gray as acting director until his successor has qualified, and then the idea of naming a Federal judge–type to take as director and moving Sullivan in as deputy. Cleaning out all the top brass. He wants Ehrlichman to handle the Gray withdrawal with Gray, Kleindienst, and Mitchell. He thinks Ehrlichman and Dean should consider what our answer is if McCord names people on Thursday, especially if it's people in the White House. Wants to know from Dean who was the person in the White House to whom Barker gave the reports from the Watergate. I checked with Dean and he says there was nobody. It was somebody at the committee that Barker claimed he gave them to.

On declassification, he wants E to get going because the P wants to issue an order. He feels that everything should be declassified in ten years so we can open up the Kennedy stuff on Vietnam. He thinks we should get Tom Huston or someone in on this to be sure there's no cover-up and get out the story on Diem and all that sort of thing. Went back to my talking to Dean on who McCord will name, what's our action, if there's anybody on the White House regarding going to the grand jury, does he still think he should go to the grand jury, what about the Colson problem and so on, what about Caulfield's name, what does he know. Then he went back to the question of his TV speech or his use of TV and says he thinks he should do more 7:30 or 7:00 press conferences and announcements and that on press conferences he should always do them at 7:30 unless he has a major issue and then he'll go on prime time. Wants me to analyze the audience sizes at these various times. His point is that he won't have any more Vietnam announcements to make, so he's got to figure out other ways of getting on TV and getting TV domination.

Wants Colson to spin out the whole grand jury idea and have me find out why he's opposed to that.

Then late tonight I talked to Dean and there's a new problem developing, because it now turns out that McCord spent considerable time yesterday and today meeting with the counsel, *(Sam)* Dash, from the Ervin Committee and filling them in on things. Supposedly on a secret basis, but Dash had a press conference saying he had gotten a lot of information from McCord, and then the *LA Times* and *Washington Post* picked up a whole lot of supposedly what McCord told Dash and are running it in the paper tomorrow. Among other things he says that Dean was involved in the Watergate and that Magruder perjured himself and that he will be providing them with a lot more information, based on what he's heard from other people as well as what he knows himself. This, of course, gives Dean a whole new set of things to worry about.

Monday, March 26, 1973

The P had me over again at 10:00 this morning for another six-hour session. I talked to Dean on the phone first to get a reading on how the reaction to the story is going. He decided last night to hire a lawyer and to have him give notice to the papers that he would move for libel action if they went ahead with the story. They did go ahead with it, so now he's faced with the problem of whether to do anything on the libel thing.

Says that this morning he feels that Mitchell has a problem and that Mitchell may not realize it and he, Dean, doesn't really know what Mitchell's problem is. But he thinks he should go to Mitchell and ask if he really feels that everybody should go to jail except him. The point is that if he'd stepped forward, it would solve a lot of problems. For example, Jeb said that he and Mitchell were afraid Colson was going to take over the intelligence apparatus, so they went ahead, and Dean feels it was probably with Mitchell's OK. The real question is why Mitchell is going to such great lengths to keep it quiet. The only basis for his doing that would be if it goes higher than Mitchell, which Dean feels is not possible.

He says that Moore and others are working on discrediting the Ervin Committee on the basis of the press release of the meeting with Dash. He thinks he should probably wait a few days to file his libel suit, because the problem is that discovery starts with depositions and all that wouldn't be good. He thinks still that the only problem for us is the after-the-fact bailing-out; that the line of legal fees and personal expenses won't wash. The only apparent defense is blackmail. He thinks I should check with Ehrlichman to see if he feels Hunt is a threat in any way. Talked to Ehrlichman later. He said that Hunt is a real threat and that the weak link here is Colson and that's why Colson's hanging tough.

The P started in on a general review again on the whole Watergate thing. Covering the same ground. He said that on the Gray thing, we should hold until all this is out of the way. We shouldn't just cave right away on it. Wants to get a scheme developed regarding the Gray withdrawal so that we're ready to go on it next week. Thinks the key now is that we've got to change our appearance of cover-up. And the immediate question is Dean. At that point Ziegler came in and the P agreed that Ron should get out today that there are very serious allegations made by McCord, and as the P has directed, there will be complete cooperation with the grand jury and Justice and the FBI to get to the bottom of all this. He should be pursued in the judicial process. Feels we may have an opportunity now to discredit the Senate committee.

He's concerned that we've lost sight of the P's statement that he's directed complete cooperation with the grand jury, the courts, and the FBI and all those with responsibility on this. He suggested Ziegler say that this rather shocking action of the counsel to the committee making charges based on hearsay and so forth, raises serious doubts as to whether the committee's going to be bipartisan and work in a judicial manner. The charges are being put out, printed, aired on TV, and a counsel to the so-called nonpartisan committee is aiding and abetting it. But he wants Ziegler to try to get as the lead, the thing that the P orders cooperation.

He had me go out and call Dean and I had a long talk with him, as a result of which we decided not to offer Dean, the idea of Dean going to the grand jury this morning. Just to reaffirm the P confidence in Dean, and then Ziegler left.

John Dean's Report

In my phone call to Dean I raised the question of whether we should move today on announcing that he's going to the grand jury and what problems he'd have with that. He said he had no problem, but that he just talked with Jeb, and Jeb says that he'd testify differently than Dean would, in that Dean says there were two meetings and Dean turned off the intelligence operation at one of those. However, Jeb testified differently. He said there was one meeting and that it was regarding the new campaign spending law and so forth, rather than intelligence. This would be a difficulty in the fact that the two stories don't completely check out. Dean's idea was maybe that he would say that he's requested to appear and that he's waiving his privilege regarding lawyer/client. He thinks the privilege is a tough call, especially regarding the post–June 17 thing. If there's any political embarrassment, though, certainly the grand jury is the right forum rather than the Hill.

He said he wanted to review with me some of the things out of his statement in the problem areas. Then he went into a great deal of detail on what he sees as the really serious problems now. The main one is the blackmail situation. He says that he was aware that Mitchell and others were being blackmailed by those involved in the Watergate thing, and he sought to ignore this and therefore is vague on some of the specifics. He first learned of it when Mitchell was told that the defendants wanted help regarding money for their bond. This was a phone call or communication from Mrs. Hunt via Bittman to Parkinson, the committee's lawyer, who then went to Mitchell and LaRue and said they were threatening to cause general havoc if they were not helped. Parkinson said he didn't want to be involved any further in this, so Bittman used *(CRP assistant counsel)* Paul O'Brien. He was unhappy in being in it, too, but agreed to go ahead with it. O'Brien reported these threats over a period of time to Mitchell, LaRue, and Dean. Dean passed them on to some people in the White House.

After Mitchell had the original threat, he told Dean to tell Ehrlichman and Haldeman and to raise with them the question of using Kalmbach to raise the money, which Dean did, and Ehrlichman and Haldeman authorized that. Kalmbach raised the money on that authority and delivered it per instructions to LaRue. Dean thinks it was about $70,000. The next time, the threat was to the committee. There were no dollars available and Kalmbach was not able or willing to try and raise any more.

However, Stans, LaRue, Mitchell, and others of the committee were aware there was $350,000 in cash that had been moved to the White House during the campaign for polling purposes, and so forth. But the White House had not spent this money and wanted to return it. Only Strachan could spend this money, and with Haldeman's approval. And it was our desire to return that money to the campaign, but there was a problem in that $22,000 of it had been spent. We don't know for what purpose. The problem was how to return the funds without making a big deal in the press about it, because of all the attention on secret campaign funds. So the funds sat in Strachan's safe while this was to be worked out. Mitchell at this point requested Dean to ask Haldeman for some of that money to meet the demand threats and assured that it could be replenished. Dean told Haldeman, he said there was a bad situation and was growing worse. That LaRue or O'Brien, one of the two, had said there was a crisis. So Haldeman said, have Strachan get the money but clear it up as soon as possible. Get all of the money out of here and get a receipt for it. Turn it all back to the committee. Strachan did then eventually turn the money all back to the committee, but got no receipt.

Dean's summary over the phone to me of his notes regarding his areas of particular problem and concern: He says that Mitchell requested Dean to ask Haldeman for some of the money that we were holding in cash. Haldeman told Strachan to get all the money returned, which he did, but didn't get a receipt. Then Dean said he was not aware of the extent of the threats to the committee, but he was aware of two specific blackmail threats to the White House. First, Mrs. Hunt called Colson's secretary, made what Colson considered to be a veiled threat. Colson didn't know what it was about, so he referred it to Dean. Dean advised Colson to take no more calls from Mrs. Hunt and then Dean referred the whole matter to O'Brien. The second one was when O'Brien told Dean that Hunt had insisted on meeting with him and had said at that meeting that he wanted a message delivered to Dean. That he needed $72,000 for personal expenses and $50,000 for lawyers' fees, and that if they were not received within a couple of days (and this was just last week), that he would reconsider his options and disclose some of the seamy things that he had done for E and Krogh. This, of course, was the thing we were dealing with last week. Dean's record says that he advised Haldeman and E of this threat. E requested that Dean discuss it with Mitchell and Colson. Dean discussed it with Mitchell, but not with Colson. Later, in the meeting Mitchell, Dean, E, and I had, Mitchell said that there was no problem on this matter, and that's all we knew about it. Dean feels he's not in a position to fully evaluate the blackmail situation, but it's clear that all concerned felt there were dire threats to the White House, and when you're being blackmailed you imagine the worst.

Regarding clemency, he says that O'Brien told Dean that Bittman was asked by Hunt to meet with Colson. E said that Colson should meet with Bittman, and he did. Colson came back from that saying that it's essential that Hunt be given assurances regarding clemency, and E agreed. So Colson told Bittman that he could make no commitment, but as a friend he would assist Hunt. And he referred to Christmastime as when clemency actions are usually taken. Hunt was satisfied with this report back from Bittman.

Another problem was that McCord wrote Caulfield requesting that Caulfield turn off the line of defense they were developing that the CIA was involved in the case. Caulfield gave this letter to Dean, Dean told Mitchell about it, Mitchell told Dean to have Caulfield see McCord and take his pulse. This was done. Developed out of this, apparently, that there seemed to be a view that there was a one-year clemency commitment floating around, and that Dean assumes that Caulfield assured McCord that he would fight for him as a friend in the same way that Colson had agreed to fight for Hunt.

Dean feels that if he testifies before the grand jury, he would volunteer all of the information that he has prior to June 17 and lay out the details. He feels sure that they would raise the questions on the post–June 17 and we have to be prepared to answer them. He says he also has a problem on the question of why there was a delay in his turning the evidence over to the FBI, in terms of the material that he got out of Hunt's files. The story on that is that Hunt called Colson right after the Watergate incident, that weekend, and said to be sure to take care of his files. On Monday morning Colson stirred around and told E and Dean that they had to get the files. Dean was told to open the files. He had *(staff assistant to Haldeman Bruce)* Kehrli and the GSA guy do it with *(Dean assistant Fred)* Fielding also present. They found the electronic equipment and some very sensitive political documents. Dean didn't look at the documents, but Fielding did. There were some things there, like a wire regarding the Vietnam war *(a forged cable implicating JFK in the Diem assassination),* some evidence that Colson had put Hunt into the Plumbers operation to spy on Krogh, and so on. Dean was told to deep-six this material, but he felt he couldn't do it because it was destroying evidence, so he decided to give it all to Gray. Gray was called to Ehrlichman's office and given two sealed envelopes, told that they contained material from Hunt's files that did not relate to Watergate, but were highly sensitive. He doesn't know what Gray did with it, but he believes that Gray took it to Connecticut, read the material, satisfied himself that it didn't involve the Watergate, and he's not sure what Gray's done with it since then, but he feels this revelation of this would create a major problem for Gray.

Another problem is that Liddy called Krogh before Gray's confirmation hearings and wanted some assurances and advice. He was given a brush-off and was very mad at Krogh.

Krogh asked Dean to call Liddy and reassure him, tell him not to worry, which Dean did. So much for the Dean phone call.

Bill Rogers' Evaluation

The P had me call Rogers and fill him in on all those problems of Dean's and then get Rogers' evaluation as to what we ought to do. Rogers raised the question of determining clearly from Dean whether he knew anything about intelligence operations between the time in December, when he told the group in Mitchell's office to turn off what they were doing, and June, when the Watergate was revealed. Rogers feels we need to consider the full significance of Dean's testimony. The important question is how the Watergate was launched. That's the key thing. His Watergate things were to cover up for the Watergate itself, and the fact that they were done makes it look like the White House had to cover up for the Watergate. Dean's story therefore seems incredible because why did we get into the cover-up if we don't know what the real story was to begin with at the Watergate? It just isn't believable. The attempts to cover up make the basic alibi of noninvolvement of the White House inconceivable.

He feels that whatever the consequences, whoever is affected, they have to be taken. That we can't continue not to get to the bottom of this. He thinks it's hard to judge Dean's position, that he probably comes out looking like he's trying to do the best he could. Clean but naive. Then that he had an impossible situation because he's the lawyer for these people and if something is wrong he becomes an accessory after the fact. The most painful question is what happens to the P himself. It's not too bad if Mitchell's not in it, but if he is, it would really be tough. McCord's statement looks to Rogers as if he was pointing at Mitchell. On balance, he feels that Dean has to offer to testify to the grand jury. There's no other way out. He has no problem regarding the refusal to discuss his conversations with the P, but as soon as Dean opens up, they'll question the whole range of things, and he has to handle confidentiality on the individual questions. He can't just take executive privilege overall, or lawyer-client privilege. He should not count on telling part of the story.

As far as the P's interest is concerned, the best thing is to go ahead, get it out in the open, and let whoever has to take the lumps.

John Mitchell's Views

The P then had me call Mitchell to get his view on having Dean go to the grand jury. He said if we do, it gives credence to the charge, but it's much better to be at the grand jury than at the Congressional hearings. Mitchell says there would be a problem in Dean's testimony on the number of meetings, because Mitchell wasn't specific on number of meetings, but he did get into the thing of they were for the purpose of election laws. He didn't mention that there was any discussion of intelligence.

He points out that McCord's new lawyer, Fensterwald, is a mediocre law practice, rich, white, super-lib type. He used to be on Senator Long of Missouri's staff. He's in the "cause" business generally, and he's the guy who put up McCord's bond, which makes the thing a little bit fishy. He feels that Baker should be doing something on this weekend stuff and that we should be getting some action on it.

Chuck Colson's Feelings

The P also had me call Colson. Colson feels we have no options regarding the grand jury, for any of us, unless they get into the national security areas. But that, while we should go up, we should not grandstand it, and we should definitely not waive executive privilege. We should cooperate in providing all the information we can to be helpful. He feels that Dean has an obligation to the P. He cannot reveal confidences from his relationship with the P, either as the P's lawyer or as the P's staff man. Also, Dean has acted as the lawyer to staff members and he clearly has done so, so he has to treat some of his communication with White House aides as executive privilege or as lawyer-client privilege. We should say that he has the desire and willingness to give the grand jury anything he can, the P's instructed him to cooperate fully with the authorities, but we should stop it right there. Not go beyond that. He should maintain the position of cooperating fully.

Colson then raised the question of the Magruder phone call, which I had raised with him the other day on the phone. He

was worried about that. He also feels that our problem is that
we need someone who can handle our side publicly and he
urges again the special counsel to the P idea, which Rogers
shot down the other day. He reports that his contacts in the
Democratic hierarchy say the Democrats want this whole thing
to go away because they're worried about the "glass houses"
thing. He feels strongly that someone has to take on Dash and
deal with Baker and our people to try and get them to stand
up on some of this stuff.

The P then got to talking about it. He thinks Mitchell ought
to call Kleindienst, get him to step up, and get off his ass. The
P can't keep calling him. He wonders if the Campaign Committee should hire a special counsel to use as a spokesman,
along the line Colson was talking about. He wants to know
whether Dean can go to the grand jury comfortably if he
doesn't have immunity. He wonders whether Kleindienst
should name a special prosecutor. He says that Kleindienst
reported back to him yesterday and said Weicker didn't have
any names, but Kleindienst won't hit Weicker publicly on this
or follow up, which he should do. Also, Kleindienst should be
fighting Dash, instead of Ziegler having to fight him. Ziegler
was in and we agreed not to do anything on the Dean to the
grand jury deal today. We'll hold up until tomorrow on that.

He wanted me to talk to Rogers again on the question of
how we handle the special prosecutor idea. What do we do
about the Segretti statement? What about the publicizing of
the Dean report? And overall, how do we appear publicly to
be taking the offensive? He wants Moore's judgment regarding
the Segretti statement. We should recognize that all of this is
being fought in public and worry about it on that basis, not
just the legalities.

Wants me to call Kleindienst in tomorrow and make the
point that we all stood by him and he damn well better get
going on this thing himself. I called Mitchell and made a pitch
on this, and Mitchell obviously wasn't willing to take on the
Kleindienst matter. Wants me to talk to Dean, Rogers, and
Kleindienst about the special prosecutor. Question of what will
it buy us? Question of who will talk to Silbert now that Dean
is into the case as a principal. Thinks we should get E into
this privately. Wants E to make a good check on Dean's FBI
guy and be ready to go on that next week. We can't leave a

vacuum there. All that session took another six hours, during all of which the sun had come out. It's a beautiful day at Key Biscayne, which I spent inside, locked in the P's villa. We'll leave late tonight to go back to Washington.

Tuesday, March 27, 1973

The staff meeting this morning was mainly taken up with the problem of Wounded Knee because E feels the time has come that the White House has got to get into it and bust up the siege. Also Shultz is concerned about his need to meet the P on a lot of items sometime this week before he goes to California. The P had a few odd items this morning about Julie's speech to the Jewish group and some general schedule things about trips and state visits.

John Dean's Report

He shifted into the question of the Watergate again. Wanted me to talk to Dean to get Mitchell down here today and to set up a meeting with Mitchell and Magruder, as Magruder had requested. I called Dean to get the morning report on him. He said that he'd had a long conversation with O'Brien. That he's very distressed at Mitchell because he thinks Mitchell could cut the whole thing off if he would just step forward. John feels that Mitchell very definitely did sign off on the Watergate thing and so he tends to concur with O'Brien. He says that Jeb told O'Brien and *(CRP lawyer Kenneth)* Parkinson in his meeting with them yesterday that he believes the whole Liddy plan was put together—that is, the superintelligence operation—by us at the White House before it was presented to the campaign group. He thinks Dean cooked it up, probably at my instructions. Mitchell bought it, and it was an accomplished fact in December, when Liddy arrived at the committee. Then there was a hiatus. The meetings occurred in Mitchell's office, Liddy unveiled his plan, nobody bought the first plan, so they went back. Then nobody bought the second plan, and so the whole thing just kind of lingered along. Liddy was pushing to get something done, Colson got into the act, pushing to do something, and then according to Magruder, the final step was that Gordon Strachan called Magruder, saying that Haldeman had told him to get this going, the P wanted it. Magruder told Mitchell this, and Mitchell signed off on it. Also, Magruder says that at a later point

Mitchell called Liddy in and read him the riot act regarding the poor quality of stuff they were getting.

Dean's theory now is that Mitchell and Magruder have their ass in the sling and are mixing apples and oranges for their own protection; that is, they don't realize, for instance, how little Dean told Liddy about the need for political intelligence on the demonstrators and that sort of thing. The fact is that at the first meeting, everybody laughed at the plan because it was absurd. At the second meeting, Dean got Mitchell off the hook. He arrived late, but said that the plan still was impossible, and then came and told me afterward that it was impossible and we had to stay completely away from it. Dean saw the problem and wanted to get ten miles away from it. The problem then was that Liddy was never given any guidance. Mitchell was in the middle of ITT and didn't focus on it. O'Brien says that Magruder wants to meet and that that's his motive. He doesn't really believe Jeb, but he's not sure, and he does see the mixing of apples and oranges. He's very disappointed in Mitchell, but won't tell him so.

O'Brien suggested that if we want to force this thing to a head, the two lawyers, O'Brien and Parkinson, have been retained by the committee and they could waive their lawyer-client privilege and they could report to the P on all of the facts at the committee. Hunt is at the grand jury today. We don't know how far he'll go. Probably he'll get into the money question, but he's not as desperate today as he was last night, but still on the brink. Bittman called O'Brien yesterday, said that Hunt was shaky, that he saw McCord walking out free and thinks maybe it's his turn. And he might reveal the fact that he was given money.

Editor's Note: Sirica had freed McCord on bond, while Hunt got a provisional sentence of 35 years, and the other four got 40 years. Liddy received 6 years, 8 months, to 20 years, plus a $40,000 fine.

Dean feels we're not really at the crunch that we were last night. Liddy's lawyer is going to argue against immunity with Sirica. He'll probably fail. If he gets immunity, he'll stay in contempt by still not saying anything. O'Brien and Parkinson are getting very shaky themselves. They're wringing their hands. That's all for now, but there's a sort of a semithreat to step forward. Dean has asked Liddy's lawyer for Liddy to give him a private statement that Dean knew nothing in advance about the Watergate. He thinks Liddy will do this, since he knows it's the truth. He says the Mitchell office meetings were in December and January, and that Dean heard absolutely nothing more regarding intelligence until June 17. He did see Liddy five or six times, but only on campaign matters. Nothing that got into the intelligence operation.

Dean then volunteered that the reason that he called Liddy on June 19 was that Kleindienst told him that Liddy saw him, Kleindienst, on the 18th, at Burning Tree about getting the men out of jail, which Kleindienst told him he would have nothing to do with, and at that time, Liddy told Kleindienst that Mitchell had ordered the operation.

Regarding the idea of the Warren Commission–type thing, Dean still thinks that it's possible. He's been trying to pick it apart with Dick Moore. His idea is that the P says here's what's charged of the White House and the committee. He puts it all into perspective in politics, this is all bad. Fact and fiction are being confused. We're in an intense political situation. The press and the Senate committee have prejudged the matter. Quote Ervin and Weicker and so on. The FBI is falsely charged, Justice and the U.S. Attorney are falsely accused. No man is above the law, but under these circumstances, there's no possibility of a fair hearing. The public is entitled to the facts, but the people involved are entitled to fair treatment, so the P creates a superpanel, with the cooperation of all investigative agencies, all the people involved agree to tell everything. They agree to waive trial by jury, etc.

The panel can remove Federal employees, levy fines, and pose criminal sanctions, etc. The defendants can also submit to this. Anyone who does not submit would be warned that all the information developed would be turned over to the Justice Department for criminal prosecution. There would be no judgment until all the facts are received and then we'll make public all the findings and the reasons for any action taken. Proceedings in secret, decisions final. Advantages are, on the long haul, twofold. One, nothing will be done until after the '74 elections, and two, the P maintains the ultimate stroke with the power to pardon at a later point. For the panel, he suggested Earl Warren, Tom Clark, some former governor, someone who knows politics. He would call Ervin down and tell him the plan, explain why, not that the present program isn't just and that there's too much finger pointing. We'd ask him to hold his hearings in abeyance and ask him to serve on the panel.

He also suggested considering the P and Mitchell have a one-on-one talk for the P to find out Mitchell's true perception of what has gone on. So that was Dean's view this morning.

Then E, Ziegler, and I met with the P and discussed how to handle the Dean matter with the press today, and agreed that we wouldn't go for anything on that at this point, but we do need to establish that Dean will have an opportunity to clear his name. Ziegler then left and we had a long review of the Dean report and general strategy. The P gave some guidance to E on the FBI, as to going ahead and pulling out Gray. The P agreed to have Rogers come over and see him this afternoon after I give him a briefing first. We discussed Weicker's problem and some of the other general questions. The P raised his idea of an alternate to the commission approach, which would be to send everyone in the White House to the grand jury, but that the P would talk to the judge ahead of time, and expedite it. He'd call the judge in, saying he's sending all of them down, we want you to get to the bottom of this, and then the P would go out and announce that he's done that. We'd base this on the argument that here's an honest judge, and so on, rather than a kangaroo court in Congress.

He then had me call Mitchell to try and get him to come down today, but he said he couldn't, and in the process said he was meeting with Magruder at the time, so that was set up without our knowing it.

John Dean's Report

Talked to Dean a little later in the day, and he said Mitchell asked Jeb up and Mitchell is going to tell Magruder that, "I ain't going to jail. You can make your own decision." Mitchell told Dean to stiffen up, said, "If you were to go before the grand jury, you wouldn't be believed, because your story doesn't jibe with mine." Mitchell told him yesterday that his going up would just open a can of worms. Dean thinks that Mitchell is saying obliquely that Dean should rerememeber things Mitchell's way.

Jeb said that McCord did budget work for Liddy and that maybe Liddy told him that the plan was presented to Dean, Magruder, and Mitchell and they said to cut it down, which would be the way that McCord might feel that Dean did have advance knowledge. Dean thinks that Jeb did talk to Strachan ahead of the thing. He feels that Jeb now, in answer to my question, should first hire a good lawyer; second, plead the Fifth; or third, seek immunity. He thinks in the latter case, we should beat Magruder to the punch on immunity by immunizing Dean. Which is John's solution at each point now.

The problem is, Jeb's perception of the truth is bad. It changes all the time, so he doesn't really know the truth. Dean thinks the Sirica idea of the P's is bad, that it would scare everyone and there'd be no chance of a fair trial. He thinks the panel is better. They can make a fair assessment of the facts out of the public eye.

The P told E to get Kleindienst in, but John discovered later that Kleindienst is on the way to Arizona on a speaking trip.

John Dean's Report

I talked to Dean a little later. He says that Hunt is going to give a written statement at the grand jury today and then will take the Fifth on everything else, and that *(Justice Department lawyer Henry)* Petersen won't know what happens at the grand jury until later in the day, but we can probably find out from him then.

He reported a new development. F. Lee Bailey called Mitchell regarding his gold-reserve client. Then said that Fensterwald had called to request that Fensterwald be present as co-counsel when McCord talks to Sirica, and he then offered the comment that we don't give a damn about McCord. We're after Richard Nixon.

Dean is thinking maybe Bailey will have a press conference. He thinks Fensterwald has a link to Kennedy, that he was the chief counsel to the administrative subcommittee when Kennedy was subchairman and then later succeeded Long. The question is how to get the Fensterwald story out. Who's paying him, who paid McCord's bail and expenses, destroyed a witness and so on.

The P wants Dean and Moore to rethink the Sirica idea.
And as a result of the P's being with Rogers, filled him in on
the whole plan. He felt that the Sirica idea was pretty good,
and then when he talked to the P, they modified it on the basis
of Kleindienst should meet with Sirica and say that the P to
this point has relied on the statements of various people, but
the McCord charges raised a cloud on this serious issue and
the P has therefore asked Kleindienst to talk to Sirica. One,
does he want to appoint a special prosecutor; two, does he
want to appoint a new grand jury; three, in the event of
whether or not he does either of those two, there will be total
cooperation from the White House with the grand jury, including testimony from the White House staff that have been
named directly or indirectly. Now all the White House people
who have volunteered to appear and testify, there's no question
of privilege on matters leading to the Watergate, because there
was no communication with the P on this before that. Then
Ziegler would go out and announce that we've done this. The
P wanted me to check E, Dean, Moore, Kleindienst, Mitchell,
and Colson on this. He feels we need a way to blunt the committee and have to work that out.

Chuck Colson's Feelings

I talked to Colson on the phone about the Sirica plan. He said
he didn't like the idea, that up until now the assumption is that
we've hidden behind executive privilege. Now McCord blows,
so we send the Attorney General to the judge. It appears like
overreaction. We should never offer the special prosecutor. He
said he'd tell me, when he saw me, why. Then I suggested that
he come over, which he did right then. This was late this afternoon. I met with him. He said that the problem is that here's a
case for conspiracy to commit perjury and conspiracy to obstruct justice. They can be made and sustained, so the special
prosecutor or the commission idea would insure indictment and
probably convictions. You can't limit the authority of a special
prosecutor. The greatest danger is a runaway grand jury and our
objective should be to control the grand jury. Especially regarding conversations within the White House.

The problem on obstruction is that everyone is a participant
except, as Colson says, of course, Colson, who didn't say what
he was told to say and therefore isn't a participant. This is why

the P needs one independent person to advise him. A good, skilled trial lawyer. The worst thing is to overreact now.

Kleindienst going to Sirica telegraphs to the judge the proof that the Administration is in a conspiracy. He would blast the Attorney General and he would know he had succeeded in smoking us out. A criminal lawyer would say don't give any unnecessary targets and don't grandstand, so Chuck says, first, we should get the best criminal lawyer possible, because none of us can render good advice. Definitely Dean's in the soup and he should take all the privileges he can handle. Second, don't overreact this week, especially on Sirica; third, a question of a statement over the weekend that the allegations are made public. The P says that he has instructed the staff as he did last summer, to cooperate fully with the official investigating activity and on any charges of wrongdoing, any staff member is under strict orders to comply fully.

I reported this back to the P and he said I should work out tomorrow morning with Colson a statement for Ziegler, if he's pressed, to the effect that all members of the White House staff have volunteered at any time to appear before the grand jury and answer questions on these matters. We should line up the statement as what Ziegler should put out, that much and no more. How to handle the question of executive privilege at the grand jury, especially as versus the Congress, and explain how the grand jury differs from the Ervin Committee. One is a separation of powers problem, the other is regarding the criminal activity and the grand jury is the proper place to investigate that, not before the TV lights of a Senate hearing.

He feels that we should drop the Kleindienst-Sirica meeting because it just won't work and would be a bad signal, as Chuck suggests. He liked my idea of trying to hit Weicker directly, since Pat Gray has now found out that Weicker's charges all relate to the Segretti matter and his thought that he's going to get me on that.

John Dean's Report

I found out from Dean late today that McCord goes to the Senate before he goes to the grand jury. He'll go tomorrow in closed session. Dean feels that within 24 hours he will have documentation proving he didn't know anything about the Watergate ahead of time. He already has Jeb's and John Mitchell's statements and Liddy will give him a good statement, too.

Regarding the post-June activity, he thinks there's a good chance to hunker down and survive. If Dean goes to the grand jury, he has to go. The P should waive privilege as it relates to Dean personally. He then reported that Woodward, the guy who's been writing all the bad articles at the *Post,* came to Gerry Warren and said that they didn't want to be polarizers and they realized that maybe they were running some stuff that was unfortunate and all that, and they want to set things at rest, so they'd like to have an interview with the P, which is the epitome of gall.

Chuck Colson's Idea

Colson called me later with an idea, which would be that Kleindienst call in Hunt and Liddy, tell them to come clean, and if they do, Justice would consider the question of parole or commutation. They would tell Kleindienst, with a reporter, under oath, the whole story on Watergate and would get immunity from further prosecution. This would preempt the obstruction of justice issue. Colson trusts Shapiro, his partner. He tried this idea on him and he says it's brilliant. It cuts the ground from under the McCord thing. This would accomplish Dean's objective of cutting the cancer out and it's discovered by us instead of by a grand jury or Ervin. If we accept the inevitability that it's going to come out anyway, this is a good way to do it, and it extinguishes the issue of post-Watergate problems.

Wednesday, March 28, 1973

Another Watergate day. The P had his schedule cleared to work on his speech, but spent a fair amount of time with me on the Watergate. I had John Mitchell in at 8:15 and started with him. The P called me over for about 15 minutes at 8:45 to the EOB. He said, with Mitchell we need to know what he thinks about the grand jury appearance and his view regarding Colson's idea of holding all the privileges because of our concern regarding obstruction of justice, and so on, and get his legal views on obstruction. We need to decide what to do if events overrun us. The P would like a deal that would show that we're cooperating. Offer an informal session of the whole committee and take sworn testimony. Try to cut a deal with Ervin to undercut the bad rap on cover-up.

John Mitchell Meeting

I spent a long time with Mitchell. He feels it's vital that we know what the grand jury and the committee are doing and that we've got to get our sources set up to provide that. He reported on his meeting with Jeb yesterday. Says that Jeb's view is the following: That the plan was hatched at the White House by Hunt, Liddy, and Colson, Colson called Jeb twice to tell him to get going on this thing, specifically, the Larry O'Brien information regarding the Florida dealings. Liddy told Magruder later that he was in Colson's office when Colson called. Gordon Strachan probably had a lot of direct dealings with Liddy. He knows he had some. A copy of the output came here, to either Strachan or Colson. Strachan told them I had approved the plan and he feels that four people in the White House had full knowledge of the Watergate. Colson, because of the phone calls: Howard, because of conversations he had with him; Strachan, because he had copies of what Liddy passed out; and Haldeman, because Strachan told Magruder that I had approved the plan. He says the procedure was that Baldwin made notes on the tap reports, gave them to McCord, McCord gave them to Liddy, Liddy made two copies, sent one to Magruder and one to the White House. Either to Strachan or to Colson.

Mitchell further said on his own knowledge that he believes Dean agreed with Magruder, in Mitchell's office prior to the testimony, about the purpose of the meetings at the Attorney General's that they were to deal with corrupt practices and so on. Not intelligence. Mitchell also says that Magruder told him that Porter talked to Dean regarding his testimony about the accounting for the purposes of the money that was given to Liddy, and that Porter was happy to so testify. Magruder and Porter also talked to Mitchell and to their lawyers.

Regarding the Senate, the view is that the P should reserve judgment regarding sending White House witnesses to the Senate because of the apparent political circus, but we will ask them all to cooperate with the grand jury. That's Mitchell's view. On the post–June activities, there's a question of who Dean talked to. There's a question of the significance of Caulfield's meetings with McCord. What was Caulfield's purpose, and so on? At that point, we had discussed the whole thing in general and we asked Magruder to come in.

Jeb Magruder's Report

Jeb said to Mitchell and me that Liddy was ordered to prepare a plan by someone. The question is who started him? Also, there's a question as to whether Gordon Strachan told Magruder to rehire Liddy after he fired him in April. Magruder then went into his problem of the cash disbursements made by Porter which will have to be revealed, says Howard is adamant that he's got to cover up one of $8,000 given to him prior to April 7, which Jeb said was for some purpose that would be very embarrassing. I pushed him on what it was, and he said they used it to buy books, and I'm sure that's to buy the Efron book, which, of course, wouldn't be embarrassing at all *(a book by Edith Efron on politics and the media which P had decided he wanted to make a best-seller)*. There were a lot of cash payments to Colson in that period for ads, primarily. These were legal, but maybe peculiar. Also, for a Kennedy mailing in New Hampshire, which Colson said, according to Magruder, was ordered by the P.

Liddy wasn't the committee's operative during January, February, and March, while he was working there, but was doing things at other people's direction. Jeb doesn't know whose.

In an agreement that was reached at the meeting in Mitchell's office with Dean, Magruder said he had only one meeting with Mitchell and Liddy, and this was after Liddy was hired, and was to discuss his role. This was Dean's idea. Also, Dean told Magruder to destroy his diary. Mitchell says there's no question regarding the meeting. He had to testify on the meetings. Magruder has testified that there never was a meeting with Liddy, and so forth, regarding intelligence. I made a note at that point that this could be the little thing that does it. The typewriter or pumpkin of this case. That is, the discrepancy on these meetings. *(I was referring back to the Hiss case.)* Jeb says he could have said that he did have a meeting on intelligence, but he didn't, because Dean told him not to. So Dean cannot now say that there was such a meeting. Magruder feels that McCord may name Strachan because of his contact with Liddy.

The P called on the phone. Wanted a report on all this, but said while I was talking with Mitchell to go down the checklist of his views on whether we can work on an accommodation with Ervin. Second, whether we should maintain privilege before the grand jury, third, what about problems with the grand jury in New York and fourth, what do we do regarding Dean. On the New York thing, Mitchell said they're looking primarily at Vesco. Our only problem is Don Nixon and Cerni, and Ed Nixon, who was set up. They won't get into campaign expenditures. Justice will handle those down here.

Editor's Note: Mitchell and Stans would ultimately be indicted—and acquitted of charges that they tried to influence the SEC in exchange for a $200,000 contribution from international businessman Robert Vesco. There were also allegations, but no more than that, regarding the President's brothers.

P called me at home this evening to say that he has decided to read his speech tomorrow night after all rather than standing up for it. He wanted to talk about that for a little. I told him I thought that sounded fine and he seemed pleased that I agreed with it. Raised the question of whether he should praise those that stood with us on Vietnam against the flak from the people who didn't. I agreed that he should.

Wants to be sure that I fill Colson in tomorrow on Magruder's charges and his line. Wants me to give him a report if I get anything from Dean. Says he's been thinking alot about working for Republican candidates in '74 and thinks he'll really hit the stump on that.

John Dean's Report
Talked to Dean on the phone to get a progress report this evening. He says Hunt spent four hours with immunity and created no problems for us. That Sirica's changed his mind; is not going to hear McCord in court. He's going to have him go direct to the grand jury, probably on Friday.

Dean said O'Brien had a long conversation with LaRue today, which evolved into a discussion about Mitchell, and LaRue said he thinks Mitchell is on the verge of breaking, by which he means suicide.

Dean says he can't do what Mitchell and Magruder told him to do. The more he looks at it, the post-June activity, the more he thinks we can work that out. Mitchell and Magruder both told him that they had both signed off on the project, which Mitchell told me, also. Dean feels it's imperative that we get a criminal lawyer and suggests maybe he should hire one. Then he could consult with him on the whole thing, which is a good idea.

I talked to Timmons on the Branson and on getting the word from Gurney as to what went on today *(Republican Senator Ed Gurney, also on the Ervin Committee)*. He says he's got a tip, that apparently there's some guy who's on the staff of the Judiciary Committee, who leaves a package at the Senate newsstand every day at 12:00 and someone comes at 4:00 and picks it up. The girl at the stand opened it by accident today and found it full of Watergate stuff, so Timmons is going to stake that out and see if he can get any lead out of that.

Thursday, March 29, 1973

The P spent the whole day working on preparation for his TV speech tonight. I spent virtually the whole day on various Watergate matters, and did have to get to the P on a couple of points during the day, which he seemed to want to do.

Bill Timmons's Report

Timmons called Ed Gurney last night to see if he would be willing to provide us with input as to what was going on at the Committee so we'd have some reading of what we were up against. Gurney said the Committee spent a great deal of time over secrecy and that he would play by the rules and expected others to, also, which is a little absurd since the whole thing leaked in all the papers today. Bill tried a different approach by asking his view of Dean testifying and so on. He volunteered that things looked pretty bad for the White House, and that the P should take some kind of initiative on the issue, and Dean's appearance would be one way. He also suspects that Gurney would be more open in person rather than talking over the phone, and he's going to try to get to him directly.

He also was going to watch the brown package switch business at the Senate newsstand today. He's disturbed, though, because the delivery service, the man on the Senate Judiciary Committee, is a hard-line anti-Communist, so he's afraid maybe the FBI's the final beneficiary of the material.

I met with the P at 1:00 with E and reported those things and we evolved a plan that we should put out today a statement saying that what is involved here are charges of criminal conduct and the proper place for such charges is the grand jury. Therefore I'm sending Dean to the grand jury and I'll waive the executive privilege regarding any personal involvement in the Watergate crime. Told me to check this out with Mitchell, Dean, Colson, Ziegler, and so on, and then get back to him. He feels that, or we talked about the problem that the sticky problem here still is going to be the Mitchell-Magruder position regarding the meetings. I also pointed out to him that we have a problem that George Bush had called, wanted to see him, because he was concerned, too, about the reaction that's building. He said he would see Bush Friday if it was necessary.

I talked to Mitchell and he said that it—the question of making such a release of Dean to the grand jury—depends on how it's phrased, that we shouldn't get into privilege. Mitchell's main concern is that he thinks Ziegler should have hit the senators for their attack on Mitchell today.

We met again at 2:30 because the idea was to get Ziegler to put this out at 3:00. We had Ziegler in, too. He was very much opposed to putting it out today *(because of the President's speech that night on TV)*, and we worked with E, Ziegler, and the P on a statement that he then decided not to put out today, but rather wait until tomorrow. Then, a little later, Dean called to say that you can't put it out at all because the lawyers say that it would be wrong for him to offer to go to the grand jury or for the P to offer him when they haven't called him.

The P told me later in the afternoon to be sure to get ready to emphasize the three big points tonight, then he named four. First a shot across the bow at North Vietnam, and a jab on amnesty. Second, the ceiling on meat. Third, the need to support the P on the vetoes, and fourth, don't cut the defense budget.

John Mitchell's Report

Later in the afternoon Mitchell called on the phone again. He says Hunt is through with the grand jury and had no problems regarding the White House, post-June, or anything. F. Lee Bailey called. Was very pleased with his treatment at the White House. He and Alch examined McCord totally and what he said so far is all he knows. They told him not to make such statements, that he'd make a fool of himself.

Bittman told O'Brien that an *LA Times* reporter is getting information from the Committee. He says that he has the story that the meeting in February was attended also by Colson and Hunt, and in his meetings with Dash, he told him about other break-ins, including a New York doctor's apartment and some other things like that. Liddy's counsel refuses to allow him to testify. Everyone says Dean is uptight. He's not making proper judgment.

Mitchell strongly suggests that I make sure he doesn't go off the reservation without my reviewing it. I'm the only one he'll trust. His opinion of E is incredible and frightening, so I should establish contact with Dean and maintain it. He says Weicker came on with a big espionage plan in the White House. The rumor is that he's going to hit E, not Colson. He then probably has some of the earlier activities, that's what he's after.

Friday, March 30, 1973

The P had a solid round of appointments this morning, getting ready for the departure for California. On the plane out to California, the P had me up for a little while, talking almost totally on Watergate. His concern is developing in terms now of the damage to the Presidency and his ability to govern and feels that we have to take action to clear this up because of that. He's getting a lot of heat from the likes of Goldwater, etc., who have a real concern and are expressing it to him via letters, etc., which makes him feel that we've got to face up to the erosion of confidence question and take some action to get at that. E, of course, feels strongly the same way, and he spent some time with the P afterward and hit him very hard on that point. Told me later that the P comes down that the thing to do is put it to Magruder and try to draw the line there. There's a question whether that's possible.

Saturday, March 31, 1973
In San Clemente. E and I talked to Kleindienst to review the Gray question and the FBI. We agreed that he was through and had to be out. We also got into the question with Kleindienst of the Watergate handling and more particularly the need for some cooperation from him and some discussion of strategy. He feels that he probably ought to appoint a three-judge panel to replace himself as the prosecutor on the case, since he's basically disqualified.

Tonight was the John Ford dinner, which went very well. The superclimax, which nobody will probably ever know, was when after he was wheeled up to the stage, Ford did a magnificent job, of standing up by himself, walking to the podium, and accepting the Film Institute Award, then sitting down while the P made his remarks, then coming up to receive his Medal of Freedom. In his response to that, he said that he wanted to quote Captain Jeremiah Denton, who had said he was stunned by the reaction of the people, and so on, and that he felt the same way. Then he said the P had talked with him on the phone about the reaction of the POW's and he had told the P that he had cried and blubbered like a child when he saw them coming off, and then had gotten out his rosary and said a few prayers and then had said a simple little prayer himself, that was the prayer millions of Americans say in their homes—God bless Richard Nixon. It was an extremely impressive moment, and one that nobody there, I don't think, will ever forget. It really stuck it to the anti-Nixon types in the film crowd.

Last Month: April

Sunday, April 1, 1973

The big deal today was Weicker on "Face the Nation," where he hit me pretty hard on knowledge of Watergate and that's the lead out of his thing. He seems to think I had directed a master plot of sabotage and espionage, of which Watergate was only a minor part. He admitted he didn't have any evidence, but that didn't seem to stop him. The P called E several times but did not call me on the subject. I guess he did call once this morning while I was out to breakfast, but, missing me, he talked to John and then maintained his contact with John the rest of the day. We didn't get into the office.

Monday, April 2, 1973

Big story today was my involvement in Watergate as charged by Weicker. Major headline in the *LA Times,* not so big in other papers. Spent most of the morning working on that, with time out for the Thieu arrival, which went very well. Mitchell called to say that O'Brien had met with Dean and that Dean's taken a "unique stance," as Mitchell put it, and that the only salvation is for me to talk to him. What he's after is to try to get him to put his story differently regarding the meetings. Mitchell says if Dean does say what he suggests, he will unravel the whole thing, and after the meeting the other day, John thought Dean understood. But he says Dean's using me as the reason for taking the position he does, on the basis that I have to testify in the same way Dean intends to. He says some of the post-June activities will also be a problem, and we should consider the solution of having Dean not testify. That would solve several problems and we have ample grounds for doing it.

John Dean's Report

I talked right after that to Dean. He says his lawyer has told him that he must not talk to Mitchell or Magruder. He says that he would rather take the contempt citation or the Fifth Amendment than to cause anyone a problem, and if it comes down to an impossible position, that's what he'll do, but that opens the potential for indictment. He said Strachan is being worked on by Magruder, that Moore had lunch with Kleindienst and got into the special prosecutor thing, and John feels that's simply a device on Kleindienst's part to avoid Kleindienst having to do in Mitchell. If Dean has to testify and tells the truth, it'll start the whole finger-pointing exercise that he feels would be unbearable. He has no idea what Mitchell said before the grand jury, but Mitchell must consider it will conflict with Dean, or he wouldn't be so worried. O'Brien told Dean Saturday that Jeb was not now concerned with Dean's testimony. Says O'Brien knows all the facts.

After the Thieu meeting this morning, then a trip over to the house for lunch, the P came back, had E and me in for a couple hours this afternoon. The P said he wanted to make a couple of points on the whole Watergate situation that he felt were very important. First, that the P must be isolated from the discussions. That we've got to tell all parties, or that John does, that the P has other problems during April and May, with the Congress, the Soviet Summit, Vietnam, and so on, and he can't talk to the people that are concerned, that is, Dean, Mitchell, Moore, Colson, George Bush, the VP, and all of them. E must get the confidence of all those people and handle the thing for the P. He commented on the side that the schedule for the first three months of this year was all wasted as far as anything public was concerned, and that he's got to concentrate on that side of things for the next few months.

Second, that there must be no falling-out amongst our people. Having all of them going off in all different directions. We can't have a situation of every man for himself. They're all on the team. No one's going to flush anybody and they must understand that.

He then launched into a fascinating review of the Hiss case, making the point as to how he conducted the investigation and worked around to where he trapped Hiss, using that as an object lesson in terms of what we've got to watch out for, and what Weicker et al. are doing wrong in their conduct of this investigation.

He then got into a strategy review and the question of whether I should go out publicly. We agreed that I should not, but that we should consider my doing the newspaper interview with *The Washington Post,* but I should definitely not go on TV. He felt that we've crossed the bridge on Dean and he's not going to permit Dean to go up and testify, and John said, "Don't make a final decision on it," but that's basically John's position, too, as the way around conflicting testimony. He got into some personnel things. He feels that we probably should move Kleindienst out and discussed possible Attorney General, Ruckelshaus *(EPA head William Ruckelshaus)* being Ehrlichman's candidate. The P decided he should not do a press conference this week after the Thieu meetings, so he's not going to. Then we dropped that, and he spent a lot of time just going round and round on the various aspects of the whole Watergate situation as it now stands.

Wednesday, April 4, 1973
The P had no schedule today. He had E in for some general discussion on Watergate, and then it was about 10:40 and we talked a little while about my concerns and so on, and then I went out so he could have further discussion with John. I went back in to give him Dean's report.

John Dean's Report
John had called me on the phone to say that his lawyers saw the U.S. Attorneys Silbert and Glanzer, and just sat and listened to take their temperature as representatives of Dean, regarding what will happen going to the grand jury. He finds that first, he will be called, probably next week, the same as Mitchell. Same basis—no cameras, and not announced until afterward. Second, Dean is not a target of the grand jury, also Haldeman is not. They don't believe they'll have to call Haldeman except as perhaps a way to corroborate other statements. Third, Liddy has talked to the U.S. Attorney. His lawyer doesn't know it. They believe him, the U.S. Attorneys do. And in his discussions he's freed the White House from their minds, although John doesn't know what he said.

Dean's lawyers had told him he must not talk to Jeb, and this morning Jeb called him. Dean's lawyers talked to Jeb's lawyer to try and untangle this. They discussed the business on privilege and so on. Dean, according to the U.S. Attorneys this morning, can't take the Fifth Amendment. His lawyers say he may have to on technicals. U.S. Attorneys say they won't pursue that. Dean's lawyers think that in effect it'll be a practical immunity granted regarding after-the-fact technical violations.

He says there's a funny position regarding the grand jury minutes to the Ervin Commission. Sirica has heard the Justice Attorneys have filed an *amicus* brief with Sirica regarding some rule that the grand jury minutes are secret. This would violate that, and Ervin of course has returned a request for the minutes, so the government is in a good position regarding not releasing the grand jury minutes, John feels. Dean's view regarding Ervin appearances is that some arrangement has to be made on ground rules so that we talk only about firsthand knowledge, no hearsay. Regarding Dean, he thinks we should hard-line it and have no appearance at all.

He says Mitchell called Dick Moore, who was in Dean's office with Clawson, and they put Dean on the phone, too. Mitchell called to report that he had talked to F. Lee Bailey, and Alch had told him that when McCord was going to go before Judge Richey on the civil case deposition, he had a letter that he was going to file saying that Parkinson had handled the payoffs to the defendants via Mrs. Hunt. He told his lawyers that this was a lie, but that he had wanted to get Parkinson somehow, and this was the best way to do it. He and Fensterwald cooked this up. Mitchell thinks we ought to find a way to get this out. Dean still thinks Jeb is the most serious problem, but his lawyers are working with Bierbower, Jeb's lawyer.

I reported all this to the P and John and then went out. The P and John finished up about 12:15 and called me in again. Discussed Magruder and the problem of what he would do if he was given immunity. I said I thought it would be very serious, and the question was raised of whether Strachan would tell Magruder to hire Liddy, something that we need to return to. In the discussion with the P and John while I was in there, we got into the point that the Weicker attack is an approach that we've got to contend with. We should hit the press criticizing us, because we didn't campaign as a defense thing there. "Reinforce the Presidency" was our campaign concept, and it's ironic that we would be brought through the mud because of ill-advised people, since we have taken such a high-level approach, and I should condemn any excesses that took place. He then told John that he is to understand the overriding need for Haldeman on the staff. The P said, "Haldeman is more important to me than Adams was to Ike. For example, the K situation, which only he can handle. I can handle the rest, probably, but I can't do that. So protecting Haldeman, in terms of whether his testimony is raising a greater doubt about him, is a major consideration. He is the P's closest confidant, his Chief of Staff, and we can't let him be tarred as a dirty SOB, and this is a case in point."

E, Ziegler, Higby, and I then spent the rest of the afternoon going over a Q & A session to work out what might develop in my interview. It didn't work out very satisfactorily, and we're back to a general discussion of how we should approach this at this point. My feeling is that we have more problems than solutions and that we've got to really consider the desirability of my going. I'm not sure it would be productive.

Thursday, April 5, 1973

John Dean's Report

Back to Dean this morning. He felt that he had a new idea that we ought to consider, which is that we should go public, saying that we want the facts to emerge in this case, but we have trouble finding out how to do it, so we suggest that the Ervin Committee cut Watergate out of their inquiry, let the U.S. Attorneys summarize that later, when the appeals are not jeopardized, and at that time commit to releasing a full report. Then Ervin could go ahead on all but the Watergate, because really the rest of it's all "BS" anyway. The point is, we have nothing to hide, but we can't handle Watergate properly with the Committee without jeopardizing the defendants' rights, and so on, in a legal action. He suggests maybe the VP take the lead on this. He says Jeb Magruder now thinks that he's going to be indicted, but that he can beat it on trial, or at least his wife is telling Bart Porter's wife that.

Dean goes to the grand jury one day next week and feels we need a plan for how to handle that. He'll first have a session with the U.S. Attorneys to discuss the parameters. He feels we should hold any release of the Segretti material until we work out the plan for the Senate Committee.

The P's told E to tell Harlow to make it clear to the VP that he can follow his own course and the P will follow his own course. The P's very disturbed because of the VP's unwillingness to step up on the executive privilege matter unless the P will talk to him.

K talked to the P this morning. His theory is that Mitchell is responsible and should come forward and say so. The P feels we need someone to have talks with Mitchell, Magruder, and Dean, persuade them that we have to show some motion, that we just can't sit in a bomb shelter, that we can do some things that won't hurt them. Wants me to talk to Magruder and tell him that this is all coming through on the jungle telegraph full circle, and he's got to quit talking.

We talked to George Bush, who said he had a one and a half hour meeting with Connally and wanted to talk to the P. Raised this with Rose Woods and one of the things Bush raised, well, his primary thing, was the Connally matter. He's concerned that Connally feels we've got to get the Watergate thing cleared up (which hardly comes as a surprise). Bush says that Connally wants something done drastically, that someone has to walk the plank and some heads have to roll. The P told me to call Connally and tell him he wants to see him in Washington next week, that there's nothing the P's greater concerned about, but frankly he doesn't have answers to how to deal with it. Who does he think ought to walk the plank?

I had a bunch of miscellaneous phone calls. Elliot Richardson all concerned about personnel in the Defense Department and things being held up there, especially on the Air Force Secretary where we vetoed his man. Bob Hope was worried about the guest list and stars for the POW dinner. I talked to Pat Gray this evening at the P's request. We removed him as FBI nomination. The P wanted me to call him and just say we were all thinking of him and so on, which I did. Talked to Finch, who says he's made his decision. He's going for the Senate, but he has to extract commitments. He has a list of concerns, such as how to play it against '76, what did you do with Connally, what did you do about Nelson Rockefeller vs. Reagan vs. Connally, and so on. He can't go to the ball game with the P Friday night because he's speaking at Marymount, but wants to see the P on Saturday, which I later set up. He feels he needs a capability of having input on appointments in California. He wants to work as if he were a senator with the White House. Probably he won't announce until the first of the year, but he'll do some dramatic things now and get out of the governorship hassle. He's going to talk to Reagan and all the other candidates next week. Feels this must be closely held because he's got to get commitments, especially from Younger and Reagan.

John Connally's Analysis

Had a long talk with Connally on the phone tonight. He says the Watergate thing's gone too far to back off of, that we have to view it not only as the Watergate, but Segretti and the whole thing. He says that we ought to pose the Segretti approach on an attack basis, that we did it in order to counter what we were confronted with by the Democrats. Go on the offensive. Use the examples of what they did. He thinks the P should waive executive privilege on the grounds that the Senate Committee is so partisan and demagogic they've impaired the government's function. That as many of us as can should go up there, they should get it away from Haldeman and away from the White House. He says they won't let it rest until someone else is brought in, involved, and hung. There's no way to stop it, so we should get divorced from it. We should be outraged at their demagoguery. Take them head-on in open session and grandstand it.

On a purely hypothetical, and he never mentioned his name, he said if it gets to Mitchell, people would never believe that the P didn't know it. He says if we don't know the facts, we should get a good trial lawyer and then tell him all the facts and get his advice as to the possibilities. He thinks we could say that at any cost the P has to sacrifice anybody in order to clear the Presidency, but if one particular individual is involved (and he's referring to Mitchell), then you can't get the taint off unless the P himself delivers him up. It's entirely possible that there's a middle road, such as E going up and saying to the Committee, "We know you're after Haldeman, so we'll waive privilege for him if you'll agree to shut down after that." He then agreed with me that wouldn't work.

He says assume Haldeman, E, Dean, Colson, Chapin all go up and really put on an act, take the Committee on, try to nail them, that they'd been on a witch-hunt. You need some phrases. You need to be coached and rehearsed, each one of you. You might, by that, screw the Committee in people's minds and destroy it, or at least pull its teeth. But you should definitely get there at the beginning. Be the first ones on. He's very worried about Wall Street and the uneasiness in the country, and feels we have to deal with it one way or another, and, in a way, it's related to the whole Watergate business, too.

Saturday, April 7, 1973

K came bouncing in today to report that the P keeps telling him that he's under great pressure to dump me, and that it's his feeling that he should do so, but he wants Henry's view on it, that this is especially coming from Connally and he asked K what he thinks. K says he thinks this is the worst possible choice of alternatives, that this would accomplish nothing and would create monumental problems and that there's no way if I'm guilty that the P can separate himself from this, and therefore that would be the strongest argument for his not dumping me, in K's view; the next strongest being that he needs me, and that it isn't worth paying that price. Henry claims he wants to be helpful in all this, and that he's very concerned that the P's going to make the wrong move on it.

I covered this with E and he said he could explain that. Yesterday the P said he thinks what Connally was suggesting to me when he was saying we couldn't save Mitchell was that I had to fall, and that's what he's basing it on. He hasn't talked to Connally. He's going on the basis of my report. E, too, told him that he thought that was ridiculous and he says the P agreed, that we can't survive Bob's falling, and we must all hang together. And he says, in the car going to the ball game, that the P got into his historical mood and said this is the day we all go down defending Haldeman.

Dean called later today, said his lawyers had met with U.S. Attorneys again, that they only want to get the facts on the Watergate and that they do not expect to go beyond that. Dean believes this, says that Liddy has told them everything he knows, they don't believe Hunt and are going to push him harder, they want to meet with Dean tomorrow off the record with no action, to discuss the problems of how he would testify at the grand jury and questions of the Fifth Amendment, attorney-client relations, and all. Dean feels we're at the moment of truth, in that he should go and that we've got to decide it right away. He says the grand jury's scope is not broad in what they're trying to cover, and they want what happened pre-Watergate. They're not interested in post-Watergate, which they think is a can of worms. They want Dean because of his knowledge, want to get those points laid out so that they can move on their investigation of others to nail someone on the pre-Watergate planning.

Dean called again later today and thought it was imperative that he decide. E wanted him to wait until we got back on Monday. Dean called later yet and said that he wanted to meet with us tomorrow night when we get back, so he's obviously really uptight on it. I'm going to try to keep that in Ehrlichman's ballpark where it belongs. We keep going round and round on various approaches, and I think E still comes down on the side of my testifying. He had a long talk with Baker today, and Baker agrees that we should move to go up soon, that would work very much to our advantage, would be the smartest move that we could make at this point, and that the Committee would have to go along with it, so John's idea is to try that in his meeting with Baker and Ervin Monday evening. In any event, I think we've got to come to a final decision on strategy on the plane tomorrow and just see what we can do from there.

Monday, April 8, 1973

Got into the Watergate issue as usual. The P's gone over the whole thing and we have to hang together. Feels now that we're faced with three basic problems—Watergate, prices, and foreign policy—but that all of them added up don't equal the problem that the war was until we ended it, as far as the public is concerned with regard to the P. He says we've got to remember that we won the election and we shouldn't get so disturbed about the problems. We should be on the positive.

After we got back, E and I met at the White House with John Dean to go over his problems. He's about to go to the grand jury and wanted to discuss his approach to the prosecutor.

Tuesday, April 9, 1973

We got back into the Watergate discussion, of course, as we do all the time. Had a long discussion about the monitoring facilities in his offices and he wants them all taken out, but then he later changed his mind and said to leave them in on a switch *(activated)* basis. He's obviously concerned about having everything covered and wants to set up some kind of limited means of coverage. I spent most of the day, as usual, working on the Watergate. The P had a fairly involved schedule that kept him otherwise occupied.

Wednesday, April 10, 1973

The VP called me over today and said he had a real problem, because Jerome Wolff, who used to work for him back in Maryland, was about to be called by the United States Attorney who was busting open campaign contribution cases and kickbacks to contractors. It seems that Wolff kept verbatim records of meetings with the VP and others, back over the years, concerning fund-raising, and has a lot of quotes about how much we ought to get from a certain contractor, and so on, who has had good jobs. It wasn't shakedown stuff, it was merely going back to get support from those who had benefited from the Administration, but the way it's worded, the VP feels it would sound bad. He made the point that *(Baltimore prosecutor)* George Beall is *(Senator)* Glenn Beall's brother, and that if Glenn Beall would talk to him, he could straighten it out. The VP's tried to get him to, but apparently not successfully, so he wanted me to talk to Glenn Beall, which, of course, I won't do, in order to verify a White House awareness and concern. He feels that publication of this stuff would finish the VP, because Wolff was with him for so long and is very much concerned. He agreed he'd probably get Colson into it, and that it would be the best way to handle it.

Editor's Note: On October 10, Agnew would plead nolo contendere to one count of having knowingly failed to report income for tax purposes—and resigned as Vice President.

Wednesday, April 11, 1973

I was out most of the morning. Mitchell called, which I returned from home. He wanted to talk about the settlement of the civil suits. He'd been talking to Strauss of the Democratic National Committee and he said this morning that he had cleared the whole thing with Mansfield and Albert and so on, and we could go ahead and settle, but Mitchell said after two hours with Stans, he's still holding out for damages in the O'Brien libel suit, and we need to turn that off. That he had talked with E and thought he had that taken care of.

He also was concerned that Dean's testimony would be the one thing that could really unscramble the whole operation. We should try to get Dean not to go to the grand jury, in his opinion. I mentioned this to the P. He's quite concerned about it. Told me to talk to E. He was raising the question of whether that is the linchpin in the whole thing, and the P had Ziegler come in and we went through the whole question of the White House going up to the Senate. Ron argues strongly that we should not. His real fear is that it's going to focus the whole thing onto me and hang it on me and destroy me, and he feels that would be extremely harmful to the P. The P made the point again that the key here is to protect Haldeman, but Ziegler feels that Ehrlichman's moves to lock up the Senate deal with Ervin are going to basically haul me in.

Chapin and Strachan both testified at the grand jury today, and both said that I had agreed to their approaching Segretti, and Chapin said afterward that some assistant DA that's working with Silbert made the point that this was a real bombshell and was probably going to destroy the P, because it laid the whole thing right at the White House doorstep and really right at the P.

In the Ziegler meeting, E came in and there was general agreement that we should put out a preemptive statement of some kind. In other words, that I should make my statement ahead of going to the grand jury, so that we get our story out in writing separately from the Q & A session story. Try and establish our own position first, so I'm going to work on getting my statement ready with that thought in mind.

The P still obviously very concerned about the whole issue and spending quite a little time on it. E meets this evening again with Ervin and Baker to try to resolve the ground rule question of whether we go up to the Senate and how. Dean is still concerned on the whole grand jury question. Magruder called and wanted guidance from me on what to do, and I had

Larry call him back and say I couldn't give him any guidance, that he should do what his lawyer tells him to, and he apparently wasn't satisfied with that and said, well, he hated to do it, and he wanted us to know he was still on the team, but he was going to have to go ahead, if that's what we said, and he was going up to tell Mitchell that tomorrow. Looks like we're nearing the moment of truth and everybody's getting a little panicky in the crunch.

Thursday, April 12, 1973

The P was pretty well tied up all day with NSC, other meetings, a couple of long sessions with E on Watergate strategy, and a follow-up with K on the problem in SE Asia, plus a Congressional thank-you reception for those who supported him on the vetoes in the House and Senate. I had only a short session with him at midday, and that was mainly a Watergate discussion as usual.

K came in late in the day and had a long session with me. He's very concerned, because he thinks there's a serious strategic mistake in putting me out front on this, because it will put all the focus on me and therefore render me practically ineffective, and he went into all kinds of threats that if the P dumped me or set it up so that I had to leave, he would leave, too. He won't going to stay if I wasn't there; and he thinks E should be sacrificed, or someone else, rather than me. I tried to explain that it wasn't either/or and that I didn't feel I was being sacrificed. That I felt I had to have the opportunity to clear myself, but he feels that no matter what the merits of the facts are, whoever goes out front on this is going to be killed by it, and that, at any cost, it should not be me. So that's another factor to weigh in the equation. I am going to have to get my statement redone, which I keep talking about but never doing, and get ready to put it out, maybe the first of next week. Ehrlichman's pushing me for even getting it out this week, but everyone else feels strongly, that is, everyone being K and Ziegler, and, of course, my staff feels strongly, that I shouldn't get out front, so I may hold up on that for the time being.

Friday, April 13, 1973

Another long Watergate day. As I spent a good part of the day locked in my office working on my revised statement, for whatever purpose we decide to use it. There were, however, several major external developments.

Chuck Colson's Report

Colson reported to E this morning that he had reports that Jeb Magruder had met with two different reporters and with Mitchell this week, and that he was putting out the story that Mitchell was not involved at all in Watergate, and that he had discussed specifically with me both the idea of bugging and the Watergate in particular. He claims he also had the same discussions with Colson. Chuck's conclusion from this was that Magruder and Mitchell were conspiring together to sink Colson and me in their own self-defense, on the theory that if they could get that much blood, the whole effort would be dropped and Mitchell would be clear.

This he covered in some detail with John, and John reported to the P and to me and that started the whole track of revised thinking and emotion. Then, a little later, while I was over talking that over with the P, John was meeting with John Dean and he came over to report a whole new chain of events, which was that—

John Dean's Report

Dean's lawyers had met with the U.S. Attorneys and come up with a whole new insight into the process of the case at the grand jury. According to this theory, they have the case totally made on Magruder and almost totally on Mitchell and they have no doubt that they will complete it, and they intend to bring indictments on both of them about May 15.

The indication from them is that they have nothing on anyone in the White House, which, of course, there's no way that they could have, and that they have no intention of trying to develop anything in that direction. They are interested in the post-June area and will be trying to develop the material in that as they go along, and they apparently feel they have some pretty good leads into that.

Jeb Magruder's Report

In the process, I had Larry check with Magruder, and he came back with an extremely interesting telephone conversation which fortunately he taped, in which Magruder denied meeting with the reporters, denied having talked with Mitchell yet, but then spelled out his position, which is the recognition that he's had it and the decision to tell the story, or, at least, probably to. He hasn't made the final decision, but if he talks at all, he will tell the true story, which will be rough for Mitchell, but it will, of course, clear the White House, specifically me. As would the current grand jury development.

In a follow-up conversation, Jeb admitted to Larry that he had a conversation with a reporter, but he had covered the same old ground, denying anything and telling the standard story, which doesn't jibe with Colson's information.

Colson originally, though, told E he had a tape recording of this interview, but when I called him to say I'd like to hear the tape, he said he didn't have a tape, he had a transcript, so I said he should bring the transcript over and we'd review it, and he said, well, he didn't actually have the transcript, but someone else did, so I asked him if he'd get it, and he backed off on that and said he'd try but wasn't sure he could. Which sort of shoots some holes into his story.

The thing was boiling along in that direction, with the Magruder tape being the best thing we've gotten yet on clearing things up at our end, although he does say he will, to a degree, implicate Dean, and to a minor degree, Strachan, and, of course, to a major degree, Mitchell. While we were working on that, E got a call from Colson, who said that he and his lawyer partner, Shapiro, needed to come over immediately and see John. They came over and reported that they've learned that Hunt is going to tell the whole story to the grand jury on Monday at 2:00, which set in a new chain of events, at least on the thinking side, as to whether we can get out in front of them, whether there's a way to bring the whole thing to a focus now, have Mitchell step forward and clean the whole thing up, or have Magruder do his pitch early and get things moving in that way. They apparently also—that's Colson and his partner—have some information about the results of the Vesco grand jury, which is also probably going to indict Mitchell, as is a grand jury in Washington that's hooking into some contractor who supposedly gave money to Mitchell. That is involved in some way in the VP matter that he raised with me the other day.

So right now we're in the midst of pursuing a whole range of alternatives. E and I met with Dean for quite a while this afternoon to try to run out some of the possibilities and figure whether there's any way we actually can bring the thing to a head this weekend. Ehrlichman's main goal in it seems to be to try to get the thing on the record as having come from the White House, so the P breaks the case and cleans the thing up.

My view is that it's better to let it run through the grand jury, get the case broken, and then the P can say that this shows, as it certainly does, that he was following the right course right from the beginning of letting the legal process run in the proper way, so that it brings the guilty people to account and protects the innocent people, which all of these hearings and innuendoes have not done. I strongly feel that's the best route for us, but we'll get back at it tomorrow and see what we can develop.

Henry Kissinger's Viewpoint

Henry made the interesting comment that if the P does let me down, or does let the situation develop to the point where I have to get out, he too will leave because he would refuse to serve in a White House that would permit such a thing to happen. I think he really feels that his own position would be untenable without me here, and also that the same chain of events that would permit that to happen could also get him, and that he'd be better off to get out ahead of time. Besides that, I think he has some desire to get out anyway, and would use this as a means to do so. In any event I don't think the P has that in mind, because his conclusion generally comes out that they've got to keep me covered.

In any event, I don't see how there's any way that they can gain anything by dropping me anyway, because the case simply does not hold, especially now, of course, but I mean even before the developments of today. Today's developments pretty well lock the thing on Magruder and Mitchell, with a few others possibly falling with them. The P now is very concerned, as would be expected, about Mitchell, and Jeb, but especially Mitchell and is adamant that we are not to be the ones to bring him down, which, of course, we won't be, since the case is 90 percent made already. As everybody's been saying, we come closer and closer to the moment of truth, and this finally may well be it. We'll determine tomorrow morning what immediate steps to take, and there's a strong feeling that now is the time to take them.

Saturday, April 14, 1973

The P agreed last night that he'd let E and me work out alternatives. Henry reported to him about 11:00 or 11:30 this morning, but he called us over at 9:00. He kept us there for two and a half hours, reviewing his notes on alternatives and so on. The point he was concerned about was the question of the P's involvement, whether anything had developed on that, and he said that E had told him that Colson argues that the P should persuade Liddy to talk, so that the P will appear to crack the case. Based on doing that, this weekend, prior to Hunt coming out on Monday or going to the grand jury on Monday, the P felt we need to put all the pieces together, such as the question of Magruder going to the press and all the other stories we've got, as to whether they've really worked out. E then said that he had stayed up a good part of the night writing out what would be his report to the P on his overall findings, and he wanted to review that with the P. The P obviously didn't particularly want to hear it, although he listened to several points on it. His interest was reviewing the checklist that he had prepared. The Magruder question to the press was one item, the question of clemency to Hunt and whether that had actually been promised, he is concerned about. The point that the P is trying to determine with E and me is, who should talk to Mitchell to tell him the jig is up, and that the only way for this to be a plus is for you to go in and volunteer a statement. Ken Rush, Bill Rogers, Haldeman, the P, Elliot Richardson, Kleindienst, Rebozo and then got to Ehrlichman. It was agreed that really Ehrlichman was probably the only one that could do it. On his checklist he also had the point that Rogers must be told now that it's essential that he delay his departure until the whole Watergate thing is over; that we can't have him leaving in the middle of it. During all this, the P kept interrupting, wouldn't let us spin out any line at all. He had all these notes with his questions, especially regarding Hunt and Colson that he kept coming back to, and insisted that we work with those.

We did zero in then on the need to talk to Mitchell, and I suggested that I ought to call him so as to set Ehrlichman up right and that Ehrlichman should talk with him. So I went out, called Mitchell, told him that we had been reviewing things with the P and the P felt that it was important that he come down immediately, if possible, to meet with Ehrlichman and review where we presently stand. Mitchell immediately said he would do so and that was at, I believe, 11:00. He arrived by around 1:30.

We went over some other items, and the P agreed that E should also call Magruder in and review things with him. The point of E's review with each of them would be to say that he had been conducting an investigation of the entire situation for the P for the last couple of weeks and that it had come to his attention that it was possible that some people were laboring under the assumption that their not testifying was in some way a service to the P, and that the P wanted them to know they should not restrict themselves out of that option. If they wish to say anything or take any action, they should not refrain from doing so because of any concern that it would be harmful to the P. The point here being to try to get the basic point to Mitchell that the time has come for him to speak up.

I had trouble reaching Jeb, and when I finally did get him, he said he had made his decision late last night to tell everything and that he was going ahead with that. Then he sort of spelled out to me that he concluded now that there was no hope for him. There were witnesses on top of witnesses and there was nothing he could do now but tell the truth, and hope that would lighten his punishment. I told him the same pitch we gave Mitchell, that E wanted to talk with him and review the P's thing. He said fine and he would come over at 4:00 P.M. and do that. E felt that when I reported to him that Jeb had already made his decision that he didn't need to see Jeb, but in talking with the P a little later to report on the Mitchell meeting, it was agreed that E should see Jeb so that we'd be on the record.

It was further agreed that E should talk with the Attorney General following these meetings and turn over what information he had gained to him, so that the P would be clear on having cooperated fully with whatever information he had.

E had his meeting with Mitchell, which lasted about an hour, and the upshot of it was that Mitchell says he feels completely clear in his own heart and in his own mind, that he has no guilt and has no intention of stepping forward. That he has his reputation and position to protect and he's going to have to defend that in every possible way and will do so. E apparently lobbed in a number of sort of veiled allusions to Mitchell on things that might come up, problems we might have and all if people started talking and totally stonewalled any questions of his own involvement.

The next development was E's meeting with Magruder, at which Magruder told him he not only had made his decision but had carried out his act and that he and his attorneys had met with the U.S. Attorney and had given them the full story. Jeb's attorneys were with him when he met with John and they said they'd be happy to give E the same story—the same full report—that they gave the U.S. Attorney. They proceeded to do so, spelling out the step-by-step development of Watergate and related matters and follow-up.

It almost totally and precisely confirmed what E had written down last night in terms of how, based on the hearsay he picked up, he saw the thing as having unfolded and very totally and clearly implicates Mitchell as part of the planning, approval, review and so on of the Watergate, which is directly contrary to Mitchell assertions, and will give Mitchell a serious problem when they call him in, which now they will have to do, of course.

Jeb also implicates John Dean in the earlier planning meetings, which is no problem because Dean intended to do that himself, but he also ties Dean into the ongoing stuff and very heavily into the activity postdiscovery, post-June. He ties Strachan in fairly heavily on knowledge, saying he had a copy of the budget for the final and approved activity and that since he had no objection from me assumed it was approved over here. He has no reason to believe that I had seen the budget, which I didn't, and he apparently completely clears me of any involvement. But it creates a problem, indirectly, by his involvement of Strachan.

E reviewed the whole story with me. Then we went over and reviewed it with the P, and the general feeling is that pretty well settles things.

The P called me at home late tonight after the *(White House*

Correspondents') dinner to talk through it. He felt it had gone pretty well. Laughed about the quote he had used from David Lawrence because he said he never told me that, but it's the kind of thing he might have said anyway, the only tougher job than that of the P's waging war was that of the P's waging peace. Then he sort of reviewed our situation, made the point that when you think about it, the hopes for peace in the world really depend on the office of the P, and we can't be compromised in carrying out that office by lack of confidence in the P arising out of Watergate, and that really overrides the consideration of any individual or any other problems.

Sunday, April 15, 1973

I talked to the P at 3:30 this afternoon on the phone. He said that Kleindienst and Petersen had met with him. That Kleindienst feels it's going to take four or five years for Mitchell to run the full legal course on trials and so forth. He still feels we should have a special prosecutor and the P also has come to that conclusion. Not for this case, but to look at the indictments and review them to be sure that we cover all the people. Even *(Deputy Attorney General U.S. Justice Department Joseph)* Sneed is compromised on this. So we'd have to use someone like Wright from Texas. He referred to telling E about Magruder, that two weeks ago Magruder tried to get Strachan to concoct a story and he feels that Magruder's defense is that he was under pressure from higher-ups. The problem is that Magruder doesn't know the truth. He feels Rogers may have a point. That if we get a big fish, that takes a lot of the fire out of the case. Says the idea that the P has to go and make a new Checkers speech, which he feels he won't do. He feels the idea of a special prosecutor does help get someone in between the P and the case. He told me to talk to E, because he thinks that Rogers thing makes sense. Then he said also they told him that, on E, there was some connection on the conversation regarding the contents of Hunt's safe, and on Haldeman, there was some connection with the $350,000 and that those were the only leads they had to us. Kleindienst recommends that E and Haldeman take a leave of absence on this. The P said you ought to come up with a better recommendation.

At about 7:00 the White House switchboard called and said the P wanted E and me to meet him in the EOB office at

7:30. I got to the White House at 7:30. The P wasn't back from dinner and boat ride he had taken with Bebe. At 7:45 he arrived at the EOB, and E and I went over, and P was very cheery about what a beautiful day it was and all, and then sat down and said, well, he had his second talk with Kleindienst and Petersen, and that Dean had been in an all-day meeting with the U.S. Attorney and that Petersen will report to the P tomorrow at noon on the full details of that. But that the P will call him while we're there to get an updating on anything new he's got this evening. He's now ordered Kleindienst out of the entire operation and is dealing directly with Petersen. Instructed Petersen that he is to report directly to the P.

Henry Petersen's Report

He says that Petersen says now that the combination of Dean's and Magruder's testimony means that E and Haldeman will have to be called to the grand jury.

They told Dean that they'd do the best they can for him, offer them their good offices if he cooperated. The P's not sure what that means. He was obviously very awkward in getting into all this and is hedging around, not knowing quite how to get to the point. He said Dean talked to the U.S. Attorney all afternoon in Maryland and they want him to testify, to corroborate the Magruder thing. The plan now is to get Magruder to plead tomorrow and then immediately put out a statement that involves himself and others, certainly Mitchell. They're moving fast to avoid being forced into this by Ervin. They want to be sure they get the credit, rather than appearing that the Ervin stuff forced them into taking action. The plan is to take Magruder in the morning and Strachan in the afternoon, and they're going to be very rough on Strachan, going for corroboration and trying to tie in bigger fish.

Petersen thinks Dean lied to him and to us. He says Dean hits E regarding the line that they should deep-six the material in Hunt's safe and get Hunt out of the country and about the documents that Gray has. On Haldeman, there's a conflict between Magruder and Strachan involving three or four things: the $350,000, the document furnished to Strachan that I supposedly approved which was the budget for the bugging, and the point that I had papers indicating Liddy was in the eavesdropping business. This is totally different than what Magruder told E he had said, so we have an interesting point there.

Kleindienst says that Liddy has not talked, that they don't have anything on Colson. The problem is what will LaRue say that he got the $350,000 for, that there is a problem there, they feel. The P was troubled, because they said they don't want Haldeman and E until they hear the others. He said to them, if they have anything on Haldeman and E they should call them immediately and clear it up. Petersen said no, he didn't want to do that until he heard all the others and got the case built. He feels Petersen is crusading on this. They'll give Strachan a very hard time. One point they want to hit him on is that logs of the bugging were given to Strachan, they claim. Magruder says he won't lie for E, that he might lie for the P.

Some discrepancy arose on the question that on June 17, after a meeting in Washington, Kleindienst and Dean were supposed to come out and report to the P and then there was a call saying that only Dean was to come, which apparently bothered Kleindienst. The question is where we were June 17. I thought we were in Florida, but the P has it as San Clemente. Petersen said to the P, Dean did not serve us well.

Now Petersen's set up to report only to the P, not to Kleindienst. They say the Magruder deal may break tomorrow. Mitchell will be accused and there will probably be a tangential reference to Haldeman. Dean makes a prima facie case against both Haldeman and Ehrlichman on obstruction of justice. The P will tell Dean he owes it to him to come into the P and tell him what he's doing.

The P thinks Magruder is lying to reduce his penalty. He has a lot of loose stuff, like the question of Gray's documents from home. E says LaRue told Moore today that he's going to testify and that he's inclined to open up completely, and the P came back to the deep-six and Hunt leaving the country question again, saying that troubled him.

At 8:15 the P called Petersen and he said he had nothing further. He said Liddy wants a signal to come clean, that Liddy talked to Mitchell today and is waiting for a signal from Mitchell, but Petersen says the P should give Liddy some sign, and Liddy apparently told Mitchell he would tell everything if he got a signal from Mitchell, and now Petersen says the signal from the P will do it.

The P hung up on that and was trying to figure out what to

do, when I got a call from Larry and he said that Dean had called him to say that he wanted to deliver a message through me to the P, that he did not want to talk with me, and his message was number one, I hope you understand that the actions that I'm taking are motivated totally out of loyalty to you (Haldeman) and the P, and if that's not clear now it will become clear. Second—Ehrlichman requested to meet tonight, but I feel it is inappropriate at this time. Third—I'm ready and willing to meet with the P at any time to discuss these matters. Fourth—the P should take his counsel from Henry Petersen, who I assure you does not want the Presidency hurt.

Right after that, the P called Petersen back and said to tell Liddy that the P wants everybody to tell everything they know and he told him to do it tonight. The P then decided he should get Dean in to talk to him and so had me call the operator and tell Dean to be in his office at 9:00. We discussed it somewhat further and at 9:00 Ehrlichman and I left the office and went over to E's office. At 9:20, Dean arrived at the P's office.

In the meantime, E and I talked to Ziegler to discuss the PR plan. Ron makes the point that with the information now, the P must relieve Dean of his Watergate assignment, at least. The P should receive assurances from any other staff that have been implicated that what we've told them is correct and then we'll have an opportunity to cover it with the grand jury. The P should announce a special prosecutor who is not an Administration man. On Magruder, the information he has says that he has to ask Magruder to resign.

John Dean's Report

At 10:15 the P called us back over to the EOB and had finished with his meeting with Dean and he was obviously quite disturbed, or seemed to be, or he was probably also tired. He said Dean will either testify or be subpoenaed, he's not sure which. He's told his lawyers and apparently he told the U.S. Attorney that none of us at the White House, especially Haldeman and Ehrlichman, had any knowledge of the bugging, but on obstruction he feels both Haldeman and E are involved. Whether or not they intended to obstruct and whether or not they knew what they were doing, they have conspiracy by circumstance.

He doesn't think that Kalmbach knew the reason for the

money he was raising. Dean says the $40,000 that went over first out of the $350,000 was preelection, which doesn't check with Strachan. LaRue says there was no question what it was for, but Dean knew and that Mitchell knew. The question is whether any of us knew and I still argue that we knew it was for defendants, but not in any sense for obstruction of justice.

Dean made the point that he had briefed Ehrlichman and me every inch of the way. On Petersen, he said that was just a daily report on the grand jury and there was nothing improper. (We've made the point to the P that Petersen was supplying Dean with all kinds of information out of the grand jury and Dean's trying to put a cover-up on that.) Regarding clemency he says there was a meeting with Colson, Ehrlichman, and Dean, and E at that meeting said to make no commitments for clemency. On the contents of Hunt's safe, Colson was the one who was worried. The bogus wire—there was apparently a bogus wire implicating Kennedy in Vietnam—and so on. Dean thinks Gray may have destroyed it. Hunt told Colson to get the stuff out of the safe. Dean believes that he's the most vulnerable on obstruction, and that Haldeman and Ehrlichman are less vulnerable, and Dean thinks he has a good chance to beat any rap on it, but in the meantime the evidence is so overwhelming that it will probably require Haldeman and Ehrlichman to take leaves. Dean had something on the bug on Kraft and other newsmen that he lobbed in, but doesn't intend to use it.

At 10:45, Ehrlichman got Gray at home about the envelope. Gray said that he was going to say he knew nothing about it and he told E he had destroyed it. At 11:05 John called him back and said he's got to tell the truth. He should state the facts and not get crosswise on this. Gray says he didn't know where the papers came from, he didn't open the envelope, he simply destroyed it, but that Dean had told him they were politically sensitive papers—although not what the source of them was.

Editor's Note: It was a stunning admission. Pat Gray, as Acting Director of the FBI, had destroyed potential evidence in a criminal case.

With this, the evening pretty well came to an end. The P made a semivaliant attempt to buck us up and then to say that we're going to beat this and that it's an unfair thing, that we're being had, and that we just have to deal with it as we go along.

The P called about 12:30, after I got home. He said that he had talked to Petersen again tonight after we left, to report on his meeting with Dean, and they talked about the question of legal obstruction of justice, and Petersen admitted it's a very tough case to prove; that it's not so much the legal case as it is the appearances and the moral situation. He makes the point that Ehrlichman and Haldeman are only involved, not as actors but just exposed to it, and that that's the problem that they have. He says this is the point where you need a lawyer and you should go ahead and talk to Rogers. The P said maybe you ought to get Edward Bennett Williams, but then he said no, as long as there's no indictment, there's no point in doing that, and I feel sure there won't be an indictment. The problem dealing with a Williams will come afterward. I didn't like that idea, because of the publicity it would create. He says he's really confounded by Mitchell, who must be in a dream world on this, but when you boil it down, he's taking the only route he can if he doesn't accept taking the rap and going to jail. The P said he had been sitting there making some notes and thinking about the whole thing. He obviously wanted to talk on and on about it, but I didn't encourage that. He said Petersen had indicated they would not get to Ehrlichman and me until next week. They won't take us this week, because they want to build all the rest of the case. So the P basically is in a position of just trying to sort it all out and having trouble in doing so.

Monday, April 16, 1973

Another all-Watergate day, as they generally tend to be now. The P had me in at 9:30 and asked that Ehrlichman and I spend some time today putting down what we think our vulnerabilities are and a game plan for dealing with them. He then had Ehrlichman come in, too, and told him he's getting Dean in to have him sign the letters. They agreed he should sign both the resignation and the leave of absence letter. Then he said again he wanted Ehrlichman and me to put down our cases at the worst, and he says he'll make no decisions until he's had his responses.

Also he wanted a scenario on his role, what he did as he found out—Dean, the Camp David, the Ehrlichman report, and so on. Had a PR plan as to how we disclose the P plans. He also told Ehrlichman to talk to Moore and have him talk to

Gray and Fielding about the Hunt safe problem. We went out because he had to meet with John Dean, and then he brought us in after the Dean meeting, and he said he had asked for his resignation, but Dean then said, well, what about Haldeman and Ehrlichman. The P said I have their resignations in hand always and that's no problem, and then Dean asked to have the letters to redraft them, so that they wouldn't do him any harm in his hearing. His lawyers think that his criminal liability is very limited, because it's very hard to prove because he's just a conduit. They say it's the same with Haldeman and Ehrlichman, because it's tangential and that Justice may very well come out with no White House indictments at all.

He says Colson's involved in three areas. The P couldn't remember what they were, Bittman and Hunt and something else; and the P says the PR was the real concern, not the legal thing. Said he'd like to meet with Rogers this afternoon at 4:00. Wanted me to meet with him first and brief him, and that he would see Garment after that. Garment is of the opinion that the P has to make a massive move and cut the whole thing out in one blow, which means getting rid of Ehrlichman, me, and Dean, and anybody else that may be at all involved. That kind of thinking sort of rambled on through the day.

The Ervin Committee decided today to hold off in starting their hearings until May 15. So we've got some time there, and by then Justice will probably have something out. It turns out, however, the P met with Petersen, and he says that they're having a problem with Dean and Magruder because their attorneys in both cases are holding out for complete immunity, which the prosecutors aren't, at least now, going to grant. Dean's lawyers apparently have threatened that they're going to pull the case in and take on everybody, right on up to and including the P, if he isn't given immunity. So everybody is playing a pretty tough game at this point, and it could get pretty bloody in the process. Magruder, too, is holding out for complete immunity, so they couldn't make the deal with him and get him on his guilty plea with a big public announcement today. They may not be able to work that deal out either. They hauled Gordon in and really roughed him up apparently. Gave him all kinds of threats about his family and disbarment and that sort of thing—then told him to go away and get a lawyer and come back when he was ready to get down to business.

So they got him a little shook. Ehrlichman and I are trying to locate a lawyer, and other than that no major developments.

Tuesday, April 17, 1973

Today was another major Watergate day. This time super-major. The P called me in at 9:45 and said that he wanted to meet with Ehrlichman, Rogers, and me.

He made the point that he agreed we'd probably have to move today. He said you and John should be thinking in terms, not just of the Presidency and all that crap, which I know you think about all the time; but also think in terms of yourselves and the question of this dragging out bit by bit and whether it's not better to cut it off. He said the incentive with the U.S. Attorney and everybody else in this case is to nail the highest people they can get. The prosecution is very clever, that this had to come out and it's just as well that it's coming this way.

Dean is the one who surprises and to some extent disappoints him. I found the latter rather shocking, considering the fact that Dean has turned total traitor, and he shouldn't be surprised and disappointed. He should be shocked and furious. Then in discussing this during the morning with Ziegler, I spun out a theory that I think has proven to be correct. Which is that the P's concerned about additional knowledge Dean has and threats that Dean is making to reveal that, or that perhaps Dean has already revealed it to Petersen, and the two of them are working together in threatening in order to try and nail us.

These suspicions were confirmed when Ehrlichman and I met with the P at 12:30, and Ehrlichman reported on his meeting with Colson, who says Dean must be dealt with summarily. The key is that Dean must not get immunity, and the P, Colson feels, has total control over that. Colson told Ehrlichman he must see the P to pass this thinking on to him. The P said he didn't want Colson to come in and didn't want to see him, and that John should tell him that the P has his message and there's no need for him to come in to cover it. Then the P said the problem here in dealing with that is we have to look at what Dean has. He has threats on other things in government. If he gets immunity, he will pay the lowest price he can. In other words, if they give him immunity, he will give them the least amount of information he can and still get the immunity. That's what he tells the P obviously, but the key to that is that it has to reach all of us. That is, Ehrlichman and me, as well as Dean. The P talked to Dean about his resignation, and Dean made the point that Haldeman and Ehrlichman would have to resign if he was going to.

Petersen told the P that his view is that it's all going to come out. So Haldeman and Ehrlichman should resign, not because there's any legal exposure, but because they'll be eaten alive. So they should get a leave now and get away from the White House. The P says there will be a big hassle and that's on who is lying. Also the problem of what Dean said to the P regarding the need for the $120,000, and the problem continuing down the road on that apparent blackmail route which would, in Dean's estimate, cost a million dollars.

The P discussed that conversation, although I reminded him that I was in it, which I think startled him some. He says we have to figure that Dean could put out that story to someone else. For example, the press. He then said to John and me, you are the two most valuable members of my staff and that's why they're trying to reach you. You're also the two most loyal and the two most honest. I don't want a public clamor, as there was with Sherman Adams, where the ultimate result is that he has to be asked to leave. So we have to figure what kind of blackmail Dean has.

Dean apparently rewrote his resignation the P gave him yesterday on the basis that if Haldeman and Ehrlichman resign, I will. The P said I think I'm trapped, because I told Dean that Haldeman and Ehrlichman are willing to go if that's needed. Also Dean has an ally in the U.S. Attorney and the Assistant Attorney General. He then said, and I'm quoting, "The problem I've got is that I think maybe I've trapped myself." The P says he told Petersen that letting Dean off is an incentive to him to lie. Petersen said that's what you do, Mr. P, in criminal cases. He said that they have to have corroborating testimony on the value of Dean's evidence. And that's why he's calling Strachan, Colson, Kalmbach and so on.

The point they make is that the White House staff kept Dean's highly sensitive information from the P. That's another lie. They say that Strachan had reports that were clearly identified as wire tap material and also that he had plans regarding the wire taps.

Then we got back to the problem of Hunt's materials and reworked that ground. The P said in both Colson and Dean, I think he meant Magruder and Dean, we have clever liars that we're dealing with. He then said, in going back and agonizing over this, that there's no sense in aggravating Dean. This was in the question of suspending or canning him. He'll do anything to save his own ass.

Then we get into the question of the date of Hunt's threat and when the Dean-Haldeman meeting with the P was, where that came up. And the P says how do I handle the problem of the Assistant Attorney General telling me that he has charges against Haldeman and Ehrlichman and says that they're of such nature that he must put them on leave? So why doesn't he do it? The answer is that he can say, when you tell me you're going to file charges or indict them, then I'll suspend them. Until then, I have no basis for it. He said the real problem is what if we end up in the gray area, with no charges filed, just implications, such as knowledge in advance and so on. Then what action do we take? The P raised the question of why can't we just leave Dean in his office, but tell everybody not to have any further dealings with him.

Ehrlichman urged the special prosecutor to take over from Petersen and made his case again on what a bad guy Petersen was, and the need for the P to get special counsel, but the P didn't buy it, I don't think.

Gordon Strachan's Report

Later I got a report from Strachan. He had a conference with Silbert and Glanzer and his lawyer and they convinced him that they have enough on Dean on all kinds of things that they can indict him on perjury on two counts. One, on the discrepancy on the amount of cash. The $350,000 vs. $328,000, and second his knowledge of Liddy's activities and spying and so on. The question then is whether he continues his present lines and gets indicted or takes the Fifth and goes to jail. This is the way the message came through, which doesn't make sense. He said they won't let him correct his statement regarding the $350,000 and that they have information regarding another expenditure from the fund which Strachan doesn't know about. He said to check the seven points he covered with Ehrlichman, but that's where the things are vulnerable, and the deal they are trying to make with him is that if he goes through all those points he covered with Ehrlichman Sunday, the seven items, and everything else he knows, including some of which they say they already have, so this would just be to corroborate, then he'll have a chance of getting out, which means he'll become a witness and not a defendant. But they do not guarantee immunity. He says obviously they're trying to make a deal with him and they're not really offering him very much. The problem is that Strachan bared his soul to Dean, and so now it's all coming back to haunt him.

At 4:00, after the P had a long meeting with Petersen, he called Ehrlichman and me back in and said he went the rounds with Petersen again. That Petersen agrees on Dean, that he ought to be dismissed and has argued that point with the U.S. Attorneys. But they say that they suppose that's the only way, that Dean's the only way to get at Ehrlichman and Haldeman, and they can't jeopardize that.

The new elements are, first, the P told him immunity was out. In other words, he would not tolerate immunity for Dean, and he told him he had discussed this with Bill Rogers, who said it was totally wrong to give Dean immunity. Second, regarding the leaks by Petersen from the grand jury, he said Mitchell was aware that Dean had leaked this material and so on. Petersen said that it didn't get very far and was no problem. Third, Petersen's talked to Gray, and Gray says he destroyed the material and that he's going to have to bring that out. Gray was told there was no Watergate material, just political, but there's still the problem of destruction of evidence on Gray's part.

The P says the situation on Ehrlichman and Haldeman finally comes out. First, they don't have the Magruder deal, but they will give the P twelve hours notice when they make it. They will say that they're hauling him into court to plead guilty, and then put out a statement which would be both as broad and as narrow as possible. They'll say he's named certain people, and that other people are nonindicted co-conspirators that will be named as a group. This will include Dean, but Petersen says it will not include Ehrlichman and Haldeman if they take a leave. The P said, are you saying that if Haldeman and Ehrlichman take a leave you won't prosecute them? He said no, it just means they aren't on the list. They'll still appear at the grand jury and I'll have to make their case there.

Petersen says it will appear bad if Haldeman and Ehrlichman are left off the list and were not suspended prior to that, and that Sirica will hit them on that, and it will appear that the Justice Department is covering for the two top White House people. The P said he was concerned about our vulnerability, he doesn't think they can make a case against us. Petersen's really saying that we'll be on the list unless we decide to take a leave. Dean's lawyers said that Dean will try this Administration if they don't give him immunity. In other words, he's going to nail the P, supposedly.

Ehrlichman and I then took a break for an hour to meet with our new attorney, Mr. Wilson. This was a very satisfactory meeting just to give him the preliminaries. I think he's going to work out very well. We regrouped at 6:00 in the EOB with Rogers and the P, and went back over the point that Kleindienst and Petersen are pushing the P that Ehrlichman and Haldeman should resign. But the conclusion is that we should not go on a leave or resign or anything at this point until there's some reason for it in terms of action. Rogers then left.

The P says we were right in not following Garment's course of dumping you guys. It would have made the prosecution case for Dean's immunity, and that we don't want. Regarding Dean, I'll either make a deal or not, and when it's done he has to be dismissed. The P raised the question of whether he should see Dean again and thought he should not.

He said we should consider libel suits; especially I should, that I should get the most vicious libel lawyer in the country and sue right down the line, including Weicker, and depose him fast. The P was obviously extremely awkward and upset during this conversation. He made the point that I'm not emotional, as you know, and I won't be now, but you guys have been through hell and we've got to fight this rap all the way. He said there's a real problem in the area that you may beat the rap, but may not be able to come back to government. If that's the case, I want the two of you to take over the foundation and get that set up if you have to leave. Then we said we appreciated that thought. Ehrlichman said if he gets indicted, whether or not he's convicted, he feels he's through as far as any career is concerned, as well as in government and that he'd be through as a lawyer. The P said, well, you can be my partner. John said, yes, and then we can try traffic cases out in San Clemente.

He talked over ideas for a new counsel to the P and some ideas on Attorney General, referring to Kleindienst as a bowl of jelly. The P also told us that he had available some contributed gift funds that could be made available to us for legal fees. This would be via Bebe and could be up to a maximum of $250,000. He does not want us to have to take care of our own fees.

He then looked at me and said, if all this takes place, how do I replace Haldeman? Then I suggested that he shouldn't try to, that he would just have to set up a new structure and work without him. Replacement for me would just work in a different way. Which I honestly believe he can do. My position at this point is that we've just got to ride this out. Take whatever comes, however it comes, and handle it as best we can at the time. It's very hard to tell what that'll be, but there's every reason to believe that at some point the right result will develop and that we can have confidence in that. In the meantime, we have to contend with whatever comes along.

The P called me at midnight after the Italian dinner and said, well, I just wanted to say keep the faith. I kind of laughed and said, how was the dinner. He said it was fine, then he said, as a matter of fact, it was one of the worst I've ever had, because of what's on my mind. He said John and you and I should meet again tomorrow morning to go over what's coming, look at the names that are involved and be prepared for it. There's a question of whether someone should talk to Dean. Maybe the P should. Obviously, Dean's trying to save himself, and the P thinks the U.S. Attorney will give him immunity. If he tells the truth, that doesn't bother him. If it's an incentive to lie, that's another problem. We have to get some kind of line regarding the defendants on their fees and support, because we don't make our case clearly enough on that. He says we should think over and talk with Moore about the one thing that troubles him about Dean when he came in with the information from Bittman, because the argument is that the P should have turned it over to the U.S. Attorney. Which is a real problem that we should give hard thought to. Of course, it isn't really a problem. He says if Dean has immunity, he'll go with that.

The problem is the P talked freely with him on the blackmail point and all that because he was trying to draw him out. He then said he wished there were a way to separate Ehrlichman out, because the vulnerability of the lawyer in this kind of thing is enormous. He said let's see now, they've got clear cases apparently on LaRue, Mitchell, Mardian and Magruder, O'Brien and Parkinson. It's important to know what Ehrlichman's investigation was that triggered it. We have to figure how we can save what there is left of the Presidency. The White House is involved apart from Ehrlichman and Haldeman. There would be Strachan, possibly Colson and Fielding. Then he asked, it doesn't touch Higby, does it? They haven't subpoenaed him, have they? I said no. Said the real tragedy is Mitchell, why doesn't he step up? He's going to get it without any question. We don't think he can stall it out. He should assume the responsibility, which is, of course, what we said all along.

Wednesday, April 18, 1973

The P had me in at 8:00 this morning. Said that if this thing goes the way it might, and I have to leave, he wants me to take all the office material from his—ah—machinery there and hold it for the library.

Reviewed some of the items; wants to figure out when the meeting was with Dean. Make the point that the P had no knowledge until he got into this, which is, of course, true, but we have to be objective on Dean, don't get carried away with our attitude on him. At that point he had Ziegler in to discuss Dean's threat to Ziegler. Ziegler should tell Dean that no one's hitting him. The P is obviously very concerned about how he handles Dean. Not to appear to be hitting him. Dean said to Ziegler, I can't take this rap. We'll have to call in some friendly reporters and so on. Wanted Ehrlichman to fill the P on the circumstances regarding putting him on the case. Ziegler kept coming back to the point, you don't need to worry about Dean because he's completely lost his credibility. Which was missing the P's point. He doesn't want Ron to hit Dean on his loss of credibility or confidence in him. The P told Ziegler to say today to Dean that the P said specifically no one is to be thrown off on the basis of hearsay. We're not throwing anyone to the wolves. The "full of holes" line in the paper regarding the Dean report did not come from the White House. We're not going to characterize anything from here. And he sent Ziegler out to call Dean, and made the point that where Dean has the gun to our head is on the pre-Watergate stuff on national security, and on the Hunt blackmail report, which is also national security.

Ehrlichman and I have to figure out how to handle the Dean thing. Ziegler came back in, said Dean said the P is out front in this. Ziegler reassured him there was no focus on any individual and he seemed to be in pretty good shape. Dean said he understood, but you have to keep in mind the Dean report also involved the *(March)* 21st discussion with the P. The P said, don't leave the impression the Dean report was false. Told Ron that. And Dean said, I understand the position you're in. The important thing is we now have the P out in front on this. The P wants to get Dean in with Ziegler, but I think we talked him out of that.

Then at noon we talked about what Ron should say and decided that he should take the position of no comment now, because he's been advised by the legal authorities that any comment on this case could prejudice the prosecution or the rights of defendants. Therefore he will make no further comment, period.

The P had Ehrlichman and me come up to Camp David with him for dinner and to spend the night tonight. Talked about it in general terms on the way up, and while we were waiting for dinner, Ziegler called. Said that Henry Petersen had called him to say Carl Bernstein from the *Post* had called him and talked to Burke, his assistant, and told him to tell Petersen that they have the whole story. The Magruder aspects and the O'Brien/Bittman aspects, they said. And Petersen thinks this refers to the McCord statement and on the thing that Hunt's lawyer presented demands to the White House, which were met to keep Hunt's silence. Petersen said to Ziegler that he has held this up, the fact they have it, for ten days now trying to pursue it through the process of the grand jury. Ziegler asked him what it meant by the O'Brien aspects, what names were involved, and Petersen said we didn't ask the *Post,* because we didn't want to have to respond. But he would assume it would be Mitchell, LaRue, Dean, and principal White House people. Ziegler said what principal White House people, and Petersen said it pains me to refer to it and didn't give him the names. Petersen told him to let the P know, and he said he'll know what we're talking about. Ziegler then also talked to Dick Burke on a callback and he said Petersen was talking to Bernstein again at that time. Ziegler told him to call back.

Petersen called him back, said that Bernstein said he had

information from three sources that he was going to run tomorrow, naming Mitchell and Dean, with no reference to anyone else. Saying they were involved in large amounts of cash payments to keep the defendants silent. Thus, it's likely that this will involve Mitchell, Dean, O'Brien, Bittman. He doesn't know if they have Haldeman and Ehrlichman. Bernstein was calling various people at the White House also to get comment. Says he's running the story and wants to check it before it's played, so we told Ziegler to talk to him, and he did.

Petersen referred to the fact that O'Brien and Bittman are lawyers and they're terribly distressed. He said we'd hoped to beat the press on this. I went over to Aspen for dinner with the P and reported this to him. He had already had the same report from Petersen, whom he had called to raise Cain with him, on ordering him not to get into the testimony on what Hunt was involved in with national security. Petersen told the P Dean had already told him about the Hunt break-in in California.

Ziegler then called and said they're also going to say that Magruder has been before the U.S. Attorney and will testify at the grand jury tomorrow. That he will directly implicate Mitchell and Dean in the preplanning and directly implicate them in the payments to the defendants after the fact.

Garment talked to Bernstein to see what he could get out, and he says basically the same thing. That Magruder on Saturday over the weekend gave a full statement and so on, and also that an attorney came out to California on April 3 and discussed the whole thing with Ehrlichman, this not in a negative way. This would relate to postpayment activities. Bernstein volunteered that the story will say that the P had no knowledge, that indictments are expected shortly on Dean and Mitchell. Didn't mention the Magruder indictment.

The dinner was rather painful because the P got into the whole problem of whether John and I should go. He said the points to consider are, 1) whether we're nailed in open court by Magruder, which we can't let happen. Or, 2) if we leave, will it buy them off on the indictment. And, 3) by constant nibbling as we stay here, we can be destroyed. We don't want to be destroyed, therefore we have to move. We have to figure out another strategy. Get out and then fight like hell. We have to deal in two dimensions. First, the court, and second, the Ervin Committee. The P will not allow Weicker and Scott to force him to move on us. We should move ahead of them and fight it.

The P keeps saying during this that he hasn't decided. But he went through quite a thing in an emotional way about how Ehrlichman and I would always have the use of Camp David regardless of what happens, for the next three and a half years, and that he wasn't emotional, but he really is and that this was a terribly painful thing and so on and so on. I think it really was, and it is, hard for him, but it's also counterproductive for us. I mean the time going around and around on the same ground with him, when we should be developing our own case for our interest and his. It was clear, though, that his feeling was that there was no real way out, except for us to pull out and fight rather than trying to stay.

Thursday, April 19, 1973

At Camp David. Ehrlichman and I spent the night up here last night with the P after a painful sort of farewell dinner. At least, I think that's what he had in mind. Kissinger called first thing this morning. Said that the P had called him Tuesday night late after the Sinatra dinner and said that he thought Ehrlichman and Haldeman would be destroyed by what is going to happen. And Kissinger said that we should, in his view, pull the wagons around the White House and fight. On Wednesday, the P asked Kissinger again. Henry said that if we were going to be destroyed, that we should be given a way to get out without being implicated. One way I could leave was on the grounds I was implicated. The other is that on the grounds that I didn't know, and this only I should do if we're going to fall eventually anyway. Kissinger believes every effort should be made to keep me, and probably I'll end up stronger. But if I'm going to be destroyed anyway, I must be sure that I get out before the slow erosion starts. The course now would be to pull the wagons around until the hysteria subsides. Haldeman should not be lumped with Magruder and Dean and should not be bled to death. If I stay, I should start asserting command, giving orders. If not, everything is going to go on leaking around the White House. The leaks will stop if they think I'm out or if they think I'm in. You need one or the other.

On the chopper in today, the P talked about the question of our lawyers. Wondered about the question of what kind of immunity Ervin can give Dean. What effect the resignation would have on the prosecution and on the Dean deal. What kind of a bargain can we make. He made the point over and over that the thing we must avoid at any cost is being indicted. Went into the question of the grand jury leak and the legal possibilities there, and our idea of a libel action against Weicker for what he said about me on TV last night.

The P is trying to get Dean nailed down. He makes the point that we relied on Dean for both supervision and advice. That is, he'd say you don't want to know that, because of a deposition of a civil case and so on. Ehrlichman argues that the prosecution of Dean is what we need to destroy his credibility. After we got back from Camp David, he had us in the Oval Office. Made the point that he can't run the White House without a strong person, and that if Ehrlichman can survive, that will solve it. If not, and we both have to leave, then he's going to put Lynn over here to replace me. He feels we should not let the day come when the grand jury comes out and the P has to be forced to move on us. It's getting to the point where we have to bite the bullet. He had thought we should separate the innocent from the guilty, Mitchell, Magruder and so forth. So Haldeman and Ehrlichman should step out and say they want to fight this battle. We must fight all the way with every legal device to avoid prosecution legally. He wants us to think of the PR side in terms of ourselves and the Presidency both.

John and I then pulled out of there to meet with our lawyers and go over the things. They feel strongly we should not leave and, having covered that ground, it was decided it would be a good idea for the P perhaps to meet with the lawyers this evening. Which he decided to do. He spent the afternoon pondering this with other people over at the EOB. Then went out for dinner on the *Sequoia*, alone. Came back and met with our lawyers for about an hour. In the meantime Ziegler called me at home to say that the *Post* has another story for tomorrow. Saying Dean's associates have said that Dean will implicate people above and below himself, and that Haldeman engineered a cover-up to hide the involvement of Presidential aides in the bugging matter, and he goes on with other details of the story. We checked this back and forth, and Ziegler finally checked it with Dean, who said that he suspects who it is who put it out. That he has things scrambled, that he never mentioned Haldeman. That there's some fact and some fiction in the story. Eventually, Dean agreed to have Ziegler say that he denied mentioning Haldeman. And so we're going to try that to see if it'll help any.

The P called me at 9:30. Said he had talked to the lawyers and I told him about the *Post* story. He liked the lawyers and felt that they had been a good meeting. He sounded much more relieved than he has up to now. I told him about the *Post* story and he said, well, we've just got to expect that kind of thing, don't we? He said the lawyers don't buy Garment's idea. That is, Haldeman getting out. He feels now we have to play it day by day. The P warned them about the news stories and said it's going to be tough to ride, but we'll see what we can do. Wilson, the lawyer, called, said he had a good meeting with the P. He's a little concerned about word getting out as to why we have counsel and suggested the line that we simply say we thought we should get the advice of competent counsel.

Friday, April 20, 1973

The P had me in first thing this morning. Read me a note Julie had written, talking about how great he is and the family all stand behind him. We had a quick discussion on Watergate, and the P then had to go into the head and had me come in with him while standing in the hall, and we continued this discussion. Mainly about the need to hunker down following up on last night.

The P had us in at 11:00, said he had talked with Bush. He wants to be helpful but he's a worrywart. He brought up Rietz *(Ken Rietz, member of CRP staff)*. He was involved in the dirty tricks department and has hired a lawyer now, because he's into this thing, so Bush is going to fire him. He says 15 people in the White House, past or present, are involved, according to *Newsweek,* who talked to him. Wants to know what we do with it the way it's burgeoning. He thinks the P has done the right thing, but needs more and he reflects concern.

The P won't ask Petersen about Hunt's testimony. He feels the critical point now is the Presidential posture and the public perception of it. The P pushed Petersen on speeding the grand jury. Doesn't think it will do any good. They still have only arm's length arrangement with Dean. He thinks we should have a talk with Moore about the LaCosta thing. He's Special Counsel to the P and can't reveal conversations.

Dean says no one in the White House is involved. That he's

not trying to obstruct justice. He had no exposure himself and no one in the White House. Did not know anybody was obstructing justice. (Don't know where that comes from. Dean said that somewhere.) Dean told us that Mitchell and LaRue were raising the money, but he had no knowledge of corruption or improper purpose. We had a suspicion, but Dean kept from us any knowledge. (This is Ehrlichman's basic outline, I guess.)

The P then says I wonder where we stand on "Operation Surgery." That is, letting us go. Our lawyers convinced the P it's not the right course. He then says, though, if eventually, why not now. Both legally and in the public gray area. The theory is the White House staff has to accept the responsibility as stewards. We argued we should take one step at a time. First, the legal, then the public decision on stepping down, and then the *New York Times* theory on stewardship.

Ron Ziegler's Report

The P left at noon for Key Biscayne. Ehrlichman and I came up to Camp David. Ziegler called tonight to say that he had painfully thought through the whole thing, and especially after watching the news tonight with Mitchell coming out of the grand jury and stonewalling charges and countercharges. He feels that if I'm dragged in, not on a legal basis but public opinion, and this applies to Ehrlichman also, that if we don't move voluntarily to get out front and make it seem voluntary, they will have a very negative impact on me as a man. Then he doesn't want to see me as he saw Mitchell tonight. The more I'm weakened by dragging it out, the more it will weaken the P. If I take a voluntary leave of absence, that will have a bad impact on the P; but if I'm forced by public opinion to leave later on, that will have a far greater bad impact. So both from the human and P's viewpoint, not only considering legal but also public opinion, he thinks I ought to take the leave.

He can't sense the P's mood and tone, although he had to spend a lot of time with him this afternoon after they got to Key Biscayne and he's had four or five phone calls since. He says he's moving all over the lot. Buchanan wrote him a memo making the point that those who can't maintain their viability, for their own sake and the P's, should be leaving at their own initiative. Ziegler thinks it is inevitable from a PR standpoint, especially with the Dean factor and Mitchell's decision to stonewall. Even if there is no grand jury action, the PR will drag me down and the P along with me. I should consider a voluntary leave with forceful action afterward. Not a resignation in any way. Action on my part so as not to burden the Presidency with charges and so on.

If I'm mentioned at the grand jury, the ballgame's over. So I should take the leave, clean it up, and then come back to work. He also says you've got to consider the P's frame of mind in this. The problem is the timing, and you've got to work it against when you think the grand jury findings will come out. I should say that my name is mentioned and that puts me on the defensive. The tough call is when to do it. I go under a stronger negative if it's after my name is raised, than if I go ahead on the high ground and on the offensive. The critical point is timing. The more I'm drawn in, the weaker I become.

Saturday, April 21, 1973

The P is still in Key Biscayne. Ehrlichman and I are still at Camp David. We spent the day working on our background material for the lawyers and the factual data. Wilson called me to say he was bombarded by reporters. He had stated that he had been retained by the two of us to consult on references to us in the media. He won't say that it's in the Watergate case. Said he had no comment on the question of whether he saw the P Thursday night. Said he was not retained by the government or the P. That he had no other connection with the case. He said the press is concentrating on the exact moment that he was retained. Whether it was before or after the P's speech, and he says it was after. He had said he had met with the prosecutors and they asked him if there's anything in the case that involves us. He said I could say no comment, but I will say that there is nothing that they're involved with that gives me any concern. WTOP called him and said they were recording when he answered the phone. So he said that's the damnedest impertinence I've ever heard of. He said it's really building up on the when and what question.

Sunday, April 22, 1973

The P called this morning from Key Biscayne. Said I didn't want this Easter to go by without reminding you of how much

tougher it was last Easter, and just remember you're doing the
right thing. That's what I used to think when I killed some
innocent children in Hanoi. Then he got into the general Watergate problems. Said the question is whether I can say anything publicly. The one factor on the political side is that the
Senate comes back Wednesday, and there's a question of
whether the senators pass a resolution or something that will
create a problem for us. He thinks it was good for Ziegler to
get Chappy Rose (*a Nixon personal legal consultant*) and Pat
Buchanan down. Thinks Garment shouldn't come because he's
too emotional. Thinks that times have overrun Garment's view,
but he would probably say the same thing this week. Thinks
the Dean thing is very hard to figure. Can't figure out what
his lawyers told him.

Then he reviewed the whole question of what we talked
about before, the detail on the blackmail and all that. Said
Krogh should clearly say that his motive and involvement was
national security. The P says he's aware of all the options and
there's no good choice, but we have to do the best we can.
We should look down the road to the critical question which
Ziegler raises. That is, that we don't want Haldeman or Ehrlichman to be in the position that Mitchell is in, to be named.
The question is whether the P, after all, is looking into the
matter. Now what do Haldeman and the aides do? Wait until
they're named or move ahead? If we take a leave of absence
we must fight, but not within the White House. There'd be no
consideration of resignation, only a leave. And it's obvious
that that's the direction he tends to push in at the moment.
Other than that, we had Easter Sunday with the families at
Camp David. Spent a lot of time working on the background
material for the lawyers. Families went down this evening and
Ehrlichman and I went back through my chronological files
while he pulled out notes to be typed up.

Monday, April 23, 1973

Ehrlichman and I stayed at Camp David all day today. Worked
on the background material for the lawyers and some discussion of strategy regarding leave of absence and so forth. Came
down for dinner at home. Ziegler called me early this evening
and was obviously in a very emotional state and covered things
as follows:

Ron Ziegler's Report

He said well, I have to say that his mind is made up, as far as I can see. It was made up at Grand Cay last night. It's not decided finally, but I think he's really set. He feels there are no good choices. He returned today from Grand Cay and had a six-hour meeting with Chappy Rose and Buchanan in the whole session. And the P, at the conclusion, said there are no good choices, and he talked to Ron sort of on the way out and had tears in his eyes. Went out for a boat ride, then came back. Called Ziegler and told him to call me and tell me. Ron thinks he's going in the direction, and he said he had talked to Rogers and others, and he's aiming in the direction, although he says that he's not decided, that there's no choice but for Ehrlichman and Haldeman to move away and above it in the appropriate way.

He bases this on the argument of three premises that he evaluates. First, the legal standpoint, where he thinks we will survive. Second, public opinion probably won't make the case in the long run. Then he goes into a long dissertation on that, agonizing. Ron says everybody fought it, but something has to be done. The P feels guilt. As P, he must get this out of his mind. He has an obligation to run the nation and he cannot, as a human being, run the country with this on his mind. He told Ziegler he knows what it means, and that's why he's fought it and so on. He told Ziegler to call me and tell me that from the standpoint of the Presidency, and from my own standpoint, I should consider seriously that the P has no alternative and that I should resign and fight this, as I know how to fight it.

Ron said the separability idea was argued at length and the view is that it can't be separated. Ehrlichman and I both have to go. The P said these two men are strong enough to deal with this, to move on their own to make their case. But the Presidency cannot be encumbered by it. The points of history, separability, won't go away anyway, no guilt and so on were all argued, and the P argued the most strongly; then got up and walked out the door. And Ron realized that basically it was done. He's leaned on Rogers heavily. Rogers argued the case the other way, but he thinks this is the right decision.

Then Ron read from his notes as to various things the P said, which is what follows. There's no good way to handle this. It will in no way separate Ehrlichman and Haldeman from me, and this is irrelevant anyway. They did no wrongdoing, but they cannot assume that they will not be in the swirl of controversy. I know now the grand jury won't act for another month. There's no way that this will not go down in history as a very bad chapter, that the Presidency is seriously hurt, and I must accept responsibility for this. But Haldeman and Ehrlichman are strong men that have served the Presidency as dedicated a way as any man has served the Presidency. Probably the strongest men in terms of dedication who have ever served the Presidency. But as we look at the political forces, the forces against the Presidency, the country must have a P moving in a direction. He realizes there will be clamor. This will not pass, I'm still involved. Charges and claims are still made that I knew about it and was aware of it. But I must make a decision and move ahead in a new tone and a new way. The best thing I can do is make the decision, but I just can't do it because I can't prejudice their rights. I believe in these two men, I love these two men. The White House can't respond and can't operate with this force against us, though.

Ron says then after Rose and Buchanan left the P said, I will face this on my own. I will make these points to the men involved. They have to realize where we are in all this. Ziegler again said he was sure he had decided on this in Grand Cay last night. Ziegler says he raised the question of resignation vs. leave of absence. Gave all the arguments. The P said there's no choice, a leave is not a viable choice. They have to make their case and I must separate the Presidency from them. Then they discussed who should talk to Haldeman and who should talk to Ehrlichman. Ziegler raised the point that this would prejudice their legal case. The P said he's convinced we have no legal concern. May not even have a public opinion concern. But he then says I am not the type of man who can run this country with this force against us, and then went into a 20-minute dissertation on the problems of the Middle East and all that. Ziegler said what if they relieve themselves of their duties. The P pointed to his own head and said, I can't relieve myself of it. Ziegler emphasized this can't be separated from the P. He said I must go out to the public and say that I can't run the Presidency with this burden. That's why I've accepted this.

He feels the way to do this is for each of us to submit our resignation at our own request. The question of Dean's resignation and how to handle that has to be determined. Ron says he's very concerned about Colson. Told Ziegler he talked to Colson yesterday and had Ziegler call him a couple of times today. Then told Ziegler not to talk to him again at all. Said I now know what kind of a man Colson is. He started into the whole "What'll I do now without them" business, and Ziegler said don't talk about that now. The P wants to move immediately. He was going to have Rogers talk to us tomorrow. Then said to Ron, what if Haldeman and Ehrlichman roll him. Ron said they wouldn't try.

The P raised the point about keeping Higby in. Ziegler said I don't think he'd stay. Then Ziegler said if I stay, I don't know how I'll handle things, and the P was horrified at the thought of Ron leaving, but Ron made the point that he may have to, but Ron said he couldn't in any way replace me. He pushed Kehrli and Parker and all those people as able to take on many of the tasks, and said the P responded favorably to that. In the P's summation, he said he can't separate himself from this, his true responsibility. He argued a long time about the buffer theory and the lightning rod idea, but said it doesn't matter. I have to make a decision, I have to make a move, and I have to go on.

I called Larry and told him, which was quite a shock. Also called Ehrlichman, who took it very hard. He thought I ought to call Wilson, the lawyer, which I did. He felt it was a great surprise and will definitely have an effect on the legal case. Said they had discussed this, but had no indication that it was a real possibility. He understands the P's concern, but wonders if this is the right way to handle it. I called Ehrlichman back to report on that. He said he was having a very hard time with this. I said, why? He said it seems unfair. Which, of course, it does.

I made a long speech to Ziegler, a medium one to Larry, and a short one to John, on the need to treat this as a progressive step and approach it on that basis, recognizing that each step takes us ahead in some way, even though we don't perceive that at the time. Ron was obviously flabbergasted by my reaction and the way I tried to deal with him and strengthen him, and he kept saying someday he wanted to tell me what he really thought of me or something. It's obviously very hard on him, because he's had to take all the long sessions over the weekend, plus delivering the final news which must have been very rough to face up to, but he did it very well. Larry called back later to say he would be happy to do anything he could to help and so on. Obviously disturbed, and we'll see where it goes from there.

Tuesday, April 24, 1973

This is another Watergate day. The P in Key Biscayne returning tonight. Ehrlichman and I spent the day working on various Watergate matters. Ziegler called this morning. Said the decision still hasn't been made. That he talked to Rogers and that the P is going to talk to Rogers again today.

Henry came in and had a long talk with John and me this afternoon, and his view is strongly that if it's inevitable we're going to fall eventually, then we should get out as soon as we know it's inevitable, but definitely not before. Which is different than the way the P expresses Henry's view. Henry went through some of what he feels are the problems if we do go. He came up with the very sound idea for me that, if I go, I should not make a full statement trying to explain my role. I should go above the battle and say that I'll clear my name in the courts and the other processes and at the appropriate point after the dust has settled, I'll make a full public disclosure of my position in total. But it would serve no useful purpose to do so now. I think this might be a very good move.

John and I have both come down gradually, as the day rolls on, on the basis that we're going to confront the P pretty strongly tomorrow with the challenge that if he has something that is going to come out on us, he must tell us about it and we'll act on that basis. If he doesn't, then there isn't a case to be made for our going, at least at this point. We'll just have to see how that works out. The lawyers ought to soften him up some ahead of time on that.

Wednesday, April 25, 1973

VP called this morning and said he was going out in public today, which I said was his first mistake, and he laughed and agreed. Said there is a question on how to handle the Watergate thing. Says he'll say he has full confidence the P will handle it properly and he feels that we're going to have to stiff-arm them from there on. That this thing is driving the same lousy people to say things. He feels the P has to make clear that the rights of people involved can be jeopardized, and more so by the P than anybody, if he speaks out improperly. He also said if he can be of any assistance, to let him know.

Ehrlichman and I met with Ziegler at 9:30 to get a fill from him before we got into the Watergate round for the day. Ron said we should be prepared to work on the basis that the P feels we should leave, and thinks we should in order to permit this matter to be ironed out outside the White House. And the problem is how to assess the situation from the standpoint of the Presidency and the serious impact against the Presidency. It requires a shift of atmosphere and a shift of tone to move it away from the Presidency. And it's assumed from the press that the force will continue against the White House and specifically against Haldeman and Ehrlichman. So we were in positions that, if we were not aware of the legal impropriety, at least we could have stepped in and stopped it all. If we remain, it's virtually impossible for the P to do what he must do, which is to disengage himself to the degree that he can and move on with the business of the Presidency. Everyone realizes Haldeman and Ehrlichman didn't do anything. Because of the weight of public opinion, a voluntary departure is necessary. The real question is, can the Administration function in the future with the presence of two advisors who fall under the cloud? And we do fall under this cloud? And so he made basically the pitch that what the argument is for resigning, which we basically don't and can't buy because it just doesn't add up.

We met briefly with our lawyers to go over their plans for meeting with the P, and then met again with them after they had an hour and a half with the P. They said that they made the point that an amputation isn't going to get the gangrene out of the White House, and the P agreed, but said that if the patient survives, then maybe it's still worthwhile. They pushed him hard on Petersen to clamp down, get him the charges, get him moving fast and all that. Told him they cannot time the removal of Dean with Haldeman and Ehrlichman, and the P agreed with this. Said timing was extremely important. They didn't support the idea of leave of absence. They said the P's position was there's no real distinction between a leave and a resignation. Said the P was very apprehensive. They have no doubt that the P feels resignations are in order, but he's unresolved as to timing. And the lawyers argued that indictment is the only real excuse for a resignation. They felt they made some progress with him.

Ehrlichman and I then went over and met with him for a

couple of hours at the EOB. I reviewed the Connally and Rogers views, as expressed to me last night, and the P said now we need to look at the facts. First the legal vulnerability. Then he got off the facts. Said everybody agrees that we must do something, that we need an overt act, both for our own sakes and for the Presidency. Otherwise the crescendo keeps beating at us. We need to say that we want to be heard and cleared and we're innocent. We can't just sit and wait until the grand jury goes through the whole process. The prosecution now has a maximum incentive to hit pay dirt, especially since they're being criticized for the grand jury leaks and all that stuff.

The P says he will push Petersen hard to wind up the hearings, to hear Haldeman and Ehrlichman soon, to examine them and report to the P, and to put down for the P what is the case against Haldeman and Ehrlichman, and against Dean. Then he said let's turn to the Dean problem. That's damn tough at the moment. Ehrlichman said Dean is obviously trying to manipulate the P. The P said he sure is. Ehrlichman said this is the key, Dean's threat to the P. Ehrlichman then says let me spin out a far-out point. It's conceivable that if Dean is out of control and not handled adroitly, he could lead us to the resolution of impeachment on the ground that the P committed a crime and there's no other legal process available. So we have to consider that. What is the crime, how serious, is Dean a threat, what do we do about it? He feels that what Dean has in terms of evidence is short of a crime, but we don't know. But he may be building corroboration on it. The only solution is to listen to the tapes. If it didn't come out of those meetings, then it's manageable. If it did, we'd better know what Dean's hole card is. Ehrlichman's not afraid of Dean himself, he says; and he doesn't feel Haldeman should be. The P told me to get the conversations and listen to them. The P says he thinks he remembers especially regarding the Bittman conversation, regarding blackmail of a million dollars and all that.

The P asked Petersen if he should talk to Dean before he pleads, but feels he should not. Ehrlichman says we have to deal with the P's ultimate problem. The question of whether he's involved. The P says Dean could have described the payoffs during his "Cancer on the Presidency" speech. Ehrlichman said, then we have to decide how to decide on Dean. The P said we can't run the risk of Dean saying something regarding the P. If immunity is the price, we have to pay it. I made the point that that's the one thing you can't do, is pay any price to Dean and let him hold the permanent level of blackmail over the Presidency. You've got to destroy Dean. The P said how, and Ehrlichman said, well, you could call Petersen in. Tell him that Dean talked to Liddy and that I talked to Dean, and I have no concrete evidence of blackmail, but that is a distinct impression. This P is not subject to blackmail. You must turn this on Dean and trap him and drop the full weight of the law on him. We have to assume that Dean is also blackmailing Petersen, or trying to. We had considerable discussion of this and obviously concerned the P greatly. He kept coming back to it.

Then he said get back to subject A. A lot hinges on the Dean problem. We can't put Dean, Haldeman, and Ehrlichman in one bag. It would be wrong from an individual standpoint, and from what we know Dean is culpable without question. Dean claims that Haldeman and Ehrlichman knew all the way. Dean makes the point that the $40,000 was paid before the election, which has to be checked out. Petersen told the P, and said you must not tell anybody this, they gave Strachan and Magruder lie detector tests. That Strachan didn't pass and Magruder did, regarding the information, according to Strachan, regarding the budget and the output of the Watergate.

Regarding us, the P made the point that we could consider a leave, coupled with a statement by the attorney to the P. That was one of the ideas the attorneys came up with, is that they'd give the P a letter saying that they saw no criminal liability on our part. So we consider a leave. The P makes a statement or we put out the statement by the attorney to the P saying that we'd asked to go to the grand jury. We need to prepare for that, and the essential business of the government must go forward. Therefore, it's imperative, until cleared up, that we step out because we feel our ability to carry on our duties is impaired. This poses a problem down the road but buys time, keeps the option open, and we're able to see what does come out. Then the P can say he's not going to judge the case or anyone in it until it runs the process. The P would probably have to include Dean at this point, he feels.

Ehrlichman has a different approach. He says we really have three situations. First, you have Dean, that type, who will be indicted or given immunity, and the P in that case can say he's advised that Dean has indicated sufficient involvement that he must ask for his resignation. The second category is people in the White House openly charged, such as me, but without determination by the judicial process. So we ask them to take a leave until cleared. Third is the group that's not publicly charged but has some direct or indirect involvement. I know and they know who they are, but I'm going to leave them in place for the time being with the expectation that the facts will become available. Ehrlichman said you should treat Dean differently than Haldeman, and Haldeman differently than Ehrlichman. So fire Dean, Haldeman take leave, Ehrlichman stay, but ready to go if anything comes up. John also points out this also divides him PR-wise from Dean and Haldeman, which is to his interest. He feels there's a real practical problem with the resignation, which is, how can he live?

The P said, the more I think of the resignation, which is the option everyone comes down on (Harlow comes down on that too), the less I think it works. The difficulty is at this point it condemns us and doesn't clean up the problem, and so Haldeman and Ehrlichman leave. We were cleaning house, we put in a new team. Rush replaces Haldeman, Cole replaces Ehrlichman, Garment replaces Dean. But the P can't go through the whole White House and fire everybody. So he feels we should not move this week in any event. We can't do us before we do Dean.

Then I left to review the tapes. Did that and went back over and went over what's on the tapes, which had the P again very concerned because of the implications that are in there. The actual facts work out pretty well because he did a superb job of getting the information out of Dean, which is what he was after. But he's concerned that Dean may have had a tape recorder on him and would use the tape itself, which could be made to appear more damaging than the facts would actually testify.

He then met with Petersen for quite a long time. Called me at home afterward, said the prosecutor now is not about to give Dean immunity. That he's too much involved as a principal. He told him about the need to expedite. Told him about the paper he wants from him regarding Ehrlichman and Haldeman, which he says he'll have by Friday afternoon. Said he wants Haldeman and Ehrlichman at the earliest opportunity to meet with the prosecutor, and he said they'll have counsel request it. He said he wanted us to go to grand jury now and he said he may have us twice, then the P said OK but go fast on it. Then he gave me *(the P)* a paper regarding a note they had sent to the prosecutor in the Ellsberg case, making the point of the break-in at Ellsberg's psychiatrist by the Watergate people. And Petersen says I *(the P)* was blackmailed by Dean on them and they had to send it out to avoid cover-up in the Ellsberg thing, although it will not blow the Ellsberg case because it wasn't used.

The P says he leveled with Petersen regarding our conversation and told him he will not be blackmailed on it, and that was the interview in which I *(the P)* started my investigation. And the P wants me to hold that conversation to the P and me, not discuss it with Ehrlichman. Petersen said Dean always indicated that he won't lie for Ehrlichman, but he will never hurt the P, which would imply that he's trying to set up a semiblackmail of the P.

The P feels there's no choice but to fight him. He agrees that you can't temporize with Dean to try and keep him from putting out any public stuff.

He learned from Petersen that Dean's likely to be called in the Vesco grand jury because he made a phone call to quash an indictment on Vesco. They're trying to make Dean's lawyers come to them, and that's what they're waiting for. There can't be any move on Haldeman or Ehrlichman until Dean is resolved, and he told Petersen this. The P gave him the impression that he wasn't going to act on us anyway, but wants to see his paper on us. The belief now is to stand firm through the weekend.

Petersen doesn't know when he'll meet with Dean to get his big threat. (The P had learned from Kleindienst apparently this afternoon that Dean had some big threat he was going to deliver to Petersen when he met with him.) There's no way to stay with Dean on this, but we have to try to keep him from becoming a total enemy, so we treat him decently.

When Ehrlichman talks about impeachment, I don't see that based on the word of Dean. The P's worried that he may have made a tape recording, as I mentioned. The P then said, well, this is April 25. Put this down as the day we start up. He agrees with the lawyers that the resignation just won't work. Leave of absence question really doesn't buy us anything.

The P called a little later to see whether I thought there was a way I could find out if Dean had a tape recorder on him, and I explained there was no way. Wanted me to listen to the rest of the tape. Ziegler informed me later that Dash called Len Garment and said the Senate committee wants to see Ehrlichman and me next week in their private discovery process, apparently. So that poses a new bit of excitement.

Thursday, April 26, 1973

Another all day shot on the Watergate. The P had me in at 9:00 for an hour and a half. Said we've got to be sure that we go to the grand jury first, not to the Senate committee, and that we should request an opportunity to see the committee as soon as we're through with the grand jury. This arises because the committee counsel has notified Len Garment that they want us up there next week. He said on Segretti, that Petersen told him that he apparently had something to do with the Jackson thing on Muskie (that's the sex letter), and also that they're questioning whether he did the Canuck letter.

Editor's Note: Shortly before the Florida primary, letters on Muskie campaign stationery accused Senator Scoop Jackson of fathering an illegitimate child—and of being arrested on homosexual charges. The "Canuck" letter insulted Canadians.

He wants to be sure Buchanan is preparing a counterattack on their campaign tactics and get ready to hit them. Said I should tell Ehrlichman that they may call Dean out to the Ellsberg trial and he'll have to reveal the Hunt operation on that psychiatrist office break-in. Says Ehrlichman and I should put together, for Ziegler to put out, the Presidential initiatives within the staff to get this out. Says that I should be prepared before the Ervin Committee to defend the White House and the campaign, and defend the campaign itself, and that Ehrlichman has to get out the Nixon record in the Watergate, and why his effort to try and get the record out.

On the tapes, he says that he's given me the directive that the tapes are only made for national security information. All other stuff will not be transcribed. The question he has is, did the P at that time order Dean to do anything? And the answer is no. Regarding clemency, he said the matter was discussed. There was talk about pre-Christmas, but we couldn't even consider it until '74. The P may have called Dean. The question about what's been done on that. But he's trying to find out how deep this ran. The question is why the P didn't go right to the Attorney General with this information. The reason of course was he was running an investigation and that this was not related to the Watergate, in any event.

Raised the question of when McCord's hush money story was to be put out. Says Ehrlichman and I have to develop a game plan on how we handle Dean. The question is how Dean will be most vindictive—as a witness with immunity or as a defendant. Also the question of when did Dean's attorneys go to the U.S. Attorney and when did he get an attorney? In no way can Dean now do any more to Ehrlichman and me than he is. So Ehrlichman's theory of firing Dean has to be examined. The question of whether it unnecessarily gives Dean a motive to go wild, and that it's no problem against Haldeman and Ehrlichman, because he already is, but the question is against the P, and we have to look hard at that. So we can't fire him and put the blame on him. That would justify Haldeman and Ehrlichman, but it wouldn't help except to discredit Dean, which of course would be valuable, but not to the P. We can't give him immunity and let him blackmail, but the question is how to deal with him.

Dean apparently was lobbing threats at Petersen. Dean told the P when he talked to him on Easter that he may want to see the P before his pleading. Petersen's told the P not to see him. The only purpose of bringing Dean in to see the P, which he still thinks maybe he should do, is the human factor, which he says you, oddly enough, understand better than Ehrlichman. Dean says that he expresses the greatest respect and affection for the P and maybe it would do some good to see him. Petersen doesn't see Moore as a defendant. Also, he doesn't see Kalmbach as a defendant, except possibly on the money stuff. Moore was very close to Dean, how about having him talk with Dean and see what he has in mind. I didn't think that was too good an idea, but the P wanted at least to have it thought about.

John and I met with the lawyers from 10:30 to about 1:30. Wilson said that Hersh of *The New York Times* called him this morning, just before he came over, and said that Hersh, the press, has investigated Wilson thoroughly and he's clean. Second, and Wilson thought he was giving notice on this probably, that Mitchell, in an off-the-record statement which Hersh heard with his own ears, said that Haldeman and Mitchell engineered the cover-up. Also they reported to us that the P told them yesterday about the fact that Dean told him of the blackmail threat and that surprised them substantially.

I then spent considerable time listening to the tape. At 4:00 went over to the EOB, reviewed the tape findings with the P, reviewed my files through the whole March 20–28 period, and we had a general discussion of Watergate. The P called Kleindienst to get a report on the Ellsberg break-in deal. And Kleindienst had no report. Then the P called Ehrlichman, to tell him that, and Ehrlichman reported to him that *The New York Times* has the Pat Gray story. That is, that Gray had destroyed the evidence out of Hunt's safe. So the P told Ehrlichman to come over to the EOB.

Then the P called Kleindienst regarding Gray and said, don't you feel under these circumstances Gray has to resign? Also told him to find out what Petersen thinks we should do about it. The P says I want the whole thing out. These things have happened, I as P have to get them out. It's my responsibility. The P then called Petersen regarding his reaction to the Gray situation in *The New York Times*. Then he said he's a needless casualty in doing a dumb thing. He asked him what Gray's line is regarding why, and apparently he will say that he had explicit confidence in Ehrlichman and Dean. The P said that won't wash, they didn't tell him to destroy it. He will say he was told that the papers should be destroyed. The P asked Petersen what his view is as to what Ziegler should say. And Petersen told him that Gray now says, I was told to destroy them.

By this time it's 6:20 and the P calls Kleindienst and says there's a story to the effect that Gray came to Ehrlichman's office and recommended or received documents and was told by Ehrlichman or Dean to destroy them, and that's not true. What happened is that he was told they were not Watergate, they were political, and he must not say something that's not true. He's in a bad enough situation already. Dean apparently says there was discussion regarding destroying them, but it was not done. It's bad enough for the Director to say he destroyed them, but if he says he was ordered to, it would be terrible. By then Ziegler's in, and the P told Ziegler to call Dean and see what he's going to say on it. The P's view is that Gray has to resign tomorrow. The problem is who do you move in

as acting director. Ziegler left to make the Dean call, came
back in and said he couldn't reach Dean. A little later, the P
told him not to try. Ehrlichman suggested Ambrose as acting
FBI director and the P suggested Ruckelshaus. In this process,
the P picked up the fact that Magruder is ready to plead, but
they need Dean, too, and they're trying to get Dean to plead.
So they're still talking to Dean's lawyers, and he guesses Dean
lobs that stuff in to increase his bargaining power on the plea.
There's not going to be any blackmail, though. We've crossed
that bridge.

By this time Ehrlichman's left the meeting, and the P gets
into a discussion of whether this changes our situation regarding
the leave of absence, in view of the barrage of innuendo and the
kind of thing we have to now expect from Dean. He says on a
leave, we'd put out a lawyer's statement that there's no criminal
liability. However, because of the charges made, the leaks in the
grand jury, the stories in the press and so on, my ability to conduct my responsibilities has been seriously impaired. The only
course is for me to take a leave until I am completely cleared of
any wrongdoing. That it would be inconsistent with the high
standards of integrity that you have insisted on the White
House. I believe under the circumstances, for proper functioning, you should appoint a replacement, and so on.

At that point, the P stopped and called Petersen. Said he
had checked his notes, and so on, and Gray was not told to
destroy this, and he must not say that or the P will have to
say he lied. Petersen suggested that Gray should not necessarily leave.

Then we got back to the discussion of the replacement. He
feels Rush is the only possible replacement, the real problem
is getting the White House run. It won't work with Ehrlichman
and me here, and so a leave becomes imperative for running
the White House in terms of morale, and so on. Maybe let
Larry stay to break Rush in.

Then Ehrlichman called to say he had given his statement
to Clifton Daniel of *The New York Times,* and Daniel asked
him two questions, first does Dean know you're putting this
out? Second, the way we got the story is that you said to Dean,
you live across the river, why don't you throw the stuff in the
river on your way home tonight? Also we had the report that
Woodward has the story in the *Post* that Ehrlichman and Haldeman were told by Dean on March 20 that the jig was up

and they should be prepared to go to jail if necessary and that we agreed.

Then we got back to the discussion of the leave. P said everyone else feels that there should be a resignation, the P doesn't agree. He won't condemn on unsubstantiated evidence. That would mean everyone under fire should resign. The P's responsible to see that all in government, especially in the White House, meet a higher standard than just not doing anything illegal, and that's the test I will apply.

By then it's 7:45 and Kleindienst calls back, gives a long report to the P, who says, mmhhmm mmmm—as he goes through it. I picked up some bits and pieces.

Dick Kleindienst's Report

Gray should say nothing tonight. Regarding Dean immunity: no one's advising it, and there's no way to give it regarding suborning to perjury. Petersen told the P that Gray would say that Ehrlichman ordered him to destroy the documents. Now Kleindienst has given a different story, so the P says I know that Petersen hates Ehrlichman, and that's okay, but I don't want him to mislead me. I like Petersen myself, you trust him, don't you? I'm talking to him as if he's my counsel. Your judgment is that he should do it because he's due to change. He should say exactly what happened. The documents were sensitive, not related to the Watergate case. He didn't open it. That's why his destruction line won't work. Why didn't he look in and see what they were? No, no, Pat must not ever say that publicly. If he says the White House counsel ordered him to destroy, or that he drew that conclusion, he looks like a fool and the two would be conspiring to destroy evidence. He should not impute that to Dean, and he can't impute it to Ehrlichman, because he didn't say it. He was there, however. He's interested in the Presidency, and the worst thing he could say was that he was ordered or had the impression that he should destroy. He would resign tomorrow because of this charge. Under the circumstances, put it this way: this matter is to be heard before the grand jury, I don't think the grand jury will indict. Why not? Not of the view that he should resign because of the newspaper story. He'll be out shortly, anyway, so do nothing on the basis of the newspaper story. Tell Petersen I appreciate his hard work, but Dean floated this story. Dean's trying to sink everybody, I'm glad I never saw him. (It's obvious from the reaction there that Dean had given Kleindienst the impression that he saw the P frequently on Watergate.) He said, I don't want Gray's resignation in conflict with Ehrlichman. Gray will say nothing, he will appear before the grand jury, and he will say to the grand jury that he came over to Ehrlichman's office, that Dean handed him a packet of highly sensitive national security papers, absolutely nothing to do with the Watergate, that should not see the light of day, therefore they should not go to the FBI. Gray gathered from that that they should be destroyed, and he made the mistake of bad judgment and destroyed it. They don't feel he's guilty of a crime, just bad judgment.

P then resuming the discussion, said regarding Ehrlichman, his vulnerability is that he was there and heard this. There was never any intent of destroying it, he was amazed when he heard they had been destroyed, which we know, because we were watching him when he was on that phone conversation Sunday night of the 15th. On the resignation argument, the P says what they say is that we need to clean house, cut our losses, Caesar's wife, Presidency more important than any man, P cleans his own house. But the argument against it is that the P is then judging the case himself, on noncorroborated statements. Therefore he should wait for the grand jury.

On the other hand, the leave is imperative from the standpoint of running the joint, and our own well-being. How to handle the problem of being paid, of course, until this is determined, we go on paying him. Problem of Dean in the same bag is a difficult one. Can't take a leave from us without him. He'll soon separate one way or the other. Kleindienst is totally opposed to immunity. Dean is thrashing out at everybody.

Told us to write leave-of-absence letters, get them out on Saturday, before the weekend, and go before Dean goes, not with him. Have to avoid having Congress demand we go, just don't have any hard-liners that will stand up for us.

He went on some more in this vein, and then as I was trying to leave, got into sort of the usual sentimental discussion of how he told Rogers he was tempted, because he had to tell Adams to go, that Rogers should tell us to go, but then said no, I totally reject that out of hand, I'll tell them myself. (Of course, he's never gotten around to doing that. He had Ziegler tell me, and then I told Ehrlichman. Which is even worse than having Rogers doing it.) Another sidelight on the Adams story, he said Len Hall had written him saying that not only did Eisenhower make Nixon call Adams in and tell him to leave, but when Adams went in to see Eisenhower, Eisenhower said he wanted to keep him. To a degree, the P is doing the same thing in getting the word to us indirectly and then backing off when we hit him with it frontally, although now he's down to raising it on terms of a leave of absence, which he obviously thinks is going to be permanent, because his idea in bringing Rush in would be to put him permanently in the job, which I argued would do away with the leave of absence idea. Then he thought maybe he would just go without a Chief of Staff and see how that worked. Or be his own Chief of Staff.

After I got home, he called and said well, just wanted to let you know that I just had some corned beef hash, a couple of eggs, and some bacon, and I told him that I just had some corned beef hash, a couple of eggs, and some creamed spinach. He suggested I check Connally about the leave-of-absence idea, that he feels it's the right decision at this time, and he feels best about it. I should tell him that, and see what he thinks. Also thought maybe I should check Rogers. I wasn't able to reach Connally, and the P called me a little later, and said what about Connally for Attorney General, would he be approved by the Senate? It would be part of a bold move. I told him I didn't think Connally would take it. He says that Connally says he'll do anything that he has to do, so we'll see.

Friday, April 27, 1973

P had me in at 7:55 this morning before our staff meeting. Wanted to raise the question of what was the meeting with Ehrlichman, Dean, and Haldeman on the 20th that was reported in the *Post* this morning. And wanted me to discuss Ruckelshaus with Ehrlichman, thinks it's important to move on Gray.

At the staff meeting, I tried to turn the thing to constructive approaches on the non-Watergate base, but Henry went in to how the P has to give a speech on Watergate, and that turned everybody into that, and I couldn't turn it off.

Then on the plane to Mississippi, he had me up, said he had talked to Ehrlichman about Ruckelshaus, and that temporary isn't the answer, we've just got to lay it to Ruckelshaus that he's got to take the job on a permanent basis. Then he said we've got to come down on the leave business, like today. Wants me to talk to Ehrlichman in very direct terms, say there are no good options, but we can't wait until next week and let Congressional problems develop. It's obvious the P expects us to leave. So there's no hiatus, we believe the positions should be filled, and we have a desire to serve in some other position in the future. In asking for a leave, we say it's important there be no hiatus in the work of the government, make the leave effective not immediately, say three-or-four-day transition period working with our successor. That we'd be glad to serve in any capacity in the future, but we would not want to return until we're fully cleared. Question of toughing it out until the grand jury acts.

What really brought it home to him was last night on Ehrlichman and the FBI stuff, and the question of who would put out the news story.

He had a chat with Stennis, and Stennis' talk was rather alarming to the P. He feels time is running out. Made the point that down their way they have a saying that the rain falls on both the just and the unjust, and if the rain falls on people, they've got to go, whether they're just or not.

Then the P had us up on the way back from Mississippi, with John in, too. Went into how to handle the question of why we didn't fire Gray on the 15th and John had the answer to that. In the meantime, while we were down there, I got word from Larry that Gray wanted to resign today, and we approved that. Decided to put Ruckelshaus in as Acting Director, and I set up an appointment for Ruckelshaus at 4:00, for the P to sell him on that, which he later did.

We had a discussion of how they should handle the Pentagon Papers story, make it on national security, that there was a national security investigation as a result of serious leaks of highly sensitive national security secrets, that this was an aspect of that, and we can't discuss it beyond that, except to say this act was never authorized. Then it was agreed that we couldn't say that the act was never authorized. P makes the point that we've got to be forthcoming. Ehrlichman makes the point that Petersen has known about this for a long time.

Then we talked about the leave question again. P arguing that we move now, taking the high ground, because we want the P to carry on, so we want a leave of our duties. Physically, we would stay in our offices, use our files, and so on, remain

to work with our successor, etc. Say we and the P looked at
this and took action. We could wait until the grand jury finds
some technical illegality, but then it's not our decision, we got
caught. Or we could wait until our blowups, which hang us
publicly and the clamor is so great that we have to go under
fire. Then the problem is if we take the leave and the grand
jury doesn't indict, what do we do? We have the problem of
the committee, and maybe so much stuff out then that it becomes a close call as to whether we can survive. After the
grand jury, we can say I've been cleared, but there should be
a new team and step out. It's obvious he's still thinking that
we've got to go out and that this is just a temporary measure
in that process.

At this point Ehrlichman lobbed in that we're meeting with
the U.S. Attorneys at 9:00 Thursday, which I hadn't known.
He says he told me yesterday, but I missed the message if he
did. Then after we got back to the White House, P talked with
Petersen who says he can't make a deal with Dean, so he
cannot any longer ask the P to wait on taking action on him.
Problem now is how mad the P makes Dean, and he has to
take a hard look at that.

They've set up a meeting for us with Dash of the Senate
Committee at 1:30 on Thursday, so we have the DA in the
morning. They think this is a good program. Ehrlichman suggested we take a vacation instead of a leave, which they
thought at first was a great idea, but it isn't really. Strickler
thought it was worth another run at the P, which I decided to
do. I came up with the idea of taking a 30-day leave, and they
thought that was a good idea, too.

P says he should fire Dean tomorrow or Monday, and then
hold us through next week. He doesn't see the leave as a result
of the Senate and DA being too bad. There's some merit to
leaving before these meetings, though, he agrees. He gets back
to Dean and says that's a real problem, the P must take Dean's
resignation, he must make a distinction between Dean and us,
he can't sweep Dean under the rug. If we go now, what will
the press think? It gives Dean the fair-haired boy aspects because he's the one who made the revelations. These are the
hard questions.

After that, I went in to meet with the P again, by then it
was 6:45, and I spent about an hour and a half in there. He
wanted to clarify one point on the critical conversation of

(March) 21st. He questioned me again on whether Dean had any basis to feel that he'd been instructed by the P to go out and get the money and I said no. That wasn't the case.

P had a long meeting with Petersen, he didn't report much of it to me, but he said O'Brien is scared and is the key to the whole payoff scheme. They think they're going to break him. P feels the 30-day idea won't operate, it's too gimmicky, it should just be a leave couched in the right words. He will handle Dean differently.

The P has decided on his own thing, that he will go to Camp David tomorrow morning, work Saturday and Sunday, and try to be ready Monday night, and try to get it all out. Then he went through a long moaning process about how he has no one to help him and all. He feels we've got to take the lead, and he says he'll take care of Dean. Why not accept the voluntary leave for Dean? Who can tell Dean this? I told him I didn't know. He came up with Garment, which is probably the best bet, although not very good. What the P would prefer is that Haldeman and Ehrlichman take the high road, we leave because of the situation and we're asking for the leave. The P then gets Dean in, and under these circumstances, asks him to take a leave. He says if that's too prejudicial, that's too bad. Meaning if it's too prejudicial to us to follow that route, then it's too bad. In other words, he's made up his mind. Then he says I have to help him on the Dean deal, not to make his lying against the P infinitely worse. Dean's lawyers said they're going to tie in the P on other matters than Watergate. Hersh of the *Times* apparently has from O'Brien the point that the P is involved in other than Watergate.

He then started pushing for having us go on Saturday, to get more separation, and thinks that's better. Based on that, I had a talk with our lawyer Wilson tonight. He says that he thinks we're better off to go on Sunday, that Saturday gives Dean too much time. He thinks our deal is not too good, but it's better than some of the other options. He's convinced, though, that this is going to mean to the public that this is the first move toward getting rid of us.

Saturday, April 28, 1973

P phoned first thing this morning from Camp David. Was really upset about the Vesco story on Ehrlichman, which is a really lousy shot. Then said what time would John and I be up there today, he wants to move today on our leave of absence because he's got to get to working on his speech. I explained to him that we had gone into this in considerable detail with the lawyers and all last night, and felt strongly that we wanted to do it tomorrow instead, and explained to him why, and he agreed to that.

Told me to get the statements written in the best possible way. Says he isn't going to mention our names in his TV talk Monday night. He thinks it will be a pretty good talk, and he's convinced now it's the right time. He thinks it's good that we didn't move earlier, that it's best to hit after they've thrown a big chunk of their wad. He obviously has a cold, and was coughing into the telephone, and saying he was pretty run down, and going through the "Feeling sorry for himself" bit.

On Dean, he says he has a very tough plan on him, that it will be handled properly, that he's got it all worked out, it will be very peremptory, he won't see him, so on. He's going to tell Garment that the Assistant Attorney General said that the P should not see Dean and that Garment must ignore any threats that he makes and be very firm with him. Says it's interesting that no one ran the story about Dean's implicating the P, although the P is confident that they do have the story, which I am too, since we picked it up from a number of sources. On the decision, he said we do have to go forward. The decision's made, I want to talk to Rogers today, because I'm going to move on trying to get him to take the Attorney Generalship. Then I'm going to go to work on the speech on that basis.

So as of 9:00 this morning, he said now, if I can understand that the decision is made, I'm going to go ahead and write on that assumption, and it's okay to put this off until tomorrow, and I said the decision is made, we will take a leave, and so on. Then I talked to Ziegler on the phone and outlined my idea for the P's speech, making the point that he should move now, and put Rogers into Justice, make that change, and then make the point that the P's moving off of the Watergate case, and away from it, and that someone else will be handling it from here on, and so on.

We had a long meeting with our lawyers, mainly going over the leave-of-absence statements. Wilson feels very strongly that Dean isn't nearly as dangerous as we think he is. I agree with that, it's the P who thinks he's dangerous. There was

hours of going back and forth on the letters themselves, working out all the details. We finally ironed that out and closed
down for the day. I came home, went to an early dinner and
a movie with Jo.

Ron Ziegler's Report

When I got back, Ziegler called and covered a few things
on the P's mood, which he said was very bad, he was feeling
sorry for himself and so on. He said, would you like me to
tell you what I really think at this point on a personal basis,
and I said sure, and he said I think you're making a very major
mistake, that you should resign rather than taking a leave, that
if you take a leave you're simply setting yourself up as a su-
pertarget for the press, and they're going to bore in on you
mercilessly and force you to resign anyway, and then you'll
have to do it under pressure, and under much worse circumstances than you're doing it now. He made this argument quite
strongly, fairly effectively, and over and over, to the point
where I felt there was some merit to it.

John Wilson's Analysis

Called Wilson, made the points to him. He said nothing that
I've said appeals to him, that he doesn't think this will appeal
to Ehrlichman either, and that Ehrlichman would probably still
take a leave, even if I decided to resign. He makes the point
that you can always resign, and if you do it under exterior
pressure, this is not the P doing it, so it can't be interpreted
as the P's knowledge of guilt. He says a public clamor for
resignation doesn't convict you, because the public doesn't
know the facts, but a Presidential acceptance of a resignation
is much worse. Also he feels that Ehrlichman, Dean, and Haldeman would go out together, it all happens at once, the day
apart idea is a fiction, and that hurts us. His point is that you
don't amputate if there's any chance for anything else. He feels
the resignation may be better for the P, but not for me. If when
you go back, it will be a different world, but still, for now,
the leave of absence is better. If this is prompted by the fiction
of payroll problems and all that, then go without pay on a
leave. The hue and cry for a resignation that the press will
raise will be at the P, not at you, so that isn't a problem either.
His theory really boils down to the fact that a leave implies

> that the P has confidence in you, where the acceptance of a
> resignation shows no confidence and implies that he knows
> things that make this necessary.

Then we're up to about 10:30 and Gerry Warren calls, saying the *Post* has a story referring to two White House officials, saying that Dean was under the direction of Haldeman and Ehrlichman on the cover-up thing, has been reporting to us, and has knowledge of other illegal acts, including wiretapping. That this is all being delayed because officials in the White House are trying to mount a counterattack against Dean. He and Gerry both wanted us to answer that, but we declined to do so. Ehrlichman felt Ziegler ought to handle it because it goes beyond us. Says the only blessing in that is that it may persuade the P about Dean. He thinks he and I have to consider going for a TV play next week. So we went full cycle tonight, and ended up back where we were. We'll go tomorrow for the leave of absence.

Sunday, April 29, 1973

The papers today are full of columns and analysis calling for resignations and all, which caused me, after reading through them quickly, to say to Jo first thing this morning, if the P really gets a hold of this thing, what's he going to do is call us up there today and tell us that he's concluded that we have to resign, and from his viewpoint that's where he has to come out. It'll be interesting to see whether he does. I still at that point had the feeling that there could very well be a better course for us also.

Kissinger called just to say I'm thinking of you. Says the Restons and all those people are out for blood. He rambled on a bit. Obviously he is out of the play and sort of feeling sorry about it. P called at noon, right after I got home from church, from Camp David, said he was wondering if we could get up there at 1:30, and that John had said he wanted to meet with the P alone, and the P felt he should do that, and also he would of course meet with me alone. Felt it was appropriate for him to do so, in view of the decisions that I want to present to you, and then he said that all I can say is that I hope that Ehrlichman's as big a man as you are when I talk with him. He said everybody's trying to get at him to give him advice, but he's talked to no one, except that he spent virtually all day yesterday with Rogers. He's concluded that we've got to face up to what's right for the Presidency, and he was sure I would agree with that. Said he would talk to me first when we got up there.

Ziegler then called on the phone, said he wanted to tell me that the P's feeling very strongly now is that both Ehrlichman and I should volunteer a resignation, and that he's going to ask us to do that. He's thought it through. Ziegler argued with him last night and this morning. He's not concerned about my stepping up to it. And if Ehrlichman comes in and fights him, he's going to stick to it and force him to do it. He feels that if we take a leave we'll be eaten alive, and it won't work. A resignation will work. Wants a letter saying that we considered leave, but asked for resignation instead, so there won't be a period of uncertainty. He's confident we'll be cleared and will show our innocence, but at this time he feels we must resign. He's also made the firm decision that he will fire Dean tomorrow. So his plan is one, to accept the voluntary resignations of Haldeman and Ehrlichman, and then tomorrow, fire Dean. He definitely will separate Dean totally out. Will say that he accepts the responsibility, he's going to try and bring this back.

Apparently said to Ron, "I made this decision in Florida last week." I called Wilson and reported this to him, and he said Ehrlichman should not put himself in a position where the P has to remove him, he hopes he will do what the P wants him to do, he should not fight it, it won't help him. I told Ehrlichman that on the helicopter on the way up to Camp David, and he said he wanted to think about it, and we didn't talk any further on the helicopter.

When we got there, Ziegler said he wanted to see me and he came out, went for a walk while we were waiting over at Laurel. He was quite alarmed, because he said the P has made another firm decision that he communicated to Ron this morning, which is that he, too, is going to resign. Ron said he's deadly serious and absolutely firm on it. I told him that I was sure that was not the case, that it was part of his steeling himself for meeting with us, that he's creating a big crisis that he knew he couldn't meet, in order to be able to meet the lesser crisis that he has to meet.

I told Ron to go over to the P and tell him I was ready to meet with him. Ron said, "I'll tell him you're going to go along," and I said you can't tell him that, he's got to ask me, and I've got to say it to him, don't give him any indication, simply tell him I'm ready to meet with him.

When I got to Aspen, the P was in terrible shape. Shook hands with me, which is the first time he's ever done that. Told me to come look at the view out the window, then stepped to the door and said let's go outside and look at the flowers and all. So we were looking at the tulips from the Aspen porch, talking about the beauty and all, and as we started back in, he said, well, I have to enjoy it, because I may not be alive much longer. We got inside and he went through a discourse, saying that while nobody knows it, and he's not a publicly religious man, that it's a fact that he has prayed on his knees every night that he's been in the Presidential office. He's prayed hard over this decision, and it's the toughest decision he's ever made. He made the points on why he had to do it, but he's come to the conclusion that he has to have our resignations. He wants us to stay on to handle the transition. Then he went through his whole pitch about how he's really the guilty one. He said he's thought it all through, and that he was the one that started Colson on his projects, he was the one who told Dean to cover up, he was the one who made Mitchell Attorney General, and later his campaign manager, and so on. And that he now has to face that and live with it, and that for that reason, after he gets his other things completed, that he too will probably have to resign. He never said that directly, but implied it.

I made the pitch that he can't make that kind of a move, that Ehrlichman and I are expendable, and where there's a problem, we can step out and deal with it, but he can't do it. He doesn't have that luxury. He's got to stay in the office, he's got to pull things back together, and move them upward, and that he can. He said he thinks Ehrlichman feels he should resign, and he got that impression on the phone last night. Apparently Ehrlichman told him that he had evidence that the P knew about the fake cable about Diem, and that the P really was the one who had ordered all these acts, and that he's got to face up to that fact. I guess that really jarred him, which well it might. He says he's going to make Elliot Richardson Attorney General, he's going to force Kleindienst to resign today, he's going to announce both of those Monday night.

He told me about Tricia, that he had told the family not to come up to Camp David, but when he walked out last night nto the living room, there was Tricia sitting there. She said he and David and Julie had stayed up most of the night before, talking about this, and she had just come up to tell him that they all loved him. He's getting very sentimental—went through the whole thing about how Ehrlichman and I are the two best men he knows, and goes through all that kind of thing. On that note, I left, having assured him that I disagreed with this decision, as I had with a few other decisions he'd made, but that I had my input, and that I would abide by the decision, I would do everything I could to implement it, and make sure it came out right.

I went back over to Laurel, and Ehrlichman went over to Aspen to meet with him. Ehrlichman was over there about a half hour, then the P called me back, and Ehrlichman left. P reviewed the E meeting with me. He said he's concerned because he thinks that E wants him to admit that he ordered illegal acts, but apparently E agreed to the resignation. So he was pretty relieved about that.

Then E and I had our phone call with Wilson from Laurel while we were working out our letters of resignation. He suggested, first, that we insist Dean be fired tonight in the same breath as us, because if he's as smart as he might be, he'll get his resignation in in time for the papers tomorrow if we resign but ahead of him. Second, that both of us should announce in our letters our meeting with the U.S. Attorney and the committee counsel.

He told E to strike his words in his letter about his appreciation for his opportunity to serve the P—he feels it's his burden to appreciate us, not us him. Feels that we must now move on a very affirmative, open basis. Our meetings should be at the lawyer's office, they have a good room to do it. We should come and go openly and not sneak around or hide. He hit hard on the point that the P must not say anything complimentary about Dean, that that's absolutely essential. I think we've got that point through.

P called John and me back over at 5:30, we reviewed our letters and the release plan and all of that. He had Bill Rogers come in at six. P said that he had emphasized the National Security area with Elliot, and the fact that they must not get into that in the investigation. Then he had us read our letters of resignation, Rogers had a few points of correction, and that was the end. P got into somewhat of the emotional mood again

as John and I were leaving, but we finally got out, and h•
remained to have dinner with Rogers, and then to get back t
work on his speech. So today, the 29th, is the end of my Whit•
House career. Jo notified the families. I called them all thi•
morning to say I was going to take a leave, and Jo called ther
to say we had changed it to a resignation. Covered the base•
with them on that.

Monday, April 30, 1973

Resignation day. We finished up our resignation statement•
this morning, I had a meeting with Bull, Parker, Larry, an
Kehrli to impress on them the need to carry on the ongoin•
system just as it is until a new system was worked out an
ready to put into place, and urged that they not fall into th
trap of any sort of internal struggle for position. And explaine
the importance of their holding everything tightly together dur•
ing the interim period while the P would be in very toug•
emotional and physical shape, and so on.

Ehrlichman and I then met with the senior staff. Shult•
couldn't be there because he was testifying on the Hill, bu
we had Ash, and Kissinger, Timmons, and Ken Cole, and tol•
them what our decision was, and made something of the sam•
points. John was quite emotional in that session, broke dow•
or was on the verge of it at least, several times. Everybody,
think, was genuinely shocked, and I think we successfully im•
pressed on them also the need to deal very carefully with thi•
interim period.

I made a number of phone calls, talked to Billy Graham
He seemed to feel it was the right thing to do, said that h•
didn't believe that in government he had met two finer me•
than Ehrlichman and me, that we have his full support—h•
feels we've been caught in a web of evil that will ultimatel•
be defeated. He has great affection and love for me as a mar•
that I should count him as a friend, and that what I'm doin•
is going to help the P.

Called the VP, he said he had almost called me yesterday•
wanted to let me know about the charges that came out then
that they were tremendously unfair, and that they were nothin•
but smoke. Said he'd like to see me before I actually left. Tha•
he would like to be as helpful as he can, and thinks this i•
probably the right move.

Talked to Connally, he says I think this is the right thing t•

do at this time, although I'm awfully sorry that it came out this way. Then emphasized the great opportunity I would have to influence the P on who follows in my footsteps and in the staff restructuring. He emphasized the need to implore the P to get top people and go at the restructuring right.

The announcement plan hit a snag when Ehrlichman and Jerry Jones were unable to reach John Dean to inform him that the P was requesting his resignation, so there was a little flap at 11:00 about that, but Ron went ahead with the announcement anyway. The first lead out of it was rather unfortunate because it implied that Dean, Ehrlichman, and I had all resigned. But Ron worked all afternoon and got that corrected, so that by the time of the evening news, it came out that Ehrlichman and I had resigned, as had Kleindienst, and that Dean had been fired. There was no reaction from Dean all day.

P called in the afternoon from Camp David, where he was working on his speech for tonight. Sounded terrible, said, well, I just wanted you to know I still love you. Commented on the problem of reaching Dean, and said so be it. Said basically I have all resignations in hand anyway, don't I? And I said that he did. Told me to tell Ehrlichman that he was in the middle of the speech draft, but to tell him the same as he had told me, and also to tell him (he said you won't understand this, but John will) that I think he's a great man, and his wife is a great lady, and I won't let her down tonight. This was because Jeanne had written the P a letter which John left with him yesterday when we were up at Camp David.

John and I then spent the afternoon with our lawyers, going through the whole process of how to approach our appearances. P's TV speech tonight was, to say the least, not one of his finer efforts, but it probably was effective, because he was obviously shaken, and as the commentator said, didn't exhibit the normal confidence we associate with him. He's obviously in heavy weather, and so on. He sure showed that. It was interesting that I called him, and they said he wasn't taking calls, but he called back a little after ten. I said well, you've got it behind you now, and you should approach it that way. He said it was a very tough thing, and I'll never mention it again. Then he got feeling sorry for himself. He said Cap is the only Cabinet officer who's called. I told him that the operators were telling people that you weren't taking calls. Said to me you're a strong man, you've got to keep the faith, you're going to win this, God bless you.

Then he asked me if I thought I could do some checking around on reaction to the speech as I had done in the past, and I said no, I didn't think I could. He realized that was the case. He called again about midnight, rather bitter. Said Kissinger's reaction is typical, he's waiting to see how it comes out. Said again, keep the faith, and that was that.

Earlier this evening we'd gotten into something of a flap because Garment had met with Richardson and Ruckelshaus, and they had all decided that it was imperative that they put FBI guards on all of our files so there couldn't be any charge that we had destroyed anything, destroyed any evidence and so on. Ehrlichman didn't like that, but we went round and round and it was agreed that they were just there as guards, not as custodians, and so they said they would do it on that basis.

End of April 30 and the end of my official career in the White House.

Afterword
by Stephen E. Ambrose

When Nixon announced the resignations of Haldeman and Ehrlichman, he called it "one of the most difficult decisions of my Presidency." He referred to his aides as "two of the finest public servants it has been my privilege to know." He went on to say that the resignations were not to be taken as an implication of any personal wrongdoing on their parts, but rather that their ability to function had been impaired by rumors, accusations, and charges generated by the Watergate investigations.

In a statement, Haldeman said he had "hoped and expected to have had an earlier opportunity to clear up various allegations and innuendos that have been raised," but it had become "virtually impossible . . . to carry on . . . regular responsibilities in the White House."

A couple of months later John Dean, fired by Nixon the night he accepted the Haldeman and Ehrlichman resignations, testified to the Ervin Committee that as early as September 15, 1972, Nixon was well aware of the various ongoing cover-up activities. This contradicted directly Nixon's claim that he knew nothing about the cover-up until his "cancer on the Presidency" meeting with Dean on March 21, 1973. So it came down to Nixon's word vs. Dean's word—but Nixon had a tape. He asked Haldeman, who had moved to California, to review the September 15, 1972, tape, which Haldeman did on July 10, 1973.

Six days later Alexander Butterfield revealed to the Ervin Committee the existence of the White House taping system. That meant the evidence existed to decide who was telling the truth, Nixon or Dean. The different reaction of the two men immediately convinced most Americans: Dean was overjoyed and wanted the tape made public right away; Nixon was angry and insisted that the tape was covered by executive privilege and would never be made public.

Nixon assumed that the tapes were as sacrosanct as any Presidential document, that they were his personal property and that he could use them as he saw fit. Right there is the answer to why he didn't burn the tapes. Haldeman later said in a CBS interview that he had committed a "failure in judgment in advising Nixon not to destroy the tapes after their existence became known. I never—stupidly—did really think the thing through. . . . Nor did I think through the enormous damage that would be done to me and to Richard Nixon and to all the other participants. I thought it was a good idea to keep them for the historical value. And beyond that, because at that time Watergate was developing, I thought they would be valuable to the President knowing what had actually been said at various meetings in his office."

At that time, in fact, mid-July 1973, Haldeman was listening to the tapes, and although there was at times damaging language, Nixon was certain they were covered by executive privilege and that Nixon could use them selectively. As Nixon wrote in his memoirs, "Haldeman said that the tapes were still our best defense, and he recommended that they not be destroyed." Haldeman believed strongly that if the tapes were listened to in their entirety, the White House would indeed be vindicated.

So confident was Haldeman in his belief that when he returned to Washington to appear before the Ervin Committee two weeks after Butterfield revealed the existence of the tapes, he said he had listened to the September 15, 1972, tape and could confirm Nixon's version—i.e., that Nixon had known nothing of a cover-up. He declared, "President Nixon had no knowledge of or involvement in either the Watergate affair or the subsequent efforts to a 'cover-up.' " He said he was certain of his facts because he had listened to the March 21 tape, and could swear that Dean had lied. Haldeman said that the President had not indicated that he had discussed clemency for the burglars, nor had he given any indication that he was aware of payments to silence the conspirators.

He put the blame on John Mitchell at the CRP. "At the White House, at least," he said, "John Dean was the only one who knew that the funds were for 'hush money' if, in fact, that is what they were for." In his concluding statement, he spoke of the "high standards Nixon set for the White House staff and of his deep regret and sorrow that in a few instances there was a failure to live up to them."

In March 1974 Haldeman, Ehrlichman, and Mitchell were indicted. Haldeman was charged with conspiring to impede the Watergate investigation through the improper use of government agencies, the covert raising and distribution of payoff funds, and the concealment or destruction of records and documents. He was also charged with three counts of perjury relating to his testimony before the Ervin Committee.

Eventually, the Congress, the courts, and the Special Prosecutors forced Nixon to turn over some of the tapes. This in part led to the conviction of Haldeman for perjury, for allegedly protecting his old boss. More important, they led to an irresistible move to impeach the President. To forestall that fate, Nixon decided to resign.

On August 7, 1974, Nixon called Haldeman in California. "Bob," he opened, "I want you to know that I have decided I must resign because of its effect on the office of the Presidency." Haldeman urged him to stay on and fight. Later Haldeman conveyed through others to the President that if in fact he had to resign, "I firmly believe that before you leave office you should exercise your Constitutional authority and grant pardons to all those who have been or may be charged with any crimes in connection with Watergate and at the same time to grant amnesty to the Vietnam War draft dodgers. I think it's imperative that you bring Watergate and the Vietnam unrest to an end before you leave—for the sake of the country and especially for your successor."

Nixon said he would think about a blanket pardon. Haldeman followed with a written recommendation. He called it in to his lawyers in Washington, who typed it up and got it to the White House that night. It read, in part:

"On a personal basis—better to close the chapter now than to have to sit by helplessly for the next several years and watch trials and appeals.

"Historically—would be far better to grant the pardon and close the door to such a process than to let it run and have the trials become a surrogate impeachment. . . .

"Solves problems of potential prosecutor access to files and tapes by eliminating basis for further prosecution—also solves problem of defense forcing access to files.

"The only way to wipe the slate clean is to shut down the prosecution totally. . . . As long as it is there, there is a possibility of other things."

At one level Haldeman's memo was straightforward, businesslike, convincing, just like the man himself. The points he made were logical, indeed obvious. At another level Haldeman might be said to be continuing the cover-up, trying to protect Nixon—and himself—from whatever damaging material there was on the thousands of hours of unreleased tapes or the tens of thousands of documents in the files. On a third level it's possible Haldeman was making a disguised threat. That "possibility of other things" line might be read as a warning that Haldeman would implicate Nixon if he did not get a pardon.

Nixon did not flinch. He rejected the idea coldly. Amnesty for the draft dodgers was "unthinkable," while a blanket pardon for Watergate defendants could cause a "hysterical" political reaction.

On August 9, 1974, Nixon resigned and went into exile in San Clemente. He was never put on trial, because President Gerald Ford pardoned him. He was never asked in a court of law about his actions, because a life-threatening illness kept him away from the trials of Haldeman, Ehrlichman, and Mitchell. The only time he answered questions in public about Watergate was on television, with the questions being asked by David Frost and Nixon receiving a handsome fee for his answers. Nixon depicted himself as a man done in because he was too loyal to his subordinates. He blamed Haldeman, Ehrlichman, and Mitchell for the cover-up.

Haldeman, meanwhile, was convicted on January 1, 1975, in a U.S. district court in Washington, D.C., of one count of conspiracy, one count of obstruction of justice, and three counts of perjury. He was originally sentenced to from two and a half to eight years, but this was later reduced to from one to four years. Eventually he was paroled after serving eighteen months in the Federal minimum-security facility at Lompoc, California.

In prison, Haldeman wrote a book (with Joseph Di Mona as coauthor) entitled *The Ends of Power*. In it Haldeman theorized that it was Nixon who had erased the eighteen and a half minutes of incriminating tape and who was ultimately responsible for the cover-up. When the book was published in mid-1978, Nixon was miffed at Haldeman for the compromising position he had taken.

Haldeman was released on December 20, 1978. Nixon called him in Los Angeles. "Merry Christmas," Nixon said when Haldeman answered, "and welcome back."

They talked, easily and smoothly. Nixon discussed his travels and the new book he was writing. Haldeman said he was thinking of going into business on his own; Nixon offered to put him in touch with friends who could help. He invited Haldeman to drop by whenever he could; he wanted to hear Haldeman's views on the current political scene.

Haldeman began putting out the word that it was Joseph Di Mona who was responsible for the negative things *The Ends of Power* said about Nixon. By 1990 Haldeman was repudiating the book and saying that it was his hope to someday write another one. He read everything published on Watergate, including my own work; he told me that if he ever published another book, he wanted to make certain he had every fact exactly right.

In early 1993 he decided to publish his diaries instead. It was a wise decision. The diaries are invaluable. A book arguing that he was innocent would have had little impact. The diaries are certain to have a major impact on historians and scholars, and the general public.

Haldeman's diaries, taken as a whole, remind us that there is much more to the Nixon Administration than Watergate. Bob Haldeman was the insider's insider on some of the great events of the second half of the Twentieth Century. He was proud of his role as a participant in the opening to China, in achieving détente with the Soviet Union and the beginning of the end of the arms race, and in ending American participation in the Vietnam War. He was right to be proud, and he was courageous to publish this record of what he did, saw, and said.

After his release from prison, Haldeman made a successful career as a businessman, gaining an interest in hotels, development, real estate, and restaurants in Florida, among other investments.

He did not hide from his own past. Although he rarely gave interviews to reporters, he frequently met with students and scholars. In 1987, when I was teaching in a mini-semester at Whittier College, Haldeman came to my undergraduate seminar on Watergate. I had told the students they could ask anything they wanted to, and they did, tough questions about the cover-up. Haldeman was open, forthcoming, informative, gracious in his replies. The students came into the seminar hostile; after two and a half hours they were Haldeman fans.

I have been on panels on the Nixon Administration with Haldeman on a number of occasions, most notably at Hofstra University's conference on Nixon, and I always found him to be polite, charming, honest, absolutely free of any bitterness. Indeed, it was impossible not to like him. In 1987 I asked him to read the manuscript of the second volume of my biography of Nixon, which covered the first term. He did, and he made hundreds of comments in the margins, sometimes agreeing with my point, sometimes disagreeing with an interpretation, sometimes pointing out errors of fact, thus putting me deeply in his debt.

H. R. Haldeman died at his home in Santa Barbara, California, on November 12, 1993. He was survived by his wife of almost 45 years, the former Jo Horton, and four children, Susan, Hank, Peter, and Ann.

Nixon issued a statement: "I have known Bob Haldeman to be a man of rare intelligence, strength, integrity, and courage. . . . He played an indispensable role in turbulent times as our Administration undertook a broad range of initiatives at home and abroad."

The obituaries in the major newspapers (especially Haldeman's least favorite ones, *The New York Times* and *The Washington Post*) focused almost exclusively on Watergate and were hostile if not actually snide, which was a pity, because as every reader of Haldeman's diaries can attest, there was a great deal more to H. R. Haldeman's career as Chief of Staff than Watergate.

Final Note

For four years following Bob's resignation as Chief of Staff, he concentrated solely on his legal battles brought on by Watergate. While it would have been far easier—financially and emotionally—to plea-bargain, he was convinced of his innocence and fought to prove it. Throughout the long ordeal he remained at peace with himself, believing that his actions had been proper, legal, and in the best interests of the nation. He had hoped for a verdict which would exonerate him, at least legally, if not in the minds of the public.

Ultimately, however, he was convicted of three counts of perjury—which was particularly painful for him, and ironic to those who knew the value he placed in honesty—as well as the more intangible charges of obstruction of justice and conspiracy to obstruct justice. The prosecution, having proved there had been a conspiracy, succeeded in tying Bob into it as an *intending* member.

In this regard Bob always placed great emphasis on the distinction between "containment" and "cover-up," or obstruction of justice. He knew of no organized cover-up and certainly never approved of one. However, he did recognize containment, wherein steps are taken to minimize the political damage of an issue, as a legal, political reality—and an ongoing practice of all presidents and political figures. Given the adversarial tenor of the times—the animosity between the President and the national press, the vehemence of the opposition between the two parties, the divisiveness and domestic violence sparked by Vietnam, and the intensity of the power struggle between the Executive Branch and the Congress—containment was critical for effective leadership.

Bob believed that the break-in and bugging of the Democratic National Committee Headquarters was neither legal nor acceptable. He considered it a worthless endeavor and never knew who gave the orders to set it up. When the break-in was first reported, it was merely a minor incident amidst many major issues in which the Administration was involved; negotiations with China, the SALT Treaty, Paris negotiations regarding Vietnam, reorganization of the Executive Branch, and the reelection campaign.

Much has been written about Watergate, including Bob's own book, *The Ends of Power*. He read almost everything on the subject, searching for a better understanding of its complexities, but became resigned to the fact that no one really knew the whole story. At the same time, he became equally convinced of the greater historical importance of having the full story of the Nixon years told. It is to this end that he decided to publish his diaries. They are not the entire story, but they do contribute to it by documenting in detail the daily operation of the Nixon White House for four and a quarter years.

As the unexpurgated reflection of what was happening at the time it happened, they provide one insider's view of the trivial and the momentous, the mistakes and the triumphs— "warts and all."

Bob has stated in his foreword that he believed that the diaries can be a valuable resource to historians in their struggle to understand one of the more tumultuous times in our century. For the general reader, he hoped that they would help put the Nixon Presidency into more complete perspective and thereby continue the healing process which must follow the national trauma of the late 1960s and early 1970s.

Jo Haldeman
March 1994

Index